Sydney

timeout.com/sydney

Published by Time Out Guides Ltd, a wholly owned subsidiary of Time Out Group Ltd.
Time Out and the Time Out logo are trademarks of Time Out Group Ltd.

© **Time Out Group Ltd 2006**
Previous editions 1997, 2000, 2001, 2004.

10 9 8 7 6 5 4 3 2 1

This edition first published in Great Britain in 2006 by Ebury Publishing
Ebury Publishing is a division of The Random House Group Ltd,
20 Vauxhall Bridge Road, London SW1V 2SA

Random House Australia Pty Limited 20 Alfred Street, Milsons Point, Sydney, New South Wales 2061, Australia
Random House New Zealand Limited 18 Poland Road, Glenfield, Auckland 10, New Zealand
Random House South Africa (Pty) Limited Isle of Houghton, Corner Boundary
Road & Carse O'Gowrie, Houghton 2198, South Africa

Random House UK Limited Reg. No. 954009

Distributed in USA by Publishers Group West
1700 Fourth Street, Berkeley, California 94710

Distributed in Canada by Penguin Canada Ltd
10 Alcorn Avenue, Toronto, Ontario, Canada M4V 3B2

For further distribution details, see www.timeout.com

ISBN
To 31 December 2006: 1-904978-97-5
From 1 January 2007: 9781904978978

A CIP catalogue record for this book is available from the British Library

Colour reprographics by Wyndeham Icon, 3 & 4 Maverton Road, London E3 2JE

Printed and bound in Germany by Appl

Papers used by Ebury Publishing are natural, recyclable products made from wood grown in sustainable forests.

North Sydney Olympic Pool.
See p113.

Time Out Guides Limited
Universal House
251 Tottenham Court Road
London W1T 7AB
Tel + 44 (0)20 7813 3000
Fax + 44 (0)20 7813 6001
Email guides@timeout.com
www.timeout.com

Editorial
Editor Cath Phillips
Deputy Editor Julian Richards
Listings Editor Sarah Craske, Sarah Love, Lisa Doust
Proofreader Sam Le Quesne
Indexer Anna Norman

Editorial/Managing Director Peter Fiennes
Series Editor Ruth Jarvis
Deputy Series Editor Lesley McCave
Business Manager Gareth Garner
Guides Co-ordinator Holly Pick
Accountant Kemi Olufuwa

Design
Art Director Scott Moore
Art Editor Pinelope Kourmouzoglou
Senior Designer Josephine Spencer
Graphic Designer Henry Elphick
Digital Imaging Dan Conway
Ad Make-up Jenny Prichard

Picture Desk
Picture Editor Jael Marschner
Deputy Picture Editor Tracey Kerrigan
Picture Researcher Helen McFarland

Advertising
Sales Director Mark Phillips
International Sales Manager Ross Canadé
International Sales Executive Simon Davies
Advertising Sales (Sydney) Uptime Marketing Australia
Advertising Assistant Kate Staddon

Marketing
Group Marketing Director John Luck
Marketing Manager Yvonne Poon
Marketing & Publicity Manager, US Rosella Albanese

Production
Group Production Director Mark Lamond
Production Manager Brendan McKeown
Production Coordinator Caroline Bradford

Time Out Group
Chairman Tony Elliott
Managing Director Mike Hardwick
Financial Director Richard Waterlow
TO Magazine Ltd MD David Pepper
Group General Manager/Director Nichola Coulthard
TO Communications Ltd MD David Pepper
Group Art Director John Oakey
Group IT Director Simon Chappell

Contributors
Introduction Cath Phillips. **History** Juliet Rieden (*Walk into history* Cath Phillips). **The Other History** Miranda Herron. **Sydney Today** T Wong. **Where to Stay** Genevieve Paiement. **Sightseeing Introduction** Cath Phillips, Juliet Rieden. **Central Sydney** T Wong (*The return of the architect* Eoghan Lewis; *Time travel* Cath Phillips). **Eastern Suburbs** Kerry McCarthy (*Join the club* Hannah Rand). **Inner West** Prue Rushton (*Sydneysider spotting guide* Kevin Airs). **North Shore** Kevin Airs (*Walk 2: Cremorne Point* Cath Phillips). **Northern Beaches** Kevin Airs. **Parramatta & the West** Ed Gibbs (*The best Aboriginal Sydney* Miranda Herron). **The South** Prue Rushton. **Sydney's Best Beaches** Katie Ekberg. **Restaurants** Pat Nourse. **Cafés** Pat Nourse. **Bars & Pubs** Pat Nourse (*Fancy a game?* Prue Rushton). **Shops & Services** Hannah Rand. **Festivals & Events** Sarah Craske (*And they're off!* Hannah Rand). **Children** Lisa Doust. **Clubs** Prue Rushton. **Film** Ed Gibbs (*Lights, camera, Aussies!* Ed Gibbs, Juliet Rieden). **Galleries** Ian Gould. **Gay & Lesbian** David Mills. **Music** Ed Gibbs. **Sport & Fitness** Nick Scott. **Theatre & Dance** Stephen Dunne. **Short Trips** Kevin Airs (Blue Mountains: Stephen Dunne). **Directory** Sarah Craske, Katie Ekberg.

Maps JS Graphics (john@jsgraphics.co.uk). **Map on p335** reproduced with kind permission of Sydney Ferries Corporation. **Map on p336** reproduced with kind permission of CityRail.

Photography Héloise Bergman, except: page 10 Topfoto; page 13 Advertising Archives; page 15 Newspix; page 18 Bettmann/Corbis; page 20 Baci/Corbis; pages 25, 243 Getty Images; page 26 Rex Features; page 114 Adam Eastland; page 131 Hamilton Lund/Tourism New South Wales; page 225 Arclight Films; page 267 Robert McFarlane; page 269 Steve Lunam; page 270 Cameron Baird; pages 273, 288 Tourism Australia; page 275 Hideo Kurihara/Alamy; pages 279, 282, 289 photolibrary.com.
The following images were provided by the featured establishments/artist: pages 181, 196, 233, 249, 255, 262, 264, 271.

The Editor would like to thank Diane Glasson at Tourism NSW, Kim Salt at Seal Communications, Tim Benzie, Katie Ekberg, Juliet Rieden, Mike Harrison, the Culross family and all contributors to previous editions of *Time Out Sydney*, whose work forms the basis for parts of this book.

Contents

KT-394-652

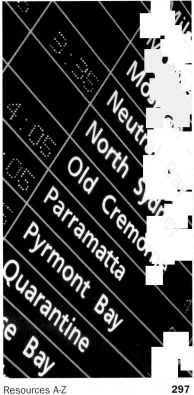

Introduction

Recent statistics from Tourism Australia, the country's official tourist outfit, show that Sydney is the most popular destination in Australia, with more than four million visitors a year. The NSW capital is top of the list for international travellers, whose average stay is just over two weeks. Of course, none of this comes as a surprise to Sydneysiders, who already know that they live in one of the loveliest cities on the planet.

The list of pluses is long. Foremost is the natural setting. There's the beautiful harbour, lush parklands, more than 50 beaches, and stunning views of water and sky at almost every turn. And the climate is enviable. Summers are long and warm, with blue skies; winters are mild, with temperatures rarely dropping below 12°C (54°F). Throughout the year you can expect over seven hours of sunshine a day.

Then there are the man-made attractions. The Opera House and Harbour Bridge remain the city's icons – the former finally making it on to the National Heritage List in 2005 as recognition of its importance to the Australian psyche. Sophisticated bars and revamped pubs abound, the gay and lesbian scene is the biggest in the southern hemisphere, and the restaurants are among the best – some would say *the* best – in the world, making the most of fantastic local produce, especially seafood, and an ethnic diversity that matches London and New York. Such diversity is a product of Sydney's multicultural make-up, its residents representing 180 different nations.

Admittedly, cultural institutions suffer in comparison with other major cities – but who wants to be indoors when sun and surf beckon? Most of the city's popular activities happen outside – be it eating and drinking alfresco, lazing on the beach, yachting or swimming in the harbour, surfing or playing sport. Sydneysiders' care-free approach to life is all part of the charm too.

As Australia's largest city, Sydney is first in many national arenas – banking, business, movie-making – but it's increasingly strutting its stuff under a global spotlight too. Literally so in the case of Australian fashion designers, whose work is appearing on catwalks and in stores in London and New York. The city's self-confidence is evident in recent large-scale inner-city developments, including the huge, high-rise World Square project and the mega-bucks revamp of the Hilton Sydney hotel.

Yes, it's a long way from anywhere else, but more airlines are offering direct flights to Sydney – Virgin Atlantic is the latest, running a daily service from London Heathrow. So what are you waiting for?

ABOUT TIME OUT CITY GUIDES

This is fifth edition of *Time Out Sydney,* one of an expanding series of Time Out guides produced by the people behind the successful listings magazines in London, New York and Chicago. Our guides are all written by resident experts who have striven to provide you with all the most up-to-date information you'll need to explore the city or read up on its background, whether you're a local or a first-time visitor.

THE LIE OF THE LAND

Sydney is a sprawling mass of suburbs clustered around a compact city centre, and at first the sheer number of suburbs can be baffling. The central area, however, is much easier to fathom, and small enough to explore on foot. Alternatively, public transport, in the form of ferries, buses, CityRail trains, LightRail and the Monorail, is excellent and accessible. Travelling to and from the suburbs is also easily done on public transport, and we've included full transport details with each listing. The options given are the most direct routes, but other routes may also be possible.

ESSENTIAL INFORMATION

For all the practical information you might need for visiting Sydney – including visa and customs information, details of local transport, advice on disabled facilities and access, and emergency telephone numbers – turn to the Directory at the back of the guide. It starts on page 292.

THE LOWDOWN ON THE LISTINGS

We have tried to make this guide as easy to use as possible. Addresses, phone numbers, websites, transport information, opening times, admission prices and credit card details are all included in the listings. And, as far as possible, we've given details of facilities, services and events, all checked and correct as we went to press. However, businesses can change their arrangements at any time. Before you go out

of your way, we strongly advise you to phone ahead to check opening times, ticket prices and other particulars. While every effort has been make to ensure the accuracy of the information contained in this guide, the publishers cannot accept responsibility for any errors it may contain.

PRICES AND PAYMENT
We have noted where venues such as shops, hotels and restaurants accept the following credit cards: American Express (AmEx), Diners Club (DC), MasterCard (MC) and Visa (V). Many shops, restaurants and attractions will also accept other cards, including JCB, as well as travellers' cheques issued by a major financial institution (such as American Express).

The prices in the guide should be treated as guidelines, not gospel. If they vary wildly from those we've quoted, ask if there's a good reason. If there isn't, go elsewhere. Then please let us know. We aim to give the best and most up-to-date advice, and want to know if you've been badly treated or overcharged.

TELEPHONE NUMBERS
The international dialling code for Australia is 61, and the code for Sydney is 02 (drop the zero if calling from overseas). Standard Sydney phone numbers have eight digits. The 02 area encompasses the whole of New South Wales, and if you're calling from within NSW you don't need to use the area code (so we haven't included it in the listings). Call rates depend on distance – the further away you're phoning, the more it will cost. Generally, calls within a 25-kilometre (16-mile) radius are charged at local rate, and anything further afield at long-distance rates.

1800 numbers are free when dialled within Australia, but are not necessarily accessible countrywide, and cannot be dialled from abroad. 13 and 1300 numbers are charged at the local rate or less throughout Australia.

MAPS
The map section at the back of the guide – which starts on page 320 – includes orientation and overview maps of New South Wales and the Sydney metropolitan area. Detailed street maps to the centre of Sydney are on pages 326-333, with maps of the suburbs of Bondi, Manly and Newtown on page 334.

The street maps now pinpoint specific locations of hotels (❶), restaurants (❶), cafés (❶) and bars and pubs (❶). We've also marked key beaches (❶). Map references in the guide indicate the page number and, where appropriate, the grid square on those maps. There's also a street index, starting on page 317. On page 335 you'll find Sydney Ferries routes, and on page 336 the CityRail train network in suburban Sydney.

LET US KNOW WHAT YOU THINK
We hope you enjoy *Time Out Sydney* and we'd like to know what you think of it. We welcome tips for places you consider we should include in our future editions, and take note of your criticism of our choices. You can email us at guides@timeout.com.

Advertisers

We would like to stress that no establishment has been included in this guide because it has advertised in any of our publications and no payment of any kind has influenced any review. The opinions given in this book are those of Time Out writers and entirely independent.

There is an online version of this book, along with guides to over 100 international cities, at **www.timeout.com**.

In Context

Features

Sydney Opera House. *See p68.*

Captain Cook at Botany Bay in 1770, as painted by Emmanuel Fox in 1902.

History

Sydney may be youthful, but it's got a torrid past.

People have inhabited the area now known as Sydney for tens of thousands of years. When Captain James Cook turned up in 1770 with orders that he should 'with the consent of the natives take possession of convenient situations in the name of the king', he noted that those natives 'appear to be the most wretched people on earth. But in reality they are far happier than we Europeans'. Not surprisingly, the first words the Europeans ever heard from the Aboriginal inhabitants of the Sydney area were 'Warra! Warra!' – meaning 'Go away!'

On 29 April 1770 Cook landed at Botany Bay, which he named after discovering scores of plants hitherto unknown to science. Turning northwards, he passed an entrance to a harbour where there appeared to be safe anchorage. Cook called it Port Jackson after the Secretary to the Admiralty, George Jackson.

Back in Britain, King George III was convinced that the east coast of the island, which had been claimed for him and called New South Wales, would make a good colony. For one thing it would help reduce Britain's overflowing prison population. For another, a settlement in the region would be convenient both as a base for trading in the Far East and in case of a war with the French or Dutch.

THE FIRST FLEET

On 13 May 1787 Captain Arthur Phillip's ship, *Sirius*, along with three provisions ships, two warships and six vessels of convicts, set sail from Portsmouth. On board were some 300 merchant seamen, their wives, children and servants, and nearly 800 convicts. Thirty-six weeks later, on 18 January 1788, after stops in Tenerife, Rio de Janeiro and the Cape of Good Hope, the *Sirius* arrived at Botany Bay. The rest of the First Fleet arrived a couple of days later. Fewer than 50 passengers had perished en route – not a bad rate for the period.

At that time of year, Botany Bay turned out to be a grim site for the new colony: there was little fresh water and it was exposed to strong winds and swell. One plus was that the naked 'Indians' seen running up and down the beach 'shouting and making many uncouth signs and gestures' turned out to be relatively friendly. Eager to make a good impression, Phillip and a small party of frock coats took a rowing boat to meet their new subjects. The meeting went well: the British exchanged a looking glass and beads for a wooden club.

Probably relieved that his first contact with the locals had not gone awry – when William Jansz of the Dutch East India Company had met Aboriginal people in 1606 he reported back that they 'killed on sight' – Phillip decided to search for Port Jackson. He returned with glowing reports: it was 'one of the finest harbours in the world, in which a thousand sail of the line might ride in perfect security'. This is one of the earliest descriptions of Sydney Harbour.

'In those early days, capturing Aborigines to turn them into honorary white men was all the rage.'

That same day, Phillip's men caught the improbable sight of two ships approaching from the sea. These were the French frigates *La Boussole* and *L'Astrolabe*, commanded by Jean-François de Galaup, Count de la Pérouse, who was on a voyage of discovery through the southern hemisphere. Surprised by the old enemy, Phillip decided to up-anchor the whole fleet the following morning and lead it to Sydney Cove – named after Viscount Sydney, the minister responsible for the colony.

The First Fleeters set to as soon as they arrived. Trees were felled, marquees erected, convict shacks constructed from cabbage palms, garden plots dug and a blacksmith's forge set up. On 7 February the settlers gathered to hear Phillip declared the first governor of the state of New South Wales and its dependencies. It wasn't long, though, before convicts started to disappear. Several were found clubbed or speared to death, probably in revenge for attacks on the locals. Food ran dangerously low, scurvy took hold and the settlers' small herd of cattle began to diminish.

During the next few weeks the animosity between the settlers and the indigenous people came to a head, and the disappearance of

several more convicts and a marine provoked Governor Phillip to try to capture some natives in a bid to force talks. Two boats were sent to Manly (named after the 'manly' nature of the undaunted Aborigines seen there). Following courteous overtures, the settlers suddenly grabbed an Aboriginal man, called Arabanoo, and rushed him to a boat under a hail of stones and spears. Arabanoo's hair was cut, his beard shaved and he was bathed and dressed in European clothes. But despite attempts by the settlers to persuade him to tell his compatriots that they meant no harm, no ground was gained on the path to friendship.

In those early days, capturing Aborigines to turn them into honorary white men was all the rage. Two such captives, Bennelong and Colbee, were rough-and-ready types, scarred from warfare and smallpox. Colbee soon bolted, but Bennelong stayed for five months and eventually, dressed in top hat and tails, travelled to London to have tea with the royal family. He gave his name to the point of land where a hut was built for him – and on which the Sydney Opera House now stands.

Early in 1789 the local Aborigines began to succumb to smallpox contracted from the British or from sailors on the French vessels that had put in at Botany Bay. Hundreds were soon dead, among them Arabanoo. The epidemics fuelled a belief among white settlers, then and later, that the Aboriginal peoples were doomed to extinction.

THE RUM CORPS
If conditions were bad for the settlers at first, they got worse as the seasons progressed. Two years and two months after the First Fleet had sailed, Britain sent its first relief to Sydney. Carrying a small stock of provisions, the *Lady Juliana* arrived in 1790 with more than 200 convicts on board. Most were women, and almost all were too weak to work. This Second Fleet also brought a regiment known as the New South Wales Corps (NSWC), which had been formed to replace the marines. They found the settlement short of clothes, while rations had become so meagre that it was feared that everyone might starve to death.

Both soldiers and convicts were so frail through lack of food that the working day had to be shortened. Thefts became commonplace, and penalties for stealing increased. Meanwhile, the Aboriginal peoples were prospering on the food that grew, leaped or swam all around them, but the first settlers were so bound by the diet of the mother country that they would rather have starved than 'eaten native'.

By the end of June 1790, four more ships had sailed into Port Jackson, carrying with them a

Walk into history

Sydney may be a young whippersnapper compared to the ancient metropolises of Europe and Asia, but that doesn't mean it's lacking in historical interest. The **Museum of Sydney** in the CBD is a good starting point for history buffs, but if you want a more personal, hands-on approach, especially if the weather is good, get out in the streets and see for yourself.

To this end, the **City of Sydney History Program** has produced a series of leaflets detailing self-guided historical walking tours, mainly around the city centre. Each focuses on a particular area and aspect of Sydney's history – so 'Colony' covers early settler life around the Rocks and Millers Point; 'Passion' delves into the bohemian past of Kings Cross; and 'Port' explores the often-ignored industrial heartland of Pyrmont and Ultimo. There are six walks in all, each designed to take an hour or two. A map shows the route and points of interest along it, plus possible detours if you're in strolling mode.

You can pick up the leaflets at tourist offices or download copies from the City of Sydney's website: go to www.cityofsydney. nsw.gov.au/aboutsydney and then 'Visitor guides & information'.

convicts to do it for them. Thanks to a shortage of money, rum rapidly became common currency, and as the NSWC ruled the rum trade it became known as the Rum Corps.

Things progressed slowly until 1808, when Governor William Bligh (of *Mutiny on the Bounty* fame) was deposed in a military coup. Bligh's evil temper and his attempts to deal with the corruption of the NSWC, which had bullied his predecessors through their control of the colony's rum, led to his downfall. The Rum Corps arrested the governor and imprisoned him for a year – the only time in Australian history when an established government has been overthrown by force.

The Corps ruled until Bligh was sent back to England and a new governor, Lachlan Macquarie, arrived. Macquarie later wrote that on his arrival he found the colony 'barely emerging from a state of infantile imbecility, and suffering from various privations and disabilities: the country impenetrable beyond 40 miles from Sydney'. A great planner, Macquarie oversaw the building of new streets and the widening of others. He named three of the largest streets: George Street, after the king, Pitt Street, after the prime minister, and the grandest of all he named Macquarie Street, after himself. With the help of convict architect Francis Greenway, he set about building a city to be proud of, with a hospital, several churches, a sandstone barracks and Macquarie Lighthouse (still on South Head) to guide ships into the harbour.

TAKING ROOT

With the discovery of the fertile hinterland beyond the Blue Mountains in 1813, the colony advanced in earnest. The flow of migrants increased after the end of the Napoleonic Wars in 1815, and soon farms and settlements dotted the regions around Sydney and Parramatta. In 1822 Macquarie was forced from the colony by powerful landowners; he died in London in 1824.

There still remained the issue of defence: Sydney was seen as prey to any passing foe. The city's vulnerability and its isolation from the distant motherland was confirmed in 1830 when its citizens woke to find that, in the night, four American frigates had passed through the Heads and sailed up to Sydney Cove without anyone noticing. Since that day, Australia has been paranoid about attack, whether from the Russians during the Crimean War, Yankee privateers or the Spanish. Fear of an invasion from Asia has been a constant undertone of government policy in more recent times.

Finding transportation ruinously expensive, the British government sought to have the infant colony subsidise the cost. Convict labour was increasingly used to generate income. As in all

stock of convicts transported in abominable conditions. Some 267 people had died en route, and of the 759 who landed, 488 suffered from scurvy, dysentery or fever. Between 1791 and 1792, the death rate matched London's at the height of the Great Plague. Those remaining alive were forced to struggle on. Men faced a lashing from the cat-o'-nine-tails if they didn't work hard. The women had it little easier and were forced into long hours of domestic work or kept busy weaving in sweatshop conditions. Finally, though, the arrival of yet more transports from England, bringing with them convicts, free settlers and supplies, meant that life in the colony began to pick up. In October 1792 Phillip reported that nearly 5,000 bushels of maize had been harvested and around 1,700 acres were under cultivation. In December that year, Phillip returned to England convinced the settlement would last.

It was almost three years before another governor arrived to take Phillip's place. The commanders of the NSWC used this interim period to their own advantage by granting officers rights to work the land and employ slave societies, the workforce was inefficient, and the colony soon became the dumping ground for England's unemployed working classes rather than her criminals. Most of these free immigrants were bonded to their colonial employers, their passage paid for by the sale of land. In 1840 transportation of convicts to New South Wales was abolished. A total of 111,500 convicts – of whom just 16,000 were women – had arrived in NSW and Tasmania.

By 1849 the population of convicts was outnumbered by free settlers. A new type of vessel, the clipper ship, had cut the sailing time from England to Australia by 49 days, to just 91. In the 1850s gold was discovered in New South Wales and Victoria, and prospectors rushed to Australia from all over the world. During the 1880s more than 370,000 arrived, mostly of British or Irish descent. Rich British businessmen poured money into the country and mine owners and farmers profited.

Governor Phillip had ensured as far back as 1790 that some physical distance was maintained between the government precinct to the east of what is now known as Circular Quay, and the barracks and convict quarters to the west. Built into the steep sandstone cliffs, this no man's land – now known as the Rocks – quickly became as degenerate as the worst of London's slums. Tiers of narrow streets and sandstone stairs crammed with makeshift shacks led up from waterfront pubs and cheap lodging houses to comfortable terraced houses inhabited by sea captains and stevedores. The massive influx of immigrants in the mid 1800s meant housing was scarce, a problem exacerbated by many inner-city homes being converted into storehouses and offices.

By the late 19th century, the Rocks was known as Sydney's worst den of iniquity. Prostitution, drunkenness, theft and street gangs were rife. Sailors ashore after months at sea were robbed of everything they owned or press-ganged straight on to another vessel.

The increasingly squalid goings-on and the build-up of rubbish, silt and sewage made conditions in the Rocks perfect for rats and the bubonic plague carried by their fleas. In the first nine months of 1900 the plague killed 103 people. Crowds stormed the Board of Health's offices demanding a share of the colony's meagre supply of anti-plague medicine. The Rocks and Darling Harbour were quarantined and in 1902 the Sydney Harbour Trust was set up to clean up the harbour: it later announced that it had pulled from the water 2,524 rats, 1,068 cats, 283 bags of meat, 305 bags of fish, 1,467 fowl, 25 parrots, 23 sheep, 14 pigs, one bullock, nine calves and nine goats.

CIVILISING MISSIONS

In the 1880s Sydney's remaining Aboriginal inhabitants were rounded up into a camp at Circular Quay and given government rations in a bid to keep them off the streets. In 1895 an Aboriginal reserve was set up at La Perouse, near Botany Bay – far from the centre of the city. By the end of the 19th century most of the area's indigenous inhabitants were restricted to reserves or in missions, where they were introduced to the supposed benefits of Christianity and European civilisation.

By this time it was apparent that, though the Aboriginal population was in decline, the mixed-descent population was increasing. The fact that the latter group had some European blood meant that there was a place for them – albeit a lowly one – in society. Many children of mixed race were forcibly separated from their parents and placed in segregated 'training' institutions before being sent out to work. Girls were sent to be domestic servants to satisfy the nation's demand for cheap labour. It was also held that long hours and exhausting work would curb their supposed promiscuity.

In Australia, I will...

That Australia is booming is hardly news. But here is a fresh thought: it's been, is and will be the sheer determination of the individual that keeps up the pace, strengthens the nation and places Australia firmly amongst the world's leaders.
There's been no shortage of Britons with such strong will. We still need more professional men, and women, who are searching for real scope–people who feel hemmed in for any reason.
You will be respected for your quali-fications, ability and experience; there are no crushing limits on, say, research facilities: natural resources are being developed with all stops out. There's an acute sense of freedom throughout Australia–you'd notice it at once and find it most stimulating.

Rewards? There are plenty. And they are big and worth striving for, for you and every member of your family.
They all stem from saying to yourself 'In Australia, I will...'
Why not join the others who are making Australia a great place for families.

In Australia, where there's a will there's a wonderful life

Ambitious Brits were wooed by migration ads like this in the 1970s. See p14.

The Commonwealth of Australia came into existence on 1 January 1901. The country had 3.8 million inhabitants, and more than half a million of them crowded on to the streets of Sydney to celebrate the inauguration of the nation. The Aboriginal peoples weren't recorded in the first census, however. They had to wait until 1967, when 90 per cent of the public voted to make new laws relating to Aboriginal people. This led the way for them to be recognised as Australian citizens, and to be included in the census of 1971.

THE NEW CENTURY AND WAR

After a lull following the 1890s depression, migration revived. In the years leading up to 1914, 300,000 mainly British migrants arrived, half of whom came on an assisted-passage scheme. In 1908 a Royal Commission set up to advise on the improvement of Sydney concluded that workers should be moved out of the slums to the suburbs. Six years later, though, World War I broke out. Around 10,000 volunteers in Sydney queued to go on the 'big adventure'. Most were sent to Gallipoli – a campaign that became synonymous with the Australian collective memory with British arrogance, callousness and incompetence. By the time the Allied forces were withdrawn in January 1916, the combination of lacklustre Allied leadership and stiff Turkish resistance meant that casualties were well above 50 per cent, with little to show for thousands of lost lives. After the disaster of Gallipoli, Australia was not going to return to a subservient colonial role: the nation had come of age.

With the end of World War I it was reasoned that to defend Australia properly the country needed more people. A further 300,000 migrants arrived in the 1920s, mostly from England and Scotland, a product of the policy known as 'White Australia'. The origins of the policy can be traced to the mid 19th century, when white miners' resentment towards Chinese diggers boiled over in violence. The 1901 Immigration Restriction Act placed 'certain restrictions on immigration' and provided 'for the removal from the Commonwealth of prohibited immigrants'. For example, applicants were required to pass a written test in a specific, usually European, language – with which they were not necessarily familiar. It was not until 1974 that Australia eliminated such official racial discrimination from its immigration policy.

Australia's vulnerability to attack came back to haunt it during World War II. On 31 May 1942, three Japanese midget submarines powered through the Heads and into Sydney Harbour. The first got tangled in a net across the harbour mouth, but the others slipped past. The third midget was spotted and attacked, but

the second took the chance to fire two torpedoes at the US cruiser *Chicago*. Both missed, but one sank the depot ship HMAS *Kuttabul*, killing 19 Australian and two British naval ratings asleep on board. Except for Aborigines and settlers killed in early skirmishes, these 21 men have been the only victims of enemy action on home ground in Sydney's history.

After the war, Australia once again decided it needed to boost the size of its population. The slogan 'populate or perish' was coined, and a new immigration scheme organised. In 1948, 70,000 migrants arrived from Britain and Europe. By the late 1950s most migrants were coming from Italy, Yugoslavia and Greece.

'The Queen's portrait was removed from post office walls and her insignia on mailboxes painted out.'

In 1951 the concept of assimilation was officially adopted as national policy, with the goal 'that all persons of Aboriginal descent will choose to attain a similar manner and standard of living to other Australians'. Eradication of Aboriginal culture was stepped up during the 1950s and '60s, when even greater numbers of Aboriginal children were removed from their families. Many Aboriginal babies were adopted at birth and later told that their true parents had died. The removal of children from their parents was halted in the 1970s, but the scars remain. The 'stolen generations' became the subject of fierce debate in Australia. Expat director Phillip Noyce's 2002 film *Rabbit-Proof Fence* – the story of three stolen children who run away from a camp and attempt to walk home over 1,000 miles of inhospitable country – brought the story to the world.

In 1964 Australian troops joined their US counterparts in action in Vietnam. As in the States, anti-Vietnam War sentiment became a hot issue, and tens of thousands of Australians blockaded the streets of the major cities. A new Labor government, led by Gough Whitlam, came to power in 1972 after promising a fairer society and an end to Australia's involvement in the war. Within months the troops were brought home. Not long afterwards 'Advance Australia Fair' replaced 'God Save the Queen' as the national anthem, the Queen's portrait was removed from post office walls and her insignia on mailboxes painted out. Land rights were granted to some Aboriginal groups, and in 1974 the government finally put an end to the White Australia policy that had largely restricted black and Asian immigration since

1901. Two years later the official cord to Britain was cut when the Australian Constitution was separated from that of its motherland.

Ties with Britain loosened further in 1975 during a messy political wrangle, when the Conservative opposition moved to block the government's supply of money in the upper house. Without a budget, Gough Whitlam's government was unable to govern, so the Queen's representative, Governor-General John Kerr, sacked it and made opposition leader Malcolm Fraser prime minister. There was fury that an Australian-elected government could be dismissed by the monarch's appointee, and resentment towards Britain flared.

INTO A THIRD CENTURY

Immigration continued throughout the 1980s and '90s, but now there were quite a few new faces among the crowds hoping for a better life in the 'lucky country'. Hundreds of thousands of migrants began arriving from Asia. Today, on average, around 90,000 people emigrate to Australia each year, from more than 150 countries. Of settlers arriving in 2002/3, the biggest groups were those born in the UK (13.3 per cent), New Zealand (13.1 per cent), China (7.1 per cent), India (6.1 per cent), South

Africa (4.9 per cent), the Philippines (3.4 per cent) and Indonesia (3 per cent). With such a multicultural mix you'd think it was time to reconsider the 'self-governing republic' option – but you'd be wrong. In a close-run national referendum in 1999, 55 per cent of the electorate voted to keep the Queen as head of state.

Some 460,000 Aborigines and the ethnically distinct people from the Torres Strait Islands off northern Queensland live in Australia today, but a rift still exists between them and the rest of the population. Aboriginal life expectancy is 20 years lower than that of other Australians; the infant mortality rate is higher; the ratio of Aboriginal people to other Australians in prisons is disproportionately high, and many are still restricted to the fringe of society.

In 1992 the 'Mabo decision' marked a breakthrough in Aboriginal affairs: the High Court declared that Australia was not *terra nullius* ('empty land') as it had been termed since the British 'invasion'. This decision resulted in the 1993 Native Title Act, which allowed Aboriginal groups and Torres Strait Islanders to claim government-owned land if they could prove continual association with it since 1788. Later, the Wik decision determined that Aboriginal people everywhere could make

Cambridge Street in the Rocks' squalid heyday in the late 19th century. *See p13*.

claims on government land that was leased to agriculturists. But Prime Minister John Howard's Liberal coalition government, under pressure from farming and mining interests, curtailed these rights.

In response, Aboriginal groups threatened (but did not mount) major demonstrations during the 2000 Sydney Olympics. The Olympic opening ceremony paid tribute to the country's Aboriginal origins, and the flame was lit by Aboriginal runner Cathy Freeman. To outsiders it seemed that Australia was embracing its past rather than marginalising it, but indigenous Australians themselves were less impressed. John Howard, in particular, has come in for harsh criticism for his refusal to apologise for the actions of past generations.

IN HOWARD'S ASYLUM

With the reconciliation issue bubbling in the background, Howard's government turned its attentions to stemming the influx of refugees. In the late 1990s asylum seekers from Iraq and Afghanistan landed in Australia only to face a grim, prison-like existence in detention centres in the middle of the South Australian desert – most notoriously, at Woomera (now closed). Processing their cases has taken years, and many are still in virtual incarceration, with their future prospects unresolved.

In 1999 when victims of war-ravaged Kosovo came knocking, the Australian government was slow to respond. Eventually, local and international pressure forced Howard's hand and the refugees were admitted, but only for a short respite on newly created 'safe haven' (ie temporary) visas. In August 2001 Howard played tough guy once again, turning away a Norwegian cargo ship carrying 400 Afghan and Iraqi asylum seekers, whom the captain had rescued from a leaky ferry. As the ship neared Australian shores, Howard – with one eye firmly on the voters – steeled himself for a showdown. 'I believe it is in Australia's national interests that we draw a line on what is increasingly becoming an uncontrollable number of illegal arrivals in this country,' he asserted.

Much unseemly to-ing and fro-ing followed. At one point, the government claimed that the refugees were blackmailing the Australian navy into rescuing them by throwing their children overboard. Later – after Howard had won the 2001 election – it was revealed that the pictures that had been flashed across the news had been taken a day later and were actually shots showing the bona fide rescue of the asylum seekers after their boat had sunk. Ultimately, the refugees weren't allowed to set foot on Australian soil: most ended up on the tiny Pacific island of Nauru.

Although heavily criticised internationally, Howard's strong-arm – and, say many, racist – policies proved popular at the ballot box and he won a third term in office in 2001, sending the opposition Labor party into free fall. Howard's government was returned once more in 2003, although NSW has remained a Labor stronghold under Bob Carr, who lasted ten years as premier before retiring in 2005, to be replaced by Morris Iemma.

Australia may be geographically removed from the centres of world affairs, but it is increasingly involved in some of the 21st century's key military issues. Australian troops led the UN peacekeeping force in East Timor in 1999 and in 2003 led a force to put down a rebellion in the Solomon Islands. More controversially, the Australian army has been heavily involved backing up US adventures in both Afghanistan and Iraq.

The nation has suffered for it: the 2002 Bali nightclub bombings killed 88 Australians (out of a death toll of 202), while another attack in Bali in 2005 killed four Australians. The Australian embassy in Jakarta, Indonesia, was also bombed in 2004, though none of the 11 dead was Australian. Jemaah Islamiah, a militant South-east Asian Muslim group, has been blamed for all three attacks.

Perhaps to calm that perennial sense of national vulnerability, in 2004 the Howard government announced a cruise missile programme to give Australia the region's 'most lethal' air combat capacity.

Antagonism towards Australia's Muslim communities grew after the bombings, and fears of more violence were raised when 15 people were arrested in November 2005 for allegedly planning bomb attacks in Sydney and Melbourne. All this may or may not have helped stoke up race riots in Cronulla and other oceanside suburbs south of Sydney a month later. The immediate spark was a hard-to-substantiate story that two surf lifesavers had been beaten up by men of Middle Eastern appearance. What is certain is that, encouraged by inflammatory talk radio and a racist texting campaign, 5,000 white 'Anglos' poured into Cronulla on 11 December to have a go at any 'Lebs' – people of Lebanese origin – they could find. There were also reports of young men of Middle Eastern or Mediterranean appearance smashing up vehicles and property. Serious injuries were few, however, and most arrests were for relatively minor offences.

The climate has been hotting up too: the worst bush fires for more than 20 years killed nine people in South Australia in 2005, and the 1 January 2006 was Sydney's hottest day since 1939, with a high of 44.3°C (111°F).

Key events

40,000BC The Aboriginal Dharug tribal group occupy the area that is now Sydney.
29 April 1770 James Cook and Joseph Banks sail the *Endeavour* into Botany Bay.
26 January 1788 Settlement of the First Fleet at Sydney Cove.
1789 Smallpox epidemic among local Aboriginal people.
1808 NSWC officers, known as the Rum Corps, overthrow Governor William Bligh.
1810-21 Governor Macquarie instils order.
1813 WC Wentworth, George Blaxland and William Lawson are the first Europeans to cross the Blue Mountains.
1840 The transportation of convicts to NSW is outlawed by the British government.
1842 The city of Sydney is officially incorporated; the first councillors are elected.
1851 A gold rush begins and Sydney's population rises to 96,000 by 1861.
1855 The colony's first steam railway, the Sydney to Parramatta line, is completed.
1858 Men are granted the vote in NSW.
1878 Seamen begin a six-week strike over the use of Chinese labour, setting in motion a movement that would lead to the White Australia policy.
1900 Bubonic plague in Sydney. More than 100 people die in eight months.
1901 Ceremony of united Commonwealth of Australia as an independent monarchy in the British Commonwealth, in Centennial Park. Edmund Barton is sworn in as prime minister.
1902 Women get the vote in NSW state elections.
1906 The world's first surf lifesaving club is founded at Bondi. Laws banning daylight beach bathing are scrapped.
1908 Canberra becomes Australia's capital.
1914-18 Of the 330,000 Australians sent to fight in World War I, 60,000 perish.
1922-30 The Empire Settlement Scheme moves thousands of working-class families from the industrial towns of the UK to Sydney.
1932 Sydney Harbour Bridge is opened.
1942 Three Japanese subs steal into Sydney Harbour and torpedo a ferry with Allied naval officers on board, killing 19.
1960-67 Aboriginal peoples are granted the vote and included in census figures.
1965-72 Australian troops sent to Vietnam.
1972 The Australian Labor Party gains power.
1973 Sydney Opera House is opened by the Queen and declared a wonder of the world.

1975 Governor-General Sir John Kerr, the Queen's representative, sacks the country's Labor government. The seeds of a serious Australian republican movement are sown.
1978 Hundreds of thousands of Vietnamese refugees enter the country; the first arrivals are illegal, stealing into Darwin by boat. The first gay and lesbian Mardi Gras ends in violence after police attack 1,000 marchers.
1985-6 A gang war for control of Sydney's prostitution, gambling and drug rackets rages. A web of business connections between the underworld and the police is exposed.
1988 One million celebrate bicentennial at Sydney Harbour. Aboriginal peoples protest.
1992 Sydney Harbour Tunnel opens. The Mabo case inserts the legal doctrine of native title into Australian law, allowing Aborigines to claim traditional rights to land.
1996 Liberal coalition government under John Howard wins power, ousting Labor Party.
1998 John Howard's coalition government narrowly wins a second term.
1999 Australian troops lead a peacekeeping force in East Timor. Referendum proposals to make Australia a republic are defeated.
2000 The Olympic Games, held at Sydney's Homebush Bay, are deemed the 'best ever'.
2001 A Norwegian ship carrying rescued refugees is refused entry to Australia and sent to a remote Pacific island. John Howard elected prime minister for a third term.
2002 Bombs explode in Bali nightclubs, killing 202, including 88 Australians. Australian troops join UN peacekeeping forces in Afghanistan.
2003 NSW Premier Bob Carr's Labor government is re-elected for a third successive term. Australian troops sent to the Iraq war.
2004 Riots in Sydney's Redfern district follow the death of an Aboriginal teenager. Parliamentary committee clears government of lying about Iraqi weapons of mass destruction. Government announces cruise missile programme. Fatal bomb attacks outside Australian embassy in Jakarta. John Howard wins fourth term.
2005 Bob Carr retires; Morris Iemma takes over as NSW premier. Another bombing in Bali kills 23, including four Australians. Fifteen are charged with planning bomb attacks in Sydney and Melbourne. Riots in Cronulla involving white and Lebanese youths.

The Other History

Why are indigenous people still fighting for justice?

Australians like to think of themselves as easy-going, egalitarian and willing to give anyone a fair go. However, this hasn't extended to the 'first Australians'. It is only relatively recently that Australia's violent, oppressive and discriminatory treatment of its indigenous people has been acknowledged or taught in schools. Histories and folklore glossed over the impact of Europeans on Aboriginal people and focused almost entirely on the heroism and tenacity of white explorers and settlers. In this version of history, the few hapless natives were swept away quietly on the tide of progress.

This 'out of sight, out of mind' attitude largely continues today, with 120,000 of 430,000 Aboriginal people and Torres Strait Islanders living in remote communities, often in desperate conditions. White Australia frequently sees their complex problems as self-perpetuated or just too unpleasant to contemplate. Happy to donate millions to victims of natural disasters overseas, many Australians resent the 'special treatment' given to some in their own backyard.

On a more positive note, the status of Aboriginal people has improved in the past 50 years. They were once the invisible underclass, but it's now usual to preface public events with an acknowledgement of the 'traditional owners' of the area. Their culture is widely celebrated: the red, black and yellow Aboriginal flag is flown on public buildings; some important sites, such as Uluru (formerly Ayer's Rock), have been handed back to Aboriginal ownership, and more and more indigenous people are appearing in most walks of life, from arts and sport to public services, law and politics.

IN THE BEGINNING

It's estimated that the first people arrived in Australia 50,000 to 70,000 years ago, travelling by foot from the north across land bridges and later by boat. Australian Aboriginals have one of the oldest continuous cultures and religions in the world, but there was never a unified nation or state: instead, people grouped into an estimated 500 clans or tribes, speaking some 250 languages and living a mainly nomadic life.

One of the hardest things for the individualist, capitalist Europeans and their system of law to understand when they colonised Australia –

and still even today – is the indivisible interrelationship of land, spirituality and culture to Aboriginal people. According to traditional indigenous laws, no individual can own, sell or give away land. Land belongs to all members of the community, and they in turn belong to the land. Ownership of a particular region was established during the Dreaming or Dreamtime – the time of creation. The details differ across the country, but the shared thread of creation stories tells of spiritual ancestors who came from the sky or earth, creating the world, giving life to animals and people, and establishing laws.

As custodians of a particular region, tribe members have a responsibility to maintain the stories, songs and rituals – also called the Dreaming – that signify ownership. Chants and songs 'map' the land, identifying natural features and defining tribal boundaries. Knowledge of law and culture is passed from elders down to initiated men and women; there is also secret knowledge and sacred locations that are entered only by the initiated.

The first Europeans saw the indigenous Australians as backward and barbaric because they did not grow crops, use metal or make pottery. What they could not see was the complex and environmentally sensitive way Aboriginal people had adapted to the vagaries of the climate: travelling light with portable tools and weapons to the best hunting and gathering grounds; managing grassland with fire to promote plant growth, thereby attracting animals; and harvesting the abundant seafood in coastal areas. Far from scrabbling a mean existence, they had a far more diverse diet than the Europeans did at that time – and there was time left over from the daily essentials for artistic and cultural pursuits.

THE ARRIVAL OF THE EUROPEANS

As the settlement of Sydney staggered through its first years, the local indigenous population was almost wiped out by diseases such as smallpox. Those who survived were then caught in a cycle of dispossession, violence and armed resistance – a pattern that continued as settlers spread across the continent. The best farmland was also the best hunting area, so with restricted ability to hunt and gather, Aboriginal people took settlers' livestock and outbreaks of guerrilla war ensued. The Aborigines used their bush skills to evade the settlers, but in the end the gun, force of numbers, disease, infertility and malnutrition ravaged populations.

The conflict didn't go unnoticed. Evangelical Christian groups in England petitioned the government, and in the 1830s and '40s various

edicts regarding the protection and rights of Aboriginals were issued. However, at the lawless frontier, where squatters simply took whatever land they wanted without payment or government consent, such ideals were ignored.

Murderous hostility was not universal. Aboriginal workers became crucial to the farming industry and were exploited as a source of cheap and skilful labour, particularly as stockmen. By the 1880s it is estimated that they represented half the rural workforce. In many cases, the Aboriginal farmhands' extended families were allowed to remain on their traditional lands, working as domestic servants in return for rations.

'From the early days, it was widely assumed that Aboriginal people were doomed as a race.'

Most indigenous Australians, however, lived in a state of physical and legal limbo. Those who had been forced off their land were relocated to reserves. Some were able to cultivate food and make a basic living; others languished in dismal conditions on the edge of settlements. Religious missions were also set up to protect, educate and 'civilise' the indigenous population. But the founding of the Commonwealth of Australia in 1901 almost completely ignored Aboriginal people, excluding them from the national census.

This was not an oversight. From the early days of settlement it was widely assumed that Aboriginal people were doomed as a race. In 1901 it was estimated that they numbered 76,000, down from a population of between 500,000 to a million in the 1780s. By the 1930s, however, it seemed that, remarkably, they had resisted extinction. In 1939, assimilation became federal government policy, aiming to raise the status of indigenous people so they could live as whites did. The paternalistic protection boards that administered this policy also controlled every aspect of life: where people lived, their employment, who they married and freedom of movement. Indigenous people were expected to abandon their own culture and fit into white society. But they still faced entrenched legal and social discrimination that kept them marginalised, disenfranchised and trapped in a cycle of poverty.

The most heartbreaking and controversial aspect of the policy, however, was the forcible removal of children, known now as the 'stolen generations'. Aboriginal 'half-caste' children were seen as having more potential for

The Block

It may be a tiny part of Sydney, a one-hectare area of run-down Victorian terraces bounded by Eveleigh, Vine, Louis and Caroline Streets in Redfern, but the Block has a huge reputation. In February 2004 the area hit the headlines around the world when 17-year-old Aboriginal Thomas Hickey was killed after falling from his pedal bike and being impaled on a fence. Locals claimed police had been chasing him, and this event was a catalyst for a backlash against the police that erupted into riots. Subsequent investigations cleared the police, but the event refocused attention on the area, which is struggling to rise above entrenched problems of poverty and drugs.

Aboriginal people have lived in the area since the 1920s, when they found cheap rent and work at the local railway workshops. The liberating effect of the 1967 referendum, which gave them citizenship rights, saw the population balloon.

The Block was due to be redeveloped, but in 1973 the federal Labor government took the unprecedented step of buying the land and giving it to the Aboriginal Housing Company (AHC) for housing.

The area has also been a centre for Aboriginal activism, such as the creation of Australia's first legal, medical and social services controlled by indigenous people, the establishment of the Aboriginal Tent Embassy in Canberra, and the 1998 bicentennial protests. The influx of heroin in the 1990s saw an increase in crime and poverty; many of the uninhabitable houses on the Block were demolished and today it remains in a state of desperate disrepair.

Developers have long been eying up prime real estate close to the CBD, and gentrified pockets have sprung up around Redfern. Plans for a multi-million dollar redevelopment of the area, including handing over parts of the Block to private developers, have been discussed. The Block remains, however, a thorn in the developers' side. The executive director of the Property Council of Australia (NSW), Ken Morrison, has said, 'There is no way Redfern is going to be that commercial mini-centre with Aboriginal housing and the Block still in place. We need to sort that out before private investors will be interested.'

This attitude has been met by outrage from the Aboriginal community, to whom the Block is not just a geographic location. Michael Mundine, CEO of the AHC, has described it as a modern sacred site. 'It's like the main watering hole for our people who have been travelling for years and years. They'll always come back here.'

Meanwhile the AHC has its own plan for the Block. The Pemuluwuy Project, described as 'self-determination in action', proposes 62 new homes plus an Aboriginal business college, artists' markets and community centre. Mundine believes a revitalisation of the Block will create positive effects that 'will flow on to the rest of the Aboriginal communities around the country'.

At the time of writing, the project has sparked hostility between the AHC and Frank Sartor, the Minister for Planning and for Redfern Waterloo, who says the plans could 'repeat the problems of the past'. As a result the AHC has refused to work with him.

'improvement' than 'full bloods', and so began what has been described as a policy of cultural genocide, with children placed in institutions or fostered out to white homes.

The impact on the cultural and social fabric was devastating, and the effects are still being felt today. Children were divorced from their home, culture and language, often losing contact completely with their families. Many were not even aware of their Aboriginal background. Poor records make it impossible to give precise numbers, but it is thought that 100,000 people were affected from 1910 to the 1970s, when the policy was halted.

FIGHTING BACK

During the 18th and 19th centuries, many indigenous Australians pursued campaigns of armed resistance. The 20th century was marked by the growth of political activism, which led to an acknowledgement of the past and the beginning of a process of reconciliation.

Aboriginal communities in the 1920s and 1930s campaigned for the abolition of the paternalistic protection system. Actions of dissent – such as an Aboriginal elder protesting at the opening of Parliament House in Canberra in 1927, and the establishment in Sydney of a Day of Mourning on 26 January 1938, while Australia celebrated 150 years of white settlement, were the beginning of a movement that would gain momentum.

In the 1950s, as the appalling conditions endured by many Aboriginal people became known, sympathetic white Australians, church groups and unions opened a public debate. 'Freedom rides' across New South Wales in 1965 exposed the unofficial but prevalent exclusion of Aboriginals from schools, shops, bars, swimming pools and cinemas. The following year, the Gurindji people at Wave Hill cattle station in the Northern Territory went on strike for better wages and conditions. This turned into demands for land rights and self-determination, and is seen as the beginning of the modern land rights movement. When the Aboriginal Tent Embassy was set up in 1972 outside Parliament House in Canberra, flying the newly designed Aboriginal flag, it became apparent to white Australia that the days of 'putting up and shutting up' were over.

After years of activism and lobbying, attitudes slowly, and often reluctantly, began to shift. In 1967, more than 90 per cent of Australians voted in a national referendum to empower the federal government to make legislation in the interests of indigenous people and to count them as citizens in the census.

In 1987 Prime Minister Bob Hawke set up a Royal Commission into Aboriginal Deaths in Custody in response to the disproportionate scale of indigenous incarceration and deaths in prison. It became the fullest study of Aboriginal experience in Australia's history. The resulting 1991 report made 339 recommendations, one of which was the establishment of a formal process of reconciliation.

The idea of reconciliation was fine for most Australians, but it was a different story when it came to land. The 'Mabo' court case in 1992 sent shock waves through Australian society. The British had claimed Australia without treaty or payment because they categorised it as *terra nullius* – land belonging to nobody. The Mabo decision recognised for the first time that indigenous Australians were the original inhabitants of the land, and British settlement did not necessarily extinguish their native title or ownership. This precedent gave farmers and mining interests the heebie-jeebies, and a scare campaign insinuated that everything from the Sydney Opera House to the family home could be clawed back. The 1993 Native Title Act allowed indigenous people to claim government land, excluding freehold title, if they could prove continuous connection with it since 1788.

Fear and uncertainty about potential land claims grew in 1996 when another high court decision, known as Wik, indicated that native title claims could be lodged on some farmland. Under pressure from business interests, the Howard government watered down these rights. To the relief of many, land-claims cases get tied up in court for years, and the predicted wave of land grabs has never materialised.

SORRY BUSINESS

In 1997 a state-sponsored enquiry into the 'stolen generations' produced a startling and controversial report, *Bringing Them Home*. The response of the federal government was decidedly lukewarm. Unwilling to risk compensation claims, and reflecting the contemporary wave of racially inflammatory nationalism, Prime Minister Howard declined to apologise. Instead, he issued a statement of regret. The government did, however, cough up an initial reparations package of $63 million.

Many other Australians, however, were shocked and ashamed, and a wave of reconciliation activity ensued. In 1998 over a million people signed 'sorry books' and the first national Sorry Day was set up on 26 May. Two years later, the People's Walk for Reconciliation saw an unprecedented 300,000 people march across Sydney Harbour Bridge.

Since this short-lived flurry of reconciliation fervour from white Australians, Aboriginal issues have largely fallen off the public agenda. Current mainstream media coverage of indigenous affairs is generally confined to sensational reporting of bad-news stories such as petrol sniffing or the 2004 Redfern riots.

Admittedly, there is a lot of bad news to be had. An indigenous young person is 21 times more likely to go to prison than his or her non-indigenous peer. Aboriginal people can expect to live 20 to 25 years less than the rest of the population. They suffer persistent problems of economic disadvantage, substance abuse, domestic violence and discrimination, exacerbated by limited access to employment, education, health facilities and social services in the remote areas where many live.

There is a simmering tension present in many communities that is frequently turned inwards but occasionally explodes outwards. The Palm Island riots in November 2004 (which began after a coroner's report into a death in custody cleared the police of any wrongdoing) highlights in an extreme way the kinds of problems found in remote communities. Off the coast of Townsville in North Queensland, Palm Island was established as a reserve in 1918 and became a de facto prison for Aboriginal people from across Australia. Today it is reported to have 95 per cent unemployment and 90 per cent illiteracy, with 3,500 people living in about 220 houses and a disturbingly high rate of youth suicide and domestic murders.

THE NEW DEAL

Within the indigenous community there are heated voices and often contradictory views on the way ahead, with claims that there has been too much of an emphasis on land rights and apologies, an unhelpful sense of victimhood and not enough economic self-determination. Passively accepting government handouts, 'sit-down money', is seen by some as perpetuating the problems, as is the unfocused tinkering by successive governments and overbearing bureaucracy. The emphasis now is on targeting money, finding innovative long-term social solutions and involving the indigenous community fully in decision-making.

Small-scale innovations include 'circle sentencing', in which Aboriginal offenders face a panel of members of their community, and sometimes their victim, who collectively decide the sentence. This has proved highly successful, with the rate of re-offence far below average. Some communities have become alcohol-free. Others have campaigned for funding to support non-sniffable petrol in their region.

On a political level, Prime Minister John Howard's conservative government has firmly steered debate away from contemplation of past wrongs, which he has dubbed 'the black armband view of history', and symbolic

gestures such as an official apology, preferring to concentrate on 'practical reconciliation'.

This has proved extremely contentious. In 2005 Australia's first and only directly elected national indigenous body, the Aboriginal and Torres Strait Islander Commission (ATSIC), and its regional councils were abolished, with the support of the opposition Labor party. Set up in the late 1980s, ATSIC was supposed to open a new era of self-determination, but was plagued by accusations of financial mismanagement and poor leadership that overshadowed its successes. The creation in 2004 of the National Indigenous Council (NIC), its 14 members hand-picked by the government, has further infuriated many indigenous people.

'Radical initiatives are under discussion, such as private ownership of land within communities.'

Many see the shift from a national approach, represented by ATSIC, to a tactic of direct negotiation with individual communities as a return to the patronising and paternalistic relationships of the past. For instance, under the new 'shared responsibility agreements' (SRAs), communities agree to behavioural change in return for government money. The 'no school, no pool' rule is one such deal, in which school attendance is tied to the construction and use of a swimming pool. These trials have been hailed a success, with pools helping reduce skin and eye diseases and school attendance rates soaring, but critics see the SRAs as poorly researched PR exercises that solve only part of the problem. In one town, a sudden influx of hundreds of extra children found the under-funded local school without enough desks or teachers, and half the new children had to be sent home for that year.

Other radical government initiatives under discussion, such as introducing private ownership of land within communities, have been met with concern. Many also ask why the indigenous community has been singled out and made to sign 'incentive and sanctions' deals to get services that other Australians regard as a right rather than a privilege.

Whatever governments do, the increasing number of well-educated indigenous people able to navigate bureaucracy and better able to represent their communities is offering hope for the future. Aboriginal communities are getting on with the job, trying to solve their own problems independently, a process that is beginning to see pockets of success.

Sydney Today

Race riots, real estate and roads: is the strain showing?

Everything you've read is true: Sydney really is vibrant, bursts with creativity and sprawls lazily around a handsome sun-kissed harbour. For many of its four million-plus inhabitants, it offers a standard of living that few other cities can hope to match. It's Australia's premier place to live: nowhere else comes close, not even Melbourne, fated to be the perpetual bridesmaid to Sydney's bride. It's popular with overseas visitors too, being regularly voted one of the world's favourite holiday destinations. In 2005 the *Los Angeles Times* proclaimed it the best place on earth to eat out, causing locals to smile contentedly at what they've known for years, only later to snarl in frustration as their favourite restaurants filled up with out-of-towners.

However, as 2005 drew to a close the kind of publicity Sydney was getting in the local and world media was something it could well have done without. Lurid stories of race-related violence, the threat of terrorist attacks, collapsing infrastructure and the strain put on the environment by population growth and increased development: the bad news combined to leave Sydneysiders wondering if their lucky city was so lucky after all.

TWO TRIBES GO TO WAR

Churchill's rallying cry 'We will fight them on the beaches' came to haunt Sydney in December 2005 when race riots swept through the southern beachside suburbs of Cronulla, Brighton-le-Sands, Miranda, Rockdale and Maroubra. The focus was Cronulla, where only 13 per cent of residents are foreign-born, as opposed to a greater Sydney average of 31 per cent. Here thousands of predominantly white, Anglo-Celtic males gathered on the beach ostensibly to protest against the reported bashing of two Cronulla lifesavers by men said to be of a Middle Eastern background.

A dangerous combination of alcohol, heat and jingoism resulted in rampaging attacks on anyone suspected of being of Lebanese descent – a 'Leb' – women included, and the smashing up of cars and property. This behaviour was later seen as the inevitable result of brewing ethnic tensions and the clash between what one commentator dubbed the 'yobbo beach tribes and the Lebanese gangsta tribes'.

A foretaste of such social unrest had occurred earlier in the year, when riots flared in the south-west suburb of Macquarie Fields after a police chase of a stolen car led to the deaths of two popular teenagers. Those with longer memories, however, knew that beachside violence was not a new phenomenon. Back in the 1960s the self-same Sydney beaches saw gang warfare between local surfies and the so-called 'rockies' from the western suburbs, a Down Under replay of the Mods and Rockers skirmishes in Britain of the same era. If Kathy Lette and Gabrielle Carey's cult 1979 novel *Puberty Blues*, also set in Cronulla, is anything to go by – and there are many who attest it is – by the 1970s surf culture had hardened into a dangerously tribal and sexist mould that manifests itself today in groups such as Maroubra's Bra Boys. Rub these mean surfer guys up the wrong way and the results can be very nasty – just ask the 30 police injured in a brawl with them at Coogee RSL in 2002.

Two days after the worst of the riots, the Bra Boys did their bit for racial harmony, standing side by side with their rivals, the Comancheros (which has a large Lebanese membership), and spokespeople for the Lebanese community to appeal for calm and an easing of tension. Meanwhile, a gulf in perceptions of the events persisted between the prime minister, John Howard, who insisted that Australians by and large were not racist, and Keysar Trad, president of the Islamic Friendship Association of Australia, who was adamant that the riots had been 'the ugliest manifestation of racism' seen so far in the country.

TERRORISM FEARS
Relations between Sydney's Muslims and the rest of the population were already under strain when the riots kicked off. In November 2005, hundreds of police swooped on houses in predominantly Muslim areas of Sydney and Melbourne, arresting 15 people believed to be involved in plotting a bomb attack. It's alleged that the group, six of whom were in Sydney, had stockpiled enough chemicals to make at least 15 large bombs similar to those detonated in London in July 2005: one target is thought to have been Sydney's Lucas Heights nuclear reactor. Bizarrely, one of the suspects, 28-year-old Omar Balajdam, who was shot during his arrest and charged with the attempted murder

of two police officers, had once had a small role in the soap opera *Home and Away*. While apprehensive at the events, few locals were surprised: given Australia's shoulder-to-shoulder stance with the US and UK during the Iraq war it was only a matter of time before Sydney became a theatre of the 'War on Terror'.

'There was public outrage when John Brogden referred to Bob Carr's Malaysian-born wife as a "mail-order bride".'

The riots were a wake-up call for Sydney, though, a timely reminder that despite it being a very multicultural city, populated with immigrants from 180 nations, there was no room for complacency when it came to race relations or encouraging greater acceptance of diversity. It's not been all bad news on the race-relations front, though. When the Socceroos, the national soccer team, qualified for the 2006 World Cup in November 2005 at Sydney's Telstra Stadium, the crowd who cheered them on contained many immigrants, all proud Australians that day whether of European, Middle Eastern, African or Asian descent.

Sydneysiders of all cultural backgrounds also united with other Australians to campaign (unsuccessfully) for the reprieve of Nguyen Tuong Van, a former Vietnamese boat child and Australian citizen, from his death sentence in Singapore for drug smuggling. And there was public outrage when NSW Liberal party leader John Brogden drunkenly referred to former NSW premier Bob Carr's Malaysian-born wife Helena as a 'mail-order bride'. Brogden resigned and subsequently attempted suicide.

GETTING REAL ABOUT REAL ESTATE
Sydney's race-relations issues may be challenging, but a far worse headache for many Sydneysiders has been the downturn in property prices following an extended boom. In a city where no one blinks an eye at asking, or readily revealing, the cost of a property (it's all published in the newspapers anyway) there was a communal groan when it was reported that prices had slid by an average of ten per cent since the peak in 2003. Mortgage industry heavyweight John Symonds proclaimed now was the time to sell or risk losing even more money on property, while the OECD – the global club for rich democracies – reported that Australia had the most overvalued houses of all its members, with prices 52 per cent higher than what is justified by rental values.

With several high-profile residential blocks just, or soon to be, completed in the city centre, developers and real estate agents, fearful for their investments and commissions, begged to differ about the state of the property market. They perhaps have a point. The state government envisages the city's population swelling to 5.3 million by 2031: in the CBD area alone it's reckoned that the number of residents will almost double from 150,000 to 280,000. Where all these people will live is anyone's guess, especially as Sydney's city government aims to limit residential development in the CBD and concentrate on providing for business. To this end, it's spending over $50 million in the next four years to improve facilities and services across such southern suburbs as Redfern, Darlington, Waterloo and Everleigh.

'The Cross City Tunnel is a flop, as motorists squeeze into the few roads allowed to traffic in the city centre.'

The likely increase in a city-centre customer base came as cold comfort to Gowings, the male outfitters and department store beloved by generations of Sydneysiders. On 29 January 2006, after 138 years in business, the doors closed on Gowings' landmark site on the corner of George and Market Streets after the bankrupt company failed to find an investor to bail it out.

ON THE ROAD TO GRIDLOCK
Some three-quarters of Sydney's commuters currently use their own transport to get to work, which translates into one enormous traffic problem for the city. In an effort to deal with the growing congestion, investment has been made in new public transport routes, although projects such as the airport rail line (built for the Olympics), the Epping-to-Chatswood rail link in the north of Sydney and a bus-only route from Liverpool to Parramatta are notorious for their budget blow-outs rather than for their success in easing traffic. Lord Mayor Clover Moore (*see p26* **The sweet smell of Clover**), wants a city-centre congestion tax, similar to the one that has been so successful in London. But she can't introduce such a tax without state government agreement, and so far this hasn't been forthcoming.

Instead, the state government remains fixed on providing more roads and tunnels, with the eventual aim of creating an orbital motorway encircling the city – all of which, many point out, will inevitably lead to increased traffic. A parliamentary inquiry was launched in November 2005 into the brand-new Cross City Tunnel, an electronic-tag toll road designed to ease east-west travel through the CBD, and a key infrastructure project of Bob Carr's administration. The tunnel is considered a flop, since it is clocking up between 20,000 and 30,000 vehicles a day compared to the envisaged 90,000. Instead of easing congestion it has led to even more chaos, as toll-avoiding motorists squeeze into the few roads allowed to traffic in the city centre. At the inquiry Carr and his former treasurer Michael Egan stood by their decision to back the tunnel, built with private money, which they believe will eventually be better patronised. Carr's successor as premier, Morris Iemma, however, is less than enamoured with the project and has repeatedly urged the company operating it to cut the toll to encourage more drivers to use it.

ELECTION JITTERS
Transport policy isn't the only controversial hangover from the Carr regime that Iemma has had to deal with. Droughts have meant Sydney has long battled to provide a steady supply of water for its citizens. Carr's team favoured building a $1.3-billion desalination plant,

Trouble brewing at **Cronulla Beach**, 11 December 2005. *See p23.*

The sweet smell of Clover

It was all change on Sydney's political scene during 2005, with the Labor party's Morris Iemma taking over as NSW premier following Bob Carr's retirement and Peter Debnam replacing John Brogden as leader of the NSW opposition Liberal party, not to mention Mark Latham resigning as the leader of the federal Labor party. Practically unscathed, though, was Clover Moore (www.clovermoore.com), independent member of the inner-city parliamentary constituency of Bligh, as well as lord mayor of the City of Sydney.

A former teacher and mother of two university-age children, Moore is a striking figure, rarely seen without her trademark spiky black hair and a generous dash of red lipstick. She's been a state MP since 1988, although she cut her political teeth as a city councillor long before that. Her amazing popularity stems from her defiant independence from all political parties and championing of many public causes. One of her current campaigns is fighting Sydney

Airport's plans to develop a large commercial complex on its land: she supports local residents who know that the area cannot handle the traffic it already has, let alone what a new shopping mall would bring.

Moore's most memorable victory came in 2004 when she was elected lord mayor, the highest-profile council job in Sydney. Labor had thrown $1 million and its formidable party machine behind the candidacy of former federal arts minister Michael Lee, but he limped away with 25 per cent of the primary vote compared to Moore's 39 per cent. The result was in part a reaction against the forced merger by the state government of Sydney and South Sydney councils. However, it was also a personal milestone for Moore, who had failed to secure the mayor's post the last time she ran, back in 1987.

In a challenge to critics who doubted she could successfully juggle her roles as a state MP and mayor, Moore set up a trust to distribute her mayoral salary to charitable and social causes. It's this kind of publicity-grabbing, populist approach that endears her to the public – and she's seen as something of a saint by Sydney's gay community, many of whom Moore represents in her state constituency. The more conservative end of Sydney's political spectrum, though, loathe her and waste no opportunity to pick faults: one memorable grumble was over her supposedly Scrooge-like approach to the city's Christmas decorations in 2004.

Moore pretty much takes it all in her stride – she is in one of Sydney's top political jobs, after all, in charge of the central core of one of the world's top cities. However, her future could be shakier. She's lost some support on the city council and is likely to be challenged by her current deputy for the lord mayorship in 2007. That could be a double-whammy year for the seemingly unsinkable Moore, who will also be fighting to hang on to her state parliamentary seat in the NSW election.

capable of producing 125 megalitres of drinking water a day – around nine per cent of the city's needs – at Kurnell on the southern Sydney coast. Public outcry over the cost and environmental impact of the plant, not to mention the draconian planning laws used to push the project through, has since caused Iemma to put the project on hold indefinitely. The NSW government will still spend $120

million on the project, though, including buying the Kurnell site and building a pilot plant – a sum that could be used, for instance, to provide around 1,200 extra police officers.

With state elections slated for March 2007, Sydney is going to be hearing a lot more about these kind of trade-offs, not to mention how best to tackle transport congestion, law and order, and the need for greater social harmony.

Where to Stay

Where to Stay

When you're tired of being out, Sydney has a great indoors too.

That old saying 'only the strong survive' certainly applies to the hotel game, especially in a city like Sydney. For a long time after the 2000 Olympics bubble burst, things seemed to be going downhill, with many hotels closing or being converted into apartments. But now the good times seem to be back again. Sydney is once more swarming with all kinds of visitors, from long-term backpackers looking for bargains to middle-of-the-road conference delegates to visitors on an Aussie-wide tour. In 2004 Tourism New South Wales launched a $4 million 'There's no place in the world like Sydney' international ad campaign, and by September 2005 the state had recorded its highest accommodation takings in three years. Also in 2005, the Hilton Sydney reopened, showing off a $200 million face-lift – the largest single-site investment ever made by the global hotel mega-brand. It looks like lots of people see a bright future for this city.

From ultra-deluxe five-star palaces to boutique zones of slickness, convenient serviced apartments, contemporary mid-priced hotels and a host of budget options, Sydney has rooms to suit every pocket. Many of the four-star-plus hotels are strung around the central sightseeing areas: the Rocks, Circular Quay, George Street, Hyde Park and Darling Harbour. Meanwhile, a swag of backpacker joints congregate around Kings Cross, nearby Potts Point and Darlinghurst, and at Elizabeth Bay. Staying in these areas means you'll have access to plenty of restaurants and bars, but if you want to see the tourist sights you'll need to catch a CityRail train back into town.

The inner west suburbs, such as Newtown and Glebe, are likewise a short train or bus ride from the city centre, but have the advantage of good pubs and a student atmosphere, if that's more your scene. Newtown's bustling King Street can be noisy and traffic-polluted, but that's just part of its charm.

If you fancy staying near the beach, you can't go wrong with Bondi, Coogee or Manly. The bus journey from Bondi and Coogee into the city can be a pain, but the beach atmosphere is

fabulous. If you stay in Manly (a popular option with British visitors), you're limited by the ferry service from the city, which stops around midnight. For the full seaside experience, head for the northern beaches, such as Newport or the stunning but pricey Palm Beach.

In the end, though, where you stay may depend on when you come. The busiest tourist times are between November and May. The beach areas are packed from mid December to late January, when the school holidays are in full swing. If you want a room during Mardi Gras (February/March) or a harbour view at New Year, you'll have to book well in advance.

Serviced apartments are listed at the end of the chapter, after the hotels and hostels. For assistance with finding the right place at the right price, *see p47* **Room service**.

KEEP IN MIND

● Room prices vary greatly, but in general Sydney is less expensive than many European cities, and you should be able to get a decent double room in the city for around $150 a night.
● In Australia pubs are also called 'hotels'. Many pubs do have rooms at reasonable prices, but standards are mixed, so ask to see the accommodation first. Also check that there is adequate soundproofing.
● Despite increased government intervention, there are still a number of illegal backpacker hostels operating all over Australia. Their flyers are pasted on lamp-posts or pinned to backpacker bulletin boards. While the prices may be tempting, these places can be cramped fire traps that flout accommodation laws. For an up-to-date list of recommended legal hostels, see **www.hostelaustralia.com**, **www.visitnsw.com.au** or **www.yha.com.au**.

ABOUT THE LISTINGS

Most hotels are air-conditioned, but not all – check first if this is an important requirement. Rates quoted below are 'rack' rates, standard prices that are often higher than what you'll pay. It's always worth asking for standby prices, weekly rates or special deals – you may well get them, even in the peak season. Top hotels also often offer discounts at weekends, when business people with a life are sleeping in their own beds. A ten per cent Goods & Services Tax (GST) applies to all hotels and hostels (as well as tours, internal

---

❶ Blue numbers given in this chapter correspond to the location of each hotel as marked on the street maps. *See pp326-334.*

Money well spent: experience designer luxury at the revamped **Hilton Sydney**.

air fares and restaurant meals), and by law it has to be part of the advertised price.

Note that 1800 telephone numbers are toll-free, and 1300 numbers are always charged at a local rate – but these only work within Australia, not if you're dialling from abroad.

The CBD & the Rocks

Deluxe

Four Seasons Hotel Sydney

199 George Street, at Essex Street, CBD, NSW 2000 (1800 221 335/9238 0000/fax 9251 2851/ www.fourseasons.com). CityRail/ferry Circular Quay. **Rooms** 531. **Rates** $350-$555 single/ double; $530-$4,300 suite. **Credit** AmEx, MC, V. **Map** p327 F4 ❶

The former Regent Hotel (some taxi drivers still know it by that name) was bought by Canadian chain Four Seasons in the early 1990s and since then has been quietly delivering an extremely high level of service within very plush digs indeed. It was the official Olympic headquarters in 2000. The decor is expensive-looking in a modern way, with a kind of pared-down opulence. All the rooms are spacious and have marble bathrooms; some overlook Walsh Bay, the Harbour Bridge and the Opera House, while the rest have city views. The 32nd-floor Executive Club caters to high-flying business types with its

corporate concierge, separate check-in and added goodies such as meetings facilities and complimentary refreshments.

Services *Bar. Business centre. Concierge. Disabled-adapted rooms. Gym. Internet (high-speed/wireless pay terminal). No-smoking floors. Pool (outdoor). Restaurants (2). Parking ($33). Room service. Spa. TV (cable).*

Hilton Sydney

488 George Street, between Park & Market Streets, CBD, NSW 2000 (9266 2000/reservations 9265 6045/fax 9265 6065/www.hiltonsydney.com.au). CityRail Town Hall. **Rooms** 577. **Rates** $290-$450 standard room; $315-$475 deluxe room; $635-$1,450 suite. **Credit** AmEx, DC, MC, V. **Map** p327 F6 ❷

After a two-year, mega-million-dollar refit, the Hilton reopened in July 2005 – to universal acclaim. From the light-filled, four-storey high lobby with its spiralling aluminium sculpture (by Australian artist Bronwyn Oliver) to the 31 'relaxation' rooms and suites, this is a classy experience. Some consider the standard rooms to be too small, though the suites are huge. The design throughout is impeccable, with limestone flooring, plush fabrics, mood lighting and (in the suites) open-plan spa bathrooms. Eating and drinking spots include Luke Mangan's Glass brasserie (*see p145*) and wine bar (*see p176*), Zeta cocktail bar (*see p177*) and the historic Marble Bar (established 1893) in the basement, left untouched

during the refurbishment. There are also extensive conference and business facilities, and a top-end health club with gym, indoor pool, saunas and steam rooms. Great views too from the higher floors over nearby Sydney Tower. **Photo** *p29*.
Services *Bars (3). Business centre. Concierge. Disabled adapted rooms. Gym. Internet (high speed). No-smoking rooms. Parking ($32). Pool (indoor). Restaurants (2). Room service. Spa. TV (cable/ DVD/VCR).*

InterContinental Sydney

117 Macquarie Street, at Bridge Street, CBD, NSW 2000 (1800 221 335/9253 9000/fax 9240 1240/www.sydney.intercontinental.com). CityRail/ ferry Circular Quay. **Rooms** 509. **Rates** $680-$830 single/double; $1,100-$4,400 suite. **Credit** AmEx, MC, V. **Map** p327 G4 ❸

This five-star heritage-listed property emerged from a $30 million refurbishment in 2004, and then won a number of prestigious awards the following year. Built in 1851, the building now features such hi-tech extras as high-speed internet access and digital TV in all rooms, plus two TV broadcast and video-conferencing studios. Rooms have a classic-contemporary feel and come with either harbour or city views. Sleek restaurant-lounge bar Mint Bar & Dining serves contemporary cuisine, the sandstone-arcaded Cortile café dispenses traditional high tea and Café Opera offers a seafood buffet. The luxurious rooftop lounge, with its uninterrupted harbour views, is only accessible to Club Inter Continental members, who pay extra for such privileges as a personal concierge service. The vistas from the top over Sydney Harbour are spectacular, and available to all guests from the indoor swimming pool on the 31st floor.
Services *Bars (2). Business centre. Concierge. Disabled-adapted rooms. Gym. Internet (high-speed). No-smoking floors. Parking ($30). Pool (indoor). Restaurants (2). Room service. Spa. TV (cable/ pay movies).*

Observatory Hotel

89-113 Kent Street, between Argyle & High Streets, Millers Point, NSW 2000 (9256 2222/fax 9256 2233/www.observatoryhotel.com.au). CityRail/ ferry Circular Quay. **Rooms** 100. **Rates** $450-$755 single/double; $780-$2,790 suite. **Credit** AmEx, DC, MC, V. **Map** p327 E4 ❹

A consistent favourite among well-heeled visitors, this service-oriented hotel offers pet-friendly rooms, a 'specs box' if you've forgotten your glasses, and even two goldfish companions, Basil and Sybil, who can share your room if you're feeling lonely. Owned by Orient-Express, the hotel's general vibe is one of refined elegance. Rooms are outfitted with colonial Australian antiques and original artworks, plus marble bathrooms, stereo TVs, CD players and high-speed internet points. Most rooms have views of Walsh Bay or Observatory Hill. The hotel's renowned spa, with its indoor pool complete with a sparkling night-sky ceiling, was refurbished and expanded in late 2005.

Services *Bar. Business centre. Concierge. Disabled-adapted rooms. Gym. Internet (high-speed). No-smoking floors. Parking ($40). Pool (indoor). Restaurant. Room service. Spa. TV (cable/pay movies).*

Park Hyatt Sydney

7 Hickson Road, The Rocks, NSW 2000 (9241 1234/fax 9256 1555/www.sydney.park.hyatt.com). CityRail/ferry Circular Quay. **Rooms** 250. **Rates** $475-$555 single/double; $685-$5,500 suite. **Credit** AmEx, DC, MC, V. **Map** p327 F3 ❺

Since opening in 1990 the Park Hyatt has played host to a steady stream of celebrities, heads of state and international jet-setters with money to burn. The jaw-dropping, close-up vista of both the Opera House and the Harbour Bridge is a major selling point, but you get what you pay (a lot) for – cheaper rooms offer just glimpses. Extras include a rooftop swimming pool, deluxe spa and 24-hour butler service. The rooms were redesigned in 2004 and now feature extra windows, mood lighting and sleek leather, marble and stainless steel surfaces. There are also LCD TVs, CD/DVD players, fast internet connections and marble bathrooms. The chic harbour

The best Hotels

For the strictly boutique

Want contemporary style, and don't mind paying for it? Try the **Blacket** (*see p33*), **Establishment** (*see p33*) or **Medusa** (*see p41*). Cheaper are the **Kirketon** (*see p41*) and **Hotel Altamont** (*see p43*).

For visiting the past

Sleep with the rough ghosts of the Rocks at the **Lord Nelson Brewery Hotel** (*see p35*) or the **Russell Hotel** (*see p36*).

For a superior hostel

All the services you could hope for and very low prices at **Footprints Westend** (*see p36*), **Railway Square YHA** (*see p36*) and **wake up!** (*see p37*).

For unassuming style

Surry Hills now has a hotel to match its restaurants: the **Crown**. *See p41*.

For location, location, location

If you fancy cinemas, bookshops and the Oxford Street scene on your doorstep, try **Sullivans Hotel**. *See p44*.

For a wild encounter

Look out for wallabies, kookaburras and possums while staying at the remote and beautiful **Pittwater YHA**. *See p50*.

Park Hyatt Sydney: a rooftop pool and jaw-dropping harbour views. *See p31.*

kitchen&bar restaurant offers yet more amazing views (through floor-to-ceiling glass doors), while the harbourbar is a good spot for cocktails, and the more old-school Club Bar caters to cigar and whisky fans. **Photo** *above*.

Services *Bars (2). Business centre. Concierge. Gym. Internet (high-speed). No smoking. Parking ($26). Pool (indoor). Restaurant. Room service. Spa. TV (cable/DVD/pay movies/satellite).*

Shangri-La Hotel

176 Cumberland Street, between Essex & Argyle Streets, The Rocks, NSW 2000 (9250 6000/ fax 9250 6250/www.shangri-la.com). CityRail/ferry Circular Quay. **Rooms** 562. **Rates** $292-$362 single/double; $605-$3,294 suite. **Credit** AmEx, DC, MC, V. **Map** p327 E4 ⑥

Ideally located between the Opera House and the Harbour Bridge, this is another five-star spot with undeniably breathtaking views – from every room. A $37 million refurbishment was completed in 2005. New features include the Horizon Club executive lounge on the 30th floor, with its 18m/60ft-high glass atrium, and the swanky Blu Horizon cocktail bar and Altitude restaurant on the 36th floor, both of which offer unbeatable picture-postcard views of the Harbour Bridge, the harbour itself stretching north, and the Opera House. The generously sized rooms have a work desk and high-speed internet access, plus marble bathrooms with separate bath and shower. There's also a gym and indoor swimming pool. **Photo** *p33*.

Services *Bar. Business centre. Concierge. Disabled-adapted rooms. Gym. Internet (high-speed). No-smoking floors. Pool (indoor). Restaurants (2). Room service. Spa. TV (cable/DVD).*

Sheraton on the Park

161 Elizabeth Street, between Market & Park Streets, CBD, NSW 2000 (1800 073 535/9286 6000/ fax 9286 6686/www.sheraton.com). CityRail St James. **Rooms** 557. **Rates** $270-$590 single/double; $555-$3,630 suite. **Credit** AmEx, DC, MC, V. **Map** p327 F6 ⑦

Overlooking bucolic Hyde Park, this award-winning hotel is huge, with 557 rooms and suites, and occupies a prime location in the central business and shopping district. The grand lobby screams luxury with its massive black marble pillars and curved staircase, and the rooms have a refined, modern and quasi-nautical design theme (all stripes and circles), and feature black marble bathrooms. There's a spacious pool and fitness centre on level 26, the Conservatory Bar on level 21 and a tea lounge off the lobby, which offers 'contemporary' high tea served by stylish black-clad waiters. The Meetings on 5 is an executive meeting centre with outdoor terraces and concierge services.

Services *Bar. Business centre. Concierge. Disabled-adapted rooms. Gym. Internet (high-speed). No-smoking floors. Parking ($40). Pool (indoor). Restaurant. Room service. Spa. TV (cable).*

Westin Sydney

1 Martin Place, between Pitt & George Streets, CBD, NSW 2000 (1800 656 535/8223 1111/ fax 8223 1222/www.westin.com). CityRail Martin Place. **Rooms** 416. **Rates** $525-$625 single/double; $900-$3,500 suite. **Credit** AmEx, DC, MC, V. **Map** p327 F5 ⑧

Here you get the best of both worlds – a sense of history married to some very contemporary design and deluxe service. Located in pedestrianised Martin

Place, smack-dab in the middle of the CBD, the Westin is partly housed in what used to be the General Post Office, built in 1887. Rooms in the heritage-listed building feature high ceilings and period details, while tower rooms have floor-to-ceiling city views and a more contemporary look (think stainless steel and pale wood). There is a renowned spa and a spectacular atrium as well as a selection of restaurants and bars in the GPO building. Exercise addicts take note: since October 2005 the hotel has offered 'Workout Rooms', which cost only a little extra, complete with treadmill, weights, a yoga mat and other fitness paraphernalia.
Services *Bar. Business centre. Concierge. Disabled-adapted rooms. Gym. Internet (high-speed). No-smoking rooms. Parking ($35). Pool (indoor). Restaurant. Room service. Spa. TV (cable/pay movies).*

Expensive

Avillion Hotel

389 Pitt Street, at Liverpool Street, CBD, NSW 2000 (1800 838 830/8268 1888/fax 9283 5899/ www.avillion.com.au). CityRail Central or Town Hall/Monorail World Square/LightRail Central.
Rooms 443. **Rates** $350-$410 twin/double; $480 family; $690-$750 suite. **Credit** AmEx, DC, MC, V.
Map p329 F8 ❾
Located in the new shopping and entertainment precinct World Square, the Avillion is a dependable four-star option within walking distance of Darling Harbour, Chinatown and the Queen Victoria Building. There's a large fitness centre and a retail plaza connects to the lower lobby. On Fridays, the hotel restaurant, Avery's, presents live jazz. Next door are cocktail lounges V Bar and Uber. Check the website – there are deals to be had.
Services *Bar. Business centre. Concierge. Disabled-adapted rooms. Gym. Internet (high-speed). No-smoking floors. Parking ($30). Restaurant. Room service. TV (cable/pay movies/satellite).*

Blacket

70 King Street, at George Street, CBD, NSW 2000 (9279 3030/fax 9279 3020/www.theblacket. com). CityRail Martin Place or Wynyard.
Rooms 41. **Rates** $210-$230 single/double; from $285 apartment. **Credit** AmEx, DC, MC, V.
Map p327 E6 ❿
A boutique hotel, with a typically boutique aesthetic: muted colours, running the gamut from charcoal to beige, match the clean lines and minimalist furniture. Opened in 2001, the Blacket is housed in a 19th-century bank building designed by architect Edmund Blacket, so there are a few period flourishes here and there. But the hotel's restaurant, Level Three, is very 21st-century – all glass, chrome and white leather booths – while the Privilege Bar in the basement draws a young urban crowd with its drink specials and DJs.
Services *Bars (2). Concierge. No-smoking rooms. Parking ($25). Restaurant. Room service. TV.*

Establishment

5 Bridge Lane, at George Street, CBD, NSW 2000 (9240 3100/3110/fax 9240 3101/www.establishment hotel.com). CityRail Circular Quay or Wynyard/ ferry Circular Quay. **Rooms** 35. **Rates** $330-$385 single/double; $970-$1,150 suite. **Credit** AmEx, DC, MC, V. **Map** p327 F5 ⓫
Though it has only 33 rooms and two two-storey penthouse suites, the Establishment's cool clout far outweighs its capacity. Exceedingly stylish, this place would be perfectly at home in the smarter districts of London or New York. Catering to celebrities, fashionistas and those with deep pockets, the complex incorporates two critically acclaimed restaurants, Sushi e (*see p143*) and est. (*see p147*), three bars including Hemmesphere (*see p176*) and a popular nightclub, Tank (*see p222*). As for the guest rooms, half are all sharp angles, minimalist Japanese elements and flashes of bright colour, while the others are more subdued – choose what suits your mood. Expect luxurious touches at every turn (think Philippe Starck taps, Bulgari toiletries, Bose stereo systems).
Services *Bars (3). Business centre. Concierge. Gym. Internet (high-speed). No-smoking floor. Restaurants (3). Room service. TV (cable/DVD).*

Shangri-La Hotel See p32.

Where to Stay

Four Points by Sheraton Darling Harbour

161 Sussex Street, at Market Street, CBD, NSW 2000 (1800 074 545/9290 4000/fax 9290 4040/ www.fourpoints.com). CityRail Town Hall/ferry Darling Harbour/Monorail Darling Park. **Rooms** 630. **Rates** $225-$360 single/double; $290-$2,100 suite. **Credit** AmEx, DC, MC, V. **Map** p327 E6 ⑫

With 630 rooms including 45 suites, this place caters to large tour groups, executives and the international conference crowd: the Sydney Convention & Exhibition Centre is a stone's throw away, and the hotel is within walking distance of several museums as well as Chinatown and the central business and shopping districts. All mod cons are provided, such as high-speed wireless internet, large work desks and cable TV. Some rooms have balconies overlooking Darling Harbour. There are high-tech conferencing facilities, a fitness centre and a sprawling shopping centre with a food court. The glassed-in Corn Exchange restaurant offers an elaborate seafood buffet, while the historic Dundee Arms pub, built in the 1850s, specialises in barbecued pub grub and locally brewed beer.

Services *Bars (2). Business centre. Concierge. Disabled-adapted rooms. Gym. Internet (wireless). No-smoking floors. Parking ($34). Restaurant. Room service. TV (cable/pay movies).*

Grace Hotel

77 York Street, at King Street, CBD, NSW 2000 (9272 6888/fax 9299 8189/www.gracehotel.com.au). CityRail Martin Place or Wynyard. **Rooms** 382. **Rates** $410-$450 single/double; $585 suite; extra $49.50 per person for triple. **Credit** AmEx, DC, MC, V. **Map** p327 E6 ⑬

This charming hotel is housed in an 11-storey corner block – a loose copy of the Tribune Tower in Chicago – that began life in 1930 as the headquarters of department store giant Grace Brothers. During World War II it was where General MacArthur directed South Pacific operations. A total refurbishment was completed in 2005, but many of the original features, such as the lifts, stairwells, marble floors and ornate ironwork, have been retained and restored to great effect. Rooms, however, are modern, large and comfortable, and all have bathtubs. The indoor heated lap pool is small, but there is a sauna and a steam room, plus a sun-filled fitness centre and rooftop terrace. Check the website for special offers; there are often deals to be had.

Services *Bars (2). Concierge. Disabled-adapted rooms. Gym. Internet (high-speed). No-smoking floors. Parking ($30). Pool (indoor). Restaurant. Room service. Spa. TV (pay movies).*

Sebel Pier One

11 Hickson Road, on Dawes Point, Walsh Bay, NSW 2000 (1800 780 485/8298 9999/fax 8298 9777/www.mirvachotels.com). CityRail/ ferry Circular Quay then 15mins walk. **Rooms** 160. **Rates** $440-$600 single/double; $760 suite. **Credit** AmEx, DC, MC, V. **Map** p327 F2 ⑭

Another successful marriage of historic architecture and contemporary design, this sleek, chic boutique hotel has water views in the most unexpected places, including beneath your feet: the glass floor in the lobby is quite the showpiece. Located in a converted warehouse at the quiet end of the Rocks, you can almost reach out and touch the Harbour Bridge. Rooms have views over serene Walsh Bay or partial Bridge views, wireless internet connection, original wooden beams and modern furnishings. The refurbished Front restaurant and wine bar offers alfresco dining and cocktails on the water, while the private pontoon is highly convenient for those travelling by water taxi or private yacht.

Services *Bar. Business centre. Concierge. Disabled-adapted rooms. Gym. Internet (high-speed). No smoking. Parking ($25). Restaurant. Room service. TV (cable/pay movies).*

Moderate

Central Park Hotel

185 Castlereagh Street, at Park Street, CBD, NSW 2000 (9283 5000/fax 9283 2710/ www.centralpark.com.au). CityRail Town Hall/ Monorail Galeries Victoria. **Rooms** 35. **Rates** from $160 single/double; from $170 studio; from $210 suite. **Credit** AmEx, DC, MC, V. **Map** p329 F7 ⑮

With its motto 'hip on a budget', the Blacket's (*see p33*) less expensive little sister is perfect for those who love to be in the heart of the action. Located on the busy corner of Park and Castlereagh Streets, this compact hotel has standard en suite rooms, 'studios' with an additional double sofa bed and a spa bath, and seven airy, two-storey loft apartments that can sleep up to four people. Some rooms overlook Hyde Park. Perched above a busy bar, restaurant and gaming room complex, the noise is kept to a minimum with soundproofing and window seals.

Services *Concierge. Disabled-adapted rooms. Internet (dataport). No-smoking floors. Parking ($40). TV (cable/DVD).*

Lord Nelson Brewery Hotel

19 Kent Street, at Argyle Street, Millers Point, NSW 2000 (9251 4044/fax 9251 1532/ www.lordnelson.com.au). CityRail/ferry Circular Quay. **Rooms** 9. **Rates** $120-$180 double. **Credit** AmEx, DC, MC, V. **Map** p327 E3 ⑯

Time marches on, but you wouldn't know it at the Lord Nelson. Though the clean and relatively spacious Victorian-style rooms were refurbished in 1999 and are air-conditioned these days, the look and feel of the place is pure 19th-century colonial – the pub opened in 1841 and claims to be the oldest in the city. There are only nine guest rooms, all with original bare sandstone walls, and most en suite. The laid-back downstairs brasserie serves contemporary Australian cuisine, while the bar and microbrewery (*see p176*) draw a lively crowd.

Services *Bar. Internet (dataport). No smoking. Restaurant. TV.*

Palisade Hotel

35 Bettington Street, at Argyle Street, Millers Point, NSW 2000 (9247 2272/fax 9247 2040/ www.palisadehotel.com). CityRail/ferry Circular Quay. **Rooms** 11. **Rates** $123-$128 single/double. **Credit** AmEx, DC, MC, V. **Map** p326 D3 🔞

Things are pretty basic at the Palisade – no air-conditioning, lift or private bathrooms – but if you're looking for views and old-time charm at very affordable prices, this is a good choice. Another historic Rocks property, the Palisade was built in 1916, and behind its imposing brown brick façade are a popular pub, with crackling log fires in winter, and a seriously good restaurant (*see p147*) that attracts the pre-theatre crowd. Hot tip: when booking, request one of the rooms on an upper floor, as these provide the best harbour views.

Services *Bar. No smoking. Payphone. Restaurant.*

Russell

143A George Street, at Globe Street, The Rocks, NSW 2000 (9241 3543/fax 9252 1652/ www.therussell.com.au). CityRail/ferry Circular Quay. **Rooms** 29. **Rates** $140-$195 double shared bath; $235-$270 double en suite; $280 suite. **Credit** AmEx, DC, MC, V. **Map** p327 F4 🔞

With a great location in the middle of the Rocks, just a stroll away from the hustle and bustle of Circular Quay, the Russell feels like a cosy country B&B. Housed in a turreted 1840s building, rooms feature such period flourishes as ornate fireplaces, antique brass beds, marble washbasins, pine dressers and floral bedspreads and wallpapers. Some rooms are en suite and some have portable air-conditioners. There's also the pleasant Acacia restaurant-cum-breakfast room on the ground floor, the historic Fortune of War pub and a tiny rooftop garden.

Services *Bar. Internet (shared terminal). No smoking. Parking ($30). Restaurant. TV.*

Budget

Footprints Westend

412 Pitt Street, between Goulburn & Campbell Streets, CBD, NSW 2000 (1800 013 186/9211 4588/fax 9211 5312/www.footprintswestend. com.au). CityRail Central or Museum/LightRail Central. **Rooms** 90. **Rates** $23-$30 dorm; $70 twin; $80 double. **Credit** MC, V. **Map** p329 F8 🔞

Who says backpackers have it rough? Located just around the corner from Central Station, this clean and modern award-winning budget option was completely refurbished in 2005. There are laundry facilities, a commercial-grade kitchen and extras geared toward working holidaymakers such as an in-house employment and travel agency. Rooms (most with air-con) are either en suite or have a private bathroom adjacent. Reception is open 24 hours, beakfast is just two dollars and airport transfers are offered to guests staying for three or more nights.

Services *Café. Disabled-adapted room. Internet (high-speed pay terminal). Kitchen. Laundry. No smoking. Payphone. TV (TV room).*

Pensione

631-635 George Street, between Goulburn & Campbell Streets, CBD, NSW 2000 (1800 885 886/ 9265 8888/fax 9211 9825/www.pensione.com.au). CityRail Central/Monorail World Square. **Rooms** 68. **Rates** from $99 single; $115 double/twin; $140 triple; $165 quad. **Credit** AmEx, DC, MC, V. **Map** p329 E8 🔞

The Pensione, which opened at the end of 2004, is part of the Eight Hotels group of affordable, stylish hotels in central Sydney. The location's good if noisy: on the edge of Chinatown opposite the new World Square development, so it's handy for Darling Harbour and the main sights in the city. The layout is somewhat confusing as the hotel straddles two buildings (one an old post office, the other a former hotel) over four levels, with entrances on both Sussex and George Streets. The rooms – all decorated in neutral tones (mushroom, grey, white) vary in size: there are around 15 family rooms, the largest sleeping up to six, but some are tiny. All have private bathrooms, a mini fridge, TV, air-con and phone. There's also a sunny lounge with sofas, a kitchen, laundry facilities and lockers. **Photo** *p37.*

Services *Bar. Disabled-adapted rooms. No smoking. Internet (high-speed). Parking ($22). Restaurant. TV.*

Railway Square YHA

8-10 Lee Street, at Railway Square, Haymarket, NSW 2000 (9281 9666/fax 9281 9688/ www.yha.com.au). CityRail/LightRail Central. **Rooms** 64. **Rates** $28-$34 dorm; $82-$92 twin. **Credit** MC, V. **Map** p329 E9 🔞

This YHA hostel, built in a former parcels shed, is very near its Central hostel (*see below*). The design incorporates a real disused railway platform with some dorms housed in replicas of train carriages (very Harry Potter), with bathrooms in the main building adjacent. Most dorms have four beds and lockers, and there are a couple of en suite double rooms. It's a very clean and bright place, with a large open-plan communal area dotted with red and orange sofas, a big kitchen and an internet café. Mod cons include a small spa pool and air-conditioning. It's very popular, so book ahead. **Photo** *p44.*

Services *Café. Disabled-adapted rooms. Internet (high-speed pay terminals). Kitchen. Laundry. No smoking. Payphone. Pool (outdoor). TV (DVD/TV room).*

Sydney Central YHA

11 Rawson Place, at Pitt Street, CBD, NSW 2000 (9281 9111/fax 9281 9199/www.yha.com.au). CityRail/LightRail Central. **Rooms** 151. **Rates** $31-$35 dorm; $86-$102 twin/double. **Credit** MC, V. **Map** p329 E9 🔞

The largest of the YHA properties in Sydney, this place has it all: kitchen, laundry, separate games, dining and TV rooms, high-speed internet terminals, mini supermarket, café, underground bar and a recently renovated rooftop pool, sauna and barbecue area with panoramic city views. Popular activities include pub crawls, big-screen movie nights and walking tours. All this is housed in an imposing, heritage-listed building opposite Central Station. There are around 50 twin rooms, some en suite, and dorms that sleep up to eight.

Services *Bar. Disabled-adapted rooms. Internet (high-speed pay terminals). Kitchen. Laundry. No smoking. Parking ($12-$14). Payphone. Pool (outdoor). Restaurant. TV (TV rooms).*

wake up!

509 Pitt Street, at George Street, Haymarket, NSW 2000 (1800 800 945/9288 7888/fax 9288 7889/www.wakeup.com.au).CityRail/LightRail Central. **Rooms** 500 beds. **Rates** $24-$34 dorm; $88-$98 double/twin. **Credit** MC, V. **Map** p329 E9 ㉓

This award-winning hostel is part of that new breed – big, clean, efficiently run and with very proactive security despite the party atmosphere. A major refurbishment is planned for 2006, which will see a revamp of the reception area, more flat-screen TVs throughout the common areas, and a wireless internet hotspot. Located opposite Central Station, the air-conditioned dorms sleep four, six, eight or ten, and some are women-only. There are also double and twin rooms, some with private showers. Bedlinen is provided, and services include a travel agency, postage service, digital photo processing, high-speed internet portals and 24-hour check-in. The bar is a popular backpackers' pick-up spot. **Photo** *p43*.

Services *Bar. Disabled-adapted rooms. Internet (high-speed pay terminals). Kitchen. Laundry. No smoking. Payphone. Restaurant. TV (DVD/ TV room).*

Y Hotel Hyde Park

5-11 Wentworth Avenue, at Liverpool Street, CBD, NSW 2010 (1800 994 994/9264 2451/fax 9285 6288/www.yhotel.com.au). CityRail Museum. **Rooms** 121. **Rates** $33 dorm; $74-$116 single; $88-$132 double/twin; $110-$145 triple. **Credit** AmEx, MC, V. **Map** p329 G8 ㉔

Run by the venerable old YWCA, this spot attracts all kinds (and both sexes), from budget-conscious business travellers to families and young singles. Deluxe rooms, corporate and studio rooms are all en

The **Pensione**: for travellers who want low-priced style. *See p36.*

suite and come with TV, fridge and high-speed internet connection. Family rooms have three beds, while backpacker rooms sleep four. All are clean and contemporary and have basic furniture. Rates include continental breakfast. The location, just south of Hyde Park, is fantastic.

Services *Internet (high-speed). Laundry. No smoking. Parking ($17.50). Payphone. TV (TV room).*

Darling Harbour & Pyrmont

Deluxe

Star City Hotel & Serviced Apartments

80 Pyrmont Street, between Jones Bay Road & Union Street, Pyrmont, NSW 2009 (1800 700 700/ 9657 8393/fax 9657 8345/www.starcity.com.au). LightRail Star City/Monorail Harbourside/bus 443, 449. **Rooms** 482. **Rates** $550-$1,020 apartment; $550-$4,000 suite. **Credit** AmEx, DC, MC, V. **Map** p326 C6 ⑮

Gambling's big in Australia. And nowhere is it bigger than at this little slice of Las Vegas, Oz-style. The numbers are dizzying: 306 standard rooms, 43 suites with 24-hour butler service, two penthouses, 131 fully serviced apartments, 13 restaurants and bars, two theatres and – of course – a casino that's open 24 hours a day. Facilities include a spa and health club and an indoor-outdoor pool with panoramic views of the city. In 2005 the serviced apartments and Astral (*see p151*), the modern French restaurant on the 17th floor of the hotel, emerged from multi-million-dollar redesigns.

Services *Bars (6). Business centre. Concierge. Disabled-adapted rooms. Gym. Internet (high-speed). No-smoking floors. Parking ($34). Pool (outdoor). Restaurants (7). Spa. Room service. TV (cable/pay movies/satellite).*

Expensive

Novotel Sydney on Darling Harbour

100 Murray Street, at Allen Street, Darling Harbour, NSW 2009 (/1300 656 565/9934 0000/fax 9934 0099/www.novotel.com). CityRail Town Hall/Monorail/LightRail Convention. **Rooms** 525. **Rates** $199-$425 single/double; $450-$700 suite. **Credit** AmEx, DC, MC, V. **Map** p328 D7 ⑯

Another option next door to the Sydney Convention & Exhibition Centre and aimed mainly at business travellers. All the rooms should have been refurbished by September 2006. Updated features include LCD TVs, new bathrooms, broadband and wireless internet access, and mobile phone and laptop charging stations. The panoramic harbour and city views are as lovely as they ever were. There are five 'boardrooms' and four 'multi-function' rooms, all equipped with the necessary internet and audio-

visual capabilities. The hotel also has a bar, restaurant, pool, tennis court, gym and sauna.

Services *Bar. Business centres. Concierge. Disabled-adapted rooms. Gym. Internet (high-speed). No-smoking floors. Parking ($20). Pool (outdoor). Restaurant. Room service. TV (cable/pay movies).*

Moderate

Hotel Ibis Darling Harbour

70 Murray Street, at Allen Street, Darling Harbour, NSW 2009 (1300 656 565/9563 0888/fax 9563 0899/www.accorhotels.com.au). CityRail Town Hall/Monorail/LightRail Convention. **Rooms** 256. **Rates** From $149 city view; from $175 harbour view. **Credit** AmEx, DC, MC, V. **Map** p326 D6 ⑰

This is a no-frills, get-what-you-pay-for option in a good location. The rooms are rather basic and on the small side, but considering where you are, it's still good value for your money, especially if you can get a deal – check the website before you book. Some rooms have views of Darling Harbour and the city, others look over Pyrmont. The Skyline bar and restaurant has an outdoor terrace.

Services *Bar. Disabled-adapted rooms. Internet (high-speed). No-smoking floors. Parking ($20). Restaurant. TV (cable).*

Kings Cross, Potts Point & Woolloomooloo

Deluxe

Blue, Woolloomooloo Bay

Woolloomooloo Wharf, 6 Cowper Wharf Road, opposite Forbes Street, Woolloomooloo, NSW 2011 (1800 969 825/9331 9000/fax 9331 9031/ www.tajhotels.com). Bus 311, 312. **Rooms** 100. **Rates** $575-$875 single/double; $775-$2,000 loft. **Credit** AmEx, DC, MC, V. **Map** p330 H6 ⑱

In February 2006 the über-stylish W hotel in the historic Woolloomooloo Wharf was bought by India's luxury hotel and resort chain Taj and renamed Blue. Though small changes are planned here and there, the management maintains it will continue to be the same kind of consistently groovy, five-star property that it's been since opening in 2000. The plush rooms still feature original elements from the old wharf building, and there's still a fitness centre, small indoor pool and the popular Water Bar (*see p183*) – and still no restaurant, though there's an array of high-class, high-priced eateries along the marina edge of the wharf. Rooms on the marina side have the best views. The hotel occupies only part of the swanky wharf development; there's also a complex of exclusive apartments (Russell Crowe owns a pied-à-terre here) and a deluxe holistic spa.

Services *Bar. Business centre. Concierge. Disabled-adapted room. Gym. Internet (high-speed). No-smoking floors. Parking ($35). Pool (indoor). Room service. Spa. TV (cable/DVD/pay movies).*

Fashionable Surry Hills newcomer **Crown Hotel**. See p41.

Moderate

Boutique-hotel group Eight Hotels (www.eight
hotels.com)– which owns **Hotel Altamont**
(see p43), the **Kirketon** (see p41) and the
Pensione (see p36) – is opening a new
flagship hotel in Kings Cross, the **Diamant**
(14 Kings Cross Road, www.diamant.com.au),
in early 2007. The 16-storey, 78-room operation
will offer low-key deluxe accommodation
with king-size beds, 42in plasma-screen TVs,
wireless internet access and a bar/restaurant.
A deluxe room will cost from $200.

Simpsons of Potts Point

*8 Challis Avenue, at Victoria Street, Potts Point,
NSW 2011 (9356 2199/fax 9356 4476/
www.simpsonshotel.com). CityRail Kings Cross.*
Rooms 12. **Rates** $145 single; $175-$315 double;
$325 suite. **Credit** AmEx, DC, MC, V.
Map p330 J6 ㉙
A very elegant and charming place, combining the
stylishness and comforts of a boutique hotel with
the informal sociability of a B&B. Located at the
quieter end of a tree-lined street in Potts Point, the
lovingly restored mansion was built in 1892 and
still retains many of its original arts and crafts
details such as mouldings and fireplaces. The 12
high-ceilinged guest rooms (all en suite and with air-
con) are old-fashioned, but elegantly so, and by no
means dowdy. This is the life: sipping a free sherry
by an open hearth in winter (OK, the fires are gas-
powered imitations), tucking into a continental
breakfast in the conservatory, thumbing through the
hardbacks in the library… Book well in advance as
Simpsons gets a lot of repeat business, and note that
it's hasn't got a licence to sell alcohol.
Services *Internet (wireless). No smoking. Parking
(free). TV.*

Victoria Court Hotel

*122 Victoria Street, between Orwell & Hughes
Streets, Potts Point, NSW 2011 (1800 630 505/
9357 3200/fax 9357 7606/www.victoriacourt.
com.au). CityRail Kings Cross.* **Rooms** 22. **Rates**
$88-$250 single/double. **Credit** AmEx, DC, MC, V.
Map p330 J6 ㉚
Leafy Victoria Street is an interesting mix of posh
restaurants, ramshackle youth hostels and converted Victorian mansions – all just around the corner from the strip clubs and general sleaze of Kings
Cross. This small hotel, formed from two 1881 terraced houses, is a celebration of Victorian extravagance, from the four-poster beds to the floral-printed
everything (carpeting, curtains, wallpaper). All
rooms are air-conditioned and have private bathrooms; some have marble fireplaces and wrought-
iron balconies. Breakfast is served in the gorgeous
plant-filled conservatory.
Services *Internet (dataport/high-speed pay terminal).
No smoking. Parking ($11). TV.*

Budget

Eva's Backpackers

*6-8 Orwell Street, at Victoria Street, Kings Cross,
NSW 2011 (1800 802 517/9358 2185/fax 9358
3259/www.evasbackpackers.com.au). CityRail Kings
Cross.* **Rooms** 28. **Rates** from $28 dorm; $75
double/twin. **Credit** MC, V. **Map** p330 J6 ㉛
With its laid-back atmosphere and reputation for
being very clean and quiet (rare for a backpackers'
hostel in this neighbourhood), Eva's has rightfully
gained a following. There are twin, double and dorm
rooms, some en suite, some with air-conditioning.
Extras include free breakfast, a laundry room with
free washing powder, wake-up calls, luggage storage facilities, broadband internet access and a
rooftop terrace and barbecue area with fabulous

views over Sydney. Located at the (less dodgy) Potts Point end of Kings Cross, it's on a quiet street, but close to everything.
Services *Barbecue. Internet (shared terminal). Kitchen. Laundry. No smoking. Payphone. TV (DVD/TV room).*

O'Malley's Hotel

228 William Street, at Brougham Street, Kings Cross, NSW 2011 (1800 674 631/9357 2211/ fax 9357 2656/www.omalleyshotel.com.au). CityRail Kings Cross. **Rooms** 15. **Rates** $71.50 single/double; $93.50 triple; $104.50 suite. **Credit** MC, V. **Map** p330 H7 ⓬
It may be attached to a popular Irish pub and live music venue, and, yes, it's dangerously close to everything that's wrong with Kings Cross, but don't write off O'Malley's. The 1907 building's 15 en suite and non-smoking rooms have lovely period touches and old-fashioned charm, and the location is quite convenient, just two minutes from the rail station. The Harbour View suite has a kitchen. On Sunday nights between 7.30pm and 8.30pm, try the 'toss the boss' competition: if you guess the flip of a coin right, the drinks are on the house.
Services *Bar. No smoking. Payphone. TV*

Original Backpackers Lodge

160-162 Victoria Street, between Darlinghurst Road and Orwell Street, Kings Cross, NSW 2011 (9356 3232//fax 9368 1435/www.original backpackers.com.au). CityRail Kings Cross. **Rooms** 35. **Rates** $25 dorm; $70 twin/double. **Credit** MC, V. **Map** p330 J7 ⓭
Established in 1980, this sprawling hostel in a Victorian mansion may look a little lived-in, but it's got plenty of character and lots of extras such as a lovely and spacious courtyard, free bedlinen and towels, 24-hour check-in and free airport pick-up. There are single, double and family rooms as well as ten-person dorms, some of which are women-only. All rooms have TVs and fridges, some have balconies. Most bath facilities are shared. Most nights, something's happening in the courtyard, whether it's pizza and beer, quiz night or a barbecue.
Services *Internet (pay terminal). Kitchen. Laundry. No smoking. Payphone. TV (cable/DVD/ TV room).*

Darlinghurst & Surry Hills

Expensive

Medusa

267 Darlinghurst Road, between Liverpool & William Streets, Darlinghurst, NSW 2010 (9331 1000/fax 9380 6901/www.medusa.com.au). CityRail Kings Cross. **Rooms** 17. **Rates** $270-$385 single/double. **Credit** AmEx, DC, MC, V. **Map** p330 H8 ⓬
What's not to love about a heritage-listed Victorian mansion that's been painted bright pink? Embodying a very Darlinghurst sense of urban chic, the Medusa is an ode to colour and design, all inter-

esting angles and bright flourishes of imagination. The lobby's (bubblegum) pink too, with bulging floral mouldings and an oversized paper chandelier. Sweet. All rooms have luxe touches like Aveda toiletries and monogrammed bathrobes. The expansive Grand Rooms feature period fireplaces, groovy chaises longues and sitting area. All rooms are en suite, with kitchenette, CD player and minibar. There's a diminutive courtyard at the back, which has a water feature and seating area.
Services *Business centre. Internet (wireless). No smoking. Room service. TV (cable/DVD).*

Moderate

Crown Hotel

589 Crown Street, at Cleveland Street, Surry Hills, NSW 2010 (9699 3460/fax 9318 1299/www. crownhotel.com.au). Bus 301, 302, 303, 372, 393, 395. **Rooms** 8. **Rates** $120-$200. **Credit** MC, V. **Map** 329 G11 ⓭
This very hip yet thoroughly unpretentious complex opened in 2005, and there's nothing quite like it in Surry Hills, land of fab restaurants but very few hotels. On the ground floor is Players, an airy pub with shiny hardwood floors and white walls, and an upscale wine shop. Level two features Dome, a sexy cocktail bar complete with chandeliers, glass bar and a gold ceiling and a huge mural based on François Boucher's baroque painting *Girl Reclining*. Finally, there are the hotel rooms up top, equally stylish and featuring deluxe extras such as L'Occitane bath products, Egyptian cotton bedlinen and wall-mounted 42in plasma screen TVs. Not bad for the new kid on the block. **Photo** *p40*.
Services *Bars (3). Disabled-adapted rooms. Gym. Internet (high-speed). No smoking. TV (cable/DVD).*

Kirketon

229 Darlinghurst Road, between Farrell & Tewkesbury Avenues, Darlinghurst (9332 2011/ fax 9332 2499/www.kirketon.com.au). CityRail Kings Cross. **Rooms** 40. **Rates** $139-$189. **Credit** AmEx, DC, MC, V. **Map** p330 H8 ⓭
This boutique hotel feels very European, from its compact stature (not an inch is wasted) to its understated *Wallpaper**-ish design and mood lighting. Flanked by the cool cafés, boutiques and restaurants of Darlinghurst Road, it's the perfect base to discover everything this hip and happening neighbourhood has to offer. Launched by the same owners as the Medusa (*see above* – hoteliers Terry and Robert Schwamberg) in 1999, it was bought in 2003 by the Eight Hotels group, owner of various budget boutique operations in Sydney, and prices were dropped dramatically to boost occupancy. Happily, the excellent service and style have not gone the same way. A new restaurant, Kirketon Bar & Dining Room is due to open in mid 2006 (taking over from celebrity chef Luke Mangan's Salt) . It will be a suitably swish mod French venture combined with a champagne cocktail bar.

Services *Bar. Concierge. Internet (wireless).*
No smoking. Parking ($15). Restaurant. Room
service. TV (cable/DVD/VCR).

Budget

Hotel Altamont

207 Darlinghurst Road, between Liverpool &William
Streets, Darlinghurst, NSW 2010 (1800 991 110/
9360 6000/fax 9360 7096/www.altamont.com.au).
CityRail Kings Cross. **Rooms** 14. **Rates** $109-$139
double; $119-$149 loft suite. **Credit** AmEx, MC, V.
Map p330 H8 ⑰
The hotel equivalent of Stella McCartney designing
a collection for H&M – luxury on a budget. The
Altamont (part of the Eight Hotels stable) is housed
in a colonial Georgian mansion that has been given
an elegant, contemporary makeover. There are sky-
lights throughout, a glass-fronted, light-filled lobby
and lounge with a pool table, heavy custom-built
wooden beds and dressers in the very spacious bedrooms, and a lovely, ornate roof terrace. The Rolling
Stones and Madonna stayed here when it used to be
attached to the infamous Cauldron nightclub. Rooms
range from an airy loft suite with soaring ceilings
and walk-in wardrobe to dorm rooms with bunk
beds. There are four of the latter, sleeping six or
eight, all with private bathrooms, air-conditioning
and a TV. Unsurprisingly, it's hugely popular, so
book well in advance.
Services *Bar. Internet (high-speed). No smoking.*
Parking ($10). TV (cable/DVD).

wake up!
See p37.

Paddington, Woollahra & Double Bay

Deluxe

Stamford Plaza Double Bay

33 Cross Street, between Bay Street & New South
Head Road, Double Bay, NSW 2028 (1300 301 391/
9362 4455/fax 9362 4744/www.stamford.com.au).
Ferry Double Bay/bus 323, 324, 325, 326, 327.
Rooms 140. **Rates** $500-$550 single/double;
$1,250-$3,500 suite. **Credit** AmEx, DC, MC, V.
Map p331 N7 ㊳
Both the look and vibe of the Stamford Plaza Double
Bay is very old money – think poodle-toting ladies-
who-lunch and white-haired gents in polo shirts
perched on overstuffed furniture. When it was still
the Ritz-Carlton, INXS frontman Michael Hutchence
ended his life here, but such unfortunate associations have all but disappeared, replaced with visits
from 'American presidents, European royalty and
entertainment celebrities' (that's what the brochure
says). Rooms feature traditional furniture, 18th-
century paintings and balconies overlooking the
courtyard or the yachts in Double Bay. There's a
rooftop (heated) pool and terrace, and high tea in
the antiques-filled lobby lounge is a very chic affair.
The Bay Grill restaurant offers smart dining, while
Winston's Lounge, with its chandeliers and grand
piano, has the aura of an old-fashioned private club.
There's also a kosher kitchen.
Services *Bar. Business centre. Concierge.*
Disabled-adapted rooms. Gym. Internet (high-speed).
No-smoking floors. Parking ($20). Pool (outdoor).
Restaurant. Room service. TV (cable/pay movies).

Expensive

Sir Stamford Double Bay

22 Knox Street, at New South Head Road, Double
Bay, NSW 2028 (1300 301 391/9363 0100/fax
9302 4100/www.stamford.com.au). Ferry Double
Bay/bus 323, 324, 325, 326, 327. **Rooms** 72.
Rates $350 double; $420 loft; $525-$770 suite.
Credit AmEx, DC, MC, V. **Map** p331 N8 ㊴
Less flouncy and old-world than the nearby
Stamford Plaza, the Sir Stamford is nestled among
the exclusive boutiques in Double Bay village, the
playground of meticulously groomed and moneyed
locals. Rooms vary from sleek, New York-style lofts
to more classic royal-blue-painted deluxe queen or
parlour rooms with silk curtains and four-poster
beds. There's a Roman-themed indoor pool, spa,
sauna and gym, all open 24 hours, and interesting
decorative touches such as prints by the late
Australian artist Norman Lindsay and imposing
Biedermeier furniture in the lobby.
Services *Business centre. Disabled-adapted*
rooms. Internet (high-speed). No smoking. Parking
($15). Pool (indoor). Room service. Spa. TV (cable/
pay movies).

PARCEL SHED CAFE

Funky **Railway Square YHA**. See p36.

Moderate

Hughenden Hotel

14 Queen Street, at Oxford Street, Woollahra, NSW 2025 (9363 4863/1800 642 432/fax 9362 0398/ www.hughendenhotel.com.au). Bus 352, 378, 380, L82. **Rooms** 36. **Rates** $148 single; $178-$268 double; from $328 four-bed annex house. **Credit** AmEx, DC, MC, V. **Map** p332 L11 ⑩

This four-star boutique hotel was thought to be a lost cause when sisters Elizabeth and Susanne Gervay bought it in 1992. But the crumbling, grand 1870s mansion was transformed into what it is today: an award-winning hotel offering 'the charms of yesteryear with the comforts of today'. All rooms are en suite, and there's also an attached four-bed terraced home that can be rented in its entirety. Elizabeth is an artist and Susanne an author, so literary events and art exhibitions take place regularly. There's a cosy lounge, an old-fashioned bar with a baby grand piano – put to good use by the talented night porter, Sir Victor, on Friday and Saturday evenings – and a sun terrace. Quaife's restaurant is named after the original owner, founder of the colony's medical association. Three rooms are designated as 'pet friendly'.

Services *Bar. Disabled-adapted rooms. Internet (dataport/wireless). No smoking. Parking (free). Restaurant. TV.*

Sullivans Hotel

21 Oxford Street, between Greens Road & Verona Street, Paddington, NSW 2021 (9361 0211/ fax 9360 3735/www.sullivans.com.au). Bus 352, 378, 380, L82. **Rooms** 64. **Rates** $145-$160 single/double; $160-$195 family. **Credit** AmEx, DC, MC, V. **Map** p332 H9 ㊶

This exceedingly friendly, family-run hotel has a great location in Paddington, with fab independent cinemas and bookshops right next door, and a short bus ride away from both the central business and shopping district and the eastern suburbs' beaches. All rooms have private bathrooms, with some inter-connecting family rooms available. There's wireless internet, a solar-heated pool, fitness room, free secure parking and free bicycles, and a ground-floor break-fast room that looks out on to Oxford Street. The owners also rent out their alpine chalet (three beds, two baths) in the Blue Mountains to guests.

Services *Disabled-adapted rooms. Gym. Internet (high-speed). No-smoking rooms. Parking (free). Pool (outdoor). Refrigerator. TV.*

Vibe Rushcutters

100 Bayswater Road, next to Rushcutters Bay Park, Rushcutters Bay, NSW 2011 (1300 300 232/8353 8988/fax 8353 8999/www.vibehotels.com.au). CityRail Edgecliff or Kings Cross. **Rooms** 245. **Rates** from $165 twin/double; from $265 suite. **Credit** AmEx, DC, MC, V. **Map** p330 K7 ㊷

The Vibe hotel chain is trying to be many things at once: stylish, affordable, young. It even released a chill-out compilation CD recently, with songs by

Morcheeba and Groove Armada. Rooms are on the small side but get lots of light, and facilities include a spacious fitness centre with steam room. The rooftop pool is a little exposed on windy days, but the panoramic views of Rushcutters Bay Park (great for jogging), the water and the city are striking. There's a cocktail bar, and a restaurant with a pleasant covered terrace. There are two other Vibes in town: one in North Sydney and one on Goulburn Street in the city.
Services *Bar. Concierge. Disabled-adapted rooms. Gym. Internet (high-speed/wireless). No-smoking floors. Parking ($16.50). Pool (outdoor). Restaurant. Room service. Spa. TV (cable/pay movies).*

Budget

Golden Sheaf Hotel

429 New South Head Road, at Knox Street, Double Bay, NSW 2028 (9327 5877/fax 9327 8581/ www.goldensheaf.com.au). Ferry Double Bay/bus 323, 324, 325, 326, 327. **Rooms** 9. **Rates** $88. **Credit** AmEx, MC, V. **Map** p331 N8 ⓭
This art deco pub is known mainly for its lovely, leafy beer garden, a very popular meeting spot for posh young eastern-suburbs types. A refurbishment a few years ago saw the creation of nine handsome and large en suite rooms, all pared down and modern in design, though some original details remain. All have fridges and cable TV. Such cheap accommodation is rare in pish-posh Double Bay, but don't expect much peace and quiet, especially in summer – there are DJs and live music performances nearly every night of the week.
Services *Bars (5). No-smoking rooms. Parking (free). Restaurant. TV (cable).*

Bondi & Coogee Beaches

Expensive

Swiss-Grand Hotel

180-186 Beach Road, at Campbell Parade, Bondi Beach, NSW 2026 (1800 655 252/9365 5666/fax 9365 5330/www.swissgrand.com.au). CityRail Bondi Junction then bus 380, 381, 382, L82/bus 380, L82. **Rooms** 203. **Rates** $220-$450 single/double; $260-$850 suites. **Credit** AmEx, DC, MC, V. **Map** p334 ⓬
The Swiss-Grand does a mean imitation of a wedding cake (all gleaming white columns and tiered levels), but it's the classiest hotel in Bondi – which says something about the state of the area's accommodation, since parts of the Grand were looking a little tired recently. But change is in the air: seven new private courtyard suites (with their own barbecues) are now open, and six new family suites should be ready by the end of 2006. The lobby has also been completely refurbished, and all the ocean view suites redesigned. Rooms are spacious, with two TVs, separate bath and shower, minibar and bathrobes. There's a rooftop pool and an indoor lap

pool, a very good fitness centre, and the renowned Samsara Day Spa, offering Balinese treatments.
Services *Bars (3). Business centre. Concierge. Disabled-adapted rooms. Gym. Internet (high-speed). No-smoking rooms. Parking (free). Pools (1 indoor, 1 outdoor). Restaurants (2). Spa. Room service. TV (cable/pay movies).*

Moderate

Coogee Bay Hotel

Corner of Arden Street & Bay Road, Coogee Beach, NSW 2034 (9665 0000/fax 9664 1576/ www.coogeebayhotel.com.au). Bus 372, 373, 374. **Rooms** 25 Heritage; 50 Boutique. **Rates** $130-$200 Heritage; $220-$260 Boutique. **Credit** AmEx, DC, MC, V.
The award-winning Coogee Bay Hotel has been operating on the same site since 1873 – though it's had a few face-lifts in that time. Not exactly a quiet beachside retreat, this complex is very big and very busy. The brasserie serves hearty fare for breakfast, lunch and dinner seven days a week, there are six different bars (*see p183*), a beer garden, a large drive-through bottle shop, a gaming lounge and a conference and function venue. The Boutique wing has spacious and modern rooms with marble bathrooms, balconies and, in some, kitchenettes. The Heritage wing in the main part of the pub is more basic.
Services *Bars (6). Disabled-adapted rooms. Internet (dataport). No-smoking floor. Parking (free). Payphone. Restaurant. TV (cable/VCR/in-house movies).*

Dive Hotel

234 Arden Street, opposite the beach, Coogee Beach, NSW 2034 (9665 5538/fax 9665 4347/ www.divehotel.com.au). Bus 372, 373, 374. **Rooms** 14. **Rates** $165-$250. **Credit** MC, V.
A smart and elegant guesthouse with a contemporary design theme that's all bold colours, polished wood and crisp bedlinen. The cosy, sun-filled breakfast room and kitchen give on to a bamboo-bordered garden. All rooms are en suite, with a microwave, fridge, TV and VCR, and the spacious front rooms have ocean views. Bathrooms are small, but stylish with tiny blue tiles and stainless steel sinks. The annex – a three-bed house two blocks from the beach – accommodates families. Dive is a disarmingly welcoming place, thanks to the gracious owners Terry Bunton and Mercedes Mariano and their poodle (Babe) and husky (Stella), who help take the sharpness off the style.
Services *No smoking. Internet (wireless/high-speed). Parking (free). TV (cable).*

Hotel Bondi

178 Campbell Parade, at Curlewis Street, Bondi Beach, NSW 2026 (9130 3271/fax 9130 7974/ www.hotelbondi.com.au). CityRail Bondi Junction then bus 380, 381, 382, L82/bus 380, L82. **Rooms** 50. **Rates** $75 single; $110-$150 double; $160 family suite. **Credit** AmEx, MC, V. **Map** p334 ⓭

The fun never stops at Hotel Bondi, where a bewildering amount of distractions are on offer, from snacking at the Bondi Grill restaurant to partying at the Starfish, Sand or Bombora bars – worryingly, the hotel's website describes the latter as 'catering to the '90s social scene'. It may not be cutting-edge, but it's very convenient – plus there are pool tables, a gaming room, big-screen TVs showing sporting events, two bottle shops, a beer garden and, of course, guest rooms. Many have beach views, others have verandas, and most are en suite with air-conditioning. The decor was recently updated to be less kitschy, and fear not: all rooms are soundproofed.

Services *Bars (3). No smoking. Payphone. Parking (free). Restaurant. TV.*

Ravesi's

118 Campbell Parade, at Hall Street, Bondi Beach, NSW 2026 (9365 4422/fax 9365 1481/www.ravesis. com.au). CityRail Bondi Junction then bus 380, 381, 382, L82/bus 380, L82. **Rooms** 16. **Rates** $125-$295 double; $260-$450 suite. **Credit** AmEx, DC, MC, V. **Map** p334 ⑯

Ravesi's is known primarily for its noisy street-level bar, a very popular meeting place, especially on Sunday afternoons in summer when young locals flock here to flirt over cocktails until well after sunset – the glass frontage is perfect for people-watching. Upstairs, the guest rooms have a distinct style-mag look. All have private bathrooms and are impeccably furnished, continuing the hotel's white-and-brown theme. The six breathtaking split-level suites have private terraces and superb sea views.

Services *Bars (2). Internet (high-speed/wireless). No smoking. Parking ($8 each entry). Restaurant. Room service. TV (cable/DVD).*

Budget

Indy's Bondi Beach Backpackers

35A Hall Street, between Gould & O'Brien Streets, Bondi Beach, NSW 2026 (9365 4900/fax 9365 4994/www.indysbackpackers.com.au). CityRail Bondi Junction then bus 380, 381, 382, L82/bus 380, L82. **Rooms** 27. **Rates** $24 dorm. **Credit** MC, V. **Map** p334 ⑰

You might feel out of place here if you're over 25. Indy's caters to young, fun-loving backpackers from around the world who are willing to overlook the terrible artwork in the hallways (cartoonish drawings of topless beach babes). It also helps anyone keen to conquer the waves, supplying free beach equipment, including surfboards, bodyboards, fins, masks, snorkels and rollerblades. A small fee is charged for wetsuits. Dorms come with six, eight or 12 beds. Other facilities include a fully equipped, recently renovated kitchen, laundry service and air-conditioned TV room (with a wide-screen TV and 400 movies on DVD/video). There's also a spacious back garden with picnic tables and a barbecue.

Services *Kitchen. Internet (pay terminal). Laundry. No smoking. Parking (free). Payphone. TV (DVD/TV room).*

Lamrock Lodge

19 Lamrock Avenue, at Consett Avenue, Bondi Beach, NSW 2026 (9130 5063/fax 9300 9582/ www.lamrocklodge.com). CityRail Bondi Junction then bus 380, 381, 382, L82/bus 380, L82. **Rooms** 52. **Rates** $23 dorm; $25-$40 single; $48-$60 double/twin. **Credit** AmEx, MC, V. **Map** p334 ⑱

This might be a better bet for more mature backpackers. Located on a quiet street 100m from Bondi Beach, the Lamrock is very clean and well maintained. All rooms have TVs, microwaves and fridges. There are four-bed dorms, singles and doubles, and rates get better the longer you stay. Furniture and decor are the usual hostel style, but bedlinen, quilts and pillows are supplied, and there are lots of vending machines. Plus, there's 24-hour security, and staff are very friendly and helpful.

Services *Internet (pay terminal). Kitchen. Laundry. No smoking. Payphone. TV (cable).*

Inner West

Moderate

Tricketts Luxury B&B

270 Glebe Point Road, opposite Leichhardt Street, Glebe, NSW 2037 (9552 1141/fax 9692 9462/ www.tricketts.com.au). LightRail Jubilee Park/bus 434. **Rooms** 7. **Rates** $176-$198. **Credit** AmEx, DC, MC, V.

A haven for antiques lovers, Tricketts has spared no detail, from the ornate moulded ceilings and imposing original cedar staircase to the cut-crystal glassware in the bedrooms and persian rugs – practically everything is a collectable. A wealthy merchant's house in the 1880s, a boys' home in the 1920s and then a children's courthouse, 270 Glebe Point Road has been many things to many people, but as a B&B it really shines. The seven guest rooms (one king-, five queen- and one twin-bedded room) are decorated in different styles, but all are en suite, and the house has air-conditioning and central heating. In summer breakfast is served on the rear deck; in cooler months it is in the conservatory.

Services *Internet (high-speed/wireless). No smoking. Parking (free). TV.*

Budget

Alishan International Guesthouse

100 Glebe Point Road, between Mitchell Street & St Johns Road, Glebe, NSW 2037 (9566 4048/ fax 9525 4686/www.alishan.com.au). LightRail Glebe/bus 431, 432, 433, 434. **Rooms** 19. **Rates** $25 dorm; $88 single; $99 double; $154 family. **Credit** AmEx, MC, V. **Map** p328 B9 ⑲

Conveniently located among the cafés, bookshops and restaurants on Glebe Point Road, this converted century-old mansion is a good inner-west budget option. The spacious dining room/lounge has a black stone floor and rattan furnishings, and the very large commercial-grade kitchen is for guests to

Room service

Most visitors could use a little help when it comes to finding a room for the night. So don't rush past the **Sydney Visitor Centre** (9667 6050) in the international arrivals hall at Sydney Airport: it's a real asset. It'll negotiate last-minute room deals and can get as much as 50 per cent chopped off standard rates. All the ticketing is done on the spot – you just present a voucher at the hotel. **The Tourism NSW Visitor Information Line** (13 2077) is another option for room-hunters.

Bargain-hungry backpackers can try the board adjacent to the **Sydney Visitor Centre** (*see p306*) in the Rocks, which covers more than 50 establishments. Or contact **YHA Australia** (422 Kent Street, Sydney, NSW 2000, 9261 1111, fax 9261 1969, www.yha.com.au) for a free information pack with membership details and a list of Australian youth hostels. If you want to stay in one of the nine YHA hostels in the Sydney area, note that rates are cheaper for members and you have to be a member to stay in the double/twin rooms – but instant annual membership is available ($35 for overseas visitors).

Campers will find many options in the bush or on the beach, most with cheap, fully equipped cabins or villas. The airport branch of Sydney Visitor Centre can provide a list of cabins and campsites, but staff can't book these for you. Also check out the government's **Tourism New South Wales** website (www.visitnsw.com.au) and the **National Roads & Motorists' Association**'s excellent camping and caravanning guides (www.nrma.com.au). The **National Parks & Wildlife Service** publishes a comprehensive booklet on National Parks in New South Wales: to get one, visit **Cadman's Cottage** (*see p306*) in the Rocks.

Many universities open their doors to casual visitors at low rates during the holidays. Dates of semester breaks vary, but are usually late November to late February, during Easter and in June and July; most also have short breaks around the end of September and October. Try the **University of New South Wales** (9385 4985, www.housing.unsw.edu.au) or the **University of Sydney** (9036 4000, www.suv.com.au).

If you're interested in short-term shared accommodation, contact **Sleeping with the Enemy** (9211 8878, www.sleepingwith theenemy.com). It offers rentals in houses around Sydney's fringe from $120 per week for a minimum one-month stay. There's no deposit and all furniture is provided.

use (no meals are provided). There are dorms, simple single, double and family rooms, plus a Japanese-style twin room with low beds and tatami mats. Some rooms have private bathrooms, but there's no air-con or in-room phones.
Services *Disabled-adapted rooms. Internet (pay terminal). Kitchen. Laundry. No smoking. Parking ($5 dorm guests; free other guests). Payphone. TV (DVD/TV room).*

Australian Sunrise Lodge
485 King Street, between Camden & Alice Streets, Newtown, NSW 2042 (9550 4999/fax 9550 4457/ www.australiansunriselodge.com). CityRail Newtown. **Rooms** 22. **Rates** $59-$79 single; $79-$99 double; $20 per extra person. **Credit** AmEx, DC, MC, V. **Map** p334 ⑩
Established in 1990, this friendly, family-run inn is small and surprisingly quiet despite being located on Newtown's main drag, King Street. The decor may be nothing special, but guest rooms have a TV, fridge, microwave, tea, coffee and kitchen utensils. Some have balconies overlooking a courtyard and are en suite, but none have a telephone or air-con – though there are ceiling fans, and electric fans are available on request. There is also a communal

kitchen and lounge. The lodge is recommended by Sydney University for off-campus accommodation, so expect a studenty clientele.
Services *Disabled-adapted rooms. No smoking. Parking (free). Payphone. TV.*

Billabong Gardens
5-11 Egan Street, at King Street, Newtown, NSW 2042 (9550 3236/fax 9550 4352/ www.billabonggardens.com.au). CityRail Newtown. **Rooms** 36. **Rates** $23-$25 dorm; $49-$88 single; $66-$88 double. **Credit** MC, V. **Map** p334 ㉛
Bohemian and arty, the decor at this Newtown hostel-motel is a patchwork of bright colours, exposed brick and crazy patterns. Set just off bustling King Street, it attracts artists and musos, even offering special deals for visiting bands. The place is clean and all rooms have ceiling fans and wireless internet. Some rooms have TVs and refrigerators, but none has air-conditioning. Other pluses: a large modern kitchen, laundry, solar-heated pool, TV room and a lovely leafy courtyard. Staff are extremely friendly and more than willing to help guests with everything from organising tours to finding work on an organic farm via the World Wide Opportunities on Organic Farms association.

Services *Internet (wireless). Kitchen. Laundry. No smoking. Parking ($5). Payphone. Pool (outdoor). TV (TV room).*

Wattle House

44 Hereford Street, between Glebe Point Road & Walsh Avenue, Glebe, NSW 2037 (9552 4997/ fax 9660 2528/www.wattlehouse.com.au). LightRail Glebe/bus 431, 432, 433, 434. **Rooms** 9. **Rates** $30 dorm; $65 single; $80 twin/double. **Credit** MC, V. **Map** p328 A8 ⑫

A lovingly restored Victorian mansion, the Wattle House was recently nipped and tucked, with a new kitchen and new carpeting. It's extremely friendly, though party animals and parents might want to steer clear: it's both non-smoking and alcohol-free, and no children are allowed. Compensation comes in the form of free tea and hot chocolate in the self-catering kitchen, and all bedlinen and towels are provided. There are dressing gowns in the twin and double rooms, and plenty of storage space. The house also has a reading room with 200 books, a laundry, a TV/video lounge and beautiful land-scaped gardens. Breakfast is included.
Services *Kitchen. Laundry. No smoking. Payphone. TV (DVD/TV room).*

North Shore

Expensive

Rydges North Sydney

54 McLaren Street, between Miller & Walker Streets, North Sydney, NSW 2060 (1300 857 922/ 9922 1311/fax 9922 4939/www.rydges.com). CityRail North Sydney. **Rooms** 166. **Rates** $285-$300 double; $335-$385 suite. **Credit** AmEx, DC, MC, V.

North Sydney, with all its office towers and corporate headquarters, means business. So it's no surprise that the Rydges caters mostly to business travellers. All rooms have a private bath and shower, and many of the deluxe rooms/suites have a beautiful view over the harbour. There are also 18 'iRooms' with a computer and unlimited internet access, as well as executive boardrooms, video-conferencing facilities and even a conference concierge service. The 50 Four bar and restaurant, opened in 2005, attempts to inject some grooviness with its retro-contemporary decor and mood lighting.
Services *Bar. Business centre. Internet (high-speed). No-smoking floors. Parking ($10). Restaurant. Room service. TV (cable/pay movies).*

Budget

Glenferrie Lodge

12A Carabella Street, between Peel Street & Kirribilli Avenue, Kirribilli, NSW 2061 (9955 1685/fax 9929 9439/www.glenferrielodge.com). Ferry Kirribilli. **Rooms** 70. **Rates** $35 dorm; $60 single; $99 double; $155 family. **Credit** MC, V. **Map** p327 H1 ⑬

This convivial, three-star, harbour-front B&B is about seven minutes by ferry from Circular Quay. A pretty, rambling house, it lacks air-conditioning, but rooms do have ceiling fans and TVs, and some have DVD players. The shared facilities are spotless and there are ample bathrooms throughout. The guest lounge offers cable TV (the rooms just have standard broadcast) and wireless internet access, and the dining room serves dinner five nights a week. A hot breakfast buffet is included in the rate.
Services *Internet (wireless/high-speed). Laundry. No smoking. Payphone. TV (cable).*

Northern Beaches

Deluxe

Jonah's

69 Bynya Road, between Norma & Surf Road, Palm Beach, NSW 2108 (9974 5599/fax 9974 1212/ www.jonahs.com.au). Bus 190, L90. **Rooms** 11. **Rates** *Mon-Thur, Sun* $449 double; $499 penthouse. *Fri, Sat* $700 double; $749 penthouse. **Credit** AmEx, DC, MC, V.

If you don't happen to own a cliffside Palm Beach mansion like the one Tom and Nic used to have back in the day, Jonah's is not a bad place to spend the night in these parts. You can even fly up by seaplane from Rose Bay. There are 11 suites, including a super-luxurious penthouse. Everything is very

Barrenjoey House.

plush and contemporary in style, with stunning views over Whale Beach from private balconies, king-sized beds and limestone bathrooms with jacuzzi spas. Friday and Saturday rates include the unmissable dinner and breakfast at the renowned restaurant (see p165).
Services *Bar. No smoking. Parking (free). Pool (outdoor). Restaurant. Spa. TV (cable/DVD).*

Expensive

Manly Pacific Sydney

55 North Steyne, between Raglan & Denison Streets, Manly, NSW 2095 (9977 7666/fax 9977 7822/www.accorhotels.com.au). Ferry Manly.
Rooms 218. **Rates** $189-$519 double; $439-$609 suite. **Credit** AmEx, DC, MC, V. **Map** p334 ⑤
Formerly known as the Manly Pacific Parkroyal, this four-star hotel overlooking Manly Beach was bought out by the multinational Accor chain in 2003. Since then, 52 courtyard rooms have been added, and various refurbishments undertaken. All rooms have balconies, there's a restaurant, two bars, a heated outdoor pool and rooftop fitness centre, sauna and spa. The Corso, Manly's pedestrian shopping and café strip, is within walking distance, and central Sydney is a half-hour ferry ride away.
Services *Bars. Concierge. Disabled-adapted rooms. Gym. Internet (high-speed/wireless). No smoking. Parking ($15). Pool (outdoor). Restaurant. Room service. Spa. TV (cable/in-house movies).*

Moderate

Barrenjoey House

1108 Barrenjoey Road, opposite Palm Beach Wharf, Palm Beach, NSW 2108 (9974 4001/fax 9974 5008/www.barrenjoeyhouse.com.au). Bus 190, L90. **Rooms** 7. **Rates** $95-$155. **Credit** AmEx, DC, MC, V.
The atmosphere at the Barrenjoey is light and beachy, with white-painted walls, white furniture and the odd touch of rattan or bamboo, as well as bowls of fresh-cut flowers. A guesthouse since 1923, it has three en suite rooms, and four with shared bathrooms – all are spotless and comfortable. The front rooms are best, as they overlook sparkling Pittwater. The café/restaurant is a popular meeting spot for locals and tourists up to explore the sights of Palm Beach and environs. **Photo** below.
Services *Bar. No smoking. Restaurant. TV (TV room).*

Newport Arms Hotel

Corner of Beaconsfield & Kalinya Streets, Newport, NSW 2106 (9997 4900/fax 9979 6919/ www.newportarms.com.au). Bus L87, L88, L90. **Rooms** 9. **Rates** $150 double; $40 per extra person in family room. **Credit** AmEx, DC, MC, V.
The Newport Arms turned 125 in 2005. A firm favourite with local families for its kid-friendly restaurant and playgrounds, it's on the shores of Pittwater, about a 40-minute drive from the CBD or

15 minutes from Palm Beach. There are eight doubles, all with basic furniture and private bathrooms, and one family room that sleeps six. The hotel also houses a very popular pub (see p185), with cheap drinks and live music. The waterfront beer garden features the new Garden Bistro, two new bars and an all-weather dining area.

Services *Bars (5). No smoking. Parking (free). Payphone. Restaurants (3). TV.*

Periwinkle Guest House

18-19 East Esplanade, at Ashburner Streeet, Manly, NSW 2095 (9977 4668/fax 9977 6308/ www.periwinkle.citysearch.com.au). Ferry Manly. **Rooms** 18. **Rates** $110-$150 single; $135-$190 double. **Credit** AmEx, MC, V. **Map** p334 ⑤⑤
Perched above tranquil Manly Cove, within walking distance of the ferry wharf, this 1895 Federation building has iron-lace verandas and lots of period charm without feeling stuffy. The 18 colourful bedrooms have ceiling fans, fireplaces and cane furniture, and 12 of them are en suite. Heaters and electric blankets are provided in winter. Guests can use the kitchen and laundry, and there's a courtyard with seating and an outdoor barbecue.

Services *Kitchen. Laundry. No smoking. Parking (free). Payphone. TV (TV room).*

Budget

Pittwater YHA

Morning Bay, Pittwater, NSW 2105 (9999 5748/ fax 9999 5749/www.yha.com.au). Ferry/water taxi Halls Wharf then 15mins walk. **Rooms** 8. **Rates** $27.50 dorm; $65.50 double/twin. **Credit** MC, V.
If you're looking for a real Australian bush experience within Sydney city limits, head here. Overlooking pretty Morning Bay, this recently refurbished stone-and-wood hillside lodge is hidden in the trees in Ku-ring-gai Chase National Park. You can't get here by car, but it's worth the arduous journey – an hour's bus to Church Point, a ferry to Halls Wharf, then a steep, 15-minute climb through the bush – because the wildlife is breathtaking. Red and green rosellas, laughing kookaburras, wallabies, possums and goannas are just a few of the native Aussie animals you're likely to spot here. Guests can hire canoes and kayaks or swim in the bay, and there are women-only massage workshops once or twice a year. It's BYO food (there are no shops) and bed-linen, or you can hire the latter for $2; no sleeping bags are allowed. It's incredibly popular, so advance bookings are essential.

Services *Barbecue. Kitchen. Laundry. No smoking. Payphone.*

Sydney Beachhouse YHA

4 Collaroy Street, at Pittwater Road, Collaroy, NSW 2097 (9981 1177/fax 9981 1114/ www.yha.com.au). Bus 155, 156, L88, L90. **Rooms** 60. **Rates** $26 dorm; $64 double/twin; $104 family. **Credit** MC, V.
Who needs the glamour and glitz of Palm Beach when Collaroy's got charm to burn and much, much lower prices? This YHA is one of the best budget options in the northern beaches, with bright, clean rooms and plenty of extras. There are four-person dormitories, twins and family rooms, free surfboards, boogie boards to rent and bicycles to borrow, and a compact, solar-heated outdoor pool. You won't be bored – other facilities include a barbecue area, arcade games, pool table and internet café.

Services *Barbecue. Café. Disabled-adapted room (family). Internet (pay terminals). Kitchen. No smoking. Parking (free). Payphone. Pool (outdoor). TV (cable/DVD/free movies/TV room).*

The South

Expensive

Novotel Brighton Beach

Corner of Grand Parade & Princess Street, Brighton-le-Sands, NSW 2216 (1300 656 565/ 9556 5111/fax 9556 5119/www.novotel brightonbeach.com.au). CityRail Rockdale then bus 475, 478, 479. **Rooms** 296. **Rates** $199-$339 double; $789 penthouse. **Credit** AmEx, DC, MC, V.
The family-friendly Novotel Brighton Beach is full of extras that help to make up for the uninspiring decor – an overhead walkway to the beach, a pool with outdoor slide for the kiddies, tennis court, fitness centre and spa. Five minutes from Sydney International Airport (25 minutes from downtown), it's convenient for stopover travellers. All rooms have private bathrooms and balconies with views inland or over Botany Bay. There's a cocktail bar and restaurant with water views.

Services *Bars (2). Business centre. Concierge. Disabled-adapted rooms. Gym. Internet (high-speed/wireless). No smoking. Parking ($10). Pool (1 indoor, 1 outdoor). Room service. Spa. TV (pay movies).*

Rydges Cronulla

20-26 Kingsway, at Gerrale Street, Cronulla, NSW 2230 (9527 3100/fax 9523 9541/ www.rydges.com. CityRail Cronulla. **Rooms** 80. **Rates** $280 double; $380 suite; $460 penthouse. **Credit** AmEx, DC, MC, V.
Overlooking Cronulla Beach and picturesque Gunnamatta Bay, this mid-range option is not far from the Royal National Park, with its great bushwalking trails and wildlife. All rooms have en suite bathrooms and at least one balcony, plus a desk and TV. Facilities include a pool, sauna, spa and beauty salon. The newly renovated Raffles restaurant is open daily for breakfast, lunch and dinner, an alfresco dining space occupies a terrace overlooking the beach, and on Friday nights there's an all-you-can-eat seafood buffet.

Services *Bar. Disabled-adapted rooms. Internet (dataport). No-smoking floors. Parking (free). Pool (outdoor). Restaurant. Room service. Spa. TV (in-house movies).*

Serviced apartments

Somewhere in between a hotel suite and a rented apartment, these used to be strictly the domain of the business traveller. But no more. These days, many holidaymakers can't get enough of the comforts of home – more space, more flexibility, in-built kitchens and other conveniences, such as washing machines.

Harbourside Apartments

2A Henry Lawson Avenue, McMahons Point, NSW 2060 (9963 4300/fax 9922 7998/ www.harboursideapartments.com.au). Ferry McMahons Point. **Apartments** 82. **Rates** $225-$395. **Credit** AmEx, DC, MC, V. **Map** p327 E1 ⑤⑤
The faded and outdated decor may leave something to be desired, but the large windows (ask for one on the harbour side) offer sweeping views of the Bridge and Opera House. Kitchens come fully equipped.
Services *Internet (high-speed). Laundry. No-smoking apartments. Parking (free). Pool (outdoor). Restaurant. TV (cable).*

Medina Executive Sydney Central

2 Lee Street, at George Street, Haymarket, NSW 2000 (8396 9800/fax 8396 9752/www.medina apartments.com.au). CityRail/LightRail Central. **Apartments** 98. **Rates** $280-$490. **Credit** AmEx, DC, MC, V. **Map** p329 E9 ⑤⑦
Choose from one- and two-bed apartments, lofts and studios, most with full kitchens, housed in the heritage-listed Parcel Post building. There's a grocery delivery service and a new bar and café. Medina has nine other locations around Sydney.
Services *Bar. Gym. Internet (high-speed). Pool (indoor). TV (cable/DVD).*

Meriton World Tower

World Tower, 91-95 Liverpool Street, at George Streets, CBD, NSW 2000 (1800 214 822/8263 7500/fax 9261 5722/www.meritonapartments. com.au). CityRail Central or Town Hall/Monorail World Square/LightRail Central. **Apartments** 147. **Rates** $178-$1,000. **Credit** AmEx, DC, MC, V. **Map** p329 E/F8 ⑤⑧
World Tower, part of the new World Square development, is the tallest residential building in the city. Studios and one-bed apartments are on levels 19-36, and two- and three-bed apartments on levels 62-77; the higher you go, the better the views. Meriton also has apartments at Moore Park and Bondi Junction.
Services *Business centre. Disabled-adapted apartments. Gym. Internet (high-speed). No smoking. Parking ($25). Pool (indoor). Spa. TV (cable/DVD).*

Quay Grand Suites Sydney

61 Macquarie Street, East Circular Quay, NSW 2000 (9256 4000/fax 9256 4040/www.mirvac hotels.com.au). CityRail/ferry Circular Quay. **Apartments** 62. **Rates** $550-$800. **Credit** AmEx, DC, MC, V. **Map** p327 G3 ⑤⑨
Near the Opera House, this five-star complex of one- and two-bedroom apartments delivers the goods – spacious suites with balconies and spectacular views over the harbour, en suite bathrooms, well-equipped kitchens, two TVs and more.
Services *Bar. Gym. Internet (high-speed). No smoking. Parking ($30). Pool (indoor). Restaurant. TV (cable/DVD).*

Regents Court Hotel

18 Springfield Avenue, off Darlinghurst Road, Potts Point, NSW 2011 (9358 1533/fax 9358 1833/ www.regentscourt.com.au). CityRail Kings Cross. **Apartments** 30. **Rates** $240-$275. **Credit** AmEx, DC, MC, V. **Map** p330 J7 ⑥⓪
This swish boutique hotel of studio suites is favoured by film and arty types – they even have a writer/ artist-in-residence programme. Set in a restored 1920s building in a leafy cul-de-sac, it's furnished with design classics by the likes of Le Corbusier and Eames. The rooftop terrace has great skyline views.
Services *Bar. Internet (high-speed/wireless). No smoking. Parking ($15). TV (cable/DVD).*

Saville 2 Bond Street

Corner of George & Bond Streets, CBD, NSW 2000 (9250 9555/fax 9250 9556/www.savillesuites. com.au). CityRail Wynyard. **Apartments** 170. **Rates** $340-$490; $1,300 penthouse. **Credit** AmEx, DC, MC, V. **Map** p327 F5 ⑥①
Located in the heart of the financial district, the apartments have full business services and well-equipped kitchens. There are also women-only floors, three penthouses and a small rooftop pool.
Services *Gym. Internet (high-speed/wireless). No-smoking floors. Parking ($30). Pool (outdoor). Spa. TV (cable/in-house movies).*

Southern Cross Suites Darling Harbour

Corner of Harbour & Goulburn Streets, Darling Harbour, NSW 2000 (1800 888 116/9268 5888/ fax 9268 5666/www.southerncrosssuites.com.au). CityRail Central/LightRail Paddy's Markets/Monorail Paddy's Markets. **Apartments** 73. **Rates** $185-$345. **Credit** AmEx, DC, MC, V. **Map** p329 E8 ⑥②
The immediate location isn't very inspiring, but it is convenient, sandwiched between Darling Harbour and Chinatown. Apartments are mainly one- or two-bedroom in size; some are looking rather drab and in need of a refurb. Extras include a small pool.
Services *Concierge. Disabled-adapted apartments. Gym. Internet (high-speed). No-smoking apartments. Parking ($36). Pool (outdoor). Spa. TV (VCR).*

Trendwest Suites Sydney

Corner of Wentworth Avenue & Goulburn Streets, Surry Hills, NSW 2000 (9277 3388/fax 9277 3399/www.trendwest.com.au). CityRail Museum. **Apartments** 120. **Rates** $165-$265. **Credit** AmEx, DC, MC, V. **Map** p329 F8 ⑥③
Brilliantly located just south of Hyde Park, this complex been taken over by the Trendwest South Pacific chain. Refurbishments due in 2006 include bathroom renovations and a complete room redesign.
Services *Gym. Internet (dataport). No smoking. Parking ($30). TV (pay movies).*

Sightseeing

Features

Maps

Coogee Beach. *See p136.*

Introduction

Start as you mean to go on.

Twice as nice: Sydney's iconic pairing of the **Harbour Bridge** and the **Opera House**.

Although the centre of Sydney is relatively small and easy to navigate, the rest of the city sprawls. Add in the complications provided by that stunning harbour and many lose the plot. But it's not as hard as it looks – honestly. The Harbour Bridge separates the north from the south, east and west, while the much newer suspension bridge, the Anzac Bridge, connects the city with the western suburbs.

Arranged by area, our Sightseeing chapters start with **Central Sydney**. This begins at Circular Quay and the Rocks area, and passes through the CBD (Central Business District) with its high-rise spires, shops and historic sights; then on to Chinatown, family-friendly Darling Harbour, gay-central Darlinghurst and neighbouring Surry Hills, colourful and seedy Kings Cross, smarter Potts Point and Woolloomooloo with its slick wharf conversion. Next, in **Eastern Suburbs**, share the glamour grounds of the city's movers, shakers and just plain rich. Here you can shop till you drop in the boutiques of Paddington, Double Bay and Woollahra, and eat and drink yourself silly in a plethora of the hippest bars, cafés and restaurants. The area extends via picturesque

harbourside suburbs all the way to South Head, taking in Bondi Beach, the closest ocean beach to the centre and a unique combination of city frenzy and 'no worries' seaside languor.

Moving west is the **Inner West**, covering one-time slums renovated into quaint cottages in waterfront Balmain, new-age chic in Glebe, a feisty Italian quarter in Leichhardt and gay, studenty, innovative Newtown.

North Shore crosses the Harbour Bridge to survey well-heeled Kirribilli, Milsons Point and McMahons Point with their 'dress circle' views of the Bridge and Opera House, and the high-end suburbs of Cremorne, Mosman and Balmoral. North Sydney, the city's second business district, is also here. Manly takes us into the **Northern Beaches** as the first of a string of glorious ocean beaches, inaccessible by train, running all the way up to Palm Beach, playground of millionaires.

Parramatta & the West heads out into greater Sydney and the geographic centre of the city, Parramatta. There are a few historic sites here, thanks to the first colonial governors choosing it for their country retreat. Sports fans will be more interested in the Olympic

Park complex in Homebush Bay. Next comes the **South**, including historic Botany Bay, the site of James Cook's landfall in 1770. But today's gem of the south is Cronulla: despite some unfortunate recent history it's a burgeoning seaside suburb with the feel of a Queensland sunshine resort.

Finally comes **Sydney's Best Beaches**, a chapter devoted to the pick of the city's surfing, swimming and sunbathing spots.

WHERE TO START

If you've come by plane, you may already have glimpsed the Opera House majestically sited on Sydney's crenellated harbour. If you're one of the chosen few arriving on a ritzy cruise ship, you'll probably wake up slap bang next to it. In any case, it is this icon that most visitors gravitate towards first and, fortuitously, it is a good place to get your bearings.

The Opera House is on the east side of Circular Quay and next to the main entrance to the Royal Botanic Gardens. From Circular Quay you can catch ferries over to the north shore and Manly with its ocean beach, or other destinations on the south side of the harbour, including Darling Harbour, Balmain and Watsons Bay. The cute gold-and-green ferries are a great way to see the city; tickets cost a little more than the bus or train, but the journey is a delight. Also at Circular Quay is a CityRail station for trains, and numerous bus stops for routes throughout the city.

The best way to start your exploration, though, is on foot. Begin around the Quay, the neighbouring Royal Botanic Gardens, and past the Quay's west side to the Museum of Contemporary Art and the Overseas Passenger Terminal with its cool bars and restaurants. Behind the latter two places is the historic area of the Rocks, where you can find the more obvious souvenirs and visit the Harbour Bridge. Next, jump on a harbour cruise – there are numerous options (*see p58*) – to see around the harbour and spot some of the city's more desirable waterfront homes.

Now you can dive into the CBD. From Circular Quay a series of parallel roads lead through Sydney's commercial and shopping areas to the Town Hall. They are serviced by buses and trains, and at some points by the Metro Monorail (an expensive, tourist-oriented service that circles the CBD at first-floor level), but are also easily walkable: a slowish walk including a bit of window-shopping from the Quay to the Town Hall will take about 30 minutes. From here you can walk west to bustling and very touristy Darling Harbour or catch a train or bus to Kings Cross, the city's sinful heart, or a host of other suburbs.

TRANSPORT AND INFORMATION

The CityRail system is, in general, easy to understand and services most of the main points of interest – apart from Manly (best reached by ferry or JetCat) and Bondi Beach (by bus from Bondi Junction or Circular Quay). Better, though, are the buses, partly because you can look out of the window (much of the train line is underground) and partly because they go everywhere and are more frequent. The driver or other passengers will be more than happy to tell you where you need to get off: Sydneysiders like nothing more than showing off their city. The ferries are the best – and most fun – way to get to the north shore and other harbourside spots.

There are lots of good-value travel passes covering a combination of transport types or specific areas or journeys. If you're pressed for time, consider one of the two **Explorer** buses (*see p57*): with these you can visit most of the sights in quick succession and pile a lot into a day. A **SydneyPass** (*see p57*) offers even more options. For details on all methods of public transport, *see p293*.

Also visit the information desk at Circular Quay, next to the CityRail station, or the **Sydney Visitor Centre** in the Rocks. You could call at nearby **Cadman's Cottage** (for both, *see p306*) to learn about Sydney's impressive national parks. There's a map of **Sydney by Area** on p325.

Tours

Tickets for many tours are available from **Australian Travel Specialists** (9211 3192, www.atstravel.com.au), which has outlets at Wharf 6 at Circular Quay and the Harbourside Festival Marketplace at Darling Harbour. The **Opera House** (*see p68*) runs its own guided tours. For a look at Sydney's seamier side, try an evening walking tour through the Rocks with **Ghost Tours** (1300 731 971, www.ghosttours.com.au) or a drive in a 1960s Cadillac hearse with **Destiny Tours** (9943 0167, www.destinytours.com.au).

General

See Sydney & Beyond Smartvisit Card

1300 661 711/www.seesydneycard.com. **Rates** *1-day* $65. *2-day* $119/$159. *3-day* $149/$205. *7-day* $209/$275. Concessions for 5-15s. **Credit** AmEx, DC, MC, V.

This swipe card plus guide booklet gives you free entry to over 40 attractions across Sydney and the Blue Mountains. It's certainly handy, but you'll need to cram in a lot to save money, so check what's on offer first. The higher-priced rates also include free transport on ferries, buses and CityRail. Available from various outlets, including the visitor centres, there are similar cards for Melbourne and Tasmania.

On foot

The **Australian Architecture Association** (8297 7283, www.architecture.org.au) runs occasional architecture walks, plus cruise and bus tour options, some led by local architects. For details of the city council's self-guided walking tours that explore Sydney's past, *see p12* **Walk into history**.

Margret's Aboriginal Walkabout

Depart from Aboriginal Art Shop, Sydney Opera House, Bennelong Point, Circular Quay (9240 8788). CityRail/ferry Circular Quay. **Tickets** $40-$65; $25-$50 concessions. **No credit cards.** **Map** p327 G3.
Margret Mhuragun Campbell and her husband offer tours that explore the history of the local Gadigal Aborigines and their relationship to the harbour and foreshores, and the use of native foods and medicines. The tours (one and two hours) traverse the area around the Opera House, Botanic Gardens and the Rocks. Tours are for eight or more people only and it's best to book 48 hours in advance.

The Rocks Pub Tour

Depart from Cadman's Cottage, 110 George Street, at Argyle Street, The Rocks (1800 067 676/ www.therockspubtour.com). CityRail/ferry Circular Quay. **Tours** 4.55pm Mon, Wed, Fri, Sat. **Tickets** $34.50. **Credit** MC, V. **Map** p327 F3.
A civilised alternative to a pub crawl, this two-hour tour pops into some of Sydney's heritage pubs for a cleansing ale and a dose of local history.

The Rocks Walking Tours

Depart from 23 Playfair Street, Rocks Square, The Rocks (9247 6678/www.rockswalkingtours. com.au). CityRail/ferry Circular Quay. **Tours** 10.30am, 12.30pm, 2.30pm Mon-Fri; 11.30am, 2pm Sat, Sun. **Tickets** $20; $10.50-$16 concessions; $50.50 family. **Credit** AmEx, MC, V. **Map** p327 F3.
Discover the picturesque heritage area of Sydney on lively 90-minute guided tours.

Sydney Architecture Walks

Depart from Museum of Sydney, corner of Bridge & Phillip Streets, CBD (8239 2211/www.sydney architecture.org). CityRail/ferry Circular Quay. **Tours** 10.30am Wed, Sat. **Tickets** (incl entry to the Museum of Sydney) $20; $15 concessions. **Credit** AmEx, MC, V. **Map** p327 F4.
These two-hour tours conducted by young architects reveal the diversity of Sydney's architecture, from its gritty industrial past to controversial contemporary structures. There are two regular tours – 'Sydney' on Wednesdays, 'Utzon' (the Opera House) on Saturdays – plus two others held intermittently: call for details.

By bike

Bonza Bike Tours

Depart from Circular Quay (9331 1127/www. bonzabiketours.com). CityRail/ferry Circular Quay. **Tickets** $70-$125; $50-$100 concessions. **Credit** AmEx, DC, MC, V. **Map** p327 F4.
What better way to get about a beautiful city in gorgeous weather than by bike? Bonza's most popular tour, the half-day Sydney Classic, takes in the major sights including the Opera House, Darling Harbour, Chinatown, Hyde Park and the Botanic Gardens. There are also day-long options: to Manly and North Head, and a Harbour Bridge ride. Bike, food, drink,

helmet and guide included. If you'd prefer to explore on your own, you can also hire bikes ($55 a day).

By bus

Sydney Buses

13 1500/www.sydneybuses.info.
The government-run Sydney Buses offer a great range of tourist services. For more information on travelling by bus, *see p293*.
DayTripper *1-day* $15; $7.50 concessions.
This one-day pass gives you access to ordinary rail, bus and ferry services, but not premium services such as the Explorer buses and Manly JetCat.
Sydney Explorer *1-day* $36; $18 concessions; $90 family.
This red bus offers unlimited travel around the highlights of Sydney. The route covers Sydney Cove, the Opera House, Royal Botanic Gardens, Mrs Macquarie's Chair, the Art Gallery of NSW, Kings Cross, Chinatown, Powerhouse Museum, Star City Casino, Darling Harbour, under the Harbour Bridge, Queen Victoria Building, the Rocks and more. Jump on and off as you please. Services (every 20 minutes or so) start at Circular Quay, but can be picked up at any of the red stops en route. The full circuit takes about 100 minutes. You can buy tickets from the driver (no credit cards).
Bondi Explorer *1-day* $36; $18 concessions; $90 family.
A blue bus, concentrating on the eastern side of town, stopping at Kings Cross and Rose Bay Convent before hitting the beaches of Bondi, Bronte, Clovelly and Coogee. A short run northwards takes in Watsons Bay and the Gap. The bus departs daily every 30 minutes from Circular Quay, but you can board anywhere you see the blue signs and buy tickets from the driver (no credit cards).

Sydney Explorer & Bondi Explorer *2-day* $62; $31 concessions; $155 family.
Allows unlimited travel on both the Sydney Explorer and Bondi Explorer buses for any two days in a seven-day period.
SydneyPass *3-day* $100; $50 concessions; $250 family. *5-day* $130; $65 concessions; $325 family. *7-day* $150; $75 concessions; $375 family.
The best-value package if you want to cram in a lot; available for three, five or seven days, it gives unlimited access to the Sydney Explorer, the Bondi Explorer and all Sydney Ferry cruises, as well as standard bus, ferry and CityRail services and return travel on the AirportLink train.

By coach

Gray Line Tours

Depart from various locations including Wharf 4, Circular Quay (9252 4499/www.grayline.com.au). CityRail/ferry Circular Quay. **Tickets** $58-$140. **Credit** AmEx, DC, MC, V. **Map** p327 F4.
Gray Line offers a variety of sightseeing tours in and around Sydney, including the Blue Mountains, Hunter Valley and a trip combined with a wildlife park sortie where you can cuddle a koala.

Sydney by Diva

Depart from outside Oxford Hotel, Taylor Square, at Oxford Street, Darlinghurst (9360 5557/ www.sydneybydiva.com). Bus 352, 378, 380, 382. **Tours** *All year* 5pm Sun. *Oct-Mar* 6pm Fri. *Wk before Mardi Gras* 6pm daily. **Tickets** $65 economy; $85 first-class. **Credit** AmEx, MC, V. **Map** p329 G/H9.
Climb aboard a luxury coach for an outlandish and memorable three-hour comedy tour of Sydney's tourist spots, hosted by one (or two) of the city's top drag queens.

By boat

Perhaps Sydney's greatest attraction is its harbour, and the best way to see it is from the water. For more on travelling by ferry, *see p294*, and for visits to the harbour islands, *see p68* **Island life**.

Captain Cook Cruises

Depart from Wharf 6, Circular Quay (9206 1111/ www.captaincook.com.au). CityRail/ferry Circular Quay. Tickets $22-$375. **Credit** AmEx, DC, MC, V. **Map** p327 F4.

In business for more than 30 years, Captain Cook is one of the biggest cruise operators, with over 20 sightseeing and dining tours departing daily. Options range from the basic Coffee Cruise (10am and 2.15pm, $44) to the Opera Dinner cruise (Thur and Sun only, $109, live on-board arias included) and a two-night cruise where you stay on the boat. The vessels are huge and modern, but lack the atmosphere and intimacy of the Sydney ferries.

Matilda Cruises

Depart from Wharf 6, Circular Quay (9264 7377/ www.matilda.com.au). CityRail/ferry Circular Quay. Tickets $24-$63. **Credit** AmEx, DC, MC, V. **Map** p327 F4.

Matilda's get-on/get-off sightseeing tours run eight times daily. The one-hour Rocket Harbour Express ($24) stops at Darling Harbour, Circular Quay, Watsons Bay and Taronga Zoo, and there are also coffee, lunch and cocktail cruises, plus combined tickets for a cruise and a visit to Taronga Zoo or Sydney Aquarium (both $43). You can also charter one of Matilda's boats, including sailing catamarans.

Sydney Ferries

Depart from Wharf 4, Circular Quay (13 1500/ www.sydneyferries.info). CityRail/ferry Circular Quay. Tours *Morning* 10.30am daily. *Afternoon* 1pm Mon-Fri; 12.30pm Sat, Sun. *Evening* 8pm Mon-Sat. Tickets *Morning* $18; $9 concessions; $45 family. *Afternoon* $24; $12 concessions; $60 family. *Evening* $22; $11 concessions; $55 family. Free under-4s. **Credit** AmEx, MC, V. **Map** p327 F4.

The cheapest sightseeing cruises are with Sydney Ferries. On offer are a one-hour morning cruise, a two-and-a-half-hour afternoon cruise – which visits the harbour's remoter reaches – and a 90-minute evening cruise, good for gazing at the city lights, which travels east as far as Shark Island and west to Goat Island.

By air

Sydney's love affair with the ocean extends to aviation, with the harbour's Rose Bay serving as a natural runway for seaplanes. From there, numerous outfits offer aerial sightseeing trips (from $135 per person) and hops up the coast to Palm Beach for a posh lunch. Longer trips are possible as well.

Operators include **Sydney Harbour Seaplanes** (1300 732 752, 9388 1978, www.seaplanes.com.au), **Sydney by Seaplane** (1300 656 787, 9974 1455, www.sydneybyseaplane.com), **Southern Cross Seaplanes** (1300 780 284, 9371 7605, www.southerncrossseaplanes.com.au), **Seaplane Safaris** (1300 732 247, 9371 3577, www.seaplanesafaris.com.au) and **SeaWing Airways** (1300 720 995, 9974 1455, www.seawing-airways.com.au) .

Cloud Nine Balloons

1300 555 711/www.cloud9balloonflights.com. **Credit** AmEx, MC, V.

Lifting off at dawn (weather permitting) from Parramatta Park, enjoy a tranquil one-hour balloon ride with views over the city followed by a champagne breakfast. Prices start at $240, plus breakfast and one-way transfer from the city. Other tours are available too.

Sydney HeliTours

9317 3402/www.avta.com.au/sydney.html. **Credit** AmEx, MC, V.

Flit over Sydney Harbour, skim along the northern beaches, watch the sun set from on high or, if the thrill's the thing, zoom along the coast with the doors off. Prices start at $189, and other tempting but expensive options are available – the website has route maps. Departures are from Kingsford Smith Airport, but they can collect you from your hotel.

By motorbike

The way to see Sydney close up – the wind in your face and a throbbing Harley between your legs, while you clutch the waist of a manly Aussie. Take your pick from **Eastcoast Motorcycle Tours** (1800 800 184, www.eastcoast-mc-tours.com.au) or **Easy Rider Motorbike Tours** (1300 882 065, www.easyrider.com.au), which offer everything from a quick 15-minute thrill for $35 to overnight outback adventures.

With added adrenaline

Whether you climb over it, speed through its waters or fly high above it, Sydney's famous harbour is licensed to thrill.

BridgeClimb

5 Cumberland Street, between Argyle & George Streets, The Rocks (8274 7777/www.bridgeclimb.com). CityRail/ferry Circular Quay. Tickets $165-$295; $100-$195 concessions. No under-12s. **Credit** AmEx, MC, V. **Map** p327 F3.

The three-and-a-half-hour climb to the top of the Harbour Bridge is, thankfully, less arduous and much safer than it appears. At 134m (440ft) above sea level, the views from the top of the arch are stunning, and the commentary on the history of the bridge is fascinating. It's hugely popular so book well ahead, especially for night and weekend climbs. Night-before revellers should note that all climbers are breath-tested and must have a blood alcohol level under 0.05%. Climbs leave every ten to 20 minutes daily from early morning to night, with dawn climbs during the summer.

Harbour Jet

Depart from Convention Jetty, between Convention Centre & Harbourside shopping centre, Darling Harbour (1300 887 373/www.harbourjet.com). CityRail Town Hall/ferry Darling Harbour/Monorail Convention. **Tickets** $60-$95; $40-$65 concessions. **Credit** AmEx, MC, V. **Map** p326 D6.

If you haven't whizzed about on a 420-horsepower jet boat before, be prepared for some serious high-speed fun, pumped up with rock music. Choose from a 35-minute Jet Blast Adventure, a 50-minute Sydney Harbour Adventure – both departing three times a day – and an 80-minute Middle Harbour Adventure departing once a day. Life jackets are provided for the wild (and wet) ride.

Ocean Extreme

Depart from Convention Jetty, between Convention Centre & Harbourside shopping centre, Darling Harbour (0414 800 046/www.oceanxtreme.com.au). CityRail Town Hall/ferry Darling Harbour/Monorail Convention. **Tickets** $95. **Credit** AmEx, MC, V. **Map** p326 D6.

Take a spin around the harbour in 'Australia's only commercially operated Special Forces vessel'. There is usually one tour a day (one hour), with room for eight passengers.

Skywalk

Centrepoint Podium Level, Sydney Tower, 100 Market Street, between Castlereagh & Pitt Streets, CBD (9333 9222/www.skywalk.com.au). CityRail St James or Town Hall/Monorail City Centre. **Tours** 9am-9.30pm daily. **Tickets** $109-$139; $85-$105 concessions. **Credit** AmEx, DC, MC, V. **Map** p327 F6.

The latest addition to the city's high-rise thrills, Skywalk takes you to the top of the the tallest building in town, Sydney Tower. You'll stand on a glass platform 260m (850ft) above the ground – twice the height of the Harbour Bridge – with great views of the CBD, and potential vertigo. But don't worry: you're clipped to a safety rail at all times. As with BridgeClimb, you'll be breath-tested for alcohol before they let you up, and you can't take your own camera (in case you drop it).

Sydney Harbour Parasailing

Depart from near Manly Wharf, Manly (9977 6781/www.parasail.net). Ferry Manly. **Tickets** $79 solo; $129 tandem; $15 boat passenger. **Credit** AmEx, MC, V. **Map** p334.

Get strapped into a harness and flung 150m (490ft) above the water while being towed along by a speedboat for ten minutes. The season runs from November to April, and there are several departures a day.

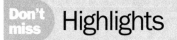

Highlights

Don't miss

Go house hunting

The **Sydney Opera House** is so much better close up than in any photo. Take in a performance in its hallowed theatres, join a daytime tour or simply wonder at its amazing structure. *See p67.*

Bridge the gap

Cross the **Sydney Harbour Bridge** – on foot, by car or by train – or even climb to the top of it. *See p64.*

Jump on a ferry

The best way to explore spectacular Sydney Harbour. The half-hour journey on one of the double-ended green-and-golders to Manly is always a winner. *See p58.*

Hit a beach

From surfie heaven to picnicking paradise, there's no shortage of options. For the full lowdown, *see pp133-139* **Sydney's Best Beaches**.

Have a party

Buy some feathers, pull on a pair of sparkly shorts and join in the fun at Mardi Gras, Sydney's famous gay festival. *See p242* **New Mardi Gras**.

Go wild

Go face-to-teeth – safely – with a shark at **Sydney Aquarium** (*see p82*) or marvel at marsupials at **Taronga Zoo** (*see p114*).

Take a walk

For the ultimate beach crawl, walk along the coast starting at Bondi Beach and winding past Tamarama Beach, Bronte Beach, Clovelly Bay and Gordons Bay to Coogee Beach. *See p96* **Walk 1: Bondi to Coogee**.

Feast on fish

Make the most of Sydney's first-class dining scene, and savour some of the greatest seafood in the world. *See p146* **The best Restaurants**.

Make a splash

Take a dip in one of Sydney's beautiful harbourside pools: the **North Sydney Olympic Pool** (*see p113*) and **Andrew (Boy) Charlton Pool** (*see p70*) are both gorgeous.

Sightseeing

Central Sydney

Explore the birthplace of modern Australia.

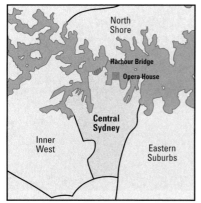

North Shore

Harbour Bridge

Opera House

Central Sydney

Inner West

Eastern Suburbs

Sightseeing

From crowd-pleasing Circular Quay and the Rocks to the rapidly gentrifying backblocks of Redfern and Waterloo, central Sydney is where to find the city's main sightseeing and recreational action. Glorious harbour views and lush parklands abound, supplemented by the cream of Sydney's cultural institutions. This is where the bulk of tourist accommodation is located and a very respectable slice of the city's premier places to wine, dine and shop. Practically the only thing missing is a beach (though you don't have to travel too far from the city's heart to find that, either – the closest is Seven Shillings Beach in Double Bay).

Circular Quay, which wraps around Sydney Cove and is bookended by the icons of the Harbour Bridge and Opera House, is central Sydney's starting point, a perpetually bustling nexus for tourists and Sydneysiders alike. As you arrive here, preferably on one of the city's much-loved green-and-cream ferries, mull over how things have changed since the First Fleet set up shop in 1788. That said, the societal split that arose in those early days of the colony – the bigwigs in their grand sandstone buildings to the east, the convicts and carousing sailors in their tumbledown cottages and seedy drinking dens to the west, in an area known as the Rocks – is still evident today. Little remains of the Cadigal people, the cove's original inhabitants, however (save for displays at various museums).

The evolution of the Rocks from inner-city slum to tourist-friendly precinct set the blueprint for other parts of central Sydney to smarten up their act. Darling Harbour and the adjacent CBD, aka Central Business District, have both benefited from major refurbishments and building programmes over the last decade. Some might bemoan that the CBD is becoming a gusty midtown Manhattan with its sprouting skyscrapers (of which **World Tower** – *see p81* **World domination** – is the largest), but there's no denying that the previously morgue-like atmosphere at night and at weekends has been replaced by the vibey buzz of party-goers and diners in search of the next big Sydney restaurant. None of this has hurt the established party strips of neighbouring Potts Point, Darlinghurst and Surry Hills, ground zero for Sydney's gay and bohemian communities, all of which are more vibrant than ever.

The CBD is easily walkable, or there are CityRail trains travelling underground around the City Circle loop – covering Central, Town Hall, Wynyard, Circular Quay, St James and Museum stations.

The CBD

Map pp326-330. **Transport** *Ferry Circular Quay/ CityRail Circular Quay, Martin Place, Museum, St James, Town Hall or Wynyard/Monorail City Centre, Galeries Victoria, Paddy's Markets or World Square/LightRail Capitol Square or Paddy's Markets.*

The Rocks & around

In January 1788, after an eight-month voyage from Plymouth, England, the First Fleet stumbled ashore (after a short visit to Botany Bay) at Sydney Cove. Their brief was to 'build where you can, and build cheap'. Hence, the Rocks. Named after its rough terrain, the area survived as a working-class district for almost two centuries until the 1960s, when it was nearly demolished to create an Australian Manhattan. Civic protest saved the day and the 'birthplace of the nation' was finally restored for posterity in the mid 1970s. Now safe under the wing of the Sydney Harbour Foreshore Authority, the Rocks still has to pay its own way, and many historic buildings have been turned to commercial use.

The resulting combination of period buildings, tourist shops, restaurants and pubs, along with harbourside vistas, has made the

View from **Sydney Tower** over the CBD and Royal Botanic Gardens. *See p77.*

Rocks one of the city's major sightseeing attractions. As a result, locals tend to shun the area, writing it off as a place filled with noisy boozers and tacky souvenirs neatly packaged for tour groups. But a clutch of good restaurants, the development of the Walsh Bay finger wharves and the installation of groovier retailers are now attracting Sydneysiders back.

Head first for the excellent **Sydney Visitor Centre** in the Rocks Centre (corner of Argyle & Playfair Streets; *see p306*), where you'll also find the new **Rocks Discovery Museum** (*see p63*). Across George Street – the Rocks' central thoroughfare – is **Cadman's Cottage**, one of the nation's oldest houses. Now home to the **Sydney Harbour National Park Information Centre** (*see p306*), it's the place for info on getting to some of the harbour's islands (*see p68* **Island life**).

The **Rocks Market** (*see p192*) appears like magic every weekend, with souvenir stalls selling all manner of arts and crafts, puppeteers and other street performers. For a top Sydney meal, there's Neil Perry's **Rockpool** (*see p147*) and David Thompson's **Sailors Thai** (*see p143*). If you'd like a cocktail with your view, try the stylishly revamped Blu Horizon Bar on the 36th floor of the **Shangri-La Hotel** (*see p32*) on Cumberland Street.

Historic buildings include the handsome sandstone **Garrison Church** (9247 1268, www.thegarrisonchurch.org.au, open 8.30am-6pm daily), on the corner of Argyle and Lower Fort Streets. Officially named the Holy Trinity Church, this was the colony's first military church; regimental plaques hang on the walls and there's a brilliantly colourful stained glass window overlooking the pulpit. You can also take a peek at how 19th-century working-class families lived at the **Susannah Place Museum** (*see p64*), a row of four brick terraces on Gloucester Street.

Still, much has been lost. The site of Sydney's first hospital, which struggled to care for 500 convicts who disembarked from the Second Fleet in 1790 suffering from typhoid and dysentery, is now an unprepossessing row of shops. Several galleries, including that of well-known Aussie artist Ken Done, now occupy the site of the **Customs Naval Office** (100 George Street), where one of the colony's most flamboyant customs officers, Captain John Piper, made money mismanaging taxes. He went on to build Sydney's finest mansion of its day at Eliza Point – now Point Piper – where he held extravagant parties until his maladministration came to light. He then had his crew row him beyond the Heads and play a Highland lament as he threw himself overboard. To his embarrassment, they dragged him from the sea and he died, impoverished, in 1851.

Off the main drag, under the thundering Bradfield Highway that feeds the **Sydney Harbour Bridge** (*see p64*) and towards Walsh Bay and Millers Point, the area has a quieter and gentler feel, with tiny cottages, working wharves and a few pubs vying for the honour of Sydney's oldest: the **Lord Nelson Brewery Hotel** (*see p176*) on Kent Street, the **Hero of Waterloo** (81 Lower Fort Street, 9252 4553) and the **Palisade** on Bettington Street, which also has a fine restaurant (*see p147*). **Glover Cottages** (124 Kent Street) – built by stonemason and surveyor Thomas Glover in the 1820s – were the first example of terraced housing in the colony. The charming Victorian **Sydney Observatory** (*see p65*), perched on the hill of the same name, offers views of the heavens above and the harbour below. Immediately below the observatory, **Argyle Place** has the air of an English village green and is one of the most picturesque and least touristy parts of the Rocks.

From Windmill Street, walk down the Windmill Steps past the striking modern sculpture of a giant egg in a nest to Hickson Road and **Walsh Bay**, where the first wharves were built by a South Sea Islands trader in 1820. The area's grandest vision was realised by the Sydney Harbour Trust from 1901-22 when Hickson Road was carved through the sandstone, a massive sea wall was built and buildings and piers were erected. As shipping methods changed, however, the Walsh Bay wharves became obsolete and were finally abandoned in the 1970s.

The area's revitalisation is now well under way, having kicked off back in the 1980s with the development of Piers 4/5 to house various cultural institutions, including the **Sydney Theatre Company** (*see p268*). An additional 850-seat theatre for the company – the **Sydney Theatre** (*see p272*) – opened in 2004 in an artfully converted bond store on Hickson Road. All the piers have now been developed, with several new watering holes, including the chi-chi wine bar **Firefly** (*see p176*), espresso bar **Senso** (No.23, 9241 1248) and the **Hickson Road Bistro** (No.20, 9250 1990) attached to the aforementioned theatre, serving the well-heeled residents of the swish waterside apartments.

A public boardwalk now stretches from Pier 1 – where the **Sebel Pier One** hotel (*see p35*) has prime position – to Piers 8/9. So you can now walk along the foreshore from Circular Quay, past the Museum of Contemporary Art, behind the Overseas Passenger Terminal, in front of the **Park Hyatt Hotel** (*see p31*), under the Harbour Bridge, around Dawes Point Park, then past the piers all the way to Millers Point.

Dawes Point Park contains the remains of **Dawes Point Battery**, Sydney's first permanent fortification. Built in 1790 against a feared Spanish invasion, it was rebuilt in 1820 by pioneer architect Francis Greenway and renovated in the 1850s and '60s. The battery was demolished in 1925 when the Harbour Bridge was built, but excavation has uncovered some remains. These include the floor of the original powder magazine, the circular battery with evidence of four gun emplacements, underground magazines, a stone ramp and the footings of the officers' quarters.

Rocks Discovery Museum

The Rocks Centre, Kendall Lane, at Argyle Street, The Rocks (1800 067 676/www.rocksdiscovery museum.com). CityRail/ferry Circular Quay. **Open** 10am-5pm daily. **Admission** free. **Map** p327 F3.

 Viewpoints

Garden Island

Climb to the roof of the old Signal Station for an admiral's-eye view, with one of the best city, Opera House and Harbour Bridge panoramas going. *See p88.*

Jonah's

It's not just for the food that clued-up visitors head to Jonah's restaurant (*see p165*) at Palm Beach. The uninterrupted view over Whale Beach and the wide ocean beyond has to be seen to be believed.

Observatory Hill

Up behind the Rocks with the Harbour Bridge so near you feel you could touch it, Observatory Hill offers some wonderful harbour views. Go at night when everything twinkles. *See p65.*

Rose Bay

The lookout at the junction of Bayview Hill and New South Head Road opens up stunning views over the waving masts of boats in Rose Bay, with the Harbour Bridge in the background. *See p99.*

Sydney Harbour Bridge

You don't have to do the BridgeClimb to get a view, though it really is priceless from the top. Alternatively, climb the Pylon Lookout or stay roadside on the pedestrian path over the bridge. *See p64.*

Sydney Tower

Right in the middle of the CBD and 250 metres (820 feet) above street level, the Sydney Tower offers a different perspective. For the ultimate thrill, try the new Skywalk. *See p79.*

Sightseeing

Jump on a ferry at **Circular Quay**, gateway to Sydney Harbour. *See p65.*

Housed in a restored 1850s coach house, this new museum covers the Rocks' history from the time of the indigenous Cadigal people to the 1970s demonstrations that saved many of the historic buildings from avaricious developers. It's a small space, but there's quite a bit packed in; amid the broken plates and bottles, and tarnished jewellery, look out for the mummified rat with a curious collar of Chinese newsprint, a remnant of the Rocks' less sanitary past.

Susannah Place Museum

58-64 Gloucester Street, at Cumberland Place Steps, The Rocks (9241 1893/www.hht.nsw.gov.au). CityRail/ferry Circular Quay. **Open** 10am-5pm Sat, Sun (daily in Jan). **Admission** $8; $4 concessions; $17 family. **Credit** (over $10) MC, V. **Map** p327 E4.
Built in 1844, this terrace of four houses, including a corner shop, original brick privies and open laundries, gives an idea of what 19th-century community living was really like.

Sydney Harbour Bridge & Pylon Lookout

Bridge & Pylon Lookout accessible via stairs on Cumberland Street (9240 1100/www.pylonlookout. com.au). CityRail/ferry Circular Quay. **Open** 10am-5pm daily. **Admission** *Pylon Lookout* $8.50; $3 concessions; free under-7s. **Credit** AmEx, DC, MC, V. **Map** p327 F3.
Long before the Opera House was built, Sydney had 'the coat hanger' as its icon. Locals had dreamed for decades of a bridge to link the north and south harbour shores before construction of the 'All Australian Bridge' began in 1924, by which time Sydney's ferries were struggling to carry 40 million passengers a year. The winning design came from English firm Dorman, Long & Co, but used Australian steel, stone, sand and labour. Families

within the path of the new bridge and its highways were displaced without compensation, and 800 houses were demolished. A total of 1,400 workers toiled on the structure, which is 134m (440ft) high and 1,149m (3,770ft) long, and was when first built the world's largest single-span bridge. It took eight years to build, and workers grafting without safety rails took great risks: 16 of them died. The opening ceremony in 1932, broadcast around the world, was interrupted by a lone horseman – disaffected Irishman Francis de Groot – who galloped forward and slashed the ribbon with his sword, declaring the bridge open in the name of 'the Majesty the King and all the decent citizens of New South Wales'. De Groot's organisation, the New Guard, resented the fact that a representative of the King hadn't been asked to open the bridge. After the police had removed him (he was later fined £5), the ribbon was retied, and the ceremony resumed.

The refurbished Pylon Lookout, in the south-east pylon, is well worth a visit. Climb 200 steps past three levels of exhibits celebrating the history of the bridge and its builders. Stained-glass windows feature a painter, riveter, stonemason, rigger, concreter and surveyor. Original bridge memorabilia from the 1930s is also on display; more up-to-date souvenirs are available in the shop on level two. And the open-air views from the top are magnificent. The more intrepid can take a guided tour to the top of the bridge itself (*see p58* BridgeClimb), with only a harness between you and a plunge into the harbour.

The bridge has been declared 'one of the seven wonders of the modern world' – though not everyone admires it. Writer James Michener commented in the 1950s that it was 'big, utilitarian and the symbol of Australia… But it is very ugly. No Australian will admit this.'

Sydney Observatory

Watson Road, off Argyle Street, Observatory Hill, The Rocks (9241 3767/www.sydneyobservatory. com.au). CityRail/ferry Circular Quay. **Open** *Museum* 10am-5pm daily. **Admission** *Museum & gardens* free. *Day tours* $6; $4 concessions; $16 family. *Night tours* $15; $10-$12 concessions; $40 family. **Credit** MC, V. **Map** p327 E3.

Built in 1858, Sydney Observatory gained international recognition under Henry Chamberlain Russell, government astronomer 1870-1905, who involved Sydney in the *International Astrographic Catalogue*, the first complete atlas of the sky. The Sydney section alone took 80 years to complete and filled 53 volumes. Increasing air pollution made the observatory ineffective, and it became a museum in 1982. It's been revamped recently, and a new exhibition celebrates the long tradition of Australian astronomy, including the Aboriginal use of southern constellations over thousands of years to navigate land and sea, and in ceremonies. Interactive displays include a virtual-reality tour over the surfaces of Venus and Mars, and there are lessons on how telescopes work. Night tours (booking essential) include a talk and tour, 3-D Space Theatre session and viewing through a 40cm (16in) reflecting telescope.

Circular Quay

Circular Quay (more of a semi-circle, in fact) is the hub of Sydney's ferry system, where the charming green-and-cream vessels leave for all points around the harbour. Commuters and day-trippers board and disembark from a constant stream of ferries, JetCats, RiverCats and water taxis at the Quay's five wharves, while tourists and teenagers idle in the cafés drinking cappuccinos, listening to buskers and admiring the view. Fast-food kiosks abound, but you'll also find **City Extra** (9241 1422), one of the few 24-hour restaurants in town, and the delicious gelati of **Gelatissimo** (9241 1566). Information stands proffer free literature, and sightseeing cruises and tours leave from here. The view back to the city is blocked by the CityRail Circular Quay station and Cahill Expressway, but the view out over the harbour is particularly lovely at night, when the Opera House, the Harbour Bridge, the Overseas Passenger Terminal and Fort Denison are all lit up.

On the west side of the Quay, with the Rocks stretching behind, is the grand sandstone facade of the **Museum of Contemporary Art** (*see p67*), housed in the deco-style former Maritime Services Board Building. Just beyond it is the striking **Overseas Passenger Terminal**, where international cruise liners dock. Not only an award-winning piece of architecture, it's also one of the city's coolest night-time hangouts with its clutch

of restaurants and bars, including Mod Oz specialists **Quay** (*see p147*) and **Cru** (*see p147*), newcomer **Ocean Room** (*see p147*), buzzy **Wildfire** (8273 1222, www.wildfiresydney. com) and mega **Cruise** (9251 1188, www. cruiserestaurant.com.au).

On the opposite side of the quay is **East Circular Quay**, a bland strip of modern buildings dubbed 'the Toaster' by wags during their construction phase several years ago. Nonetheless, it's a popular spot, not least because of its anchor tenant, the arty cinema **Dendy Opera Quays** (*see p225*), various shops and a string of popular restaurants including elegant **Aria** (*see p145*) and the high-rise **Bridge Bar** (Level 10, 2 Macquarie Street, 9252 6800, www.bridgebar.com.au).

As you walk around the Quay, look out for a series of round metal plaques set into the promenade, each one dedicated to a famous writer. Forming **Writers' Walk**, these offer brief quotations on Sydney and human nature. Many (but not all) of the writers are Australian, including Germaine Greer, Peter Carey, Barry Humphries and Clive James.

Sydney Opera House (*see p68*), the city's modern icon, stands in lone majesty on Bennelong Point at the tip of the eastern side of Circular Quay. All the photos in the world cannot prepare you for how stunning it is. The site is where Governor Phillip provided a hut for an Aboriginal man, Bennelong, in 1790. Phillip had captured Bennelong – one of the governor's more foolish moves – and planned to use him as a mediator. Some of the key events in Bennelong's sorry life are depicted in a series of paintings by Donald Friend on display in the Opera House. From the steps in front of the Opera House you can walk east along the harbour foreshore and into the Royal Botanic Gardens.

Behind the Quay, across Alfred Street, is the city-owned **Customs House** (*see p67*), which has recently undergone a spectacular refurbishment and is now Sydney's main public library. Two blocks over, on the corner of Albert and Phillip Streets, is the **Justice & Police Museum** (*see p67*). Look up and you'll spy the terracotta spine and wrapped-glass front of the 41-storey **Aurora Place**, designed by Italian architect Renzo Piano and one of Sydney's most appealing modern buildings. Opposite Aurora Place is **Chifley Tower** on one corner and **Governor Phillip Tower** on the other.

Architecturally, these are three of the more interesting late 20th-century additions to the skyline and, sitting so close together, are a reminder that this is the so-called 'big end' of town. Governor Phillip Tower stands

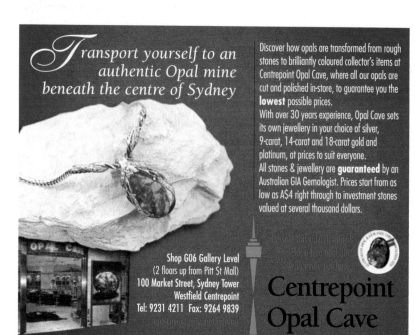

on the site of the first Government House, and inside is Trevor Weeke's towering bust of Governor Macquarie. The excellent and informative **Museum of Sydney** (*see below*), which also has a very good shop and café (*see p169*), is in front of it.

Customs House

31 Alfred Street, between Loftus & Young Streets, Circular Quay (9242 8592/www.cityofsydney.nsw. gov.au). CityRail/ferry Circular Quay. **Open** 8am-7pm Mon-Fri; 10am-4pm Sat; noon-4pm Sun. **Map** p327 F4.

Built in 1885, Customs House was one of government architect James Barnet's finest works. Its double-pillared colonnade, wrought-iron panels and long clean lines give it a feeling of space and majesty, underlined by the open area in front. The building is heritage-listed, but its use continually changes: the latest revamp saw the City of Sydney lavish $18 million on an internal refurbishment to turn it into a highly stylish public library, with decor slick enough to make boutique hotel junkies drool. There's a fantastic scale model of the city under glass on the ground floor, as well the library's newspaper, magazine and computer room (including lots of foreign publications), and the tasty pizzeria and café Young Alfred. Fashionable eaterie and jazz venue Café Sydney retains its enviable location on level five, with amazing views.

Justice & Police Museum

Corner of Albert & Phillip Streets, Circular Quay (9252 1144/www.hht.nsw.gov.au). CityRail/ferry Circular Quay. **Open** 10am-5pm Sat, Sun. **Admission** $8; $4 concessions; $17 family. **Credit** (over $10) MC, V. **Map** p327 G4.

Fittingly, the Justice & Police Museum has been a Water Police Court (1856), Water Police Station (1858) and plain old Police Court (1886). Death masks of some of Australia's more infamous crims are on display, as well as mugshots, assorted deadly weapons and newspaper reports of sensational wrongdoings. Also on view is a recreated 1890s police charge room, a dark and damp remand cell, and a restored Court of Petty Sessions with its notorious communal dock, which could hold up to 15 prisoners at a time.

Museum of Contemporary Art

140 George Street, between Argyle & Alfred Streets, Circular Quay (9245 2400/24hr recorded information 9245 2396/www.mca.com.au). CityRail/ferry Circular Quay. **Open** 10am-5pm daily. **Tours** 11am, 1pm Mon-Fri; noon, 1.30pm Sat, Sun. **Admission** free. **Credit** AmEx, DC, MC, V. **Map** p327 F4.

The MCA is the only major gallery in Sydney with a serious interest in contemporary art. After a long period during which its funding was under threat, it's now on much more secure ground under the directorship of Elizabeth Ann Macgregor, a Scot who's spearheaded the museum's renaissance. As

well as the always interesting temporary shows, many from key overseas institutions and artists, the MCA has added a new gallery on level four to display its permanent collection, which includes some fine Aboriginal works and pieces by leading Australian contemporary artists. The MCA Café (*see p168*), facing Circular Quay, is worth a look.

Museum of Sydney

Corner of Bridge & Phillip Streets, CBD (9251 5988/ www.hht.nsw.gov.au). CityRail/ferry Circular Quay. **Open** 9.30am-5pm daily. **Admission** $10; $5 concessions; $20 family. **Credit** AmEx, MC, V. **Map** p327 F4.

This modern building stands on one of the most historic spots in Sydney, site of the first Government House, built in 1788 by Governor Arthur Phillip and home to the first nine governors of NSW. In 1983 archaeologists unearthed the original footings of the house, which had survived since the building's 1846 demolition: these remains are now a feature at the museum. Run by the Historic Houses Trust and opened in 1995, the MOS offers a mix of state-of-the-art installations and nostalgic memorabilia – it's definitely worth a visit. A giant video spine spans the full height of the building and charts the physical development of the city; elsewhere a trade wall features goods on sale in Sydney in the 1830s. This area was the first point of contact for the indigenous Cadigal people and the First Fleet, so the museum

History lesson: **Museum of Sydney**.

Island life

Port Jackson, as Sydney Harbour is properly called, is sprinkled with islands. Some, such as tiny **Spectacle Island**, a domain of the Royal Australian Navy, and **Goat Island**, one-time nerve centre of port operations, are currently off limits to the public. On others, though, you can cast yourself away, or take a historical tour.

The largest island, at 18 hectares (44 acres), is **Cockatoo Island**, managed by the **Sydney Harbour Federation Trust** (8969 2131, www.harbourtrust.gov.au). The trust runs informative two-and-a-half-hour walking tours on weekends ($25, $15 concessions), which depart from Circular Quay and must be pre-booked. Cockatoo Island was once a convict prison and later a gigantic shipbuilding and ship repair operation: buildings associated with both these eras still stand like ghostly sentinels to an alternately dark and industrious past. Although there are plans to introduce facilities on the uninhabited island, such as a café and possibly boat-building again (on a small scale), for now Cockatoo remains refreshingly commercial-free.

The other islands that can be visited are under the auspices of the **National Parks & Wildlife Service** (NPWS, 9247 5033, www.nationalparks.nsw.gov.au), which has an office at **Cadman's Cottage** (see p306) in the Rocks.

Fort Denison, just off Mrs Macquarie's Point, served as an open-air prison and was called Pinchgut Island after the starvation rations – bread and water for a week – served to its inmates. Its first resident, Thomas Hill, was marooned for seven days in 1788 as punishment for taking biscuits. In 1862 a fort with a distinctive Martello tower was added and the island was renamed Fort Denison after then-governor William Denison. Again, it's only accessible by pre-booked tour (standard $22, $18 concessions; weekend tours with brunch at Fort Denison café $47, $43 concessions).

Shark Island, off Point Piper, **Clark Island**, near Darling Point, and **Rodd Island**, west of the Harbour Bridge in Iron Cove, are open to day-trippers year-round, with a $5 landing fee per person. Visitor numbers are limited, and you must book in advance with the NPWS and arrange your own transport by a private boat, chartered ferry or water taxi from a NPWS list of licensed operators. Boats are allowed to drop off and pick up at the island wharfs, but not to tie up. There's also a weekend ferry service ($16, $13.50-$14.50 concessions, $53 family) to Shark Island run by NPWS in conjunction with **Matilda Cruises** (see p58). Toilets and picnic tables are provided, but you must take your rubbish home. Swimming is not recommended, except from Shark's sandy beach (though there's no lifeguard).

---

also explores colonisation, invasion and contact. The Cadigal Place gallery honours the clan's history and culture, while, outside the museum, the *Edge of the Trees* sculpture by Fiona Foley and Janet Laurence symbolises that first encounter as the Cadigal people hid behind trees and watched officers of the First Fleet struggle ashore. **Photo** *p67*.

Sydney Opera House

Bennelong Point, Circular Quay (box office 9250 7777/information 9250 7111/tours 9250 7250/ www.sydneyoperahouse.com). CityRail/ferry Circular Quay. **Tours** every 30mins 9am-5pm daily. **Tickets** $23; $16 concessions; $63.25 family. **Credit** AmEx, DC, MC, V. **Map** p327 G3.

Set in a heavenly harbour, its cream wings reminiscent of the sails of the First Fleet, the Sydney Opera House is the city's most famous asset. It took 14 troubled years and $102 million to build – $95 million more than was anticipated. In true Aussie style, the shortfall was met by lotteries. The cultural cathedral has never been visited by its creator, Danish architect Jørn Utzon, who resigned halfway

through the project following a clash with the Minister of Public Works. On its opening night in 1973, an impromptu appearance was made onstage by two small possums.

In its five auditoria the Opera House holds 2,400 opera, concert, theatre, film and dance performances every year, attended by some 1.5 million people. The first performer was Paul Robeson who, in 1960, at the invitation of the militant builders' union, sang Old Man River at the construction site. The building is currently undergoing a 'venue improvement programme' under the guidance of Utzon and his architect son and partner Jan (*see p74* **The return of the architect**).

Attend a performance if you have the chance; otherwise, take one of the daily guided tours. It's also a great place to while away a few hours: eateries range from the haute-cuisine (and haute-priced) Guillaume at Bennelong (*see p147*) to the very stylish Opera Bar (*see p177*), with indoor and outdoor seating and live entertainment, and the Sidewalk Café. For information on concerts, *see p254*; for theatre events, *see p271*. **Photo** *p69*.

Macquarie Street, Royal Botanic Gardens & Hyde Park

Tree-lined **Macquarie Street** – named after Lachlan Macquarie, the great reformist governor of NSW, who served from 1809 to 1821 – is the closest thing the CBD has to a boulevard. It fairly drips with old money and resonates with history: on one side you'll find Sydney's main public buildings, on the other handsome apartment blocks belonging to medicos, the well-heeled and the 'squatocracy' (a sarcastic term for Australia's 'landed gentry'). A notable recent addition is Norman Foster's **Deutsche Bank Place** on the corner of Hunter and Phillip Streets, a sleek, 39-storey tower that is instantly recognisable by the triangular-shaped lattice structure on top.

To the west of Macquarie Street, the 30 broad green hectares (74 acres) of the **Royal Botanic Gardens** (*see p73*) – site of **Government House** (*see p71*), the home of NSW governors – form a green and pleasant rump to the city, leading down to the water at Farm Cove. This was the site of Australia's first vegetable patch; you can still see the spot where, two centuries ago, Governor Arthur Phillip first planted his big yams. In summer a huge screen rises from the water on the cove's eastern side, and seating is erected in the gardens so that locals can catch a movie at the **Open-Air Cinema** (*see p228*).

South of the Botanic Gardens, across Cahill Expressway, is another spacious green retreat, the **Domain**. Home to Sunday soap-box orators, the Domain has long been the place for civic protest: huge crowds gathered in 1917 to protest against World War I conscription, more than 100,000 demonstrated in 1931 against the governor's dismissal of Prime Minister Jack Lang, and in 2003 up to 50,000 demonstrated against the invasion of Iraq. It is also the site of one of the key public events on the city's annual calendar, the free **Symphony & Jazz in the Domain** concerts, part of January's **Sydney Festival** (*see p214*). If you're in town at this time, don't miss these fabulous communal picnics and concerts, topped off by fireworks.

The Domain is also where you'll find the **Art Gallery of New South Wales** (*see p70*) and memorials to poets Robert Burns and Henry Lawson. The park itself, mainly open space, offers few surprises, but hold your breath for the final sensational view: **Mrs Macquarie's Chair** overlooking the harbour. The Domain used to be Governor Macquarie's private park, and its tip was the favourite spot of his wife, Elizabeth. A seat has been shaped in the rock – hence the name – and the view is still one of Sydney's finest. On the Woolloomooloo Bay side of the Domain is **Andrew (Boy) Charlton Pool** (*see p70*), a popular outdoor lap pool for city workers, and a favoured sunbaking spot for trim gay men.

Sydney Opera House, with the popular Opera Bar in the foreground. *See p68.*

Heading south down Macquarie Street stand a row of impressive historical buildings: the **State Library of New South Wales** (*see p74*), **Parliament House** (*see p73*), **Sydney Hospital** (*see p75*), the **Mint** (*see p73*) and the **Hyde Park Barracks Museum** (*see p71*). Notable churches in the area include **St James** (corner of King and Phillip Streets, 9232 3022, www.stjameschurchsydney.org.au), designed by Francis Greenway the oldest church in Sydney (completed 1824), and **St Stephen's Uniting Church** (197 Macquarie Street, 9221 1688, www.ststephens churchsydney.org.au).

At Macquarie Street's southern end, between Elizabeth and College Streets, is gracious **Hyde Park**, named after its much larger London counterpart. It used to have a rowdy reputation, and was more a venue for sideshows, wrestling and boxing matches than a park; until the late 1820s it also served as Sydney's racecourse. Now it's a tranquil green space and fitting home to elegant Australian memorials, including the famous art deco **Anzac Memorial** (*see below*), and the graceful **Archibald Fountain**, commemorating the Australian-French Alliance of 1914-18.

During the Sydney Festival, the park erupts with free entertainment and, in summer, office workers flop down on the grass, while ibis pick their long-legged way around the supine bodies. Hyde Park is a fine sight at night, with fairy-lights in the trees, and possums scampering up trunks and foraging among the plants. The main avenue of Hills fig trees running north through the park is especially striking, though less so since 34 of them had to be removed in 2005 after being blighted by disease and decay.

On the **College Street** side of the park are **St Mary's Cathedral** (*see p74*), the **Australian Museum** (*see p71*), **Sydney Grammar School** and the **Cook & Phillip Park** aquatic and sports centre (*see p258*). Even if you don't fancy a dip, at least pop in to see Wendy Sharpe's wonderful murals above the 50-metre pool depicting the life of 19th-century swimming star Annette Kellerman, who went on to become Australia's first Hollywood movie star. On Elizabeth Street facing Hyde Park sits the elaborate **Great Synagogue** (*see p71*).

Opposite the south-eastern corner of Hyde Park on Liverpool Street is the block-long **Mark Foy's Building**, with its distinctive gold trim and green turrets. Once a department store, completed in 1917, it was converted to a court complex in 1991: you'll often see a huddle of lawyers, clients and, depending on the case, members of the fourth estate, outside here.

Francis Foy, one of the seven siblings who established the original store, took his architect to look at department stores around the world before settling on the design: the lower levels feature a special glazed brick shipped from Scotland. Unable to decide whose name the store should carry, the Foys settled the dispute by naming it after their father, Mark.

Andrew (Boy) Charlton Pool

Mrs Macquarie's Road, The Domain (9358 6686/ www.abcpool.org). Bus 411, 422. **Open** 6am-8pm daily. **Admission** $5.20; $3.40-$3.60 concessions. **Map** p330 H5.

A $10 million refurbishment has made this harbourside pool *the* place for inner-city summer swimming. It was a popular bathing spot long before the British arrived, and public sea baths first opened here in 1860. In the early 1920s famous Aussie swimmer Andrew 'Boy' Charlton achieved many of his triumphs here – including, as a 16-year-old, beating European champ Arne Borg, setting a new world record in the process. Today, the baths offer an eight-lane, heated 50m pool, learners' and toddlers' pools, sundeck and café. The pool's harbourside edges are glazed, allowing swimmers unparalleled views across the sparkling bay.

Anzac Memorial

Hyde Park, between Park & Liverpool Streets, CBD (9267 7668). CityRail Museum. **Open** 9am-5pm daily. **Admission** free. **Map** p329 F7.

Sydney architect Bruce Dellit was only 31 when he won the 1930 competition to design this beautiful grey-pink granite memorial to the Australian and New Zealand troops who fell in World War I, particularly those involved in the bloody battle for the Gallipoli peninsula. His art deco vision caused a sensation when it opened in 1934. The striking bas reliefs are by Rayner Hoff, who also made the central bronze sculpture in the 'Well of Contemplation' of a Christ-like naked figure held aloft on a shield by three women, symbolising the sacrifices of war. Over the next few years $2.4 million is being spent to shore up the monument in time for its 75th anniversary in 2009. An act of remembrance is held here at 11am daily and guided tours can be arranged at the reception desk in the monument's base, where you'll also find a small museum dedicated to Australia's military.

Art Gallery of New South Wales

Art Gallery Road, The Domain (9225 1700/ www.artgallery.nsw.gov.au). CityRail Martin Place or St James then 10mins walk/bus 441. **Open** 10am-5pm Mon, Tue, Thur-Sun; 10am-9pm Wed. **Admission** free; charges for some exhibitions. **Credit** AmEx, MC, V. **Map** p327 H6.

NSW's main art gallery moved to its present site in 1885. It includes a solid collection of 19th- and 20th-century Australian artists, as well as Aboriginal and Torres Strait Islander art, big names of European art history and international contemporary artists,

The green fields of the **Domain**. *See p69.*

plus a fine Asian art collection. There are also regular blockbuster touring shows from overseas galleries. One of its most popular, and controversial, exhibitions is the annual Archibald Prize, a portraiture competition, which is complemented by the Wynne (landscape and sculpture) and Sir John Sulman competitions (best 'subject/genre paintings' and murals). Wednesday is late-opening night, with free talks, debates and performances, and there are regular events for kids. Tours of the general collection are held two or three times a day.

Australian Museum

6 College Street, at William Street, CBD (9320 6000/www.austmus.gov.au). CityRail Museum or St James. **Open** 9.30am-5pm daily. **Admission** $10; $5 concessions; $25 family. **Credit** AmEx, MC, V. **Map** p329 G7.

The Australian Museum (established 1827) houses the nation's most important animal, mineral, fossil and anthropological collections, and prides itself on its innovative research into Australia's environment and indigenous cultures. Displays cover the Pacific Islands, Asia, Africa and the Americas, with items ranging from Aboriginal kids' toys to a tattooed chalk head from the Solomon Islands. Any serious museum-tripper should see a few of the local stuffed animals, and the displays should answer all your questions about Australian mammals. If you're at all interested in Aboriginal culture and beliefs, visit the Indigenous Australia section, which tackles such

contentious issues as the 'stolen generation', deaths in custody and problems facing indigenous people today. Around 1,000 Aboriginal objects of a secret and/or sacred nature are held separately from the main collection: access to these can be arranged through the Aboriginal Heritage Unit.

Government House

Royal Botanic Gardens (9931 5222/www.hht.nsw. gov.au). CityRail Circular Quay or Martin Place/ ferry Circular Quay. **Open** *House* guided tour only; every 30mins 10.30am-3pm Fri-Sun. *Garden* 10am-4pm daily. **Admission** free. **Map** p327 G3/4.

Designed in 1834 by William IV's architect, Edward Blore, the plans for Government House (the official residence of the NSW governor) had to be modified to take account of local conditions, such as the Australian sun being in the north rather than the south. However, the original Gothic Revival concept remained, and today's visitors can still enjoy the crenellated battlements and detailed interiors. Past governors have dabbled in redecorating and extensions with rather weird results, but the marvellously restored State Rooms are now the best example of Victorian pomp in the country. The current governor doesn't live here, but it's still used for state and vice-regal functions. Don't miss the exotic gardens.

Great Synagogue

166 Castlereagh Street, between Park & Market Streets, CBD (9267 2477/www.greatsynagogue. org.au). CityRail St James or Town Hall. **Open** *Services* 5.30pm (winter), 6.15pm (summer) Fri; 8.45am Sat. *Tours* noon Tue, Thur. **Admission** $5. **No credit cards**. **Map** p329 F7.

Sydney's Jewish history dates back to convict times – there were around 16 Jews on the First Fleet – and the Great Synagogue, consecrated in 1878, is deemed the mother congregation of Australian Jewry. Designed by Thomas Rowe, the building is a lavish confection of French Gothic with large amounts of Byzantine thrown in. The superb front wheel window, facing on to Hyde Park, repeats the design of the wrought-iron gates outside, while, inside, the cast-iron columns holding up the balcony where women sit are capped with intricate plaster designs. The ceiling, deep blue with gold-leaf stars, depicts the Creation. Twice-weekly tours (entry from the back of the synagogue on Castlereagh Street) include a short video about the history of both the synagogue and Australia's Jewish community. A small museum is also open before and after tours.

Hyde Park Barracks Museum

Queens Square, corner of Macquarie Street & Prince Albert Road, CBD (8239 2311/www.hht.nsw.gov.au). CityRail Martin Place or St James. **Open** 9.30am-5pm daily. **Admission** $10; $5 concessions; $20 family. **Credit** MC, V. **Map** p327 G6.

Designed by convict architect Francis Greenway, the barracks were completed in 1819 to house 600 male convicts, who were in government employ until 1848. Subsequently used as an immigration depot and an asylum for women, they eventually

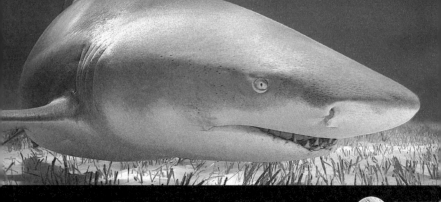

metamorphosed into a museum. On the top level are re-created convict barracks: rough hammocks hang side by side in the dormitories, while recorded snippets of conversation surround you. A computer database allows you to follow the official records of various convicts, from conviction via much flogging to, in some cases, eventual rehabilitation. The women's section on level two is no less thought-provoking – these (mostly Irish) women were escaping an awful existence to start what must have been an equally burdensome new life in a harsh colony. The quiet courtyard houses a pleasant café.

The Mint

10 Macquarie Street, between Queens Square & Martin Place, CBD (8239 2211/www.hht.nsw. gov.au). CityRail Martin Place or St James. **Open** 9am-5pm Mon-Fri. **Admission** free. **Map** p327 G6.
This attractive building with its bright yellow façade and two-storey, double-colonnaded veranda was built between 1811-16 as the southern wing of the Sydney Hospital. It turned into a coin-making operation – the first branch of the Royal Mint outside London – in the 1850s, following the discovery of gold in NSW, and continued to churn out money until 1926. Numismatists, be warned: there aren't any coins to gawp over, just a small historical exhibit and an upstairs café overlooking Macquarie Street. The building also houses the headquarters of the Historic Houses Trust.

Parliament House

6 Macquarie Street, opposite Hunter Street, CBD (9230 2111/tours 9230 3444/www.cityof sydney.nsw.gov.au). CityRail Martin Place or St James. **Open** 9.30am-4.30pm Mon-Fri. *Tours* (groups only) 9.30am, 11am, 12.30pm, 2pm, 3pm non-sitting days; individual tours available on demand between opening hours. **Admission** free. **Map** p327 G5.
Known to locals as the Bear Pit, the NSW Parliament is said to be the roughest, toughest parliament in the country. Its impressive sandstone home was built between 1811 and 1814 as the northern wing of the Rum Hospital, but was commandeered in 1829 to house the new colony's decision makers. Only the Legislative Assembly (lower house) existed until the 1850s, when the parliament became bicameral. The Legislative Council (upper house) meets in a building originally intended for use as a church; the cast-iron prefab was being shipped from Glasgow to Victoria when it was diverted mid-voyage to Sydney. The parliament is largely modelled on its mother in London: there's a Speaker and Black Rod, and even the colour scheme follows the British tradition of green for the lower chamber and red for the upper. Legislative sessions are open to the public, with viewing from a public gallery; booking is essential for the tours. **Photo** *right*.

Royal Botanic Gardens

Mrs Macquarie's Road, CBD (9231 8111/weekends 9231 8125/www.rbgsyd.nsw.gov.au). CityRail Circular Quay, Martin Place or St James/ferry Circular Quay. **Open** *Gardens* 7am-sunset daily. *Visitor Information* 9.30am-4.30pm daily. *Tropical Centre* 10am-4pm daily. *Shop* 9.30am-5pm daily. **Admission** *Gardens* free. *Tropical Centre* $2.20; $1.10 concessions. **Credit** (shop only) AmEx, MC, V. **Map** p327 G/H3/5.
The beautiful Royal Botanic Gardens, established in 1816, make a sweeping green curve from the Opera House to Woolloomooloo Bay. It's a gorgeous spot, full of majestic trees, spacious lawns, bird-filled ponds and ornamental flowerbeds. The Domain surrounds the gardens: in colonial times this land acted as a buffer between the governor's home and the penal colony, but by 1831 roads and paths had been built to allow public access, and it has remained a people's place ever since. The Palm Grove area is a good place to start: there's a shop and visitor information counter, café, restaurant and toilets. Highlights include the Tropical Centre, spectacular rose gardens, cacti collection, the large colony of fruit bats (aka flying foxes) near Palm Grove, and the 'living fossil' Wollemi pine, one of the world's rarest species, discovered in 1994 by a ranger in the Blue Mountains. The Fleet Steps provide a classic Opera House/Bridge photo-op.

There are free guided walks (10.30am daily) – or you can take the 'trackless train' ($10), which stops at areas of interest around the gardens, ending up at the Opera House. To learn more about Aboriginal life in the area, visit the Cadi Jam Ora garden or book a walk with an Aboriginal guide (details on 9231 8128, $16.50 per person).

Parliament House.

Sightseeing

The return of the architect

The **Sydney Opera House** (*see p68*) had curious beginnings. A dying premier commissions an international architectural competition in 1957, with no budget and no time frame. The jury consists of four architects; there are no engineers and no politicians on the panel. The site is dramatic but extremely surprising, given the industrial nature of the city's harbourside in the 1950s. The winning scheme, famously plucked from the reject pile by the late-arriving judge Eero Saarinen, is by an unknown Danish architect, 38-year-old Jørn Utzon, who has only a few small houses to his name.

Working from navigational maps of Sydney Harbour and a film urging Europeans to 'become Australian', Utzon absorbed and translated the essential elements of land, sea and sky in his billowing ceramic and concrete clouds hovering above the heavy geology of a stone platform. After four years and $7 million, stage one – the platform – was complete. A further five years and $21 million later, stage two – the shells –

was finished. Wranglings over the project and a political change in 1965 led to Utzon's demise; when he left in April 1966 (owed many hundreds of thousands of dollars in unpaid fees) the building was four times over budget and five years over time. The team of local architects that took over stage three – the interiors – spent an additional $74 million (four time what Utzon spent) finishing the job.

What you see today is only partly Utzon's creation. The platform and the shells are his, but the interiors – which he spent six years working on, even down to the cutlery and furniture – are nothing like his original design. This includes the windows, described by Utzon as 'hanging curtains of plywood, glass and bronze', and the Drama Theatre, Playhouse and Studio, which were were never part of the original brief.

Architecturally, the Opera House was way ahead of its time; just getting it built required pioneering technical and engineering methods, notably in the construction of the shells – made from pre-cast concrete

St Mary's Cathedral

Corner of College Street & Cathedral Square, CBD (9220 0400/www.sydney.catholic.org.au). CityRail St James. **Open** 6.45am-5.30pm Mon-Fri; 9am-6pm Sat; 7am-6pm Sun. *Tours* noon Sun; also by arrangement. **Admission** free. **Map** p327 G6.

St Mary's is the seat of the Roman Catholic archbishop of Sydney (currently the controversial Cardinal George Pell) and stands on the site of Australia's first Catholic chapel. William Wilkinson Wardell's design replaced the original cathedral, ruined by fire in 1865. Constructed from local sandstone, it's the largest Gothic cathedral in the southern hemisphere – 106m (348ft) long with a 46m (150ft) central tower – dwarfing many of the European models from which it took inspiration. Wardell's original twin spires, initially not erected due to funding problems, were lowered into place by helicopter in 1999. Don't miss the cathedral's crypt,

which is decorated with a beautifully designed terrazzo floor depicting the six days of Creation.

State Library of New South Wales

Corner of Macquarie Street & Cahill Expressway, CBD (9273 1414/www.sl.nsw.gov.au). CityRail Martin Place. **Open** *Library* 9am-9pm Mon-Thur; 9am-6pm Fri; 11am-5pm Sat, Sun. *Exhibitions* 9am-5pm Mon-Fri; 11am-5pm Sat, Sun. *Tours* 11am Tue; 2pm Thur. **Admission** free. **Map** p327 G5.

The State Library is essentially two libraries in one: the modern General Reference Library (GRL) provides access to five million books, CD-Roms and other media stored over five floors below ground, while the 1910 Mitchell Wing (closed Sundays) holds the world's greatest collection of Australiana, including James Cook's original journals and the log book of Captain Bligh. The latter wing has fine bronze bas-relief doors depicting Aboriginal peoples and European explorers, a grand mosaic and terrazzo

Sightseeing

segments held in place by steel tendons – and the million-plus ceramic tiles that cover the shells. Half matt, half shiny, these create a 'living' skin that changes with the light.

Queen Elizabeth II opened the Opera House in October 1973 to much fanfare, but the architect was not mentioned. It took another 20 years until Utzon's name appeared at the site, and until 2005 before the building was included on the National Heritage List.

In 1998, faced with embarrassing acoustic and orchestra-pit issues in the Opera Theatre, several local architects were interviewed to deal with these problems. A reluctant Richard Johnson (of Johnson Pilton Walker) went to the interview with two conditions. The first was to offer the job to Utzon, who had been living in Mallorca since the 1970s, in self-imposed exile from both Australia and Denmark, and was still producing remarkable buildings. The second was to use every change as an opportunity to go back to Utzon's original intent, so that any new work would respond to his ideas and strategies.

This approach received Utzon's blessing and, since 1999, Johnson, Utzon's architect son Jan and Utzon himself (now aged 87) have been working together on the interiors. Famously, Utzon has never returned to Australia since 1966 and never seen his completed masterpiece.

Have a look at the public toilets across from the ticketing booth in the platform, as well as the polished concrete slabs under the platform – some of the most beautiful concrete work in the world. The two most obvious new elements are the refurbished and renamed Utzon Room, featuring a large, brightly coloured tapestry by the architect; and the Colonnade on the Harbour Bridge side, which reflects Utzon's original inspiration, the pre-Columbian stone platforms in South America and their surrounding colonnades. Officially opened by Queen Elizabeth II in March 2006, the 45m/148ft-long Colonnade creates nine openings in the façade, allowing views across the harbour. It's the first external change to the Opera House since it was built.

vestibule, stained-glass windows and extensive amounts of Australian stone and timber. Its Shakespeare Room is a fine example of mock-Tudor style, with a ceiling modelled on Cardinal Wolsey's closet in Hampton Court and stained glass windows depicting the 'seven ages of man'. The GRL's very popular Family History Service offers free courses to help people trace their family history, and changing exhibitions highlight the library's large and fascinating collection of historic paintings, photos, manuscripts and rare books. There are free guided tours of both libraries.

Sydney Hospital & Sydney Eye Hospital

8 Macquarie Street, opposite Martin Place, CBD (9382 7400/www.sesahs.nsw.gov.au/sydhosp). CityRail Martin Place. **Open** *Museum* 10am-3pm Tue. **Admission** *Museum* $6. *Tour* $10. *Both* $14. **Map** p327 G5/6.

Originally known as the Rum Hospital, because its construction was paid for by government-controlled rum sales, Sydney Hospital is the city's only early institutional building still performing its original function. The current structure is a grandiose, late Victorian edifice, which thoughtlessly replaced the centre of what was once an eye-catching trio; cast your eyes to Parliament House on one side and the Mint on the other to get an idea of what the hospital originally looked like. Outside stands the *Il Porcellino* bronze boar sculpture, a copy of the famous original in Florence; its snout is shiny from people rubbing it for good luck. Inside, the marble floors, magnificent windows and colour scheme have been carefully restored. The lobby lists those who donated to its construction and the respective amounts – Dame Nellie Melba kicked in £100, as much as some of the business giants of the day. You can't just walk into the hospital itself, but you can book two weeks ahead

Sydney Hospital, built on the proceeds from rum sales. *See p75*.

for guided tours (groups only, minimum eight). The Lucy Osburn-Nightingale Foundation Museum is open to the public on Tuesdays. But the courtyard is open to all and has a very good café, with views over the Domain and an elaborate and colourful cast-iron fountain commemorating British comedian Robert Brough, who endeared himself to Australian audiences in the 19th century. **Photo** *above*.

Martin Place, Centrepoint & Town Hall

Squashed between the green spaces of the Domain and Hyde Park and the waterside promenades of Darling Harbour is the CBD proper. Apart from walking, one of the best ways of getting around this central area, as well as to Darling Harbour and Chinatown, is on the elevated Monorail system.

The CBD's historic epicentre is **Martin Place**, a pedestrian boulevard lined with monumental buildings running west from Macquarie Street to George Street. The largest non-garden open space in the CBD, it houses the **Cenotaph** – which commemorates Australian lives lost in World War I – and, in December, a Christmas tree wilting in the Sydney sun. Lunchtime concerts and a fountain make this an outdoor mecca for office workers, and huge screens are often erected here during big sporting and cultural events.

At the George Street end of Martin Place you'll find the grand **General Post Office** (*see p77*), outside which crowds gathered to celebrate the end of the two world wars. This very fine Victorian building has been wonderfully renovated: in the basement you'll find several good restaurants, a sushi bar and a very upmarket food court. The upper floors contain showy retail outlets, and a rather formal luxury/business hotel, the **Westin Sydney** (*see p32*). The sandstone banks and office buildings erected along the southern edge of Martin Place during the economic boom of wool and wheat now jostle with the odd elegant skyscraper and modern monstrosities such as the **MLC Centre** (*see p190*), which houses designer shops, a huge electrical store and some great outdoor cafés.

North of Martin Place, on the western side of George Street, is **Wynyard Station**, the main train and bus interchange for travelling across the Harbour Bridge to the north shore and northern beaches.

At night the CBD used to be quite dull, but twenty- and thirtysomething hangouts like the **Establishment** complex – home of **Tank** nightclub (*see p222*), **Hemmesphere** cocktail bar (*see p176*), **est.** restaurant (*see p147*) and a swanky hotel (*see p33*) – and the newly renovated **Sydney Hilton** hotel (*see p29*) with its fashionable **Zeta Bar** (*see p177*) and Luke Mangan-helmed **Glass** restaurant (*see p145*), have introduced a fresh after-hours vigour. Much of this resurgence in the CBD's party status can be credited to Justin Hemmes, the young dynamo behind the Establishment as well as the trendy bars and bistro of **Hotel CBD** (corner of York and King Streets, 8297 7000, www.merivale.com), and **Slip Inn** (*see p222*). His most ambitious venture, Ivy, is a vast complex on George Street housing shops, bars, restaurants and a new hotel due to open in 2007.

The main shopping district of the CBD – roughly bounded by Hunter, Elizabeth, George and Park Streets – orbits Sydney's two department stores, thoroughly modern **Myer** and majestic **David Jones** (for both, *see p189*). Nearby are the grandiose **State Theatre** (*see p271*) and the stately **Queen Victoria Building** (*see p79*). Pedestrianised Pitt Street Mall is always jammed with shoppers and has lots of buskers but never enough seats. Make sure you take a turn through the elegant **Strand Arcade** (*see p190*), packed with designer fashion and gift shops.

The **Sydney Tower** (*see p79*) – also known as Centrepoint after the shopping centre that it crowns and as the AMP Tower after the ad sign on its turret – rises 305 metres (1,000 feet) between Pitt Street Mall and Castlereagh Street. It's the tallest structure in the city. Despite its spindly appearance, the tower, which is held in place by 56 cables, is capable of withstanding earthquakes and extreme wind conditions – as the publicity blurb goes, 'if the strands of these cables were laid end to end, they would reach from Sydney to New Zealand'. Now do you feel safe? In 2005 the tower underwent a glitzy revamp, adding OzTrek, a virtual-reality adventure tour, and Skywalk, a heart-thumping open-air walk around the roof.

The intersection of George, Park and Druitt Streets is a major crossroads surrounded by the QVB, the chic **Galeries Victoria** shopping mall (*see p189*), and **Sydney Town Hall** (*see p79*). Beneath them all is bustling Town Hall train station and a warren of subterranean shopping alleys linking up the various above-ground buildings. It's a hectic area, particularly during the day when office workers and students gather on the Town Hall steps to chat, eat lunch and wait for buses. Next door is the Anglican **St Andrew's Cathedral** (*see p79*).

If Sydney's mayor Clover Moore and her council colleagues have their way, this area will see striking changes in the coming decade: they are on a mission to buy up the George Street block facing the Town Hall so that it can eventually be demolished to create a grassy public square. Currently, it's far from a pretty part of town. The multiplex cinema on George Street, surrounding burger bars and late-night pubs keep folk hanging out well into the early hours: be prepared to jostle with teenagers streaming in to play video games at several louche amusement arcades, and rowdy backpackers and boozers heading for drinking dens such as the perpetually lively, round-the-clock Irish bar **Scruffy Murphy's Hotel** (43 Goulburn Street, 9211 2002, www.scruffy murphys.com.au).

One more 'genuine' pocket is the 'Spanish quarter', the tiny stretch of Liverpool Street between George and Sussex Streets, where you can have tapas and a cerveza at the **Spanish Club** (No.88, 9267 8440) or take home Spanish chorizo, olives and rioja from the **Torres Cellars & Delicatessen** (No.75, 9264 6862, www.torresdeli.com.au).The area used to be quite down at heel, but a clean-up has encouraged previously lacklustre restaurants to lift their game; best of the crop is the upmarket **Don Quixote** (9264 5903, 545 Kent Street).

A few doors down, **Tetsuya's** (one of Sydney's superstar restaurants – *see p147*) hides behind the **Judges House** (531 Kent Street), built in 1827 and a rare example of a colonial Georgian bungalow with verandas. It's now occupied by an office, but you can admire it from the street.

The area immediately south of Liverpool Street has been transformed by the arrival – after years of delay and building work – of **World Square**, a mega shopping, office and residential complex that takes up a whole city block (*see p81* **World domination**). Large-scale musicals and suchlike are often playing at the **Capitol Theatre** (*see p269*) on Campbell Street. A block south lies **Central Station**, Sydney's main train and bus nexus, surrounded by backpacker hostels and internet cafés.

General Post Office

1 Martin Place, between George & Pitt Streets, CBD (8224 1111). CityRail Martin Place or Wynyard. **Map** p327 F5.

The GPO's foundations were laid in 1865, but workers' strikes and complications from building over the Tank Stream (the colony's first water supply) meant that it didn't open until 1874. The grand clocktower was added in 1891, its chimes based on London's Big Ben, with both the clock mechanism and bells made in England. The building's Italianate flourishes dominated the young city's skyline for decades before it fell into neglect; by 1989 the building was no longer adequate for the needs of Australia Post and in 1990 it was boarded up. A deal between the city authorities and the Westin Hotel group rescued the building, restoring the original cast-iron staircase, the clocktower and two ballrooms, and transforming the offices into hotel rooms. The GPO hall is now a light-drenched atrium that forms part of the hotel lobby and leads down to a very classy food court and collection of restaurants. The colonnaded Martin Place entrance is flanked by upmarket shops. Much of the GPO's beauty is in the details: the stencilling on the walls, the moderne windows, and the gold leaf ceiling patterned with leaves – spot the

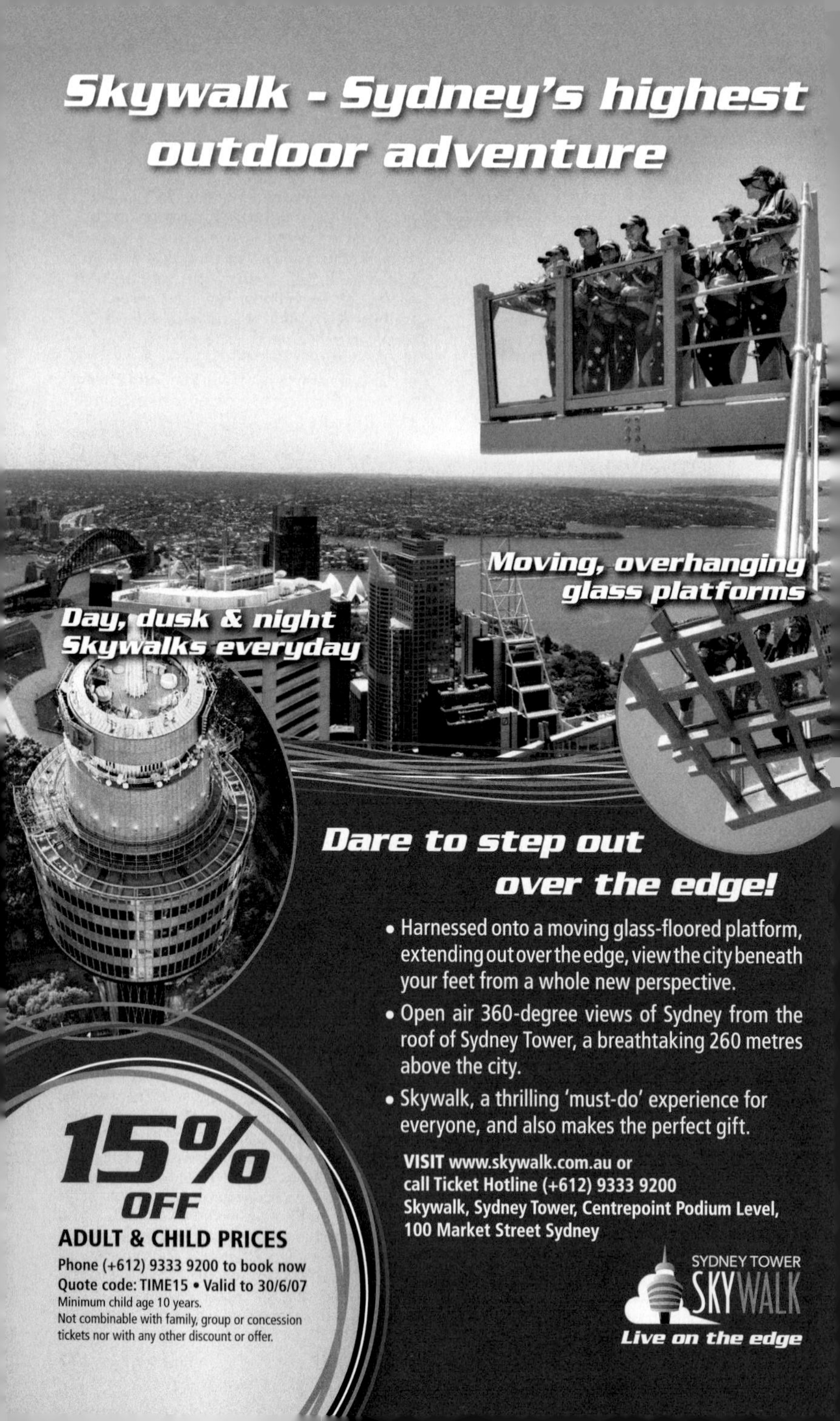

Skywalk - Sydney's highest outdoor adventure
Moving, overhanging glass platforms
Day, dusk & night Skywalks everyday
Dare to step out over the edge!
• Harnessed onto a moving glass-floored platform, extending out over the edge, view the city beneath your feet from a whole new perspective.
• Open air 360-degree views of Sydney from the roof of Sydney Tower, a breathtaking 260 metres above the city.
• Skywalk, a thrilling 'must-do' experience for everyone, and also makes the perfect gift.
VISIT www.skywalk.com.au or
call Ticket Hotline (+612) 9333 9200
Skywalk, Sydney Tower, Centrepoint Podium Level,
100 Market Street Sydney
15% OFF
ADULT & CHILD PRICES
Phone (+612) 9333 9200 to book now
Quote code: TIME15 • Valid to 30/6/07
Minimum child age 10 years.
Not combinable with family, group or concession tickets nor with any other discount or offer.
SYDNEY TOWER
SKYWALK
Live on the edge

English rose and the Irish shamrock, as well as the Australian wattle and gum. The Tank Stream viewing room is open daily to visitors.

Queen Victoria Building (QVB)

455 George Street, between Market & Druitt Streets, CBD (9264 9209/www.qvb.com.au). CityRail Town Hall/Monorail Galeries Victoria. **Tours** 11.30am, 2.30pm daily. **Tickets** $10. **Map** p327 E6.

Designed by George McRae to resemble a Byzantine palace, the QVB occupies an entire block on George Street, and once dominated the Sydney skyline with its dramatic domed roof – an inner glass dome encased by a copper-sheathed outer one. Completed in 1898 to celebrate Queen Victoria's golden jubilee, it originally housed street markets. It has suffered, and gamely survived, long periods of neglect, and demolition threats were finally quashed in the 1980s when a $75 million budget restored the building to its former grandeur. It now houses 200 outlets, including shops (*see p190*), cafés and restaurants. Of particular note are the coloured lead-light wheel windows, the cast-iron circular staircase, and the original floor tiles and lift. The ballroom on the third floor is now the Tearoom (*see p169*). On the hour, shoppers gather on gallery two to watch the Royal Automata Clock display a moving royal pageant. The execution of Charles I goes down a storm.

St Andrew's Cathedral

Sydney Square, corner of George & Bathurst Streets, CBD (9265 1661/www.cathedral.sydney.anglican.asn. au). CityRail Town Hall. **Open** 10am-3pm. **Tours** by arrangement daily. **Admission** free. **Map** p329 E7.

This huge late-Gothic edifice, the oldest cathedral in Australia, was started with astonishing confidence by Governor Macquarie (who named it after the patron saint of his native Scotland) when Sydney was still the size of a small village. The first stone was laid in 1819, and the cathedral was consecrated in 1868. Three architects contributed to it, the most notable being Edmund Blacket, city architect 1849-54. Special elements link the cathedral to the motherland, including a marble floor from Canterbury Cathedral and two stones from the Palace of Westminster. Military commemorations honour the landings at Gallipoli and the prison camp at Changi in Singapore. Recent conservation work has restored the interior (altered in the 1950s) to its original glory.

Sydney Tower

Centrepoint Podium Level, 100 Market Street, between Castlereagh & Pitt Streets, CBD (9333 9222/www.sydneytoweroztrek.com.au/www.skywalk. com.au). CityRail St James or Town Hall/Monorail City Centre. **Open** *Tower & OzTrek* 9am-10.30pm Mon-Fri, Sun; 9am-11.30pm Sat. *Skywalk* 9am-9.30pm daily. **Tickets** *Tower & OzTrek* $23.50; $14-$17.50 concessions; $41-$69 family; free under-4s. *Skywalk* $109-$139; $85-$105 concessions. **Credit** AmEx, DC, MC, V. **Map** p327 F6.

Three high-speed lifts take approximately 40 seconds to travel to the golden turret of this well-known city symbol, which provides two levels of restaurants, a coffee lounge and an observation deck at 250m/820ft with 360° views. Skywalk, the latest of the city's 'thrill' tours, opened in 2005, allowing visitors to wander around the outside of the turret. Harnessed to a range of skyways and viewing platforms, participants have the whole of Sydney at their feet: on a clear day you can see distant headlands up and down the coast, and as far west as the Blue Mountains. You're only just above the observation deck and safe at all times, but being outside is a definite buzz – it's a good alternative to BridgeClimb (*see p58*). Vertigo sufferers might prefer OzTrek, a virtual-reality ride through Australia's cultural history and geography, including climbing Uluru, a game of Aussie Rules footy and a tussle with a saltie (saltwater crocodile). Every year there's a race up the 1,504 stairs of the tower: the record, set in 2002 by Paul Crake, is six minutes, 52 seconds.

Sydney Town Hall

Corner of George & Druitt Streets, CBD (9265 9189/ concert information 9265 9007/www.cityofsydney. nsw.gov.au). CityRail Town Hall. **Open** 8am-6pm Mon-Fri. **Admission** free. **Map** p329 E7.

Built on a graveyard and completed in 1889, Sydney Town Hall is an impressive High Victorian building, topped by a clocktower with a two-ton bell. It has retained its original function and interiors, including the council chamber and lord mayor's offices. The stunning vestibule, its colourful domed ceiling hung with a huge crystal chandelier, has some of the earliest examples of Australian-made stained glass. Behind it, Centennial Hall is dominated by a magnificent 8,000-pipe organ: with a capacity of 2,048, it was once the largest concert hall in the world. It's still used for organ recitals and other musical events.

Chinatown & Haymarket

Chinese people have been in Sydney since the First Fleet landed in 1788: two of the ships' cooks were said to be Chinese. By 1891 the Chinese population had reached 14,000, but dwindled to 4,000 as the 'White Australia' policy peaked in the 1950s. Today, Chinese migrants make up the third-largest group of immigrants coming to New South Wales. Vietnamese refugees (including many of Chinese descent) arrived in the wake of the Vietnam War, while dissident students sought asylum after the 1989 Tiananmen Square debacle. In the years leading to the handover of Hong Kong to China, many Hong Kong Chinese also left for Australia.

When you hit Chinatown, the vitality and energy of the Chinese community is obvious. Sino-Sydneysiders do not live in a ghetto – there are also established suburban enclaves in Strathfield, Willoughby and Ashfield, and many are simply integrated into the community – but Chinatown is the commercial and culinary hub. Once confined to **Dixon Street**, a somewhat tacky pedestrianised mall created in the 1980s, it continues to expand and change at a phenomenal rate. It now extends well into Haymarket, over Hay Street, down Thomas and Ultimo Streets, and across George Street.

Around the ornate gates in Dixon Street, soil, sand and rock from Guangdong province has been buried. For the Chinese, it symbolises that Australia is their home and they can be buried there. **Sussex Street** has now taken over from Dixon Street as the main strip; the brightly lit section from Goulburn Street to Hay Street – where **Paddy's Market** (*see p192*) and the Market City shopping centre reside – bustles with activity from early morning to late at night. There are restaurants, supermarkets, shops, Chinese-language cinemas and some well-hidden gambling spots, and this is one of the few places in Sydney where you can get a meal and a drink at 2am.

In daylight hours, chic shops sell (real and ersatz) Agnès B and Katharine Hamnett watches, Versace and Romeo Gigli perfumes, Jean-Paul Gaultier bags and a range of bewilderingly hip gear: the Chinese community is not only growing in size, it's also increasingly affluent. The days of wall-to-wall sweet-and-sour pork have been left far behind. Nowadays, little Chinatown diners serve Peking-style dumplings, while others specialise in handmade noodles, barbecued duck or seafood, and grand Hong Kong-style dining rooms with over-the-top chandeliers are always packed with Chinese and Anglos choosing delicacies from yum cha (dim sum) trolleys. For standout restaurants in the area, *see pp149-150*.

Darling Harbour, Pyrmont & Ultimo

Map p326, pp328-329. **Transport** Darling Harbour *Ferry Darling Harbour/CityRail Central or Town Hall/Monorail Convention, Darling Park or Harbourside/LightRail Convention or Exhibition/bus 443*. **Pyrmont** *Ferry Pyrmont Bay/LightRail Fish Market, John St Square, Pyrmont Bay or Star City/bus 443, 449*. **Ultimo** *CityRail Central/Monorail/LightRail Exhibition or Paddy's Markets*.

The reclaimed waterfront of Darling Harbour, on the western side of the CBD, boasts some acclaimed modern architecture (courtesy of architect Phillip Cox) and a huge retail complex (courtesy of global capitalism). The area is geared very much towards tourists, and can feel pretty soulless compared to other parts of Sydney. So many attractions are here –

the **Sydney Aquarium**, the **Australian National Maritime Museum**, the **Chinese Garden of Friendship** (for all, *see p82*), **Sydney Entertainment Centre** (*see p249*) and the **IMAX** cinema (*see p227*) – that it's easy to overlook the most basic one: the view of the western cityscape from the Pyrmont side of Darling Harbour, one of the best in Sydney. And it's free. There's also the **Harbourside** shopping centre (*see p189*), a bit of a tourist trap but good for souvenirs if you don't want to search too hard.

Darling Harbour hosts a stream of free festivals, concerts and other events at weekends and in school holidays throughout the year. New Year's Eve and Australia Day, in particular, are occasions for giant parties: call the **Darling Harbour Information Line** for details (1902 260 568, www.darling harbour.com.au). There's also a branch of the **Sydney Visitor Centre** (*see p306*), behind the IMAX cinema.

Cockle Bay Wharf (so named because of its original abundance of shellfish), on Darling Harbour's eastern shore, houses an array of cafés, restaurants and clubs spread across an epic space designed by populist American architect Eric Kuhne, who also designed the public areas in adjoining **Darling Park** (and the enormous Bluewater development in Kent, England). Initially written off by many as a failure, Cockle Bay has become a hugely successful entertainment precinct and a fun place to dine and hang out. By day, it's a haven for teens and families; at night, tourists and twentysomethings move in, many heading for the sail-like glass building of mega nightclub **Home** (*see p221*).

Further north, past the Sydney Aquarium, the party continues along the newly created **King Street Wharf** at yet more restaurants, cafés and a clutch of waterside apartments. A good place to be on a sweltering summer's night, if you're under 30, is the **Cargo Bar** (*see p219*), a rowdy outdoor venue with pumping music and great waterside views, or stylish bar **Loft** (*see p179*) at the far end of the promenade.

Pyrmont, to the west of Darling Harbour (reached by the pedestrian Pyrmont Bridge), was once a mix of working-class cottages, refineries, quarries and engineering works. Now it's filling with apartment buildings and office blocks (including Rupert Murdoch's pay TV station, Foxtel) as the city spreads ever westward. It's also home to **Star City** (*see p82*), Sydney's casino – a gaudy, vulgar, Las Vegas-like creation (also by Phillip Cox) with a deluxe hotel (*see p39*). **Jones Bay Wharf**, at the top end of the peninsula, has

World domination

When construction workers started digging foundations in a huge CBD block bounded by George, Liverpool, Pitt and Goulburn Streets in 1988, the dream was to create a high-rise inner-city neighbourhood on the former site of the Anthony Horden & Sons department store. Just two years later, a property market crash and industrial disputes left the proposed development little more than a giant hole in the ground tacked on to a shabby car park. And so it remained for the next decade. No wonder it's taking Sydneysiders some time to adjust to the gleaming towers and vast shopping mall of the reborn **World Square** (9262 7926, www.worldsquare.com.au), which finally opened in 2005.

The complex comprises two residential towers, an office tower and a huge shopping centre (*see p190*). Its centrepiece is the 203-metre (666-foot), 73-storey **World Tower**, designed by Melbourne-based architects Nation Fender Katsalidis. It's the tallest residential building in the southern hemisphere and, apart from great views, offers three gyms, spas, saunas and swimming pools (including one on the 61st floor), two theatres and two golf ranges. The developer claims the complex caters for 35,000 workers, 16,800 residents and 9,000 tourists – who can stay in serviced apartments in World Tower or at the **Avillion Hotel** (*see p33*). Several new restaurants, cafés and bars include the **Equilibrium Hotel**, which has 64 beers on tap, and the chi-chi Melbourne-style **Liverpool Lane**, a collection of small eateries along a narrow passage leading off Liverpool Street and into the central open piazza – which features a slinky metallic dragon sculpture, a nod to nearby Chinatown.

The developers involved in World Square now have their sights set on enticing even more Sydneysiders to inner-city high-rise living. Across the road on George Street, the 58-storey **Meriton Tower** is taking shape, as is neighbouring **Regent Place**, which incorporates the 56-storey Lumiere, a sleek, Norman Foster-designed tower that's being touted as Australia's first 'vertical village'. Eventually this district – bounded by Park Street to the north, Central Station to the south, Darling Harbour to the west and Hyde Park to the east – will be the most densely populated area in the country. Already there are calls to give the area its own name and identity, with the clumsy Sybepa – SYdney BElow PArk – in the running.

undergone a sleek renovation into classy offices, topped off with the fabulous seafood restaurant **Flying Fish** (*see p151*).

Pyrmont's biggest draw is **Sydney Fish Market** (*see p83*), one of the best in the world, on the edge of Blackwattle Bay. From its auction rooms premium-grade tuna goes to Japan, and a dozen or more outlets sell fresh-off-the-boat seafood. Browse among enticing mounds of salmon, snapper and yabbies (freshwater crustaceans), then pick up some rock oysters and find a sunny wharfside seat at which to picnic. But watch out for the pelicans: they're partial to seafood too.

Ultimo – south of Pyrmont and west of Chinatown, which is creeping towards it – has evolved into a strange meeting place of media, academic and museum life. Once notorious for some of Sydney's most squalid housing, and later the site of the municipal markets, it's now home to the sprawling **University of Technology**, the headquarters of the **Australian Broadcasting Corporation** and the masterfully converted **Powerhouse Museum** (*see p82*). Late in 2006, when the **Ian Thorpe Aquatic Centre** on Harris Street opens, the 'Thorpedo' joins an elite group of Aussie swimmers with pools named after them.

The complex, housing a 50-metre pool, leisure pool, hydrotherapy pool, sauna, fitness centre and café, was one of the last jobs by top Sydney architect Harry Seidler, who died in 2006.

Australian National Maritime Museum

2 Murray Street, Harbourside, Darling Harbour (9298 3777/www.anmm.gov.au). Ferry Darling Harbour or Pyrmont Bay/LightRail Pyrmont Bay/ Monorail Harbourside/bus 443. **Open** 9.30am-5pm (6pm Jan) daily. **Admission** free; fee for special exhibits & vessels. **Credit** AmEx, MC, V. **Map** p326 D6.

For a city whose history has always been entwined with its harbour, the sea and water travel, it comes as no surprise that this museum is one of the finest and most unabashed when it comes to maritime treasures. An exhibition traces the history of the Royal Australian Navy, but the biggest exhibits are the vessels themselves, among them *The Spirit of Australia*, the world's fastest boat, designed by Ken Warby on his kitchen table and built in his backyard in 1974. Other craft include the 1888 racing yacht *Akarana*, 1950s naval destroyer HMAS *Vampire* and traditional Vietnamese junk *Tu Duo* ('Freedom'), which sailed into Darwin in 1977 with 39 refugees. A café offers seafood-oriented, open-air eating at the water's edge, while the shop sells books, nautical knick-knacks and, if you really want to splash out, sailing packages with qualified skippers. In January the museum stages Wetworld – a wet-fun centre for kids aged five to 12.

Chinese Garden of Friendship

Corner of Pier & Harbour Streets, Darling Harbour (9281 6863/www.chinesegarden.com.au). CityRail Central or Town Hall/Monorail Paddy's Markets or World Square/LightRail Paddy's Markets. **Open** 9.30am-5pm daily. **Admission** $6; $3 concessions; $15 family. **No credit cards.** **Map** p329 E8.

Unless you're prepared to arm-wrestle for your share of tranquil spots, avoid this place at the weekend when it's full of grimly determined tourists. Designed in Sydney's sister city, Guangzhou, China, to commemorate the 1988 bicentenary, the Garden of Friendship symbolises the bond between the two. The dragon wall features two dragon heads, one in gold for Guangzhou, one in blue for NSW, with a pearl in between. There are waterfalls, weeping willows, water lilies, 'wandering galleries' and wooden bridges. Head up to the tea room balcony, order a cup of shui-hsien tea and enjoy the best view of all: the entire park reflected in the Lake of Brightness, stuffed full of chubby carp. Not surprisingly, the garden is a big hit with brides, so be prepared to be muscled aside by a wedding party.

Powerhouse Museum

500 Harris Street, between William Henry & Macarthur Streets, Ultimo (9217 0111/ www.phm.gov.au). CityRail Central/Monorail/ LightRail Paddy's Markets. **Open** 10am-5pm daily.

Admission $10; $6 concessions; $25 family. **Credit** AmEx, DC, MC, V. **Map** p328 D8.

This former power station opened as a fun and funky museum in 1988 and is the largest in Australia, with a collection of 385,000 objects, 22 permanent and five temporary display spaces, and more than 250 interactive exhibits. It covers science, technology, creativity, decorative arts and Australian popular culture, resulting in exhibitions on such diverse topics as Tokyo street style and childhood memories of migration. Taking a fresh, hands-on approach, with banks of computers and interactive video screens, the Powerhouse is a joy to visit – the kids' interactive spaces will keep under-tens involved for hours.

Star City

80 Pyrmont Street, at Foreshore Road, Pyrmont (9777 9000/www.starcity.com.au). LightRail Star City/Monorail Harbourside/bus 443, 449. **Open** 24hrs daily. **Map** p326 C6.

It's easy to get lost at this huge casino complex – though that's probably a deliberate ruse to keep you gambling. Opened in 1997, Star City is both slick and tacky – marble toilets, cocktails, champagne, fine dining, then fish and chips, beer and miles of pokies. There are 1,500 slot machines, a huge sports betting lounge and sports bar, and 200 gaming tables featuring everything from blackjack and roulette to Caribbean stud poker. Elsewhere are invitation-only private gaming rooms for the high-rollers, many of whom fly in from Asia. The Lyric Theatre (*see p269*) and Showroom cabaret venue stage glittery shows, Astral restaurant (*see p151*) offers great views alongside its French food, and the revamped luxury hotel with its impressive spa means you don't ever have to leave – or you're trapped.

Sydney Aquarium & Sydney Wildlife World

Aquarium Pier, Wheat Road, Darling Harbour (8251 7800/www.sydneyaquarium.com.au). Ferry Darling Harbour/CityRail Town Hall/Monorail Darling Park. **Open** 9am-10pm daily. *Seal sanctuary* 9.30am-sunset daily. **Admission** $27; $14-$19 concessions; $30-$70 family. **Credit** AmEx, DC, MC, V. **Map** p326 D6.

This fantastic aquarium comprises a main exhibit hall, two floating oceanariums – one dedicated to the Great Barrier Reef (and the largest collection of sharks in captivity), the other a seal sanctuary – and two touch pools. Watch out for the saltwater crocs in the northern river section and those elusive platypuses in the southern river section. Underwater viewing tunnels mean visitors can watch sharks and rays gliding past, and seals frolicking close up. In late 2006 the adjacent Sydney Wildlife World is scheduled to open. The concept is a kind of mini-zoo and bird and butterfly sanctuary, where you'll be able to view many native flora and fauna including possums, quolls, yellow-footed rock wallabies and those eternal crowd-pleasers, koalas. Allow at least half a day to appreciate everything. **Photo** *p83*.

Sydney Fish Market

Corner of Pyrmont Bridge Road & Bank Street,
Pyrmont (9004 1100/www.sydneyfishmarket.
com.au). LightRail Fish Market. **Open** 7am-4pm
daily. **No credit cards**. **Map** p326 C6.

This working fishing port – with trawlers in
Blackwattle Bay, wholesale and retail fish markets,
shops, a variety of indoor and outdoor eateries, and
picnic tables on an outdoor deck – is well worth the
trek to Pyrmont. To enjoy the full experience, get up
early and catch the noisy wholesale fish auctions;
they start at 5.30am, with the public allowed in from
7am. It's the largest market of its kind in the southern hemisphere, and you won't find more varieties
of fish on sale anywhere outside Japan: it trades
more than 100 species a day and over 15 million
kilos of fish a year. There's even the Sydney Seafood
School (9004 1111), which offers classes (from $70)
in handling and cooking seafood – everything from
sushi and sashimi to tapas and paella.

East Sydney & Darlinghurst

Map pp329-330. **Transport Kings Cross side**
CityRail Kings Cross/bus 311, 312, 324, 325, 326,
327. **Oxford Street side** *CityRail Museum/bus*
352, 378, 380, 382, L82.

Stand with your back to Hyde Park at Whitlam
Square facing down Oxford Street towards
Paddington, and you're on the edge of the CBD
and the inner city. The lower end of **Oxford
Street** up to and around Taylor Square attracts
a colourful crowd of down-and-outs and all-
night hedonists. It's also the eastern-suburbs
hub of gay Sydney, and as night falls the street
fills with perfectly pumped boys in regulation
tight Ts and high-haired drag queens flitting
between shows in the huddle of pubs and clubs
along 'the Strip'. This area is lively well into the
early hours and can get a little edgy, so watch
your back – although there's always someone
willing to help if you do find yourself in trouble.

As with the rest of Sydney, apartment blocks
are forever popping up between the trad
Victorian terraces, and with them an influx
of cashed-up DINKs (double income no kids).
Consequently, the previously drab shops
have perked up – the clothes shops are more
innovative and you can buy candles and
minimalist homeware. Still, Darlinghurst and
East Sydney are not yet a second Paddington
or Double Bay – the wonderful queer-central
Bookshop Darlinghurst (*see p193*) proudly
stamps its identity on the Strip, as do the wig
and fetish-wear shops and tattoo parlours.

Some consider **Taylor Square** to be the
heart of gay Sydney and the epicentre of the
Strip, though there's not a lot to see here save
for a pocket patch of greenery (dubbed
Gilligan's Island, after the US TV show), some
arty bollards (several vandalised) containing
local memorabilia and a lacklustre fountain –
all courtesy of an extended and ultimately
disappointing upgrade in 2003. City planners
have now turned their attention to the Oxford
Street strip itself, widening the pavements and
planting a few more trees.

Just beyond Taylor Square, on the north side
of Oxford Street, **Darlinghurst Road** begins
its downhill run to Kings Cross. The Victorian
and art deco mansions here give a good idea
of what the area used to be like, while
Harry Seidler-designed Horizon residential
tower, looming over it all, typifies the present
face. Take the time to wander through the old
Darlinghurst Gaol, a magnificent collection
of sandstone buildings dating from the 1820s,
now a campus for the Sydney Institute of
Technology and one of the city's best art schools.
Incongruously, it also houses a butchery school,
so don't be surprised to see arty types one
minute and men in bloodied aprons the next.
The jail was built on a hill as a conspicuous
reminder to all that Sydney was a penal colony.

Sightseeing

Sydney Aquarium. *See p82.*

Back then, instead of negotiating the hustling hordes and screeching traffic of Darlinghurst Road, you'd have reached the Cross by scrambling through scrub and sand drifts, past farms and sandstone quarries, before clambering down wooden ladders to Woolloomooloo Bay. The Darlinghurst ridge, where the Coca-Cola sign now stands at the top of William Street, was once the site of the city's windmills – walk past on a blustery August day and you'll see why. Another place worth visiting is the **Sydney Jewish Museum** (*see below*): Jewish immigrants have played a vital part in Australia's history and their story is told here.

Running roughly parallel to Darlinghurst Road on its east side is **Victoria Street**, a lively mix of cafés, restaurants, shops and a few residential homes. The restaurants here and on Darlinghurst Road are generally better than those on Oxford Street. For a great French night out, head to **Sel et Poivre** (No.263, 9361 6530). For ice-cream and sorbet, queue up at the rightfully popular **Gelato Messina** (No.241, 8354 1223): one spoonful and you're hooked. To find the beautiful people, seek out the **Victoria Room** cocktail bar (*see p179*). A stone's throw from each other on Darlinghurst Road are the stylish boutique hotels **Medusa** and **Kirketon** (for both, *see p41*). Also nearby is that great Sydney breakfast and lunch institution, **bills** (*see p169*).

Time travel

The **Historic Houses Trust** (8239 2211, www.hht.nsw.gov.au) manages 11 houses and museums around Sydney: **Elizabeth Bay House** (*see p98*), **Elizabeth Farm** (*see p125*), **Government House** (*see p71*), **Hyde Park Barracks** (*see p71*), **Justice & Police Museum** (*see p67*), **The Mint** (*see p73*), **Museum of Sydney** (*see p67*), **Rose Seidler House** (*see p115*), **Rouse Hill Estate** (*see p127*), **Susannah Place Museum** (*see p64*) and **Vaucluse House** (*see p100*). Together they provide an overview of the history of the European settlement in the city. If you're planning to visit a few of these – and you should – consider buying a Ticket Through Time ($30, $15 concessions, $60 family), which permits unlimited entry to all properties for three months from the date of purchase. Members ($67 for one year) get free admission. The trust's events calendar has details of new exhibits, historic walks and other activities.

Sydney Jewish Museum

148 Darlinghurst Road, at Burton Street, Darlinghurst (9360 7999/www.sydneyjewish museum.com.au). CityRail Kings Cross/bus 311, 378, 380, 389. **Open** 10am-4pm Mon-Thur, Sun; 10am-2pm Fri. **Admission** $10; $6-$7 concessions; $22 family. **Credit** (shop only) MC, V. **Map** p330 H8.

After World War II, over 30,000 survivors of the Holocaust emigrated to Australia, settling mainly in Sydney and Melbourne. This museum opened in 1992 in Maccabean Hall, originally built to commemorate the Jews of NSW who had served in World War I. The hall has been the centre of Jewish life in Sydney ever since, so it was apt to transform it into a permanent memorial to victims of both world wars. There are two permanent displays – 'Culture and Continuity' and 'The Holocaust' – plus excellent touring exhibitions.

Surry Hills

Map p329. **Transport** *CityRail/LightRail Central/bus 301, 302, 303, 352.*

South of Oxford Street is Surry Hills, an increasingly des-res area and nirvana for Sydney foodies and imbibers – a dozen new cafés, restaurants and revamped bars seem to open here every week. Its main thoroughfare is north-south **Crown Street**, an interesting mix of the very cool and the tatty. At night the vibe is heady and laid-back, with watering holes to suit every taste and pocket. The Oxford Street end is a tad more chic; witness the recently renovated **Dolphin on Crown** pub (No.412, 9331 4800, www.dolphinhotel.com.au). Opposite is **Medina on Crown** (No.359) a smart, serviced apartment block popular with short-stay business types, beneath which you'll find hip restaurants **Billy Kwong** (*see p152*) and **Marque** (*see p155*).

Moving a block further south, the very stylish **White Horse Hotel** (Nos.381-385, 8333 9900, www.thewhitehorse.com.au) is providing strong competition to the long-established **Clock Hotel** (No.470 Crown Street, 9331 5333, www.clockhotel.com.au), with its dining room and wraparound balcony.

The **Shannon Reserve**, a tiny park between these two hotels, hosts a lively flea market on the first Saturday of the month, but all through the week shoppers are well served by established premises such as the oriental curio shop **Mrs Red & Sons** (No.427, 9310 4860) and **Mondo Luce** (No.439, 9690 2667), one of a number of modish lighting shops. The **Book Kitchen** (*see p171*), one of Sydney's best combined book and café operations, and the **Bourke Street Bakery** (*see p171*), on the corner of Devonshire and Bourke Streets, are delicious and highly popular new additions.

Sightseeing

Bourke Street itself, running parallel to Crown a block to the east, remains largely residential but is also sprouting some interesting shops and restaurants, spurred on by the transformation of the old St Margaret's maternity hospital into a swanky apartment complex that also includes the **Object Gallery** (*see below*). All this activity is gradually and inevitably gentrifying Surry Hills, as has happened to previously funky Paddington, now too chi-chi for words. Bourke Street is also the site of a museum dedicated to acclaimed Sydney-born artist **Brett Whiteley** (*see below*).

Brett Whiteley Studio

2 Raper Street, off Davies Street, Surry Hills (9225 1881/www.brettwhiteley.org). CityRail Central then 10mins walk/bus 301, 302, 352. **Open** 10am-4pm Sat, Sun. **Admission** $7; $5 concessions. **Credit** AmEx, MC, V. **Map** p329 G11.

Brett Whiteley was one of Australia's most exciting artists. In 1985 he bought a warehouse in Surry Hills and converted it into a studio, art gallery and living space. Following Whiteley's death in 1992 – in the motel room he was rumoured to have used for his drug and alcohol habit – the studio was converted into a museum. Managed by the Art Gallery of NSW, it offers a singular insight into the artist through photos, personal effects, memorabilia and changing exhibitions of his work.

Object Gallery

417 Bourke Street, between Albion Street & Campbell Street, Surry Hills (9361 4511/www.object. com.au). Bus 301, 302, 303, 352. **Open** 11am-6pm Tue-Sun. **Admission** free. **Map** p329 G9.

Occupying the circular chapel building of the former St Margaret's Hospital and designed by eminent Australian architect Ken Woolley in 1958, the Object Gallery promotes contemporary craft and design in Australia. Its shows, which in the past have featured dressmaker Akira Isogawa and the moulded resin jewellery and bowls of Dinosaur Designs, are always worth checking out. If you like what you see here, hop over to its shop, Collect in the Rocks (88 George Street, 9247 7984).

Redfern & Waterloo

Redfern *CityRail Redfern/bus 305, 309, 310, 352.* **Waterloo** *Bus 301, 302, 303, 355, 343.*

Surry Hills peters out in the west at Central Station (just beyond the rag-trade centre on and around Foveaux Street) and in the south at **Cleveland Street**, the border with Redfern. Aboriginal people from rural areas started moving into Redfern in the 1920s because of its proximity to Central Station, cheap rents and local workshops offering regular work. More arrived during the Depression of the 1930s, and by the '40s the area had become synonymous

with its indigenous population. Following the 1967 national referendum, which gave indigenous people citizenship rights, Redfern's Aboriginal population increased to 35,000, causing mass overcrowding.

In the decades that followed, government programmes (some helpful, some not) have disseminated the area's indigenous people and today it's undergoing intensive reinvention, with some pockets hurtling upmarket. But the central patch of run-down terraces in a one-hectare area bounded by Eveleigh, Vine, Louis and Caroline Streets – which make up the **Block**, the beleaguered heart of a black-run Aboriginal housing co-operative – remains an indigenous enclave (*see p20* **The Block**).

The area's problems – poverty, drugs and alcoholism – haven't gone away, but there's an increasingly smarter edge to Redfern as artists' galleries take up residence, and those who can't quite afford Surry Hills turn their eyes south of the Cleveland Street border looking for residential bargains. The City of Sydney is pouring money in too, with an $11 million revamp of **Prince Alfred Park**, between Central Station and Cleveland Street, under way, including a renewed 50-metre outdoor pool, as well as a proposed $19 million restoration of Redfern Park and stadium, training ground of the popular footy (rugby league to you) team South Sydney Rabbitohs.

In neighbouring Waterloo, development is also rife. **Danks Street**, at the heart of a previously industrial area, now brims with a fine range of eateries, interior design shops, art gallery complex **2 Danks Street** (*see p235*) and the top-quality **Fratelli Fresh** Italian grocers topped off by delicious **Café Sopra** (*see p171*). Further south, if all goes to plan (and it's a 20-year plan), **Green Square**, focused around the Green Square train station and bordered by Botany Road and Bourke Street, is slated to house over 5,000 people in 2,800 new apartments and houses, plus parks, shops and recreation centres. How this, Australia's largest urban renewal project, actually develops remains to be seen.

Kings Cross, Potts Point & Woolloomooloo

Map p330. **Transport** *CityRail Kings Cross/bus 311, 312, 324, 325, 326.*

Kings Cross, formed by the intersection of Darlinghurst Road and Victoria Street as they cross William Street, has long been the city's sex quarter, although today it's dominated as much by drugs as by prostitution. The seedy

Wolloomooloo Wharf.
See p88.

action is pretty much confined to 'the Strip', stretching along **Darlinghurst Road** from William Street to the picturesque **El Alamein** fountain, although visitors should stick to the main streets, especially at night when the winding roads leading back towards Potts Point and the Cross tend to become drug alleys. Along Darlinghurst Road you'll find Australia's first legal 'shooting gallery', a monitored, fully staffed injecting room opened in 2001. Despite much controversy, the centre has just been granted a second term, and many in the know say it has reduced the number of heroin deaths in the area, and provided desperately needed support for the growing number of users.

Community and local government efforts in recent years to clean up Kings Cross, spurred on by the influx of cashed-up residents to the swanky new apartments that have been created on the sites of several of the area's former hotels, have made a difference. Today's Cross is a pale hangover from the days of the Vietnam War, when thousands of US soldiers descended for R&R with fistfuls of dollars and the desire to party the horrors of war out of their consciousness. Their appetites tended towards the carnal, and the dreary parade of seedy strip clubs and massage parlours – now frequented mostly by suburbanites, out-of-towners and international sailors – is evidence of how they got their kicks. Nonetheless, the Cross's neon lights still pull in hordes of backpackers, sustained by a network of hostels, internet cafés and cheap and cheerful restaurants. The good

news for tourists is that there are plenty of police on the beat, and when the night turns ugly, as it inevitably does for some, you needn't get caught in the trouble.

At the beginning of the Cross, the inconspicuous **Crest Hotel** (111 Darlinghurst Road, 9358 2755, www.thecresthotel.com.au) has perhaps the only bona fide straight sauna in the area – the **Ginseng Bathhouse** (*see p206*), a traditional Korean bathhouse with an impressive range of therapeutic treatments. Another place that has succumbed to the ubiquitous glass-and-white refurb is the **Bourbon** (*see p181*). Previously the legendary Bourbon & Beefsteak Bar, it used to be the chosen watering-hole for stalwart locals, sailors and some of the area's more colourful characters, but is now aiming for the youth style set. The somewhat rocky transition has seen the old crowd turned away by doormen and the media running with their cause.

Beyond the El Alamein fountain you're into Potts Point proper. In contrast to the Kings Cross Strip's wall-to-wall neon lighting, **Macleay Street**, with its columns of cool plane trees, is made for slow strolling and offers architectural and culinary pleasures. Tall impregnable apartment buildings such as the neo-Gothic Franconia (No.123) offer a glimpse of the grandeur of the old Cross. Orwell Street, running west off Macleay, houses one of Sydney's finest art deco buildings, the old Minerva theatre, now called the **Metro** (Nos. 26-30), while at 3 Manning Street the **Royal**

Sightseeing

Australian Institute of Architects (9356 2955, www.architecture.com.au) helped rescue **Tusculum**, a grand villa dating from the 1830s.

Potts Point has many fine eateries and good coffee shops. It's a far cry from the desperate world of the Strip. You seem to be on another planet: one populated by chic, wealthy Sydneysiders. If you turn off Macleay Street and into Challis Avenue (also dotted with cafés), you'll soon enter the northern end of **Victoria Street** and a handful of the grand 19th-century terraces that formerly made it one of the city's most elegant thoroughfares. Victoria Street backs on to a cliff that drops down to Sydney's oldest suburb, Woolloomooloo, which stands partly on land filled with the remains of scuttled square-riggers, and is now a mix of public housing (incorporating many original buildings) and swish new developments.

You can walk down from Victoria Street via Horderns, Butlers or McElhone Stairs. Alternatively, Italian restaurant **Mezzaluna** (123 Victoria Street, 9357 1988, www. mezzaluna.com.au) offers a spectacular view over Woolloomooloo Bay to the city skyline. **Embarkation Park**, atop a navy car park at the corner of Victoria Street and Challis Avenue, provides an equally magnificent vista, particularly midweek around twilight when the office towers are lit up.

Macleay Street becomes Wylde Street, which runs out of puff at the **Garden Island Naval Base** on Woolloomooloo Bay, where you are greeted by the surreal sight of the Royal Australian Navy's fleet moored at the side of the road. The US Navy also regularly docks here, disgorging fodder for the strip joints and massage parlours of the Cross. The newly opened **Royal Australian Navy Heritage Centre** (*see below*) is at the very tip of the base on Garden Island – although you can't access it on foot; instead you have to catch a ferry from Circular Quay.

Woolloomooloo was named by the Womerah people who lived here before European colonisation. The area's Aboriginal roots are celebrated in several colourful street murals, although you should wander with care around this public housing estate: it doesn't have Sydney's best reputation for safety. Jutting into the bay is **Woolloomooloo Wharf** (also called Cowper Wharf), constructed in 1910 as a state-of-the-art wool and cargo handling facility. Over the years the wharf fell into disuse, and it seemed destined to crumble into the harbour until Premier Bob Carr slapped a conservation order on the site. As the largest remaining timber-pile wharf in Australia, and a rare example of industrial Federation architecture, it had to be saved.

In 2000 a stylish mix of eateries, apartments, an upmarket hotel (formerly the W, now **Blue**; *see p39*) and private marinas opened. Those who can't afford to eat in the snazzy restaurants that line the finger wharf promenade on the boardwalk in the sun. And just up Cowper Wharf Road is **Harry's Café de Wheels**, Sydney's most famous pie cart, here since World War II, and practically an obligatory fuel stop after a night's boozing in the Cross or 'Loo.

Opposite the wharf is **Artspace** (*see below*), an extraordinary government-run art gallery, and, on the corner of Bourke Street, the **Woolloomooloo Bay Hotel** (9357 1177). This large traditional pub with outdoor seating, restaurants, a balcony and bands is always lively, and from Thursday nights on it's packed with old neighbourhood faces and rowdy youngsters who don't care for the Blue bar peacocks over the road. Around the corner on Nicholson Streeet the **Tilbury Hotel** has a great restaurant and a stylish bar that's popular with a gay crowd (*see p240*) on Sunday night.

Artspace

The Gunnery, 43-51 Cowper Wharf Road, between Forbes & Dowling Steets, Woolloomooloo (9368 1899/www.artspace.org.au). Bus 311, 312. **Open** 11am-6pm Tue-Sat. **Admission** free. **Credit** MC, V. **Map** p330 H6.

This government-funded contemporary art gallery presents edgy, experimental and challenging work. Five galleries and 12 studios (for local and international artists) are housed in the historic Gunnery building. Prepare to be 'shocked, stimulated, inspired and entertained' – or so the gallery claims.

Royal Australian Navy Heritage Centre

Garden Island (9359 2003/www.navy.gov.au/ranhc). Ferry Garden Island. **Open** 9.30am-3.30pm daily. **Admission** $5. **No credit cards. Map** p330 K3.

For close on a century Garden Island, home to the Royal Australian Navy (RAN), has been off-limits to the general public. In late 2005 the very tip of the one-time island, long since connected to Potts Point, was reopened, with the only access via a five-minute ferry ride from Circular Quay. It's worth a visit, if only to enjoy the relative quiet of the grounds and the odd collection of monuments and giant naval objects, including radars, a propeller and 21in torpedoes, which constitute a bizarre outdoor sculpture exhibition. The view from the former Main Signal Building is spectacular – it's easy to see why this was the nerve centre for controlling the movement of naval vessels around the harbour. The Heritage Centre, occupying what was the Gun Mounting Workshop (dating from 1922) and an ex-boat shed (1913), includes an oceanic range of items that provides plenty of insight into navy life. Bring a picnic or enjoy lunch or afternoon tea at the Salthorse Café with a lovely view across Elizabeth Bay.

Eastern Suburbs

Head east for wealth, glamour – and Sydney's most famous beach.

Whether you're looking for beautiful beaches, must-have fashions or just a sneaky peek at how the other half live, there's no doubt that you'll find it in eastern Sydney.

Home to some of the city's best-heeled residents, areas such as Rose Bay, Double Bay, Vaucluse, Woollahra and Point Piper have always had the smell of wealth lingering along their leafy streets. Old money is still evident in various colonial-style mansions with English gardens and pretty summer houses.

Meanwhile, younger cash has replaced any hint of slum dwellings in Paddington. What Paddo loses in terms of an ocean view is made up for in its proximity to the city and its superior shopping and stylish nightlife. The area's skinny town houses are now home to the hip, rich and gorgeous and their small dogs. Other areas too have experienced gentrification and the rising real estate prices that accompany it. The beaches of Bondi, Tamarama, Bronte and Coogee – though still popular with a transient backpacker population – are now overlooked by austere glass palaces that dwarf the older bungalows. With this prime property have come some of the city's best bars, shops, restaurants and cafés to answer the call of the cool.

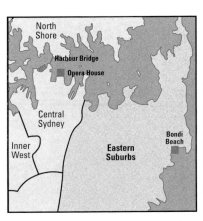

Paddington

Map p332. **Transport** Bus 378, 380, 389, L82.

There's nowhere in Sydney quite like Paddington and it's easy to see why the area has attracted a wealth of young, trendy professionals, eager to pay high rents in exchange for the aspirational zip code. Unlike Darlinghurst and Surry Hills, its neighbours to the west, Paddo has managed to create a fashionable chic without a seedy underside, but hasn't gone so far as its easterly neighbours Woollahra and Centennial Park in becoming so overpriced that the young and impressionable can't afford to live there.

Walking up the main drag of **Oxford Street**, with the city behind you, Paddington proper starts just after Taylor Square, the heart of gay Sydney. The scene gets straighter (but no less fabulous) the further up the hill you go until the reach Centennial Park at the top. Banks, bottle shops, boutiques and beautiful boys and girls happily co-exist on

Oxford Street, and it's a great place to spend a few hours just walking and taking in the buzzing atmosphere.

Just past South Dowling Street are two of Sydney's best art-house cinemas, the Palace chain's **Academy Twin** and **Verona** (for both, *see p226*). Nearby are two of the city's best bookshops, **Berkelouw Books** and **Ariel** (for both, *see p193*), open late for pre- and post-movie browsing.

Further on, on the south side of Oxford Street, is **Victoria Barracks** (*see p91*). Built by convicts to house soldiers and their officers (some of the contemporary NCO housing is visible in nearby Underwood Street), the complex predates most of Paddington, and its strict Georgian lines are more than a little at odds with the area's current cosmopolitan atmosphere. From the Barracks to Centennial Park, Paddington's best-dressed come out in force in the ever-changing mix of designer shops, one-off boutiques and chain stores. The cafés, pubs, bars and gift shops get their fair share of trade too.

Paddington Town Hall & Library (built in 1891) on the corner of Oatley Road and **Paddington Post Office** (1885) provide an elegant edge and are a reminder of the days when these grand Victorian buildings – the Town Hall in typical Classical Revival style with a 106-foot (32.5-metre) clock tower – dominated the skyline, and steam trams rattled up Oxford Street. Next to the Post Office is

Sightseeing

Welcome to **Paddington**: Oxford Street, and a typical house with iron-laced balcony.

the delightful **Juniper Hall** (about 1824), probably the oldest surviving villa in Australia. Built as a family home for gin distiller Robert Cooper, it was named after the berry used in making gin. Cooper, nicknamed 'Robert the Large' for his size, was a colourful character, a convict who smuggled wine from France, fathered 28 children and founded Sydney College, which later became Sydney Grammar School. In 1984 the property was restored by the National Trust and is now privately leased to local businesses.

The imposing **Paddington Inn** (338 Oxford Street, 9380 5913, www.paddingtoninn. com.au) is the area's best-known pub. It has good bar-bistro food and a heaving mix of locals, tourists and the transitory overseas population that washes through Paddo. The **Light Brigade** on the corner of Jersey Road (2A Oxford Street, 9331 2930, www.light brigade.com.au) is also worth checking out for its recently refurbished upstairs restaurant.

Each Saturday you can sample the wares at the popular **Paddington Market** (*see p192*), on the corner of Oxford and Newcombe Streets. You'll find an assortment of local crafts, reasonably priced clothing (a number of Sydney designers started out here), fortune tellers, masseurs and just about every other knick-knack you could hope for.

The streets off Oxford Street also hold much of interest. **William Street**, to the north just before the Paddington Inn, has a cluster of Sydney's best local fashion designers. Duck down and check out **Collette Dinnigan**, **Leona Edmiston** (for both, *see p195*), the **Corner Shop** (*see p198*) and **Sylvia Chan** (No.20, 9380 5981, www.sylviachan.com).

Back towards the city, opposite the Barracks, is **Glenmore Road**, flanked by the girlish **Alannah Hill** boutique (*see p195*) on one corner and a new **Scanlan & Theodore** store (*see p197*) on the other. Wander down Glenmore Road and you'll be treated to a smattering of art galleries and high-class boutiques, which tail off to some of the area's most extravagantly and expensively refurbished Victorian terraces. Don't be fooled by the cramped exterior of many of the terrace-lined streets. Behind the front doors and delicate, iron-laced balconies – typical of Paddington – interior designers have gone to work creating bright, modern pads with the use of the odd skylight thrown in here, a spiral staircase there.

Five Ways, which is indeed the junction of five roads surrounding a mini-roundabout, is the popular villagey heart of the area. You're spoilt for choice for somewhere to eat here. There's the excellent Japanese restaurant **Wasavie** (*see p158*); **Tapenade** (2B Heeley

Built with local sandstone between 1841 and 1849, the Regency-style Victoria Barracks were designed by Lieutenant-Colonel George Barney, who also built Fort Denison and reconstructed Circular Quay. Sydney's first barracks had been at Wynyard Square, where the soldiers of the 11th (North Devonshire) Regiment of Foot had been able to enjoy all the privileges of living in the city: the pubs, the eating houses, the brothels. So there were groans of despair when they were uprooted to the lonely outpost that was Paddington. The site had been chosen because it had borehole water and was on the line an attacker from the east might use, but its main feature was scrub: heath, swamp and flying sand from the adjacent dunes, which caused conjunctivitis (known as 'Paddington pink-eye'). And while the main building and parade ground were (and still are) quite stunning, the soldiers' quarters were cramped, and British regiments dreaded being posted to Australia. Nowadays, the barracks is used as a military planning and administration centre. The museum is housed in the former 25-cell jail, also home to a ghost, Charlie the Redcoat, who hanged himself while incarcerated for shooting his sergeant. There are uniforms, guns and medals galore, and helpful, friendly staff. Well worth a visit.

Centennial Park & Moore Park

Map pp332-333. **Transport** Centennial Park *Bus 352, 355, 378, 380, L82.* **Moore Park** *Bus 339, 373, 374, 376, 377, 392, 393.*

If it's greenery you're after, head to the top of Oxford Street where **Centennial Park** (*see p92*) awaits. It's hard to believe that such a huge and lush expanse of breathing space and picnic spots is so close to the inner city. Filled with artificial lakes, fields, bridle paths and cycle tracks, the park attracts families looking for the perfect spot for a toddler's birthday party, outdoor fitness fanatics and casual strollers. Rolling all the way down to Randwick Racecourse and across to **Queens Park** and **Moore Park** (the site of Sydney's first zoo), Centennial Park was created in the 1880s on the site of the Lachlan Swamps as part of the state celebrations to mark the centenary of the landing of the First Fleet. The three parks (Centennial, Moore and Queens) encompass 3.8 square kilometres (1.5 square miles) and are collectively known as Centennial Parklands.

The former Royal Agricultural Society Showground on the west side (Cook Road) of Centennial Park has been controversially and expensively redeveloped by Fox Studios Australia into a film studio and entertainment complex, the **Entertainment Quarter** (*see p92*). Next to the complex (approached from

Street, 9360 6191), a tapas bar with a lovely outdoor courtyard; French bistro **Vamps** (227 Glenmore Road, 9331 1032); the gorgeous suntrap terrace at breakfast spot **Local** (No.211, 9332 1577); upmarket fish 'n' chips den **A Fish Called Paddo** (No.239, 9326 9500); plus **and the dish ran away with the spoon** (No.226, 9361 6131), a favourite hangover stop where you can get your teeth into organic burgers and roast chook.

Overseeing the lot is the majestic **Royal Hotel** (*see p184*), built in 1888 in a grand classical style. On the ground floor is a busy pub with pokies and TV screens; upstairs there's a restaurant with a wrap-around balcony, which gets packed, especially on Australian high days and holidays. There's also a new roof terrace with some killer views.

If you carry on down Glenmore Road you'll find **White City Tennis Club** (9360 4113) on your left, and eventually **Trumper Park** with its cricket oval. Behind is native bush, and a fairly steep and mosquito-ridden walkway up to Edgecliff on the left and Woollahra, via tennis club Palms, on the right.

Victoria Barracks

Oxford Street, between Greens & Oatley Roads (9339 3170). Bus 352, 378, 380, L82. **Open** *Museum* 10am-1.30pm Thur; 10am-3pm Sun. *Tour* 10am Thur. Closed Christmas holidays. **Admission** *Museum* $2; $1 concessions. *Tour* free. **Map** p332 J10.

Sightseeing

Moore Park Road or Driver Avenue) the huge white doughnuts that form **Sydney Cricket Ground** and **Aussie Stadium** (*see p261*) light up the skyline for miles around at night. South of the cricket ground, **Moore Park Golf Course** (*see p257*) is one of the most popular and best public golf courses in the city.

Centennial Park

Between Oxford Street, York, Darley, Alison & Lang Roads (9339 6699/www.cp.nsw.gov.au). Bus 352, 355, 378, 380, L82. **Open** *Pedestrians* 24hrs daily. *Vehicles* Sunrise to sunset daily. Car-free days last Sun in Mar, May, Aug, Nov. **Map** pp332-333.

A weekend trip to Centennial Park, especially in summer, is a fine example of Aussies at their leisure best. Every kind of fitness fiend – walking, jogging, cycling, rollerblading – is on display. There's an outdoor gym, and you can hire rollerblades and bikes and even go horse riding. Cyclists used to be a bit of a menace, but these days most adhere to the 30km/hr speed limit and will dodge a pedestrian if at all possible. But don't be scared off by all this activity: the park is also teeming with those just looking for a shady spot to snooze or read a good book. Even in peak season, when it seems every Sydneysider wants a piece of the park, the vast lawns mean that there's always a secluded spot to make your own. Statues, ponds and native Australian flowers make it one of the prettiest places to spend a day, and there's a fantastic restaurant and café, a favourite with yummy mummies during the week. Ranger-led walks include Tree Tours, Frog Pond Workshops and the excellent night-time Spotlight Prowl, and don't miss the Moonlight Cinema (*see p227*) from December to March.

Entertainment Quarter

Driver Avenue, Moore Park (9383 4333/ www.entertainmentquarter.com.au). Bus 355, 373, 374, 376, 377, 391, 392, 396. **Map** p332 J/K12.

Fox Studios Australia (www.foxstudiosaustralia. com) opened in May 1998. Since then, Sydneysiders have become used to having US movie stars in their city; some, such as Keanu Reeves and Tom Cruise, have become regular visitors, returning to film sequels to the *Matrix* and *Mission: Impossible* blockbusters. Regrettably, Australia's first (and only) Hollywood-style film studios are not open to the public any more, even for tours. What the public gets instead is the super-slick Entertainment Quarter complex, with cinemas, shops, a barrage of eateries and some huge entertainment spaces. There's a weekend crafts market and a farmers' market on Wednesday and Saturday (both 10am-4pm). Kids will have a ball at the two state-of-the-art playgrounds, seasonal ice-rink, ten-pin bowling centre, crazy golf course and the popular Bungy Trampoline. Channel [V], Australia's first interactive television studio, is based here; teenagers can watch live recordings from Tuesday to Saturday afternoons and even get involved.

Woollahra

Map p333. **Transport** *Bus 200, 389.*

If a long day of being fashionable on Oxford Street proves too much, you'll find a welcome escape opposite the Paddington Gates of Centennial Park. **Queen Street** is the closest thing in eastern Sydney to an old-fashioned English high street, and the villagey feel will make you think the city is hours rather than minutes away. Pricey antique shops, galleries, delis, homeware stores and boutiques line the first stretch, leading down to the upmarket, if rather twee, suburb of Woollahra. The antique shops are not for the bargain hunter, but are surprisingly rich in wares – there's everything here from a Louis XVI mantel clock and late Ming-dynasty furniture to delicious art deco jewellery.

Walking along Queen Street, turn left at the traffic lights into Moncur Street at French restaurant **Bistro Moncur** (*see p158*), past posh deli **Jones the Grocer** (*see p204*), round to the right into Jersey Road and you'll come to the **Lord Dudley Hotel** (No.236, 9327 5399, www.lord dudley.com). The Dudley is an oasis for nostalgic Poms looking for a touch of home; it positively screams English pubdom, from its ivy-clad exterior down to its cosy bar with British beers on tap. It's also popular with mature moneyed locals and revellers from the nearby **Palms Tennis Centre** (Quarry Street, Trumper Park, 9363 4955) and **Paddington Bowling Club** (2 Quarry Street, 9363 1150), who meet at the pub for a leisurely post-match schooner.

A walk from the east end of Queen Street via Greycairn Place and Attunga Street to Cooper Park – which runs east into the suburb of Bellevue Hill – is a pleasure in the jacaranda season (late November to December), when the streets are flooded with vivid purple blossoms. At the east end of Cooper Park, across Victoria Road, you'll find small **Bellevue Park**, which has some unbeatable views of the harbour.

The eastern suburbs, from Woollahra to Double Bay, Bellevue Hill, Bondi Junction and Bondi, are home to Sydney's Jewish community. On Friday evenings and Saturday mornings the streets are alive with the devout walking to and from the various synagogues dotted through the area, including the liberal **Temple Emanuel** in Woollahra (7 Ocean Street, 9328 7833, www.emanuel. org.au) and the beautifully designed, light-filled **Central Synagogue** in Bondi Junction (15 Bon Accord Avenue, 9389 5622, www. centralsynagogue.com.au).

Bondi Junction

Map p333. **Transport** *CityRail Bondi Junction/bus 200, 352, 378, 380, L82.*

While the almost mythical appeal of Bondi Beach is what draws the crowds to this part of Sydney, Bondi is in fact its own sprawling suburb, made up of four distinctly individual areas. **Bondi Junction** is the buzzing shopping and transport mecca bordering Paddington, Woollahra and Queen's Park to the west. **Bondi** proper is really just Bondi Road, the suburban and commercial road that links the Junction to **Bondi Beach**. That famous beach heads north by way of its main drag, Campbell Parade, and leads straight into the quieter area of **North Bondi**, home of many an expat veteran Sydneysider and the Bondi Golf Course.

While it's the beach that is the focus for most, the Junction now puts up many tourists looking for a safe spot to stay while they explore, thanks to an infestation of high-rise apartment blocks and the arrival of the **Westfield Bondi Junction** shopping centre (*see p188* **Mall monster**) as the place to shop in eastern Sydney. After years of development, the centre opened just in time for Christmas 2004. It boasts every brand-name shop from Oxford Street and the city, supermarkets, restaurants, a multiscreen cinema and even a state-of-the-art gym with great views over the city. The proximity to the city by train or bus has turned Bondi Junction into a booming area of commerce and property, and although the older parts now look relatively shabby in the shadow of the Westfield, on the whole the area has finally come into its own.

From the Junction, there are two roads that lead to Bondi Beach. **Old South Head Road** turns away from the ocean and heads north to Watsons Bay – so take the turn-off at O'Brien Street or Curlewis Street. It tends to be quieter than the other route, **Bondi Road**, which can be thick with buses; in summer, when the crowded buses trundle at a snail's pace, it's often quicker to walk (about 30 minutes).

Snaking through Waverley into Bondi (increasingly called 'Bondi Heights' by estate agents keen to exploit its trendiness), Bondi Road is a mixed bag of alternative shops and international restaurants. **Kemeny's Food & Liquor** (Nos.137-147, 13 8881, www.kemenys.com.au) is the best place to buy cheap but good wine, and you can take your pick from a variety of casual eateries, including **Laurie's Vegetarian Takeaway** (No.286, 9365 0134) and well-known fish restaurant **The One That Got Away** (No.163, 9389 4227). A rabble of tattoo parlours, bakeries and the majority of Sydney's kosher food outlets also call this road home.

Join the club

RSL (Returned Services League) clubs exemplify the camaraderie and mateship Aussies are so famous for. They're found all over Australia – there are over 90 in Sydney alone – and in more rural areas serve as a community centre and local pub in one. Most people know them as a place for cheap beer and food, but RSLs have more honourable beginnings. They originated to serve as a financial support network for Diggers returning from World War I and to preserve and honour the memory of those who suffered and died.

Anyone who has served in the Australian Defence Forces is entitled to free membership, anyone else living within a five-kilometre (three-mile) radius has to join (usually for a nominal fee of around $20 per year). Otherwise, you'll need to take ID to prove that you live outside the membership zone – overseas visitors should take a passport or driving licence.

Two great examples are in Bondi, both housed in striking modern buildings with outoor balconies from which to soak up the panoramic views across the beach and ocean. **North Bondi RSL** (118-120 Ramsgate Avenue, 9130 3152, www.northbondirsl.com.au) is at the northern end of the beach; the **Icebergs Club** (*see p95*) occupies the iconic Icebergs building at the southern end – just one floor below the ritzy Icebergs Dining Room & Bar. At both you'll get surprisingly decent food for between $10 and $20, a schooner of beer for around $3.50, plus events such as live music, film screenings and quiz nights. And, of course, million-dollar views for a fraction of the price the punters are paying in Bondi's private beachside restaurants.

Bondi Beach to Coogee Beach

Map Bondi Beach p334. **Transport** Bondi Beach *CityRail Bondi Junction then bus 380, 381, 382, L82/bus 380, L82.* Coogee Beach *CityRail Bondi Junction then bus 313, 314/bus 372, 373, 374, X73.*

Bondi Beach is anything but a romantic, stroll-in-the-moonlight sandy spot. It's the closest ocean beach to the city and at first glance could easily be dismissed as a tacky tourist trap. But don't be fooled: there's a reason that some die-hard Sydneysiders wouldn't live anywhere else and rarely venture out unless they absolutely have to. Everything you hear about Bondi Beach is true, including the fact that it's too noisy, too crowded and, thanks to the influx of visitors and backpackers each year, mostly overpriced. It's also the funkiest beach in town, boasts some of the best eating and drinking holes in the city and Sydney's beautiful people wouldn't be seen anywhere else.

The main thoroughfare is noisy, four-lane **Campbell Parade**, which runs parallel to the beach and is lined with restaurants, cafés, swimwear and souvenir shops that are usually packed at weekends. Below that is dinky Bondi Park – housing the 1928 **Bondi Pavilion** and the **Bondi Surf Bathers' Life Saving Club** (the first of its kind in the world) – and then the sand itself. Bondi is a good surfing beach, and there are plenty of places to hire wetsuits and surfboards along Campbell Parade; check out **Bondi Surf Co** (see p200) and **Krack Surf & Skate** (No.68, 9130 8101). You can get info on surf lessons too. Summer nights bring in punters by the carload, particularly around Christmas and on New Year's Eve, when Bondi is best given a wide berth.

Key restaurants on the thumping, pumping Parade include **Hugo's** (see p160), a Bondi institution, but many eateries are merely reasonable rather than remarkable. To get a feel for why some people live and die in Bondi, you really need to look round the corners.

Hall Street is the villagey heart of Bondi Beach, with such everyday necessities as banks, a post office and travel agents, as well as a gaggle of cafés and restaurants that have changed it from a daytime strolling location to a funky nightlife strip. The new vibe has spread to the surrounding streets. Visit **Hurricanes** (126 Roscoe Street, 9130 7101) for steak, and **Brown Sugar** (106 Curlewis Street, 9130 1566) for its famous breakfast eggs blackstone. **Gould Street** has a small but significant collection of designer shops, many of whose keepers started selling their wares at the famous **Bondi Market** (see p191), which takes place every Sunday. Clothes, books, food, flowers and paintings – all are available, but don't skip the inner courtyard, where vintage items are a fraction of the price of most trendy second-hand stores in the city.

Bondi is popular with backpackers for good reason: it's loud, crowded and anything goes. Most of the budget accommodation is on or around Campbell Parade, Hall Street and nearby Lamrock Avenue and Roscoe Street. Further north is the favourite drinking spot of all out-of-towners, **Hotel Bondi**. It has guest rooms (see p45) and is a fun and feisty spot for watching sport, dancing into the wee hours or enjoying a mid-afternoon schooner, but give it a wide berth if you want to meet anyone local. Australians prefer the **Beach Road Hotel** (see p218), previously known as 'the Regis' and still called that by genuine Bondi-ites. On the corner of Hall Street, **Ravesi's** (see p46) hotel and bar is still a fashionable flame drawing the pretty people in from the suburbs to drink and get very merry.

The north end of the beach has its fair share of cafés and eating establishments – including **Sean's Panaroma** (see p160) and **North Bondi Italian Food** (see p159) – but a quieter vibe. The outdoor gym, which is really just a collection of bars set up for manly pull-ups and grunting, is now generally acknowledged as the number one spot for tanning, posing and mutual admiration among Sydney's gay men.

Further on is the pricey Ben Buckler headland and the shops of North Bondi. Beyond that is the small but pretty **Bondi Golf Course**, site of some Aboriginal rock engravings, and **Williams Park**, a favourite spot with North Bondi residents to watch the sunset or New Year fireworks. Watch out, though: civilised North Bondi has a sometimes unpleasant side when the smell from the sewage treatment plant, heralded by the large chimney on the headland, drifts down. Gunk from the plant runs via a network of tunnels to an outlet five kilometres (three-and-a-half miles) into the ocean.

Bondi is also home to the famous **Bondi Icebergs Club** (see p95), housed in a striking, four-storey modern building at the southern end of the cove. Throughout the winter, members of the Icebergs swimming club (formed in 1929) gather every Sunday morning for their ritual plunge into the icy waters of the outdoor pool. The club also houses the upmarket **Icebergs Dining Room** (see p159) **& Bar** (see p184) on the third floor – both ideal for panoramic views over the beach.

Past the Icebergs complex is the start of a stunning walk along the cliffs to **Tamarama Beach**, **Bronte Beach** and beyond (see p96 **Walk 1: Bondi to Coogee**). The views are fabulous from Bondi's southern headland, which turns inwards to show off Bondi Beach in all its glory. Past Waverley Cemetery, the coastal walk continues south to lovely **Clovelly Beach** and then on to dramatic **Coogee Beach**, with its historic Wylie's Baths and the deservedly popular women's pool.

Bondi Beach: home of sun-worshippers and the Icebergs outdoor pool.

Generally acknowledged to be Bondi's poorer cousin in terms of fashion, restaurants, bars and even the beach, Coogee has raised its game in the past few years. Although still littered with backpackers, who find the cheaper rates preferable to overpriced Bondi, it's answered a need for more palatable eating and drinking spots. The travellers' faves, **Coogee Bay Hotel** (*see p183*) and the **Beach Palace Hotel** (169 Dolphin Street, 9664 2900, www. beachpalacehotel.com.au), are still thumping every weekend, but trendy **Cushion Bar** (242 Arden Street, 9315 9130) provides a slightly more swanky place for a drink. **A Fish Called Coogee** (229 Coogee Bay Road, 9664 7700) is a casual-looking gem, and there are also Indian, Thai and Japanese restaurants, plus breakfast spots aplenty, which are always packed at weekends.

Bondi Icebergs Club

1 Notts Avenue, Bondi Beach (café 9130 3120/gym 9365 0423/pool 9130 4804/www.icebergs.com.au). CityRail Bondi Junction then bus 380, 381, 382, L82/bus 380, L82. **Open** *Bar* 10am-midnight Mon-Fri; 8am-midnight Sat; 8am-10pm Sun. *Café* 10am-10pm Mon-Fri; 8am-10pm Sat, Sun. *Gym* 6am-8.30pm Mon-Wed, Fri; 6am-8pm Thur; 8am-5pm Sat; 9am-5pm Sun. *Pool* 6am-7pm Mon-Wed, Fri; 6.30am-6.30pm Sat, Sun. **Admission** *Gym* $15. *Pool* $4; $2.50 concessions; $10 family. **Map** p334.
Although most famous for its all-weather swimming club, Icebergs houses a number of other attractions. There's a pool, gym, sauna and deck (all open to the

public) on the ground floor, plus the national head-quarters of Surf Life Saving Australia and a small museum on the first floor. The stunning Italian restaurant and cocktail bar are on the top floor, but you can get equally good views (and cheaper booze and nosh) from the Icebergs Club bar and Sundeck Café on the second floor (*see p93* **Join the club**).

Elizabeth Bay & Rushcutters Bay

Map p330. **Transport** *CityRail Kings Cross/bus 200, 311, 323, 325.*

Back on Sydney Harbour, **Elizabeth Bay** begins beyond Fitzroy Gardens at the southern end of Macleay Street. Gone are the backpackers and crowded streets: here the calm, quiet streets are lined with impressive residences that date from the 1930s. Worth a peek are **Elizabeth Bay House** (*see p98*) and **Boomerang** (corner of Ithaca Road and Billyard Avenue), a 1930s Alhambra-esque fantasy that has been home to some of Sydney's highest flyers – and fastest fallers. On the edge of Elizabeth Bay is **Beare Park**, one of many little green Edens that dot the harbourside.

The next inlet east is the romantically named **Rushcutters Bay**, so called because of the convicts who really did cut rushes here: two of them were the first Europeans to be killed by the local Aboriginal inhabitants, in May 1778. Now there is a large and peaceful park lined

Walk 1: Bondi to Coogee

Character The definitive coastal walk, with dramatic ocean views.
Length 5km (3 miles) one way.
Difficulty Easy, with a few uphill climbs and steps.
Transport CityRail Bondi Junction then bus 380, 381, 382, L82/bus 380, L82.

This coastal walk through some of the prettiest beaches in suburban Sydney will take about two and a quarter hours. You don't have to go all the way to Coogee; you can stop at any of the beaches en route, and you can, of course, do the walk in reverse.

Start at the southern end of Bondi Beach, where steps take you up to Notts Avenue

and past the stylish **Icebergs** clubhouse and outdoor pool. The path starts to the left of Notts Avenue, dropping down then up some steep steps to **Marks Park** on the spectacular cliff-top **Mackenzies Point**, with its 180-degree views along miles of coastline.

This first stretch – as far as Tamarama Beach – is the site of the annual **Sculpture by the Sea** festival (*see p213*) in November. It's a fantastic sight, but attracts huge crowds. After another headland the path drops down to Tamarama, which has a park, a little café next to the beach and its fair share of surfers.

At the southern end of Tamarama, steps lead up to the road, which in a few hundred coast-skirting metres will take you

to **Bronte Beach**. Bronte is popular with surfers and families (especially the southern end, around the outdoor pool), and good for picnics and barbecues. There are also shower and toilet blocks and a kiosk (prices go up on a Sunday, by the way), plus a cluster of cafés and restaurants on the road just behind the beach.

Walk through the car park and take the road uphill through a cutting, via steps through Calga Reserve, to **Waverley Cemetery**. Spreading over the cliffs, the cemetery is a tranquil, well-kept area, and the view out to sea makes this a fitting resting place for any soul. Take the oceanside path through the adjoining **Burrows Park** to the warm welcome of **Clovelly Beach**. Equipped with a café and a pub just up the hill, this is one of the prettiest of the walk's beaches and a great place to stop for a bite to eat or a swim. At the end of a long, narrow inlet, the waves are small and manageable – making it popular with families.

Continuing on round the next headland, the last patch of sand before Coogee is **Gordon's Bay**; there's not much in the way of beach, but the view over the water is stunning. Then comes **Dunningham Reserve**, where a sculpture commemorates all those who died in the 2002 Bali bombings. Two plaques nearby list the victims from Sydney: six from the local Dolphins rugby league club, and 20 from the eastern suburbs. Then it's down

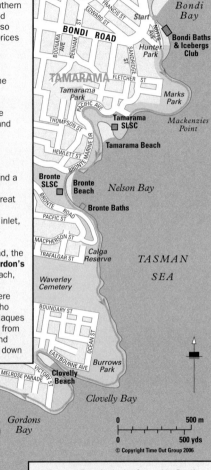

to **Coogee Beach**. At the far end is South Coogee, where you'll find **Wylie's Baths**, a pretty nature walk and dog park. To get back to the city, catch bus 372, 373 or X73 from Arden Street.

A word to the wise. Avoid the walk at all costs if it's a windy day, as the cliffs are exposed. If you insist on going in the midday sun, take plenty of water and a hat. Oh, and watch out for the joggers!

by huge Moreton Bay figs. The bay is home to the **Cruising Yacht Club of Australia** (CYCA) on New Beach Road: its marinas are a frenzy of activity every December when the club is the starting point for the **Sydney Hobart Yacht Race** (*see p214*). If you fancy trying your hand at some sailing, or simply want to sit back, glass of wine in hand, while someone else steers you around the harbour, **Eastsail** (d'Albora Marinas, New Beach Road, 9327 1166, www.eastsail.com.au) close to the CYCA will make life easy for you.

Elizabeth Bay House

7 Onslow Avenue, Elizabeth Bay (9356 3022/ www.hht.nsw.gov.au). CityRail Kings Cross/bus 311, 312. **Open** 10am-4.30pm Tue-Sun. **Admission** $8; $4 concessions; $17 family. **Credit** (over $10) BC, MC, V. **Map** p330 K6.
No expense was spared on this handsome Greek Revival villa, designed by John Verge for NSW colonial secretary Alexander Macleay in 1839: it boasted the first two flushing toilets in the country, the finest staircase in Australian colonial architecture, and breathtaking views of Elizabeth Bay and the harbour. But Macleay's extravagance proved fatal, and his debt-ridden family were forced to move out. Over the years the grand old house was vandalised, partly demolished and finally divided into 15 studio flats, garrets for the artists who flocked to Kings Cross. From 1928 until 1935 it acted as a kind of cheap boarding house for the Sydney 'Charm School' artists, who included Wallace Thornton, Rex Julius and Donald Friend. The gardens, on which Macleay lavished so much love, have long since gone to property developers, but the beautiful house (now run by the Historic Houses Trust) still breathes noblesse, wealth and good taste – and a good sniff of decadence to boot. Rooms are furnished as they would have been in its heyday, 1839-45.

Darling Point & Double Bay

Map p331. **Transport** Darling Point *Ferry Darling Point/bus 324, 325, 326, 327.* Double Bay *Ferry Double Bay/bus 324, 325, 326, 327.*

Bordered by Rushcutters Bay Park to the west and Edgecliff to the south, **Darling Point** is another of Sydney's most salubrious suburbs, none of which would be complete without spectacular views – the best of these can be sampled free from **McKell Park** at the northern tip of Darling Point Road. Head south down the street to the corner of Greenoaks Avenue to see **St Mark's Church**, designed by the acclaimed Gothic Revival architect Edmund Blacket, consecrated in 1864 and still de rigueur for showy society, showbiz and celebrity weddings.

The next suburb to the east is **Double Bay**, also known as 'Double Pay' as it's home to

Sydney's luxury shopping precinct. Migration after World War II turned 'the Bay' into a sophisticated European-style village of cafés, restaurants, delicatessens and ritzy boutiques. Don't wander through here unless you look the part: you'll feel out of place in less than a well-put-together outfit and will have to cope with scathing looks and bad service in cafés.

It's no surprise that cosmetic surgeons prosper in the area – take a look at the ladies who lunch and you'll see the results. Despite the snob quota being fairly high, it's still a good place to grab a coffee or a bite to eat amid the pretty streets and lanes. The stunning purple blooms of the jacaranda tree set Double Bay ablaze in springtime, and for good reason: Michael Guilfoyle, one of the area's earliest professional gardeners, whose own nursery of exotic plants could be found on the corner of Ocean Avenue in the mid 1800s, was responsible for first acclimatising the Brazilian species to Australia.

New South Head Road is the main thoroughfare through the Bay. The **Golden Sheaf Hotel** had a major renovation a few years ago and is now even more of a popular watering hole with drinkers of all ages and tastes. The bistro is exceptional, and the busy beer garden is especially fun on Sunday afternoons when bands perform. It's also got hotel rooms (*see p45*). At the western end of New South Head Road you'll find real estate agents, upmarket tea specialist **Taka Tea Garden** (*see p205*) and **Lesley McKay's Bookshop** (Queens Court, 118 Queen Street, 9328 2733). There are also two beaches at Double Bay, but only one of them is suitable for swimming. The beach next to Steyne Park and the Sailing Club wharf is not, but it's a nice place to wander and always bustling with yachties. On summer weekends you can see the famous 18-footer sailing boats that compete in the annual Sydney-to-Hobart race rigging up and practising their moves, ready for battle.

If you do want to wet your feet and have a swim, continue east for ten minutes on New South Head Road to **Redleaf Pool** (a shark-netted swimming area) and **Seven Shillings Beach**. This adorable little harbour beach is well hidden from the road, has a lovely garden setting and welcomes everyone. Behind the beach, next to Blackburn Gardens, is the attractive Woollahra municipal council building. On the other side of the gardens is **Woollahra Library** (548 New South Head Road, 9391 7100), undeniably the quaintest library in Sydney, set on two levels with views of the harbour and surrounded by English cottage-style gardens. It's a good place to read the newspapers for free.

Point Piper, Rose Bay, Vaucluse & Watsons Bay

Map Point Piper p331. **Transport** Point Piper *Bus 323, 324, 325.* **Rose Bay** *Ferry Rose Bay/bus 323, 324, 325.* **Vaucluse & Watsons Bay** *Ferry Watsons Bay/bus 323, 324, 325, 386, 387.*

Even if you can't match the hefty wallets of the people who live in these stunning harbourside suburbs, they are still easily enjoyed on the cheap. By ferry from Circular Quay you can take in Darling Point, Rose Bay and Watsons Bay – though not every ferry stops at every destination, and there's no service to Darling Point at weekends.

From Double Bay, small harbour beaches dot the shore up to **Point Piper**, which is full of stunning high-walled mansions. You can enjoy the multi-million-dollar views for free from the teeny **Duff Reserve** on the edge of the harbour, a good picnic spot if you manage to beat the crowds.

Lyne Park in **Rose Bay** is where the city's seaplanes land (for flights, *see p58*). Watch them in more comfortable surroundings at the bayside restaurants **Catalina** (*see p159*) and **Pier** (*see p160*) – both great (and expensive) places to eat. On the other side of New South Head Road is **Woollahra Golf Course**, which is very charitably open to the general public, unlike the snooty Royal Sydney Golf Course right next door.

The streets from Rose Bay to **Vaucluse** feature yet more millionaire mansions: for the jealously inclined, the hidden jewels of the Hermitage Foreshore Reserve and an arm of Sydney Harbour National Park, which run around the peninsula, come as compensation. They are reached by a walking track that starts at Bayview Hill Road, below the imposing stone edifice of **Rose Bay Convent**, and offer fine views of the Harbour Bridge, as well as picnic spots aplenty and glimpses of the lifestyles of the rich and incredibly comfortable. The walk emerges at **Nielsen Park** (*see p100*), off Vaucluse Road, where there is an enclosed bay, **Shark Beach** – particularly beautiful on a summer evening – and a popular restaurant plus cheaper café, the **Nielsen Park Kiosk** (9337 1574, www.npk.com.au).

Further along, on Wentworth Road, the estate that became **Vaucluse House** (*see p100*) was bought by newspaperman and politician William Charles Wentworth in 1827. It's open to the public, along with its fine tearooms. Next to Vaucluse Bay, **Parsley Bay** is a lesser-known, verdant picnic spot popular with families.

It is claimed that **Watsons Bay** was the country's first fishing village. Now largely the province of **Doyles on the Beach** seafood restaurant (11 Marine Parade, 9337 2007, www.doyles.com.au) and rowdy weekend pub **Doyles Palace Hotel** (*see p183*) – both owned by one of the bay's original fishing families – it has stunning views back across the harbour to the city, particularly at night, and retains vestiges of its old charm, including original weatherboard houses and terraces. These are best seen by walking north to the First Fleet landing spot at **Green Point Reserve** and on to Camp Cove and Lady Bay beaches, and the Hornby lighthouse on the tip of South Head.

On the other (ocean) side of the peninsula from Watsons Bay beach is the bite in the sheer cliffs that gives the **Gap** its name – and from which many have jumped to their doom. **Gap Park** is the start of a spectacular cliff walk that runs south back into Vaucluse. Along the way, hidden high above the approach to Watsons Bay at the fork of the Old South Head Road, is another fine Blacket church, **St Peter's** (331 Old South Head Road, 9337 6545, www.stpeterswb.org.au), home to

Ever-popular Doyles, in **Watsons Bay**.

Australia's oldest pipe organ, which dates from 1796 and was once loaned to the exiled Napoleon. The church gates commemorate the Greycliffe ferry disaster of 1927 when 40 people (including many schoolchildren) died in a collision at sea.

You can hire put-put boats for a spot of fishing, or just messing around, from **Jimmy's Boat Hire** (Block 2, Unit 3 Bell Street, 0407 462 738).

Nielsen Park
Greycliffe Avenue, Vaucluse (9337 5511/ www.nationalparks.nsw.gov.au). Bus 325. **Open** *5am-10pm daily.*
Generations of Sydneysiders have been flocking to Nielsen Park for family get-togethers since the early 1900s. They sit on Shark Beach or the grassy slopes behind or climb the headlands either side of the beach for a great view across the harbour. With its abundance of shady trees, gentle waters, panoramic views and the excellent Nielsen Park Kiosk (serving à la carte meals, plus snacks and ice-creams), it's the perfect picnic spot. It's also a favourite New Year's Eve viewing point for the harbour fireworks. Nestled in the grounds to the rear of the grassy slopes lies Greycliffe House, a Gothic-style mansion built in 1862 as a wedding gift from the co-founder and first editor of the *Australian* newspaper, William Charles Wentworth, for his daughter Fanny and her husband

John Reeve. In 1913 it became a baby hospital, then a home for new mothers. Nowadays it's a NSW National Parks & Wildlife Service office, providing info on parks throughout the state. Watch out for the seaplanes that take off in neighbouring Rose Bay and begin their ascent over the waters of Shark Bay.

Vaucluse House
Vaucluse Park, Wentworth Road, Vaucluse (9388 7922/www.hht.nsw.gov.au). Bus 325. **Open** *House* 10am-4.30pm Tue-Sun. *Grounds* 10am-5pm Tue-Sun. **Admission** $8; $4 concessions; $17 family. **Credit** (over $10) BC, MC, V.
The oldest 'house museum' in Australia nestles prettily in a moated 19th-century estate, surrounded by ten hectares (28 acres) of prime land, with its own sheltered beach on Vaucluse Bay. From 1827-53 and 1861-2 this was the opulent home of William Charles Wentworth. The house originally stood in a much larger estate, and 26 servants were required to look after the master's seven daughters and three sons, not to mention his vineyards, orchards and beloved racehorses. The Historic Homes Trust has endeavoured to keep the place as it was when the Wentworths were in residence. In the kitchen a fire burns in the large grate and hefty copper pans line the walls; a tin bath, taken on European travels, still displays its sticker from London's Victoria Station; the drawing room is sumptuously furnished, and has a door that hides a secret (just ask a guide to open it).

Randwick & Kensington

Map p323. **Transport** Randwick *Bus 314, 316, 317, 371, 372, 373, 374, 376, 377.* Kensington *Bus 391, 392, 393, 394, 399.*

For a flutter on the horses or just an excuse to get dressed up for a day, head to the **Royal Randwick Racecourse** (*see p263*). It's on Alison Road bordering Centennial Park, and the the Spring Carnival in November is especially popular, giving all the fillies – both on and off the track – a chance to show off their finery. Check www.ajc.org.au for race dates. The **University of NSW** campus lies south of it, while, across the road, the **National Institute of Dramatic Art** (NIDA) – alma mater of such stars as Nicole Kidman and Mel Gibson – has its headquarters and theatre.

Anzac Parade is one long highway, but will lead you to **Grotta Capri Seafood Restaurant** (Nos.97-101, 9662 7111). Hardly convenient for the city, the only reason to make the trip out is to gaze in wonder at the decor of this bizarre but wonderful eatery. Decked out like an undersea fantasy, it's well worth the taxi ride. Just up the road is the pinkest department store you'd ever hope to see, **Peter's of Kensington** (*see p189*). Avoid it like the plague at Christmas or during sale season, unless you like to queue.

The aptly named **Gap**. See p99.

Inner West

Head inland to discover a noisy multicultural playground.

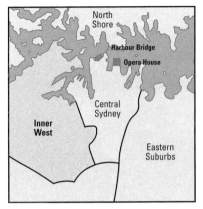

North
Shore

Harbour Bridge

Opera House

Central
Sydney

Inner
West

Eastern
Suburbs

The west hasn't yet become quite the 'destination' the opening of the Cross City Tunnel in 2005 promised to make it. With the tunnel dogged by high tolls and alleged shady deals, those east of the city still largely regard the western interior as the dark side, shuddering at its 'distance' – about ten minutes' drive. Perhaps it's more a gaping cultural divide that separates west and east. While the east is all shiny surfaces and water views, the west gets down and dirty (and noisy – it's got the city's worst air traffic pollution). Yes, there are pockets of glamour thanks to ever-increasing gentrification – minimalism meets flashes of trash with chandeliers and Florence Broadhurst wallpaper. And die-hard foodies do head across the Anzac Bridge in search of the multicultural mix of delis, bakeries, cafés and restaurants in Balmain, Rozelle, Glebe, Leichhardt, Haberfield and Petersham. But even so, the west tends to attract the sort of lip-curling rebuff from outsiders that suggests 'don't go there'.

Curiously, house prices don't reflect the apparent undesirability of the area. First-time buyers arrived in squadrons in search of a bargain a few years back, but now prices are nearly Paddington-sky-high. Even Newtown, specialised home to goths, students and musos, has not escaped the sheen or the bursting mortgages of the Sydney property market. In general, though, the west remains the domain of a bohemian and multicultural mix.

Balmain, Birchgrove & Rozelle

Map p322; Balmain p326. **Transport** Balmain *Ferry Balmain, Balmain West or East Balmain/bus 442, 434.* **Birchgrove** *Ferry Birchgrove/bus 441.* **Rozelle** *Bus 432, 433, 434, 440, 441, 442, 500.*

Snuggled in the inner west's harbour, a six-minute ferry ride from Circular Quay or a 20-minute bus trip from the city centre, Balmain was settled in the 1830s by boatbuilders; today it's increasingly home to on-the-make moneyed types. **Darling Street** – the spine of the area – starts at Balmain East ferry wharf and curves uphill past the sandstone **Watch House** (built in 1854, it was once the police lock-up and is now the headquarters of the Balmain Historical Society). For an easy ferry-and-food experience, walk a couple of minutes up from the wharf to **Relish at Balmain Bug** (55 Darling Street, 9810 5510). Housed in a cute a, um, bug, stone cottage, this restaurant mixes traditional Australian with an Asian edge.

Further up in central Balmain, Darling Street is lined with more food options interspersed with homeware and clothing shops, all winding along in a pleasingly low-key, two-storey way. A cluster of impressive Victorian buildings – the Post Office, Court House, Town Hall and Fire Station – are testament to Balmain's prosperity in the 1880s. **Balmain Market** (*see p191*), held on Saturdays in the grounds of St Andrew's Church, opposite Gladstone Park, is worth a browse, as is **Bray Books** (No.268, 9810 5613).

Pockets of urban cool include **Chopsticks** (No.264, 9818 3551), a dark, devil's-lair cube that serves pho, laksa and noodles at good prices. **Kazbah on Darling** (No.379, 9555 7067) transports you to Morocco, while **Tuk Tuk Real Thai** (No.350, 9555 5899) offers fast and funky Thai. **Blue Ginger** (No.241, 9818 4662) specialises in modern Asian cuisine, and **L'Unico**, just off the main drag (79 Elliott Street, 9810 5466), serves Italian food in a contemporary indoor/outdoor setting.

Cafés abound too, including the modern and spacious **Canteen Café** (*see p173*) and current fashion hotspot **Bertoni Casalinga** (No.281, 9818 5845) with its crates-on-the-footpath seating and Italian food. **Circle Café**

It's a dog's life in **Glebe** – with the Anzac Bridge in the distance. *See p103.*

(No.344, 9555 9755) recalls Balmain's simpler, eccentric 1970s period: it houses a Uniting Church service on Sunday mornings. To create your own meal, head to French bakery **Victoire** (No.285, 9818 5529), a 25-year-old institution, for sourdough baguette and cheese, or **Dockside Seafood** (No.314, 9810 6587) to order mandarin scallops or spicy prawns.

Pubs are still the lifeblood of Balmain. Glamour couples head for the refined surroundings of the **London Hotel** (234 Darling Street, 9555 1377) or the **Exchange Hotel** (corner of Beattie and Mullens Streets, 9810 1171) – never mind the incongruity of a ping pong tournament and Martini club on Thursday nights. Ageing funsters patronise the **Unity Hall Hotel** (292 Darling Street, 9810 1331), while the **Town Hall Hotel** (No.366, 9818 8950) hovers oddly between pleasing pool sharks and house music lovers. A variety of bands play the ever-popular **Cat & Fiddle Hotel** (*see p251*).

On the northern side of Darling Street is Birchgrove, flanked on three sides by water. The somewhat ramshackle **Sir William Wallace Hotel** (31 Cameron Street, 9555 8570) features a large autographed poster of a kilted Mel Gibson in *Braveheart* mode. Locals claim that Gibson, who lived in the area as an up-and-

coming actor, was first inspired by the Scottish patriot while drinking at their bar. On Sundays the owners throw a free barbecue lunch. There's also the **Riverview Hotel** (29 Birchgrove Road, 9810 1151), for years owned by legendary Olympic gold medal-winning swimmer Dawn Fraser; her name lives on at the carefully restored harbourside pool at the edge of charming **Elkington Park.** The park overlooks **Cockatoo Island**, the largest of the harbour's islands and a former prison and shipyard.

Another park can be found at the tip of the narrow finger of Louisa Road, which is lined with half-hidden, multi-million-dollar homes. The peninsula was originally an abattoir of sorts, where Aboriginal people used to kill kangaroos. Its name was officially changed from Long Nose Point to **Yurulbin Point** in 1994 to reflect its indigenous heritage, but most people still use its former name. The wharf at its end is where the Birchgrove ferries arrive.

To reach Rozelle, simply continue west along Darling Street. If you're driving, let the overall-clad lads fill 'er up at Balmain's oldest service station, **Bill's Garage** (418 Darling Street, 9810 2611), established in 1915 and still with its original fixtures. For years the weekend **Rozelle Market** (*see p192*) was about the only thing that brought people here, with bargain stalls selling CDs, plants, ceramics and collectables. That was, of course, until food became such an integral part of Sydney life.

The first figure to make local folk think beyond lentils was Tetsuya Wakuda, the internationally renowned Japanese chef, who opened his first restaurant (now closed) in the area. These days there are two hulking hangars that have become monuments to modern cuisine. First to arrive was **Barn Café & Grocery** (731 Darling Street, 9810 1633) with its mix of restaurant, café and 'supermarket' of hard-to-find, beautifully packaged, pricey ingredients. Next came **About Life** (No.605, 8755 1311), a self-styled 'natural marketplace' – a posh mix of café, caterer and naturopath. Across the road, the **Organic Trading Company** (No.584, 9555 9991) is a toned-down rival selling yet more organic lotions and funky baby clothes.

The rest of this stretch of Darling Street is a smattering of cafés, nurseries, antiques stores and gift shops. Chocolatier **Belle Fleur** (see p204) injects some wicked indulgence into the somewhat earnest, upmarket-hippie scene. But it's **Orange Grove Farmers' Market**, held on Saturdays at Orange Grove Public School at the junction of Darling Street and Balmain Road, which has the last word with its organic produce and multinational cuisines (Ethiopian, Japanese, Dutch) that are good – and cheap – enough to lure Bondi dwellers across town.

Back out along Victoria Road to the north, the **Balmain Leagues Club** (138-152 Victoria Road, 9556 0400), one of two venues belonging to local rugby battlers the Wests Tigers, is a good place for a cheap steak and beer, rivalled only by the **Red Lion Hotel** (726 Darling Street, 9555 7933), which caters to travelling backpackers. Bringing back a smidge of Tetsuya glamour to this part of the strip is **La Grande Bouffe** (758 Darling Street, 9818 4333), a modern take on the classic French bistro. Back down Victoria Road towards the city is new arrival the **Restaurant at Three Weeds** (see p162), specialising in Mod Euro flavours. Housed in the Three Weeds Hotel, a former rock haven, it's a revamped, remodelled testimony to redemption.

Glebe

Map p328. **Transport** *LightRail Glebe/bus 431, 432, 433, 434.*

Directly to the west of central Sydney and shaped by its proximity to Sydney University on Parramatta Road, Glebe is an incongruous but atmospheric mix of grand, turn-of-the-20th-century mansions flanking quaint terraces

and drab 1970s flat lets, with most streets still sporting their original rusty street signs. There are probably more cheap takeaway joints per capita than anywhere else in Sydney – Glebe is land of the $5 pad Thai.

The main drag is **Glebe Point Road**. Walking along it is akin to crocheting as you weave in and out between students and travellers, who are well catered for by several budget hotels, including **Alishan International Guesthouse** (see p46), **Wattle House** (see p48) and the large and leafy **Glebe Village Backpackers** hostel (256 Glebe Point Road, 9660 8133). Become as one with them at **Toxteth Hotel** (No.345, 9660 2370) or bond with Brits at **British Sweets & Treats** (No.85, 9660 9912), which has helpfully collected together all the faves needed to console homesick Poms.

You will never go hungry in Glebe, with its overwhelming array of Indian, Chinese, Thai and Vietnamese eateries. Expect quick-fill, rather than gourmet. But the retail landscape is changing, with the likes of the **Sonoma Woodfired Baking Co** (No.215A, 9660 2116) for brilliant baked-on-the-premises spelt breads, and **Le Mille-Feuille Pâtisserie** (No.95, 9552 2234) for cakes and designer biscuits delicately arranged like jewellery in glass cases. For organic takeaway, try Moby's favourite Sydney haunt **Iku** (see p162) – think brown rice, miso, tofu and tahini-type offerings wrapped up in little brown paper parcels. And it's worth opening your wallet to try out Mod Euro newcomer **Restaurant Atelier** and oyster specialist the **Boathouse on Blackwattle Bay** (for both, see p162).

For bestsellers and books to impress, head to **Gleebooks** (see p193), something of a literary institution with user-friendly extended opening hours and two branches. Duck next door for a cheaper browse in **Sappho Books** (see p195), which peddles second-hand books and the extra lure of coffee. You'll probably find cheaper still across the road on Saturdays at **Glebe Market** (see p191). Sprawling out through school grounds, it deals in everything from clothes to CDs, with a small army of Asian food stalls to keep you going.

Traditional pubs include the British-style **Nag's Head Hotel** (see p185), and Irish pub the **Friend in Hand Hotel** (68 Cowper Street, 9660 2326), which is stuffed with street signs, number plates and even a surfboat hanging from the ceiling, and hosts live crab races every Wednesday night.

For a feel of what Sydney used to be like before money took over, visit **Wentworth Park Greyhound Track** (see p263), Sydney's premier dog-racing venue, which has meets

Sightseeing

Norton Street, Leichhardt.

every Monday and Saturday night. It's a great night out – there are bars and a bistro – and the betting ring here is about the only place where you'll still see pork-pie hats worn without a trace of irony.

At the Rozelle Bay end of Glebe Point Road is the large expanse of **Jubilee Park** and **Bicentennial Park** and adjoining **Harold Park Raceway** (*see p263*), home of 'the trots'. At the time of writing, the park area was undergoing a major face-lift to become a pleasantly marshy play zone that will see all manner of canoes and watercraft at its edge. Construction has also begun on a two-kilometre foreshore walk from the Bicentennial Park round to the Fish Markets in Pyrmont.

If you're in town in November, look out for the one-day **Glebe New Music Festival & Street Fair** (*see p213*), the city's longest-running street party.

Annandale

Map p322. **Transport** *Bus 436, 437, 438, 440, 470.*

Annandale was once earmarked as a model township – hence the look of the main throughfare: broad, tree-lined **Johnston Street** (named after Lieutenant George Johnston, the first man to step ashore from the First Fleet in 1788, albeit on the back of a convict). Located between Glebe and Leichhardt, it soon became a predominantly working-class district. These days it's

gradually upping its foodie quotient on Booth Street to cope with the growing influx of residents decamping from the east.

Leading the charge is **Zenith on Booth** (No.37, 9660 6600) with Mario Percuoco at its helm (he's the son of Italian food giant Armando, of the acclaimed Buon Ricordo restaurant; *see p158*). Down the road at **Three Clicks West** (*see p162*), the mood is Mod Oz at medium prices. Providing a quick fix in its red-chair surrounds is eat-in/take-away **Bar Asia** (No.101, 9571 9919), where it's noodles, rice and curry in a box at five paces. **Bar Sirocco** (No.62, 9660 3930) picks up the pieces with brilliant breakfasts after a night out at the **North Annandale Hotel** (corner of Booth and Johnston Streets, 9660 7452).

Relaxed to the point of horizontality, Annandale has a gentle vibe that smacks of parents with two-point-five kids. However, at the Parramatta Road end of the district, the **Annandale Hotel** (*see p250*) punks up the atmosphere with some of Australia's best rock bands, and low-budget 16mm movies on Monday nights.

Leichhardt

Map p322. **Transport** *Bus 436, 437, 438, 440.*

Further west still lies Leichhardt. Formerly the 'Little Italy' of the west, it's long outgrown that title and the suburb's main thoroughfare, **Norton Street**, pumps to a whole new

a four-screen art-house specialist with a very good licensed bar and restaurant called Martini, a café, a bar and a CD shop that pulls the crowds. Readers should look to **Berkelouw Books** (*see p193*) across the road for a great selection of titles, and a café to read them in.

Haberfield

Map p322. **Transport** *Bus 436, 437, 438, 440.*

Situated to the west of Leichhardt, Haberfield is the more recently discovered 'Little Italy' of the west – 'little' being the operative word. It remains the heartland of homeland authenticity.

Foodies make a beeline for the main thoroughfare, **Ramsay Street**, where you'll find **Paesanella** delicatessen (No.88, 9799 8483) for arguably the best antipasti and cheeses in Sydney; **Haberfield Bakery** (No.153, 9797 7715) for fresh pasta and 17 types of bread; and **A&P Sulfaro Pasticceria** (No.119, 9797 0001) for ice-cream, biscotti and hand-made chocolates.

Trattoria **Il Locale** (No.94A, 9797 8966) is a newcomer to the scene. A simple tiled shell with wooden tables, its pizza is proving popular with the masses. Book ahead or prepare to queue. Also recently opened is **Dolcissimo** (Nos.96-98, 9716 4444). Choose from the bright café or the smarter, low-lit restaurant – though it's somewhat of a bloodsport trying to get a seat in either. And still going strong is old favourite **Napoli in Bocca** (73 Dalhousie Street, 9798 4096): the red-checked tablecloths and pizza and pasta menu are as much an institution as the bustling, old-style service.

Newtown, Erskineville & Enmore

Map p334. **Transport** Newtown *CityRail Newtown/bus 422, 423, 426, 428, 352.* Erskineville *CityRail Erskineville.* Enmore *CityRail Newtown/bus 426, 428.*

You can throttle it with renovators and young families, you can tart up the rough edges with smart shops, but Newtown somehow manages to remain stubbornly and comfortably down-at-heel, like an old drag queen in her glitter rags. Lying to the south of Annandale and Glebe, Newtown has it all: few other areas accommodate so many subcultures – grungy students from the nearby University of Sydney, young professional couples, goths, spiky punks, gays and lesbians – and in such apparent harmony. See the community in all its glory during the **Newtown Festival** (*see p213*) in November.

nightlife vibe, while still retaining some of the old. Young, slick Italians have a firm grip on the territory, but lately it seems as if Chinatown regulars have decamped further west in a reverse of Marco Polo's noodle-discovery tour.

Two stalwarts of the Italian dining scene are recently revamped **Elio** (159 Norton Street, 9560 9129) offers an elegant modern take on old favourites, while **Grappa** (*see p161*) has barn-like proportions that would happily house the entire crew from *The Sopranos* – great big-night-out stuff.

Get down with old-Med boys at **Bar Italia** (*see p173*) to snap up cheap focaccia and great ice-cream. Drive the kids into **Café Gioia & Pizzeria** (No.126A, 9564 6245), housed in a renovated service station, or visit the **Italian Forum** shopping mall. The architecture isn't to everyone's taste, but the enclosed piazza is a boon for parents with wandering offspring – they can eat and watch at the same time. **La Cremeria Sorbetteria** (No.106, 9564 1127), still shifts great gelati, while **Glace** around the corner (27 Marion Street, 9569 3444) sexes it up with champagne sorbet. For a serious caffeine hit, you can always rely on **Bar Sport** (2A Norton Street, 9569 2397).

A cluster of Australian heritage buildings includes the two-storey **Leichhardt Town Hall** (107 Norton Street), built in 1888, which often hosts visiting art exhibitions, the former **Post Office** (No.109) and **All Souls Anglican Church** (No.126). But it's the **Palace Norton Street Cinema** (*see p226*),

Sightseeing

You could easily spend a day wandering along the main drag, **King Street** (and it's faster to stroll than drive, since the traffic can be notoriously bad). Intriguing and often eccentric specialist shops include one dedicated solely to buttons, another to ribbons and braids. A major player in the area is the **Dendy Newtown** four-screen cinema (*see p225*); next door is a good dance and alternative music shop, **Fish Records** (*see p208*), which opens late, as does bookshop **Better Read Than Dead** (No.265, 9557 8700). There's also **Goulds** (*see p193*), one of the largest and most popular second-hand bookshops in the city. Maybe it's because of the wild mix of humanity that makes up Newtown, but it's the perfect place to find anything for anyone. **Pentimento** (No.249, 9565 5591) has an exquisite range of books, homewares and handbags, while **Eastern Flair** (No.319, 9565 1499) offers exotic jewellery and homeware. For divine teas, visit **T2** (*see p205*), while funky bags of all kinds are available at **Crumpler** (No.305, 9565 1611).

You'll have no trouble finding somewhere to linger over a cappuccino – every second shopfront houses a café, and new places seem to open every week. The **Old Fish Shop Café** (No.239, 9519 4295) is a popular open-sided affair with strings of garlic and dried chillies hanging from the roof. There's also **Bacigalupo** (No.284, 9565 5238) for organic coffee, and **El Basha Café** (No.233, 9557 3886) for Lebanese sweets and pastries.

The restaurants on the strip veer to pan-Asian bland, but are satisfying for the price. **Thanh Binh** (No.111, 9557 1175) is a stand-out Vietnamese, while **Sumalee Thai** (No.324, 9557 1692), at the back of gay-friendly pub **Bank Hotel** (*see p237*), injects authenticity to its dishes – note that at time of writing the pub was undergoing a major makeover. For a quick dinner, try funky **Simply Noodles** (No.273, 9557 4453) or **Italian Bowl** (No.255, 9516 0857), which offers a nifty, choose-your-own selection of pastas and sauces. For a contemporary take on Australian cuisine, duck off King to newcomer **Oscillate Wildly** (*see p162*).

Newtown also has no shortage of pubs, each with its own distinctive slant. Check out bands at the **Sandringham Hotel** (*see p252*), still adorned with its original green and yellow tiles. New on the block for jazz and blues is the **Vanguard** (*see p252*) – more of a moody club than a pub, with sit-down dining during performances. The **Newtown Hotel** (*see p239*), remains an ever-popular gay haunt, but has a tarted-up lounge bar on the first floor. Also freshly nipped and tipped and back on the

scene is the **Marlbrough Hotel** (No.145, 9519 6500), which has a wide deco balcony upstairs. For near-24-hour comfort, try **Zanzibar** (No.323, 9519 1511): with pool downstairs and a cushion room upstairs, it relies on low lighting and beads to fulfil its name's exotic promise.

The bottom end of King Street, south of the railway station, has always been heaven for fans of antiques, junk and second-hand clothes, but edgy fashion shops are now beginning to predominate – look for **Dragstar** (No.535A, 9550 1243), **Lenny & Kate** (No.473, 9557 1604) and **Zukini** (No.483, 9519 9188). Kids get similar treatment at **Shorties** (No.537, 9550 5003), while louche retro glamour can be found at **Vintage Glamour & Alterations** (No.481, 9516 0012). **Fiji Market** (No.591, 9517 2054), offers Indian/Pacific Islander produce as well as cheap sari fabrics and fabulously kitsch Hindu icons and posters. For a coffee break, the locals head to the grungily hip **Chocolate Dog Café** (No.594, 9565 2526). Get the total Lebanese experience at **Arabella's** restaurant (No.489-491, 9550 1119) where a small clutch of Beirutians seem to be in permanent celebration mode. On Friday and Saturday nights there's bellydancing.

While in Newtown it's also worth ducking off King Street to the two E suburbs, Erskineville and Enmore. To reach the former – which is rapidly expanding into a own crowd-puller in its own right – turn off King Street at Erskineville Road and keep walking. You may recognise the landmark art deco **Imperial Hotel** (*see p237*) from the movie *Priscilla, Queen of the Desert*. If drag shows are your thing, head here on Thursday to Saturday nights to see one of the best.

On Swanson Street – a continuation of Erskineville Road – is music club the **Rose of Australia** (*see p252*), which has been revved up to become a bar and restaurant with pavement seating. Across the road, **Stir Crazy** (128 Erskineville Road, 9519 0044) is creating its own noise with twists like pumpkin stir-fry and chilli jam seafood. For well-priced, good all-round food (and chai lattes, of all things), try the **Big Boys Café** (106 Erskineville Road, 9557 9448) before heading down for a seriously strong espresso at **Café Sofia** (7 Swanson Street, 9519 1565). It's worth walking a little further down the road (which changes its name again, to Copeland Street) for the gourmet **Bitton Café** (*see p173*). Despite its somewhat out-of-the-way location, Bitton has thrived under French-born chef David Bitton and his Indian wife, Sohani. You can buy sauces, dressings and oils to take home, and David also offers cookery classes.

Sydneysider spotting guide

Some people claim you are what you eat, but in Sydney you are where you live. Not only is there a distinct divide between those who live north and south of the Harbour Bridge, but each area of the city has its own tribe, characterised by specific attitudes and ambitions, likes and dislikes.

Want to be able to pinpoint a Sydneysider's regional affiliations at a glance? Here's a handy field guide.

Eastern Suburbs

Wears Something designer, expensive and conspicuous.
Drives Yellow Lamborghini or red Ferrari.
Hangs out On the party pages of the Sunday papers and the coffee shops of Double Bay.
Loves Themselves and their bank balance.
Hates Having to travel beyond the Harbour Bridge for anything.
Wants This to never end.

Inner West

Wears Black. Probably jeans, jumper or T-shirt and a beanie in the winter… but always black.
Drives Probably doesn't, actually, it's very bad for the environment.
Hangs out On King Street, in record shops and cafés.
Loves Tofu, music, meetings, intimate chats and social revolution.
Hates Racists, homophobes, Liberals and sunshine.
Wants The rest of Australia to be just like Newtown.

North Shore

Wears Blue shirt and chinos for men, baby-sick-stained summer frocks for women.
Drives Mercedes.
Hangs out Local rugby club, golf club or a friend's house for dinner – if they can get a babysitter.
Loves The north shore. Feels the rest of Australia should be exactly like it.

Hates The rest of Australia for not being like the north shore.
Wants A new car, a bigger house and a regular, reliable babysitter.

Northern Beaches

Wears Wetsuit in winter, swimmers in summer.
Drives An old Holden stationwagon for their surfboard.
Hangs out At the beach, as often as possible.
Loves The beach, man. And the surf. And that, like, perfect wave.
Hates Hassle.
Wants To get paid for this.

Parramatta & the West

Wears 'Trackie dacks' (tracksuit trousers), singlet and baseball caps. Both sexes.
Drives Something 15 years old but with a dustbin for an exhaust pipe.
Hangs out At leagues clubs and fast-food restaurants.
Loves Rugby league, their bro.
Hates Surfies.
Wants Respect.

The South

Wears Designer fakes.
Hangs out In their backyard and at barbies.
Drives Early-model BMW.
Loves Their property portfolio.
Hates That their mortgages mean they haven't had a holiday in 20 years.
Wants To be able to afford to live on the north shore.

North-west Suburbs

Wears A cross and man-made fabrics.
Drives Holden Commodore or Ford Falcon.
Hangs out In church and shopping malls.
Loves Their neighbour and their family.
Hates They have no room for hate in their life, but they're not that keen on abortion, drugs, porn or the Middle East.
Wants The world to be a better place for their kids.

To get to Enmore, return to Newtown and then turn off King Street on to Enmore Road. Bands and DJs occupy the renovated **@Newtown RSL** (*see p250*), two large levels of slink with beads, funky wallpaper and chandeliers. Also check out the **Enmore Theatre** (*see p248*), a renovated deco-style theatre popular with local and international

rock bands and stand-up comedy acts. For a pre-gig dinner, try out any of the Thai restaurants – **Banks Thai** (91 Enmore Road, 9550 6840) has raised, cushioned seating. More food can be found at late-opening **Saray Turkish Pizza** (No.18, 9557 5310). In fact, there's no need to stop there, as there are still more dining options among the cluster of

King Street, the main drag of funky, grungy Newtown. *See p106.*

high-quality Lebanese restaurants on the street. Try **Fifi's** or head off the main track to **Emma's on Liberty** (for both, *see p162*). The **Duke of Edinburgh Hotel** (No.148, 9550 3452) is also great for cheap food, drinks and a game of pool. Perhaps one of the oddest yet coolest additions to the Sydney nightlife scene is the **Sly Fox** (*see p221* and *p239*); the music varies nightly, while Wednesday brings Sydney's lesbians and drag kings out in force.

Petersham

Map p322. **Transport** *CityRail Petersham/bus 428.*

Petersham lies north-west of Enmore; if you're driving, turn right off Enmore Road into Stanmore Road, which becomes New Canterbury Road, the main thoroughfare. Until very recently the neighbourhood was tainted by the Oxford Tavern that hulks at its gateway, flashing '24 hour lingerie waitresses' in screaming neon. It took some time to see that within the cloud of choking fumes of the main road, a 'Little Portugal' was already born. It's a tiny strip that lacks the glamour of Leichhardt or the more villagey vibe of Haberfield, both just over Parramatta Road to the north, but makes up for it with authenticity.

A fleet of excellent traditional Portuguese restaurants and pâtisseries line the few blocks of New Canterbury Road from Audley Street to West Street. Picking up occasional honours is

Gloria's Café (82 Audley Street, 9568 3966), which serves homely Portuguese bites (pork and clam stew or cod cakes), both indoors and out on the pavement seating – a vague attempt at turning on some southern charm. There's often a trail of prettily dressed Portuguese families heading into **Silvas Portuguese Traditional Charcoal Chicken** (82-86 New Canterbury Road, 9572 9911). At first glance, it looks like a Portuguese McDonald's, only with alcohol, but scratch the surface and you'll find seafood specialities and table service alongside the takeaway chook and chips. At the sweetly named **Honeymoon Pâtisserie & Coffee Lounge** (No.96, 9564 2389) elderly Iberian gents gather for Portuguese snacks, while the barn-like **Petersham Liquor Mart** (No.41, 9560 2414) offers shelves of red, white and rosé wines imported from Portugal.

To experience the full flavour of the area's cuisine and culture, visit during Audley Street's annual **Bairro Português** festival, held on a Sunday in March.

Finally, don't miss Petersham's main claim to fame on the food front – even though it's Greek, not Portuguese. Modern taverna **Perama** (*see p161*) has soaked its way so completely into the touchy taste buds of Sydney's foodie elite that they don't mind the trek out to plane-traffic territory. Its signature dish of crisp kataifi pastry with bastourma, warm ricotta and figs is regularly eulogised on critics' lists of the best eats in Sydney.

North Shore

Funfair, zoo – it's family fun in the city's traditional breeding grounds.

For those who enjoy the edgy glamour of Sydney's eastern suburbs, the mantra 'Don't go beyond the Harbour Bridge' is almost the basis of a religion. But when they start getting broody, there is only one place for them to move – the north shore. The eastern suburbs aren't ideal for bringing up children, but the sedate sophistication of the north shore most definitely is, and families flock there in such numbers the area could almost be called the Breeding Fields.

The north shore's waterside suburbs boast the best views in town – the Opera House and Harbour Bridge in one frame from your living room, say, or kookaburras and rainbow lorikeets nestled in weeping figs along the Cremorne foreshore. Add to this a clutch of pretty harbour beaches, numerous delis, cafés and coffee shops, and family homes echoing with early 20th-century heritage and the appeal is obvious.

The north shore is not an officially designated area: rather, it's a term to lump together the suburbs on the north side of the harbour that are south and/or west of the northern beaches. Many of these suburbs are not actually on the shore, nor are they especially interesting to tourists, being suburban enclaves. Those that are worth visiting – **Kirribilli**, **North Sydney, McMahons Point, Milsons Point, Mosman, Balmoral, Cremorne** – are all on the water.

The loosely termed 'northern suburbs' link the north shore with the western suburbs and include middle-class neighbourhoods such as Cheltenham, Epping, Beecroft and North Ryde. The north shore stops at Hornsby in the north, Lane Cove in the west and Belrose in the east. It is punctuated by sprawling commercial centres at places like North Sydney, Chatswood and Hornsby.

Getting around the north shore is not easy. Its size and sprawl mean that you're best off in a car, and many of its hidden beaches can only be reached by car, on foot (if you're prepared for the hills) or by charter boat (if you're not). But there is public transport available in the form of the north shore CityRail train line from North Sydney to Hornsby, a wide range of buses and the green-and-gold ferries from Circular Quay. The latter offer the most picturesque way to travel and capture

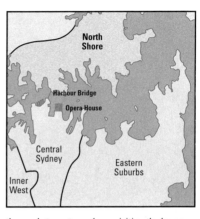

the area's true atmosphere, visiting the lower north shore suburbs. Take a seat outside at the front or back of the ferry and ogle the waterfront houses and foreshore flora and fauna. Each of these suburbs has a centre, usually with clusters of cafés and speciality shops, plus stunning harbour views and harbourfront walks. The region is also home to **Taronga Zoo**, a famous Sydney landmark and the world's only harbourside zoo.

Today the north shore is largely the homeland of Sydney's well-heeled whites, and while the multicultural landscape is slowly changing with Japanese, Chinese, Korean and South African immigrants moving in, the original Aboriginal population is long gone. The early north shore settlers in the first decades of the 1800s were land grantees, among them Billy Blue, James Milson and Edward Wollstonecraft, and its development into a place of white estates and family homes stems from that time.

The Cammeraygal and Wallumedegal tribes who inhabited the area when the First Fleet arrived in Sydney Cove in 1788 had largely been driven out of the region by the 1860s. The Cammeraygal, recorded as being a powerful and numerous tribe, 'most robust and muscular', lived along the foreshore, in the bushland and cliffs, and in rock shelters. Places such as Berry Island, Balls Head, Kirribilli, Cremorne and Cammeray are dotted with cultural remains of the tribe.

Have a laugh at **Luna Park** funfair.

Kirribilli

Transport *Ferry Kirribilli.*

The north shore starts at Kirribilli and Milsons Point, tiny suburbs nestled on either side of the Harbour Bridge and boasting sweeping vistas of the city and the Opera House (dubbed 'dress-circle views' by estate agents). Despite the apartment blocks that have sprung up in between the old houses, both suburbs are Victorian in feel, with many original buildings still standing. The southern tip of Kirribilli is home to the official Sydney residences of the prime minister – **Kirribilli House** – and the governor-general – **Admiralty House**, where British royals and other foreign dignitaries also stay. The latter is the most impressive, a classic colonial mansion built in 1844-5 by the collector of customs, Lieutenant-Colonel Gibbes. Originally called Wotonga, it was bought in 1885 by the NSW government to house admirals of the fleet, hence its name today.

Kirribilli House next door, with its rolling, manicured lawns, was built in 1855 in a Gothic Revival style by a rich local merchant. After a series of owners it was acquired by the government in 1956 for use by the prime minister, his family and important guests. Since taking office in 1996, John Howard has used the house as his principal home, rather than the official prime ministerial residence, the Lodge

in Canberra. It's a choice that opposition parties claim is costing the taxpayer dearly, but Mr Howard is not about to give up his harbour view – and when you see it you'll understand why. To get the best views of Kirribilli House and Admiralty House (neither are open to the public), hop on a ferry from Circular Quay.

There's a distinctly villagey feel to Kirribilli, and its good-life residents continue to fill the cafés and restaurants around the hub of Fitzroy, Burton and Broughton Streets. Try upmarket Mod Oz fare at **Milsons** (*see p164*), seafood at **Garfish** (*see p165*) or Japanese cuisine in a traditional setting at newcomer **Ainoya** (34 Burton Street, 9922 1512). Or there's laid-back **Freckle Face** (32 Burton Street, 9957 2116), **Trio's Harbourside Café** (12 Fitzroy Street, 9955 3738) for pasta, seafood or steak by the water, and the renowned **Kirribilli Hotel** (35 Broughton Street, 9955 1415) with its outdoor terrace. The famous **Ensemble Theatre** (*see p269*), built over the water at Careening Cove, serves up new and classic theatre.

A particularly good time to visit Kirribilli is on the fourth Saturday of the month, when one of Sydney's oldest markets is held on the former Kirribilli Bowling Club site on the corner of Burton and Alfred Streets. All sorts of stuff is on sale, but it's best known for upmarket bric-a-brac and antiques – and occasionally plays host to the odd Australian celebrity clearing out some space in their attic.

Despite appearances, not everyone in Kirribilli is rolling in cash. In among the multi-million-dollar mansions and swanky apartment blocks lurk some Housing Commission blocks and older, cheaper homes. It's not quite a case of rich and poor rubbing shoulders, since the shoulder pads around the big homes tend to stretch some distance, but it does mean that the area retains some balance of old-world character and modern reality.

Milsons Point, McMahons Point & North Sydney

Transport Milsons Point *CityRail/ferry Milsons Point.* **McMahons Point** *Ferry McMahons Point.* **North Sydney** *CityRail North Sydney.*

On a sunny day, treat yourself to a ferry trip from Circular Quay's Wharf 4, gliding past the Opera House to Milsons Point wharf (Alfred Street South). From here, you can take the harbourside walk in either direction. The ferry pulls up right in front of the grinning face and huge staring eyes of the newly reopened **Luna Park** funfair (*see p111*). To the right (with your back to the water) is the revamped **North Sydney Olympic Pool** (*see p113*), perhaps the most stunningly located swimming pool in the world: it's at the water's edge, beneath the northern pylon of the Harbour Bridge. The pool also houses a couple of snazzy eateries popular with the media and advertising crowd who work in North Sydney. The less formal **Ripples** (corner of Alfred Street and Olympic Drive, 9929 7722) is bang next to the pool and has outdoor tables. On the other side, in a glass box overlooking the pool, is the pricey **Aqua Dining** (*see p164*). The same people run both restaurants, and both are open for lunch and dinner.

If you walk along the boardwalk in front of the pool, you can peek in through the glass-sided bay windows at the swimmers and sunbathers. The colourful art deco façade has fabulous mouldings of frogs and cockatoos. Carry on under the bridge and continue past the green lawns of **Bradfield Park** with the rather ugly *Australian Angel*, the Swiss cultural contribution to an exhibition of sculpture and graphic art at the 2000 Olympics. There's also a plaque commemorating the deaths of 51 people from typhus aboard the quarantined ship *Surry*, which was anchored here in 1814. Third Mate Thomas Raine was the only officer to survive, and his grandson Tom Raine founded the wealthy Sydney estate agents Raine & Horne – a fitting north shore tale. The foreshore walk ends at **Mary Booth Lookout**, a patch of green with a fab view that's perfect for picnics.

In the other direction from Luna Park the foreshore walk winds around **Lavender Bay**: it's especially dazzling at sunset when the city lights shimmer in the golden glow. Walk up the Lavender Bay Wharf steps to Lavender Street, turn left and after another couple of minutes you'll reach **Blues Point Road**, which slices down from North Sydney through the heart of McMahons Point. It's one of Sydney's great people-watching strips, and an influx of magazine publishers and advertising agencies has turned the locale into Sydney's answer to London's Clerkenwell. There are numerous cafés, pubs, delis and restaurants from which to take in the view; try **Blues Point Café** (No.135, 9922 2064) or the **Commodore Hotel** (No.206, 9922 5098, www.commodore hotel.com.au), a popular after-work haunt with a large outdoor terrace. Allow time to walk down to **Blues Point Reserve**, a swathe of open parkland at the southern tip of Blues Point that provides a great photo op for that obligatory Sydney Harbour holiday snap.

The northern end of Blues Point Road merges into Miller Street, dominated by North Sydney office blocks – this is Sydney's main business district after the CBD. A little way up on the left-hand side of Miller Street is Mount

Street and the bizarre **Mary MacKillop Place** (*see p112*). This homage to Australia's only saint stands on the site of her former convent and is worth a visit, if only for its zany exhibition. To get a sense of the history of the area, visit the nearby **Don Bank Museum** (*see below*), located inside one of North Sydney's oldest houses. Further up Miller Street is **North Sydney Oval**, one of the oldest cricket grounds in Australia (established 1867), now used for rugby (league and union) as well as cricket matches.

The heart and main commercial centre of the lower north shore is **Military Road**, a low-slung, seemingly endless and faceless strip of shops, cafés and restaurants that heads east through Neutral Bay to Balmoral. At No.118, in Neutral Bay, the popular **Oaks** pub (*see p185*), with its tree-covered courtyard, is a hangout for local movers and shakers, who order steaks and fish by the kilo and then make for the outdoor barbecue to cook up a storm. Further up the road is the unmissable **Pickled Possum** pub (No.254, 9909 2091), a genuine taste of a small Outback pub in the centre of the city. Stubbies are served straight from an esky and the only way to tell the electricity hasn't actually been cut off is the nonstop karaoke on the extremely kitsch – and tiny – stage. Opening hours are erratic and entirely at the whim of the owner. If you can catch it open, it's a great night out – as long as you're not shy.

Don Bank Museum

6 Napier Street, off Berry Street, North Sydney (9955 6279). CityRail North Sydney. **Open** noon-4pm Wed; 1-4pm Sun. **Admission** $1; 50¢ concessions. **No credit cards**.
It's not known exactly when this house was built, but parts are thought to date from the 1820s. Originally called St Leonards Cottage (most of North Sydney, as it now is, was once called St Leonards) it was part of the Wollstonecraft Estate granted to Edward Wollstonecraft in 1825. The house was bought by North Sydney Council in the late 1970s and restored with assistance from heritage groups: it is now a community museum. As well as visiting exhibitions, its permanent displays include kitchen objects from the times of the early settlers and other historical items. The building itself is significant, being one of the few surviving examples of an early timber-slab house.

Luna Park Sydney

1 Olympic Drive, at the foreshore, Milsons Point (9922 6644/www.lunaparksydney.com). CityRail/ ferry Milsons Point. **Open** 11am-6pm Mon-Thur; 11am-10pm Fri; 10am-11pm Sat; 10am-6pm Sun (later in school holidays). **Admission** *Entry* free. *Rides* individual rides vary. *Unlimited ride passes* $18, $29, $39; free under-5s. **Credit** AmEx, DC, MC, V.

Walk 2: Cremorne Point

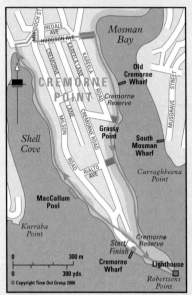

The paved track around Cremorne Point is hardly taxing, but the spectacular vistas are quite breathtaking, and if the idea of picnicking to the laughter of kookaburras against a backdrop of Sydney red gums appeals, this is one for you. Signs chart the history of the area from its Aboriginal roots as Wulwarrajeung to the present-day efforts to put indigenous flora and fauna back into the bushland between the lovingly manicured gardens along the way.

The walk is signposted from Bogota Avenue down to Cremorne Point wharf at the tip and then back up. However, transport-wise, it's easiest to catch a ferry to the wharf and start from there. The path dives off to the left, leading north past a series of manicured lawns (good for picnics) and the backs of properties on Milson Road: an electic mix of federation, art deco and more modern styles. Don't miss the side path to historic **MacCallum Pool** (*photo*), a narrow little harbourside pool with fantastic views back towards the Harbour Bridge and city.

At the top of Shell Cove, there's a couple of hundred metres of tarmac to cross to the other side of the peninsula: turn right on to Bogota Avenue, go up the hill, cross over Murdoch Street and walk along Hodgson Avenue to its end, where you'll find steps taking you down to the path along the shore of Mosman Bay.

Character Great harbour views and bushland.
Length 3km (2-mile) loop.
Difficulty Easy.
Transport Ferry Cremorne Point/bus 225.

The huge laughing clown's mouth that marks the entrance to Luna Park is visible from Circular Quay. Walk through that mouth and you'll find Sydney's venerable funfair back in full stomach-churning swing after a troubled few decades. The park opened in 1935, on the site of the Dorman Long workshops used to build the Harbour Bridge, and its heyday lasted until well into the 1950s. A slow decline into the '70s ended in sudden closure in 1979 following a fatal fire on the Ghost Train. After an abortive 1990s relaunch, a new plan took off in 2000. Now Luna Park lives again, this time as a 1930s-style fun park and a performance venue. Some of the park's traditional rides are still around, as are many of its old-fashioned sideshow games, and there's no shortage of fixes for addicts of high speeds and vertigo. There are great views from the top of the 40m/131ft-high Ferris Wheel. Modern additions include the Big Top, used for concerts, and the revamped Crystal Palace, now a banqueting and conference hall. Foodwise, it's unapologetic funfair fare: fish and chips, hot dogs, pies, ice-cream, pizza, candy floss… unwise (before a ride, at least) but irresistible.

Mary MacKillop Place

7 Mount Street, between Edward &William Streets, North Sydney (8912 4878/www.marymackillopplace. org.au). CityRail North Sydney. **Open** 10am-4pm daily. **Admission** $7.50; $3-$5 concessions; $15 family. **Credit** MC, V.

Mary MacKillop (1842-1909) was the founder of the Sisters of St Joseph, an order initially devoted to educating poor Australian children. Often referred to as 'the people's saint', MacKillop's pioneering work lead to her beatification in 1995 when the Pope visited and blessed the site, giving Australia its first – and only – saint to date. She died on 8 August 1909 and the eighth day of each month has become a day of pilgrimage to the museum for devout Catholics. It includes MacKillop's home, Alma Cottage, and the chapel housing her tomb. A curious mix of humble 19th-century artefacts and high-tech wizardry, the displays of MacKillop's possessions – including crucifixes, rosary beads, figurines and scraps of her habits – are jazzed up with talking dioramas, videos and other surprisingly cool special effects, all of which take you on a journey through the saint's life.

After **Old Cremorne Wharf** there's an uphill stretch to **Grassy Point** and its outstanding views, which account for this being the site of the Laurels. This huge house (now flats), set back from the bushland, is one of Sydney's best examples of the early 20th-century federation style – characterised by decorative timberwork, coloured glass and bay windows. You'll then pass the stunning **Lex & Ruby Graham Gardens**, first maintained by this local couple and now taken on by the National Trust. You may also see magpies, kookaburras, lizards and rainbow lorikeets.

The finger of land at the bottom of the peninsula is **Robertsons Point**, named after the Scottish watchmaker who lived here in the first half of the 19th century. Pleasure gardens, with a shooting gallery, fireworks and masked balls, operated here in the 1850s. Walk down to the whitewashed 1904 **lighthouse** at its end and gaze west to Kurraba Point and Kirribilli, south to the city and Woolloomooloo, and east to Double Bay and Watsons Bay, looking over Taronga Zoo. There are toilets, a children's play area and picnic tables here. Then it's a short walk back to the ferry wharf.

If all this has whetted your appetite for more urban bushland exploration, or you want to discover more about the history of North Sydney, the council has devised an impressive range of self-guided walks. You

can get leaflets from Stanton Library (234 Miller Street, 9936 8400) or the council itself (200 Miller Street, 9936 8100), or download them from www.northsydney.nsw.gov.au – click on 'recreation'.

North Sydney Olympic Pool

4 Alfred Street South, at the foreshore, Milsons Point (9955 2309/www.northsydney.nsw.gov.au). CityRail/ ferry Milsons Point. **Open** 5.30am-9pm Mon-Fri; 7am-7pm Sat, Sun. **Admission** *Pool* $4.90; $2.30-$4 concessions. *Sauna, spa & swim* $9.30. **Credit** AmEx, DC, MC, V. **Map** p327 F2.

This unique outdoor swimming pool, situated between the Harbour Bridge and Luna Park, holds a special place in Sydneysiders' hearts. Built on the site where much of the construction work for the bridge was carried out, it opened in 1936. Hailed as the 'wonder pool of Australasia' because of the high standard of its facilities and the sophistication of its filtration system – at the time one of the most advanced in the world – the building has wonderful intact art deco styling and decorative plasterwork. A total of 86 world records have been set here by such swimming greats as Jon Konrads, Shane Gould and Michelle Ford. Thanks to a revamp in the early 2000s, a 25m indoor pool, state-of the-art gym, spa and sauna have been added to the famed 50m heated outdoor pool. The views from the pool itself, and the

terraced concrete seating above it, are stupendous; if you're going to swim in only one pool in Sydney, make it this one.

Cremorne, Mosman, Balmoral & the Spit Bridge

Transport Cremorne *Ferry Cremorne Point then bus 225/bus L88 to Neutral Bay then bus 225.* **Mosman** *Ferry South Mosman, Old Cremorne or Mosman Bay/CityRail Milsons Point then bus 228, 229, 230.* **Balmoral** *Ferry Taronga Zoo then bus 238/CityRail Milsons Point then bus 229.*

If you continue east along Military Road (an extension of the busy main route that links the suburbs of the lower north shore), you will arrive at some of Sydney's richest suburbs: Cremorne, Mosman and Balmoral, where the heavily moneyed live in conspicuous splendour.

Cremorne Point, a sliver of a peninsula, offers one of the finest panoramas of Sydney

Visit **Bathers' Pavilion** for first-rate seaside dining at Balmoral Beach.

Harbour. It's the perfect setting for a scenic harbourside stroll – *see p112* **Walk 2: Cremorne Point**. You can then hop back on the ferry to Mosman Bay wharf, where an uphill walk or bus will take you into Mosman village (alternatively, the Cremorne Point walk leads around Mosman Bay). Stop at the friendly **Rowers Restaurant** (3 Centenary Drive, 9953 7713, www.mosmanrowers.com) for lunch, dinner or (on Sundays) breakfast. Part of the Mosman Rowing Club, it's right on the water, with a great outdoor seating area and reasonably priced DIY barbecue options.

Further east lies **Taronga Zoo** (*see below*), which occupies a splendid vantage point overlooking Bradleys Head. North of the zoo, Mosman's commercial centre runs along Military Road – a good place to people-watch and shop, if your wallet can cope. Many of the main chain stores are here, plus a clutch of Australian designers, plenty of shabby-chic homeware shops and endless delis and cafés.

Beyond Mosman is Balmoral, one of Sydney's prettiest harbour suburbs. Boasting not one but two beaches, lots of green space, a Romanesque bandstand (the venue for many local events) and a couple of excellent restaurants – **Watermark** (2A The Esplanade, 9968 3433, www.watermarkrestaurant.com.au) and **Bathers' Pavilion** (*see p164*) – plus a pretty decent fish and chip shop for a promenade snack, Balmoral offers a more relaxed version of north shore life. The two arcs of sand, Edwards and Balmoral Beaches,

are separated by Rocky Point, and part of Edwards is protected by a shark net. If you come on a Saturday before 10am you're likely to spy members of the Spit Amateur Swimming Club pounding the water. This family-friendly club is a local institution and has been using Balmoral's outdoor baths since 1916.

Head further north and you hit the **Spit Bridge**, the beautiful bottleneck faced by those wanting to head towards Manly and the northern beaches. The view driving down Spit Road from Military Road is one of Sydney's most delicious, with boats bobbing in the marina either side of the narrow bridge causeway and swanky mansions clinging to the rocky cliffs. Traffic comes to a halt when the bridge lifts to let boats pass beneath. If you're driving though and get a clear run, watch your speed: the area is circled by speed cameras.

Taronga Zoo

Bradleys Head Road, Mosman (9969 2777/www.zoo. nsw.gov.au). Ferry Taronga Zoo/bus 247. **Open** 9am-5pm daily. **Admission** *Zoo only* $30; $16.50-$21 concessions; $79 family; free under-4s. *Zoopass* $37; $27 concessions. **Credit** AmEx, DC, MC, V.
Only 12 minutes by ferry from Circular Quay, the 'zoo with a view' covers 30 hectares (74 acres) on the western side of Bradleys Head. The zoo moved here from Moore Park in Sydney's eastern suburbs in 1916. The animals arrived by ferry – the story goes that Jessie the elephant actually walked from Moore Park to Circular Quay before gingerly climbing aboard ship. The zoo contains 2,600 animals of more than 340 species: best of all, especially for foreigners,

are the native ones, including koalas, kangaroos, platypuses (twins were born recently), echidnas, Tasmanian devils and lots of colourful, screechy birds (follow the Wild Australia Walk to see them all). Visitors are no longer allowed to cuddle koalas, but a 'koala encounter' (11am-3pm) lets you have your photo taken beside one of the sleepy critters.

Other highlights include the Free Flight Bird Show, the Capral Seal Show, Giraffes in Focus – meet the giraffes face to face, listen to a keeper talk and grab a close-up photo – the huge Komodo dragon and the Gorilla Forest. New exhibits include Backyard to Bush (a journey from an Aussie backyard through an adventure-packed farmyard into a bush wilderness) and construction is finally nearing completion of the much-delayed and controversial Asian Elephant Rainforest, which has been plagued by rows over the wisdom of turning more elephants into zoo exhibits.

The zoo is on a hill, so if you're coming by ferry, take the Sky Safari cable car to the main zoo compound at the top and then walk back down to the wharf. You can buy a Zoopass at Circular Quay to cover the return ferry trip, cable car and zoo admission. It's a huge place and tricky to find your way around (the free map is pretty poor), so allow at least three to four hours for a visit. There are several cafés, but the food isn't great, so it's more agreeable to take your own picnic.

Waverton

Transport Waverton *CityRail Waverton.* Wahroonga *CityRail Wahroonga.*

While it's true that the north shore's most spectacular vistas are found on the harbour foreshore, there are a couple of other areas worth visiting for something a little different. A train ride across the Harbour Bridge to Waverton (one stop past North Sydney) will deliver you to **Balls Head Reserve**, a thickly wooded headland overlooking the start of the Parramatta River. Turn left out of the station down Bay Road, which runs into Balls Head Road; it's a five- to ten-minute walk. From here you can look west to Gladesville, south to the city, Balmain and Goat Island and east to McMahons Point and beyond. Until 1916 this area was the home of a local Aboriginal community – an engraving of a six-metre (20-foot) whale with a man inside is still preserved – but during World War I the Australian army claimed the land and a Quarantine Depot (still standing) was established. Wildlife is abundant, and on summer nights you might see flying foxes feeding on the Port Jackson fig trees, dragon lizards, geckos, brush-tailed possums and up to 68 species of bird. There are free gas barbecues, so you can take your own steak or prawns and dine out at one of the finest window seats in Sydney. (Check there isn't a fire ban in place first, though, especially in midsummer.)

West of Balls Head, around the next cove, **Berry Island Reserve** is the best place to see remnants of the north shore's Aboriginal heritage. The island was originally a camping area for Aboriginal communities, and evidence of their way of life, including shell middens, axe grindings and a rock hole that would have stored water, are still visible. In the early 19th century Edward Wollstonecraft attached the island to his land by building a stone causeway over mud flats (now reclaimed as lawns); the area became a public nature reserve in 1926.

Wahroonga

Transport Wahroonga *CityRail Wahroonga.*

Wahroonga is a quiet, leafy suburb on the north-west fringe of the north shore, and the place where you'll find **Rose Seidler House** (*see below*). This was the first building that the Viennese-born architect Harry Seidler designed in Australia. He went on to become one of Sydney's most celebrated architects, and his unusual buildings around the city continue to provoke admiration and controversy in equal measure. The house itself is impressive enough on its own, but do check out the amazing panoramic views of Ku-ring-gai Chase National Park from almost every window – you'll see why Seidler chose this spot.

Rose Seidler House

71 Clissold Road, at Devon Street, Wahroonga (9989 8020/www.hht.nsw.gov.au). CityRail Wahroonga. **Open** 10am-5pm Sun; and by appointment. **Admission** $8; $4 concessions; $17 family. **No credit cards**.

Harry Seidler built this house, his first commission, in 1948-50 for his parents, Rose and Max. The ambitious architect came over from New York, where he had been working for Bauhaus guru Marcel Breuer, specifically to build the house; it was the first local instance of 'mid-century modern' domestic architecture. In basic terms, the house is a flat single-storey box resting on a smaller box, with a section cut out to form a sun deck and floor-to-ceiling windows. The open-plan interior is divided into two distinct zones: the living or public areas, and the sleeping or private areas. The original 1950s colour scheme has been restored, and the furnishings are by important post-war designers such as Charles Eames and Eero Saarinen. The kitchen had all mod cons – the very latest refrigerator, stove and dishwasher, plus a waste-disposal unit and exhaust fan – which were then utterly new to Australia and added to the house's allure locally. Max and Rose Seidler lived in the house until 1967. It's now run by the Historic Houses Trust, and guided tours are available on request. Seidler died in March 2006.

Sightseeing

Northern Beaches

If you're serious about sea and sand, you'd better get out of town.

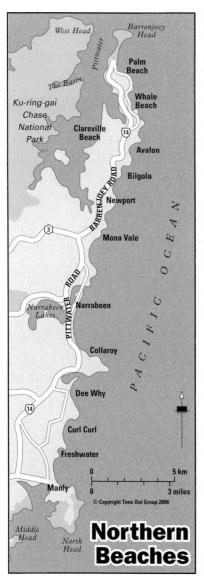

West Head
Barrenjoey Head
Pittwater
Palm Beach
The Basin
Whale Beach
Ku-ring-gai Chase National Park
Clareville Beach
(14)
Avalon
Bilgola
BARRENJOEY ROAD
Newport
(3)
Mona Vale
ROAD
PITTWATER ROAD
Narrabeen Lakes
Narrabeen
PACIFIC OCEAN
Collaroy
Dee Why
(14)
Curl Curl
Freshwater
0   5 km
0   3 miles
© Copyright Time Out Group 2006
Manly
Middle Head
North Head

Northern Beaches

Sightseeing

No trip to Sydney is complete without a visit to Bondi and Manly. But if you really want to see the finest beaches on offer, head north to where the real surfie's heart lies. Beyond the city reaches, over Spit Bridge, past Manly and further up the northern coastline sits a string of stunning golden sand and surf, with many beaches all but empty on weekdays – just you, the sea, the sun and your board.

The northern beaches officially start at busy, touristy Manly, but it is the more distant suburbs such as Collaroy, Narrabeen, Newport and Avalon that set the tone for the area. The secret of the northern beaches' character (dubbed the 'insular peninsula' by some) lies in their relative inaccessibility: there's no suburban train line that services the area. This means that residents of the northern beaches must either drive to the city in the crawling rush-hour traffic, sit on a sweaty bus or charter their own boat. This prospect has largely kept city workers from living around the northern beaches, and allowed the area to develop in a special way: it's a unique blend of genuine locals with not too much spare cash and wealthy newcomers (think the late Kerry Packer) who breeze in and snap up the prime property sites – the ones with eye-popping ocean views and space for a helipad.

The presence of rich folk has encouraged the opening of a smattering of cool restaurants, upmarket shops and classy businesses, while the locals have fought to preserve the beaches, parklands and countrified atmosphere. But the tide is turning. Real-estate price hikes have put pressure on every Sydney suburb, and as the city sprawls further outward even the northern beaches have succumbed to the invasion of apartment blocks and shopping centres that has become the norm elsewhere.

Take the 190 or the faster L90 bus from Wynyard up Pittwater Road (the easiest way to tour the northern beaches if you don't have a car – if you take the ferry to Manly first, you have to take another two buses to get up to Palm Beach) and you'll immediately spot the changes: family suburbs such as Dee Why,

▶ For more details on some of the beaches mentioned here, see pp133-139 **Sydney's Best Beaches**.

Narrabeen, Mona Vale and Newport are awash with imposing developments. Palm Beach became a millionaires' playground long ago, and the coastline is now cluttered with more and more designer palaces, while Avalon, always the protected heart of the northern beaches, is growing far quicker than the outspoken 'Save Our Avalon' locals would like: with its homeware shops, sushi and juice bars, it's in danger of turning into a mini Mosman.

For the tourists, though, the development is not all bad. There are far more places to stay than there used to be – cute B&Bs, pub-style accommodation, youth hostels and four-star hotels – and a greater choice of eateries and watering holes. And while locals may whinge about the changes, this is still an undeniably stunning stretch of coastline.

Manly

Map p334. **Transport** *Ferry Manly.*

A summery explosion of shops, restaurants, cafés, surfboards, people and colour, this famous beachside suburb nestles on its own peninsula, boasting both ocean and harbour beaches, and views from every corner. Since its first days as a resort in the 1920s, Manly's catchphrase has been 'seven miles from Sydney and a thousand miles from care' – actually an advertising slogan coined by the once-famous Port Jackson & Manly Steamship Company. Hearing it might cause the locals to cringe a little these days, but the sentiment still remains.

Just a few years ago Manly was slipping into decline and had the feel of a fading British seaside resort. But it has rejuvenated itself and is now a vibrant and dynamic suburb with a bevy of great bars, restaurants, cafés and clubs (although a campaign by local councillors to rein in licensing hours could curtail its appeal).

The suburb was given its name by Arthur Phillip, the first governor of New South Wales, when he saw a number of 'manly' Aboriginal men of the Kay-ye-my clan on the shore of what he later called Manly Cove. Now it's a centre for such macho pursuits as surf lifesaving, bodysurfing, kayaking and the Australian Ironman Championships, so the name still fits.

Sydneysiders have mixed feelings about Manly, but its perennial holiday atmosphere and one-and-a-half kilometres (one mile) of tree-lined ocean beach are irresistible to visitors. The tourists who head for Manly are a curious mix of the well-heeled, who stay at the area's expensive hotels, a burgeoning (predominantly British) backpacker brigade holing up in cheap hostels and pubs, and day-trippers delivered by ferry from the Sydney suburbs.

To get to Manly, take one of the large Manly ferries (30 minutes) or the pricier but faster JetCats (15 minutes) from Circular Quay to Manly Wharf on secluded **Manly Cove**, where you'll find a peaceful patch of harbourside sand (though no surf, of course). Stop in at the **Visitor Information Centre** (*see p120*) in front of the wharf for maps and brochures. The recently upgraded **Manly Wharf Hotel** (*see p166*) with its outside deck is one of Sydney's finest waterside drinking and eating spots. Nearby, at the western end of the cove, is popular **Oceanworld Manly** (*see p120*), **Manly Art Gallery & Museum** (*see p119*) and **Manly Waterworks** (9949 1088, www.manlywaterworks.com), a small water park that's open from September to April. Further west is the start of a fine ten-kilometre (6.25-mile) walk through bushland and along clifftops to **Spit Bridge** (pick up a self-guided walk leaflet at the Visitor Information Centre).

The main pedestrian precinct, the **Corso**, links Manly Wharf with Manly Beach on the oceanfront, and is lined with restaurants, surf shops, fast-food joints and tourist shops. A recent influx of new businesses, including a clutch of high-street chains, plus cool clothing and footwear shops, has made this strip a popular shopping destination in its own right. The Corso's amphitheatre is used regularly for live entertainment and has been known to draw enormous crowds, particularly for the fantastic **Manly International Jazz Festival** (*see p212*) in October and the equally popular **Food & Wine Festival** in June. The **Manly Arts & Crafts Market**, worth a browse for hand-made jewellery and unusual souvenirs, is held every weekend on the lower end of Sydney Road, just off the Corso.

The suburb's main attraction, though, is **Manly Beach** itself, a long, pale crescent of sand and ocean surf, fringed by a promenade lined with giant Norfolk pines that is a mecca for surfers, sunbathers, cyclists, in-line skaters and beach volleyball enthusiasts. The pines were planted in the 1850s by Henry Gilbert Smith, a wealthy English immigrant who decided to turn Manly from a tiny fishing village into a holiday resort for Sydneysiders. He built the first pier in 1855 and set up the first permanent ferry service in 1859. It was here too that local newspaper editor WH Gocher flouted the law prohibiting daylight bathing in 1902, a symbolic act that probably marked the beginning of Manly's – and Sydney's – love affair with sun, sea, sand and surf. The services of Eddie and Joe Sly, the first lifesavers to patrol the beach, were soon needed, as the holidaymaking crowds failed to understand the danger of the surf. The Slys staged a lifesaving

Manly by name, surfie by nature: surf lifesavers have patrolled **Manly Beach** for a century.

demo in 1903 to raise money for their service. Surfboards, wetsuits and beach umbrellas are for hire on the beach; novice surfers can hone their skills with **Manly Surf School** (9977 6977, www.manlysurfschool.com).

Head south along the beachfront road to find a row of laid-back bars and cafés with lovely ocean views on South Steyne. Busy most of the time, they are perfect spots in which to enjoy a meal or coffee, or just watch the world cruise by. Some of the most popular spots include **Blue Water Café** (28 South Steyne, 9976 2051), **Zinc Café** (Nos.30-31, 9977 9199) and **Rouge Mediterranean Café** (No.33, 8966 9872). Or there's the chic **Manly Ocean Beach House** (Ocean Promenade, South Steyne, 9977 0566) slap bang in the middle of the beachside promenade, so close to the surfers you can almost touch them.

A must is the 15-minute walk to **Shelly Beach**. Walk south on the beachfront from Manly Beach to Marine Parade and follow the winding path around the headland known as Fairy Bower, passing magnificent cliff-top homes along the way. Watch out for the beautiful, and carefully hidden, sea-themed artworks of the Sculpture Walk sited along the way. En route are a couple of eateries: the

Bower Restaurant (7 Marine Parade, 9977 5451) is a good spot for breakfast, lunch or an early dinner, while, at Shelly Beach, the sandstone **Le Kiosk** (1 Marine Parade, 9977 4122/2956) is a smart restaurant with a cheaper takeaway kiosk next door.

Another must is the spectacular view from **North Head**, the northern of the two Heads that form the gateway to Sydney Harbour. It's a five- to ten-minute drive via Darley Road (running south-east from the middle of the Corso) and North Head Scenic Drive. North Head is also home to the historic **North Head Quarantine Station** (see p120) and **North Fort** (see p120). You can take bus 135 from Wentworth Street, but be aware that the service operates in the daytime only. Keep your eyes peeled on the walk and down at the harbourside: you might spot some of Sydney's famous fairy penguins, tiny versions of their Antarctic cousins, living in the heart – and the heat – of the city. Don't approach them, though, as they're a protected species.

Manly Art Gallery & Museum

West Esplanade (9949 1776). Ferry Manly. **Open** 10am-5pm Tue-Sun. Closed public holidays. **Admission** $3.60; $1.20 concessions. **Credit** MC, V. **Map** p334.

Although Manly is not exactly synonymous with high culture, you can pop into this small gallery/museum if all the surfer lingo starts to curdle your brain. Opened in 1930, it has an 800-strong collection of paintings by Australian artists, some impressive ceramics and edgy exhibitions by local students and photographers. The museum is devoted to the history of Manly and has a marvellously kitsch collection of beach memorabilia, including vintage swimming costumes. The shop sells leaflets describing two Heritage Walks around Manly.

Manly Visitor Information Centre

Manly Wharf (9976 1430/www.manlytourism.com). Ferry Manly. **Open** 9am-5pm Mon-Fri; 10am-4pm Sat, Sun (5pm summer). **Map** p334.
Situated at the front of the wharf, this is the place to find brochures, bus timetables, free maps and the handy mini magazine *Manly Seaside Observer*.

North Fort

North Fort Road, off North Head Scenic Drive (9976 6102/www.northfort.org.au). Ferry Manly then bus 135. **Open** 11am-4pm Wed, Sat, Sun. **Admission** $11; $5-$8 concessions; $25 family. **Credit** MC, V.
The remote location of North Fort means its landscape has changed little since early colonial paintings of the spot. Wind-blown sand dunes cover the headland, with hillside 'hanging' swamps among the coastal shrub. Today it is home to the Royal Australian Artillery National Museum, once part of the School of Artillery, constructed between 1935 and 1938 in the shadow of war and the need to defend Sydney Harbour from naval attack. You can still tour the fortifications, underground tunnels and a memorial walkway – the last undergoes continual upgrades as more and more inscribed paving stones are added.

North Head Quarantine Station

North Head Scenic Drive (bookings 9247 5033/www.manlyquarantine.com). Ferry Manly then bus 135. **Open** (pre-booked tours only) *Public tour* 1.15-3pm Mon, Wed, Fri-Sun. *Adults' ghost tour* 7.30-10.30pm (8-11pm summer) Wed, Fri-Sun. *Kids' ghost tour* 6-8pm (7-9pm summer) Fri. **Admission** *Public tour* $11; $7.70 concessions; $30.80 family. *Adults' ghost tour* $22 Wed; $27.50 Fri-Sun. *Kids' ghost tour* $13.20. **Credit** MC, V.
The ghost tours at the North Head Quarantine Station are possibly the creepiest sightseeing you'll ever do. Built in 1828, the station was the prison – and burial place – of scores of unfortunate souls, who were quarantined here for a minimum of 30 days if their ship was suspected of carrying an infectious disease, such as smallpox, bubonic plague or influenza. The station was overcrowded, the treatment often degrading and many who died were buried in unmarked graves. Closed in 1972 (though, incredibly, it was used as emergency housing for Vietnamese orphans in 1975), the station is currently a top attraction for ghoulish tourists. They are led through its black streets, old fumigation rooms, shower blocks and cemetery by a guide with a

kerosene lamp. Several visitors claim to have seen the resident ghosts – a moustachioed man in a three-piece suit and a stern matron – and others have reported feeling nauseous after getting a whiff of putrid and inexplicable smells. If you take a night tour, bring a torch and wear flat shoes. Despite its grim past the Quarantine Station is much revered by locals. Protests in recent years have prevented it from being leased to a private developer, but its future remains uncertain.

The complex occupies an ancient Aboriginal ceremonial site and is home to many threatened species of flora and fauna: bandicoots nest at Spring Cove, and the only breeding colony of fairy penguins in mainland NSW is here.

Oceanworld Manly

West Esplanade (9949 2644/www.oceanworld. com.au). Ferry Manly. **Open** 10am-5.30pm daily. **Admission** $18.50; $9.95-$13.50 concessions; $30.95-$44.95 family; 15% discount after 3.30pm. **Credit** AmEx, MC, V. **Map** p334.
Located a couple of hundred metres from Manly's ferry terminal, Oceanworld is about as good as aquaria get. The three-level attraction has a floor devoted to dangerous Australian creatures (poisonous snakes, funnel-web spiders, giant monitor lizards, crocodiles) and another to tropical fish, corals and venomous sea creatures. The main attraction, on the lower level, is the oceanarium, which holds the largest sharks in captivity in Australia, plus giant rays and sea turtles. You can view them via a 110m-long underwater viewing tunnel. Fish and sharks are fed at 11am on Mondays, Wednesdays and Fridays and there's a Dangerous Australian Animals show at noon daily. Other attractions include the 'touch pool' where you can get up close and personal with hermit crabs and starfish. For the really adventurous there's Shark Dive Xtreme ($175-$235), a chance to swim with huge grey nurse sharks.

Freshwater to Whale Beach

Transport Dee Why, Collaroy, Narrabeen & Mona Vale *Bus 188, 190, L88, L90.* Newport & Avalon *Bus 188, 190, E88, E89, L88, L90.* Whale Beach *Bus 190, L90 then bus 193.*

From Manly, the other northern beaches stretch out like a golden necklace and the names – Freshwater, Curl Curl, Dee Why, Collaroy, Narrabeen, Newport and Avalon – slip off the tongue like a surfer on the crest of a wave. This is serious surf territory, where Sydney's pros limber up. Here the air smells of sea salt and coconut oil, and every second teenager hides under a mop of matted bleached blond hair, with a surfboard in tow. But people live here too: scattered communities of holiday homes are gradually turning into suburbs as increasing numbers of Sydneysiders from all classes opt to put up with a long drive home for the sybaritic pleasures of life on the northern beaches.

The best way to explore is by car, allowing you to stop, take in the view, and swim at leisure at whichever beach you fancy. Otherwise, the L90 bus from Wynyard will take you all the way to Palm Beach – the journey takes about 90 minutes if you don't stop – calling in at various beaches (but not Manly) en route. The road becomes steeper and more winding after you've passed Newport and the views get increasingly breathtaking.

You can pick up the useful and informative **Sydney's Northern Beaches Map**, produced by the Northern Beaches Visitors Association, from Sydney Beachhouse YHA (4 Collaroy Street, Collaroy, 9981 1177); much of the same information is on the association's website, www.sydneybeaches.com.au. Also useful is www.sydneynorthernbeaches.com.au.

If you want to try one of the best meat pies in Sydney head for **Upper Crust** (1003 Pittwater Road, 9971 5182) at the crest of the hill in Collaroy. Sylvia and Fran's legendary pies have amassed such a devoted following there's always a jostle for a parking spot outside the shop: be prepared to fight for your place in the queue with barefooted surfies who dash across the busy street for a bite between waves. And for a cool beer in spectacular surroundings pop into the **Surf Rock Hotel** (1064 Pittwater Road, 9982 3924) with its balcony overlooking the seashore and sensational interior design.

Visitors with a car can take a detour to **Garigal National Park** (9451 3479, www.national parks.nsw.gov.au), which links Sydney's north shore suburbs with the northern beaches. Covering more than 20 square kilometres (nearly eight square miles) of rugged bush, sandstone outcrops and waterways, it's divided into various sections. The western section hugs Middle Harbour Creek, which leads into Sydney Harbour; a walking track by the creek offers historical interest (and four picnic areas), and some rare native ash and stringybark trees. Further north is the much larger **Ku-ring-gai Chase National Park** (see p123), on the western shore of Pittwater. It has the classic Greater Sydney mix of sandstone, bush and water vistas, plus walking tracks, horse-riding trails and picnic areas.

On the south-eastern edge of Ku-ring-gai Chase, inland from Mona Vale, is a striking domed white building. This is the **Bahá'í House of Worship** (173 Mona Vale Road, Ingleside, 9998 9221, www.bahai.org.au), a temple for members of the Bahá'í faith, a religion founded in the 19th century that has five million members worldwide. The temple's design, with nine sides and nine entrances,

represents the unification of the human race under one God. Whatever your religious views, it's a lovely spot, with beautiful grounds and great views of the ocean.

North of Mona Vale is Newport, worth a stop for it great delicatessen, **Tongue Teasers** (339 Barrenjoey Road, 9997 3557) – a top spot to load up for a picnic – and the **Newport Arms Hotel** (see p185), a much-loved pub with a fantastic beer garden overlooking the tranquil ocean inlet of Pittwater.

The final community before Palm Beach is **Avalon**, once something of a secret but now a thriving shopping centre and booming residential village, getting bigger by the year. It's approached via a slightly unnerving steep, winding road, which offers stunning, dramatic ocean views for whoever is in the passenger seat but one hairy ride for the driver. On the right, you'll pass the jaw-droppingly steep decline that leads to **Bilgola Beach**. Take time to turn off, follow the signs for the beach and drive around breathtaking bends – the road's not called the Serpentine for nothing – that lead you down and then back up the hillside. Just before you rejoin the main road, the lookout point on Bilgola Head is well worth a stop – it offers unique views right down the coastline towards Bondi and up to Barrenjoey Lighthouse at Palm Beach. Watch out for the hang-gliders

Sightseeing

A light hike

Barrenjoey Lighthouse

Character Rugged bushland and incredible ocean views.
Length 700m one way.
Difficulty Moderate.

The starting point, at the northern end of Barrenjoey Beach (on the Pittwater side), is marked by a sign next to a rust-coloured shed. There's a choice of routes to the top: the left-hand one, the Service Road, is the least steep and has the best views back over Palm Beach. But don't let the short distance mislead you – you'll work up quite a sweat climbing to the grassy summit plateau. From here, a 360-degree vista takes in the Pacific Ocean, Pittwater, Palm Beach and Lion Island, a deserted rocky outcrop that guards the entrance to Broken Bay. The 1881 lighthouse, built from Hawkesbury sandstone, is 113 metres (370 feet) above sea level and visible from 35 kilometres (22 miles) out at sea. It's open only on Sundays (11am-3pm) for guided tours ($3).

soaring within a couple of feet of your head as they cruise the thermals off the hillside.

On the upward ascent into Avalon, look out for the traditional birthday and anniversary greetings that locals pin to the trees. **Avalon Beach** is down the hill on the right. This beautiful surf beach was once considered as a possible new location by the makers of *Baywatch*, but the locals weren't having any of it. Today Avalon surfers still jealously guard their waters; they're in their combies from dawn until dusk, waiting for that perfect wave.

The town itself has two main strips: Avalon Parade, which runs from the beach up towards the Pittwater side of the peninsula, and the Old Barrenjoey Road, which crosses Avalon Parade and leads to Palm Beach in one direction and Sydney in the other.

On Old Barrenjoey Road there's an old favourite, the **Ibiza Café** (No.47, 9918 3965), which does a roaring trade: it's got an open pavement area for summer and a warm, friendly feel in winter. **Bookoccino** (No.37A, 9973 1244) is one of the best bookshops on the northern beaches, with an excellent range of children's books, cookery, biographies, history, Australiana and much more; as the name suggests, there's a café here too. There's also the traditional and well-established **Avalon Toys** (No.33, 9918 9106).

To get to the idyllic stretches of **Clareville Beach** on the calm shore of Pittwater, sheltered from ocean waves, head up Avalon Parade keeping the post office on your left. Avalon Parade becomes Hudson Parade and hooks left to run parallel to Pittwater; when you reach the bottom of the hill, turn right into Delecta Avenue – 20 minutes' walk from Avalon, a few minutes in the car. The sandy beach is not good for swimming, but it's popular with locals for meet-and-greet Sunday barbecues. Many also moor their boats here. **Clareville Kiosk** (27 Delecta Avenue, 9918 2727, www.clareville kiosk.com), a delightful beach-house-style restaurant, is open from Wednesday to Sunday for dinner and on Saturday and Sunday for lunch. Be sure to book ahead.

There's one more treasure to be seen before you reach Palm Beach, the end of the northern beaches road. For many locals, **Whale Beach** is closer to paradise than glitzier Palm. Its inaccessibility helps, making it a definite 'those in the know' bolt-hole. You can get there by bus – the 193 from Avalon Parade in Avalon – or by walking from Careel Head Road where the L90 bus stops. Head along Careel Head Road then turn left into Whale Beach Road and continue until you reach the beach itself; it's a long (at least half an hour) and hilly trek through residential roads lined with wonderful beach houses, but it's worth the effort. The pinky sand, rugged surf and rocky headland have a quality all their own, and there's an oceanside swimming pool.

And if you're feeling peckish – and flush – on the way home, stop in at lovely **Jonah's** (*see p165*), to mix with the area's swankier denizens and enjoy five-star food on a coastal hilltop. There are guest rooms too (*see p49*). You might want to bring a change of clothes, though – beachside gear won't cut it here.

Palm Beach & around

Transport *Bus 190, L90.*

Finally to Palm Beach, the well-heeled tip of the northern beaches, where you'll find more multi-million-dollar mansions than seagulls. As a result, there aren't as many cabbage tree palms around as there were when they gave the place its name. It's worth at least a day's exploration. The community itself is reserved and somewhat quiet, although at the time of writing a small shopping complex on Ocean Road, which runs alongside the beach, was close to completion.

If you haven't time for the road trip from the city, splash out and do it in style by seaplane. Planes fly from Rose Bay to Pittwater on the sheltered western side of the Palm Beach peninsula. For companies offering sightseeing and gourmet dining packages, *see p58*.

Don't mistake **Palm Beach Wharf** on the western side of the peninsula for the main beach. Palm Beach proper is on the eastern, ocean side. At the southern end of the beach – the safest place to swim – the colonial-style buildings of the Palm Beach Surf Club and private Palm Beach Pacific Club sit majestically, their picturesque wooden balconies surrounded by stately palms. It was this beautiful corner of Australia that Governor Arthur Phillip first passed in his cutter before entering Broken Bay in 1788; a plaque commemorates his voyage. Now Palm Beach Surf Club is *the* surf club to join for wannabe socialites in Sydney – and as a result one of the pickiest. The reason is that membership also grants you access to the prestigious Cabbage Tree Club next door, hangout of Sydney's real movers and shakers.

Soap fans might want to head further up to **North Palm Beach**, where, if you're lucky, the kids from *Home and Away* will be filming by the North Palm Beach Surf Club (ironically, one of the easiest surf clubs to join, as it is at the unfashionable end of Palmie). When the 'Summer Bay SLSC' sign is hanging on the side of the building, the Channel Seven crew are in business and you may well spot wily old Alf

If you haven't got a surfboard or a mansion, try not to feel left out at **Palm Beach**.

Stewart (aka actor Ray Meagher) ordering a latte from the kiosk or younger cast members learning their lines. Right at the top of the peninsula is **Barrenjoey Head** and its historic lighthouse, which can be reached by a short but steep walk (*see p121* **A light hike**).

If the sun gets too hot – there's not much shade, particularly at the southern end of the beach – head to the wharf and take a boat trip instead. The **Palm Beach Ferry Service** (9918 2747, www.palmbeachferry.com.au) runs every day (including Christmas Day) across Pittwater to the Basin, an area within **Ku-ring-gai Chase National Park** (*see below*), where you can walk to some excellent Aboriginal rock carvings. Cool off afterwards with a swim in the spookily dark and seriously deep bay that, thanks to its shape, gave the Basin area its name. **Palm Beach & Hawkesbury River Cruises** (0414 466 635) offers a trip that crosses Pittwater into Broken Bay, stops at Patonga (a pleasant beach village) and then cruises up the beautiful lower Hawkesbury River into Cowan Waters, stopping at Bobbin Head for lunch. The boat leaves Palm Beach

daily at 11am, returning at 3.30pm, with more cruises at the weekend and during school holidays. Alternatively, splash out on a **Peninsula Water Taxi** (0415 408831) for a bespoke cruise for up to six people.

Ku-ring-gai Chase National Park

NPWS office 9472 9300/www.nationalparks.nsw. gov.au. **Open** sunrise-sunset daily. **Admission** $3 arriving by boat/ferry; $11 per vehicle. **Map** p321. Occupying nearly 150sq km (58sq miles) of dense forest, hidden coves and sheltered beaches where the Hawkesbury River meets the sea, Ku-ring-gai Chase was designated a national park in 1894. It is located in one of Sydney's wealthiest municipalities, stretching from the suburbs of St Ives North and Wahroonga in the south to Broken Bay in the north. Every visitor to Sydney should take in the West Head lookout, with its views over the mouth of the Hawkesbury, the beginning of the Central Coast, Barrenjoey Lighthouse and Palm Beach. Walking tracks lead to significant examples of Aboriginal rock art. Guided walks and canoe and boat tours can also be arranged. There are various routes into the park depending on where you want to go: contact the park office for more info.

Parramatta & the West

For a fuller picture of Sydney's cosmopolitan melting pot, head west.

Sightseeing

Although inhabitants of the western suburbs were involved in ugly beachside riots between Lebanese and Caucasian Australians at the end of 2005, the reality of this 'other Sydney' is very different. A fascinating spread of cultures is represented in these often misunderstood suburbs, which sprawl out from the inner city to the foothills of the lush Blue Mountains. A visit to the Harbour City wouldn't be complete without an exploration of the key districts of Parramatta and Cabramatta at the very least.

Back in the 19th century, the area now called Greater Western Sydney was a series of rural farming communities, which is why some of the oldest white settlement buildings can be found there. These days, the 'settlement' story is very different, of course. The western suburbs cover more than two thirds of the metropolitan area and house a third of the city's population (1.4 million), with a mix of blue-collar Aussies, Asians, East Europeans, Latinos and others. The melting pot of the west also attracts three-quarters of the 50,000 people who migrate to Sydney each year, making it the fastest-growing area of the city. According to local government estimates, the west will house over two million by 2031, by which time Sydney's population will be around the 5.3 million mark.

Parramatta – the 'capital' of the west – boasts an historical importance to rival any area in Sydney, as well as housing the city's second business district. Closer to the city, the Olympic Park in Homebush Bay was where the Aussies proudly held the 2000 'best ever' Olympic Games, and they haven't forgotten it. The area has since been turned into a family-oriented sports complex, with adjacent Newington (a new suburb created from the athletes' Olympic Village) feeding the facilities with people, cash and the retail outlets to go with it. Further west is the Asian centre of Cabramatta, a food and clothes shopper's delight that draws visitors with its market life and spirit.

The so-called 'Westies' are often snobbishly dismissed by their eastern-suburb cousins as unsophisticated, beer-guzzling gamblers, but in compensation they enjoy more spacious surroundings and greater value for money in their property. Racial tensions may challenge future community leaders, but the tourist areas remain unaffected by such issues.

For a map of Greater Sydney, *see p321*.

Parramatta

Transport *CityRail/RiverCat Parramatta.*

Parramatta may be the gateway to the west, but it's also the geographic centre of the Sydney sprawl. There are various ways of getting there: the nicest is by RiverCat ferry from Circular Quay along the pristine Parramatta River (a stunning route – just under an hour). For those in a hurry, there's the train (25 to 30 minutes) or car (35 to 40 minutes).

Historically, western Sydney belonged to the Dharug, Dharawal and Gandangara people before the white settlers moved in, and the word Parramatta is, like many Sydney place names, Aboriginal in origin. In fact, the Aboriginal warrior Pemulwuy kept the people of Parramatta in fear of their lives for more than a decade before he was eventually killed in 1802 and his head sent to England. More than 1,000 descendants of the Dharug still live in western Sydney, and altogether there are over 10,000 Aboriginal people in the district, many having moved in from rural areas. Others have been forcibly relocated to outposts such as Minto, in a failed effort to 'clean up' inner-city Redfern.

Parramatta's rich heritage as Australia's second-oldest white settlement makes it an important tourist stop. You can learn more about its history, and what to see, at the **Parramatta Heritage & Visitor Information Centre** (*see p126*) on the north bank of the river, next to **Lennox Bridge**, which was built by convict labour in the 1830s. The centre is a short stroll from the ferry wharf via the **Riverside Walk**, designed by Aboriginal artist Jamie Eastwood, which explores the story of the Parramatta River and the traditions of the Burramatta people, Parramatta's first inhabitants.

Once known as the 'cradle city', Parramatta is the site of many Australian firsts: its first jail, land grant, successful farm (which saved the First Fleet from starvation in 1788), orchard, train line to Sydney and wool mill. Many of the first settlers were buried in **St John's Cemetery**, on O'Connell Street between St John's Cathedral and spacious Parramatta Park.

Parramatta also contains New South Wales's second-largest business district (after the CBD to the east), and thus has a dynamic mix of old and new, with towering skyscrapers next door to heritage-listed huts. **Elizabeth Farm** (*see below*), built in 1793 by wool pioneer John Macarthur and named after his wife, is the oldest colonial home still standing in Australia. Nearby is **Experiment Farm Cottage** (*see below*), a beautiful colonial cottage built on the site of Australia's first land grant.

Also open for viewing is **Old Government House** (*see p126*), the oldest public building in Australia. Standing in the grounds of Parramatta Park, the spot was chosen by the colony's founding governor, Arthur Phillip, within months of the establishment of the penal settlement at Sydney Cove in January 1788, and was used by NSW governors until the new residence opened in the centre of Sydney in 1845. Old Government House and Experiment Farm Cottage are both run by the National Trust; buy a combined admission to both and you'll also get a ten per cent discount in the visitor shops and restaurant.

Parramatta was also the site of Australia's first recorded race meeting and first legal brewery – and Westies still love a beer and a bet. **Rosehill Gardens Racecourse** (*see p263*) on Grand Avenue is a citadel of both pursuits, particularly during Autumn Carnival when the $2 million Golden Slipper – the world's richest race for two-year-olds – is held.

Cultural attractions include the **Parramatta Riverside Theatres** (*see p270*), which hosts stand-up comedy, various arts events and part of the Sydney Festival each January. The **Roxy** (69 George Street, 9687 4219) is the hip hangout where hot local bands play. **PJ Gallaghers Irish Pub** (74 Church Street, 9635 8811) prides itself on being the finest drinking hole in the west (it's not, but it's not bad), while other old Parramatta pubs with character include the **Woolpack** (19 George Street, 9635 8043), said to be Australia's oldest licensed hotel and dating back to 1796 (though it was on a different site till 1821), the **Commercial** (2 Hassall Street, 9635 8342) and the **Albion** (135 George Street, 9891 3288), which is undergoing extensive refurbishment in 2006.

Those seeking retail therapy during their tour of the west should head to the gargantuan mall **Westfield Parramatta** on Church Street, near the station. And for kids, in the nearby suburb of Merrylands, just south of the Great Western Highway, is the entertaining **Sydney Children's Museum** (*see p216*).

Elizabeth Farm

70 Alice Street, between Arthur & Alfred Streets, Rosehill (9635 9488/www.hht.net.au). CityRail Parramatta then 15mins walk. **Open** 10am-5pm daily. **Admission** $8; $4 concessions; $17 family. **Credit** MC, V.

Elizabeth Farm is notable for being the birthplace of the Australian wool industry – John Macarthur imported merino sheep for breeding at the site – and for the farm's main building. With its deep, shady verandas and stone-flagged floors, it became the prototype for the Australian homestead. Parts of the original 1793 construction – the oldest surviving European building in Australia – remain. The interior has been restored to its 1830s condition, with a recreated Victorian garden to match. The farm is run by the Historic Houses Trust, which looks after various museums and historic sites in Sydney.

Experiment Farm Cottage

9 Ruse Street, Harris Park (9635 5655/ www.nsw.nationaltrust.org.au). CityRail Harris Park then 10mins walk/RiverCat Parramatta then 20mins walk. **Open** 10.30am-3.30pm Tue-Fri; 11am-3.30pm Sat, Sun. **Admission** $5.50; $4 concessions; $14 family. *Joint admission with Old Government House* $10; $7 concessions; $25 family. **Credit** (over $20) MC, V.

In 1789 Governor Phillip set up an experiment 'to know in what time a man might be able to support himself'. The guinea pig was convict James Ruse, who became self-sufficient in two years and was given the colony's first land grant here as a reward, thereby becoming Australia's first private farmer. He then sold the land to a surgeon, John Harris, who built this modest cottage in 1793.

Colonise the kitchen at **Elizabeth Farm**.

Sightseeing

Old Government House

Parramatta Park, Parramatta (9635 8149/ www.nsw.nationaltrust.org.au). CityRail/RiverCat Parramatta then 15mins walk. **Open** 10am-4pm Mon-Fri; 10.30am-4pm Sat, Sun. **Admission** $8; $5 concessions; $18 family. *Joint admission with Experiment Farm Cottage* $10; $7 concessions; $25 family. **Credit** MC, V.

Set in extensive parkland, Old Government House was built between 1799 and 1818 on the foundations of Governor Phillip's 1790 thatched cottage, which had fallen down. Previously a vice-regal residence and, at the turn of the 20th century, a boarding house for a local boys' school, it has been restored to its former glory by a recent multi-million-dollar revamp. It also boasts the nation's most important collection of Australian colonial furniture.

Parramatta Heritage & Visitor Information Centre

346A Church Street, next to Lennox Bridge, Parramatta (8839 3311/www.parracity.nsw.gov.au). CityRail/RiverCat Parramatta then 10mins walk. **Open** 9am-5pm daily.

Homebush Bay

Transport *CityRail Olympic Park/RiverCat Sydney Olympic Park.*

If you've got even the tiniest sporting spark in your body, do visit the site of the triumphant 2000 Olympic Games. **Sydney Olympic Park** (*see below*) is in Homebush Bay, eight kilometres (five miles) east of Parramatta. The site features a huge range of sporting and entertainment facilities, including the mammoth **Sydney SuperDome** (*see p249*) and the **Sydney Showground** (9704 1111, www.sydneyshowground.com.au), which plays host to the annual Big Day Out music festival and other large-scale events.

An arm of the Parramatta River, the bay is surrounded by 1.8 square kilometres (0.7 square miles) of wetlands, woodland and grassland, which provide sanctuary for 160 bird species. **Bicentennial Park** (open sunrise to sunset daily), the largest of the bay's five main parkland areas, is one of the best places to go for specialist birdwatching excursions. A waterbird refuge and salt marsh are out on the water, with a fine viewing tower at their north-easterly tip. You may recognise the Brickpit, at the park's heart, as Mad Max's Thunderdome. There's a café and restaurant, and it's also a pleasant spot for picnics.

Sydney Olympic Park

Visitor Centre *1 Showground Road, at Murray Rose Avenue (9714 7888/www.sydneyolympic park.com.au). CityRail Olympic Park/RiverCat Sydney Olympic Park then bus 401.* **Open** 9am-5pm daily.

Spoilt for sports at **Sydney Olympic Park**.

If you're time-rich, hop on the most scenic route to Olympic Park: the RiverCat ferry from Circular Quay to Sydney Olympic Park (50 minutes). Bus No.401 meets the boat and takes you to the visitor centre. If you prefer to travel by train, the station you want is Olympic Park, bang in the middle of the complex – but be warned: frustratingly, there are few direct CityRail services (even when an event is being staged); your best bet is to go to Lidcombe and pick up the Sprint train from there.

To see the stadia rising out of the flat landscape as you approach is awe-inspiring. The size and scope of the biggest – Telstra Stadium – dwarfs everything else in the vicinity. The park is big but easily walkable if the weather isn't too hot; even better, you can explore by bike (for hire at the visitor centre). At the Aquatic Centre you can go for a dip, marvel at the indoor water slides and get a faint tingle of what it must be like to perform before thousands of cheering spectators (swim meets continue to be held here). It's free to visit the Sports Centre and stroll down the gallery's Hall of Champions, covering athletes from the 1890s to the present. To get into the other key venues, you'll need to take an organised tour (there are many – ask at the visitor centre). The one-hour Telstra Stadium tours are particularly good, including the new interactive Explore tour, in which you follow in the footsteps of heroes of the the 2000 games. Check out the website before you go; it's rammed with information.

Blacktown & around

Transport *CityRail Blacktown.*

Blacktown, 11 kilometres (seven miles) north-west of Parramatta, earned its name from being home to the Native Institution, established by the early colonial authorities to educate Aboriginal children. Today, it has the largest urban Aboriginal population in Australia. For a unique insight into Australian taste through the years, head north of Blacktown to historic **Rouse Hill Estate** (*see p127*). You can visit the house only on a guided tour, and it's wise to book in advance. And if you want to see native wildlife, including a face-to-face encounter with a koala, visit the excellent, family-run **Featherdale Wildlife Park** (*see below*).

In keeping with local tastes, western Sydney boasts more social clubs than any other suburb in the area. League clubs, golf clubs, bowling clubs, workers' clubs, returned servicemen's clubs – they're absolutely everywhere, providing community services, cheap food and drink, and live entertainment, subsidised by row upon row of poker machines. Two of the biggest and best around here are **Blacktown Workers Club** on Campbell Street (9830 0600, www.bwcl.com.au) and **Rooty Hill RSL Club** (9625 5500, www.rootyhillrsl.com.au) on the corner of Sherbrooke and Railway Streets in Rooty Hill. Blacktown is also home to one of Sydney's last two remaining drive-in movie theatres – though unfortunately not the better one – the **Greater Union Drive-In** (*see p227*).

Public transport is generally poorer in the west than in the east, so Westies tend to have a special attachment to their cars. Rev-heads love **Eastern Creek Raceway** (Brabham Drive, Eastern Creek, 9672 1000, www.eastern-creek-raceway.com), Sydney's biggest automotive venue, which regularly hosts touring car, motorbike and drag races.

Featherdale Wildlife Park

217-229 Kildare Road, Doonside (9622 1644/ www.featherdale.com.au). CityRail Blacktown then bus 725. **Open** 9am-5pm daily. **Admission** $18.50; $9-$14.50 concessions; $45 family; free under-3s. **Credit** AmEx, DC, MC, V.

Kangaroos, koalas and Tasmanian devils all feature in this well-kept wildlife park, which houses one of Australia's largest collections of native animals. The huge diversity of birds includes the bizarre cassowary (which lives in the rainforests in the tropical far north, but is rarely spotted by locals) and some scary-looking owls.

Rouse Hill Estate

Guntawong Road, off Windsor Road, Rouse Hill (9627 6777/www.hht.net.au). CityRail Riverstone then bus 741R or taxi. **Tours** Mar-Nov every hr 10am-2pm Wed, Thur, Sun. Closed Dec-Feb. **Admission** $8; $4 concessions; $17 family. **Credit** MC, V.

This two-storey Georgian sandstone house, set in a 15 hectare (37 acre) estate, was the home of the Rouse family for six generations. Free settler Richard Rouse built the original house in 1813-18, and his last direct descendant left in 1993. There are also some 20 outbuildings, ranging from a pretty Victorian summerhouse to a corrugated iron cottage annex, and a very early 'dry weather' garden.

Cabramatta & Bankstown

Transport Bankstown *CityRail Bankstown.* **Cabramatta** *CityRail Cabramatta.*

Cabramatta, Bankstown and their neighbours are the country's multicultural heartland. Given Sydney's dominance over the country's other state capitals, it's hardly surprising that it remains the most popular destination for immigrants entering Australia, and the vast majority of them go to live in the western suburbs. In some south-western suburbs, more than half the population was born overseas: in Italy, Greece, Vietnam, Cambodia, the Philippines, China, Serbia, Croatia, Poland, Latin America, Lebanon and the Pacific Islands.

One of the consequences of this multicultural mix is that there's high-quality, inexpensive dining to be had. Cabramatta, in particular, has developed a name for itself as the culinary centre of the western suburbs. It also suffers from a reputation as heroin central in Sydney, thanks to various Asian gangs, and tends to hit the headlines for drug- and gang-related deaths. For a grittily honest portrayal of the lives of the homeless and disadvantaged in the Asian centre of Sydney, check out local director Khoa Do's raw, no-holds-barred film *The Finished People* (2003) or the more recent star-studded, downbeat drama *Little Fish* (2005), starring Cate Blanchett and Hugo Weaving.

When visiting Cabramatta, it's important to keep things in perspective. True, as a casual tourist, you should remain vigilant and savvy when wandering about – it's better to visit during the day rather than after dark – but if you like dining and shopping, don't miss the area's exotic mix of Aussie suburbia, Saigon, Shanghai and Phnom Penh.

From Cabramatta CityRail station, cross over the road to Arthur Street and pass through the ornate Pai Lau Gate into **Freedom Plaza**, the main marketplace. It's like stepping into Asia, with the authentic flavours of Thai, Laotian, Cambodian, Filipino and Chinese cuisines on offer at numerous stalls. There's plenty of discount fabrics, clothing and jewellery too: on Park Road, John Street, Hughes Street and around the main plaza, direct importers and wholesalers ply their wares for all their worth in typical Asian bazaar fashion (haggling is the norm). Other attractions are the nearby **Tien Hau** and **Kwan Zin** Buddhist temples.

The best time to visit is when the Chinese and Vietnamese communities hold their New Year celebrations (around February), with wild dragon parades and more firecrackers than you can shake a match at. Some lucky visitors may experience the annual Moon Festival, held

You can visit Asia without leaving Australia in **Cabramatta**. See p127.

on the 15th day of the eighth lunar month –
August or September, depending on the year.

Sport is a key feature of life in the west too.
It's thanks to the high number of immigrants
that soccer (or 'wog ball', as some rugby
supporters disparagingly call it) is a bigger
sport than rugby in this part of the city. Sydney
soccer fans follow their teams with a fiery
passion based along ethnic lines, and the games
can be boisterous and spectacular affairs.
Local teams in the NSW premier league include
the Parramatta Eagles, Marconi Stallions,
Blacktown City Demons and Bankstown City
Lions. Bankstown is also the home town of
the famous cricketing Waugh brothers (now
retired), and boasts an impressive cricket team,
which you can catch on summer weekends at
the **Bankstown Oval** (Bankstown District
Sports Club, 8 Greenfield Parade, 9709 3899,
www.bankstownsports.com).

Penrith

Transport *CityRail Penrith.*

At the foot of the Blue Mountains and perched
on the banks of the Nepean River, Penrith lies
50 kilometres (31 miles) west of central Sydney.
It's a sprawling modern suburb distinguished
by beautiful rural and bushland scenery as well
as history and modern culture.

At its heart is Panthers, Australia's largest
licensed club, and the rugby league team it
supports. The huge **Panthers World of**
Entertainment on Mulgoa Road (1300 666747,
4720 5555, www.panthersworld.com.au)
resembles an Antipodean Butlins resort; you'll
find not only a vast array of 24-hour bars,
gaming facilities, restaurants, nightclubs and
live music, but also a motel, swimming pools,
water-skiing, water slides, tennis courts, beach
volleyball, a golf driving range and more. This
staggering creation rakes in more than $100
million a year, with the profits being ploughed
back into the rugby club and the community.
You might catch the Panthers training at winter
weekends in **Penrith Park**, just opposite the
club centre. Or try to attend one of their home
games in **Penrith Stadium** against one of the
western suburbs' other first-class rugby league
teams, the Parramatta Eels, the Canterbury-
Bankstown Bulldogs and the Wests Tigers.

Penrith also offers dogs and trots at **Penrith**
Paceway (corner of Ransley and Station
Streets, 4721 2375, www.harness.org.au/
penrith). On a more cultural note, there's the
long-running and well-respected **Q Theatre**
Company (www.railwaystreet.com.au), with
which Toni Colette made her professional stage
debut in 1990. The company moved into its
new home, the striking, glass-fronted **Joan**
Sutherland Performing Arts Centre
(597 High Street, 4723 7611, www.jspac.com.au),
at the end of 2005. Also worthy of your time is
the beautiful **Penrith Regional Art Gallery**
(86 River Road, Emu Plains, 4735 1100,
www.penrithregionalgallery.org).

Sightseeing

The best Aboriginal Sydney

For more ideas, get hold of *Aboriginal Sydney: A Guide to Important Places of the Past And Present* (Aboriginal Studies Press), by Melinda Hinkson and Alana Harris. It covers 50 places to visit from ancient rock carvings to points of modern significance.

Art Gallery of New South Wales
The Yiribana gallery houses the best selection of traditional and contemporary indigenous works in Sydney. It also hosts free dance, song and storytelling performances. *See p70.*

Australian Museum
The indigenous section holds artefacts and an exhibition that explores the pre- and post-colonial history of indigenous people, and issues such as the 'stolen generations'. Every Sunday there is a didgeridoo performance and dancing. *See p71.*

Boomalli Aboriginal Artists' Co-op
Established in 1987, Boomalli specialises in contemporary art from local indigenous artists. All the proceeds go back to the artists. *See p235.*

Gavala Aboriginal Cultural Centre
Aboriginal-owned and staffed, this Darling Harbour emporium sells both traditional and contemporary art and artefacts ranging from boomerangs and prints to jewellery. *See p206.*

Museum of Sydney
This innovative museum's collections meander from the archeological to the anthropological, and include a stunning Aboriginal sculptural installation outside the entrance (*photo*), an exhibit on the Cadigal clan on whose land Sydney stands, and a video montage celebrating Aboriginal culture in the city. *See p67.*

Powerhouse Museum
The Koori exhibition focuses on contemporary Aboriginal culture featuring objects of interest, oral histories, literature, music, decorative art and sport. *See p82.*

Royal Botanic Gardens
The Cadi Jam Ora native plants garden has a 50 metre (164 foot) 'storyline' mapping local history and explaining the traditional uses of plants. Tours with an Aboriginal guide are available. *See p73.*

Websites
Gadigal (**www.gadigal.org.au**) is a community-based website providing a media, arts and information service about local Koori radio, arts, sport and indigenous newspapers. The City of Sydney (**www.cityofsydney.nsw.gov. au/barani**) has thoughtful articles on topics ranging from pre-colonial Sydney to the effect of the church and science on Aboriginal culture, plus biographical sketches of local Aboriginal people of historical significance.

If you want to get away from urban life for a bit, you'll find a waterborne solution in the form of the historic paddle-wheeler **Nepean Belle** (The Jetty, Tench Avenue, 4733 1274, www.nepeanbelle.com.au), which offers lunch and dinner cruises up the spectacular Nepean Gorge. The Penrith area is also home to several vineyards, among them **Vicary's Winery** in Luddenham (1935 The Northern Road, 4773 4161, www.vicaryswinery.com.au). Sydney's oldest working winery, it runs tastings and uses a converted woolshed for weekend bush dances.

North of Penrith, the Nepean River becomes the Hawkesbury River, which forms the lifeline of another unique part of western Sydney. For the historic towns of Richmond, Windsor and Wilberforce and more on the delights of the Hawkesbury, *see p278.*

The South

Welcome to the good life of the sunny, surfie suburbs.

Sightseeing

South of Sydney, there's **Brighton-le-Sands** and then an area collectively known as 'the Shire', inhabited by a people who call themselves 'the locals'. **Cronulla** is the stronghold of the Shire, championing a lifestyle of sun, surf, fair hair and anything (preferably motorised) that allows you to travel on water. Brighton-le-Sands involves a different hair colour, having largely been claimed by generations of Greeks. Neither the noisy swoop of planes into Sydney Airport at next-door Mascot, nor the view of billowing smoke from the oil refinery at Kurnell across Botany Bay, can dim their enthusiasm for recreating the spirit of a Greek coastal town.

During the week the Shire remains a relatively insular peninsula with few interlopers. On Sundays, families from the outer southern and western suburbs catch Sydney's only train-to-beach service to picnic under the beachside trees. After an incident where boys 'of Middle-Eastern appearance' (as labelled in the news) supposedly roughed up two volunteer lifesavers in the dying days of 2005, one of these Sundays saw Cronulla erupt in what were beamed around the world as race riots. While Australia has been left to debate whether it is racist or not, the event has certainly shown how effective text messages are at mobilising a crowd, with everyone from gang members to outer Sydneysiders turning up at the trouble spot.

Languishing across Port Hacking from Cronulla, oblivious to any tension, is the former artists' colony of **Bundeena**. Here, inside the **Royal National Park**, life carries on much as it always has – with private picnics, swimming spots and much home- and pool-building.

Brighton-le-Sands

Map p321. **Transport** Kurnell *CityRail Cronulla then bus 987.* **Brighton-le-Sands** *CityRail Rockdale then bus 475, 478, 479.*

From the air, the first thing you notice about Brighton-le-Sands is the oversized pyramid of the Novotel. Set on the west side of Botany Bay, just below the airport, this hulking hotel doesn't look much prettier from the ground. Fortunately, the swankier end of the Greek community is bent on transforming the busy car-laden, beachfront drag of **Grand Parade** into, well, a grand parade, and has lined it with

sleek cafés. Anyone who knows the coastline near Athens will have and idea what they're aiming at. On Friday and Saturday evenings and all day Sunday, Grand Parade is bumper to bumper with traffic and crowds visiting the eating and drinking establishments of 'Little Athens'. The stretch starts at the north end with **Gecko** (Shop 18, Bayside Plaza, 9567 3344), a long charcoal line of indoor/outdoor café chic. Next door is **Mezes** (Shop 36, 9567 2865), a bustling mix of café, restaurant and ice-cream-loaded dessert bar that seems to capture the young crowd. Further down, **Eurobay** (86 Grand Parade, 9597 3300) goes for an ultra-smooth, Greco-Italian blend of food and style, while nearby restaurant/café **Kamari** (No.82, 9556 2533) is more rustic, with its whitewashed walls and terracotta floors.

The cafés and restaurants along Bay Street around the corner attract a slightly older, more glam Greek crowd, sunning themselves in Gucci shades. There's **One Bay** (376 Bay Street, 9599 5775) and **Zande Brasserie** (No.380, 9567 6475). The most upmarket restaurant (price-wise, but not necessarily style-wise) is **Le Sands** (Grand Parade, 9599 2128) with its panoramic views of Botany Bay – never mind the planes landing to the left and the pipes and towers of the oil refinery to the right. Back across the road, **Enigma** (88 Grand Parade, 9556 3611) touts, of all things, Greek yum cha with all-you-can-eat servings of dips, halloumi, dolmades and other traditional Greek dishes.

The bay itself is usually awash with colour as windsurfers and kitesurfers take advantage of the continuously near-cyclonic weather. To have a go yourself, contact **Long Reef Sailboards & Surf** (116 Grand Parade, 9599 2814, www.longreefsailboards.com.au).

To learn more about the beginnings of colonial Australia, head further south around the bay to the tip of **Kurnell Peninsula**, where the British first landed in 1770. Under the command of James Cook, and with botanist Joseph Banks leading a party of scientists, the crew of HMS *Endeavour* spent a week exploring the area and recording information on the flora and fauna they found (hence the bay's name). Eighteen years later, when the newly appointed governor of New South Wales, Captain Arthur Phillip, arrived with the First Fleet, he relinquished the base at Kurnell in favour of a deeper bay further north, which was named Sydney Cove. But Kurnell's historical significance was not forgotten, and in 1899 more than a square kilometre (half a square mile) of land was set aside as a public area.

Captain Cook's Landing Place is now a regular school excursion: on weekdays it's crowded with children visiting the Cook Obelisk, Cook's Well and Landing Rock. To find out more about the history of the area and the young colony, visit the **Discovery Centre** (Captain Cook Drive, Botany Bay National Park, 9668 9111, open 11am-3pm Mon-Fri, 10am-4.30pm Sat, Sun, $7 per car).

Cronulla

Map p321. **Transport** *CityRail Cronulla.*

It helps to have 'the look' when you're visiting **Cronulla Beach**. This largely revolves around a tan, blond/e hair and as little else as modesty will allow – imagine the love children of Jessica Simpson and David Hasselhoff. If that doesn't describe you, you might find it more comforting to hang with the multicultural Sunday crowd picnicking beneath the trees. But despite what the 2005 riots might suggest, the locals are a relatively friendly lot, perhaps just a little too in love with their machines.

Cronulla is a much longer beach than its more famous city counterparts Bondi, Coogee, Clovelly and Maroubra. It takes at least four hours to walk its length from South Cronulla northwards to Green Hills and beyond. There's also a walking track that starts at the end of South Cronulla and wends its way southwards around the cliff of Port Hacking, past sea pools to **Darook Park**, where you can swim in calm, clear water. Halfway along the track is **Bass & Flinders Point**: from here you can stare across the water to Jibbon Beach on the edge of the Royal National Park.

Serious surfers head to the northern end, to Eloura, Wanda and Green Hills Beaches, where there's often the background churn of 4WDs playing on the sand hills behind the beach. Revs are big in these parts – especially on the water. Jet skis, speedboats and waterskiers create chaos in the otherwise sleepy arms of the Port Hacking river every weekend. For more water action, contact **Cronulla Surf School** (9544 0895, www.cronullasurfschool.com) for surfing lessons, and **Pro Dive** (9544 2200, www.prodivecronulla.com) to discover what lies beneath the waves.

In Cronulla itself, the pedestrianised strip of Cronulla Street is jammed with surf shops. For great coffee and corn cakes, duck into **Surfeit** (2 Surf Road, 9523 3873) – you might even see

Seaside fun at **Cronulla Beach**.

swimming supremo Ian Thorpe having breakfast here. Better coffee still can be found closer to the beach at **Grind** (Rydges Hotel, 20-26 The Kingsway, 0403 844 533) where Richard Calabro is almost a one-man Little Italy with his coffee-only, hole-in-the-wall café that offers everything from *affogato* to *caffè romano*. It's worshipped by the locals, who send back photos from overseas trips holding banners that howl 'I'd rather be at Grind'.

If your wallet stretches to city prices, head to **Summer Salt** (Eloura Surf Club, 66 Mitchell Road, 9523 2366) for uninterrupted beach views and a mix of tapas and seafood. More city chic can be found at the **Nun's Pool** (103 Ewos Parade, 9523 3395), named after a little rock pool across the road through Shelley Park. Open only for breakfast and lunch, its take on contemporary Australian features Moroccan-spiced Atlantic salmon and chermoula-marinated lamb. On the Kingsway, views can be found at mid-market prices at **Stonefish** (Shop 3, Nos.8-18, 9544 3046), which offers a mix of stir-fries, steaks and seafood, while **Bella Costa** (9544 3223) in the same complex specialises in modern Italian. For fish and burgers try **Joe's Fish Bar** (Nos.4-6, 9544 5522), though it's worth hiking up the road to **Peter Michaels Seafoods** (No.47, 9544 0033) for first-rate seafood kebabs and grills.

On summer nights the electric-coloured interiors of **Northies-Cronulla Hotel** (corner of Elouera Road and the Kingsway, 9523 6866, www.northies.com.au) spill over with energy. For a slower vibe, try **Brass Monkey** (115A Cronulla Street, 9544 3844), where you can hear live jazz and blues bands.

Bundeena & around

Map p321. **Transport** *CityRail Cronulla then ferry Bundeena.*

A 20-minute ferry ride from Cronulla's Tonkin Street wharf across Port Hacking delivers you to Bundeena, a small township (population 2,700) that spreads out along the top of the north-eastern section of the **Royal National Park** (*see below*). Its charm is that it's quiet. Very quiet. But the increasing numbers of people hungry for such solitude could soon turn it into a suburban sprawl.

Established in 1879, the Royal was Australia's first national park – and only the second in the world, after Yellowstone in the US. Covering 150 square kilometres (58 square miles) on the southern boundary of the Sydney metropolitan area, it offers stunning coastline, rainforest, open wetlands, estuaries and heath. You can spend days bushwalking, picnicking, swimming and birdwatching. The depths of the park are best explored by car, though Bundeena is a handy haven from the wilds, especially if you're fed up with camping.

Bundeena, which means 'noise like thunder' in the local Aboriginal language, was named after the sound of the surf pounding on the east coast. The Aboriginal Dharawal people used the area as a camping ground, and were sometimes joined by other large clans for feasting and ceremonies. In the 1820s white settlers arrived in the 'village', as locals call Bundeena, to build a few fishing shacks. More came during the 1930s Depression, but it was only after World War II that a substantial number of permanent houses and holiday homes began to appear.

There are three main beaches, two of which fall within the national park. The main strip of sand is **Hordens Beach**, which you'll see to your right as you approach by ferry.

Walk up the hill from the wharf to find a small supermarket, a newsagent, a couple of inexpensive cafés and a fish and chip shop.

To reach **Jibbon Beach**, walk left from the ferry, past a toilet block and the RSL club (which serves very cheap drinks with brilliant views and has a retro Chinese restaurant open Tuesday to Saturday). Follow the road to its end, turn downhill and through a cutting to the magnificent, forest-edged, orange-sand beach. At the far end, hop up the rocks and take the track through the bush to **Jibbon Head**, about 20 minutes away, where there are awe-inspiring views out to sea. A sign en route points to Aboriginal rock engravings of whales and fish. From Jibbon Head you can walk further down the coast on a well-worn track; it's about a three-hour return walk to Marley Beach, six hours to Wattamolla. Take plenty of water, sunscreen and insect repellent in summer.

The third beach, **Bonnie Vale**, is to the right just before you leave the village; you can walk to it in about 15 minutes via Bundeena Drive. Edged by swamp and ponds, it's an exceptionally long and pristine beach, with very shallow water that's ideal for kids.

The ferry to Bundeena leaves Cronulla every hour on the half-hour from 5.30am to 6.30pm weekdays (there's no 12.30pm service), returning on the hour from 6am to 7pm. On weekends, the first ferry leaves at 8.30am and the last returns at 7pm. It costs $4.50 each way. It's around a 20-minute drive to Bundeena through the national park if you come by road – about an hour in total from the city.

Royal National Park

9542 0648/www.nationalparks.nsw.gov.au. **Open** *Park* 7am-8.30pm daily. *Visitor centre* 9.30am-4.30pm Mon-Fri; 8.30am-4.30pm Sat, Sun. **Admission** $11 per vehicle.
You can get to the Royal by following walking paths from various nearby CityRail stations – Engadine, Heathcote, Loftus, Otford, Waterfall – but driving is the easiest way to explore its vast expanse. The park's nerve centre is at Audley, on the Hacking River, once the heart of the park's Victorian 'pleasure gardens'. There you'll find the main visitor centre, spacious lawns, an old-fashioned dance hall and a causeway. You can hire a canoe or rowing boat from the Audley boathouse and head upstream to picnic spots at Ironbark Flat or Wattle Forest. If you're a surfer, Garie Beach provides the waves, while further south is Werrong Beach, located among littoral rainforest and the park's only authorised nude bathing spot. At secluded Wattamolla Beach you can often see migrating whales. Walking trails include Lady Carrington Drive, an easy 10km (six-mile) track along the Hacking River, and the more arduous 26km (16-mile) Coast Track, which hugs the coastline from Bundeena to Otford.

Sydney's Best Beaches

Stock up on vitamin sea.

Summer, winter, after school, after work, with a bunch of mates or just plain solo, beaches are where Sydneysiders head to chill out. And with more than 50 beaches along Sydney's coastline, from posey Palm Beach in the north to family magnet Cronulla in the south, each one has its own character. The protected harbour beaches inside the Heads are smaller and have no surf, but are great for views and picnics – after heavy rain they're not ideal for swimming though, as pollution floats in through the storm pipes. Instead, locals often take their daily dip in the outdoor seawater pools cut into the rocks on many beaches – both harbour and ocean. The bigger, bolder ocean beaches attract hordes of surfers and serious swimmers.

From September to May nearly all Sydney's ocean beaches are patrolled at weekends by local volunteer lifesavers and during the week by lifeguards – hours vary with the beach and time of year. The famous surf lifesavers wear red and yellow uniforms and an unmistakeable skullcap. The council-paid lifeguards (who are sometimes also hired on harbour beaches) wear different colours – usually a more sober blue or green – and in surfing hot spots such as Bondi and Manly work 365 days a year.

Rules on Sydney's beaches are stringent: alcohol and fires are banned, and on many beaches ball games, skateboards, rollerblades, kites and frisbees are also illegal. Smoking is also forbidden on many beaches, including Bondi, Tamarama, Bronte, Manly and the northern beaches up to Palm Beach, and the beaches on the north side of the harbour. That said, rules are regularly flouted by 'no worries' regulars, especially off-season. Locals love to fish on the beach, but you need a licence and there are catch limits. Dropping rubbish is

▶ ❶ Orange numbers given in this chapter correspond to the location of each beach as marked on the **Greater Sydney** map on p321 or the **Sydney Harbour** map on pp322-323. There's also a more detailed map of the **northern beaches** on p117.
▶ For more information on many of the beaches listed here, see the relevant **Sightseeing** chapters.

Whale Beach.
See p138.

Sightseeing

also an offence – 'Don't be a tosser, take your rubbish with you!' is the motto – and recycling a must in the provided bins. And don't expect to find deckchair touts, donkeys or even an ice-cream seller, because Sydneysiders are fiercely protective of their unspoilt beaches – and intend to keep them that way.

WATER TEMPERATURES
The water at Sydney beaches can turn icy without warning, so take the following as a guide only. As a general rule, the water temperature lags a couple of months behind the air temperature. So when the weather is warming up in October and November, the ocean is still holding its winter chill of 16-17°C

Balmoral Beach: two beaches, a bridge and an island. *See p135.*

(61-63°F). Only in December does the sea become a nicely swimmable 18-19°C (64-66°F). The ocean is a balmy 20-21°C (68-70°F) from February to April, sometimes until May. It can even reach 23-24°C (73-75°F) if there's a warm current running from the north.

Below are Sydney's best beaches: the harbour beaches are listed from east to west; the northern ocean beaches heading north; and the southern ocean beaches heading south. For information on the latest surfing conditions, visit www.coastalwatch.com.

Harbour beaches

South

Shark Beach
Nielsen Park, Vaucluse Road, Vaucluse. Bus 325. **Map** p323 ③④
Locals swim in the smooth warm waters of this sheltered harbour inlet all year round. In summer it's as packed as an Australian beach can get, with families swarming the narrow 300m beach or picnicking in the shade of the Moreton Bay fig trees on the grassy slopes. Part of leafy Nielsen Park, the beach also boasts fabulous views of Manly, Shark Island (hence its name) and, from the upper parklands, the Harbour Bridge. If you don't swim, you can watch the ferries, yachts, kayakers, seaplanes and oil tankers vie for space in the harbour, or you could just grab a bite to eat. Sergio and Lucia Lieto run the renowned Nielsen Park Kiosk, an Italian restaurant that's been there since 1914 and offers spectacular sunset views. In summer its adjoining café serves home-made gelati to the chic children of Vaucluse.

Services *Café (closed winter Mon-Fri). Changing rooms. Child-friendly. No dogs. Parking. Picnic area. Restaurant. Shade. Shark net (Sept-May). Showers. Toilets.*

Parsley Bay
Horler Avenue, Vaucluse. Bus 325. **Map** p323 ㉙
Since the 1970s Parsley Bay's expansive picnic lawn has been a popular venue for weddings; indeed, it's the grass, not the tiny beach, that is the big draw here. Nestled at the foot of a steep road of million-dollar mansions, the bay is part of a 5.7-hectare (14-acre) nature reserve with its own ranger and an abundance of birds, fish and insects. It's great for small children, who can play safely on the lawns and in the well-equipped recreation area, and there are excellent walks through the bush and even across a suspension bridge over the water. The small crescent-shaped beach (approx 70m long) leads into what are often murky waters: after heavy rain, rubbish floats into the bay from storm pipes. Nevertheless, the millpond-like swimming area is popular with snorkellers and scuba divers, thanks to its array of tropical fish.
Services *Café. Changing rooms. Child-friendly (play area). No dogs. Parking. Picnic area. Shade. Shark net (removed for repairs 1mth winter). Showers. Toilets.*

Camp Cove
Victoria Street, Watsons Bay. Ferry Watsons Bay/bus 324, 325, L24, L82. **Map** p323 ④
Serious sun-seekers love this 200m strip of bright yellow sand, which runs in a thin curve against a backdrop of designer cottages. It's also a gay haven, which probably has more to do with its secluded ambience than its name. The beach is not great for surfing, but it's a fine place for a dip and provides

fabulous views of the city's skyscrapers. At the southern end of the upper grasslands is the start of the South Head Heritage Trail. Camp Cove has just one small kiosk, but plenty of parking spaces.
Services *Café (Oct-May). Lifesavers (Oct-May). No dogs. Parking. Toilets.*

Lady Bay Beach
Corner of Victoria & Cliff Streets, Watsons Bay. Ferry Watsons Bay/bus 324, 325, L24, L82.
Map p323 ㉒

Sydney's first nudist beach, Lady Bay is just below South Head and a short walk along the South Head Heritage Trail from Camp Cove. Steep iron steps lead down to the 100m beach, which is reduced to virtually nothing when the tide comes in: you're better off sunbathing on one of the rocks. It's popular as a pick-up place for gay men, but Lady Bay offers scenic thrills as well as sexual ones, namely, spectacular views of the city and, if you walk around the headland to Hornby Lighthouse, the open sea to the east. In fact, it's the last southern beach inside the harbour.
Services *No dogs. Toilets (located on clifftop above beach).*

North

Balmoral Beach
The Esplanade, Balmoral. Ferry South Mosman then bus 233/ferry Taronga Zoo then bus 238.
Map p323 ➊

Home to Sydney's seriously rich, Balmoral has been a popular bathing spot since the late 1900s. Its beach promenade and Bathers' Pavilion (now one of Sydney's most sought-after eateries) were both built in the late 1920s and retain a genteel air from that era. Hundreds of families flock here at weekends to enjoy the sheltered waters of its two large sandy beaches, which together stretch for about 1.5km (one mile). The beaches are separated by Rocky Point, a tree-covered picnicking island accessible by a footbridge. To the south, Balmoral Beach has an enclosed swimming area surrounded by boardwalks, excellent for kids. To the north, Edwards Beach is bigger and less protected, but has rock pools with shells, fish and anemones. You can hire boats from Balmoral Boathouse. **Photo** *p134.*
Services *Boat hire. Cafés. Changing rooms. Child-friendly (play area). Danger: underwater rocks. No dogs. Parking. Picnic areas. Restaurants. Shade. Shark nets. Shops. Showers. Toilets.*

Chinamans Beach
McLean Crescent, Mosman. Bus 175, 178, 249.
Map p323 ➏

A real Sydney secret, Chinamans Beach in Middle Harbour is stumbled upon through dunes on the edge of the Rosherville bushland reserve. It's a quiet paradise, with 300m of beautiful sand, gently lapping waters and huge, strikingly designed homes perched on the hills above. Located right opposite busier Clontarf Beach, Chinamans has plenty of

recreational facilities – a play area, picnic tables nestled under pepper trees, and rolling lawns where you can play ball games – but no shop, café or restaurant. Children love the mass of barnacle-encrusted rock pools at the southern end, but there's a $500 fine for taking any crustaceans home.
Services *Changing rooms. Child-friendly (play area). No dogs. Parking. Picnic area. Shade. Showers. Toilets.*

Clontarf Beach
Sandy Bay Road, Clontarf. Bus 171, E71.
Map p323 ➑

With around 600m of great sand, a large grassy picnic area, an excellent playground, outdoor pool and all the facilities, Clontarf is a very popular family spot. It's situated right opposite the Middle Harbour Yacht Club, so there are good views of the Spit Bridge with boats sailing underneath and cars racing over the top. And it's worth stopping at Balgowlah Heights en route to pick up a picnic – the fantastic Gourmet Deli on Beatrice Street is open from 7am to 7pm daily.
Services *Barbecues. Café. Changing rooms. Child-friendly (play area). No dogs. Parking. Picnic area. Pool. Restaurant (closed July). Shade. Shark net (Sept-May). Showers. Toilets.*

Ocean beaches

South

Bondi Beach
Campbell Parade, Bondi Beach. CityRail Bondi Junction then bus 380, 381, 382, L82, X84/bus 380, L82. **Map** p323 ➋

Australia's most famous beach, Bondi is believed to have been named after an Aboriginal word meaning 'the sound of breaking waves'. Certainly, its crashing breakers attract a huge fraternity of urban surfies as well as ubiquitous Britpackers and new-generation hippies strumming guitars on the sand. When the volleyball stadium for the 2000 Olympics was temporarily constructed on the beach, locals went bananas – but the pay-off has been a much-needed clean-up job. Today the elegant Bondi Pavilion, built in 1929 as a changing area, houses showers, toilets, a community centre and some cafés. Two lifesaving clubs patrol the 1km (half-mile) beach – 'Ready Aye Ready' is the motto of the North Bondi Surf Life Saving Club. The central area near the Pavilion is the safest swimming area; surfers favour the southern end, with its strong rips. Also at this end is a skateboard ramp and the famous Bondi Icebergs' pool and club. Be vigilant: 'Thieves go to the beach too' warn big NSW police signs. Lockers are available in the Pavilion – use them. For a local area map, *see p334.*
Services *Barbecues. Cafés. Changing rooms. Lifeguards/savers. No dogs. Parking. Picnic area. Play area. Pool. Restaurants. Shark net (Sept-May). Shops. Showers. Toilets.*

Tamarama Beach

Pacific Avenue, Tamarama. CityRail Bondi Junction then bus 361. **Map** *p323* ⓰
A 100m sheltered cove, Tamarama is neither easy to get to by public transport nor to park at should you decide to drive there. Once you arrive, it's not particularly accessible either: you have to climb down 40 steep steps to reach the water. And with its tricky surf and deep rip, it's not a swimming spot. That said, it's got a serious fan base of macho surfers who like to live dangerously and equally dedicated sun-seekers (there's absolutely no shade to be found on the sand). The latter consist mostly of air stewards, who have dubbed the beach Glamarama. Britpackers play Sunday soccer matches on the large grassy picnic area. The small kids' play area with swings and slide is within eyeshot of the excellent Tama café, which serves wonderful gourmet vegetarian and non-vegetarian sandwiches as well as refreshing power juices.
Services *Barbecue. Café (closed May-Sept Mon-Fri). Changing rooms. Danger: underwater rocks. Lifeguards/savers (Sept-May). No dogs. Parking. Picnic area. Play area. Shark net (Sept-May). Showers. Toilets.*

Bronte Beach

Bronte Road, Bronte. CityRail Bondi Junction then bus 378. **Map** *p323* ❸
Bronte is absolute bliss for local parents – pack the kids, the swimsuits and the boogie boards, and this 300m stretch of sand will babysit all day long. Though the water has a strong rip and is great for surfing, the outdoor Bronte Baths at the southern end – and the adjacent community centre – are the preserve of kids. There's plenty of shade under the sweeping sandstone rocks and scores of covered picnic benches (some with inlaid chessboards) to enjoy the traditional Aussie tucker served at the Bronte Kiosk – meat pies and hot chips aplenty.
Services *Barbecues. Cafés. Changing rooms. Child-friendly (play area). Danger: underwater rocks. Lifeguards/savers (Sept-May). No dogs. Parking. Picnic area. Pool. Restaurants. Shade. Shark net (Sept-May). Shops. Showers. Toilets.*

Clovelly Beach

Clovelly Road, Clovelly. CityRail Bondi Junction then bus 360/bus 339, X39. **Map** *p323* ❾
Once known as Little Coogee, tucked around the corner from the more famous Big Coogee (now simply Coogee), Clovelly is an idyllic spot, swathed in natural beauty. The tiny square of sand slopes into a long inlet of calm water, surrounded by a boardwalk and a concrete promenade. It's a favourite with scuba divers and snorkellers, but it's the wheelchair access that weaves the real magic. The Clovelly Bay boardwalk boasts specific entry points to the water with locking devices for a submersible wheelchair, on loan from the Beach Inspector's office (weekdays) or the SLSC (weekends). On the south promenade sits a chic 25m three-lane lap pool, built in 1962 and nicely revamped in 2002.
Services *Barbecues. Café. Changing rooms. Child-friendly. Lifeguards/savers (Sept-May). No dogs. Parking. Picnic area. Pool. Restaurant. Shade. Showers. Toilets. Wheelchair access.*

Coogee Beach

Beach Street, Coogee. CityRail Bondi Junction then bus 313, 314/bus 372, 373, 374, X73, X74. **Map** *p323* ⓬
This excellent family swimming beach is 400m long, with old-fashioned pools carved into the rocks at both ends. It's not great for surfing, but at least you don't have to worry about getting munched: in 1929 it was declared Australia's first shark-proof beach when nets were introduced. There are plenty of fast-food restaurants, cafés and places to picnic, and it's very much a tourist attraction. In 2003 the northern headland was renamed Dolphin Point, in memory of the six Coogee Dolphin rugby league players who were killed in the Bali bombings. Two memorial plaques, plastered with photographs, list the 26 victims from the local community (from a total Australian death toll of 88). **Photo** *p137.*
Services *Barbecues. Cafés. Changing rooms. Child-friendly. Lifeguards/savers. No dogs. Parking. Picnic area. Pools. Restaurants. Shade. Shark net (Sept-May). Shops. Showers. Toilets.*

Maroubra Beach

Marine Parade, Maroubra. Bus 376, 377, 395, 396, X77, X96. **Map** *p321* ❾
Maroubra was chosen as the new headquarters for Surfing NSW in 2003 – which didn't come as much of a surprise, since the waves are huge here and it's long been a top surf spot. All the outfit's coaching, judging, educational and safety programmes are now conducted at the 1.1km (0.7-mile) beach, which also picked up the Keep Australia Beautiful cleanest beach award in 2002. Much less touristy than neighbouring Coogee, it's also a favourite with joggers. There are a few local shops, showers and toilets, a well-equipped kids' play area and a sizeable skateboard park (which is packed when school's out) located next to the beach's windswept dunes.
Services *Barbecues. Cafés. Changing rooms. Child-friendly (play area). Lifeguards/savers. No dogs. Parking. Picnic area. Pool. Restaurants. Shark net (Sept-May). Shops. Showers. Toilets.*

Cronulla Beach

Mitchell Road, Cronulla. CityRail Cronulla. **Map** *p321* ❺
A vast sandy beach more than 6km (3.75 miles) long, Cronulla had a flash of worldwide notoriety in December 2005 as a race-riot battleground. To Sydneysiders, though, it has long been the south's most popular surfing and swimming spot. It has the feel of a big Queensland resort with its high-rise apartments and hotels, bars, steakhouses and carloads of young rev-heads. The southern end, a half-moon patch of sand around 100m long, is patrolled by a lifeguard all year round; with less of a rip, this is family territory for bathing, fossicking in the rock pools or swimming indoors at the Cronulla Sports

Coogee Beach. *See p136.*

Complex (located next to the lifesavers' hut). The much longer northern end of the beach has a fiercer undertow and views of a not-so-pretty oil refinery. There's a huge grassy picnic area with plenty of tables and an esplanade walkway. To get to Cronulla from the city, it takes about 50 minutes by train or an hour by car.

Services *Cafés. Changing rooms. Child-friendly (play area). Lifeguards/savers (south all year round; north Sept-May). No dogs. Parking. Picnic area. Pools. Restaurants. Shade. Shark net (Sept-May). Shops. Showers. Toilets.*

North

Shelly Beach

Marine Parade, Manly. Ferry Manly. **Map** p323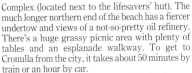

A ten-minute stroll south of Manly, small Shelly Beach is a family delight with yellow sand, gentle waters and a grassy picnic area. As you stroll south along the promenade from Manly, don't miss the Fairy Bower ocean pool, an excellent outdoor rock pool with spectacular views of the coastline. Set in Cabbage Tree Bay, Shelly Beach is best known for

good swimming conditions, but is also popular with novice scuba divers testing the deep.
Services *Barbecue. Café. Changing rooms. Child-friendly. No dogs. Parking. Picnic area. Restaurant (closed winter Sun-Mon). Shade. Showers. Toilets.*

Manly Beach

Manly. Ferry Manly. **Map** p323 ㉖

Jumping aboard a Sydney ferry is a must and a trip to Manly is the perfect excuse. Take one of the trusty old yellow-and-green giants from Circular Quay to Manly Wharf in Manly Cove, where there's a small harbour beach (about 250m long) and a netted swimming area. To reach the open sea, head across the busy pedestrianised street, the Corso, to the 1.5km (mile-long) crescent of sand known as Manly Surf Beach, but actually comprising Queenscliff in the north, followed by North Steyne, South Steyne and Manly Beaches. A mecca for mums, surfies and international tourists, Manly has all the facilities of a big resort. And plenty of history: in 1903 it was one of the first beaches to permit daylight swimming, but the crowds didn't understand the danger of the surf – there are rips along the entire length of the beach – and so fishermen Eddie and Joe Sly set up Manly's first lifesaving patrol. For a local area map, *see p334.*
Services *Cafés. Changing rooms. Child-friendly. Lifeguards/savers. No dogs. Parking. Picnic area. Pool (at Queenscliff). Restaurants. Shade. Shark net (Sept-May.) Shops. Showers. Toilets.*

Collaroy Beach

Pittwater Road, Collaroy. Bus 188, 190, E83, E84, E86, E87, E88, E89, L88, L90. **Map** p321 ➍

North of Manly lies a stretch of magnificent surfing beaches with wonderfully ludicrous names: Curl Curl, Dee Why, Long Reef, Narrabeen. At Collaroy, which lies directly south of Narrabeen, there's a 1km (half-mile) stretch of honey-coloured sand pounded by huge waves. It's also got an excellent, large ocean pool, plus a toddler pool at its southern end. The Bruce Bartlett Memorial Playground to the rear is shaded and has masses of fun equipment. The Hog's Breath Café is right on the beach and so the whole area tends to get thumping at night.
Services *Barbecues. Cafés. Changing rooms. Child-friendly (play area). Danger: underwater rocks. Lifeguards/savers (Sept-May). Parking. Picnic area. Pools. Restaurants. Shark net (Sept-May). Shops. Showers. Toilets.*

Newport Beach

Barrenjoey Road, Newport. Bus 188, 190, E88, E89, L88, L90. **Map** p321 ⑫

This 1km (half-mile) windswept beach offers good surf with easy access to a busy main road of shops, cafés and restaurants. Its accessibility makes it very popular with locals keen to catch a quick wave. There's a well-equipped, fenced-off play area in the grassland to the rear, but at dusk the beach can get rowdy and is no place for youngsters.
Services *Barbecues. Cafés. Changing rooms. Children's play area. Danger: underwater rocks.*

Lifeguards/savers (Sept-May). No dogs. Parking. Picnic area. Pool (south end). Restaurants. Shark net (Sept-May). Shops. Showers. Toilets.

Avalon Beach

Barrenjoey Road, Avalon. Bus 188, 190, E88, E89, L88, L90. **Map** p321 ➊

Once considered as the new filming location for *Baywatch*, this sandy beach (about 1km/half a mile long) gets pretty busy in the summer, especially with surfers, who arrive by the carload to tackle the generous waves. There's also good swimming and an excellent ocean pool at the southern end, and the whole beach is backed by sand dunes.
Services *Barbecues. Changing rooms. Children's play area. Lifeguards/savers (Sept-May.) Parking. Picnic area. Pool. Shark net (Sept-May). Showers. Toilets.*

Whale Beach

The Strand, Whale Beach. Bus 190, L90 to Avalon then bus 193. **Map** p321 ⑮

Approached via mind-bendingly steep roads, this 700m stretch of salmon-pink sand offers big surf and a rugged coastline. There's a 25m ocean pool at the southern end: take care when the tide comes in as the waves crash over the pool and surrounding rocks. A multi-million dollar improvement programme has been put on the backboiler after locals rebelled for fear it would attract too many outsiders to their little piece of paradise. **Photo** *p133.*
Services *Barbecue. Café (closed July). Changing rooms. Child-friendly (play area). Danger: underwater rocks. Lifeguards/savers (Sept-May). Parking. Picnic area. Pool. Restaurants. Shade. Shark net (Sept-May). Showers. Toilets.*

Palm Beach

Barrenjoey Road, Palm Beach. Bus 190, L90. **Map** p321 ⑬

Situated at the northernmost tip of the northern beaches peninsula, Palm Beach is a local paradise. Don't be fooled by Palm Beach Wharf, a busier beach on the west side that you come to first. Keep on driving up the hill and around the bend to get to the real deal on the east side: you won't be disappointed. Palm Beach is home to Sydney's rich and famous; colonial-style mansions set on the hillside possess breathtaking views of foaming ocean and nearly 2km (1.2 miles) of caramel-coloured sand. The southern end, known as Cabbage Tree Boat Harbour, is the safest spot to swim and surf. If you find the sea too daunting, there's the excellent Jack 'Johnny' Carter outdoor pool, named after the man who spent 50 years teaching local kids to swim. The Beachcomber café on North Palm Beach serves good tucker. And keep an eye out for young Aussie actors on a tea break – this is where the hit soap *Home and Away* is filmed.
Services *Barbecues (in play area). Café. Changing rooms. Child-friendly (play area in adjacent Governor Phillip Park). Lifeguards/savers (Sept-May). Parking. Picnic area. Pool. Restaurant. Shade. Shark net (Sept-May). Shops. Showers. Toilets.*

Surf, sharks and jellyfish

TO THE RESCUE

Each year Sydney's famed surf lifesavers carry out countless rescue operations. A disproportionate number are of foreigners who have underestimated the 'rips' (currents) in the surf. Waves at Sydney's ocean beaches can be up to four metres (13 feet) high and conceal powerful rips. More often, they are less than one metre; at Bondi and Manly, they're somewhere in between.

To be safe, always swim between the red and yellow flags that the lifesavers plant in the sand each day. If you stray outside the flags, the lifesavers will blow whistles and scream through megaphones at you. And don't think shallow water is completely safe. 'Dumpers' are waves that break with force, usually at low tide in shallow water, and can cause serious injury. Waves that don't break at all (surging waves) can knock swimmers over too and drag them out to sea. Finally, remember that alcohol and water don't mix – most adults who drown in NSW are under the influence.

If you do get caught by a rip and you're a confident swimmer, try to swim diagonally across the rip. Otherwise, stay calm, stick your hand in the air to signal to a lifeguard and float until you're rescued: don't fight the current by swimming toward shore.

SHARK THINKING

Shark attacks are very rare. In the past 20 years only one person in all NSW has been killed by a shark, and the last fatal attack in Sydney harbour was in 1963. It's true there have been more sharks seen in recent years,

but this is because better sewage methods have made the beaches much cleaner and so more palatable to sharks. That said, the closest most people get to a shark is in an aquarium: since beach swimming became popular, sharks have tended to shy away.

A lot of Sydney's beaches are shark-netted. The nets are 150 metres long, seven deep and are anchored to the sea floor within 500 metres of the shore. You won't spot them because they are always dropped in ten metre-deep water ensuring three metres (ten feet) of clearance for swimmers and surfers. The nets are meant not so much as a physical block to sharks but to prevent them establishing a habitat close to shore. They are moved from time to time to keep the sharks guessing.

If by some quirk of fate you do see a shark while swimming, try not to panic: just swim calmly to shore. Easier said than done, yes, but keep in mind that sharks are attracted to jerky movements. 'However,' say the experts at Taronga Zoo, 'if a shark gets close then any action you take may disrupt the attack pattern, such as hitting the shark's nose, gouging at its eyes, making sudden movements and blowing bubbles.'

Scared? Honestly, it hardly ever happens.

STINGERS

Two kinds of jellyfish are common on Sydney's beaches in summer. The jimble (a less potent southern relative of the deadly box jellyfish) is box-shaped with four pink tentacles. It is often found at the harbour beaches. On the ocean beaches you're more likely to come across bluebottle jellyfish (aka Portuguese man-of-war), which has long blue tentacles and tends to appear only when an onshore wind is blowing.

Jimbles can deliver a painful sting but are not dangerous; bluebottles are nastier, causing an intense, longer-lasting pain, red, whip-like lesions and, occasionally, respiratory problems. Even dead bluebottles on the beach can sting, so don't touch them.

Treatment for each is different. If stung by a jimble, wash the affected area with vinegar (lifeguards and lifesavers keep stocks of it) – or, if you can, pee on it – gently remove any tentacles with tweezers or gloves, and apply ice to relieve the pain. If stung by a bluebottle, leave the water immediately, don't rub the skin and don't apply vinegar; instead use an ice pack or anaesthetic spray.

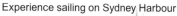

Eat, Drink, Shop

Loft. *See p179.*

Restaurants

Paradise on a plate.

Sydney is a city that loves eating out. It has restaurants every bit the calibre of London's finest, ethnic diversity on a par with New York and a dining public as passionate as those in Paris, all supported by a fraction of the total populace of any of its international rivals. It's also the most expensive place to eat in Australia and has a reputation (only partly true) for putting things glamorous and novel above constancy and substance.

Most of the city's top restaurants wouldn't be out of place in Manhattan or Mayfair in terms of the food on the plate. While they make the best of local produce, they belong, for better or for worse, to that light, inventive, produce-driven cuisine common to the Western world's finest, albeit with a keener understanding of the flavours of Asia and fewer ties to French technique. Native ingredients appear on some menus and indeed are the focus of some restaurants, but they're regarded in much the same terms as, say, Native American foods in the States or Welsh food in the UK: more a diversion than a serious component of contemporary dining. You can eat crocodile and kangaroo and wattleseed in Sydney, but the native ingredients you'll see in the city's better restaurants tend to run more along the lines of Coffin Bay scallops, Yamba prawns, West Australian crayfish and Tasmanian oysters than Skippy and co.

And there lies one of Sydney's great strengths: seafood. It's diverse, plentiful, fresh and of excellent quality. Just as importantly, perhaps, people know how to cook it: that is, not very much – or at all. Minimal interference between hook and plate keeps the natural qualities of the fish to the fore.

Many of the city's best seafood restaurants happen to make the most of the city's other great asset, the harbour. It's another distinctive facet of Sydney dining: true, there is no shortage of waterside places that will strip your wallet in return for food and service distinguished only by their ordinariness, but a significant fraction of the view-restaurants are worth visiting for more than the eye candy – in some instances grandly so.

Nowhere else in Australia is the country's proximity to Asia better expressed on the plate. While good and authentic Cantonese, Thai, Vietnamese, Japanese, Korean and Malaysian food is readily available (truly outstanding Indian, Pakistani and Sri Lankan is another matter), the modern Asian restaurants make a much better fist of things than their Western counterparts, dispensing with the ugly forced unions of 'fusion' food in favour of dishes that remain true to their ethnic roots even as they're dressed up for the cocktail-and-couture set.

One flavour you won't get much of in Sydney restaurants is smoke. Smoking is banned everywhere indoors that food is served. The fines are steep and the laws strictly enforced, so anyone keen to spark up after a meal had best find an outside table or partake of the Sydney smokers' ritual of huddling outside the door. Bars too are following this lead, so ensure an ashtray is handy before you reach for the fags.

On the plus side, the bring-your-own (BYO) tradition is alive and kicking: even some high-flyers allow it. But it often extends only to bottled wine, so call ahead if you plan to bring beer. Some restaurants offer BYO in the week, but go in-house-only on busier nights. A small corkage fee is usually charged, either by the head or bottle. In the listings below we've indicated whether the restaurant is licensed, BYO, both or doesn't allow alcohol at all. We've also given the price range for main courses at dinner.

Tipping, meanwhile, is something Sydneysiders do to reward exceptional service, not to keep angry waiters at bay. Ten per cent on top of the bill is the local standard, but no one's likely to be offended if you up the ante, and equally they're not likely to chase you down the street if you don't tip at all (though we're mindful of the New York bartenders' mantra – if you can't afford to tip, you can't afford to drink. Or eat).

The CBD & the Rocks

Asian

Azuma

Level 1, Chifley Plaza, 2 Chifley Square, corner of Phillip & Hunter Streets, CBD (9222 9960/www.azuma.com.au). CityRail Martin Place. **Open** noon-2.30pm, 6-10pm Mon-Fri; 6-10pm Sat. **Main courses** $30-$40. **Licensed/BYO**. **Credit** AmEx, MC, V. **Map** p327 F5 ❶ Japanese

Long-standing and outstanding: Neil Perry's **Rockpool**. *See p147.*

The deluxe skyscraper setting will have you squinting and pretending you're in Roppongi Hills or some other moneyed Tokyo setting, but the lightness and boldness of the kitchen's way with traditional Japanese flavours will tell you otherwise. When Azuma-san suggests you try sashimi with a squeeze of lemon rather than the ubiquitous soy, follow his advice and experience raw fish perfection. Keep an eye out for occasional specials of *o-toro*, the prized fatty belly meat of the blue-fin tuna.

Sailors Thai

106 George Street, opposite Mill Lane, The Rocks (9251 2466). CityRail/ferry Circular Quay. **Open** *Canteen noon-10pm daily. Restaurant noon-2pm, 6-10pm Mon-Sat.* **Main courses** *Canteen* $16.50-$26. *Restaurant* $29-$39.50. **Licensed. Credit** AmEx, DC, MC, V. **Map** p327 F3 **2** Thai

Chef David Thompson now spends most of his time running Nahm, his superb, Michelin-starred Thai restaurant in London. Here you can eat food every bit as dynamic and thrilling, but for a fraction of the cost. If the relative bargain of the downstairs restaurant is still too rich for your blood, you can sacrifice a little comfort, service and range for food that is significantly cheaper yet no less impressive in the upstairs Canteen. The signature *som dtam* – nuggets of caramelised pork with peanuts, dried tiny shrimp, cherry tomatoes and a fiery sour salad of green mango – can be considered Authentic Thai Food 101 for newcomers to the cuisine.

Sushi e

Level 4, Establishment Hotel, 252 George Street, between Bridge Street & Abercrombie Lane, CBD (9240 3041/www.merivale.com.au). CityRail Circular Quay or Wynyard/ferry Circular Quay. **Open** 6-10pm Tue; noon-2pm, 6-10pm Wed; noon-2pm Thur; noon-2pm, 6.30-10pm Fri; 6.30-10pm Sat. **Main courses** $25-$45. **Licensed. Credit** AmEx, DC, MC, V. **Map** p327 F5 **3** Japanese

Shaun Presland, you're our hero. Not only are you the first *gaijin* sushi chef we've ever seen, your eel rolled in cucumber and soft-shell crab hand rolls are magnificent. This tiny polished gem of a sushi bar is part of the Hemmesphere bar (*see p176*) and also probably one of the three best sushi joints in town. It ain't cheap, but it's a very slick and satisfying caper from start to finish.

Yoshii

115 Harrington Street, between Essex & Argyle Streets, CBD (9247 2566/www.yoshii.com.au). CityRail/ferry Circular Quay. **Open** 6-9.30pm Mon, Sat; noon-2pm, 6-9.30pm Tue-Fri. **Set menu** $80, $110 tasting menu. **Licensed. Credit** AmEx, DC, MC, V. **Map** p327 E4 **4** Japanese

1 Purple numbers given in this chapter correspond to the location of each restaurant as marked on the street maps. *See pp326-334.*

KOBE JONES

SYDNEY / MELBOURNE

Kobe Jones is a modern Japanese Restaurant with a twist. Super chic and innovative - the perfect setting to indulge an ultra culinary experience.

Inspired by the best of eastern spices and the Californian flavours of the west.
The huge menu is fresh and light containing some surprising delicious dishes.

Taste one of our fabulous cocktail creations, enjoy a blend of chill-out ambient music with spectacular water views.

ON PRESENTATION OF THIS CARD WE WOULD LIKE TO OFFER A GLASS OF WINE PER PERSON OR A BOTTLE OF KOBE JONES HOUSE FOR A SPECIAL BOOKING OF 4 PERSONS

Sydney: 02 9299 5290

for bookings and reservations
Address: 29 Lime Street, Sydney NSW 2000
Fax: 02 9299 5929
Email: kobejones@kobejones.com.au

Melbourne: 03 9329 9173

All Major Credit Cards Accepted

bean
ground
&
drunk

aromatic
desirable
plentiful

Open 7 Days

Ryuichi Yoshii's dad was a sushi chef, and the genes have run true, with young Yoshii-san offering the finest sashimi in the land. Sit at the bar and watch him at work or take a table for cooked treats like the chaud-froid of egg and sea urchin roe. This is culinary inventiveness at the bleeding edge, presented in cosy but utterly civilised surrounds.

European

Bécasse
204 Clarence Street, between Druitt & Market Streets, CBD (9283 3440/www.becasse.com.au). CityRail Town Hall. **Open** noon-2.30pm, 6-10pm Tue-Fri; 6-10pm Sat. **Main courses** $34-$45. **Licensed. Credit** AmEx, DC, MC, V. **Map** p327 E6 ❺ French
Bécasse has blossomed from a Surry Hills bistro of some repute to a big city restaurant of justified acclaim. Chef Justin North trained with Raymond Blanc, and his exactitude in saucing and finesse with flavour is dazzling. From the service to the sublime wine list to the riches of dishes such as crab risotto with spring onions and a sauté of prawns, right down to the petits fours, this is the full three-star dining experience Down Under.

Bilson's
Radisson Plaza Hotel, 27 O'Connell Street, at Hunter Street, CBD (9016 0496/www.bilsons.com.au). CityRail Wynyard. **Open** 6pm-late Tue-Thur, Sat; noon-3pm, 6pm-late Fri. **Set menu** $60 2 courses; $90 3 courses; $120-$150 tasting menus. **Licensed. Credit** AmEx, DC, MC, V. **Map** p327 F5 ❻ French
A hotel dining room, Bilson's can be quiet – too quiet for some. But not for those who appreciate chef Tony Bilson's unfailingly sharp technique and good taste. The unashamedly francophile elder statesman of Sydney dining creates marvels, whether turning his hand to chicken poached in a bladder or delicately handled freshwater crayfish.

Bistro CBD
Level 1, CBD Hotel, 52 King Street, at York Street, CBD (8297 7010/www.merivale.com). CityRail Wynyard. **Open** noon-3pm, 6-10pm Mon-Fri. **Main courses** $31-$37. **Licensed. Credit** AmEx, DC, MC, V. **Map** p327 E6 ❼ French
Throw a bread roll at lunch here and you're likely to incur the wrath of one of Sydney's top CEOs: the white-collar brigade love Bistro CBD for its pace, sirloin with Café de Paris butter, and buzz. The rest of us love the 'Your usual, sir?' service, the consistency and the exemplary fish cookery.

Forty One
Level 42, Chifley Tower, 2 Chifley Square, corner of Phillip & Hunter Streets, CBD (9221 2500/ www.forty-one.com.au). CityRail Martin Place. **Open** noon-2pm, 7pm-late Mon-Fri; 7pm-late Sat. **Set menu** $125 3 courses; $140-$150 tasting/ vegetarian menus. **Licensed. Credit** AmEx, DC, MC, V. **Map** p327 F5 ❽ Modern European
While the talk of the views from the urinal in the men's room (it's glass from the waist up, with 41

floors below) is a constant, so too is the quality of chef/owner Dietmar Sawyer's cuisine. Try the braise of white asparagus with croustillant of egg and truffled creamed spinach.

Glass
2nd Floor, Hilton Sydney, 488 George Street, between Park & Market Streets, CBD (9265 6068/ www.glassbrasserie.com.au). CityRail Town Hall/ Monorail City Centre. **Open** noon-11pm Mon-Fri; 6-11pm Sat, Sun. **Main courses** $32.50-$39.50. **Licensed. Credit** AmEx, DC, MC, V.
Map p327 F6 ❾ French
Yes, it's one of those hotel dining rooms dreamed up by the damned. The same panel may have also thought that yoking culinary whizz Luke Mangan to a steak-frites-and-soufflés brasserie-by-numbers menu was a good idea. Sadly, the schismatic result does little service to either, but the room is seriously splashy and real effort has been made in the wine department. The wine bar (*see p176*) is nice, though.

Omega
Basement, 161 King Street, between Castlereagh & Elizabeth Streets, CBD (9223 0242/www.omega restaurant.com.au). CityRail Martin Place. **Open** noon-12.30pm, 6pm-late Mon-Fri; 6pm-late Sat. **Main courses** $35-$40. **Licensed. Credit** AmEx, DC, MC, V. **Map** p327 F6 ❿ Greek
Peter Conistis came to fame taking the Greek palate-palette and using it to paint in a bold, exciting Mod Oz manner at the tiny Eleni's on Bourke Street (now closed). Omega, by contrast, is a sizeable basement room, rich with designer flourishes; even so, it's the likes of the salad of roast corella pears with sheep's milk feta, almonds, rocket and pomegranate that are the real drawcards.

Modern Australian

Aria
1 Macquarie Street, East Circular Quay (9252 2555/www.ariarestaurant.com.au). CityRail/ferry Circular Quay. **Open** 12.30-2.30pm, 5.30-11.30pm Mon-Fri; 5.30-11.30pm Sat, Sun. **Main courses** $38-$45. **Licensed. Credit** AmEx, DC, MC, V. **Map** p327 G3 ⓫
You've got plush timber and leather trimmings framing views of the Bridge, Quay and Opera House on the one hand, and Matt Moran's fresh and lively bistro-gone-glam food on the other. Hit the Peking duck consommé, then the roast Murray cod, and go for broke on the outstanding wine list.

Bistro 163
163 King Street, between Castlereagh & Elizabeth Streets, CBD (9231 0013). CityRail Martin Place. **Open** 11.45am-2.30pm, 6-9pm Mon-Fri. **Main courses** $17.50-$27. **Licensed/BYO. Credit** AmEx, DC, MC, V. **Map** p327 F6 ⓬
One of Sydney's 1990s superstars, Paul Merrony has since chucked the fine dining caper (after a stint at Harvey Nichols, among other UK engagements) and gone bistro. There's barely room to swing a

Eat, Drink, Shop

Restaurants

The best

Eat, Drink, Shop

For hot stuff

The tucker at **Spice I Am** (*see p153*) can render one speechless, and not just with pleasure. Less fiery are **Longrain** (*see p152*) and **Sailors Thai** (*see p143*). For a change, try the cold burn of Sichuan pepper at **Red Chilli** (*see p150*).

For seafood

Pier (*see p160*) stands out, but you can get similarly amazing fish for less (*photo*) at **Fish Face** (*see p158*). For oysters, visit the **Boathouse at Blackwattle Bay** (*see p162*), while crab fans should head to **Flying Fish** (*see p151*), **Golden Century** (*see p149*) and **Manta** (*see p156*).

For service

There's plenty of good service on show in Sydney, but Beverley Wood at **Ristorante Riva** (*see p152*) is so natural a hostess she eclipses the rest.

For steak

Prime (*see p149*) is in a class of its own – it's even got a separate menu just for wagyu beef. Excellent cuts can also be had at **Aria** (*see p145*), **Bistro Moncur** (*see p158*) and the **Restaurant at Three Weeds** (*see p162*), and no meat discussion is complete without the salt-crusted rib-eye at **Icebergs** (*see p159*).

For sweet things

Lorraine Godsmark at **Yellow Bistro** (*see p157*) isn't known as the queen of tarts for nothing. Don't miss her famous date tart.

For vegetarians

Forget cheap and cheerful. The vegetarian tasting menu at **Claude's** (*see p159*) tears up the rulebook – and any credit cards you may have handy.

For views

You can't beat sunset over Bondi from **Icebergs** (*see p159*) or the harbour views from **Aria** (*see p145*), **Guillaume at**

Bennelong (*see p147*), **Quay** (*see p147*) and the **Wharf** (*see p149*). Alternatively, try the working harbour vista at **Flying Fish** (*see p151*) or look down from on high at **Forty One** (*see p145*). **Jonah's** (*see p165*) has a breathtaking view over Whale Beach.

For wine

Marque (*see p155*) is the winner if you want something unusual, **Aria** (*see p145*) has serious breadth, while **Becasse**'s (*see p145*) excursions into southern France are a joy.

For yum cha

Competition is fierce, with delights on offer at **Marigold Citimark** (*see p149*), **Sea Treasure** (*see p163*) and **Zilver** (*see p150*), but **East Ocean** (*see p149*) is the one to beat.

cochon's pied in Bistro 163, but that bustle and squeeze, along with minimal, faithful salades lyonnaises and prawn omelettes plus surly service, give it a decidedly Parisian feel.

Cru

Level 3, Overseas Passenger Terminal, West Circular Quay (9251 1188/www.cruiserestaurant.com.au). CityRail/ferry Circular Quay. **Open** 6-10.30pm Mon, Sat; noon-2.30pm, 6-10.30pm Tue-Fri. **Main courses** $37-$39. **Licensed**. **Credit** AmEx, DC, MC, V. **Map** p327 F3. **⑮**

Ed Halmayagi is a chef of Hungarian ancestry best known in Sydney circles for his cooking at an Italian restaurant. He's recently stepped up to the plate to do Mod Oz at this plush diner overlooking Circular Quay. Roll from a raviolo of wild wood pigeon with pickled cabbage to sautéed skate with braised celery hearts and octopus cannelloni without missing a beat.

est.

Level 1, Establishment Hotel, 252 George Street, between Bridge Street & Abercrombie Lane, CBD (9240 3010/www.merivale.com.au). CityRail Circular Quay or Wynyard/ferry Circular Quay. **Open** noon-2.30pm, 6-10pm Mon-Fri; 6-10pm Sat. **Main courses** $42-$45. **Licensed**. **Credit** AmEx, DC, MC, V. **Map** p327 F5 ⓮
To step out of the lift and into the bright, colonnaded est. dining room is to enter a bubble of total assurance. You can rely as much on the good humour and utter professionalism of the staff as you can on the food of Mod Oz maestro Peter Doyle and the thoroughly excellent wine service. Vegetarians are especially well catered for. Won the *SMH Good Food Guide*'s best restaurant prize in 2006.

Guillaume at Bennelong

Sydney Opera House, Bennelong Point, Circular Quay (9241 1999/www.guillaumeatbennelong. com.au). CityRail/ferry Circular Quay. **Open** noon-3pm Thur, Fri; 5.30-11.30pm Mon-Sat. **Main courses** $42. **Licensed**. **Credit** AmEx, DC, MC, V. **Map** p327 G3 ⓯
Given the following that Guillaume Brahimi picked up while working with Joël Robuchon in Paris, it's tempting to call his food French (not least of all his note-perfect rendition of the great Robuchon's Paris mash). But there's a lightness that is pure Sydney to his signature dish of tuna infused with basil, for example, or the crab sandwiches that are the mainstays of the bar menu. Wine and service are of a similarly high order, and the Opera House is a nonpareil setting. The Bennelong Bar (*see p176*) is a treat too.

Ocean Room

Ground Level, Overseas Passenger Terminal, West Circular Quay (8273 1277/www.oceanroomsydney. com). CityRail/ferry Circular Quay. **Open** noon-3pm, 6-11pm Mon-Thur; noon-3m, 6pm-midnight Fri; 6-11pm Sat. **Main courses** $22-$75. **Licensed**. **Credit** AmEx, DC, MC, V. **Map** p327 F3 ⓰
Japanese chef Raita Noda's wilfully out-there Japanese fusion cuisine had a loyal following at Darlinghurst's obscure Rise (*see p152*), but something has been lost in the translation to this tourist-tempting gastro-barn by the water. Noda's work is in there somewhere, along with some superb seafood, but a throw-everything-at-the-wall-and-see-what-sticks approach from the management means you'll be as likely marooned and confused as riding high on waves of inspiration.

Palisade Hotel

Corner of Bettington & Argyle Streets, Millers Point (9247 2272/www.palisadehotel.com). CityRail/ferry Circular Quay/bus 308. **Open** noon-3pm, 6-9.30pm Tue-Fri; 6-10pm Sat. **Main courses** $26-$33. **Licensed**. **Credit** AmEx, DC, MC, V. **Map** p326 D3 ⓱

A hidden gem, the upstairs dining room in this lovely old pub is certainly worth the fossick. Brian Sudek crafts food that sings with freshness, balance and simplicity. Service can be as laid-back as the atmosphere, but that's not necessarily a bad thing. Be warned – the bridgeside location doesn't necessarily translate to views for all.

Pavilion on the Park

1 Art Gallery Road, opposite Art Gallery of NSW, The Domain (9232 1322/www.pavilion.com.au). CityRail Martin Place or St James. **Open** *Café* 9am-4pm daily. *Restaurant* noon-4pm Mon-Fri, Sun. **Main courses** *Café* $8-$16. *Restaurant* $28-$36. **Licensed**. **Credit** AmEx, DC, MC, V. **Map** p327 H5 ⓲
Prehistoric-looking Moreton Bay fig trees provide the backdrop for what must be one of the best places for a leisurely, thoroughly modern lunch of lobster panna cotta with sauce vierge, or duck and foie gras pie. Breakfast at the adjoining café is a must.

Quay

Upper Level, Overseas Passenger Terminal, Circular Quay West (9251 5600/www.quay.com.au). CityRail/ferry Circular Quay. **Open** noon-2.30pm, 6-10pm Tue-Fri; 6-10pm Mon, Sat, Sun. **Main courses** $38-$46. **Licensed**. **Credit** AmEx, DC, MC, V. **Map** p327 F3 ⓳
Peter Gilmore is a singular culinary talent. He's no slouch on flavour, but has a particular gift for coaxing all sorts of pleasures from texture. The pressed suckling pig with baby turnips, black pudding and Pedro Ximénez sauce is a case in point. Desserts are little short of spectacular, as in a two-tier creation with panna cotta on the bottom and halved white nectarines set in their own poaching liquor on top. Luxury all round, with views (and prices) to match.

Rockpool

107 George Street, between Alfred & Argyle Streets, The Rocks (9252 1888/www.rockpool.com). CityRail/ferry Circular Quay. **Open** 6-11pm Tue-Sat. **Set menu** $150 5 courses, $150 vegetarian menu, $175 tasting menu. **Licensed**. **Credit** AmEx, DC, MC, V. **Map** p327 F4 ⓴
Atop the Rockpool catwalk of tables you'll sit with the Keanus and CEOs of the world, but also with plenty of regular folk who save their pennies (lots of 'em) to eat at Neil Perry's restaurant because it's such an exciting thing to do. More importantly, the food is great. Inspirations are diverse, but seafood and Asia are the kitchen's passions, and when they intersect, as in the prawn cake with kimchi, congee (rice porridge) sauce, duck confit and water chestnuts, culinary nirvana is the result. **Photo** *p143*.

Tetsuya's

529 Kent Street, between Bathurst & Liverpool Streets, CBD (9267 2900/www.tetsuyas.com). CityRail Town Hall/Monorail Galeries Victoria. **Open** 6-8.30pm Tue-Sat. **Set menu** $180 tasting menu. **Licensed/BYO**. **Credit** AmEx, DC, MC, V. **Map** p329 E7 ㉑

Eat, Drink, Shop

You must eat here. No arguments. Yes, it's a very large amount of money to pay for food. But, given that Tetsuya Wakuda is a culinary Olympian of the order of France's Alain Ducasse and the USA's Thomas Keller, it's also a bargain of sorts. Don't be put off by the numerous courses in the fixed menu; each is so light and small you're guaranteed to leave groaning only with pleasure. And don't worry: everyone ends up eating the entire dish of butter whipped with black truffle and parmesan that accompanies the bread. They'd worry if you didn't.

Wharf
Pier 4, Hickson Road, Walsh Bay (9250 1761/ www.thewharfrestaurant.com.au). CityRail/ ferry Circular Quay then 15mins walk. **Open** noon-3.30pm, 6-10pm Mon-Sat. **Main courses** $32.50. **Licensed**. **Credit** AmEx, DC, MC, V. **Map** p327 E2 ㉒

Cavernous, isn't it? A diner could almost feel lost, were it not for chef Aaron Ross's capacity to create a menu that is at once down to earth and completely gripping. Asian flavours are particularly well handled, but there's pleasure – and excellent value – to be found throughout. The bar menu is perfect for play-goers (the Wharf Theatres are here; *see p272*), and the light of wallet, while the wine list is perfect when you're feeling flush. **Photo** *p153*.

Other

Prime
Lower Ground Floor, GPO Sydney, 1 Martin Place, between George & Pitt Streets, CBD (9229 7777/ www.gposydney.com). CityRail Martin Place or Wynyard. **Open** noon-3pm, 6-10pm Mon-Fri; 6-10pm Sat. **Main courses** $32-$44. **Licensed**. **Credit** AmEx, DC, MC, V. **Map** p327 F5 ㉙ American

The closest Sydney gets to a big, New York-style steakhouse, this designer basement in the old GPO building is all about the blokey business of heavy stone, big-dollar blockbuster reds, and meat – lots of it. The red wine sauces are finger-lickin' great, and the knives are made from German surgical steel.

Chinatown & Haymarket

Asian

Chinese Noodle Restaurant
8 Quay Street, at Thomas Street, Haymarket (9281 9051). CityRail Central/Monorail Paddy's Markets/LightRail Capitol Square or Paddy's Markets. **Open** 10am-9pm daily. **Main courses** $13-$20. **BYO**. **No credit cards**. **Map** p329 E9 ㉔ North-western Chinese

Yes, those are plastic grapevines strung across the ceiling, and yes, this is definitely a Chinese restaurant. It's one of the best – and one of the cheapest – serving dishes from the north-western provinces. The noodles are handmade, the dumplings fresh and the atmosphere lively. 'Combination noodles'

resembles a bizarre Chinese parallel-universe spag bol, replete with cucumber julienne garnish. A must.

East Ocean
88 Dixon Street, at Liverpool Street, entrance at 421-429 Sussex Street, Haymarket (9211 3674). CityRail Central/Monorail Paddy's Markets or World Square/LightRail Capitol Square or Paddy's Markets. **Open** 10am-midnight Mon-Fri; 9am-2am Sat, Sun. **Main courses** $12.80-$16.80. **Licensed**. **Credit** AmEx, DC, MC, V. **Map** p329 E8 ㉕ Cantonese

The revamped East Ocean looks terribly slick (for a Hong-Kong-style, barn-sized Cantonese diner, anyway), while the food is as pleasing as ever. Ignore the printed menu and have a chat with the waiters about how best to enjoy the live seafood. The salt-and-pepper squid is particularly good, as are the baby abalone steamed with ginger and spring onion, and the yum cha (dim sum) is among the city's finest, with impressive diversity and freshness, so be prepared to queue at weekends.

Emperor's Garden BBQ & Noodles
213 Thomas Street, between Ultimo Road & Quay Street, Haymarket (9281 9899). CityRail Central/ Monorail Paddy's Markets/LightRail Capitol Square or Paddy's Markets. **Open** 9.30am-11pm daily. **Main courses** $9.50-$20. **Licensed**. **Credit** AmEx, DC, MC, V. **Map** p329 E9 ㉖ Cantonese

There are other establishments in Chinatown that dispense barbecue that's nearly as good as the Emperor's, but the hardcore of roast and barbecue pork fanciers (and their pigeon and soy chicken brethren), Westerners and Cantonese alike, still only go to one place for their fix. The Garden also does faithful renditions of stir-fried asparagus with garlic, ma po bean curd and other classics.

Golden Century
393-399 Sussex Street, between Goulburn & Hay Streets, Haymarket (9212 3901). CityRail Central/ Monorail World Square/LightRail Capitol Square. **Open** noon-4am daily. **Main courses** $15-$30. **Licensed/BYO**. **Credit** AmEx, DC, MC, V. **Map** p329 E8 ㉗ Chinese

Though the printed menu is fine, many regulars bypass it completely and flag down a member of the famously surly staff for steamed fish with ginger and spring onion, the salt-and-pepper prawns and the restaurant's top-notch signature Peking duck. After 10pm the restaurant switches down a gear, offering cheaper, one-bowl meals for owls, drunks, chefs and other miscreants. Midnight congee (rice porridge – we favour the pork and preserved egg version) at the Golden C is a Sydney institution.

Marigold Citimark
683 George Street, between Hay Street & Ultimo Road, Haymarket (9281 3388/www.marigold. com.au). CityRail Central/LightRail Capitol Square. **Open** 10am-3pm, 5.30-11pm daily. **Main courses** $15-$30. **Licensed**. **Credit** AmEx, DC, MC, V. **Map** p329 E8 ㉘ Cantonese

Visit **Zilver** for classical Chinese dining with a modern sensibililty.

There's something in the local adage that Sydney is the place for yum cha, while Melbourne rules the roost when it comes to Cantonese by night. But the Marigold comes close to confusing the issue, cunningly offering a dazzling array of snacks at lunch, and then an equally impressive line-up after dark, not least the sizzling pepper oysters.

Musashi

Corner of Pitt & Campbell Streets, Haymarket (9280 0377). CityRail Central/LightRail Capitol Square. **Open** 11.45am-2.30pm, 5.30-10pm Mon-Fri; 5.30-10pm Sat. **Main courses** $10-$35. **Licensed**. **Credit** AmEx, MC, V. **Map** p329 E8 ㉙ Japanese
Fickle as the young Japanese cool crowd in Sydney may be, this downtown-glam izakaya seems to have some staying power in the fashionable restaurant stakes. The food's certainly pretty good for the low prices. The sashimi's OK, but the cooked stuff, such as the okonomiyaki – here thoughtfully translated as 'Japanese pizza' – is where it's at.

Pasteur

709 George Street, between Ultimo Road & Valentine Street, Haymarket (9212 5622). CityRail/LightRail Central. **Open** 10am-9pm daily. **Main courses** $6-$10. **BYO**. **No credit cards**. **Map** p329 E9 ㉚ Vietnamese
Hands down the best place for phô – the beef noodle soup that is Vietnam's lifeblood – in Chinatown. Should the soups – beef or chicken, no part of the beast left unturned – not grab you, try the excellent vermicelli and grilled pork salad.

Red Chilli

51 Dixon Street, entrance on Little Hay Street, Haymarket (9211 8122). CityRail Central/Monorail Paddy's Markets/LightRail Paddy's Markets. **Open** 11.30am-3.30pm, 5.30-11pm daily. **Main courses** $15. **Licensed/BYO**. **Credit** AmEx, DC, MC, V. **Map** p329 E8 ㉛ Sichuanese
Abandon hope all ye who fear spice, for this is not the place for thee: Red Chilli is one of only a handful of Sichuan places in the whole of Australia – and one of the best. The signature deep-fried chicken served with its weight in chilli (balanced in the mouth by the cool burn of Sichuan pepper, of course) deserves its fame, and is highly indicative of the restaurant's forte.

Thainatown

91 Goulburn Street, between Castlereagh & Pitt Streets, Haymarket (9211 0090). CityRail Museum/Monorail World Square/LightRail Capitol Square. **Open** 10am-10pm daily. **Main courses** $9-$11. **BYO**. **No credit cards**. **Map** p329 F8 ㉜ Thai
To the untrained eye, this place doesn't look that radically different to any other reasonably polished Thai restaurant. But look again: see the way the room is filled with Thais? See the specials written in Thai stuck to the walls? See the dishes you've never heard of on the menu? Hit the pad kaprow for an example of a familiar dish – chicken and chilli – taken to new heights, or go the whole Thai hog and dive into a bowl of 'boat noodle' soup, brimming with livery goodness.

Zilver

Level 1, 477 Pitt Street, entrance on Hay Street, Haymarket (9211 2232/www.zilver.com.au). CityRail Central/LightRail Capitol Square. **Open** 10am-3.30pm, 5.30-11pm Mon-Fri; 9am-3.30pm, 5.30-11pm Sat, Sun. **Main courses** $12.80-$48. **Licensed/BYO**. **Credit** AmEx, DC, MC, V. **Map** p329 E8 ㉝ Chinese

It might not quite stack up against the Michelin-starred likes of Hakkasan and Yauatcha in London, but Zilver, with its newly polished dark tones, crisply uniformed staff and Peking duck pancakes, is definitely an indication of the way ahead for Sydney's yum cha palaces. And while it's a great leap forward in look and feel, the food stays true to its roots and prices are far from forbidding. **Photo** *p150.*

Darling Harbour & Pyrmont

Asian

Malaya
King Street Wharf, Darling Harbour (9279 1170/ www.themalaya.com.au). CityRail Town Hall/ferry Darling Harbour/Monorail Darling Park. **Open** noon-3pm, 6pm-late Mon-Sat; 6pm-late Sun. **Main courses** $19-$27. **Licensed. Credit** AmEx, DC, MC, V. **Map** p326 D6 **34** Malaysian
The Malaya looms large in the recent history of Sydney restaurants, having been responsible, over the course of 30-odd years and several changes of location, for introducing local palates to galangal, lemongrass and other Asian flavours. It might not be the cutting edge for Malaysian food any more, but the latest incarnation is the slickest yet: an airy establishment boasting water views.

Zaaffran
Level 2, 345 Harbourside Shopping Centre, Darling Harbour (9211 8900/www.zaaffran.com.au). Ferry Darling Harbour/Monorail Harbourside. **Open** noon-2.30pm, 5.30-9.30pm Mon-Thur, Sun; noon-2.30pm, 5.30-10.15pm Fri, Sat. **Main courses** $15.50-$25.50. **Licensed. Credit** AmEx, DC, MC, V. **Map** p326 D6 **35** Indian
Free-range chickens issuing from the tandoor? Semolina-crusted barramundi with turmeric, lime, ginger and chilli? It's an Indian restaurant, Jim, but not as we know it. And while you might not want to enter Darling Harbour expressly to visit it, should you find yourself here already, it's definitely a superior dining option.

European

Astral
Level 17, Hotel Tower, Star City Casino, 80 Pyrmont Street, between Jones Bay Road & Union Street, Pyrmont (1800 700 700/www.starcity.com.au). LightRail Star City/bus 443. **Open** 6-10am, 6-10pm Tue-Thur; 6-10am, noon-3pm, 6-10.30pm Fri; 6-10am, 6-10.30pm Sat; 6-10am Sun. **Main courses** $72 2 courses; $88 3 courses. **Licensed. Credit** AmEx, DC, MC, V. **Map** p326 C6 **36** French
OK, so Monte Carlo it ain't, and the less said about the casino setting the better, although the 17th-floor location makes for some ace views. Chef Sean Connolly makes a daube of wagyu beef, but the white wine (instead of red), salsify and asparagus to undercut the meat's riches. It's this cleverness – plus the foie-gras-and-caviar frills (and wine list) for the high-rollers – that makes Astral shine.

Coast
Roof Terrace, Cockle Bay Wharf, Darling Harbour (9267 6700). CityRail Town Hall/ferry Darling Harbour/Monorail Darling Park. **Open** noon-2.30pm, 6-10pm Mon-Sat. **Main courses** $24-$34. **Licensed. Credit** AmEx, DC, MC, V. **Map** p326 D6 **37** Italian
Chef Stefano Manfredi was one of the first to take Italian dining to the five-star level in Sydney, and here at Coast, his newest venture, things are as slick as ever, from the deluxe salumi (cured meats) platter and excellent barbecued whole rabbit to taking the rather spiffy Italian wine list for a spin.

Other

Flying Fish
Lower Deck, Jones Bay Wharf, 19-21 Pirrama Road, Pyrmont (9518 6677/www.flyingfish.com.au). LightRail Star City/bus 443. **Open** noon-2.30pm, 6-10.30pm Tue-Fri; 6-10.30pm Sat; 6-9.30pm Sun. **Main courses** $36-$42; crabs/crayfish $60-$140. **Licensed. Credit** AmEx, DC, MC, V. **Map** p326 C4 **38** Seafood
Flying Fish is the name and fish (albeit bound to the plate) is the game. This newish, showy establishment at the far end of the wharf, wears its designer looks on its sleeve, but the food, from Tasmanian mussels with harissa and flatbread to the outstanding chilli Northern Territory mud crab, is the real deal. Service has yet to really hit the mark, but the location is interesting enough to bridge the gap. Flying Fish & Chips, the cheaper, spin-off kiosk, is worth a gander too.

Nick's Bar & Grill
King Street Wharf, Darling Harbour (9264 1212/ www.nicks-seafood.com.au). CityRail Town Hall/ferry Darling Harbour/Monorail Darling Park. **Open** noon-3pm, 6-10pm Mon-Sat; noon-10pm Sun. **Main courses** $25.50-$38.50. **Licensed. Credit** AmEx, DC, MC, V. **Map** p326 D6 **39** Seafood
You can eat brilliantly at Nick's or you can not. The trick is simple: order fish from the extensive selection (don't ever pass up an opportunity to eat red emperor) and get it cooked as simply as possible, with other basics – salads, mash and whatnot – on the side. Follow these simple instructions, add a sunny day and a chilled riesling, and you won't find a better alfresco seafood experience.

East Sydney & Darlinghurst

Asian

Oh! Calcutta!
251 Victoria Street, at Burton Street, Darlinghurst (9360 3650/www.ohcalcutta.com.au). CityRail Kings Cross/bus 389. **Open** 6pm-midnight Mon-Sat. **Main courses** $16.90-$26.90. **Licensed. Credit** AmEx, MC, V. **Map** p330 H8 **40** Indian

Easily the most glamorous Indian in town, Oh! Calcutta!'s fit-out, by local design legends Burley Katon Halliday, marries comfort with edgy good looks in a manner that echoes the kitchen's gift for clarifying the tastes of the subcontinent and applying them to upmarket ingredients. Take, for example, the excellent crab salad with puris, and rich curry of wagyu beef. Owner Basil Daniell is an engaging host, keen to lead inexpert diners through the best the restaurant has to offer.

Phamish

354 Liverpool Street, at Boundary Street, Darlinghurst (9357 2688). CityRail Kings Cross. **Open** 6-10pm Mon, Wed-Sun. **Main courses** $12.50-$19.50. **BYO. Credit** AmEx, DC, MC, V. **Map** p330 J8 ⓭ Vietnamese

Part of the movement to upgrade Vietnamese cuisine, Phamish takes lots of southern Vietnamese standards and places them in the context of a very buzzy, shiny, Darlinghurst no-bookings BYO. The food won't always knock your socks off (though the crunchy take on the rice-paper roll is intriguing, and the chilli-tamarind prawns are fun), but it's never bad and the price is right for groups.

Rise

23 Craigend Street, at Royston Street, Darlinghurst (9357 1755/www.riserestaurant.com.au). CityRail Kings Cross. **Open** 6-10pm Tue-Sun. **Main courses** $20-$35. **Licensed. Credit** AmEx, DC, MC, V. **Map** p330 J8 ⓬ Asian

Soft-shell tacos what? Gai-yang chicken huh? Fasten your seat belt and make sure you've got a firm grip on your chopsticks: Rise's Japanese chefs take the food of their homeland as their departure point and then proceed deftly to interweave international influences at a fierce rate of knots. Midweek dinners can see exceptional value in well-priced tasting menus.

European

Onde

346 Liverpool Street, between Womerah Avenue & Victoria Street, Darlinghurst (9331 8749). CityRail Kings Cross. **Open** 5.30-11pm Mon-Thur; 5.30-11.30pm Fri, Sat; 5.30-10pm Sun. **Main courses** $18.50-$26. **Licensed. Credit** AmEx, DC, MC, V. **Map** p330 J8 ⓭ French

Not so much a restaurant as the part-time dining room of half of swinging Darlinghurst, Onde is unpretentious, buzzy, well-priced and friendly – in short, the epitome of the good neighbourhood restaurant. It's duck confit and terrine territory: the steak frites with red wine butter and a sassy red will cure whatever may ail you.

Pello

71-73 Stanley Street, between Riley & Crown Streets, East Sydney (9360 4640). CityRail Museum. **Open** noon-3pm, 6-10pm Mon-Fri; 6-10pm Sat. **Main courses** $25-$34. **Licensed/BYO** (Mon-Thur only). **Credit** AmEx, DC, MC, V. **Map** p329 G7 ⓭ Modern European

In the sea of Stanley Street's red-sauce merchants, Pello stands out as a beacon of non-Italian goodness. The look is sharp and the pace is fast, but there are enough smiles from the staff and so much to engage you on chef Thomas Johns' menu that it never feels cold. A bowl of Pello's feisty chilli crab linguine is perfect for lunch.

Pizza Mario

248 Palmer Street, between Liverpool & Burton Streets, East Sydney (9332 3633). Bus 389. **Open** 6-10pm Mon-Fri, Sun; noon-2pm, 6-10pm Sat. **Main courses** $12-$23. **Licensed. Credit** AmEx, MC, V. **Map** p329 G8 ⓭ Pizza

In a setting as swish as the Republic apartment complex, we can only interpret the chequered tablecloths as a stab at irony. Happily, no one is trying to be clever when it comes to the pizza: it's thin, crisp, wood-fired and, if you order the DOC version (you should), comes topped simply with tomato and buffalo mozzarella.

Ristorante Riva

379 Liverpool Street, at Darlinghurst Road, Darlinghurst (9380 5318). CityRail Kings Cross. **Open** 6.30-10.30pm Mon-Fri; 12.30-3pm, 6.30-10.30pm Sat. **Main courses** $34-$38. **Licensed. Credit** AmEx, DC, MC, V. **Map** p330 H8 ⓭ Italian

Beverly Wood is the very model of everything you want from floor staff, not least of all in the way she can guide you through the clipped, elegant menu her husband, Eugenio Riva, crafts for the narrow room of doctors, bon viveurs and other regulars. Riva reinterprets classic northern Italian cucina for the inner-city set, making for food that is at once seductive and full of integrity. The braised oxtail will have you sucking the bones and calling for a nice big barolo.

Surry Hills

Asian

Billy Kwong

355 Crown Street, between Albion & Foveaux Streets, Surry Hills (9332 3300). CityRail/LightRail Central then 10mins walk/bus 301, 302, 303. **Open** 6pm-late daily. **Main courses** $18-$39. **Licensed/BYO** (wine only). **Credit** AmEx, MC, V. **Map** p329 G9 ⓭ Modern Chinese

It's loud, you can't book, you eat elbow-to-chopstick with other diners on three-legged stools – and it's utterly fabulous. Kylie Kwong takes the food of her Cantonese ancestry and sexes it up, keeping the emphasis on freshness, flavour and lightness. Stir-fries rock, the kingfish sashimi sings with sweet freshness and the crisp duck with blood plums has a well-deserved following.

Longrain

Corner of Commonwealth & Hunt Streets, Surry Hills (9280 2888/www.longrain.com.au). CityRail Central or Museum/LightRail Central. **Open** noon-2.30pm, 6-10.30pm Mon-Fri; 6-10.30pm

Sat. **Main courses** $18.50-$41.50. **Licensed**. **Credit** AmEx, DC, MC, V. **Map** p329 F8 Thai

The restaurant's hip and gorgeous and so's the crowd along its communal tables. Think the food's going to have less depth and integrity than your waiter's lip-gloss? Think again. Witness big, mostly Thai flavours dressed up for a big night out. Caramel pork hock with chilli vinegar is curry gone glam, the betel leaves with prawn, peanuts and pomelo are frequently imitated but seldom bested, and the salt-and-pepper squid is the finest in town. The bar is a must-visit too (*see p180*).

Maya Da Dhaba

431 Cleveland Street, between Baptist & Bourke Streets, Surry Hills (8399 3785/www.mayamasala. com.au). Bus 301, 302, 303. **Open** 11am-3pm, 5.30-10.30pm daily. **Main courses** $8.90-$15.90. **BYO**. **Credit** DC, MC, V. **Map** p329 G11 South Indian

Spawn of the city's increasingly common Maya Indian sweet shops (gulab jamin, anyone?), but where the other Maya outlets typically only augment their dessert sales with the odd masala dosai and other vego-only snackage, Dhaba has a full – and very attractive – menu of meaty delights from the subcontinent's south.

Red Lantern

545 Crown Street, between Lansdowne & Cleveland Streets, Surry Hills (9698 4355/www.redlantern. com.au). Bus 301, 302, 303. **Open** 12.30pm-3pm, 6.30-10.30pm Tue-Fri; 6.30-10.30pm Sat, Sun. **Main courses** $15-$20. **Licensed**. **Credit** AmEx, DC, MC, V. **Map** p329 G11 Vietnamese

The chef might be a white guy, but the combination of his skills and the knowledge and experience of the restaurant's young Vietnamese owners raise Red Lantern above most other purveyors of the cuisine, while the funked-up look and democratic prices give it an uncommon edge.

Sagar

423 Cleveland Street, between Crown & Bourke Streets, Surry Hills (9319 2170). Bus 301, 302, 303, 372, 393, 395. **Open** noon-10.30pm Tue-Sun. **Main courses** $11.50-$14.50. **BYO**. **Credit** AmEx, DC, MC, V. **Map** p329 G11 South Indian

It's pretty nondescript, yes, but what this narrow little room lacks in airs and graces it makes up for in chicken biriani. That and scores of other daily Indian specials keep things fresh at Sagar – one day sees a range of meat thalis, another a wealth of vegetarian dosai. The uniting factor in all this? Every special represents a total bargain.

Spice I Am

90 Wentworth Avenue, between Campbell & Commonwealth Streets, Surry Hills (9280 0928). CityRail Central or Museum/LightRail Central. **Open** noon-2.30pm, 6-10pm Tue-Sun. **Main courses** $10.90-$25.90. **Licensed**. **Credit** AmEx, DC, MC, V. **Map** p329 F8 Thai

Spice they certainly are: this unremarkable-looking bolt-hole on (appropriately enough) a fume- and backpacker-loaded street serves the most authentic Thai food in Sydney. If you want to dice with some serious chilli, just ask your waitress to take down your order in Thai. That way the kitchen will do your green mango salad, your mussel and chilli pancakes and sour curries without concession to local tastes. Be warned – food this good is addictive, and so is the value: witness the ever-present queue of would-be diners waiting for a table. **Photo** *p157*.

Uchi Lounge

15 Brisbane Street, between Goulburn & Oxford Streets, Surry Hills (9261 3524). CityRail Museum. **Open** 6.30-11pm Mon-Sat. **Main courses** $13.50-$16.50. **Licensed/BYO** (wine only). **Credit** MC, V. **Map** p329 G8 Japanese

Wharf.
See p149.

Chefs supreme

The Australian celebrity chef scene was born in Sydney, and even now, in foodie circles, names such as Neil, Tets, Armando and Bill are dropped sans surname as readily as others might speak of Russell and Nicole. Here's a quick primer of who's who.

Mark Best

The dark horse of the Sydney restaurant scene, Best (*photo below*) chucked in his career as an electrician to become a chef, worked in Europe at the likes of L'Arpege in

Paris and came back to open **Marque** (*see below*), a restaurant whose French tagline is becoming increasingly outmoded in the face of his intelligent exploration of flavour. He won the *Sydney Morning Herald Good Food Guide*'s best chef gong in 2006.

Guillaume Brahimi

With the 1980s' brightest French light, Joel Robuchon, as his mentor, Guillaume (that's 'gee-YOM') Brahimi already had a bit of an edge. Now that he's settled into **Guillaume at Bennelong** (*see p147*) in one of the sails of the Opera House, you could say his advantages over other chefs border on the unfair. Luckily for us.

Peter and Greg Doyle

Both passionate surfers and veterans of Sydney's top-end dining scene. Greg is the seafood expert nonpareil at **Pier** (*see p160*), while Peter is chef at **est.** (*see p147*), with the lightest hand in any Australian kitchen. No relation to the Doyles of Watson Bay.

Peter Gilmore

Gilmore streaked on to Sydney's three-star scene in the new millennium, becoming an overnight success at **Quay** (*see p147*) after a decade of hard slog. The master of textural interplay, he's also one of the finest dessert chefs you'll encounter anywhere.

Despite the fact that they're so hip they can barely see over their pelvises, the aggressively fashion-forward folk at this well-hidden restaurant are a surprisingly nice bunch of kids. The other surprise is how little they charge for their extremely stylish and palatable mod Japanese eats, such as the outstanding agedashi tofu. Drinks in the bar downstairs will open your eyes – and your palate – to the idea of saké as the party drink of the future.

European

Alio

3-5 Baptist Street, at Cleveland Street, Surry Hills (8394 9368/www.alio.com.au). Bus 372, 393, 395. **Open** 6-10.30pm Mon-Sat. **Main courses** $26-$32. **Licensed/BYO** (Mon-Thur only). **Credit** AmEx, DC, MC, V. **Map** p329 G11 ❸❹ Italian
You've gotta hand it to them, this gang of young chefs and restaurateurs are really making a fist of this nifty little Surry Hills eaterie. A good cut above the trattoria level, Alio nonetheless offers good value for its Italy-via-the-the-River-Café eats. Their bollito

misto, for example, finds few competitors in Australia. And they're mates with Jamie Oliver (that's a good thing, right?).

Café Mint

579 Crown Street, between Devonshire & Cleveland Streets, Surry Hills (9319 0848/www.cafemint. com.au). CityRail/LightRail Central then 10mins walk/bus 301, 302, 303. **Open** 7am-5pm Mon, Sat; 7am-9.30pm Tue, Wed; 7am-10.30pm Thur, Fri. **Main courses** $26-$32. **BYO. No credit cards.** **Map** p329 G11 ❸❺ Mediterranean
The modern takes on Mediterranean food that have been the talk of Melbourne for some years have yet to make real waves in Sydney, but there are a few noteworthy incursions – one of the best being this cool yet inexpensive caff-cum-restaurant down the uncool end of Crown Street. The food's great and the almond and grapefruit frappé is an exceptional hangover-buster. It's a tiny space, note.

La Sala

23 Foster Street, between Hunt & Campbell Streets, Surry Hills (9281 3352/www.lasala.com.au). CityRail Central or Museum/LightRail Central.

Bill Granger

From humble beginnings and an aesthetic born out of his café **bills** (*see p169*) initially not having enough refrigeration to do anything except cook produce quickly and simply, Granger is now the face of sunny Australian café fare worldwide.

Kylie Kwong

After training in Neil Perry's restaurants, this mistress of both eastern and and western flavours opened **Billy Kwong** (*see p152*), published successful books, made a fist of TV and is now a brand unto herself, the Australian-born Chinese Nigella.

Matt Moran

Son of a sheep farmer, Moran has many more strings to his bow than cooking lamb. From bistro chef to culinary superstar, his rise has brought much press attention and a keen following for his restaurant **Aria** (*see p145*).

Armando Percuoco

A mercurial Neapolitan, the local CEO of chefs and chef to CEOs, has fans and passion in number. Don't miss the truffled egg fettuccine at **Buon Ricordo** (*see p158*).

Neil Perry

The ponytailed champion of Mod Oz fine dining, Perry (*photo right*) is a master of seafood, Asian flavours and is never far from cameras and glossy pages. **Rockpool** (*see p147*) is his temple to style.

Tetsuya Wakuda

Softly spoken, highly talented Tets got his start 20 years ago washing dishes before someone assumed that, being Japanese, he could make sushi. Flash-forward to **Tetsuya's** (*see p147*), and he's chummy with such star chefs as Alain Ducasse and Thomas Keller, and the equal of Nobu Matsuhisa.

Open 6-11pm Mon-Wed, Sat; noon-3pm, 6-11pm Thur, Fri. **Main courses** $27-$35. **Licensed**. **Credit** AmEx, DC, MC, V. **Map** p329 F8 **56** Italian

Darren Simpson is an Irishman who cut his teeth at the River Café in London; Andrea Mellas is a Melbourne Greek famed in Sydney for opening Otto (*see p157*) and Icebergs Dining Room & Bar (*see p159*). Now the two of them run the sexiest Italian proposition in the inner city. Dress for success and order like the bill doesn't matter. **Photo** *p163*.

Lo Studio

53-55 Brisbane Street, at Commonwealth Street, Surry Hills (9212 4818/www.lostudio.com.au). CityRail Central or Museum/LightRail Central. **Open** noon-3pm, 6pm-late Mon-Fri; 6pm-late Sat. **Main courses** $34-$37. **Licensed**. **Credit** AmEx, DC, MC, V. **Map** p329 F8 **57** Italian

And Lo, it was good: the old Paramount Studios building is a fittingly deco home for this paean to chic 1950s Italy. Think *The Talented Mr Ripley*, only with better food and cocktails (the Corleone with fresh nectarine is an offer you can't refuse).

Marque

355 Crown Street, between Albion & Foveaux Streets, Surry Hills (9332 2225). CityRail/LightRail Central then 10mins walk/bus 301, 303, 310. **Open** 6.30-10.30pm Mon-Sat. **Main courses** $39-$47. **Licensed/BYO**. **Credit** AmEx, DC, MC, V. **Map** p329 G9 **58** French

Chef Mark Best trained with France's finest and has one eye on the pioneering work done by Spain's gastro-wizards, yet the food at his quietly luxe restaurant manages to be at once at the bleeding edge and utterly his own. Beetroot tarte (almost a tatin) with horseradish foam sits cheek by jowl with sweetbreads paired with sea urchin roe and samphire on one of the country's most exciting menus. And the outstanding – and out-there – wine list rolls with every punch.

Restaurant Assiette

48 Albion Street, at Mary Street, Surry Hills (9212 7979/www.assiette.com.au). CityRail/LightRail Central. **Open** 6.30-10.30pm Tue-Sat. **Main courses** $29. **Licensed**. **Credit** AmEx, DC, MC, V. **Map** p329 F9 **59** French

Assiette presents highly polished, lively and intelligently constructed dishes – the pan-fried barramundi with bacon lardons, smoked eel and matelote sauce and parsnip purée is da bomb – in convivial, if basic, surroundings for under $30 a main. Sensational value.

Tabou

527 Crown Street, between Devonshire & Lansdowne Streets, Surry Hills (9319 5682). Bus 301, 302, 303. **Open** noon-2.30pm, 6.30-10pm Mon-Fri; 6-10.30pm Sat, Sun. **Main courses** $26-$35. **Licensed/BYO** (Mon-Thur, Sun only). **Credit** AmEx, DC, MC, V. **Map** p329 G11 **60** French

Lots of bistros in Sydney forget that a bistro, almost by definition, needs to be a boisterous affair. Thankfully, Tabou has that requirement in hand, with dishes that almost undercut their elegance with their gutsiness. The upstairs bar, incidentally, is one of the best-kept secrets on Crown Street.

Vini

118 Devonshire Street, entrance on Holt Street, Surry Hills (9698 5131). CityRail/LightRail Central. **Open** noon-midnight Tue-Fri; 4pm-midnight Sat. **Main courses** $22-$27. **Licensed**. **Credit** AmEx, DC, MC, V. **Map** p329 F10 **61** Italian

A tiny restaurant with a whole lotta style, Vini plays off the brevity of its excellent Italian menu – two starters, two mains, two desserts and some snacks – with the richness and variety of its blackboard of Italian wines. The value on both counts is bang-on.

Other

Erciyes

409 Cleveland Street, between Crown & Bourke Streets, Surry Hills (9319 1309). Bus 301, 302, 303, 372, 393, 395. **Open** 11am-midnight daily. **Main courses** $14.90-$20. **Licensed/BYO.** **Credit** AmEx, MC, V. **Map** p329 G11 **62** Turkish

'Err-chee-ehs'. It's really not that hard, but it seems to elude most non-Turkish speakers for some reason. But no one seems to have a problem wrapping their tongue around the spicy sausage-topped Turkish pizzas, the cabbage rolls or smoky kebabs. Hit the dips and breads hard and don't leave without a Turkish coffee. Saturdays see the ante upped by, uh-huh, belly dancers.

Kings Cross, Potts Point & Woolloomooloo

Asian

Aki's

1 Woolloomooloo Wharf, Cowper Wharf Road, opposite Forbes Street, Woolloomooloo (9332 4600/ www.akisindian.com.au). Bus 311. **Open** noon-3pm, 6-10pm Mon-Fri, Sun; 6-10pm Sat. **Main courses** $18.80-$28.80. **Licensed. Credit** AmEx, DC, MC, V. **Map** p330 H6 **63** Indian

Sydney's Indian dining scene doesn't have the sophistication of London, let alone the old country. But it does have Sydney Harbour, as seen from Aki's – and that's got to count for something. Enjoy artfully presented (mostly Southern) Indian food while the water laps at the edge of Woolloomooloo Wharf.

jimmy liks

186-188 Victoria Street, between Darlinghurst Road & Orwell Street, Potts Point (8354 1400/ www.jimmyliks.com.au). CityRail Kings Cross. **Open** 5pm-midnight daily. **Main courses** $22-$35. **Licensed. Credit** AmEx, DC, MC, V. **Map** p330 J7 **64** South-east Asian

So much like its Surry Hills big bro Longrain (*see p152*) that its nickname is Shortgrain, jimmy liks has copped some flak in the past for not treating its customers particularly well. And in terms of service, it's a fair cop. But don't let that keep you from sampling the good cocktails, nor, for that matter, the full-flavoured takes on the street food of South-east Asia. The hang lae curry of lamb shank with peanuts and pickled garlic is a killer, while the pad thai with scallops and garlic chives brings new glamour to an old takeaway favourite. *See also p181.*

European

Fratelli Paradiso

12-16 Challis Avenue, at Victoria Street, Potts Point (9357 1744). CityRail Kings Cross. **Open** 7am-11pm Mon-Fri; 7am-5pm Sat, Sun. **Main courses** under $30. **Licensed. Credit** AmEx, DC, MC, V. **Map** p330 J6 **65** Italian

Gotta love that wallpaper: a pattern of big sexy lips sucking down some spaghetti strands. Expect to see a similar scene on the faces of your fellow diners – there's plenty in the way both of sexy pouts and good pasta in this dim, stylish diner. Calamari San Andrea is a favourite, and the scrambled eggs with sausage and farro braise accounts for the breakfast faithful. If you're feeling less than flush, the adjoining bakery knocks out very decent Italian pastries and savouries.

Manta

Woolloomooloo Wharf, 6 Cowper Wharf Road, opposite Forbes Street, Woolloomooloo (9332 3822/www.mantarestaurant.com.au). Bus 311. **Open** noon-3pm, 6-10pm daily. **Main courses** $29-$42. **Licensed. Credit** AmEx, DC, MC, V. **Map** p330 H5 **66** Italian

The name change – it used to be Manta Ray – reflects the new influence of celeb chef Stefano Manfredi. Seafood is still the focus, but it's now refracted through Manfredi's upmarket Italian sensibility. The buttered linguine with yabbies and sesame seeds is superb, the live seafood excellent and the wine list and service commendable.

Nove

9 Woolloomooloo Wharf, Cowper Bay Road, opposite Forbes Street, Woolloomooloo (9368 7599). Bus 311.

Tingle your taste buds at budget Thai diner **Spice I Am**. *See p153.*

Open noon-midnight Tue-Sat; noon-11pm Sun.
Main courses $16-$25. **Licensed**. **Credit** AmEx,
DC, MC, V. **Map** p330 H5 ⑰ Pizza
Buzz, buzz, buzz. What's that? Oh, it's a scene. Look
one way and you'll see celebs and water views. Turn
your head to the other for an eyeful of today's pizza
(square-cut, Roman-style) and a blackboard full of
clipped, thoughtful Italian treats. And it's not a bad
spot for just a mid-afternoon Peroni or Aranciata
Rosso. Located on Woolloomooloo Wharf, next to
Otto and various other flash eateries.

Otto

8 Woolloomooloo Wharf, Cowper Wharf Road,
opposite Forbes Street, Woolloomooloo (9368 7488/
www.otto.net.au). Bus 311. **Open** noon-3pm,
6pm-late daily. **Main courses** $32-$38. **Licensed**.
Credit AmEx, DC, MC, V. **Map** p330 H5 ⑱
Italian
Don't ask to speak to Otto – it's Italian for 'eight',
the address of this celeb-magnet. If you can fight
your way through the air-kissing and attract the
attention of the charming but wildly inconsistent
waiters, you might be in for some outstanding cucina
moderna. Or you might not – it's that sort of place.
But you'll have fun either way.

Modern Australian

Bayswater Brasserie

32 Bayswater Road, at Ward Avenue, Kings Cross
(9357 2177/www.bayswaterbrasserie.com.au).
CityRail Kings Cross. **Open** 5pm-late Mon-Fri;

3-10pm Sun. **Main courses** $25-$33. **Licensed**.
Credit AmEx, DC, MC, V. **Map** p330 J7 ⑲
An air of cultured hedonism lingers at this exceedingly pleasant landmark. Enjoy great oysters and
other French brasserie classics in the front and cocktails and luxe bar snacks – foie gras on toast, say –
in the hopping bar (*see p181*) out the back.

Lotus

22 Challis Avenue, at Mcleay Street, Potts Point
(9326 9000/www.merivale.com). CityRail Kings Cross.
Open 6pm-late Tue-Sat. **Main courses** $29.
Licensed. Credit AmEx, DC, MC, V. **Map** p330 J6 ⑳
For the perfect definition of what inner-urban dining
should be about in today's Australia, doll yourself
up and grab a banquette at this unceasingly hip little
bistro. Drinks in the speakeasy-like back bar (*see
p182*) segue neatly into featherlight crisp-fried cour-
gette flowers stuffed with ricotta and green olive,
and from there to barramundi with braised witloof
and broccolini with toasted almonds. Yum.

Yellow Bistro

57-59 Macleay Street, at Mcdonald Street,
Potts Point (9357 3400). CityRail Kings Cross.
Open noon-3pm, 6-10pm Mon-Sun. **Main courses**
$29-$42. **Licensed. Credit** AmEx, DC, MC, V. **Map**
p330 J6 ㉑
George Sinclair is an exemplary bistro chef, while
Lorraine Godsmark is the dessert chef with the
golden whisk. Together, they make beautiful food.
He serves featherlight gnocchi with fresh tomato
and pesto, she makes the legendary date tart and

Eat, Drink, Shop

Seafood with a smile at **Fish Face**.

superb macaroons. Not only can you sample their skills at breakfast, lunch and dinner, you can also take stuff home from Yellow's shop section. Cheap it ain't, but there's excellence here.

Other

Fish Face
132 Darlinghurst Road, between Liverpool & Burton Streets, Kings Cross (9332 4803/www.fishface.com.au). CityRail Kings Cross/bus 389. **Open** 6-11pm Mon-Sat. **Main courses** $24.50-$32.50. **Licensed/BYO. No credit cards.** **Map** p330 H8 ⑰ Seafood
Steve Hodges used to run half the show at Rose Bay's smart Pier restaurant (*see p160*), but now he's taken over this popular fish caff and pushed the menu upmarket without putting the prices out of reach. The sashimi bar is top-notch, while the fish and chips must be tried to be believed; the note suggesting you eat with your fingers is entirely superfluous. There is no other way. **Photo** *above*.

Eastern Suburbs

Asian

Mu Shu
108 Campbell Parade, at Hall Street, Bondi Beach (9130 5400/www.mushu.com.au). CityRail Bondi Junction then bus 380, 381, 382, L82/bus 380, L82.
Open *Restaurant* 6pm-midnight daily. *Yum cha* noon-3pm Thur, Fri; noon-5pm Sat, Sun. **Main courses** $21-$39. **Licensed/BYO. Credit** AmEx, DC, MC, V. **Map** p334 ⑲ Pan-Asian
You know you're in flash territory when male diners return to the table unsure whether they've just relieved themselves in a designer urinal or done something terrible to a water feature. Mu Shu is as big and brash as its Bondi setting, with an ambitious pan-Asian menu. It could all be a bit much, were it not for the shameless love-me attitude that is its saving grace. Don't miss the house-roasted Cantonese-style duck with featherlight pancakes or the fabulously gingery, wok-fried whole snapper.

Wasavie
8 Heeley Street, at Glenmore Road, Paddington (9380 8838). Bus 352, 378, 380, 389, L82. **Open** 6-10pm Tue, Wed; noon-3pm, 6-10pm Thur-Sat. **Main courses** $20-$25. **BYO. Credit** AmEx, DC, MC, V. **Map** p332 K9 ⑭ Japanese
This minimal little local is living proof that good, cheap Japanese food isn't a paradox. You can sear your slices of raw fish on a hot stone for a bit of theatre, abandon yourself to the pleasures of the flesh in the form of the sumptuously sticky braised pork belly with hot mustard, or walk on the wilder side with Japanese-slash-Mod Oz experiments.

European

Bistro Moncur
Woollahra Hotel, corner of Moncur & Queen Streets, Woollahra (9363 2519/www.woollahrahotel.com.au). Bus 378, 380, 389. **Open** 6-10.30pm Mon; noon-3pm, 6-10.30pm Tue-Sat; noon-3pm, 6-9pm Sun. **Main courses** $25-$40. **Licensed. Credit** AmEx, DC, MC, V. **Map** p333 M10 ⑮ French
Bistro Moncur isn't as cheap as its name might suggest, but it is one of the finest examples of a smart-casual restaurant in Sydney that really gets it right, balancing near-boisterous conviviality with food that is as satisfying as it is seductive. Damien Pignolet is the god of (seemingly) simple things done well. Bistro classics such as provençal fish soup with rouille, pork sausages with lyonnaise onions and sirloin steak with Café de Paris butter aren't just near-perfect – they're near-perfect every time. The Woollahra Hotel is also a jazz venue.

Buon Ricordo
108 Boundary Street, at Liverpool Street, Paddington (9360 6729/www.buonricordo.com.au). CityRail Kings Cross/bus 389. **Open** 6.30-10.30pm Tue-Thur; noon-2.30pm, 6.30-10.30pm Fri, Sat. **Main courses** $37.50-$44.50. **Licensed. Credit** AmEx, DC, MC, V. **Map** p330 J8 ⑯ Italian
Armando Percuoco is hospitality on two legs. Watch him: clapping a back here, kissing a hand there, his big sandpaper voice booming one minute, confidential the next. And yet he somehow runs a tight kitchen too, with Buon Ricordo's luxe fare earning it a swag of best-Italian awards over the past decade.

Go all out with the fettuccine al 'tartufovo', a rich explosion of house-made pasta with soft-poached truffled egg, or spare your arteries and delight your palate with the excellent seared beef carpaccio.

Buzo

3 Jersey Road, at Oxford Street, Woollahra (9328 1600/www.buzorestaurant.com). Bus 380, 389. **Open** 6.30pm-late Mon-Sat. **Main courses** $22-$27. **Licensed. Credit** AmEx, DC, MC, V. **Map** p332 L10/11 **77** Italian
The atmosphere of this classy osteria in Woollahra is fostered by the rustic simplicity of the blackboard menu, the relatively modest pricing and the crush of locals who storm the place. Antipasti are a highlight – the salad of celery, white anchovy and parsley, say – as are faves such as the Sicilian roast lamb and the vincisgrassi, which interleaves porcini mushrooms, prosciutto, pasta and truffle oil in a luxurious lasagne.

Claude's

10 Oxford Street, between Queen Street & Jersey Road, Woollahra (9331 2325/www.claudes.org). Bus 378, 380, L82. **Open** 7.30-9.30pm Tue-Sat. **Set menu** $135 3 courses; $165 tasting menu. **Licensed/BYO. Credit** AmEx, DC, MC, V. **Map** p332 L11 **78** French
New chef/owner Chui Lee Luk didn't just buy a landmark of Sydney dining wrapped up in a tiny, quiet, Limoges-china bedecked terrace, she bought the expectations of two generations of diners who come for a rare combination of subtlety and envelope-pushing seen nowhere else. Fortunately for her (and us), Luk is a chef of virtuosic talent and her elegant sensibility is perfectly in pitch with the restaurant's pioneering past and pristine present.

Icebergs Dining Room

1 Notts Avenue, Bondi Beach (9365 9000/ www.idrb.com). CityRail Bondi Junction then bus 380, 381, 382, L82/bus 380, L82. **Open** noon-3pm, 6.30-10.30pm Tue-Sat; noon-3pm, 6.30-9pm Sun. **Main courses** $34-$43. **Licensed. Credit** AmEx, DC, MC, V. **Map** p334 **79** Italian
Bondi Beach-flavoured eye-candy is the order of the day at this roost for the see-and-be-seen crowd. Chef Karen Martini's stripped-back menu is presented in a room bursting with contemporary Italo-Bondi style. What better way to enjoy a strikingly fresh and simple salad of grilled lobster with green peas, fingerling potatoes, tarragon and mayo than with the deep blue at one elbow and a waiter discreetly pouring you a glass of Veuve at the other. The adjoining bar (*see p184*) is fabulous at dusk, and the building also houses the famous Icebergs winter swimming club.

Lucio's

Corner of Windsor & Elizabeth Streets, Paddington (9380 5996/www.lucios.com.au). Bus 380, 382, 389. **Open** 12.30-3pm, 6.30-11pm Mon-Sat. **Main courses** $37.80-$42. **Licensed. Credit** AmEx, DC, MC, V. **Map** p332 L10 **80** Italian

Love art and food? Lucio's – where the myth of the starving artist is exploded – is the answer. The walls are festooned with works by many of the foremost Australian painters of the past 50 years, while the plates adorned with 20 years' worth of modish Italian eats. The chilli crab linguine has acquired local-legend status.

North Bondi Italian Food

118-120 Ramsgate Avenue, at Campbell Parade, North Bondi (9300 4400/www.idrb.com/northbondi). CityRail Bondi Junction then bus 380, 381, 382, L82/bus 380, L82. **Open** 5-10.30pm Mon, Tue; noon-4pm, 6.30-10.30pm Wed-Sat; noon-4pm, 6.30-10pm Sun. **Main courses** $14-$29. **Licensed. Credit** AmEx, DC, MC, V. **Map** p334 **81** Italian
Yes, it can get a bit noisy; no, you can't book and it isn't as cheap as menus printed on disposable paper place mats may suggest. But it is fabulous – fabulously busy, fabulously simple, a fabulously stylish osteria by the beach, with Coopers Pale Ale on tap and tripe with cotechino sausage, borlotti beans and peas in its own tripe section on the menu.

Pompei

Corner of Roscoe & Gould Streets, Bondi Beach (9365 1233). CityRail Bondi Junction then bus 380, 381, 382, L82/bus 380, L82. **Open** 11am-late Tue-Sun. **Main courses** $15.50-$17.90. **Licensed/BYO** (wine only). **Credit** AmEx, MC, V. **Map** p334 **82** Pizza
It's a matter of fierce debate: is the greatest thing about Pompei the creamy, all-natural gelato that comes in a range of drool-worthy flavours – or is it the pizza, Naples-thin and available topped with everything from seasonal delights, like the pizza bianco with fresh artichoke, to the timeless margarita? It's a question best examined in person, as frequently as possible.

Restaurant Balzac

141 Belmore Road, at Avoca Street, Randwick (9399 9660/www.restaurantbalzac.com.au). Bus 372, 3763, 376. **Open** 6-10pm Wed,Thur, Sun; 5.30-10.30pm Fri, Sat. **Main courses** $32. **Licensed/ BYO** (Tue-Thur only). **Credit** AmEx, DC, MC, V. Modern French
Oh, Balzac, how do we love thee? When counting the ways, factor in chef Matt Kemp's genius for combining and transforming cheaper ingredients into culinary gold, the loving service and the low-key refinement of the whole experience, from smart amuse-gueule soups to indulgent cheeses and dessert wines. The attention to detail in dishes such as risotto of beef shin with horseradish and the signature bread and butter pud with pain d'épice ice-cream is unflagging.

Modern Australian

Catalina

Lyne Park, off New South Head Road, Rose Bay (9371 0555/www.catalinarosebay.com.au). Ferry Rose Bay/bus 323, 324, 325. **Open** noon-11pm

Mon-Sat; noon-6pm Sun. **Main courses** $34-$40.
Licensed. Credit AmEx, DC, MC, V.
Arriving by boat has a certain cachet, yes, but to
really nail the sense of occasion nothing beats
pulling up in a seaplane. Catalina is pricey, showy
and not immune to occasional attitude attacks. That
said, the juxtaposition of so-Sydney water views and
superb wine is pretty special, and the food is pretty
slick. There are the offerings of a dedicated sushi
chef, plus the likes of pan-fried barramundi with
morcilla (blood sausage) and chickpeas.

Four in Hand Bistro
Corner of Elizabeth & Sutherland Streets,
Paddington (9362 1999). Bus 352, 378, 380, L82.
Open 6.30-10pm Mon-Thur; noon-2.30pm, 6.30-
10pm Fri, Sat; noon-2.30pm, 6.30-9pm Sun. **Main
courses** $29. **Licensed. Credit** AmEx, DC, MC, V.
Map p332 L9 ③
I SAID IT'S REALLY LOUD IN HERE, ISN'T IT?
That's one of the salient features of this pub dining
room. Another is the enormous painting of a squid
that takes up an entire wall. And another still is the
food: it's really outstanding, and much less expensive than it should be. So there's the trade-off –
divine eats or easy conversation. We'll take the
excellent rabbit and corn terrine with broad beans
and watercress purée, or the pineapple clafoutis with
cinnamon and star anise ice-cream any day. Sign
language has its advantages, right?

Hugo's
70 Campbell Parade, between St Thomas
Mitchell Road & Lamrock Avenue, Bondi Beach
(9300 0900/www.hugos.com.au). CityRail Bondi
Junction then bus 380, 381, 382, L82/bus 380,
L82. **Open** 6.30pm-midnight Mon-Fri; 9am-4pm,
6.30pm-midnight Sat; 9am-4pm Sun. **Main courses**
$30-$39. **Licensed. Credit** AmEx, DC, MC, V.
Map p334 ③
Yes, it's him… and don't look now, but that's her too.
Yep, Hugo's is home to a capital-S scene. But there
is some substance under all that style: subtlety isn't
the kitchen's forte, but a little showiness is to be
expected with a clientele like this. Asian dishes, such
as the Sichuan roasted duck and shiitake omelette
in duck broth, are definitely the way to go. Also
check out sister bar Hugo's Lounge (*see p181*) in
Kings Cross – beneath it is Hugo's Bar Pizza, the
latest addition to the empire.

Sean's Panaroma
270 Campbell Parade, at Ramsgate Avenue,
Bondi Beach (9365 4924/www.seanspanaroma.
com.au). CityRail Bondi Junction then bus 380,
381, 382, L82/bus 380, L82. **Open** 6.30-10pm
Wed-Fri; noon-3pm, 6.30-10pm Sat; noon-3pm Sun.
Main courses $21-$40. **Licensed/BYO. Credit**
MC, V. **Map** p334 ③
Picture an afternoon by the beach whiled away
over a glass of Billecart or three. A man striding
through the small tiled room in a dripping wetsuit
barely causes a stir. But the blackboard-menu special of lightly fried blue swimmer crab with lime

aïoli really sets tongues wagging. Sean's is one of
the most relaxed, charmingly idiosyncratic restaurants in the world. Don't miss it. **Photo** *p161.*

Other

Pier
594 New South Head Road, opposite Cranbrook
Road, Rose Bay (9327 4187/www.pierrestaurant.
com.au). Bus 323, 324, 325. **Open** noon-3pm,
6-10pm Mon-Sat; 6-9pm Sun. **Main courses** $44.
Licensed. Credit AmEx, DC, MC, V. Seafood
Jutting into Rose Bay itself, Pier is so committed to
freshness that diners are submitted to a vaguely
alarming precis of preferred fish-killing techniques
on the menu. Those troubled by phrases like 'brain
spiking' are best served by simply sampling chef
Greg Doyle's work. Witness, for example, the incom-
parable texture of the salmon 'pastrami', beautiful
orangey-pink sheets of barely cured fillet drizzled
with oil and dotted with spice. And don't miss
dessert: the soufflés are things of beauty. The lobby
area is now the 'Tasting Room', where you can perch
on a stool and try tapas-sized samples of Doyle's
work. Not cheap, but very good, and much less
expensive than the restaurant proper.

Inner West

Asian

Bay Tinh
318 Victoria Road, at Marrickville Road, Marrickville
(9560 8673). CityRail Marrickville or Sydenham.
Open 11.30am-2pm, 5.30-10.30pm Mon-Fri, Sun;
4.30-11pm Sat. **Main courses** $9.25-$11.70. **BYO.**
Credit MC, V. Vietnamese
In his former line of work – cooking for the prime
minister of Vietnam – chef Tinh was no doubt
accustomed to serving big groups: a good thing, for
the stunning value for money offered by his stalwart Marrickville restaurant is a magnet for groups,
discerning and otherwise. All order the bonfire
dishes (nothing makes the half-drunk happier than
food that's on fire), all leave full of gullet and relatively fat of wallet.

Dakhni
65 Glebe Point Road, between Francis & Cowper
Streets, Glebe (9660 4887). Bus 431, 432, 433.
Open 5-10.30pm Mon, Sun; noon-2.30pm, 5-10.30pm
Tue-Thur; noon-2.30pm, 5-11.30pm Fri, Sat.
Main courses $15.90-$18.90. **Licensed/BYO.**
Credit AmEx, DC, MC, V. **Map** p328 B9 ③
South Indian
Whether chatting over chaat or here to pay more
attention to the warm spicing of dishes from the
breadth of Tamil South India, diners are drawn to
Dakhni's simple formula of homely food cooked with
skill and served with care. Order the dosai – and the
crunchy, yoghurty fun of the bel chaat, of course –
and explore at will.

Sean's Panaroma. *See p160.*

restaurant a hit, but lucky diners occasionally have the pleasure of witnessing Wong tickling the ivories of the centrepiece grand piano.

European

Grappa
267-277 Norton Street, at City West Link, Leichhardt (9560 6090/www.grappa.com.au). Bus 445, 446. **Open** 6-10pm Mon; noon-3pm, 6-10pm Tue-Thur; noon-3pm, 6-11pm Fri; 6-11pm Sat; noon-3pm, 6-9.30pm Sun. **Main courses** $31-$48. **Licensed/BYO** (wine only). **Credit** AmEx, DC, MC, V. Italian

From toddlers sucking on strands of linguine with chilli and roasted tomato to couples exchanging looks over slices of pizza to tables of old whipper-snappers hoeing into the whole salt-baked snapper, punters of all ages and stripes find something to tempt on this barn-like restaurant's menu.

Il Piave
639 Darling Street, between Merton Street & Victoria Road, Rozelle (9810 6204). Bus 433, 434, 442, 445. **Open** 6-10pm Tue-Sat; noon-4pm Sun. **Main courses** $6-$34. **Licensed/BYO**. **Credit** AmEx, DC, MC, V. Italian

We think it might be Italian for 'clean lines and good service'. Or perhaps 'unpretentious food, full of life and good enough to eat every day'. Brush up on your Italian-language skills while grazing on the better-than-necessary bread and olives, then swoon over the fat scampi with radicchio and fennel, but be sure to leave some of the swooning and hand-waving for the outstanding desserts.

Peasant's Feast
121A King Street, between Missenden Road & Elizabeth Street, Newtown (9516 5998/ www.peasantsfeast.au). CityRail Newtown. **Open** 6-10pm Tue-Sat. **BYO**. **Credit** AmEx, V. **Map** p334 ☞ Pan-European

King Street's dining scene is a bit of a sham: restaurants, restaurants everywhere, but nothing good to eat. So dining at the Feast comes as that much more pleasant a surprise. Organic produce is brought to the fore, but flavour and presentation haven't become casualties to the kitchen's ideals. Check out gnocchi with a ragout of aubergine and mushrooms, or the 100% organic cassoulet. Good prices too.

Perama
88 Audley Street, between New Canterbury Road & Trafalgar Street, Petersham (9569 7534/ www.perama.com.au). CityRail Petersham. **Open** 6-10.30pm Tue-Sat; 11.30am-2.30pm Sun. **Main courses** $23.50-$27; banquet $45. **Licensed/BYO** (wine only). **Credit** MC, V. Greek

The whitewash and retsina are in place, yes, but there's something unusual about this Greek restaurant. That's right, it's the food: from Greek favourites such as falling-off-the-bone lamb or rabbit pie to adventures in food history like the Byzantine (in the original sense) specials – imagine honey-peppered

Faheem's Fast Food
196 Enmore Road, between Metropolitan & Edgware Roads, Enmore (9550 4850). CityRail Newtown. **Open** 5pm-midnight daily. **Main courses** $6-$15. **Unlicensed**. **No credit cards**. Indian/Pakistani

Faheem may be the man, but we reckon it's haleem who's responsible for all the repeat business. In a menu of brilliant halal and vegetarian subcontinental cheap treats, haleem – a Pakistani curry of four different kinds of lentils and boneless beef cooked to seriously flavoursome mush – still stands out. How many dishes earn a subtitle, much less one as high-falutin' as 'the king of curries'? Super cheap and open until midnight too.

WildEast Dreams
102 Norton Street, between Marion Street & Parramatta Road, Leichhardt (9560 4131/ www.wildeastdreams.com). Bus 436, 437, 438, 440, 445, 470, L38. **Open** 6-10pm Tue-Fri; noon-3pm, 6-10pm Sat, Sun. **Main courses** $13-$28. **Licensed**. **Credit** AmEx, DC, MC, V. South-east Asian

Irritating, early '90s name, it's true. But it is kinda fitting, considering the nerve it took owner Albert Wong to open a glam South-east Asian restaurant in this most Italian of neighbourhoods. He's also pulled off that rarest of tricks: the ginger soup with black sesame dumplings actually constitutes an Asian dessert worth ordering. Not only is the

Eat, Drink, Shop

figs – it's really interesting, and really good. Super-warm service, as well as superb baklava ice-cream, seal the deal.

Restaurant Atelier
22 Glebe Point Road, between Parramatta Road & Francis Street, Glebe (9566 2112/www.restaurant atelier.com.au). Bus 431, 432, 433. **Open** 6pm-late Tue-Sat. **Main courses** $28-$30. **Licensed/BYO** (wine only). **Credit** MC, V. **Map** p328 B/C10 ⑱
Modern European
Glebe Point Road has a knack for killing off restaurants that try to reach for the stars, so let's hope the curse passes the door of this modest-looking house. Darren Templeman cut his teeth in the Michelin-starred restaurants of the UK, and his command of technique is clear in everything from Berkshire pork rillettes with pickles to a 'lasagne' of blue swimmer crab, shellfish oil, basil and olives.

Restaurant at Three Weeds
197 Evans Street, at Belmore Road, Rozelle (9818 2788). Bus 433, 434, 442, 445. **Open** 6.30-10pm Tue-Sat; noon-2pm Fri. **Main courses** $29. **Licensed. Credit** AmEx, MC, V.
Modern European
Darrell Felstead could no doubt keep the well-heeled clientele who flock to this now chic pub dining room happy with the dazzling ways he learned with meat at city steakhouse-to-the-stars Prime (*see p149*). But to his great credit, he prefers to present a tight menu of Modern Euro inspiration, marrying smart sauces with deftly executed terrines, carpaccios, finely turned-out ravioli and tartes tatin. Good wine too.

Three Clicks West
127 Booth Street, between Johnston & Annandale Streets, Annandale (9660 6652/www.threeclicks west.com.au). Bus 370, 470. **Open** 6.30-10.30pm Mon-Sat. **Main courses** $26-$28. **Licensed/ BYO** (Mon-Wed only). **Credit** AmEx, MC, V.
Modern European
That's three clicks from the city's centre – not that you can tell from such an urbane menu: quail, boned and stuffed with chorizo, then pot-roasted in an onion stock, effortlessly walks the tightrope between hearty and chic. Service and pricing definitely hint at the suburban location, but in a good way, being warmer and more reasonable, respectively, than what you'd expect in their eastern counterparts.

Modern Australian

Oscillate Wildly
275 Australia Street, between King Street & Hoffman Lane, Newtown (9517 4700). CityRail Newtown. **Open** 6-10pm Tue-Sat. **Main courses** $23. **BYO. Credit** AmEx, MC, V. **Map** p334 ⑲
It's not every day you run across a restaurant named after a Smiths track, but it almost makes sense in Newtown. The restaurant doesn't share Morrissey's devotion to vegetarianism, though, as the pork belly and duck confit on white bean purée or the fish pie

attest. Tiny and pitched at a bargain price, it's not the most formal and refined of dining experiences, but there's plenty of heart.

Other

Boathouse on Blackwattle Bay
Blackwattle Bay end of Ferry Road, Glebe (9518 9011/www.boathouse.net.au). Bus 431, 432, 433, 434, 370. **Open** noon-3pm, 6.30-10.30pm Tue-Sun. **Main courses** $39-$43. **Licensed. Credit** AmEx, DC, MC, V. **Map** p328 B7 ⑳ Seafood
It's all about the oysters. Order lots of them – there are typically at least six kinds – and lash out on some quality bubbles. Now marvel at the oysters' freshness, their diverse tastes and textures, how well they go with brown bread and champagne – and at the unique glory of this most relaxing of top-tier Sydney restaurants. Crab, flown in fresh from the Northern Territory, gets minimal mucking about, cracked and tossed in a wok just long enough and with just enough salt, pepper and spring onion to bring out the meat's clean sweetness.

Emma's on Liberty
Corner of Liberty & Gladstone Streets, Enmore (9550 3458). CityRail Newtown. **Open** 6-10pm Tue-Sat. **Main courses** $9-$14; banquet $32. **BYO. No credit cards.** Lebanese
It's an even bet to say which aspect of Emma's is most memorable: the noise or the value. Smarter pundits have suggested that the two may in fact be related – the great value of the Lebanese treats contributing to diners' sense of conviviality, spurring them to greater feats of volubility, not to mention volume. The dips are a near-religious experience, and the *mjadra* (lentil stew) has enough caramelised onion to do any Lebanese mum proud.

Fifi's
158 Enmore Road, between Metropolitan & Simmons Roads, Enmore (9550 4665). CityRail Newtown. **Open** 5.30pm-late Tue-Sun. **Main courses** $10-$25. **Licensed/BYO** (wine only). **Credit** AmEx, DC, MC, V. Lebanese
It was sad to learn that Fifi's, so beloved of local couples and groups, had to discontinue its breakfast service. However, much as we miss the mind-altering coffee and the oh-so-refreshing slices of watermelon with halloumi, there's solace to be found in well-rendered classics in the cabbage roll, kebab and legume salad vein.

Iku Wholefood Kitchen
25A Glebe Point Road, between Parramatta Road & Francis Street, Glebe (9692 8720). Bus 370, 431, 432, 433, 434. **Open** 11.30am-9pm Mon-Fri; 11am-8pm Sat; noon-7.30pm Sun. **Main courses** $7-$9. **BYO. No credit cards. Map** p328 C10 ㉚
Vegan
Vegetarians, vegans, macro-eaters and diet-conscious individuals flock to Iku's sharp-looking establishments in search of nourishment that is

Eat, Drink, Shop

Stylish Italian **La Sala**. *See p154.*

entirely vegetable in origin. Pleasing tastes and textures don't always rule the day, but specialities such as the lime leaf curry laksa and the rice balls have dedicated followings.
Other locations: 62 Oxford Street, Darlinghurst (9380 9780); 168 Military Road, Neutral Bay (9953 1964); 279 Bronte Road, Waverley (9369 5022); 612A Darling Street, Rozelle (9810 5155).

North Shore

Asian

Kam Fook Chatswood

Level 6, Westfield Chatswood, Help Street, Chatswood (9413 9388). CityRail Chatswood. **Open** 10am-11pm daily. **Main courses** $5.80-$24.80. **Licensed/BYO. Credit** DC, MC, V. Cantonese
Despite being only marginally smaller than a middling football stadium, the Kam Fook manages to offer personalised service that is so condescending to *gwailos* that you'll be tempted to salute their efficiency. Argue, instead, with your waiter, that you'd like to see the real specials list, and stand firm until they acquiesce and bring you some of the most authentic Cantonese food in the land.

Mino

521 Military Road, between Gurrigal & Harbour Streets, Mosman (9960 3351). Bus 143, 144, 151, 228, 230, 243, 246, 247, 257, 289. **Open** 6-10pm Tue-Sun. **Main courses** $14-$55. **Licensed/BYO** (wine only). **Credit** AmEx, MC, V. Japanese
Military Road's many Japanese eateries range from very ordinary mass-market sushi joints to the well-hidden charms of this little restaurant. Not much to look at from the outside, Mino is quite nice once you're through the door – and though the à la carte options are wide-ranging, regulars all seem happy to put their faith in the chef's *kaiseki* menu.

Nilgiri's

81-83 Christie Street, between Pacific Highway & Oxley Street, St Leonards (9966 0636/www.nilgiris. com.au). CityRail St Leonards. **Open** noon-3pm, 6-10pm daily. **Main courses** $14-$26. **Licensed/ BYO** (wine only). **Credit** AmEx, MC, V. Pan-Indian
Okra and goat, potatoes and dosai – Nilgiri's takes dishes from all over India and imbues them with the its trademark refinement and elegance of spicing. The owners' commitment to educating Sydneysiders in the best that Indian dining has to offer is to be heartily commended.

Sea Treasure

46 Willoughby Road, at Falcon Street, Crows Nest (9906 6388). Bus 257, 273, 288, 289, 290, 291, 292. **Open** 11am-3pm, 5.30-11pm Mon-Fri; 10am-3pm, 5.30-11pm Sat, Sun. **Main courses** $18.80-$33.80. **Licensed/BYO. Credit** AmEx, DC, MC, V. Chinese
Those tanks aren't there for show: seafood – surprise, surprise – is the Treasure's area of expertise. Fat Pacific oysters come steamed on the shell with XO sauce, flounder gets the salt-and-pepper treatment, while steamed Murray cod is doused in ginger and shallot. Wok that booty. And the yum cha is among the best you're likely to find in the country.

Ying's

270 Willoughby Road, between Bruce & Shirley Roads, Crows Nest (9966 9182). Bus 257, 273, 288, 289, 290, 291, 292. **Open** 11am-3pm, 6-11pm daily. **Main courses** $18.80-$33.80 **Licensed/BYO. Credit** AmEx, DC, MC, V. Cantonese
Ying's owes much of its success to owner Ying Tam's unerring sense of hospitality and willingness to concede that great Cantonese food needn't be served by tight-lipped automatons in garish, run-down barns. The seafood banquet demonstrates the menu's highlights, including the pipis in Chiu Chow-style broth laden with Asian celery, and what appear to be the world's largest and most succulent salt-and-pepper prawns.

European

Alchemy 731

731 Military Road, between Gouldsbury Street & Belmore Road, Mosman (9968 3731). Bus 143, 144, 151, 228, 230, 243, 246, 247, 257, 289.

Eat, Drink, Shop

Beautifully crafted Mod Euro treats at **Alchemy 731** in Mosman. *See p163.*

Open 6-10pm Tue, Wed; noon-2pm, 6-10pm Thur-Sat. **Main courses** $28. **Licensed. Credit** AmEx, DC, MC, V. Modern European
What it loses in points for the name, the kitchen makes up for by over-delivering on everything from the delicacy of seared scallops with ocean trout brandade and vanilla orange oil to the intensity of lamb 'three ways' with rosemary mash and jus. The room is plain, but the service is personable, and the wine and value make this a local standout. **Photo** *above.*

Modern Australian

Aqua Dining
North Sydney Pool, corner of Paul & Northcliff Streets, North Sydney (9964 9998/www.aqua dining.com.au). CityRail/ferry Milsons Point. **Open** noon-2.30pm, 6-10.30pm Mon-Fri, Sun; noon-2.30pm, 6-10pm Sat. **Main courses** $44-$49. **Licensed. Credit** AmEx, DC, MC, V. **Map** p327 F1 ⓛ
Aussies with childhood memories of standing barefoot and dripping by the deep end while clutching a meat pie slathered in tomato sauce may be thrown by the setting of this hip diner. But there's something very appealing about looking out over North Sydney's lovely Olympic pool and across the harbour as you dine. The food isn't amazing or cheap, but that view is something else.

Bathers' Pavilion
4 The Esplanade, between Awaba Street & Mandolong Road, Balmoral Beach (9969 5050/ www.batherspavilion.com.au). Ferry Taronga Zoo then bus 238/ferry Mosman South then bus 233. **Open** *Café* 7am-late daily. *Restaurant* noon-2.30pm, 6.30-9.30pm daily. **Main courses** *Café* $10.50-$24.50. **Set menu** *Restaurant* $90 2 courses; $110 3 courses. **Licensed. Credit** AmEx, DC, MC, V.

Serge Dansereau is one of the big men of Australian cuisine. Big, that is, in terms of his contribution to Sydney dining, helping to usher in the idea of seasonality and an Australian style of cooking, not to mention numerous individual ingredients. This beautiful beachside restaurant highlights the best of his philosophy. Seared scallops snuggle up to beef-cheek ravioli in a barely-there ginger-soy sauce, demonstrating Dansereau's light touch and mastery of Asian flavours, while the veal rack with wild mushrooms, pomme purée and spinach shows the part provincial European simplicity plays.

Milsons
Corner of Broughton & Willoughby Streets, Kirribilli (9955 7075/www.milsonsrestaurant.com.au). CityRail Milsons Point. **Open** noon-3pm, 6-9.30pm Mon-Thur; noon-3pm, 6-10.30pm Fri; 6-10.30pm Sat. **Main courses** $32-$38. **Licensed/BYO. Credit** AmEx, DC, MC, V.
We've yet to see the prime minister duck in for a bite, but his Sydney residence is so close he'd be a fool (ahem) not to delve into this sharp, under-appreciated restaurant to get a taste of what his more food-savvy constituents are spending their tax breaks on. Seafood and Asian flavours are handled with particular grace.

Northbridge Bistro
Northbridge Hotel, 57 Strathallen Avenue, at Baringa Road, Northbridge (9958 5228). Bus 202, 203, 204, 205, 206, 207, 208, 209. **Open** noon-3pm, 6-10pm Tue-Fri; 6-10pm Sat. **Main courses** $18-$27. **Licensed. Credit** AmEx, DC, MC, V.
Out the back of a pub in the northern suburbs is the last place you'd expect to find food this good. John Evans is one hell of a chef, and his takes on contemporary bistro classics – tomato and rocket pasta,

crisp pork belly, roast duck – take some beating. Don't miss dessert – they're made by front-of-house manager Sonia Greig, and are of a quality that suggests she didn't get the gig purely on the strength of being married to chef Evans.

Tables

1047 Pacific Highway, between Telegraph & Gandview Streets, Pymble (9983 1047). CityRail Pymble. **Open** noon-2.30pm, 6-9.30pm Mon-Fri; 6-9.30pm Sat. **Main courses** $31.90. **Licensed/BYO** (wine only). **Credit** AmEx, DC, MC, V.
Our theory is that the creative energy the Tables team conserved coming up with the name they wisely channelled into the menu. Slow-braised pork belly arrives with seared scallops, chilli jam and a pool of beautifully aromatic, star anise-spiked braising liquor. The technicolour decor we can only put down to a rash burst of exuberance – happily, everything that appears on the plates exhibits a more even aesthetic temper.

Other

Garfish

Corner of Burton & Broughton Streets, Kirribilli (9922 4322). CityRail/ferry Milsons Point. **Open** 7.30am-11am, noon-3pm, 6-9.30pm Mon-Thur; 7.30am-11am, noon-3pm, 6-10pm Fri, Sat; 7.30am-11am, noon-3pm, 6-8.30pm Sun. **Main courses** $22-$28. **Licensed/BYO** (wine only). **Credit** AmEx, MC, V. Seafood
These guys are really into their fish. Working hand-in-fin with one of Sydney's leading seafood suppliers, the focus is on freshness. And it's great to see the fish choice going beyond the usual clichés of salmon and tuna. Try the likes of aromatic kingfish curry with aubergine pickle or choose one of the day's catch from the blackboard, select a cooking method and garnish and await satisfaction.

Vera Cruz

314 Military Road, between Winnie Street & Langley Avenue, Cremorne (9904 5818). Bus 247, 263. **Open** 6-10pm Mon-Sat. **Main courses** $25.50. **Licensed/BYO. Credit** AmEx, MC, V. Mexican
'True Cross', maybe, but it's not true Mexican cuisine – that great gap in the Australian culinary landscape. But the food on offer at this very designer boîte isn't aiming for authenticity so much as a crowd-pleasing lightness and clarity of flavour – no bad thing, either. A couple of cervezas don't go amiss with the killer chicken *mole*, for that matter.

Northern Beaches

Asian

Avalon Chinese Restaurant

74 Old Barrenjoey Road, at Avalon Parade, Avalon (9918 6319). Bus 188, 190, E88, E89, L88, L90. **Open** 11am-3pm Mon-Sat; 5-10pm Sun.

Main courses $9.80-$18.80. **Licensed/BYO. Credit** AmEx, DC, MC, V. Cantonese
Avalon is not the first place you'd go looking for a Cantonese restaurant, but once you've seen past the déshabillé arcade setting to the so-bad-it's-great gold-and-red flocked Asian-print wallpaper, you won't look back. Nothing beats the salt-and-pepper squid after a big day in the surf.

European

Alhambra Cafe & Tapas Bar

54 West Esplanade, opposite Manly Wharf, Manly (9976 2975). Ferry Manly. **Open** noon-3pm, 6-10.30pm Mon-Fri; noon-5pm, 6-10.30pm Sat, Sun. **Main courses** $20-$26. **Licensed. Credit** AmEx, DC, MC, V. **Map** p334 ⑬ Moroccan/Spanish
Moorish by theme, moreish by nature, this loud, fun restaurant in Manly does a kickin' line in tapas, as well as richly spiced tagines, fluffy jewelled couscous and luscious pastilla – shredded braised chicken in light, crisp pastry dusted with sugar. The outdoor seating and wild flamenco on Saturday nights only serve to up the ante.

Pilu at Freshwater

Freshwater Beach, Moore Road, Harbord (9938 3331/www.piluatfreshwater.com.au). Ferry Manly then bus 136, 139. **Open** 6.30-9.30pm Tue; noon-3pm, 6.30-9.30pm Wed-Sat, noon-3pm Sun. **Main courses** $32-$36. **Licensed. Credit** AmEx, DC, MC, V. Sardinian
The Freshwater in question is the beach of that name, the Pilu is talented chef Giovanni Pilu, who moved with his partner and front-of-house manager Marilyn Annecchini – from Mosman's beloved Cala Luna to present their menu of Sardinian specialities in far more becoming surrounds. Segue from a Sardinian beer to Sardinian gnocchi with bottarga di muggine, the pressed dried mullet roe Sardinians just can't get enough of. Pilu's signature roast suckling pig with apple sauce makes a triumphant culmination to any meal.

Modern Australian

Jonah's

69 Bynya Road, between Norma & Surf Roads, Palm Beach (9974 5599/www.jonahs.com.au). Bus 190, L90. **Open** noon-3pm, 6.30pm-late Mon, Tue; 6.30pm-late Wed-Sun. **Main courses** $37-$45. **Licensed. Credit** AmEx, DC, MC, V.
The setting, overlooking lovely Whale Beach, explains why Jonah's has been a favourite with wedding parties since time immemorial. Now American chef George Francisco is cooking food to match the views. It's high-falutin' stuff in part, what with crisp red mullet with caviar and pearl onion mousseline rubbing shoulders with paper-wrapped foie gras and caramelised kumquats. But it's also gutsy, encompassing the likes of roast wild boar with braised red cabbage and maple-glazed chestnuts.

Feast your eyes on the divine view at **Jonah's**. *See p165.*

Don't miss the Gaultier-bra-inspired panna cotta. You can stay overnight too (*see p48*). **Photo** *above*.

Manly Wharf Hotel

Manly Wharf, East Esplanade, Manly (9977 1266/ www.manlywharfhotel.com.au). Ferry Manly. **Open** noon-3pm, 6-10pm Mon-Sat; noon-4pm Sun. **Main courses** $28-$35. **Licensed. Credit** AmEx, DC, MC, V. **Map** p334 ⓴

The slick Manly Wharf development is a divine (if loud) place to meet for a drink (*see p185*), but it's also a really lovely spot to rendezvous for more solid sustenance. While the steaks, duck potsticker dumplings with pineapple relish and suchlike are good, the seafood is, fittingly enough for the waterside location, a big highlight. You can go à la carte – open lobster raviolo with scallops and asparagus, say – or why not just opt for the enormous seafood platter.

Parramatta & the West

Asian

Pho An

27 Greenfield Parade, between Chapel Road & Neville Lane, Bankstown (9796 7826). CityRail Bankstown. **Open** 7am-9pm daily. **Main courses** $8.70-$11.80. **Unlicensed. No credit cards.** Vietnamese

There's plenty of dissent over who does what best in Sydney's Vietnamese restaurants. But not when it comes to phô. The beef noodle soup (and the chicken version too) dispensed at this Bankstown landmark is the very coriander-accented nectar of the gods, and the toppings, from steak slices (prosaic) to wobbly bits (exciting), are without peer.

Shun Tak Inn

Corner of Macquarie & Marsden Streets, Parramatta (9635 8128). CityRail Parramatta. **Open** 10am-midnight daily. **Main courses** $25-$30. **Licensed/BYO. Credit** AmEx, DC, MC, V. Chinese Let's hear it for the Singapore-style crab. Not only does it come in a beautiful tomatoey chilli sauce that will have you licking your fingers, but it's accompanied by the traditional steamed buns to sop up the juices. Score! The yum cha too will have you in thrall to the kitchen.
Other locations: 138 Church Street, Parramatta (9635 8130).

Tan Viet

95 John Street, between Railway Parade & Hill Street, Cabramatta (9727 6853). CityRail Cabramatta. **Open** 8.30am-7pm daily. **Main courses** $9-$9.50. **BYO. No credit cards.** Vietnamese

The poultry versions of phô, the great Vietnamese soup, tend to be overshadowed by the beef style that is the nation's lifeblood. But not here: chicken gets celebrated in soup as well as some very fine fried incarnations, while the duck phô is a rare treat.

Temasek

Roxy Arcade, 71 George Street, between Horwood Place & Smith Street, Parramatta (9633 9926). CityRail Parramatta. **Open** 11.30am-2.30pm, 5.30-9.30pm Tue-Sun. **Main courses** $10-$24.80. **BYO. Credit** AmEx, DC, MC, V. Malaysian

Long held to be the purveyor of Sydney's finest curry laksa, this plastic-tableclothed palace also takes top honours in the beef rendang and Hainan chicken stakes. Call ahead for house specialities such as fishhead curry and chilli crab.

Thanh Binh

52 John Street, between Railway Parade & Smith Street, Cabramatta (9727 9729). CityRail Cabramatta. **Open** 9am-9pm daily. **Main courses** $8-$30. **BYO**. **No credit cards**. Vietnamese
John Street is full of buzzy Vietnamese restaurants, but Angie Hong's Thanh Binh is pretty much universally accepted as the mothership. The choice is typically broad, but, atypically, almost everything on the menu is interesting, with many dishes unique to this establishment. The other branches fight the good fight, but the original is still best.
Other locations: 111 King Street, Newtown (9557 1175); 33 Arthur Street, Cabramatta (9724 9633).

Woodland's

67 George Street, between Horwood Place & Parramatta Mall, Parramatta (9633 3838). CityRail Parramatta. **Open** 11.30am-2.30pm, 6-9.30pm daily. **Main courses** $11-$18. **Licensed/BYO**. **Credit** AmEx, DC, MC, V. South Indian
Consider the masala dosai: is there a bigger commonly available foodstuff? And why hasn't anybody invented plates large enough not to be dwarfed by these vast, crisp, South Indian pancakes? You may not find any answers here, but you will find blissfully light examples of the dosai genre.
Other locations: 238 George Street, Liverpool (9734 9949).

Other

Sahara

Burwood Shopping Plaza, 101 Burwood Road, Burwood (9747 4540). CityRail Burwood. **Open** 8am-midnight daily. **Main courses** $12-$28. **Licensed/BYO**. **Credit** AmEx, DC, MC, V. Turkish
Is this the fanciest kebab shop in town? It is certainly the only one with textured walls and other glam architectural quirks. The kitchen's no slouch, either – there's not a lot that will be unfamiliar to dabblers in local Turkish fare, but the quality is top-notch.

Sofra

35-39 Auburn Road, at Queen Street, Auburn (9649 9299). CityRail Auburn. **Open** 7am-midnight daily. **Main courses** $5-$16. **Unlicensed**. **No credit cards**. Turkish
In the very Turkish suburb of Auburn, on the very Turkish strip of Auburn Road, just a stone's throw from the mosque, is this very Turkish eaterie. Forget rugs on the walls and bellydancers – the look here is tiles, backlit pictures of food and fluoro strips – Sofra's cred is down to its very good charcoal-grilled kebabs and fluffy pide. And the baklava rocks.

Summerland

457 Chapel Street, between Ricard & French Streets, Bankstown (9708 5107). CityRail Bankstown. **Open** noon-10.30pm daily. **Main courses** $6-$21. **Licensed/BYO** (wine only). **Credit** AmEx, MC, V. Lebanese
Thirty-five bucks and a big appetite will take you far at this most hospitable of Lebanese restaurants. One of its many drawcards (apart from the sheer size of its banquets) is a focus on seafood. It goes well beyond the usual whitebait – a breadth not common in Lebanese eateries in Australia and something we'd love to see emulated elsewhere.

The South

Asian

Ocean King House

Corner of Princes Highway & English Street, Kogarah (9587 3511). CityRail Carlton. **Open** 11am-3pm, 5.30-10.30pm daily. **Main courses** $13.80-$26.80. **Licensed/BYO**. **Credit** AmEx, DC, MC, V. Chinese
The best yum cha, say many clued-up Sydneysiders, is no longer necessarily to be found in Chinatown, but in suburban restaurants like this one. The stunning diversity of dishes on offer in this former mansion and their overall quality (the fried dough-stick in rice noodle sheets is top-notch, for example) lends weight to that argument, while the juicy mud crab in XO sauce with vermicelli is an excellent reason to come after dark.

European

Chez Pascal

250 Rocky Point Road, at Ramsgate Road, Ramsgate (9529 5444). Bus 476. **Open** 7-9.30pm Tue-Sat. **Main courses** $16-$24. **BYO**. **Credit** DC, MC, V. French
Hankering for some old-school French fun? Make a beeline for Chez Pascal: in a room decorated with murals of a can-can chorus line you can indulge in gloriously unreconstructed coq au vin, super-rich saucisson lyonnais and garlic-laden snails. Crêpes normandes to finish are, of course, mandatory.

Modern Australian

Les Trois Freres

16 Princes Highway, between Belgrave Esplanade & Clare Street, Sylvania (9544 7609). Bus 477. **Open** 6-10pm Wed-Sat. **Main courses** $25-$27. **BYO**. **Credit** AmEx, DC, MC, V.
The Three Brothers have been largely responsible for holding the culinary fort in this neck of the woods for several years. Now it's just one of them, and though the food isn't (as you might think) French in origin, but Modern Australian, it's still worth a detour – not least for the value.

Cafés

Get a taste of the daily grind.

The city that was obsessed by coffee is now in the throes of a tea renaissance. Shops selling every imaginable tea trinket do a roaring trade; saké and soft drinks have lost favour in sushi bars to the palate-cleansing pleasures of *genmai cha*; and the close of a fine meal brings the question not of which Cohiba to spark up, but which chamomile tisane – blended privately for the restaurant in question, naturally – to savour.

That said, coffee is still the thing, and Sydney is still a vastly more accommodating city for the true caffiend than London, New York or Paris. Italianate terms and style pervade – there are short blacks, flat whites and long blacks, but you can't go wrong ordering an espresso, a latte, a lungo or, more contemporarily, a macchiato or a retro-credible cappuccino. Unlike Italy, though, prices remain the same whether you stand, sit inside or sit outside. Table service is the norm, and, unlike in other Australian states, many cafés aren't licensed to sell or serve alcohol. Be aware that many establishments aren't open in the evening. And oh, fans of the coffee-and-cigarettes concept, take note: you can't smoke indoors in any – that's right, any – café in

the state. Should you wish to multitask your nicotine and caffeine habits, you'll have to find somewhere with tables outside.

Starbucks and other chains are tempting a slice of the CBD's office business and the young and gullible but, thankfully, independent cafés still abound along caffeine arteries such as Darlinghurst's Victoria Street, Paddington's Oxford Street, King Street in Newtown and Glebe Point Road in Glebe.

Central Sydney

The CBD & the Rocks

Bambini Trust Café
185 Elizabeth Street, between Park & Market Streets, CBD (9283 7098/www.bambinitrust.com.au). CityRail Museum or St James/Monorail City Centre. **Open** 7am-11pm Mon-Fri. **Licensed**. **Credit** AmEx, DC, MC, V. **Map** p329 F7 ❶
To walk into Bambini for a breakfast meeting is to meet some serious scrutiny. To have lunch here mid-week, doubly so. Designed with echoes of Milan in its wooden Venetian blinds and dark timber against crisp linen and white tiles, this is the canteen for Sydney's media elite, not least the editors of the Australian Consolidated Press stable whose building it adjoins and who can usually be seen monopolising the back corner banquettes. The coffee is great, the food is OK, but the buzz is the real deal.

GG Espresso
175 Pitt Street, between Martin Place & King Street, CBD (9221 1644). CityRail Martin Place or Wynyard. **Open** 6.30am-5.15pm Mon-Fri. **Unlicensed**. **Credit** AmEx, MC, V. **Map** p327 F6 ❷
That's GG as in George Gregan. Not content with making his mark in the world of rugby union, the Wallabies' captain has set about making his initials synonymous with good coffee in the inner city. The food on offer is pretty basic, but the espresso has plenty of oomph.

MCA Café
Museum of Contemporary Art, 140 George Street, between Argyle & Alfred Streets, The Rocks (9241 4253/www.mca.com.au). CityRail/ferry

> ❶ Green numbers given in this chapter correspond to the location of each café as marked on the street maps. *See pp326-334.*

Eat, Drink, Shop

Circular Quay. **Open** 10am-4pm daily. **Licensed**.
Credit AmEx, DC, MC, V. **Map** p327 F4 ❸
Not for the Museum of Contemporary Art the glam
stylings of the eateries at the Guggenheim at Bilbao,
say, or the flash new MOMA in New York. The deco
design takes its cues more from the building's days
housing the Maritime Services Board than Warhol
or Emin, and while the food is no more avant-garde
than grilled swordfish with artichokes, beans and
chorizo, it's none the worse for it. The timber deck
(with umbrellas and heaters) at the front of the
museum makes this one of the best bets at Circular
Quay for under $30 a main.

MOS Café
*Museum of Sydney, 37 Phillip Street, at Bridge
Street, CBD (9241 3636/www.moscafe.com.au).
CityRail/ferry Circular Quay.* **Open** 7am-9pm
Mon-Fri; 8.30am-5pm Sat, Sun. **Licensed**. **Credit**
AmEx, DC, MC, V. **Map** p327 F4 ❹
It might be an idea for the Museum of Sydney to
move a few of its exhibits into the café. Such is the
popularity of this spot that we reckon only a modest
slice of the caff's clientele put two and two together
and make sense of the acronym. They're drawn by
the opportunity to sit in the middle of the city's skyscraper canyons overlooking a nice patch of open
space and drinking a decent cup of java (or, better
yet, a nice cold beer).

Speedbar
*27 Park Street, between Castlereagh & Pitt Streets,
CBD (9264 4668). CityRail Town Hall/Monorail
Galeries Victoria.* **Open** 7am-6pm Mon-Fri;
8am-3pm Sat. **Unlicensed**. **No credit cards**.
Map p329 F7 ❺
No, it's not much to look at, but then it ain't called
the 'Have a Seat, Take Your Time and Enjoy Our
Carefully Crafted Decor and Finely Wrought
Hospitality'. The focus here is coffee, done right, done
fast and done consistently. You want to lounge in an
armchair lingering over a dry double hazelnut frap-
pucino, there's a Starbucks up the street, pal. The
rest of us are trying to drink coffee.

The Tearoom
*Level 3, Queen Victoria Building, 455 George
Street, between Market & Druitt Streets, CBD
(9269 0774/www.thetearoom.com.au). CityRail
Town Hall/Monorail Galeries Victoria.* **Open**
11am-5pm Mon-Fri, Sun; 11am-3pm Sat. **Licensed**.
Credit AmEx, DC, MC, V. **Map** p327 E6 ❻
It's a little-known fact that this ornate, soaring space
hidden at the top of the QVB shopping complex also
does killer coffee in addition to its myriad premium-
leaf teas. Grandmothers sip single-estate Darjeelings
and attack three-tiered platters of pretty cakes and
finger sandwiches while the CBD business set
takes advantage of the widely spaced tables to talk
business over white tea, Mornington Peninsula pinot
noir and Mark Holmes's light, contemporary food.
Other locations: The Tearoom Gunners' Barracks,
Suakin Drive, off Middle Head Road, Mosman
(8962 5900).

Pyrmont

Concrete
*224 Harris Street, at Pyrmont Bridge Road, Pyrmont
(9518 9523). LightRail Fish Market or Wentworth
Park/bus 443, 449.* **Open** 7am-4pm Mon-Sat; 8am-
4pm Sun. **Licensed**. **Credit** AmEx, DC, MC, V.
Map p326 C6 ❼
Though the decor is as modern and industrial as the
name suggests, there's nothing cold about Concrete
on a sunny day. The Pyrmont peninsula's advertising and dotcom types swing by for their fresh juices,
while pram-pushers seek out the superior scrambled
eggs with goat's cheese. A fine place to laze away
an afternoon with good coffee, smiling service and
lots of magazines.

East Sydney & Darlinghurst

Bar Coluzzi
*322 Victoria Street, between Surrey & William
Streets, Darlinghurst (9380 5420). CityRail Kings
Cross.* **Open** 5am-7pm daily. **Unlicensed**.
No credit cards. **Map** p330 J8 ❽
One of Sydney's caffeinated landmarks, Coluzzi has
provided cups of high-quality, Italian-style espresso
for decades. Thronged by regulars, its wooden
streetside seating sees almost as much primping
and posing as it does good coffee.

bills
*433 Liverpool Street, at West Street, Darlinghurst
(9360 9631/www.bills.com.au). CityRail Kings
Cross/bus 389.* **Open** 7.30am-3pm, 6-10.30pm

The best Cafés

For breakfast
bills (*see above*), **Book Kitchen** (*see p171*),
Bourke Street Bakery (*see p171*), **Café
Sopra** (*see p171*), **Chelsea Tea House**
(*see p174*).

For coffee
Allpress Espresso (*see p174*), **Ecabar**
(*see p170*), **Ten Buck Alley** (*see p171*),
Toby's Estate (*see p172*).

For late-nighters
Badde Manors (*see p173*), **Café Hernandez**
(*see p172*).

For people-watching
Café Hernandez (*see p172*), **Ecabar**
(*see p170*), **Latteria** (*see p170*),
Tropicana (*see p171*), **Una's** (*see p171*).

For tea
The Tearoom (*see left*).

Eat, Drink, Shop

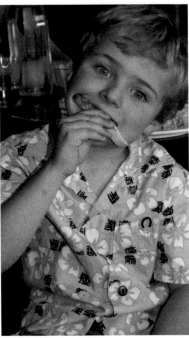

Ten Buck Alley may be small in size, but it's big in appeal. *See p171.*

Mon-Sat; 8.30am-3pm Sun. **Licensed/BYO.**
Credit AmEx, MC, V. **Map** p330 J8 ⑨
Chef Bill Granger has an ever-expanding empire of cookbooks and TV appearances, but this café is still the finest of his achievements. Its communal table plays host to his famous creamy scrambled eggs, sunrise drink and toasted home-made coconut bread at breakfast, while lunch sees the simplicity of steak sandwich with garlic cream and chicken club sandwich with roasted tomatoes. Expect to wait, expect to be seduced. If you want similar food with (slightly) shorter queues, try the sister cafés in Surry Hills and Woollahra.
Other locations: 359 Crown Street, Surry Hills (9360 4762); Queen's Court, 118 Queen Street, Woollahra (9328 7997).

Ecabar
128 Darlinghurst Road, at Liverpool Street, Darlinghurst (9332 1433). CityRail Kings Cross. **Open** 7am-5pm Mon-Sat; 9am-4pm Sun. **BYO.** **No credit cards. Map** p330 H8 ⑩
It's all about the coffee. Not that the scrambled eggs with pesto or the sliced boiled egg with tomato and avocado on rye aren't great. And not to make light of the brilliant fresh pear, apple and lime juice. It's just that the coffee at this popular, sunny sliver of a venue is really, really outstanding.

Kings Lane Sandwiches
28 Kings Lane, between Palmer & Bourke Streets, Darlinghurst (9360 8007). CityRail Museum/bus 389. **Open** 8am-2.30pm Mon-Fri; 9am-1.30pm Sat. **Unlicensed. No credit cards. Map** p329 G/H8 ⑪
To call Marcella Aebi-Nelson the sandwich dictator is not quite fair. True, she has been known to speak sharply should customers dither at the head of the inevitable lunchtime queues in her shop, but she's only looking out for everyone else hankering for one of her gigantic constructions. Top-quality ingredients, great bread and inventive condiments make for Sydney's best sandwiches, including a vegetarian offering of walnut houmous that's good enough to tempt any carnivore.

Latteria
320B Victoria Street, between Surry & William Streets, Darlinghurst (9331 2914). CityRail Kings Cross. **Open** 5.30am-7.30pm daily. **Unlicensed. No credit cards. Map** p330 J8 ⑫
Want a caffè just like mamma used to make? Check out Latteria, next door to Bar Coluzzi (*see p169*). The coffee and panini are pure Italian, sure, but it's the incredible efficiency with which the space in this cupboard-like venue is used that really makes you think you're just off the Via Tornabuoni.

Le Petit Crème

118 Darlinghurst Road, between Farrell Avenue
& Liverpool Street, Darlinghurst (9361 4738).
CityRail Kings Cross. **Open** 7am-2.30pm Mon-Sat;
8am-2.30pm Sun. **BYO**. **No credit cards**.
Map p330 H8 ⑬
Everything here, from the crêpes to the coffee to the
1980s film posters, is pure Paris. Pull up a bentwood
chair and dive into an enormous Gallic breakfast.
The milkshakes, made with French-style *chocolat
chaud* as their base, can't be beat.

Ten Buck Alley

*185A Bourke Street, between Stanley & William
Streets, East Sydney (9356 3000). CityRail Kings
Cross/bus 389.* **Open** 6.30am-6pm Mon-Fri;
8am-4pm Sat. **No credit cards**. **Map** p329 H7 ⑭
Should the carpet of coloured latex that appears
fresh each morning in the lane adjoining the café not
tip you off, we feel bound to advise you that Ten Buck
Alley takes its name from the street's somewhat insalubrious after-dark trade. But by day,
nothing is more savoury than this little space's soy
and linseed toast with avocado and tomato (with
whole soybeans in the bread, no less), its peerless
chocolate milkshakes and kick-arse coffee.

Tropicana

*227 Victoria Street, between Surrey & William
Streets, Darlinghurst (9360 9809/www.tropicana
caffe.com).* **Open** 5am-11pm
daily. **Licensed/BYO**. **No credit cards**.
Map p330 J7/8 ⑮
Forget agents and casting calls: this is where the real
business of Sydney's film and theatre industries
takes place. Against a background of reasonable coffee, adequate café food and capable service, deals
are done and names are made. Immortalised in the
name of Tropfest (*see p229*), the country's leading
short film showcase, the Trop has an energy – and
a clientele – like no other.

Una's

*340 Victoria Street, at Surrey Street, Darlinghurst
(9360 6885/www.unas.com.au). CityRail Kings
Cross.* **Open** 7.30am-10.30pm Mon-Sat; 8am-10.30pm
Sun. **Licensed/BYO** (wine only). **No credit cards**.
Map p330 J8 ⑯
It's Heidi meets *Queer as Folk* every day at this
wood-panelled Victoria Street stayer. Lederhosen-
wearing waiters flit between tables of boofy boys
fuelling up on the menu's big, meaty mainstays of
schnitzel, stews, rösti, wurst and sauerkraut. Una's
is cheap, no one leaves hungry and the little-known
upstairs bar is worth its weight in weird.
Other locations: 135 Broadway, Ultimo (9211
3805); 372 New South Head Road, Double Bay
(9327 7287).

Zuppa Uno

*166 Riley Street, between Burton & Liverpool Streets,
East Sydney (9331 7163/www.zuppauno.com.au).
Bus 373, 378, 380, L82.* **Open** 7am-4pm Mon-Fri.
BYO. **No credit cards**. **Map** p329 G8 ⑰

The sexy inner-urban face of soup kitchens, Zuppa
Uno – that's more like number one than just the one
soup, thankfully – has an ever-changing array of
fresh potages, *minestre*, broths and their liquid like,
balanced by the constants of pleasant service and
good espresso.

Surry Hills & Waterloo

Il Baretto

*496 Bourke Street, at Arthur Street, Surry Hills
(9361 6163). CityRail/LightRail Central/bus 303,
355.* **Open** 6-10pm Mon; 8am-3pm, 6-10pm Tue-Sat;
9am-3pm Sun (winter only). **BYO**. **No credit cards**.
Map p329 G10 ⑱
The popularity of the loud 'little bar' is such that
you'll often have to wait. The authentico carbonara
guanciale (that's cured pig cheek to you), gorgeous
gnocchi with gorgonzola, and specials such as
brown butter and nettle ravioli, will have you licking your plate. Best for dinner.

Book Kitchen

*255 Devonshire Street, at Bourke Street, Surry Hills
(9310 1003/www.thebookkitchen.com.au). CityRail/
LightRail Central then 10mins walk/bus 301 303,
355.* **Open** 8am-4pm Mon, Wed, Sun; 8am-4pm,
6.30-10pm Thur-Sat. **Licensed/BYO**. **Credit**
AmEx, MC, V. **Map** p329 G11 ⑲
The idea of a bookshop as a café has currency, so
why not a café selling books? Better yet, why not a
café selling cookbooks? You can browse shelves of
new, imported and second-hand cooking titles at
Book Kitchen while you wait for your excellent
hand-cut chips or home-made baked beans cooked
with ham hock. The duck club sandwich, made with
hazelnut bread from the nearby Bourke Street
Bakery (*see below*), is to die for.

Bourke Street Bakery

*633 Bourke Street, at Devonshire Street, Surry Hills
(9699 1011). CityRail/LightRail Central then 10mins
walk/bus 301, 303, 355.* **Open** 7am-6pm Tue-Fri;
8am-5pm Sat, Sun. **Unlicensed**. **No credit cards**.
Map p329 G11 ⑳
It's hard to swing a ciabatta here, let alone a cat. Yet
this slightly scruffy corner bakery still finds room
to pack shelves with ace chocolate cookies, pork and
fennel sausage rolls, pastries rich with tomato and
olive, and all sorts of wonderful bread. Get in early
to score one of the very few seats in the window and
be the envy of all who pass.
Other locations: 130 Broadway, Ultimo
(9281 3113).

Café Sopra

*1st Floor, Fratelli Fresh, 7 Danks Street, between
Young & Bourke Streets, Waterloo (9699 3174).
Bus 301, 302, 303, 355.* **Open** 10am-3pm Tue-Fri;
8am-3pm Sat. **Licensed/BYO**. **Credit** AmEx,
MC, V.
Sopra is Italian for upstairs, and this coffeehouse is
located above Fratelli Fresh, the warehouse head-
quarters of one of Sydney's top importers of Italian

foodstuffs. Simplicity is the watchword, and sparkling fresh produce and the warehouse's peerless dry goods are at the fore in dishes such as the salad of beetroot and poached eggs, or *papa al pomodoro*, the luscious peasant soup of bread and tomatoes. *Squisito*.

Danks Street Depot

2 Danks Street, at Young Street, Waterloo (9698 2201/www.danksstreetdepot.com.au). Bus 301, 302, 303, 355. **Open** 7.30am-4pm Mon; 7.30am-4pm, 6-10pm Tue-Sat; 8am-4pm, 6-10pm Sat. **Licensed/BYO** (daytime only). **Credit** MC, V.
'Melburnian' is a term oft-used in talk of this curiously warm industrial space in an increasingly arty part of Waterloo. One can extrapolate, then, that Sydneysiders associate Melbourne with good value, professional service and unpretentious food cooked with a great deal of skill and plenty of thought for flavour. The corned-beef reuben can't be beat. While here, be sure to visit some of the galleries on the premises (*see p235* 2 Danks Street), or spend some time lounging in the new bar annex.

Kafa

224 Commonwealth Street, between Foveaux & Albion Streets, Surry Hills (9280 2624). CityRail/LightRail Central. **Open** 7am-4pm Mon-Fri; 8am-1pm Sat. **Unlicensed**. **No credit cards**. **Map** p329 F9 ㉑
A fine example of how designer smarts can make a Kmart budget look a million bucks. A single large round table fills the room, while above it hangs an enormous chandelier constructed of large bucket-like… buckets. Just the thing to ponder while you knock off breakfast treats from the better-than-average menu.

Wah Wah Lounge

1 Danks Street, at Young Street, Waterloo (9699 3456). Bus 301, 302, 303, 355. **Open** 7.30am-4pm Mon, Tue; 7.30am-10pm Wed-Sat; 8am-3pm Sun. **Licensed/BYO** (wine only). **Credit** MC, V.
The new kid on the Danks Street block, Wah Wah (we're betting they're big George Harrison fans too) might not be able to compete with neighbouring Café Sopra (*see p171*) and Danks Street Depot (*see above*), but they've definitely got the edge in the cool name stakes. Team that with a pleasant sunny aspect and the street's best baristas and you're looking at some real potential.

Kings Cross, Potts Point & Woolloomooloo

Just down Cowper Wharf Road from Woolloomooloo Wharf is shiny snack van **Harry's Café de Wheels**. A much-loved Sydney institution, it's been supplying late-night meat pies with gravy, mash and mushy peas to locals, visitors, overseas sailors, cab drivers and drunks for more than 50 years.

Café Hernandez

60 Kings Cross Road, between Ward Avenue & Roslyn Street, Kings Cross (9331 2343/www.cafehernandez.com.au). CityRail Kings Cross/bus 200. **Open** 24hrs daily. **Unlicensed**. **Credit** MC, V. **Map** p330 J7 ㉒
A favourite among strong-coffee drinkers, this Spanish-inflected, 24-hour establishment just off the Kings Cross strip is also one of the few places in the city where you'll find non-alcoholic entertainment after the witching hour.

Spring Espresso

65 Macleay Street, at Challis Avenue, Potts Point (9331 0190/www.springespresso.com.au). CityRail Kings Cross. **Open** 6.30am-6.30pm daily. **BYO**. **No credit cards**. **Map** p330 J6 ㉓
A landmark on Potts Point's see-and-be-seen scene, Spring, though tiny, bounces with as much energy as its name suggests, and the menu, though brief, can be relied upon for simple pleasures. The fit-out, it must be noted, nearly out-glams the clientele. The entrance is on Challis Avenue.

Toby's Estate

129 Cathedral Street, at Palmer Street, Woolloomooloo (9358 1196/www.tobysestate.com.au). CityRail Kings Cross. **Open** 7am-5.30pm Mon-Fri; 8am-4pm Sat; 9am-4pm Sun. **Unlicensed**. **Credit** AmEx, DC, MC, V. **Map** p329 H7 ㉔
Though Toby's beans are widely available, coffee obsessives come to this Cathedral Street roastery-cum-espresso bar to worship at the scant few tables that surround the roasting machinery. Textbook espresso is guaranteed, and they have latterly branched out with some very nice teas.
Other locations: 32-36 City Road, Chippendale (9211 1459); corner of Manning & Macleay Streets, Potts Point (8356 9264).

Uliveto

33 Bayswater Road, between Kellett Street & Ward Avenue, Kings Cross (9357 7331). CityRail Kings Cross. **Open** 7am-5pm Mon-Sat; 8am-5pm Sun. **Unlicensed**. **No credit cards**. **Map** p330 J7 ㉕
The latest venture from the chap who opened the revolutionary-for-its-time Spring Espresso (*see above*), Uliveto occupies a nice indoor/outdoor slice of Bayswater Road between a gym and a strip club. Handily enough for both crowds, in addition to fine breakfast staples it does a wonderful heart-starter smoothie that's ideal if you're feeling a little dented.

Zinc

Corner of Macleay Street & Rockwall Crescent, Potts Point (9358 6777). CityRail Kings Cross. **Open** 7am-4pm Mon; 7am-4pm, 6.30-10pm Tue-Sat; 8am-4pm Sun. **Licensed/BYO**. **Credit** AmEx, MC, V. **Map** p330 J6 ㉖
Perhaps Zinc's popularity with the beautiful people is connected to the prominent role that mirrors play in its design. Or maybe it's just that the city's lovelies have a taste for just-squeezed blood orange juice, good coffee and lovely, fresh Italianate salads.

Take your time choosing from the top-notch Italian menu at **Café Sopra**. *See p171*.

Eat, Drink, Shop

Eastern Suburbs

Blue Orange

49 Hall Street, between Jacques & Consett Avenues, Bondi Beach (9300 9885/www.blueorange restaurant.com.au). CityRail Bondi Junction then bus 380, 381, 382, L82/bus 380, L82. **Open** 7am-5pm, 6.30pm-late Tue-Sat; 7am-5pm Wed, Sun. **Licensed/BYO** (wine only). **Credit** AmEx, MC, V. **Map** p334 ②
Intimate and woody, Blue Orange is a sultry restaurant by night, but its daytime incarnation as a café offers the most mileage. If a ricotta and passion fruit soufflé somehow isn't your cup of tea first thing, try your luck with smoked salmon pancakes. The Sichuan salt squid with palm sugar and lime mayo makes for a feisty lunch.

Flat White

98 Holdsworth Street, at Jersey Road, Woollahra (9328 9922). Bus 380, 389. **Open** 7am-4pm Mon-Sat; 8am-4pm Sun. **BYO. Credit** MC, V. **Map** p333 M10 ②
Gruyère and ham brioche toastie? Oh, yes please. The space isn't huge (and, between you and me, neither are the portions), but everything here is skewed towards the perfectly formed – including the clientele. European is the slant, eggs are a favourite, and the milk coffees are as good as you'd hope with a name like this.

Parc

30 Clovelly Road, between Darley Road & Avoca Street, Randwick (9398 9222). Bus 400. **Open** 7am-4pm Tue-Fri; 8am-3pm Sat, Sun. **BYO. Credit** MC, V. **Map** p333 N14 ②
Toast made with bread from the Infinity Sourdough Bakery is just the beginning. The set menu is solid – check out the salad of smoked trout with orange, baby cos lettuce and fried capers – and daily specials such as tomato and smoked ham soup thickened with arborio rice keep things interesting. Parc is popular with the cycling crowd who flock here after jaunts in Centennial Park.

Inner West

Badde Manors

37 Glebe Point Road, at Francis Street, Glebe (9660 3797/www.baddemanorscafe.com). Bus 431, 432, 433, 434. **Open** 7.30am-midnight Mon-Fri; 7.30am-1am Sat; 8.30am-midnight Sun. **Unlicensed. No credit cards. Map** p328 C9 ③
Maybe the waiters can't help themselves. Maybe it's the name. Or maybe those tattoos and piercings have unusual side-effects. Whatever the reason, their manners can, at times, be a little eccentric. But, just like the staunchly vegetarian food, the funny wooden booths and the gelato-vending window, they're only part of charm of this veteran Glebe Point Road café. So deal with it.

Bar Italia

*169 Norton Street, at Macauley Street, Leichhardt
(9560 9981). Bus 436, 437, 438, 440, L40.* **Open**
9am-midnight Mon-Thur, Sun; 9am-1am Fri, Sat.
BYO. No credit cards.
Many Sydneysiders got their first taste of gelato
within these very walls, and many more still make
the pilgrimage as soon as the weather gets even a
little warm. The savoury stuff is nothing special –
Bar Italia is all about the coffee, the vibe and the
double scoop of pistachio and tiramisu trickling
down your fingers.

Bitton Cafe

*37A Copeland Street, between Newton Street
& Mitchell Road, Alexandria (9519 5111/
www.bittongourmet.com.au). CityRail Erskineville.*
Open 7am-3pm Tue-Fri; 8am-3pm Sat, Sun.
Unlicensed. Credit AmEx, DC, MC, V.
A liberal splash of Gallic charm colours everything
in this friendly café, from the repartee of the waiters
and kitchen staff to the divine crêpes with orange
jelly. Bitton also does a roaring trade in jams,
sauces, oils and pretty much anything else that can
be bottled or put in a jar.

Canteen Café

*332 Darling Street, between Short & Phillip Streets,
Balmain (9818 1521). Ferry Balmain East then bus
442, 445/bus 433, 434, 442, 445.* **Open** 7am-5pm
Mon-Sat; 8am-5pm Sun. **BYO. No credit cards.**
Soccer mums, footy dads and dilettante creatives of
every stripe crowd this veteran of the Darling Street
café crush. The look is minimal, but thankfully
there's nothing spare about the food or the portions.
A popular spot with the superannuated theatre set
who call Balmain home too.

Vargabarespresso

*Corner of Wilson Street & Erskineville Road,
Newtown (9517 1932). CityRail Newtown.* **Open**
7am-6pm Mon-Fri; 8am-6pm Sat, Sun. **BYO.**
No credit cards. Map p334 ⊕
Forget café-laden King Street – the coolest coffee in
Newtown is just off the beaten track. Friendly staff
serve thoughtful, interesting eats in the mould of the
American diner-style meatball sandwich with
grilled cheese, and hangover-helpers such as the iced
liquorice tea or Berocca frappé. The hamburgers are
sensational, but if you're feeling more virtuous
there's much to be said for their porridge too.

North Shore

Awaba

*67 The Esplanade, at Awaba Street, Balmoral
(9969 2104/www.awabacafe.com.au). Bus 233,
238, 257.* **Open** 7.30am-3pm Mon-Sat; 6pm-9.30pm
Thur-Sat; 7.30am-5pm Sun. **Licensed/BYO.**
Credit AmEx, MC, V.
Sunglasses-on may be a very Sydney look, but in
this white-on-white sunny space on the edge of the
beach, it's pretty much a necessity. No need to
shield your eyes from the menu, however (though

it is quite bright): what's on offer is pretty upmarket fare. Buttermilk flapjacks with maple syrup and
berry compote? Yes, please.

Northern Beaches

Chelsea Tea House

*48 Old Barrenjoey Road, Avalon (9918 6794).
Bus 188, 190, E88, E89, L88, L90.* **Open** 8.30am-
4pm daily. **Licensed/BYO. No credit cards.**
Gotta love this – one of those places where you sit
down expecting little and find yourself treated to
much. Asian-style steamed eggs at breakfast should
tip you off to the fact that there are some serious
smarts in this kitchen, and the café over-delivers on
pretty much every front you'd care to name

Cook's Larder

*Shop 1, 21-23 Old Barrenjoey Road, near Avalon
Parade, Avalon (9973 4370/www.thecookslarder.
com.au). Bus 188, 190, E88, E89, L88, L90.*
Open 8am-4.30pm Mon-Thur, Sat, Sun; 8am-4.30pm,
6.30pm-late Fri. **BYO. Credit** AmEx, BC, MC, V.
Run by people who have a real passion for what
they're selling, the Cook's Larder offers quality coffee and eats running from ham and gruyère omelette
to a salad of five-spice tofu, cloud ear fungus, Asian
herbs and sesame seeds. Don't miss chef Susan
Doran's diet-blowing range of lovingly made cakes.
There are deli goods and cookery classes too, and
we love the tomato-coloured wall hung with old-
fashioned egg beaters.

Ground Zero

*18 Sydney Road, at Central Avenue, Manly
(9977 6996). Ferry Manly.* **Open** 8am-6pm Mon-
Wed, Sun; 8am-10pm Thur-Sat. **BYO. Credit** MC, V.
Map p334 ⊕
Sun, surf and… short blacks? For some reason
Sydneysiders have recently come to think that a fun-
packed day at the seaside isn't right unless it's
capped off with a cappuccino or some other decent
coffee. This loungey establishment, just a hop and
a skip from the sand of Manly Beach, is one of the
best places to get your java fix this side of the bridge.

The South

Allpress Espresso

*58 Epsom Road, between Dunning & Mentmore
Avenues, Rosebery (9662 8288/www.allpress
espresso.com.au). Bus 309, 310, 343, 345.* **Open**
7am-3pm Mon-Fri; 8am-2pm Sat. **Unlicensed.**
Credit MC, V.
Allpress's interior provides a microcosmic reflec-
tion of the evolution of this neighbourhood, with
industrial machinery (coffee-roasting and packing
equipment) juxtaposed with the forces of gentrification in the form of its customers and the swish
look of the café itself. The coffee is outstanding,
while the breads and pastries, from sister company
Brasserie Bread, are a must. Make ours a *vitello ton-
nato* roll to go, thanks.

Bars & Pubs

Friendly boozers, temples to cocktail cool and plenty in between.

The cliché is that Melbourne is the bar town, while Sydney has the pubs. As with most clichés there is some truth in this: there are lots of pubs here, while NSW's peculiarly strict licensing laws (something to do with its convict heritage, perhaps?), coupled with the city's sky-high real estate prices, mean that where any ten given art students in Melbourne, say, can pool their resources, buy a bit of second-hand furniture, whack some bottles on a shelf and hang out their shingle, in Sydney you need to drop six figures just to get your foot in the door. As a result, the city's bar scene isn't huge, and what there is tends to be pitched at the premium end of the market – all the better to recoup that colossal investment.

This may make Sydney's drinking culture sound a touch homogeneous, and compared to Melbourne's thriving bar scene it is. But that doesn't mean there isn't fun to be had. And while it's true that pubs take the lion's share of the casual drinking market, there are enough exceptions falling between the pub and bar genres to keep things interesting.

Those licensing laws also mean that you're usually required to eat if you want to drink in an establishment where dining is the focus. Anyone who wants to have a drink in a restaurant or licensed café must, in most instances, establish their 'intention to dine', whether that intention is fully borne out or not. Restaurants that have forked out the extra dough for a 'drink or dine' licence will usually go out of their way to advertise the fact.

Meanwhile, pubs – confusingly known as 'hotels' for historical reasons, though precious few in the city still offer rooms for the night – continue to do a roaring trade. And whether they're of the million-dollar-refit type or fragrantly unreconstructed, the primary trade will be in beer. Cold draught beer is bought in middies (a 285ml glass, close to a half-pint) and, more commonly, 425ml schooners. Boutique Australian beers such as Coopers, James Boag's, Cascade and James Squire are increasingly popular, but the bulk of beer drunk tends to be the big domestic names. These once divided fiercely down state lines, with Resch's and Toohey's beers being the big deal in Sydney and NSW, but lately VB (Victoria Bitter), brewed by Foster's, has become almost ubiquitous. Foster's Lager itself, it should be mentioned, rarely gets a look-in at a Sydney bar – except when tourists order it.

Smokers will be less than thrilled to learn that the state's mission to outlaw smoking pretty much anywhere except in your own home under a blanket with the lights out continues apace. Lots of bars have gone totally smoke-free in anticipation of legislation to that effect; from July 2007 smoking will be banned in all indoor areas. Drinking alcohol in bars seems, for the moment, to still be OK.

Central Sydney

The CBD & the Rocks

Attic Bar

2nd Floor, ArtHouse Hotel, 275 Pitt Street, between Park & Market Streets, CBD (9284 1200/www.the arthousehotel.com.au). CityRail St James or Town Hall/Monorail Galeries Victoria. **Open** 5.30pm-late Tue-Sat. **Credit** AmEx, DC, MC, V. **Map** p329 F7 ❶
Almost hidden atop three levels of suits drinking Becks and domestic fizz, the Attic is an eyrie of good drinking. Champion bartender and self-styled 'cocktail chef' Ben Davidson now oversees all the ArtHouse Hotel's bars, so you'll be lucky to get him in person, but his staff are well drilled in the ways of the Negroni and Manhattan, and his list is still full of curve-balls worthy of your extra time.

Australian Hotel

100 Cumberland Street, at Gloucester Street, The Rocks (9247 2229/www.australianheritage hotel.com). CityRail/ferry Circular Quay. **Open** 11am-midnight Mon-Sat; 11am-10pm Sun. **Credit** AmEx, DC, MC, V. **Map** p327 E4 ❷
Locals and tourists flock to this old-school pub just by the Harbour Bridge. There's no view to speak of, but the neighbourhood is very much olde Sydney towne, yet happily a step away from backpacker ground zero. The pizzas have a big following, and the range of local and imported draught beers is impressive – be sure to give Scharers, a very local brew sold only here and at a handful of other pubs, a good Aussie go. It also offers accommodation.

> ❶ Pink numbers given in this chapter correspond to the location of each pub or bar as marked on the street maps. *See pp326-334.*

Bars

Eat, Drink, Shop

For ale fans

Australian Hotel (*see p175*), **Lord Nelson Brewery Hotel** (*see right*), **Nag's Head Hotel** (*see p185*), **Old Fitzroy Hotel** (*see p183*).

For beer gardens

Coogee Bay Hotel (*see p183*), **Court House Hotel**, **Oaks**, **Newport Arms Hotel** (for all three, *see p185*).

For cocktails

Attic Bar (*see p175*), **Icebergs Bar** (*see p184*), **jimmy liks** (*see p181*), **Lotus** (*see p182*), **Water Bar** (*see p183*), **Zeta Bar** (*see p177*).

For late-night boozing

Baron's (*see p181*), **Bourbon** (*see p181*), **Burdekin Hotel** (*see p179*), **Coogee Bay Hotel** (*see p183*), **Hollywood Hotel** (*see p180*), **Town Hall Hotel** (*see p185*).

For views

Bennelong Bar (*see below*), **Coogee Bay Hotel** (*see p183*), **Doyle's Palace Hotel** (*see p183*), **Icebergs Bar** (*see p184*), **Newport Arms Hotel** (*see p185*), **Oaks** (*see p185*), **Opera Bar** (*see p177*), **Orbit Bar** (*see p177*).

Bennelong Bar

Sydney Opera House, Bennelong Point, Circular Quay (9241 1999/www.guillaumeatbennelong. com.au). CityRail/ferry Circular Quay. **Open** 5.30pm-late Mon-Sat. **Credit** AmEx, DC, MC, V. **Map** p327 G3 ❸

Here's one to give designer bars the world over a solid run for their money – though to be fair to the rest of the globe, plonking your bar in the smallest sail of the Sydney Opera House does give Bennelong Bar something of an unfair advantage. The soaring ceiling is stunning, the harbour views rock, the superb wine list and service make you feel grown-up and sexy, and the Saarinen chairs are God's gift to lounging. Tapas start at $40 for two: don't miss the crab sandwiches, the ultimate in bar-snacking and the perfect partner to a flute of ice-cold French. The bar is in the top level of top-notch restaurant Guillaume at Bennelong (*see p147*).

Ember

Overseas Passenger Terminal, Circular Quay West, The Rocks (8273 1204/www.wildfiresydney.com). CityRail/ferry Circular Quay. **Open** 6pm-midnight Mon; noon-1am Tue-Fri; 6pm-2am Sat; noon-midnight Sun. **Credit** AmEx, DC, MC, V. **Map** p327 F3 ❹

It's all about the Manhattans. Quite fitting, really, for a bar that adjoins Wildfire, a big, brash, American-style restaurant. Between you and me, we'll take the bar over the mothership any day. Kick back and crunch some popcorn shrimp while you peruse the selection of infused bourbons and the lengthy and distinguished cocktail list.

Firefly

Pier 7, 17 Hickson Road, Walsh Bay (9241 2031/ www.fireflybar.net). CityRail/ferry Circular Quay then 10mins walk/bus 343, 431, 432, 434. **Open** noon-10pm Mon-Sat. **Credit** AmEx, MC, V. **Map** p327 E3 ❺

We reckon they picked the name on the strength of this spot being so small and shiny. Not the sort of place you'd want to be kicking back during, say, a gale or snap frost, Firefly's indoors-outdoors shtick runs to coffee all day and good cocktails and small, smart, snacky plates of an upmarket order after dark. It's absolutely sublime on a balmy evening.

Glass Bar

2nd Floor, Hilton Sydney, 488 George Street, between Park & Market Streets, CBD (9265 6068/ www.glassbrasserie.com.au). CityRail Town Hall/ Monorail City Centre. **Open** noon-11pm Mon-Fri; 6-11pm Sat, Sun. **Credit** AmEx, DC, MC, V. **Map** p327 F6 ❻

The jury is still out on Glass (*see p145*), the restaurant proper in the shiny new Hilton, but its wine bar annex gets the big thumbs-up. Shimmering with designer gimmicks such as towering shelves of wine, and with a stunning view of the Queen Victoria Building's architectural curlicues, it's everything a big-city hotel bar should be – offering assured cocktail service, good snacking and an outstanding wine experience for greenhorns and connoisseurs alike. Upstairs is glam Zeta Bar (*see p177*).

Hemmesphere

Level 4, Establishment Hotel, 252 George Street, between Bridge Street & Abercrombie Lane, CBD (9240 3040/www.merivale.com). CityRail Wynyard or Circular Quay/ferry Circular Quay. **Open** 6pm-late Tue-Fri; 7pm-late Sat. **Credit** AmEx, DC, MC, V. **Map** p327 F5 ❼

On the ground floor of the enormous Establishment building, lots of guys – and girls – in near-identical suits shout orders for pricey beers and stare blankly at the talent. Upstairs sees a much rosier picture: couples lounge around a high-ceilinged bar, sipping luxe cocktails and discussing the various absinthe drinks on offer. Celeb-spotting is a bonus; the downside is that it's wise to book in advance. Sushi e (*see p143*), adjoining the lounge, is one of the city's finest sushi bars, while first-floor restaurant est. (*see p147*) serves fabulous Mod Oz fare.

Lord Nelson Brewery Hotel

Corner of Argyle & Kent Streets, Millers Point (9251 4044/www.lordnelson.com.au). CityRail/ferry Circular Quay. **Open** 11am-11pm Mon-Sat; noon-10pm Sun. **Credit** AmEx, DC, MC, V. **Map** p327 E3 ❽

Real ale fans, rejoice – the Lord Nello is one of the best places to explore the joys of Sydney's varying microbrews. The rest of us will be admiring the pub's colonial stonework and tucking into the seriously hearty bar plate – pickled onions, cheese, pickles, doorstop wedge of bread and all. Keep an eye out for the sign announcing the occasional treat that is Nelson's Blood, the pub's signature beer.

Opera Bar

Lower Concourse Level, Sydney Opera House, Bennelong Point, Circular Quay (9247 1666/www.operabar.com.au). CityRail/ferry Circular Quay. **Open** 11.30am-late daily. **Credit** AmEx, DC, MC, V. **Map** p327 G3 ❾

Loved by Sydneysiders and visitors alike, the Opera Bar is one of those multi-purpose venues that actually gets it right. It offers better-than-it-needs-to-be lunch for quayside rubberneckers; a lovely environment for an afternoon beer; quick, reasonably priced dinners for the pre-theatre crowd; and live music (*see p253*) and cocktails most nights for people looking to shake a little booty. The views – the Opera House above and the Bridge across the water – are particularly pretty at dusk, and this place won't hurt your wallet as much as rival Bennelong Bar (*see p176*).

Orbit Bar

Level 47, Australia Square, 264 George Street, between Hunter & Bond Streets, CBD (9247 9777/www.summitrestaurant.com.au). CityRail Wynyard. **Open** 5pm-late daily. **Credit** AmEx, DC, MC, V. **Map** p327 F5 ❿

Do not adjust your set, and don't worry, your drink hasn't been spiked: it's the bar itself that's spinning. And, 47 floors up, you get a fat eyeful of the city in plush retro-modern surrounds. The drinks are decent and the cheese twists suitably twisty, but the bill can make you dizzy if you're not careful. The building itself is a city landmark, designed by Harry Seidler, Sydney's original modernist architect.

Wine Banq

53 Martin Place, entrance on Elizabeth Street, CBD (9222 1919/www.winebanq.com.au). CityRail Martin Place. **Open** noon-late Mon-Fri; 6pm-late Sat. **Admission** free-$15. **Credit** AmEx, DC, MC, V. **Map** p327 F5 ⓫

A jug of wine, some live jazz (*see p253*) and thou. OK, so the wine comes either in Riedel crystal by the glass or in pricey (if eye-catching) boutique bottles, but the rest is bang on. In addition to one of the city's most intriguing wine lists and a more-than-serviceable menu, this swanky basement also does a fine line in cocktails and eaux de vie.

Zeta Bar

4th Floor, Hilton Sydney, 488 George Street, between Park & Market Streets, CBD (9265 6070/www.zetabar.com.au). CityRail Town Hall/Monorail City Centre. **Open** 5pm-late Mon-Wed; 3pm-late Thur, Fri; 4pm-late Sat. **Credit** AmEx, DC, MC, V. **Map** p327 F6 ⓬

Kin to London's Zeta by virtue not only of its Hilton connection and Tony Chi design, but also the handful of London bar geezers who run the place, the

Eat, Drink, Shop

High-speed service for the Hilton's movers and shakers at **Zeta Bar**.

Sydney Zeta has bright lights, big city written all over it. It's a large space, running from glam VIP areas (yours too for a hefty minimum spend) past acres of bar to a tree-shaded terrace overlooking George Street storeys below. It might not be the sort of place that wants to know you personally, but the drinks and service are good – nearly good enough to justify the prices. Beware the queues of suburbanites at weekends. There's also Glass Bar (see p176), attached to the Glass brasserie on the hotel's second floor. **Photo** p177.

Darling Harbour

Loft

3 Lime Street, King Street Wharf (9299 4770/ www.theloftsydney.com). CityRail Wynyard/ferry Darling Harbour/Monorail Darling Park. **Open** 4pm-midnight Mon-Thur; noon-2am Fri-Sun. **Credit** AmEx, DC, MC, V. **Map** p326 D5 🔞
The Baghdad Iced Tea – cucumber Smirnoff Blue voddy, Plymouth gin, apple, mint, lime and jasmine tea – is our kind of early-evening refresher. There's much to love about the Loft in general, even if the bridge-and-tunnel types pack the place out on weekends. Carved Moorish-styled ceilings, lots of squishy leather loungers and verandas opening onto water views across Darling Harbour will all conspire to keep you smiling. **Photo** p180.

East Sydney & Darlinghurst

The heart of gay Sydney – and therefore gay Australia – the 'Golden Mile' of Oxford Street stretches from mixed, occasionally sleazy business down at the Hyde Park end, becoming noticeably flasher as it goes art-house with cinemas and bookshops between Taylor Square and the Paddington Town Hall, and then much straighter and glossier in the land of moneyed boutiques and collar-up pubs for private-school kids between there and Centennial Park.

The area around Taylor Square – the locals know it as Gilligan's Island for the number of fools who find themselves hopelessly marooned there – can be a bit of a zoo on weekends, as it's the meeting point for Surry Hills cool kids, Darlinghurst hipsters, suburbanites up for a lark, bottom-feeding eastern suburbs wannabes and every flavour of homosexuality. The bars cater for all types and are, by and large, quite mixed and open. Thirst and a willingness to pay to cater to it are the common denominators. For more gay bars, *see p237*.

Burdekin Hotel

Corner of Oxford & Liverpool Streets, Darlinghurst (9331 3066/www.burdekin.com.au). CityRail Museum/bus 378, 380, L82. **Open** 4pm-4am Tue-Thur; 4pm-6am Fri; 5pm-6am Sat; 4pm-midnight Sun. **Credit** AmEx, DC, MC, V. **Map** p329 G8 🔞

One of the best Sydney bars of the early 1990s, the Burdekin may have aged, but it still has great bone structure. A range of upstairs rooms offers a world of dance options at the weekend, while the ground-floor bar feels like an upmarket pub. The tiny tiled art deco Dugout Bar in the basement, with its speakeasy cred, is the coolest bet.

Café Pacifico

1st Floor, 95 Riley Street, between Stanley & William Streets, East Sydney (9360 3811/www.cafepacifico. com.au). CityRail Kings Cross/bus 389. **Open** 6pm-late Tue-Sun. **Credit** AmEx, DC, MC, V. **Map** p329 G7 🔞
Yes, it's part of the same chain that operates Café Pacificos in London, Paris and Amsterdam; no, the Tex-Mexican food here isn't far above Sydney's relatively low standard – but Pacifico has a rockin' bar scene and the kind of random crowd mix on any given evening that makes it pleasingly unpredictable. Or maybe that's just the nation's broadest range of tequilas talking. Muy bien.

Darlo Bar

Corner of Liverpool Street & Darlinghurst Road, Darlinghurst (9331 3672/www.darlobar.com). CityRail Kings Cross/bus 389. **Open** 10am-midnight Mon-Sat; noon-midnight Sun. **Credit** AmEx, DC, MC, V. **Map** p330 H8 🔞
More properly known as the Royal Sovereign Hotel, the Darlo Bar has been a local institution for the past decade: in gay-friendly Darlinghurst it's distinguished by its reputation for being the number-one straight pick-up joint. Sure, there's plenty of boy-boy, girl-girl action to be had over its pool tables, mismatched op-shop furniture and adequate drinks, but the ease with which happy young heteros hook up here is almost freakish.

Victoria Room

Level 1, 235 Victoria Street, between Liverpool & William Streets, Darlinghurst (9357 4488/www.the victoriaroom.com). CityRail Kings Cross. **Open** 6pm-midnight Tue-Thur; 6pm-2am Fri, Sat; 2pm-midnight Sun. **Credit** AmEx, DC, MC, V. **Map** p330 J8 🔞
Victoria Street goes truly Victorian with this dim and sexy space harking back to the Raj, with much in the way of heavy baroque furnishings and classic cocktails. There's plenty to like in the way of Tom Collinses and Old Fashioneds, but no shortage of ginger and vanilla Martinis and their ilk should you wish to travel back to the future. There's a Mediterranean/Middle East-inflected restaurant too.

Surry Hills

Cricketers Arms

106 Fitzroy Street, at Hutchinson Street, Surry Hills (9331 3301). CityRail Central then 10mins walk/ bus 371, 373. **Open** noon-midnight Mon-Sat; noon-10.30pm Sun. **No credit cards. Map** p329 H10 🔞
In addition to being one of the finest places in the city to down beers, the Cricketers is everything

Eat, Drink, Shop

The **Loft**: beautiful bar, beautiful views, extraordinary cocktails. *See p179.*

that's good about Surry Hills in microcosm, remaining poised between unreconstructed flavour (read grime and the occasional thug) and moving with the times (read decent grub, a good range of beers and quality tracks issuing from the decks by the bar). The beer garden is the ideal ground on which to mount a late-afternoon assault on sobriety.

Gaslight Inn

278 Crown Street, between Oxford & Campbell Streets, Surry Hills (9360 6746). Bus 352, 378, 380, L82. **Open** noon-2am Mon-Sat; noon-midnight Sun. **No credit cards. Map** p329 G8 ⑲

By the time you read this, they'll probably have moved on, but right now this once-dingy pub, beloved of the ragged, the lost and the perpetually thirsty, is the darling of that floating world of fashion students, musicians, waiters, young professionals in denial, artists and fauxhemians that makes up a sizeable slice of Sydney's indie in-crowd. The pub itself is serviceable – dark, with lots of beer on offer and tough chicks working the bar – but it's the scene that brings it to life.

Hollywood Hotel

Corner of Foster & Hunt Streets, Surry Hills (9281 2765/www.hotelhollywood.com.au). CityRail Central or Museum/bus 301, 302. **Open** 11am-midnight Mon-Wed; 11am-3am Thur, Fri; 6pm-3am Sat. **No credit cards. Map** p329 F8 ⑳

Hooray for the Hollywood. One of the most personable pubs in town, it draws a busy mix of young and old, straight and gay, musical and less so, all under

the commanding gaze of the great Doris Goddard. A former cabaret performer, Hollywood starlet and chanteuse, the formidable Ms Goddard puts all the charm and wit of her 75-plus years into maintaining an establishment that gives performance its due without losing the sense that it should never be anything less than lots of fun. **Photo** *p181.*

Longrain

85 Commonwealth Street, at Hunt Street, Surry Hills (9280 2888/www.longrain.com.au). CityRail Central or Museum/bus 301, 302. **Open** 5.30pm-midnight Mon-Sat. **Credit** AmEx, DC, MC, V. **Map** p329 F8 ㉑

Now this is a bar. And a restaurant, for that matter, but the bar is so much part of the leading edge of Sydney nightlife that it commands equal footing with the famed Thai diner (*see p152*). Taste the greatness first in the Bloody Longrain – a winning mix of vodka, red chilli, nahm jim, cucumber and coriander – and then settle back on a low stool to contemplate the beauty of the century-old converted warehouse and the freshness and zest that informs every aspect of the business.

Mars Lounge

16 Wentworth Avenue, between Oxford & Goulburn Streets, Surry Hills (9267 6440/www.marslounge. com.au). Bus 378, 380, L82. **Open** 5pm-midnight Wed, Thur; 5pm-3am Fri; 7pm-3am Sat; 7pm-1am Sun. **Credit** AmEx, DC, MC, V. **Map** p329 G8 ㉒

Sunday night is the new Saturday. Or at least it is in this neighbourhood. Fed up with Oxford Street and its surrounds being overrun by the suburban hordes on Fridays and Saturdays, many locals now save much of their partying for Sundays. Foremost among the Sunday-nighters, the dark and spacious red-and-black Mars Lounge is famed for its mixed crowd and extensive selection of ultra-premium vodkas. Food comes as platters, pizzas and snacks.

Kings Cross, Potts Point & Woolloomooloo

The **Tilbury** (*see p240*) in Woolloomooloo is a popular gay haunt, particularly on Sunday afternoons, but its chi-chi beer garden full of mature frangipani trees is lovely at any time.

Baron's

5 Roslyn Street, between Darlinghurst Road & Ward Avenue, Kings Cross (9358 6131). CityRail Kings Cross. **Open** 6pm-4am Mon-Thur, Sun; 6pm-5am Fri, Sat. **Credit** AmEx, MC, V. **Map** p330 J7 ㉓
Of course you intend to dine. Baron's is technically the bar for the Italian restaurant downstairs (it was Thai a couple of years ago, but chips and garlic bread are the mainstay nonetheless), and the quirks of Sydney's licensing laws mean that unless you're a diner, you're really not supposed to enjoy its bizarre contrast of Teutonic hunting-lodge style (note the backgammon booths and open fires) and slice-of-late-nightlife patrons. So, of course you intend to dine, right? One of the city's finest late-nighters. Pass the garlic bread.

Bayswater Brasserie

32 Bayswater Road, at Ward Avenue, Kings Cross (9357 2177/www.bayswaterbrasserie.com.au). CityRail Kings Cross. **Open** 5pm-late Mon-Fri; 3-10pm Sun. **Credit** AmEx, DC, MC, V. **Map** p330 J7 ㉔
In the 1980s, before the Fringe Benefits Tax effectively killed the Australian version of the three-Martini lunch, the Bayz was better known as 'the Office'. And while the zenith of the expense-accounts days may have passed, the Harry's-esque bar at the back still retains a whiff of that three-o'clock-be-damned spirit, with great drinks, informed bartenders and a notable tequila selection. The Mod Oz food, with oysters a speciality, is good too (*see p157*).

Bourbon

24 Darlinghurst Road, at Macleay Street, Kings Cross (9358 1144/www.thebourbon.com.au). CityRail Kings Cross. **Open** 10am-6am daily. **Credit** AmEx, DC, MC, V. **Map** p330 J7 ㉕
Speaking of late-nighters steeped in history (is that what that smell is?), the Bourbon & Beefsteak opened in the 1960s to cater to the tastes of visiting US sailors on leave during the Vietnam war. It stayed a decidedly, uh, idiosyncratic venue until a thorough makeover (think Hercules and the Augean stables) a few years ago rendered it designer-bland cookie-cutter contemporary. It remains, however, very broad in the scope of drinkers it attracts, and is a fine last resort for any night in the Cross. It also has its own club, Plan B (*see p221*).

East Sydney Hotel

Corner of Cathedral & Crown Streets, Woolloomooloo (9358 1975/www.the-eastsydneyhotel.com.au). CityRail Kings Cross/bus 200. **Open** 10am-late Mon-Sat; noon-midnight Sun. **No credit cards**. **Map** p329 H7 ㉖
With signs proudly bearing the news that it's a poker-machine-free establishment, the East Sydney Hotel marks itself out as a breed apart. And if the friendly bar staff, roaring darts tournaments and generally genial air of this old-fashioned pub, complete with pressed-tin ceilings, are any guide, it's a breed that should be encouraged. The outdoor tables make for excellent, beer-enhanced people-watching.

Hugo's Lounge

Level 1, 33 Bayswater Road, between Ward Avenue & Kellett Street, Kings Cross (9357 4411/www.hugos.com.au). CityRail Kings Cross. **Open** 5.30pm-3am Wed-Sat; 8pm-3am Sun. **Credit** AmEx, DC, MC, V. **Map** p330 J7 ㉗
Inner-city brother of chi-chi Bondi Beach restaurant Hugo's (*see p160*), the Lounge also does dinner, but most people come here for the drinks. The drinks and the babes, that is. Male and female, they tend towards the blonde, corn-fed, moneyed (or money-hungry) end of the spectrum and prowl the Lounge's broken-glass bar, dim banquettes and canopied veranda. Mere mortals come for the peerless fresh mango Daiquiris. Downstairs is Hugo's separate pizza and pasta restaurant.

jimmy liks

186-188 Victoria Street, between Darlinghurst Road & Orwell Street, Potts Point (8354 1400/www.jimmyliks.com.au). CityRail Kings Cross. **Open** 5pm-midnight daily. **Credit** AmEx, DC, MC, V. **Map** p330 J7 ㉘
You've gotta love a list that features a drink called the Kyoto Protocol, especially when it also offers some of the finer Asian-accented cocktails in town. Chilli, saké, nahm jim, ginger and more find their way into jimmy liks' concoctions. Service is famously uneven, so arrive early, pull up a pew on the street or slide on to a stool at the long, elegant bar, and bat those lashes extra hard. *See also p156.*

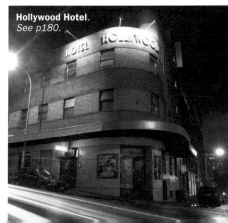

Hollywood Hotel.
See p180.

Eat, Drink, Shop

Fancy a game?

In Sydney, pool is the indoor equivalent to bonding around the barbie. Walk into most pubs and there's almost guaranteed to be at least one table in the room. It remains one of the easiest ways to meet people: whether you're a guy or a girl, stand there solo with a cue in hand and you'll probably be invited to join in on a game. Pool (usually $3 a game) is more of a social lubricant than a battleground, so if you want to play for cash you'll need to check first. Rules vary from place to place and are usually displayed near the tables. Don't make the mistake of assuming international rules: in most cases, it's the regulars who decide.

Being in the smart heart of town is no obstacle to playing pool, as you'll find at multi-faceted **Q Bar** (*see p221*), which sets its sights on being all things to everyone. Players at its five tables are surrounded by *Playboy* glamour and get to hover between cocktails, clubbing and arcade games.

Down in Surry Hills, the **Clock Hotel** (470 Crown Street, at Collins Street, 9331 5333, www.clockhotel.com.au) has a four-table pool bar plus three other smart bars, a gaming room and a restaurant in one of the more sophisticated entertainment developments in town. There is $1 pool on Tuesdays and a pool competition on Sundays at 5.30pm. Further south again is **Bar Cleveland** (corner of Cleveland and Bourke Streets, 9698 1908, www.barcleveland.com.au). It's only got two pool tables, but it's worth going for a game there to see just how classy old-style Australian pub decor actually was.

Glebe backpackers treat the **Toxteth Hotel** (345 Glebe Point Road, at Ferry Road,

9660 2370) as their very own local, and it's probably one of the friendliest get-to-meet-people places. It barely registers on the style quotient, so all attention can be focused on playing. Wednesday night's pool comp begins at 7.30pm with a $90 cash prize.

If you're staying at Bondi Beach, you don't have to stop misspending your youth (well, we can all fantasise a little) when it gets too dark to surf. Bands, bar DJs and pool tables is a dizzying combination that makes the **Beach Road Hotel** (*see p218*) one of Sydney's best all-rounders. Downstairs, the four tables buzz with a mix of backpackers and young indie beach refugees. Upstairs there are eight tables in the smarter pavilion bar; you'll need to wear more than a bikini, but the party atmosphere and cheapish drinks are hard to match. The winner of the Thursday night pool comp takes a whopping $200.

There are more options down the coast in Coogee. The **Coogee Bay Hotel** (*see p183*) has nine tables, and its huge beer garden is a firm favourite with British backpackers. The pool comp is on Monday nights. Or there's the **Beach Palace Hotel** (corner of Dolphin and Beach Streets, 9664 2900, www.beachpalacehotel.com.au) for bargain-basement pool – and we do stress the 'basement' part of that. While the upstairs level has some gobsmacking views over Coogee Beach, the four tables have been relegated to a windowless alcove in the downstairs bar. All are up for grabs at a tiny $1 per game until 6pm, when it becomes $3; the pool comp starts at 7.30pm on Tuesday. The weekday happy hour (4-7pm) makes this a cheap backpacker night out.

Lotus

22 Challis Avenue, at Macleay Street, Potts Point (9326 9000/www.merivale.com). CityRail Kings Cross. **Open** 6pm-1am Tue-Sat. **Credit** AmEx, DC, MC, V. **Map** p330 J6 ㉙

Walk into this mini-bar and ask Alexx Swainston to make you a drink. One of the best bartenders in the land, she'll look you up and down and maybe ask you about the kind of flavours you like or the mood you're in. It's not unusual to see a regular come in complaining of a sore throat and a broken heart only to have both cured in a single cocktail. You may end up with a crisp classic (a perfect Manhattan made with 18th-century style rye), a twist thereon (a tequila Old Fashioned) or one of Swainston's own subtle creations (the kaffir-lime tinged Celestial Spritzer).

This kind of bespoke mixology comes at a price, but rest assured the fit is always excellent. **Photo** *p183*.

Melt Bar

Level 3, 12 Kellett Street, at Bayswater Road, Kings Cross (9380 6060/www.meltbar.com.au). CityRail Kings Cross. **Open** 7pm-late Wed, Thur, Sun; 7pm-3am Fri, Sat. **Credit** AmEx, MC, V. **Map** p330 J7 ㉚

One of the few bars in the city and east to buck the swank-by-numbers trend, this newish establishment makes a virtue of its former status as a house of ill repute/pool hall, contrasting shiny new fittings with expanses of exposed plaster stencilled with graffiti murals. Drinks are straight down the line, but with plenty of space for lounging, eclectic tunes and an inviting programme of live entertainment, DJs and art exhibitions, Melt is a fine addition to the scene.

Old Fitzroy Hotel

129 Dowling Street, at Cathedral Street,
Woolloomooloo (9356 3848/www.oldfitzroy.com.au).
CityRail Kings Cross/bus 200. **Open** 11am-midnight
Mon-Fri; noon-midnight Sat; 3-10pm Sun. **No credit
cards. Map** p330 H7
Theatre, laksa, beer. Not uncommon to encounter
them all during a night on the town, but finding
them all under the one roof – and a particularly
comely roof, at that – is more of a talking point. Best
of all? Even without the cheap and reasonable Asian
noodle soups and the talents of the Tamarama Rock
Surfers, one of the city's more daring theatre troupes,
the pub has a rollicking charm rare for this neck of
the woods. For theatre info, *see p271*.

Water Bar

Blue, Woolloomooloo Wharf, Cowper Bay Road,
opposite Forbes Street, Woolloomooloo (9331 9000).
Bus 311, 312. **Open** 4-10pm Mon, Sun; 4pm-
midnight Tue-Sat. **Credit** AmEx, DC, MC, V.
Map p330 H6
The bar at the Taj-owned Blue (formerly the W
hotel) may be the size of a middling aircraft hangar,
but the design and placement of its booths and
ottomans is so clever that you get the sense of space
without it feeling stark, cold or empty – in fact, quite
the opposite. A 15-plus selection of vodkas is just
one virtue of the excellent bar, and this is the ideal
place for smokers and non-smokers to mingle without fear of irritating one another.

Eastern Suburbs

Coogee Bay Hotel

Corner of Arden Street & Bay Road, Coogee (9665
0000/www.coogeebayhotel.com.au). Bus 372, 373,
374. **Open** *Beach Bar* 9.30am-3am daily. *Sports Bar*
9am-3am Mon-Wed; 9am-5am Thur, Fri, Sat; 9am-
10pm Sun. *Arden Bar & Arden Lounge* noon-1am
daily (summer only). *Nightclub* 9pm-late Thur-Sat.
No credit cards.
Seating 500 (most of them visiting from the UK) the
Coogee Bay's beer garden is truly a thing to behold,
and with a cool ocean breeze waving the palms, and
Coogee Beach spread before you, it's a contender for
the best of its ilk in the east. Other bars within the
pub itself – which is enormous – offer sport, top-40
DJs, pool, a brasserie with cook-your-own steaks,
and live music, none of which come close to sup-
planting the allure of the outdoor areas.

Doyles Palace Hotel

1 Military Road, at Marine Parade, Watsons Bay
(9337 5444/www.doyles.com.au). Bus 325, L82.
Open 10am-midnight daily. **Credit** DC, MC, V.
The fish and chips are so-so. The drinks aren't
thrilling or cheap. But the Watto (as it's known) is
still on most Sydneysiders' list of the city's top pubs.
An eastern suburbs institution, there really is something to be said for watching the sun sink over the
harbour from the comfort of its capacious veranda,
surrounded by other beer-swilling day-trippers.

Lotus. *See p182.*

Eat, Drink, Shop

Cocktails

Bloody Longrain, Longrain
Themed Bloody Mary variants, all horseradish and beetroot, come and go. But the version (*photo*) at **Longrain** (*see p180*) is different: the punch packed by this concoction of cucumber-infused vodka, Thai chilli jam, coriander, fish sauce and a good wedge of fresh cue in place of the traditional celery makes for a fiery and memorable remix. Don't waste your time asking for it with less chilli.

Martini, Bayswater Brasserie
It's not for nothing that award-winning Australian novelist Frank Moorhouse acknowledged **Bayswater Brasserie** (*see p181*) in his recent Martini memoir. Ask the bar staff for a straight Martini and you can be sure that the drink delivered swiftly to your hands will be cold, crisp and dry. Make ours with Hendrick's gin for preference.

Negrita Crush, Icebergs Bar
Icebergs (*see below*) is utterly Italian – and yet utterly Bondi Beach. The brief is followed through in everything from the waiters' uniforms to this, a lighter version of the Negroni, combining campari, gin and sweet vermouth with ruby grapefruit juice and crushed ice. It might be less alcoholic than the classic formula, but don't be fooled – a couple of these while watching the sun go down over the water can see tie-loosening progress quickly to the belt area.

Old Fashioned, Lotus
Technically, the signature drink at **Lotus** (*see p182*) is the Lotus Martini. But if you really want to put the staff through their paces, the ten-minute ritual of pouring and stirring whisky-bitters-sugar-and-ice to create this most labour-intensive – and rewarding – of classic cocktails is rarely rendered better than here. If you're feeling outré, skip the rye in favour of a fine golden sipping tequila.

Icebergs Bar
1 Notts Avenue, Bondi Beach (9365 9000/idrb.com). CityRail Bondi Junction then bus 380, 381, 382, L82/bus 380, L82. **Open** noon-midnight Mon-Sat; noon-10pm Sun. **Credit** AmEx, DC, MC, V. **Map** p334 ❸❸
There is no better time to enjoy the bar adjoining the swanky Icebergs Dining Room (*see p159*) than at dusk. The rays of the dying sun swing across the length of Bondi Beach, turning the northern Heads golden, while loved-up, cash-flashing punters, some as slender and angular as the decor kick back on the bar's multi-level lounges and narrow balconies, sipping from the Campari-stained Italianate cocktail list or poppin' Veuve La Grande Dame and snacking on polenta chips and trout carpaccio.

Royal Hotel
237 Glenmore Road, at Five Ways, Paddington (9331 2604/www.royalhotel.com.au). Bus 389. **Open** 10am-midnight Mon-Sat; 10am-10pm Sun. **Credit** AmEx, DC, MC, V. **Map** p332 K9 ❸❹
Paddington is ground zero for strapping lads and lasses who love their rugby, and lots of them love the Royal too. Three levels of well-heeled conviviality are divided between the ground-floor bar, the quite reasonable Mod Oz restaurant on the first floor, and the second floor's Elephant Bar, which is stuffed with pachyderm knick-knacks and young upwardly mobiles enjoying Cosmopolitans and Caipiroskas.

Inner West

Abercrombie Hotel
Corner of Broadway & Abercrombie Street, Ultimo (9211 3486). CityRail Central. **Open** 11am-1am Mon-Wed; 11am-late Fri, Sat. **No credit cards**. **Map** p328 D10 ❸❺
There was a guy in a Greek myth whose eternal punishment involved standing in a pool of water: terribly thirsty as he was, any time he moved to drink it, it shrank from his grasp. So it is at the Abercrombie, a pleasantly studenty pub with a wide range of beers, good jukebox and a nice beer garden that

never seems to be open when you actually want to drink there (we're thinking particularly of Saturday afternoons). Finding it open, then, is a treat, and its regular indie dance, hip hop and drum 'n' bass sessions – including Purple Sneakers (*see p221*) on Friday – extra rewarding.

Clare Hotel

20 Broadway, between Regent & Abercrombie Streets, Ultimo (9211 2839). CityRail Central. **Open** 9.30am-midnight Mon-Wed; 9.30am-1am Thur, Fri; 6.30pm-3am Sat. **No credit cards. Map** p328 D10 **36**

It was the bike couriers who first colonised this place anew a couple of years back. Soon their Lycra-clad arses were being crowded off the shared-house couches by students from the nearby University of Technology, Sydney, and now the Clare runs the gamut from blow-ins here for the music to late teens to beer-loving, twentysomethings who make up its Thursday/Friday/Saturday party faithful.

Court House Hotel

Corner of Australia & Lennox Streets, Newtown (9519 8273). CityRail Newtown. **Open** 10am-midnight Mon-Sat; 10am-10pm Sun. **No credit cards. Map** p334 **37**

From the meal orders coming over the PA ('Number 14, number 14 – your T-bone is ready') to the beer garden at the back, this is the epitome of all that's good and right about drinking beer in Sydney. And what a beer garden. Whiling away a summer's arvo over a few shandies amid the nippers, mums and Newtown scruffs under the frangipani trees has got to be one of the best simple pleasures of living in this town. A great place to spend Anzac Day, by the by.

Leichhardt Hotel

95 Norton Street, between Parramatta Road & Marion Street, Leichhardt (9569 6640/ www.95norton.com). Bus 435, 436, 437, 438. **Open** 10am-midnight Mon-Thur, Sun; 10am-3am Thur-Sat. **Credit** AmEx, MC, V.

A two-storey-high reproduction of Caravaggio's *Bacchus* makes the business of this ostentatiously renovated open space all too clear. In the midst of Norton Street's Italian red-sauce merchants, the Leichhardt is a shiny beacon of things done with an eye away from the Old Country – Caravaggio notwithstanding. Downstairs you'll find cheap Asian food, upstairs darkness and layered shooters.

Nag's Head Hotel

Corner of St Johns Road & Lodge Street, Glebe (9660 1591/www.nagshead.com.au). Bus 431, 432, 433, 434, 370. **Open** 9.30am-midnight Mon-Sat; noon-midnight Sun. **Credit** MC, V. **Map** p328 A9 **38**

One of the closest approximations to a proper British pub to be found in Sydney, the Nag's has what too many wannabe boozers can't seem to manage: charm. It's got all ye olde glass, woody bits and Mother Country draught beers that any real ale fan could want, and its situation – away from the main drag of Glebe Point Road – keeps the mix of young students, old whippersnappers and locals fresh.

Town Hall Hotel

326 King Street, between Newman & Wilson Streets, Newtown (9557 1206). CityRail Newtown. **Open** 9am-2.30am Mon; 9am-3.30am Tue-Thur; 9am-4.30am Fri, Sat; 10am-midnight Sun. **No credit cards. Map** p334 **39**

Along with the Zanzibar (née Oxford) and Bank Hotel (*see p237*), the Town Hall forms what locals affectionately refer to as the Devil's Triangle of pubs near the juncture of King Street and Enmore Road. All three are popular with students, the pierced, tattooed, dyed and branded, as well as the just plain reckless, but there's a kind of mojo at work at the Townie that sees its two floors of undistinguished wooden furniture and framed train-wreck photos play host to the sort of two-fisted drinking mayhem that make it a thing of beauty unto itself.

North Shore

Oaks

Corner of Military & Ben Boyd Roads, Neutral Bay (9953 5515/www.oakshotel.com.au). Bus 175, 178, 180, 247, 263. **Open** 10am-midnight Mon-Wed; 10am-1.30am Thur-Sat; noon-midnight Sun. **Credit** AmEx, DC, MC, V.

Sydney's biggest pub? Quite possibly. A North Shore institution, the Oaks is beloved of locals young and old. The cook-your-own barbie may or may not be regarded as a plus, but the huge spreading namesake tree in the beer garden is lovely, and the fireplaces, bistro, pizza, innumerable bars and various other hooks are put to good use.

Northern Beaches

Manly Wharf Hotel

Manly Wharf, East Esplanade, Manly (9977 1266/ www.manlywharfhotel.com.au). Ferry Manly. **Open** *Public bar* 11.30am-midnight Mon-Sat; 11.30am-10pm Sun. *Jetty bar* midday-10pm daily. *Lounge bar* 5pm-midnight Thur-Sat; 4-10pm Sun. **Credit** AmEx, DC, MC, V. **Map** p334 **40**

From the bamboo-screened cocktail bar to the public bar opening on to the large timber deck and the open-air jetty bar, the Manly Wharf Hotel is all about light, water and a fresh, contemporary look. There's a good range of well-priced Margarita variants, summery stick drinks and classics. The Mod Oz restaurant is worth a gander too (*see p166*).

Newport Arms Hotel

Corner of Beaconsfield & Kalinya Streets, Newport (9997 4900/www.newportarms.com.au). Bus L87, L88, L90. **Open** 10am-11pm Mon-Fri; 10am-midnight Sat; 10am-10pm Sun. **Credit** AmEx, DC, MC, V.

This Newport landmark (est. 1880) has a mammoth beer garden out the back with a spectacular view over Pittwater and the eucalyptus-clad hills of Ku-ring-gai Chase National Park. It's the perfect spot for a post-beach beer and to contemplate your sunburn. Three restaurants, a vast outdoor screen and guest rooms are further attractions.

Eat, Drink, Shop

Shops & Services

Smart, rich, urban Australia hangs out its shingle in Sydney.

In the past ten years Australian shopping has reached new heights of international recognition. Once upon a time, the only Aussie clothing labels anyone overseas would recognise were outback outfitters Driza-Bone, Akubra or RM Williams, but nowadays home-grown designers such as jean junkies Sass & Bide, edgy Tsubi, badass Wheels & Doll Baby and super-elegant Collette Dinnigan are sold in Paris, New York and London. Such global interest has breathed new life into the shopping sectors of Sydney. Where once were suburban malls and naff tourist shops, now you'll find slick and sophisticated stores, cheeky boutiques and to-die-for designer outlets.

The **CBD** is where visitors gravitate on their first visit, and where you'll find the biggest concentration of shops. A labyrinth of arcades and malls snakes around the centre via the corner of Bathurst and Kent Streets through to Town Hall Square, connecting George, Pitt and Market Streets. Pedestrianised Pitt Street Mall (the section of Pitt Street between Market and King Streets) is a focal point, and leading departments stores David Jones and Myer (formerly Grace Bros) battle for supremacy on Market Street. A shiny new mall inside the World Square development has boosted options near Chinatown, but one landmark Sydney name – iconic menswear store Gowings – has gone; it closed in early 2006, after nearly 140 years in business.

If it's traditional souvenirs and duty-free you're after, head to the historic but touristy **Rocks** district where upmarket fashion labels and didgeridoo shops line up for 21st-century tourist dollars – a far cry from the original slums and sluice of the 19th-century immigrants who used to live in this area.

City insiders make for Oxford Street, an epically long road that acts as a spine to surrounding Darlinghurst, Surry Hills and Paddington. The city end of Oxford Street, in **Darlinghurst**, is queer Sydney central with fetish and wig shops and bookshops. In the **Paddington** area you'll find the flagships of the fashion chain stores, plus pretty boutiques harbouring smaller designers who have escaped being swallowed up by bigger brands. On Crown Street, heading south towards **Surry Hills**, you'll find offbeat clothing stores amid the numerous restaurants and arty cafés.

In **Double Bay**, ladies who lunch browse middle-of-the-road designer fashion in between meeting friends from the gym at the many good eateries. **Woollahra**'s Queen Street boasts some excellent antique shops and delicatessens, the high prices reflecting the privilege of living in the postcode. Over the Harbour Bridge, in **Neutral Bay** and **Mosman**, you'll find everything a middle-class family could need, including homeware, high-end fabric shops, kids' clothes and fashion.

On the west side of the CBD lie the suburbs of Balmain, Rozelle, Leichhardt and Glebe, all of which have become increasingly gentrified as young families move out of the eastern suburbs in the hunt for reasonably priced property. Darling Street is **Balmain's** main drag and caters for the area's funky, upwardly mobile young families. Further up Darling Street in **Rozelle** the spending changes gear with interesting bric-a-brac stores and organic

The best Shops

For all-in-one shopping
David Jones (see p189), Queen Victoria Building (see p190), Westfield Bondi Junction (see p188 Mall monster).

For cosmetic junkies
Jurlique, Mecca Cosmetica (for both, see p207), Napoleon Make-up Academy (see p208).

For groovy tunes
Birdland, Fish Records, Red Eye (for all, see p208).

For kitsch gifts
Opus Designs, Pop Shop (for both, see p205).

For second-hand book browsing
Berkelouw Books, Gleebooks, Goulds (for all, see p193).

For sweet stuff
David Jones food hall (see p189), Belle Fleur, Max Brenner, Simon Johnson Quality Foods (for all, see p204).

produce. In **Leichhardt**, revel in Italian fashion on Norton Street and at the Italian Forum complex of shops and eateries.

Backpacker-friendly Glebe Point Road in **Glebe** has numerous second-hand booksellers amid cafés, pubs and health-food shops. Further south, King Street is the main thoroughfare in studenty, multicultural **Newtown**, and home to well-priced furniture shops, great vinyl outlets and loads of vintage clothing shops.

For the best swim- and surfwear head over to **Bondi Beach** and **North Bondi**, where you can also find good vintage clothing shops and ultra-trendy boutiques. Nearby **Bondi Junction** offers an entirely different vibe, centred around the massive – and brand-new – Westfield Bondi Junction mall (*see below* **Mall monster**). It's got the major brands and a few

exclusives, plus a multi-screen cinema and an excellent food court with sensational views of the Harbour. The Westfield overshadows the shops that were here before the development, but some are still worth checking out – there's a good cobbler on Oxford Street and other stores geared towards budget-conscious families. Look out for cheap second-hand furniture and electrical goods in the area too.

Duty-free shopping abounds, particularly in the heart of the CBD. The cavernous **Downtown Duty Free** occupies the whole basement level of the Strand Arcade; make sure you take your travel documents.

OPENING HOURS

Shops open between 9am and 10am and close between 5.30pm and 6pm Monday to Friday,

Mall monster

Bondi Junction used to be little more than a transport interchange between the city and Bondi Beach. There was a cheap market, a few dusty old pubs and some budget shops. Then, in 2004, Australian mall monolith Westfield opened a whopping, $750-million shopping centre. Westfield Bondi Junction morphed three slightly shoddy malls into one hell of a shopping experience, with department stores Myer and David Jones, supermarkets Coles and Target, 450 speciality shops, six restaurants, an 11-screen cinema, 3,300 car parking spaces and a food court with some of the best views of Sydney Harbour.

There's no doubt WBJ has changed the face of the eastern suburbs. Shoppers no longer have to head into the city centre to get their retail fix. WBJ may not have the soul of funky shopping areas such as Paddington, Darlinghurst and Surry Hills, and some smaller local businesses have undoubtedly suffered in the face of such overwhelming competition, but it's bought a significant amount of cash back into an area that had been directionless since the Bondi trams stopped running in the 1960s.

The Westfield group (which employs a whopping 75 per cent of the NSW retail workforce, and also owns shopping centres in New Zealand, the UK and the States) has bigger ambitions, though. It recently purchased the CBD's Skygarden and Imperial Arcade malls for a cool $241 million, and already owns two others (Sydney Central Plaza and Centrepoint). It plans to integrate

them into one mega complex, so domination in the city beckons – assuming the council approve the development.

Westfield Bondi Junction

500 Oxford Street, at Grosvenor Street, Bondi Junction (9947 8000/www.westfield.com.au). CityRail Bondi Junction/bus 352, 378, 380, L82. **Map** p333 P11.

except for Thursday when most mainstream shopping areas stay open until around 9pm. On Saturday most places tend to shut pretty sharpish between 5pm and 6pm. Sunday trading is the norm, with most shops open between 11am and 4pm, or 5pm in the summer – though hours can vary quite a bit.

Sale time is usually at the end of summer and of winter, but department stores also hold sales to coincide with public holidays. The big ones to watch out for are David Jones's twice-yearly clearance at the end of June and after Christmas, and Myer's Boxing Day sale.

What you see on the price tag is what you pay; it includes GST (Goods & Services Tax). For details of how to reclaim your GST when you fly out, see *p303*.

One-stop shopping

Department stores

David Jones
Market Street, at Castlereagh Street; Elizabeth Street, at Market Street, CBD (9266 5544/ www.davidjones.com.au). CityRail St James or Town Hall/Monorail City Centre. **Open** 9.30am-6pm Mon-Wed, Fri; 9.30am-9pm Thur; 9am-6pm Sat; 10am-6pm Sun. **Credit** AmEx, DC, MC, V. **Map** p327 F6.
Opened in 1838 by its Welsh-born namesake, DJ's is the world's oldest department store still trading under its original name. The flagship city-centre store is on two sites at the junction of Market and Castlereagh Streets, linked by a first-floor walkway. The Market Street store has three floors of menswear, plus furniture, homewares and electrical goods. There's an appetising food hall on the lower ground floor as well as a stationer's and a cosmetics section – though the main one is on the ground floor, along with jewellery and accessories. More cosmetics, perfumes, jewellery and accessories are on the ground floor of the Elizabeth Street store. Above them are four floors of women's fashion, including a range of international designers.
Other locations: Westfield Bondi Junction (9619 1111); see website for other suburban locations.

Myer
436 George Street, at Market Street, CBD (9238 9111/www.myer.com.au). CityRail St James or Town Hall/Monorail City Centre. **Open** 9am-6pm Mon-Wed, Fri, Sat; 9am-9pm Thur; 11am-5pm Sun. **Credit** AmEx, DC, MC, V. **Map** p327 F6.
In 2004 Sydney institution Grace Bros changed its name to Myer in one of the biggest rebrandings in Australian history, although it had been owned by Coles Myer since 1983. Sidney Myer was a penniless Russian immigrant who opened his first store in Bendigo, Victoria. Now, along with David Jones (*see above*), Myer is one of the two leading department stores in the country. It positions itself as providing something for everyone, and you'll find a good range

of clothes, homewares, electrical goods and cosmetics. The brands tend to be a little cheaper than at David Jones, but everything is good quality and some designer brands are still there.
Other locations: Westfield Bondi Junction (9300 1100); 159-175 Church Street, Parramatta (9831 3100); see website for other suburban locations.

Peter's of Kensington
57 Anzac Parade, between Todman Avenue & Alison Road, Kensington (9662 1099/www.petersof kensington.com.au). Bus 393, 394, 395, 396, 397, 398, 399. **Open** 9.30am-5.30pm Mon-Fri; 9.30am-5pm Sat. **Credit** AmEx, DC, MC, V.
This old-fashioned suburban emporium is housed in a bubblegum-pink building on Anzac Parade, a couple of streets away from Royal Randwick Racecourse. Step inside and you'll see it's kept up with the times with a revamped section of high-class funky cookware alongside quality collectibles, luggage, trad children's toys and a good cosmetics section. And prices are far lower than you'd expect in a classy city department store.

Shopping centres
See also p188 **Mall monster**.

Chifley Plaza
2 Chifley Square, corner of Hunter & Phillip Streets, CBD (9221 6111/www.chifleyplaza.com.au). CityRail Martin Place. **Map** p327 F5.
Chic business workers shop at this New York-style tower complex, which stocks designer labels such as MaxMara, Pierucci and Leona Edmiston. There's also a food court, not to mention the excellent Japanese restaurant Azuma (*see p142*).

Galeries Victoria
500 George Street, at Park Street, CBD (9265 6888/ 9265 6812/www.tgv.com.au). CityRail Town Hall/ Monorail Galeries Victoria. **Map** p329 F7.
Designed by award-winning Sydney architects Crone Associates, the Tokyo-esque four-level Galeries Victoria is a welcome relief from the nearby identikit Pitt Street malls. Here you'll find Polo Jeans, Mooks, Mango and Freedom Furniture, as well as cosmetics boutique Mecca Cosmetica and Kinokuniya – Sydney's largest cross-cultural bookshop with titles in English, Japanese and Chinese – and an in-store coffee lounge.

Harbourside
Darling Drive, Darling Harbour (9281 3999/ www.harbourside.com.au). CityRail Town Hall/ ferry Darling Harbour/Monorail Harbourside. **Map** p326 D6/7.
A glitzy shopping centre on the Pyrmont side of Darling Harbour. The shops, including a good clutch that sell Australian products, are open until 9pm daily to attract as many tourists as possible after a day's sightseeing – but don't expect to nab a bargain. There's free parking if you spend $40 at any of the shops in the centre.

Imperial Arcade

168 Pitt Street Mall, between King & Market Streets, CBD (9233 5662/www.imperialarcade.com.au). CityRail Martin Place, St James or Town Hall/Monorail City Centre. **Map** p327 F6.

One of four arcades running off pedestrianised Pitt Street Mall (the others are the Mid City Centre, Skygarden and Strand Arcade), Imperial Arcade has three levels of fashion, accessories, jewellery, cafés, hair, beauty and services. Check out super-cheap teenage-chic fashion at Supre, Cotton On, Hype DC and Diva. There's also an Angus & Robertson bookshop and Lindcraft for haberdashery and crafts.

Italian Forum

23 Norton Street, between Parramatta Road & Marion Street, Leichhardt (9518 3396/www.italianforum.com.au). Bus 435, 436, 437, 438, 440, L38, L40.

A mall modelled on an Italian village complete with Romanesque piazza? Not as bad as it sounds, in fact. This suburban square of upmarket shops, restaurants, cafés and apartments does a good job of conjuring up an authentic taste of Italy. Check out the Merchant of Venice, where everything, from carnival masks to Murano glass, is imported from Venice. There's also Piccolo Toys & Books, an old-fashioned children's shop, and, for the cultural consumer, a statue of Dante in the main piazza.

Mid City Centre

197 Pitt Street Mall, between King & Market Streets, CBD (9221 2422). CityRail Martin Place, St James or Town Hall/Monorail City Centre. **Map** p327 F6.

Running between Pitt and George Streets, Mid City Centre has a big HMV, a large Rebel Sports, the Body Shop and fashion store Marcs at the front, and a den-like fast-food frenzy on the lower ground floor. If you go up the escalators at the back, you'll come across some good fashion stores. Glam girls will love the Holly Golightly boutique.

MLC Centre

Martin Place, corner of King & Castlereagh Streets, CBD (9224 8333/www.mlccentre.com.au). CityRail Martin Place/Monorail City Centre. **Map** p327 F6.

Old-timers still mourn the loss of the Parisian-style Rowe Street, which was levelled to make way for this arcade in the 1970s. Coined-up city slickers now splurge on top designer names, such as Cartier and Gucci, as well as über-boutique Belinda. The Theatre Royal is part of the complex, as is a huge Harvey Norman Technology Shop with home cinema rooms. There's a good food court too.

Queen Victoria Building (QVB)

455 George Street, between Market & Druitt Streets, CBD (9264 9209/www.qvb.com.au). CityRail Town Hall/Monorail Galeries Victoria. **Map** p327 E6.

The elegant, airy Victorian halls of this historic building pull in the tourist dollars, but there are plenty of places for Sydneysiders to shop as well. You'll find designer labels, fashion chain stores, shoe shops, florists and chocolate shops on the ground floor, and

arts, antiques and Australiana on level two. The lower ground level links through to the Town Hall Square shops and station, along with the Galeries Victoria shopping centre. **Photo** *p191.*

Skygarden

77 Castlereagh Street, between King & Market Streets, CBD (9231 1811/www.skygarden.com.au). CityRail Martin Place, St James or Town Hall/Monorail City Centre. **Map** p327 F6.

Sportsgirl and a decent-sized Borders bookshop are the main draws on the ground floor of this centre running between Pitt Street Mall and Castlereagh Street. On the first and second you'll find quality shoe shops and men's tailoring – for a bit of panache in your pinstripe, try Antons on level one. You can also connect to the Glasshouse arcade, which has furniture store Pacific East India Co, STA Travel and Mollini and Midas shoe shops.

Strand Arcade

412-414 George Street, between King & Market Streets, CBD (9232 4199/www.strandarcade.com.au). CityRail Martin Place, St James or Town Hall/Monorail City Centre. **Map** p327 F6.

This beautiful arcade is as historic as the QVB, but a hundred times cooler. There's a huge Downtown Duty Free in the basement, and touristy shops such as Haigh's Chocolates and Strand Hatters on the ground floor. But venture upwards and you'll discover the darlings of the Australian fashion scene, including Leona Edmiston, Lisa Ho, Wayne Cooper, Third Millennium, Bettina Liano, Zimmermann, Bare, and Dinosaur Designs. The prices continue to escalate as you move up again – check out the divine Alex Perry and sleek Jayson Brunsdon.

Sydney Central Plaza

450 George Street, at Market Street, CBD (8224 2000/www.westfield.com.au). CityRail Town Hall or St James/Monorail City Centre. **Map** p327 F6.

Department store Myer (*see p189*) dominates Sydney Central Plaza, but there are plenty of other decent shops worth visiting. For fashion, there's Sydney designer Morrissey, as well as Saba and the excellent chain store Witchery. The international food court on the lower ground floor is one of the city's best, and stays open until 10pm on Thursdays.

World Square

Liverpool, George, Goulburn & Pitt Streets, CBD (9262 7926/www.worldsquare.com.au). CityRail Central or Town Hall/LightRail Central. **Map** p329 E/F8.

A brand-new office, residential and retail development covering an entire block at the Central Station end of the CBD. With nearly 90 fashion, lifestyle and homeware stores, medical centres, travel agents, bars and restaurants, and a big Coles supermarket, this latest addition to the Sydney shopping scene might not be as pretty as the QVB or the Strand (for both, *see above*), or as cool as Galeries Victoria (*see p189*), but its sheer size and scope is certainly impressive. *See also p81* **World domination**.

Markets

Most Sydney markets are held in schools or church grounds. Be prepared to try things on in the toilets, and you can leave your credit cards at home as cash is preferred – plus you're more likely to get a bargain that way.

Balmain

St Andrew's Congregational Church, corner of Darling Street & Curtis Road, Balmain (9555 1791/ www.balmainsaturdaymarket.citysearch.com.au). Ferry Balmain or Balmain East/bus 433, 434, 442. **Open** 8am-4pm Sat.

Artists sell paintings and ceramics in this pretty market in the grounds of a charming 19th-century church. You'll also find good-quality vintage jewellery, hammocks and naturally made cosmetics. Check out the enamelled organ pipes inside St Andrew's church before you leave.

Bondi Beach

Bondi Beach Public School, corner of Campbell Parade & Warners Avenue, Bondi Beach (9315 8988/www.bondimarkets.com.au). CityRail Bondi Junction then bus 380, 381, 382, L82/bus 380, L82. **Open** 10am-5pm Sun. **Map** p334.

The beautiful Bondi primp and pose among the stalls of the emerging generation of Aussie fashion designers. The market can get crowded and hot, but is worth a visit if you're after either new or vintage clothing, and there's an excellent flower stall.

Glebe

Glebe Public School, Glebe Point Road, between Mitchell Street & Parramatta Road, Glebe (4237 7499). Bus 431, 432, 433. **Open** 10am-4pm Sat. **Map** p328 B9.

This used to be the most feral of Sydney's markets, but is becoming smarter as the area gentrifies. All the same, you can expect second-hand clothing, various kinds of bargain of interest to students and New-Agey stalls, plus some good crafts and bookshops. Great cafés nearby too.

Kings Cross Car Market

Kings Cross Car Park, Ward Avenue, at Elizabeth Bay Road, Kings Cross (1800 808188/9358 5000). CityRail Kings Cross. **Open** 9am-5pm daily **Map** p330 J7.

This underground car park in Kings Cross contains an area for overseas travellers to buy and sell motor vehicles. There are no professional car dealers, only private sellers, and you should be able to pick up a car, wagon, van or camper van on the spot – often complete with camping gear. You can come back and sell it again on your way out.

Kirribilli

Bradfield Park, Alfred Street, at Burton Street, Milsons Point (9922 4428). CityRail/ferry Milsons Point. **Open** 7am-3pm 4th Sat of the mth; extra markets on 1st & 3rd Sat in Dec.

This monthly market specialises in bric-a-brac and antiques, but you'll also find some great vintage dress stalls and original jewellery.

Eat, Drink, Shop

Fit for royalty: the landmark **Queen Victoria Building**. *See p190.*

There's plenty to tempt tongue and eye as you stroll through **Paddington Market**.

Paddington

Paddington Uniting Church, 395 Oxford Street, at Newcombe Street, Paddington (9331 2923/ www.paddingtonmarket.com.au). Bus 352, 378, 380, L82. **Open** 10am-4pm Sat. **Map** p332 L10.
This is the centre of Paddo shopping activity on a Saturday. Many a big-name fashion designer began by selling here. There are also masses of jewellery makers, ceramicists and artisans selling their wares, plus multicultural food stalls. The market makes a nice break from the air-conditioned stores on Oxford Street, but it does get packed. **Photo** *above.*

Paddy's

Market City, corner of Hay & Thomas Streets, Haymarket (1300 361 589/www.paddysmarkets. com.au). CityRail Central or Town Hall/Monorail/ LightRail Paddy's Markets. **Open** 9am-5pm Thur-Sun. **Map** p329 E8.
Paddy's covered labyrinth of stalls caters to bargain-hunting families and backpackers. You'll find kooky Asian clothing, shoes, CDs, electronics and fruit and veg – all at cheap, cheap prices.

The Rocks

North Precinct, George Street, at Atherden Street, The Rocks (Sydney Harbour Foreshore Authority 9240 8717/www.rocksmarket.com). CityRail/ferry Circular Quay. **Open** 10am-5pm Sat, Sun. **Map** p327 F3.
Here you'll find mainly quality arts, crafts, home-wares, antiques and collectibles, including a lot of stall selling indigenous craft and souvenirs. You might spot a bargain among the tourist prices.

Rozelle

Rozelle Public School, Darling Street, between Victoria & Merton Streets, Rozelle (9818 5373). Bus 432, 433, 434, 440. **Open** 9am-4pm Sat, Sun.
A good, old-fashioned bric-a-brac market with staples such as second-hand clothes, music and books, and plants, plus a jazz band to liven up pro-ceedings. The vintage clothing on offer is usually cheaper than at the other markets.

Surry Hills

Shannon Reserve, Crown Street, at Foveaux Street, Surry Hills (9380 5555). CityRail/Light Rail Central. **Open** 10am-5pm 1st Sat of the mth. **Map** p329 G10.
Still the hippest of all of the city's many weekend markets. There's lots to catch the eye in the form of clothes, accessories and good junk. This is also where you'll find retro revivals before anyone else realises they are fashionable.

Books

Dymocks (www.dymocks.com.au) is Sydney's best-established bookshop chain, and it also has excellent stationery and travel sections. You're never far from one of its shops, as it has branches all over town, including a big one at 424 George Street, CBD (9235 0155). There are also quite a few outlets of the nationwide chain **Angus & Robertson** (www.angusrobertson. com.au), including one on the Corso in Manly (24 The Corso, 9976 3188).

Ariel
42 Oxford Street, between Barcom Avenue & West Street, Paddington (9332 4581/www.arielbooks. com.au). Bus 352, 378, 380, L82. **Open** 9am–midnight daily. **Credit** AmEx, DC, MC, V. **Map** p332 H9.
Situated opposite NSW University College of Fine Art, Ariel stocks a lot of gorgeous hard-back (and so expensive) art, design, photography, fashion and contemporary culture books, which the laid-back staff are happy for you to leaf through for as long as you like. It also sells a range of terrifyingly hip and highbrow magazines.
Other locations: 103 George Street, The Rocks (9241 5622).

Berkelouw Books
19 Oxford Street, between South Dowling Street & Greens Road, Paddington (9360 3200/ www.berkelouw.com.au). Bus 352, 378, 380, L82. **Open** 9.30am–midnight daily. **Credit** AmEx, DC, MC, V. **Map** p332 H9.
More or less opposite Ariel, Berkelouw has an intriguing selection of new and antique Australiana and assorted rare books. It's also right next to the Palace art-house cinemas (*see p226*) and has a café upstairs – a great place to grab a soy latte and a slice of organic toasted banana bread before the movie.
Other locations: 70 Norton Street, Leichhardt (9560 3200).

The Bookshop Darlinghurst
207 Oxford Street, between Flinders & South Dowling Streets, Darlinghurst (9331 1103/ www.thebookshop.com.au). Bus 352, 378, 380. **Open** 10am–10pm Mon–Wed; 10am–11pm Thur; 10am–midnight Fri, Sat; 11am–11pm Sun. **Credit** AmEx, DC, MC, V. **Map** p332 H9.
Specialises in gay and lesbian literature and also stocks a range of rare imported books, as well as mainstream books that cater for hip inner-city dwellers. The staff are exceptionally knowledgeable.

Gleebooks
49 Glebe Point Road, between Cowper & Francis Streets, Glebe (9660 2333/www.gleebooks.com.au). Bus 431, 432, 433. **Open** 9am–9pm daily. **Credit** AmEx, DC, MC, V. **Map** p328 B9.
Highly rated Gleebooks has two branches on Glebe Point Road. No.191 specialises in second-hand and children's books, as well as more esoteric works on the humanities. No.49 sells everything else.
Other locations: 191 Glebe Point Road, Glebe (9552 2526).

Map World
280 Pitt Street, between Park & Bathurst Streets, CBD (9261 3601/www.mapworld.net.au). CityRail Town Hall/Monorail Galeries Victoria. **Open** 9am–5.30pm Mon–Wed, Fri; 9am–6.30pm Thur; 10am–4pm Sat. **Credit** AmEx, MC, V. **Map** p329 F7.
Road maps for the whole of Australia, as well as travel guides, atlases and books about such outdoor activities as four-wheel-driving and rock climbing.
Other locations: 136 Willoughby Road, Crows Nest (9966 5770).

Second-hand

In addition to those listed below, *see also above* **Berkelouw Books** and **Gleebooks**.

Goulds
32 King Street, between Queen & Fitzroy Streets, Newtown (9519 8947/www.gouldsbooks.com.au). Bus 422, 423, 426, 428, 352. **Open** 8am–midnight daily. **Credit** AmEx, MC, V. **Map** p334.
Around 3,000m (9,000ft) of bookshelves make this the largest second-hand bookshop in Sydney. It's a librarian's nightmare, but worth the rummage – and

Eat, Drink, Shop

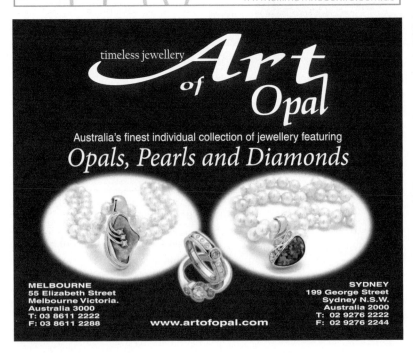

it's open until midnight. It specialises in Australian history and politics, and general Australiana.

Sappho Books
51 Glebe Point Road, between Cowper & Francis Streets, Glebe (9552 4498/www.sapphobooks. com.au). Bus 431, 432, 433. **Open** 8am-9pm Mon-Sat; 9am-8pm Sun. **Credit** AmEx, DC, MC, V. **Map** p328 B9.
A popular, friendly and immaculately catalogued second-hand bookshop that offers something for every bookworm – from Australian first editions and leather-bound tomes to art books and the latest kiddie's classic. There's also a comfortable café at the rear, with a lovely big courtyard.

Cameras & photo developing

Bondi Beach One Hour
25 Hall Street, between Campbell Parade & Gould Street, Bondi Beach (9300 9577). CityRail Bondi Junction then bus 380, 381, 382, L82/bus 380, L82. **Open** 9am-6pm daily. **Credit** AmEx, MC, V. **Map** p334.
Basic photo development and other camera-related services are provided at this handily located Bondi shop. If you've left the film age behind, you can print out digital snaps at the self-service booth too.

Paxtons
285 George Street, at Hunter Street, CBD (9299 2999/www.paxtons.com.au). CityRail Wynyard. **Open** 8am-6pm Mon-Fri; 9am-4pm Sat, Sun. **Credit** AmEx, DC, MC, V. **Map** p327 F5.
Sydney's largest independent camera retailer stocks a fine selection of digital cameras, SLRs, video cameras, lenses, digital audio gear and more. Don't be shy about asking for a discount: staff are keen to outprice arch-competitors Harvey Norman. **Other locations**: Westfield Bondi Junction (9389 6100); Westfield Parramatta, Church Street, Parramatta (9635 9696).

Fashion

Mall mammoth Westfield may be munching its way through the city, but smaller boutiques are biting back. Clusters of stylish shopping areas are nestled on **William Street** and **Glenmore Road** in Paddington, and the Oxford Street end of **South Dowling Street**.

Australian designers
For the latest Aussie fashion names, *see p196* **Stars of the southern hem**.

Akira Isogawa
12A Queen Street, at Oxford Street, Woollahra (9361 5221/www.akira.com.au). Bus 352, 378, 380, L82. **Open** 10.30am-6pm Mon-Wed, Fri; 10.30am-7pm Thur; 10am-6pm Sat. **Credit** AmEx, MC, V. **Map** p332 L11.

Akira is known for his romantic other-worldy multi-layering of transparent fabrics and bold colours. The shop has been in Woolahra since 1993, and his garments are now sold in all the world's fashion epicentres. If you're a follower of original and high-end designs, he's worth checking out.
Other locations: Strand Arcade, CBD (9232 1078).

Alannah Hill
118-120 Oxford Street, at Glenmore Road, Paddington (9380 9147/www.alannahhill.com.au). Bus 352, 378, 380, L82. **Open** 10am-6pm Mon-Wed, Fri, Sat; 10am-8pm Thur; 11am-6pm Sun. **Credit** AmEx, DC, MC, V. **Map** p332 J9.
Alannah has cornered flirty feminine style. The vintage-doll-like shop assistants look like they are having as much fun trying on the rich fabrics, velvet trims, lace and feathered hats as the customers. A good place to buy race-day accessories.
Other locations: Strand Arcade, CBD (9221 1251); Westfield Bondi Junction (9389 3066); Factory Outlet, Birkenhead Point Shopping Centre, Drummoyne (9181 4999).

Charlie Brown
178 Oxford Street, opposite Victoria Barracks, Paddington (9360 9001/www.charliebrown online.com). Bus 352, 378, 380, L82. **Open** 10am-6pm Mon-Wed, Fri, Sat; 10am-8pm Thur; 11am-5pm Sun. **Credit** AmEx, DC, MC, V. **Map** p332 J9/10.
American-born Charlie Brown provides flamboyant, innovative clothes for women who are tired of the stick-insect sizes provided by other designers. She's one of the doyennes of Australia's fashion scene, and both Jade Jagger and Jerry Hall have modelled at her shows. She stocks the Howard Showers label as well as her own. You'll also find vintage accessories and exciting costume jewellery.

Collette Dinnigan
33 William Street, off Oxford Street, Paddington (9360 6691/www.collettedinnigan.com.au). Bus 352, 378, 380, L82. **Open** 10am-6pm Mon-Sat; noon-4pm Sun. **Credit** AmEx, MC, V. **Map** p332 K10.
Models about to get married and celebs in need of a sensational gown to wear on the red carpet love Dinnigan's exquisite beading and sensual embroidery. Prices are as jaw-dropping as the designs.

Leona Edmiston
88 William Street, off Oxford Street, Paddington (9331 7033/www.leonaedmiston.com.au). Bus 352, 378, 380, L82. **Open** 10am-6pm Mon-Sat; noon-4pm Sun. **Credit** AmEx, MC, V. **Map** p332 K10.
Sydneysider Leona Edmiston once teamed up with Morrissey (*see p196*) but set up on her own in 2001 after a break-up. Now her designs couldn't be more different, with a fun and flirty collection of pretty frocks and fabulous accessories. Chic and cheeky femininity is the thing here, with delicate prints and flattering cuts.
Other locations: Chifley Plaza, CBD (9230 0322); Strand Arcade, CBD (9221 7277); Westfield Bondi Junction (9369 5399).

Stars of the southern hem

Though Australian designers such as **Collette Dinnigan** (*photo*; see p195) and **Lisa Ho** (*see below*) are creating a buzz in the front rows of international fashion shows, and ultra-trendy department stores such as London's Harvey Nicols and New York's Bloomingdale's are clamouring to stock up on Sydney's **Wheels & Doll Baby** and **Tsubi** (for both, *see p197*), there is some excellent local talent that you won't find overseas.

The heart of creative Australian fashion beats in Melbourne, but label lovers visiting Sydney for the first time are often surprised at the diversity of home-grown designers. Sure, some follow trends coming from London, Paris and Milan, but others stand out for their sheer originality.

The CBD's **Strand Arcade** (*see p190*) is home to many of these names. For high-high-end party frocks, head to **Alex Perry** or **Jayson Brunsdon**, whose Audrey Hepburn-esque eveningwear is already a couture staple even though he only opened his first boutique in 2005. Also in the arcade you'll find some of the coolest Aussie labels, such as the sumptuous **Third Millennium**, whose store manager Carmen is as saucy as the clothes, wearing fresh tiger lilies in her bleached blonde beehive. Quirky **Leona Edmiston**, jeans goddess **Bettina Liano** and super-sexy **Zimmermann** (*see p197* also have outlets there.

Newer to the scene, **Marnie Skillings**, **Josh Goot**, **Alice McCall**, **Rebecca Dawson** and **Mad Cortes** are on the brink of global recognition while driving the fashion industry forward in their home country. The **Corner Shop** (*see p198*) in Paddington is a good starting point as it specialises in emerging Australian designers: it stocks Skillings' ladylike creations, Goot's slinky jersey knits for men and women, and Cortes' feminine but edgy designs. McCall's hippy-dippy floaty numbers and fab jeans are stocked at **Capital L** (*see p197*) and **David Jones** (*see p189*),

while Dawson's dreamy eveningwear label Bare can be found in the Strand Arcade, as well as at other boutiques around town.

The annual Mercedes Australian Fashion Week trade shows (held in Sydney in April/May, and in Melbourne in October) are key events for new designers. MAFW's 'Start Up' scheme searches Australia for the next big thing: in 2005 young Brisbane designer **Gail Sorronda** (also stocked at the Corner Shop) was attracting plenty of attention from domestic and international buyers. Swimwear designers **Flamingo Sands** (www.flamingosands.com) and **High Tea with Mrs Woo** (www.highteawithmrswoo.com.au) also did well at MAFW and look set to make the big time. You can find the former at **Holly Golightly** (www.hollygolightly.com.au) in the **Mid City Centre** (*see p190*), and the latter at **Von Troska** (www.vontroska.com.au), which has four shops around town including one in the Strand Arcade. Drape yourself in their designs while no one else at home can get their hands on them.

Lisa Ho

Corner of Oxford & Queen Streets, Woollahra (9360 2345/www.lisaho.com.au). Bus 352, 378, 380, L82. **Open** 10am-6pm Mon-Wed, Fri, Sat; 10am-8pm Thur; 11am-5pm Sun. **Credit** AmEx, DC, MC, V. **Map** p332 L11.

If the prices at Collette Dinnigan seem a little steep, try equally luxurious Lisa Ho. When Australian actress Sarah Wynter wore one of Ho's creations to the Emmy awards ceremony in 2004, regard for the designs became international. Stretch fabrics and sheer chiffon are beaded and pleated with gorgeous results. Great swimwear too.
Other locations: Strand Arcade, CBD (9222 9711).

Morrissey

372 Oxford Street, between Elizabeth Street & Jersey Road, Paddington (9380 7422). Bus 352, 378, 380,

L82. **Open** 9.30am-5.30pm Mon-Wed, Fri, Sat; 9.30am-8pm Thur; 11am-5pm Sun. **Credit** AmEx, DC, MC, V. **Map** p332 L10.

Peter Morrissey began his fashion career with Leona Edmiston (*see p195*), and together they created the Morrissey Edmiston label, a hit for 14 years. Today Morrissey is owned by Oroton and his designs reflect their classic styling with vibrant colours. Good contemporary tailoring for men and women. **Other locations**: Sydney Central Plaza, CBD (9221 8002); Westfield Bondi Junction (9387 1166); Factory Outlet, Birkenhead Point Shopping Centre, Drummoyne (9719 2060).

Paablo Nevada

140 Curlewis Street, between Campbell Parade & Glenayr Avenue, Bondi Beach (9365 0165). CityRail Bondi Junction then bus 380, 381, 382, L82/bus 380, L82. **Open** 11am-6pm daily. **Credit** AmEx, DC, MC, V. **Map** p334.

A Sydney label combining urban-chic streetwear with a little bit of country. Owners Wayne Homschek and Betty Fong, curiously enough, also have a pie shop in Bondi Junction called Pie Face. **Other locations**: 15 Cross Street, Double Bay (9362 9455).

Saba

Sydney Central Plaza, 450 George Street, at Market Street, CBD (menswear 9231 2436/womenswear 9232 4666/www.saba.com.au). CityRail St James or Town Hall/Monorail City Centre. **Open** 9am-6pm Mon-Wed, Fri, Sat; 9am-9pm Thur; 11am-5pm Sun. **Credit** AmEx, DC, MC, V. **Map** p327 F6.

Melbourne designer Joe Saba's label has always been synonymous with style and sophistication. But after a heart attack in 1999 and a personal rethink, the fashion legend sold his sprawling collection of shops. Expect hip denims, cosy knitwear, shirts in sharp colours and smart suits for men and women. **Other locations**: 39 Bay Street, Double Bay (9362 0281).

Sass & Bide

132 Oxford Street, between Glenmore & Shadforth Streets, Paddington (9360 3900/www.sassand bide.com.au). Bus 352, 378, 380, L82. **Open** 10am-6pm Mon-Wed, Fri, Sat; 10am-8pm Thur; 11am-5pm Sun.* **Credit** AmEx, DC, MC, V. **Map** p332 J9.

Sarah-Jane 'Sass' Clarke and Heidi 'Bide' Middleton started selling clothes on London's Portobello Road, but struck gold when they made international headlines with their sexy, skinny low-rise jeans. This concept store is the only one in the world devoted to their label, though you'll find their clothes in many other department stores and boutiques.

Scanlan & Theodore

122 Oxford Street, at Glenmore Street, Paddington (9380 9388/www.scanlantheodore.com.au). Bus 352, 378, 380, L82. **Open** 10am-6pm Mon-Wed, Fri; 10am-5.30pm Sat; noon-5pm Sun. **Credit** AmEx, DC, MC, V. **Map** p332 J9.

If you love fashion and can only make it to one Australian designer, make it Scanlan & Theodore.

You'll find things in outrageously luxurious fabrics with creative but classy colours. **Photos** *p199.* **Other locations**: 443 Oxford Street, Paddington (9361 6722).

Tsubi

82 Gould Street, between Hall & Curlewis Streets, Bondi Beach (9300 8233/www.tsubi.com). CityRail Bondi Junction then bus 380, 381, 382, L82/bus 380, L82. **Open** 10am-6pm Mon-Wed, Fri, Sat; 10am-8pm Thur; 11am-5pm Sun. **Credit** AmEx, DC, MC V. **Map** p334.

Sydney boys Dan Single, George Gorrow and Gareth Moody launched their brand at Australian Fashion Week 2001. Making a sensation with quirky shows since then (they released 250 live rats at the first show they did in Sydney), they've since made a name for ultra-cool jeans and tees. **Other locations**: 16 Glenmore Road, Paddington (9361 6291).

Wheels & Doll Baby

259 Crown Street, at Goulburn Street, Darlinghurst (9361 3286/www.wheelsanddollbaby.com). CityRail Museum/bus 373, 374, 377, 378, 380. **Open** 10am-6pm Mon-Wed, Fri, Sat; 10am-8pm Thur; noon-5pm Sun. **Credit** AmEx, DC, MC, V. **Map** p329 G8.

Melanie Greensmith started her vampy fashion label in 1987. Her clothes became synonymous with all things rock when Michael Jackson came in browsing for a customised leather jacket for his Bad tour. Now rockers such as Deborah Harry and the Black Crowes all wear her styles on stage. Greensmith has recently launched two 'baby shops' in LA and London's Harvey Nichols, creating fans out of the likes of Kate Moss and Gwen Stefani.

Zimmermann

387 Oxford Street, opposite William Street, Paddington (9357 4700/www.zimmermann wear.com). Bus 352, 378, 380, L82. **Open** 10am-6pm Mon-Wed, Fri, Sat; 10am-8pm Thur; noon-5pm Sun. **Credit** AmEx, DC, MC, V. **Map** p332 K10.

Sisters Nicole and Simone Zimmermann launched this very successful label in the early 1990s. Swimwear has always been their calling card: bright, bold, contemporary designs for hip bodies. **Other locations**: Strand Arcade, CBD (9221 9558); Westfield Bondi Junction (9387 5111).

Boutiques

Also try funky **Kitten** (4 Glenmore Road, 9357 6480, www.kitten.com.au) in Paddington, which doubles as a shop for the Spunk records labels and **Capital L** (333 South Dowling Street, 9361 0111, www.capital-l.com).

Belinda

8 Transvaal Avenue, off Cross Street, Double Bay (9328 6288/www.belinda.com.au). Ferry Double Bay/bus 323, 324, 325, 326. **Open** 10am-6pm Mon-Fri; 10am-5pm Sat. **Credit** AmEx, DC, MC, V. **Map** p331 N7.

Eat, Drink, Shop

The pick of the crop of exquisite fashion and beautiful accessories, both local and overseas, selected by the store's stylish namesake Belinda Seper, ex-model turned fashion queen.
Other locations: 29 William Street, Paddington (menswear) (9380 8873); 39 William Street, Paddington (9380 8728); MLC Centre, CBD (9233 0781).

Corner Shop

43 William Street, off Oxford Street, Paddington (9380 9828). Bus 352, 378, 380, L82. **Open** 10am-6pm Mon-Wed, Fri, Sat; 10am-7pm Thur; noon-5pm Sun. **Credit** AmEx, DC, MC, V. **Map** p332 K10.

For this eclectic fashion venture, the Belinda team (*see p197*) scours the world's international fashion fairs to bring back the hippest and brightest of the up-and-coming designers they find. A good place to catch the newest Aussie names.

Christensen Copenhagen

2 Guilfoyle Avenue, off Bay Street, Double Bay (9328 9755). Ferry Double Bay/bus 323, 324, 325, 326. **Open** 10am-6pm Mon-Fri; 10am-5pm Sat; noon-5pm Sun. **Credit** AmEx, DC, MC, V. **Map** p331 M/N7.

The stylists' favourite. They come here to stock up on European brands such as Matthew Williamson, Johnny Loves Rosie, Burberry and Petit Bateau. Owned by Marianne Christensen, who ran a designer boutique in Copenhagen, it's the only shop in Australia to stock the gorgeous Paul & Joe label.
Other locations: Westfield Bondi Junction (9389 9055).

JAG

Westfield Bondi Junction, 500 Oxford Street, at Grosvenor Street, Bondi Junction (9387 8478/ www.jag.com.au). CityRail Bondi Junction/bus 352, 378, 380, L82. **Open** 9.30am-7pm Mon-Wed, Fri; 9.30am-9pm Thur; 9.30am-6pm Sat; 10am-6pm Sun. **Credit** AmEx, DC, MC, V. **Map** p333 P11.

The JAG label was the brainchild of Melbourne designers Rob and Adele Palmer, who shot to success in the 1970s with their casual sportswear and sharp denim designs, attracting a worldwide following that included Steve McQueen, Jackie Onassis and Bianca Jagger. Today the company is owned by Brisbane footwear group Colorado and boasts a team of funky young designers.
Other locations: Westfield Parramatta, Church Street, Parramatta (9687 1300).

Marcs

Mid City Centre, between King & Market Streets, CBD (9221 4583/www.marcs.com.au). CityRail St James or Town Hall/ Monorail City Centre. **Open** 9.30am-6pm Mon-Wed, Fri; 9.30am-9pm Thur; 9am-6pm Sat; 11am-5pm Sun. **Credit** AmEx, DC, MC, V. **Map** p327 F6.

The Marcs label launched in the 1980s when a couple of designers had the idea to make men's shirts out of women's fabrics Now it's a massively successful string of men's and women's clothes shops. The label was recently taken over by Oroton,

which also owns Morrissey and Polo Ralph Lauren. It offers cool fashion basics using lots of colour, plus imports including Diesel and Citizens of Humanity.
Other locations: 31-33 Knox Street, Double Bay (9362 5977); 645 Military Road, Mosman (9968 1298); 270 Oxford Street, Paddington (9360 5238); Westfield Bondi Junction (9369 1733).

Robby Ingham

424-426 Oxford Street, between Elizabeth Street & Jersey Road, Paddington (9332 2124). Bus 352, 378, 380, L82. **Open** 10am-6pm Mon-Wed, Fri, Sat; 10am-8pm Thur; 11am-5pm Sun. **Credit** AmEx, DC, MC, V. **Map** p332 L10.

What started out as a single men's shop is slowly building up into a small empire. Now there are individual Robbie Ingham shops catering to men, women and jeans-wearers, stocking local designers such as Helen Sherry and Sample, while imports are represented by Paul Smith and Comme des Garçons.
Other locations: MLC Centre, CBD (9232 6466).

Chain stores

Sydney has large branches of womenswear chain stores like **Country Road** (142 Pitt Street, CBD, 9394 1818, www.countryroad. com.au), which is excellent for basics; cheap and cheerful **Dotti** (356 Oxford Street, Paddington, 9332 1659, www.dotti.com.au); the funky, unique chain **Seduce** (163 King Street, Newtown, 9565 2022, www.seduce.com.au); and **Sportsgirl** (Skygarden, 77 Castlereagh Street, CBD, 9223 8255, www.sportsgirl. com.au), where many girls spend their first pay cheque before graduating to the more grown-up **David Lawrence** (Westfield Bondi Junction, 9386 5583, www.davidlawrence.com.au). **Witchery** (332 Oxford Street, Paddington, 9360 6934, www.witchery.com.au) offers well-priced designs that often copy the latest catwalk releases. For both men and women, try plain and practical **Rivers** (Town Hall Arcade, 464 Kent Street, CBD, 9264 3501, www.rivers. com.au), a sort of Aussie Gap.

RM Williams

389 George Street, between King & Market Streets, CBD (9262 2228/www.rmwilliams.com.au). CityRail Martin Place, St James or Town Hall/Monorail City Centre. **Open** 8.30am-6pm Mon-Wed, Fri; 8.30am-9pm Thur; 9am-5pm Sat; 11am-5pm Sun. **Credit** AmEx, DC, MC, V. **Map** p327 E/F6.

Reginald Murray Williams and his pardner Dollar Mick started out as a 'bush outfitters' in South Australia in the early 1930s. Now their clothes are more likely to be seen on urban cowboys than the hard-riding jackaroos they were first designed for. Boots and moleskins are the staple, but you can also get good-quality shirts, knits and shorts for men.
Other locations: 71 George Street, The Rocks (9247 0204); Chifley Plaza, CBD (9233 5608); Westfield Bondi Junction (9369 3519).

Scanlan & Theodore: colourful shop, gorgeous clothes. *See p197.*

Children

Bonds (www.bonds.com.au), **Gumboots** (www.gumboots.com.au), **Fred Bare** (www.fredbare.com) and **Mini Minors** (www.miniminors.com.au) are good Australian brands; look for them at **David Jones** and **Myer** (for both, *see p189*). Or try the markets (*see p191*) for something more original – Bondi, Balmain and Paddington are particularly good.

Fetish

Kaos Koncepts

197-199 Oxford Street, between Flinders & South Dowling Streets, Darlinghurst (9357 1699). Bus 352, 378, 380. **Open** 10am-midnight Mon-Thur, Sun; 10am-4pm Fri, Sat. **Credit** MC, V. **Map** p332 H9.
Level one is heterosexual and has a cute 'create the mood' lounge with editions of the *Kama Sutra* and 'pleasure toys', plus a small fetish section and a good DVD and video area. Level two is the gay area – men only – which has a balcony and seating area if your shopping partner gets bored (unlikely).

Reactor

Level 2, 185 Oxford Street, at Taylor Square, Darlinghurst (9385 5007/www.rubber.com.au). Bus 352, 378, 380, L82. **Open** 11am-5pm Tue-Sat. **Credit** AmEx, MC, V. **Map** p329 G/H9.

If fetish has couture, you'll find it here. Beautifully constructed corsets by Vollers Corset Co of England are available, as well as Latex Designs by Donna. Reactor's own rubberwear designs also feature heavily and cater for both guys and girls.

Tool Shed

Basement, 191 Oxford Street, at Taylor Square, Darlinghurst (9360 1100/www.toolshed.com.au). Bus 352, 378, 380, L82. **Open** 10am-1am Mon-Thur, Sun; 10am-3am Fri, Sat. **Credit** AmEx, DC, MC, V. **Map** p329 G/H9.
Should you feel the need for an extra-sexual accessory, head for Tool Shed, which stocks a vast range of appliances, protuberances and fetish wear.
Other locations: 81 Oxford Street, Darlinghurst (9332 2792).

Surfwear & swimwear

See also p203 **In the swim**.

Aussie Boys

102 Oxford Street, between Crown & Palmer Streets, Darlinghurst (9360 7011/www.aussieboys.com.au). Bus 352, 378, 380, L82. **Open** 10am-6pm Mon-Wed, Fri, Sat; 10am-9pm Thur; 11am-5pm Sun. **Credit** AmEx, DC, MC, V. **Map** p329 G8.
A fun, friendly shop selling beach towels from the cute Aussie Boys label, Dolce & Gabbana bathers and Bonds T-shirts; there's even a hair stylist downstairs. It's a one-stop shop for all that the smart gay

man needs at the beach, and there are all sorts of underwear and jockstraps to investigate too.

Beach Supplies (aka Between the Flags)

Opera Quays, East Circular Quay (9241 1603). CityRail/ferry Circular Quay. **Open** 9am-9pm Mon-Fri; 10am-9pm Sat, Sun. **Credit** AmEx, MC, V. **Map** p327 G3/4.

Have fun on the beach and give something back to those iconic Aussie lifesavers. Ten per cent of the takings of these innovative swimwear shops goes to the Bondi Surf Bathers' Live Saving Club. The Opera Quays shop has some fantastic maritime memorabilia, while the wood-lined Bondi branch has a ceiling in the shape of a boat's hull.

Other locations: Corner of Argyle & Playfair Streets, The Rocks (9247 4333); Bondi Pavilion, Queen Elizabeth Drive, Bondi Beach (9365 4063); 152 Campbell Parade, Bondi Beach (9365 5611); Harbourside, Darling Harbour (9212 5994); Westfield Bondi Junction (9388 9609).

Big Swim

74 Campbell Parade, between Lamrock Avenue & Hall Street, Bondi Beach (9365 4457/www.big swim.com.au). CityRail Bondi Junction then bus 380, 381, 382, L82/bus 380, L82. **Open** 9.30am-6pm daily (5pm in winter). **Credit** AmEx, DC, MC, V. **Map** p334.

An Aladdin's cave of bikinis, tankinis, one-pieces, G-strings and bandeau tops. Perhaps the best place in Sydney for women to buy swimwear: rack after rack of well-priced stuff in loads of different styles, plus bags, towels, sarongs and footwear. And if the big Bondi waves knock your bikini top off, the shop is right across the road from the beach. **Photo** *p203*.

Other locations: 51 The Corso, Manly (9977 8961); Warringah Mall, Brookvale (9907 3352).

Bondi Surf Co

72 Campbell Parade, between Lamrock Avenue & Hall Street, Bondi Beach (9365 0870). CityRail Bondi Junction then bus 380, 381, 382, L82/bus 380, L82. **Open** 9am-7pm daily (6pm in winter). **Credit** AmEx, MC, V. **Map** p334.

Sales, hire, repairs, surfboards, bodyboards and wetsuits for the serious surfer. Plus surfie clothing, sunglasses, watches and other accessories.

Mambo

17 Oxford Street, between South Dowling & Verona Streets, Paddington (9331 8034/www.mambo. com.au). Bus 352, 378, 380, L82. **Open** 10am-6pm Mon-Wed, Fri-Sat; 10am-7pm Thur; 11am-5pm Sun. **Credit** AmEx, DC, MC, V. **Map** p332 H9.

Launched in 1984, this flamboyant surf/skatewear label has become an institution. Founder Dare Jennings employed radical artist Reg Mombassa of the band Mental As Anything to create his trademark gnarly designs. Pick up shorts, T-shirts, swimwear, sunnies, caps and wallets.

Other locations: 80 Campbell Parade, Bondi Beach (9365 2255); 80 The Corso, Manly (9977 9171); 105 George Street, The Rocks (9252 4551).

Rip Curl

82 Campbell Parade, between Lamrock Avenue & Hall Street, Bondi Beach (9130 2660/www.rip curl.com). CityRail Bondi Junction then bus 380, 381, 382, L82/bus 380, L82. **Open** 9am-7pm daily (6pm in winter). **Credit** AmEx, MC, V. **Map** p334.

In the late 1960s Doug 'Claw' Warbrick and Brian 'Sing Ding' Singer decided to start a surfboard shaping company from their garage in Torquay, Victoria. When they started making wetsuits for surfers of the icy Victorian waters, Rip Curl became big business. The designs may be more 'street' today, but the company hasn't lost its roots. The HQ is still in Torquay and its website has weather maps for diehard surfers. Stock up on boards, boardies and everything else a surfer could wish for.

Other locations: 98-100 The Corso, Manly (9977 6622).

Surfworld

180 Campbell Parade, between Curlewis Street & Beach Road, Bondi Beach (9300 0055).CityRail Bondi Junction then bus 380, 381, 382, L82/bus 380, L82. **Open** 9am-6.30pm daily. **Credit** AmEx, DC, MC, V. **Map** p334.

Step over the threshold on to the surfboard-shaped rug and you're in surfie heaven. Every big name is on sale, including Roxy, Billabong, Quiksilver and some cool Lonsdale shirts and tops. You'll find gear for the beach (swimmers, boardshorts) and the street (men's long-sleeved shirts, canvas wallets for girls). Also an excellent place for hiring boards.

Other locations: 79 Gould Street, Bondi Beach (9300 8226).

Vintage, recycled & second-hand

Blue Spinach Recycled Designer Clothing

348 Liverpool Street, at Womerah Avenue, Darlinghurst (9331 3904/www.bluespinach.com.au). CityRail Kings Cross/bus 389. **Open** 10am-6pm Mon-Wed, Fri, Sat; 10am-7pm Thur. **Credit** AmEx, DC, MC, V. **Map** p330 J8.

If your idea of recycled clothing is more about last season's Missoni than musty-smelling cast-offs, head down to this fashion-insider spot. Run by Mark and Jayne Thompson, it's the most innovative and upmarket recycled clothing joint in town. The building is bright blue, so you can't miss it.

Puf'n Stuff

96 Glenayr Avenue, at Blair Street, Bondi Beach (9130 8471). CityRail Bondi Junction then bus 380, 381, 382, L82/bus 380, L82. **Open** 10am-6pm daily. **Credit** AmEx, MC, V.

If you want to fit in with the hip Bondi crowd, you need to come here – a short walk from the beach. If you're quick you can snap up a 1950s or '70s original. Cowboys boots, '70s denim, floaty dresses and envy-inducing vintage accessories.

Other locations: **Puf'n More Stuff** 102 Glenayr Avenue, Bondi Beach (9130 8984).

Rokit Gallery

Metcalfe Arcade, 80-84 George Street, north of Atherden Street, The Rocks (9247 1332/www.rokit. com.au). CityRail/ferry Circular Quay. **Open** 10am-5.30pm daily. **Credit** MC, V. **Map** p327 F3.

A treasure trove of vintage clothing and jewellery in immaculate condition. Most of the stock is from the 1930s to '50s, ranging from dresses, coats, skirts and blouses to cigarette cases, magazines and watches. It's like a glittering museum, and you'll be served by a shop assistant made up in full '50s eyeliner and powder, with clothes to match. Wonderful.

Route 66

255-257 Crown Street, at Goulburn Street, Darlinghurst (9331 6686/www.route66.com.au). Bus 301, 302, 303, 352. **Open** 10.30am-6pm Mon-Wed, Fri; 10.30am-8pm Thur; 10am-6pm Sat; noon-5pm Sun. **Credit** AmEx, MC, V. **Map** p329 G8.

Rockabilly heaven. A huge range of second-hand Levi's, 1950s chintz frocks and more Hawaiian shirts than you can swing a lei at.

Fashion accessories

Bags & hats

bondi beach bag co

76 Campbell Parade, between Lamrock Avenue & Hall Street, Bondi Beach (9300 0826/www.bondi beachbagco.com.au). CityRail Bondi Junction then bus 380, 381, 382, L82/bus 380, L82. **Open** 9am-6pm daily. **Credit** DC, MC, V. **Map** p334.

Exactly what it says on the front of the shop – straw bags for the beach in a shop opposite Bondi Beach. There are also beach pillows and towels.

Mimco

436 Oxford Street, between Elizabeth & Queen Street, Paddington (9357 6884/www.mimco.com.au). Bus 352, 378, 380, L82. **Open** 9.30am-6pm Mon-Wed, Fri, 9.30am-8pm Thur; 11am-4pm Sun. **Credit** AmEx, MC, V. **Map** p332 L10/11.

'Humbly understanding that nobody needs for what we do, so respectfully Mimco creates for want.' So says (rather confusingly) owner Amanda 'Mim' Briskin. Highly original and funky bags, hats, jewellery and other accessories with a nod to the vintage but an eye on the future.
Other locations: Strand Arcade, CBD (9223 1055); Westfield Bondi Junction (9387 6851).

Strand Hatters

Strand Arcade, 412-414 George Street, between King & Market Streets, CBD (9231 6884/ www.strandhatters.com.au). CityRail Martin Place, St James or Town Hall/Monorail City Centre. **Open** 8.30am-6pm Mon-Wed, Fri; 8.30am-8pm Thur; 9.30am-4.30pm Sat; 11am-4pm Sun. **Credit** AmEx, MC, V. **Map** p327 F6.

While Akubras pull the crowds in, you can also top off your look with an authentic panama or fedora, or even a replica of the pith helmet worn by dapper soldiers at Rorke's Drift in 1879. **Photo** *right*.

Jewellery

Also try the super-elegant **Melissa Harris Jewellery** (Shop 14, 2-16 Glenmore Road, 9331 8817, www.melissaharrisjewellery.com), which has some fabulously unusual designs. You might also have a look at the jewellery in gift shop **Dinosaur Designs** (*see p206*). If you want to buy opals – a popular Australian souvenir, as 95 per cent of the world's supply comes from here – it's a good idea to check that the retailer is a member of the **Jewellers' Assocation of Australia** (www.jaa.com.au): look for the JAA 'pink diamond' in the shop.

Family Jewels

46-48 Oxford Street, between West & Comber Streets, Paddington (9331 6647/www.thefamily jewels.com.au). Bus 352, 378, 380, L82. **Open** 10am-6pm Mon-Wed, Fri, Sat; 10am-7.30pm Thur; 11am-5.30pm Sun. **Credit** AmEx, DC, MC, V. **Map** p332 H9.

Silver jewellery from all over, plus fun designs from hot local designers and sparkly costume jewellery.
Other locations: 393A Oxford Street, Paddington (9331 3888); Sydney Central Plaza, CBD (9231 0009).

Akubra hats: available at **Strand Hatters**.

Victoria Spring

110 Oxford Street, between Glenmore Road & Hopewell Street, Paddington (9331 7862/ www.victoriaspringdesigns.com). Bus 352, 378, 380, L82. **Open** 10am-6pm Mon-Wed, Fri, Sat; 10am-7pm Thur; noon-4pm Sun. **Credit** AmEx, MC, V. **Map** p332 J9.

Victoria Spring's jewellery is unashamedly feminine, made from original 1930s and '40s patterns using vintage glass, pearls and crystals, and designed by a team of artisans in her Sydney and Byron Bay studios. The shops are perfumed treasure troves of accessories and homewares.
Other locations: Strand Arcade, CBD (9238 0700).

Lingerie

Some department stores also have excellent and extensive selections of lingerie: try **David Jones** and **Myer** (for both, *see p189*). For sexy sleepwear, visit **Peter Alexander** (Pitt Street Mall, 9223 3440, www.peteralexander.com.au).

Miss Amour

114 Oxford Street, between Glenmore Road & Hopewell Street, Paddington (9360 0195). Bus 352, 378, 380, L82. **Open** 10am-6pm Mon-Wed, Fri, Sat; 10am-8pm Thur. **Credit** AmEx, DC, MC, V. **Map** p332 J9.

At first sight, this boutique looks like your average upmarket lingerie shop, but delve a little deeper and you'll be surprised. The front of the shop holds plenty of high-end brands such as La Perla, while towards the back is a sophisticated section dedicated to 'feminine toys' and 'dress-up'. There's a slick beauty parlour downstairs too.

Papinelle

112 Oxford Street, between Glenmore Road & Hopewell Street, Paddington (9332 2922/www. papinelle.com). Bus 352, 378, 380, L82. **Open** 10am-6pm Mon-Wed, Fri, Sat; 10am-7pm Thur; 11am-4pm Sun. **Credit** AmEx, MC, V. **Map** p332 J9.

Pyjamas, nighties, cute camis and pretty boxers – every type of nightwear is covered by this shop in smart fabrics and flattering fits. A nice place to buy a present for a girlfriend or female relative.

Shoes

See also p189 **Department stores**.

Gary Castles Shoes

Strand Arcade, 412-414 George Street, between King & Market Streets, CBD (9232 6544/www.gary castlessydney.com). CityRail Martin Place, St James or Town Hall/Monorail City Centre. **Open** 9.30am-6pm Mon-Wed, Fri, Sat; 9.30am-8.30pm Thur; 11am-5pm Sun. **Credit** AmEx, DC, MC, V. **Map** p327 F6.

Smart, gorgeous, sophisticated styles in great colour combinations. Wait for the sales if you find the prices too close to international designer levels.
Other locations: 45A Bay Street, Double Bay (9327 5077); 328 Oxford Street, Paddington (9361 4560).

Midas

Ground Floor, QVB, 455 George Street, between Market & Druitt Streets, CBD (9261 5815/ www.midasshoes.com.au). CityRail Town Hall/ Monorail Galeries Victoria. **Open** 9am-6pm Mon-Wed, Fri, Sat; 9am-9pm Thur; 11am-5pm Sun. **Credit** AmEx, MC, V. **Map** p327 E6.

Like Mollini (*see below*), this is a great destination for well-priced, well-made and gorgeous footwear for women. It sells fun bags, belts hats and scarves to coordinate with your shoes too.
Other locations: Glasshouse on the Mall, 135 King Street, CBD (9221 5620); 17 Knox Street, Double Bay (9363 3977); Westfield Bondi Junction (9388 9359).

Mollini

380A Oxford Street, between Elizabeth & William Streets, Paddington (9331 1732/www.mollini. com.au). Bus 352, 378, 380, L82. **Open** 10am-6pm Mon-Wed, Fri; 10am-8.30pm Thur; 9.30am-6pm Sat; 11am-5.30pm Sun. **Credit** AmEx, DC, MC, V. **Map** p332 K10.

Wedges, flats, round-toes, point-toes, boots, kitten heels, mid-heels, sandals, stilettos and platforms, plus bags and belts, from around the world – phew. They come in fashionable shapes and designs, in various finishes (plaited leather, ponyskin, sequins, metallic). A fix for shoe addicts.
Other locations: QVB, 455 George Street, CBD (9261 0364); Glasshouse on the Mall, 135 King Street, CBD (9232 5191); Emporio Sydney, 182 Pitt Street, CBD (9233 1014); Westfield Bondi Junction (9386 1838).

Platypus Shoes

47 The Corso, Manly (9977 1500/www.platypus shoes.com). Ferry Manly. **Open** 9.30am-6.30pm Mon-Sat; 10am-5.30pm Sun. **Credit** AmEx, DC, MC, V. **Map** p334.

Hip brands like Diesel, Royal, Vans and Birkenstock, at reasonable prices. Plus loads of cool trainers and Aussie Blundstones, as well as clothes, hats, sunglasses, watches and more.
Other locations: 124 Campbell Parade, Bondi Beach (9365 0015); 275 King Street, Newtown (9557 4599); Market City, corner of Hay & Thomas Streets, Haymarket (9211 8499); 385 Oxford Street, Paddington (9360 1218); 468 Oxford Street, Bondi Junction (9386 0708).

Tattooing & piercing

Piercing Urge

251 Crown Street, between Oxford & Goulburn Streets, Darlinghurst (9360 3179/www.thepiercing urge.com.au). Bus 352, 378, 380, L82. **Open** 11am-7pm Mon-Wed, Fri; 11am-8pm Thur; 11am-6pm Sat; noon-6pm Sun. **Credit** AmEx, DC, MC, V. **Map** p329 G8.

A clean and smart place offering full body, facial and genital piercing, plus custom-made jewellery. There's a very good follow-up service, in case you have any problems – though staff won't do a piercing if they think it won't work.

In the swim

With 169 beaches around Sydney alone, it is not surprising that Australia leads the way in swimwear design. With surf that is liable to whip off saggy bikinis, and boardie fabrics that need to survive constant immersion in saltwater and friction from surf wax, no swimwear company can get away with shoddy merchandise. And considering many of Sydney's beaches resemble a catwalk, having a decent pair of togs is as essential as a good pair of sunnies.

The modern era for 'swimmers' began when the first 'budgie smuggler' Speedo was tested out on Bondi Beach in 1928 by one Alexander MacRae, who wanted to expand his hosiery business into swimwear. While the Speedo remains a symbol of the Australian beach and its famous surf lifesavers, for most it's as big a fashion crime as a corked hat. Instead, blokes of all ages stick to boardies. Available widely, **Rip Curl** (see p200), **Quiksilver** and **Billabong** are all great Aussie makes; they started out as bona fide surf brands and still sponsor many of the top pro surfers. Also popular, **Mambo** (see p200) has more of a street/skate edge.

For bikinis, Sydney has a wealth of boutiques run by women with fitting skills that rival the finest lingerie shops. The best outlets are found near the beaches, particularly at Manly and Bondi. Look out for brands such as **Moontide** (www.moontide.com), **Tiger Lily** (www.tigerlilyswimwear.com.au), which was started by socialite Jodie Packer, and **Seafolly** (www.seafolly.com.au).

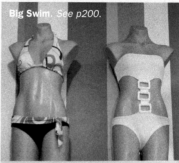

Big Swim. See p200.

Zimmermann (see p197) excels in glamorous resort-wear, while **One Teaspoon** (www.oneteaspoon.com.au) does quirky, flirty swimmers for the svelte.

Eat, Drink, Shop

Wigs

The Oxford Street strip in Darlinghurst has a number of wig shops, popular with the gay community and those after a new look. Try **Ahead In Wigs** (No.127, 9360 1230) or **Celebrity Wigs** (No.167, 9331 5240, www.celebritywigs.com.au).

Food & drink

Butchers

Jim's Butchery
211 Oxford Street, between Taylor Square & South Dowling Street, Darlinghurst (9331 1678). Bus 352, 378, 380, L82. **Open** 7am-5.30pm Mon-Fri; 7am-1pm Sat. **No credit cards.** **Map** p329 H9.

An old-fashioned butcher reminiscent of the days when now-busy Darlinghurst was just a village, Jim's has been selling meat since 1962. If you're heading to the city for a rooftop barbecue, this is the place to pick up a juicy steak or plump lamb chop.

Sam the Butcher
129 Bondi Road, between Bennett & Watson Streets, Bondi (9389 1420/www.samthebutcher.com.au). CityRail Bondi Junction then bus 380, 381, 382, L82/bus 380, L82. **Open** 7am-6pm Tue-Fri; 7am-4pm Sat; 7am-3pm Sun. **Credit** AmEx, MC, V.

Organic butcher with a mission to spread the good word about non-pesticide, free-range farming and game, and a great selection of sangers (sausages), chops, steaks and more. All the butchers are 'country boys', with a good knowledge of cuts and cooking. You can also order via the website. **Other locations**: Farmers' Market, Entertainment Quarter, Moore Park (10am-4pm Wed, Sat).

Chocolates

Belle Fleur

658 Darling Street, between Victoria Road & Nelson Street, Rozelle (9810 2690/www.bellefleur.com.au). Bus 432, 433, 434, 501, 502, 504. **Open** 9am-6pm Mon-Fri; 9am-4pm Sat; 10am-4pm Sun. **Credit** AmEx, MC, V.

Where confectionery meets art. Check out the Aussie barbecue window display, with stubbies, steaks, bread rolls, bricks and grill made entirely from chocolate. Or you might fancy a chocolate mushroom, or bolt, or mobile phone – or even just one of the exquisite conventional varieties. Jan and Lynne ter Heerdt are third-generation chocolatiers from Belgium who set up in Sydney 20 years ago. The chocolates are freshly made daily.

Max Brenner

437 Oxford Street, between Centennial Park & Elizabeth Street, Paddington (9357 5055/www.maxbrenner.com). Bus 352, 378, 380, L82. **Open** 7.30am-10.30pm Mon-Thur; 7.30am-midnight Fri; 9am-midnight Sat; 10am-10.30pm Sun. **Credit** AmEx, DC, MC, V. **Map** p332 L10/11.

There's a café at the front and an upmarket shop at the back of this branch of the international chain. You can drink frozen chocolate cocktails or thick steaming cups of hot choc, or even gorge on strawberries dipped in chocolate fondue.
Other locations: David Jones, CBD (9266 5544); Manly Wharf, Manly (9977 4931); 15 Knox Street, Double Bay (9328 2555).

Sweet Art

96 Oxford Street, between Glenmore Road & Hopewell Street, Paddington (9361 6617/www.sweetart.com.au). Bus 352, 378, 380, L82. **Open** Mon-Fri 9am-6pm; Sat 9am-5pm. **Credit** AmEx, MC, V. **Map** p332 J9.

Cake creation at its best. Check out the window displays of sculptured cakes, made to whatever shape or design you desire. Sweet Art is also a florist and an event management service – useful if you want to organise a wedding, christening or party.

Delis & gourmet foods

Delicacies on King

257 King Street, between Church & Mary Streets, Newtown (9557 4048). CityRail Newtown. **Open** 9am-7pm Mon-Fri; 9am-6pm Sat, Sun. **Credit** MC, V. **Map** p334.

A fabulous continental deli with such mouth-watering savouries as own-made moussaka, cheese pies and gourmet ravioli, as well as lots of imported products including tins of Dutch liquorice and little jars of Lebanese garlic. You can grab a coffee while you plan your meal too.

the fine food store

595 Darling Street, between Wise & Norman Streets, Rozelle (9810 2858/www.finefoodstore.com). Bus 432, 433, 434, 440. **Open** 8.30am-7pm Mon-Fri; 9am-6pm Sat; 10am-4pm Sun. **Credit** AmEx, MC, V.

The staff are surprisingly friendly and approachable in this chic gourmet food store, whose motto is 'food is our passion'. It does what it says on the label, selling pasta, frozen dim sum and tins of real English golden syrup. There's also a cheese room.
Other locations: Shop 9, The Rocks Centre, The Rocks (9252 1196).

Jones the Grocer

68 Moncur Street, at Queen Street, Woollahra (9362 1222/www.jonesthegrocer.com.au). Bus 389. **Open** 8.30am-5.30pm Mon-Sat; 9am-5pm Sun. **Credit** AmEx, DC, MC, V. **Map** p333 M10.

Known for fine cheeses, sausages, cakes and high-quality grocery, Jones is also a great place to just hang out and have a coffee.
Other locations: 91-93 Macleay Street, Potts Point (9358 3343); 166 Military Road, Neutral Bay (8905 0150).

Provedore Pelagios

235 Victoria Street, between Liverpool & Surrey Streets, Darlinghurst (9360 1011). CityRail Kings Cross/bus 389. **Open** 9am-8pm Mon-Sat; 10am-7pm Sun. **Credit** AmEx, DC, MC, V. **Map** p330 J8.

Established in 1926, this traditional Italian grocer prides itself on its knowledgeable and enthusiastic staff. The bread is divine and there are also salads, cold cuts, cheeses, organic veg and gourmet pasta. The chocolate counter at the checkout is especially tempting at Easter. You can also have a coffee in the small lounge area at the front.

Simon Johnson Quality Foods

55 Queen Street, between Oxford & Moncur Streets, Woollahra (9328 6888/www.simonjohnson.com). Bus 389. **Open** 10am-7.30pm Mon-Fri; 9am-5pm Sat; 10am-4pm Sun. **Credit** AmEx, MC, V. **Map** p333 M10.

Esteemed foodie Simon Johnson has set himself up as the nation's leading provider of Australian and imported gourmet foods. His produce comes from more than 50 key sources, all vetted for quality. This shop has a great kitchenware section, a pleasingly odorous cheese room and plenty of sweet offerings.
Other locations: 181 Harris Street, Pyrmont (9552 2522).

Health foods

Bayside Natural Health Centre

30-36 Bay Street, between Cooper & Cross Streets, Double Bay (9327 8002). Ferry Double Bay/bus 323, 324, 325, 327. **Open** 9am-6.30pm Mon-Sat; 11.30am-5.30pm Sun. **Credit** AmEx, DC, MC, V. **Map** p331 N7/8.

Lots of organic fresh and dried produce, including bread and a small deli section. A few well-placed stone buddhas and oil burners create a calming ambience in which to splurge on the herbal remedies, natural skincare cosmetics and therapeutic massages (book in advance) on offer.

Health Emporium

*263-265 Bondi Road, between Wellington &
Castlefield Streets, Bondi (9365 6008). CityRail
Bondi Junction then bus 380, 381, 382, L82/bus
380, L82.* **Open** 8.30am-7pm Mon-Fri; 8.30am-6pm
Sat, Sun. **Credit** AmEx MC, V.
As well as stocking eco-friendly cosmetics including Jurlique, Dr Hauschka and Weleda, this shop
also has a good organic and grocery section and as
many vitamins and supplements that a vegan could
need. You can also get eco-safe detergents and
'ethical' coffee from the small takeaway deli.

Oriental

Lucky Food Stores

*37 Ultimo Road, between Quay & Thomas Streets,
Haymarket (9212 4743). CityRail Central/Monorail
Paddy's Markets/LightRail Capitol Square, Central
or Paddy's Markets.* **Open** 9.30am-6.30pm daily.
No credit cards. Map p329 E9.
A fabulous store for Thai foodstuffs. Where else will
you find ten brands of fish sauce? Plus 25kg (55lb)
sacks of Thai rice, enormous bags of fresh
beansprouts, pink and white lime paste, and bottles
of chilli paste with sweet basil leaves.

TQC Burlington Supermarket

*Corner of Thomas & Quay Streets, Haymarket
(9281 2777/www.tqc-burlington.com.au). CityRail
Central/Monorail Paddy's Markets/LightRail Capitol
Square, Central or Paddy's Markets.* **Open** 9am-7pm
daily. **Credit** AmEx, MC, V. **Map** p329 E9.
A huge emporium of Chinese and other Asian gro-
ceries, including fruit and veg, and a butcher.

Tea

T2

*173 King Street, at O'Connell Street, Newtown
(9550 3044/www.t2tea.com.au). CityRail Newtown*
Open 10am-6pm Mon-Wed, Fri, Sat; 10am-9pm
Thur; 10am-5pm Sun. **Credit** AmEx, DC, MC, V.
Map p334.
In a city as coffee-mad as Sydney, tea is making
quite a comeback. T2 has everything a tea lover
could want, plus some things they didn't realise they
did. There's English Breakfast for the traditionalist,
as well as wackier types such as chocolate-chip-
cookie-flavoured tea alongside.
Other locations: Westfield Bondi Junction
(9389 5799).

Taka Tea Garden

*320 New South Head Road, between Manning &
Kiaora Roads, Double Bay (9362 1777/www.takatea
garden.com.au). CityRail Edgecliff/ferry Double Bay/
bus 323, 324, 325.* **Open** 2-6pm Tue-Sat. **Credit**
AmEx, MC, V. **Map** p331 N8.
Taka Pan and Helen Kwok opened this sophisticated tea house in 1999. It's the only place in
Australia to sell Japanese chikumedio tea, a con-
noisseur's green tea grown on the slopes of Mount

Fuji. It also has Taiwanese and Chinese green teas,
German herbal infusions and Ceylon black tea,
which you can buy loose or taste in store with a slice
of green tea cake. The website has scientifically precise brewing instructions.
Other locations: World Square, CBD (9268 0008);
Mid City Centre, CBD (9222 1577).

Furniture

In Australia most long-term rents – which
means anything more than a few weeks – are
unfurnished. For reasonably priced, brand-
new contemporary furniture, try **Freedom**
(9313 8211, www.freedom.com.au), those clever
Swedes **IKEA** (9313 6400, www.ikea.com.au)
or **Fantastic Furniture** (9663 4588, www.
fantasticfurniture.com.au), all located in Moore
Park's Supacenta (corner of South Dowling
Street and Todman Avenue).
   There are heaps of second-hand furniture
emporiums that sell (when you arrive) and
buy (when you leave) all types of furniture
from lamps to sofas, beds to washing machines.
Two reliable outlets are **Bondi Furniture
Market** (2 Jacques Avenue, Bondi Beach,
9365 1315) and **Peter Foley's Furniture**
(93-99 Bronte Road, Bondi Junction, 9387 3144).
   To rent white goods and/or furniture, look
in the *Yellow Pages* under 'Hire Household
Appliances & Furniture'.

Gifts & homeware

There is a whiff of Disneyland about the
historic **Rocks** area near Circular Quay, but
it is still a quaint and interesting place to spend
a day. There's plenty of Australiana kitsch, but
also genuinely decent souvenirs in stores large
and small, at a range of prices.
   Didj Beat (corner of Argyle & Harrington
Streets, 9251 4289, www.didjbeat.com) sells
didgeridoos, Aboriginal art and artefacts
from all over Australia. Staff can teach you
how to play a didgeridoo and tell you about
the Aboriginal artists the shop buys from.
Naturally Australian (43 Circular Quay
West, 9247 1531, www.naturallyaust.com.au)
specialises in native timber furniture and craft,
while **Australian Image Craft** (Metcalfe
Arcade, 82-84 George Street, 9241 5825) is
operated by the Society of Arts & Crafts NSW
(www.artsandcraftsnsw.com.au) and has a
wide selection of ceramics, handwoven, hand-
spun and hand-knitted garments, as well as
glass and woodwork. Also in Metcalfe Arcade,
Natural Selection Souvenirs (9247 9174)
sells Driza-Bone coats and Ugg boots. Head to
Flame Opals (119 George Street, 9247 3446,
www.flameopals.com.au) for opal jewellery,

Eat, Drink, Shop

and **Bottom of the Harbour Antiques** (104 George Street, 9247 8107, www. bottomoftheharbour.com) for artefacts that reflect Sydney's maritime past: binnacles, ships' telegraphs, diving helmets, and much more. Check www.therocks.com for more options.

The **Museum of Contemporary Art** (*see p67*) has a good gift shop, as do the **Museum of Sydney** (*see p67*) and the **Powerhouse Museum** (*see p82*).

Arte Flowers

112 Queen Street, between Moncur & Oxford Streets, Woollahra (9328 0402). Bus 389. **Open** 10am-5.30pm Mon-Wed, Fri; 9.30am-6pm Thur; 9.30am-5pm Sat; 11am-5pm Sun. **Credit** AmEx, DC, MC, V. **Map** p333 M10.

A stylish, European-feel homeware and gift shop on the busy antique-shop strip of Woollahra. Pop in for a coffee and browse the glossies at the big wooden table at the back and then take in the designer furniture, glassware and jewellery, as well as Lulu Guinness bags, Votivo candles and lovingly designed gardeners' gloves.

Dinosaur Designs

Strand Arcade, 412-414 George Street, between King & Market Streets, CBD (9223 2953/ www.dinosaurdesigns.com.au). CityRail Martin Place, St James or Town Hall/Monorail City Centre. **Open** 9.30am-5.30pm Mon-Wed, Fri; 9.30am-8pm Thur; 10am-4.30pm Sat. **Credit** AmEx, MC, V. **Map** p327 F6.

Founded in 1985 by three former art students, Dinosaur Designs makes bright, glowing resin bowls, vases, jugs, plates and other household items, as well as chunky jewellery, with ranges inspired by artists as well as by natural forms. **Photos** *p207*. **Other locations**: 339 Oxford Street, Paddington (9361 3776).

Gavala Aboriginal Cultural Centre

Harbourside Centre, Darling Drive, Darling Harbour (9212 7232/www.gavala.com.au). CityRail Town Hall/ferry Darling Harbour/Monorail Harbourside. **Open** 10am-9pm daily. **Credit** AmEx, MC, V. **Map** p326 D6/7.

Established in 1995, Gavala is Aboriginal-owned and staffed, and is a top spot to buy arts, crafts and souvenirs made by Aboriginal artists. Expect clothes, jewellery, boomerangs, didgeridoos and more, including paintings in the separate art gallery.

Morning Glory

Galeries Victoria, 500 George Street, at Park Street, CBD (9286 3098). CityRail Town Hall/Monorail Galeries Victoria. **Open** 8am-6pm Mon-Wed, Fri; 8am-8pm Thur; 10am-5pm Sat; 11am-5pm Sun. **Credit** (over $20) MC, V. **Map** p329 F7.

Kitsch key rings, Miss Kitty bags and stationery including erasers, tiny notebooks and highly coloured pencils fill the shelves in this cute little shop. The trinkets are mostly made in Korea and school kids devour them.

Other locations: 22 Goulburn Street, Haymarket (9267 7899); Market City, corner of Hay & Thomas Streets, Haymarket (9212 4088).

Opus Designs

344 Oxford Street, between William & Elizabeth Streets, Paddington (9360 4803/www.opusdesign. com.au). Bus 352, 378, 380, L82. **Open** 10am-6pm Mon-Wed, Fri; 10am-7.30pm Thur; 9am-6pm Sat; noon-5pm Sun. **Credit** AmEx, DC, MC, V. **Map** p332 K10.

This Paddo institution has been open since the 1960s, selling a kitsch collection of novelties, funky ashtrays, photo frames, beach bags, clocks and drag-queen greetings cards, plus other homeware, kitchenware and stylish furniture too.

Other locations: Octopus Design, 260 King Street, Newtown (9565 4688).

Pop Shop

153 Oxford Street, between Crown Street & Taylor Square, Darlinghurst (9332 4840/www.thepopshop. com.au). Bus 352, 378, 380, L82. **Open** 9am-6.30pm Mon-Wed, Fri, Sat; 9am-8pm Thur; 10.30am-6pm Sun. **Credit** AmEx, DC, MC, V. **Map** p329 G8.

Sydney's best queer gifts shop offers a wonderful selection of deeply camp merchandise, including kitsch clocks and colourful inflatables.

Health & beauty

Beauty salons & body treatments

Ella Baché

David Jones, Elizabeth Street, at Market Street, CBD (9266 6019/www.ellabache.com.au). CityRail St James or Town Hall/Monorail City Centre. **Open** 9.30am-6pm Mon-Wed, Fri; 9.30am-9pm Thur; 9am-6pm Sat; 10am-6pm Sun. **Credit** AmEx, DC, MC, V. **Map** p327 F6.

One of the oldest bespoke skin-therapy programmes in Australia, Ella Baché offers a host of luscious treatments, from massage to body bronzing, water therapy, waxing and body wraps – all done using its many famous products.

Other locations: David Jones, Westfield Bondi Junction (9619 1272).

Ginseng Bathhouse

1st Floor, Crest Hotel, 111 Darlinghurst Road, between William & Macleay Streets, Kings Cross (9356 6680/www.thebathhouse.com.au). CityRail Kings Cross. **Open** 9.30am-9pm Mon-Fri; 9am-9pm Sat, Sun. **Credit** AmEx, DC, MC, V. **Map** p330 J7.

This traditional Korean bathhouse offers steam treatments, ginseng baths, scrubs and masterly massage. Separate baths for men and women.

Zen Day Spa

116-118 Darlinghurst Road, between William & Liverpool Streets, Darlinghurst (9361 4200/ www.zendayspa.com.au). CityRail Kings Cross. **Open** 9am-9pm Mon-Fri; 8am-8pm Sat; 10am-7pm Sun. **Credit** AmEx, MC, V. **Map** p330 H8.

Serenity is the name of the game at this day spa, a sanctuary in the heart of bustling Darlinghurst. Options include massage, aromatherapy sessions, and skincare treatments using Dermalogica products, as well as waxes, manicures and pedicures. **Other locations**: 118-122 Queen Street, Woollahra (9328 1656).

Complementary medicine

Complete City Health
Level 14, National Mutual Building, 44 Market Street, at York Street, CBD (9299 1661/www. completecityhealth.com.au). CityRail St James or Town Hall/Monorail City Centre. **Open** 8am-6pm Mon-Fri. **Credit** MC, V. **Map** p327 E6.
One of the first centres in Sydney to bring together all major healthcare professions, with the philosophy that the body only works when it is well as a whole. You'll find a GP and dentist, as well as chiropractors, naturopaths, massage therapists, reflexologists and more.

A Natural Practice
161A Glebe Point Road, between Mitchell Street & St Johns Road, Glebe (9660 7308/www.anatural practice.com.au). Bus 431, 432, 433. **Open** 10am-5pm Mon-Sat; after-hours appointments available. **Credit** MC, V. **Map** p328 B9.
The practice has been running for over 15 years and has experts in acupuncture, homeopathy, iridology, shiatsu, reflexology, reiki, remedial massage, naturopathy, osteopathy, psychotherapy and more. Detox programmes are also on offer.

Cosmetics

Jurlique
Strand Arcade, 412-414 George Street, between King & Market Streets, CBD (9231 0626/ www.jurlique.com.au). CityRail Martin Place, St James or Town Hall/Monorail City Centre. **Open** 9am-6pm Mon-Wed, Fri, Sat; 9am-9pm Thur; 11am-5pm Sun. **Credit** AmEx, DC, MC, V. **Map** p327 F6.
This small company based in South Australia is making big news at home and overseas. It might not be cheap, but this is the real deal when it comes to 'aromatherapeutic' natural cosmetics.
Other locations: 573 Military Road, Mosman (9969 2155); 352A Oxford Street, Paddington (9368 7373).

Mecca Cosmetica
126 Oxford Street opposite Victoria Barracks, Paddington (9361 4488/www.meccacosmetica. com.au). Bus 352, 378, 380, L82. **Open** 10am-6pm Mon-Wed, Fri, Sat; 10am-8pm Thur; 11am-5pm Sun. **Credit** AmEx, DC, MC, V. **Map** p332 J9/10.
A chic cosmetic boutique with overseas brands such as Nars, Stila and Philosophy. Some branches have pedicure and make-up services too.
Other locations: David Jones, Westfield Bondi Junction (9389 4407); Galeries Victoria, CBD (9261 4911).

Dinosaur Designs. *See p206.*

Eat, Drink, Shop

Napoleon Perdis Make-up Academy

74 Oxford Street, between Comber & Hopewell Streets, Paddington (9331 1702/www.napoleon cosmetics.com). Bus 352, 378, 380, L82. **Open** 9.30am-6pm Mon-Sat; 1-5pm Sun. **Credit** AmEx, DC, MC, V. **Map** p332 J9.

Founded by Napoleon Perdis, an Australian-born Hollywood make-up artist, this shop has its own cosmetics brand and in-house make-up artists. **Other locations**: Sydney Central Plaza, CBD (9221 6277); World Square, CBD (9262 7733).

Perfect Potion

QVB, 455 George Street, between Market & Druitt Streets, CBD (9286 3384/www.perfectpotion. com.au). CityRail Town Hall/Monorail Galeries Victoria. **Open** 9am-6pm Mon-Wed, Fri; 9am-9pm Thur; 9am-5.30pm Sat; 11am-4.30pm Sun. **Credit** AmEx, MC, V. **Map** p327 E6.

These people are serious about their holistic aromatherapy, and offer a good skincare range made from essential oils, infused plant oils, cold-pressed vegetable oils, organically grown herbal extracts and other plant-derived ingredients. **Other locations**: Strand Arcade, CBD (9238 0203); Westfield Bondi Junction (9389 6120).

Hairdressers

Halt Beauty

30-40 Holt Street, between Devonshire & Cooper Streets, Surry Hills (8399 0141/www.halt.com.au). CityRail/LightRail Central. **Open** 10am-6pm Tue; 10am-7.30pm Wed, Fri; 10am-9pm Thur; 8am-6pm Sat. **Credit** AmEx, DC, MC, V. **Map** p329 F10.

A buzzing hair salon offering the sharpest cuts and blow-dries in the city. Opposite, at No.45, is the associated beauty salon, which offers body treatments, tanning, waxing and other services.

Luc Espace

Westfield Bondi Junction, 500 Oxford Street, at Grosvenor Street, Bondi Junction (9389 8080/ www.lucespace.com). CityRail Bondi Junction/bus 352, 378, 380, L82. **Open** 10am-7pm Mon-Wed, Fri; 10am-9pm Thur; 10am-6pm Sat, Sun. **Credit** AmEx, MC, V. **Map** p333 P11.

A beauty editor's favourite: Aveda products, free aromatherapy head massage and vibrating leather chairs that recline to flat while your hair is washed.

Music

The megastores are **HMV** (Mid City Centre, Pitt Street Mall, 9221 2311, www.hmv.com.au) and **Sanity** (Imperial Arcade, Pitt Street Mall, 9239 0050, www.sanity.com.au).

Ashwood's Music & Books

129 York Street, between Market & Druitt Streets, CBD (9267 7745/www.ashwoods.com). CityRail Town Hall/Monorail Galeries Victoria. **Open** 9.30am-6.30pm Mon-Wed, Fri; 9.30am-8pm Thur; 9.30am-5pm Sat; noon-4pm Sun. **Credit** MC, V. **Map** p327 E6.

This basement music emporium opposite the QVB has traded since 1932 and is a great place to find obscure CDs or vinyl. It's also good for second-hand music books and DVDs, and vintage sheet music.

Birdland

231 Pitt Street, between Market & Park Streets, CBD (9267 6881/www.birdland.com.au). CityRail St James or Town Hall/Monorail City Centre. **Open** 10am-5.30pm Mon-Wed, Fri; 10am-8pm Thur; 9am-4.30pm Sat. **Credit** AmEx, DC, MC, V. **Map** p329 F7.

Birdland is the best jazz and blues shop in the city – some claim it's one of the best in the world.

Central Station Records

46A Oxford Street, between Hyde Park & Crown Street, Darlinghurst (9361 5222/www.central station.com.au). CityRail Museum/bus 373, 375, 377, 378, 380, L82. **Open** 10am-7pm Mon-Wed, Fri; 10am-9pm Thur; 10am-6pm Sat; noon-5pm Sun. **Credit** AmEx, MC, V. **Map** p329 G8.

Want to buy that track you heard in the club last night on vinyl? Central Station's vast basement shop houses the very latest in import and domestic dance, house, hip hop, R&B and Mardi Gras compilations. It also produces dance compilations on its own label.

Fish Records

261 King Street, between Church & Mary Streets, Newtown (9557 3074/www.fishrecords.com.au). CityRail Newtown. **Open** 9am-9.30pm Mon-Wed; 9am-10pm Thur, Fri, Sat; 10am-9.30pm Sun. **Credit** AmEx, MC, V. **Map** p334.

Next to the Dendy cinema, this branch of Fish stocks mostly top-40 and dance music, with a good soundtrack section. The Balmain and Glebe outlets specialise in jazz, while the George Street branch focuses on classical music. **Other locations**: 289 Darling Street, Balmain (9810 8421); 350 George Street, CBD (9233 3371); 47 Glebe Point Road, Glebe (9692 0480); Norton Plaza, Norton Street, Leichhardt (9560 3074); 471 Oxford Street, Bondi Junction (9388 9641).

Folkways Music

282 Oxford Street, between Underwood & William Streets, Paddington (9361 3980). Bus 352, 378, 380, L82. **Open** 9am-6pm Mon-Wed, Fri, Sat; 9am-8pm Thur; 11am-6pm Sun. **Credit** AmEx, DC, MC, V. **Map** p332 K10.

The standard-bearer for folk and ethnic music.

Red Eye

66 King Street, between George & York Streets, CBD (9299 4233/www.redeye.com.au). CityRail Wynyard. **Open** 9am-6pm Mon-Wed, Fri; 9am-9pm Thur; 9am-5pm Sat; 11am-5pm Sun. **Credit** AmEx, MC, V. **Map** p327 E6.

The biggest of the indie shops, Red Eye has an excellent selection of Australian bands and labels, as well as a good selection of imports. There's also second-hand merchandise upstairs, but it's the Pitt Street branch that specialises in second-hand. You can also buy tickets for gigs here. **Other locations**: 370 Pitt Street, CBD (9262 9755).

Op shops

Op (for 'opportunity') shops are second-hand shops, the Australian version of the UK's charity shops and the US's thrift stores.

St Vincent de Paul

292 Oxford Street, between Elizabeth & Underwood Streets, Paddington (9360 4151). Bus 352, 378, 380, L82. **Open** *9.30am-5pm Mon-Wed, Fri; 9am-7pm Thur; 10am-5pm Sat, Sun.* **Credit** MC, V. **Map** p332 K10.

The proceeds of these shops – fondly known as 'St Vinnie's' – go to the St Vincent de Paul hospitals and charity work. This Oxford Street branch specialises in clothes and, thanks to the quality of its stock, turnover is quick. Look out for current-season fashion and designer labels.

Other locations: throughout the city.

Salvos Store St Peters

7 Bellevue Street, off Princes Highway, St Peters (9519 1513). CityRail St Peters. **Open** *8.30am-3.30pm Mon-Fri; 8.30am-1.45pm Sat.* **Credit** MC, V.

More department store than humble op shop, this warehouse-size emporium holds racks of clothes, enough furniture to fill an apartment block, old computers, a good collection of records and cut-price household goods. Proceeds go to the Salvation Army ('Salvos') – huge in Australia.

Other locations: throughout the city.

Opticians

K Optica

432 Oxford Street, between Elizabeth & Jersey Streets, Paddington (9331 3400). Bus 352, 378, 380, L82. **Open** *9am-6pm Mon-Wed, Fri; 9am-8.30pm Thur; 9.30am-6pm Sat; 11am-5.30pm Sun.* **Credit** AmEx, DC, MC, V. **Map** p332 L10.

A popular eyewear shop with an ever-changing collection of the latest frames, including designer lines. There's also an on-site optician service.

Pharmacies

Non-prescription painkillers commonly available over the counter include Panadol (paracetamol), Disprin, Aspro Clear (aspirin), Nurofen (ibuprofen) and Panadeine (codeine/paracetamol). There are very few 24-hour pharmacies, but plenty of the chains trade into the evening, including:

Darlinghurst Prescription Pharmacy

261 Oxford Street, at South Dowling Street, Darlinghurst (9361 5882). Bus 352, 378, 380, L82. **Open** *8am-10pm Mon-Sat; 11am-6pm Sun.* **Credit** AmEx, DC, MC, V. **Map** p332 H9.

Situated just up the road from St Vincent's Hospital, this friendly, well-stocked pharmacy has knowledgeable staff and a full prescription service.

Sport & outdoor

Kathmandu

Town Hall Arcade, corner of Kent & Bathurst Streets, CBD (9261 8901/www.kathmandu.com.au). CityRail Town Hall/Monorail Galeries Victoria. **Open** *9am-5.30pm Mon-Wed, Fri; 9am-8.30pm Thur; 9.30am-5pm Sat; 10am-4pm Sun.* **Credit** AmEx, MC, V. **Map** p329 E7.

'Live the dream, ski it, sail it, run it, climb it, surf it, walk it, paddle it, explore it, skate it': that's the motto, and this shop means it. It has everything in here: the gear, the clothes, the gadgets.

Paddy Pallin

507 Kent Street, at Bathurst Street, CBD (9264 2685/www.paddypallin.com.au). CityRail Town Hall/Monorail Galeries Victoria. **Open** *9am-5.30pm Mon-Wed; 9am-8.30pm Thur; 9am-9pm Fri; 9am-6pm Sat; 10am-5pm Sun.* **Credit** AmEx, DC, MC, V. **Map** p329 E7.

Bushwalker Paddy opened his first shop in the 1930s, selling lightweight camping and walking gear. The chain is still going strong and sells everything for the modern-day backpacker – and more.

Other locations: 74 Macquarie Street, Parramatta (9633 1113).

Toys & games

Both **David Jones Myer** (for both, *see p189*) have well-stocked toy departments.

Kidstuff

126A Queen Street, between Moncur & Ocean Streets, Woollahra (9363 2838/www.kidstuff.com.au). Bus 389. **Open** *9am-5.30pm Mon-Fri; 9am-5pm Sat, Sun.* **Credit** AmEx, DC, MC, V. **Map** p333 M10.

Grandma-friendly wooden toys and doll's houses, as well as educational toys for kids of all ages.

Other locations: 774-776 Military Road, Mosman (9960 3222); 101-103 Parramatta Road, Camperdown (9519 4848).

Toy Villa – Toy Kingdom

455 New South Head Road, between Kiaora & Manning Streets, Double Bay (9327 7558). CityRail Edgecliff/ferry Double Bay. **Open** *9am-5.30pm Mon-Fri; 9am-4pm Sat; 10am-4pm Sun.* **Credit** AmEx, DC, MC, V. **Map** p331 N8.

One of Sydney's more versatile toy shops, with everything from cheap farmyard animals, yo-yos, Lego and so on to the model kid's car that Double Bay junior might park next to his dad's BMW.

Travel agents

The reliable chains **Flight Centre** (66 King Street, between York & George Streets, CBD, 9262 6644, 13 3133, www.flightcentre.com.au) and **STA Travel** (855 George Street, at Harris Street, Haymarket, 9212 1255, www.statravel.com.au) have branches throughout the city.

Eat, Drink, Shop

Arts & Entertainment

Festivals & Events

Any excuse to get outdoors and let off some fireworks.

Melbourne may claim to be the cultural capital of Australia, but Sydney's far too busy putting on the show to worry. Rarely a week goes by without a major event or festival happening in the city, and organisers seem to always be striving to make it bigger and better than the one last year – and generally they succeed. What really sets Sydney apart, though, is the number of free events and festivals on offer year round, whether stand-alone fixtures such as Sculpture by the Sea or free elements of a major festival, such as Sydney Festival's Jazz & Symphony in the Domain events.

Top of the charts for attendance – and not to be missed if you're in town – are the **New Year's Eve fireworks**, the **Sydney Hobart Yacht Race**, **Sculpture by the Sea** and the **Gay & Lesbian Mardi Gras Parade**. But with every suburb now holding its own cultural festival, there are plenty of events that attract smaller, more manageable crowds.

For more details of what's going on when, check the daily papers or the City of Sydney council website at www.cityofsydney.nsw. gov.au. More film festivals are listed on *p229*, and sporting events are covered on *pp256-265*. For NSW public holidays, *see p307*.

Spring

Art & About

Various venues (www.cityofsydney.nsw.gov.au/ artandabout). **Date** Oct.

For three weeks in October the parks, squares, streets and shopping centres of the city become the canvas for events, exhibitions and workshops showcasing local artists both established and emerging. There's fashion, photography, ice sculpture, banners, flowers and more, and passers-by can paint their own contribution at Art in the Park. Gallery-heavy Danks Street in Waterloo had its own sub-festival as part of Art & About 2005.

Good Food Month

Various venues (http://gfm.smh.com.au/index.asp). **Date** Oct.

There's something for everyone to nibble in this *Sydney Morning Herald*-sponsored festival. The idea is that the city's best chefs offer their fare at affordable prices, and lunchtime specials are on offer at some top restaurants and there are plenty of outdoor events, including the Night Noodle markets in Hyde Park and the Food & Wine Fair.

Festival of the Winds

Bondi Beach (8362 3400/www.waverley.nsw.gov.au). CityRail Bondi Junction then bus 381, 378, 380, L82/bus 378, 380, L82. **Map** p334. **Date** 2nd Sun in Sept.

Australia's largest free kite-flying festival is staged outside the Bondi Pavilion on Bondi Beach and in the park behind the beach, attracting up to 50,000 people and hundreds of kites of all shapes and sizes. The competitions are only open to kite club members, but there are plenty of other activities for beginners and non-kiters, including music and masses of stuff for kids. The festival kicks off around 10am and finishes about 4.30pm.

Sydney Running Festival

9310 8120/www.sydneyrunningfestival.org. **Date** Sun in mid Sept.

First held in 2001 and incorporating the Sydney Marathon, the Running Festival is the only community event that closes the Sydney Harbour Bridge. It comprises four road races – the marathon, a half-marathon, a 10km (6.2 mile) Bridge Run and the most recent addition, a family fun run of 3.8km (2.3 miles). Entry is open to all, though you have to apply in advance and pay an entry fee. The marathon follows the famous 'blue line' used in the 2000 Olympics and charts a spectacular route, taking in the Royal Botanical Gardens, Centennial Park, Anzac Bridge, Sydney Olympic Park and Sydney Opera House. All four races start in North Sydney and all finish at the steps of the Opera House.

Manly International Jazz Festival

Manly (9977 1088/www.manlytourism.com.au). Ferry Manly. **Map** p334. **Date** Oct long weekend.

Australia's largest and longest-running community jazz festival attracts crowds of over 20,000. Local and international artists play on the outside stages set along the Corso, the beach and the council forecourt opposite Manly Wharf. Along with roving bands, there are more than 60 free performances from noon till sunset, as well as indoor sessions for which you'll have to pay going into the night.

Sleaze Ball

Entertainment Quarter, Driver Avenue, Moore Park (9568 8600/www.mardigras.org.au). Bus 339, 373, 374, 376, 377, 393, 395, 396. **Tickets** (plus booking fee) $120; $80 members, concessions. **Date** 1st Sat in Oct. **Map** p332 J12.

A spectacular and, of course, sleazy dance party organised as a fund-raiser for gay Sydney's main event, Mardi Gras. There's a new hot and sexy theme each year to inspire wild costumes and shows.

Though 2005's attendance of 6,500 was fewer than organisers hoped for, Sleaze still kick-starts the summer party season. For more information, *see p244*.

Sculpture by the Sea

Along the cliff walk from Bondi to Tamarama (8399 0233/www.sculpturebythesea.com). CityRail Bondi Junction then bus 381, 378, 380, L82/bus 378, 380, L82. **Map** p334. **Date** 1st 3wks in Nov.
This must be one of the world's most spectacular locations for an art event. For three weeks in November, Australia's largest free outdoor exhibition of contemporary sculpture shows off over 100 works by local and overseas artists along the coastal cliff walk from Bondi Beach to Tamarama Beach. It's incredibly popular, so go during the week to avoid the worst of the crowds. Alongside the outdoor event, 'Sculpture Inside' exhibits smaller works by the selected artists at the Bondi Pavilion Gallery and the Tamarama Surf Life Saving Club.

Newtown Festival

Camperdown Memorial Park, corner of Lennox & Australia Streets, Newtown (9519 2509/ www.newtowncentre.org). CityRail Newtown. **Map** p334. **Date** Sun in mid Nov.
Tucked behind King Street in the grounds of St Stephen's Church, this inner-west free festival boasts a dog show like no other ('Celebrity Look-a-like' is just one of the categories). If you're not into the pooches there's plenty of other stuff going on, with music, workshops, food and plenty of activities for kids. The festival runs from 10am to 6pm.

Glebe New Music Festival & Street Fair

Glebe Point Road, from Parramatta Road to Bridge Road, Glebe (9281 0024/www.glebestreetfair. com.au). LightRail Glebe/bus 431, 432, 433, 434, 370. **Map** p328 A/B9-C10. **Date** 3rd Sun in Nov.
Sydney's longest-running street festival takes over Glebe Point Road as traffic gives way to food stalls, wine-tasting booths, arts and craft stalls, clowns, stilt-walkers and music stages. Foley Park is devoted to children's activities. Expect crowds of around 100,000. The fair runs from 10am to around 5pm.

Summer

Homebake

The Domain, Mrs Macquarie's Road, Royal Botanic Gardens, CBD (tickets 9266 4800/ www.homebake.com.au). CityRail Circular Quay or Martin Place/ferry Circular Quay. **Map** p327 G/H5. **Date** late Nov/early Dec.
As the name suggests, this one-day music festival features some of Australia's (and New Zealand's) best home-grown talent. Homebake celebrated its tenth anniversary in 2005 and has grown from muddy beginnings in a Byron Bay paddock to the tens of thousands that now descend on the Domain for 12 hours of ear-splitting pleasure. A cinema tent extends the concept to new film-makers. Gates open

Christmas Day on Bondi Beach. *See p214.*

at 11am but don't expect to get a ticket on the day – they sell out well in advance. There are no age restrictions, but it's not recommended for young children. Bring photo ID if you want to drink alcohol.

Carols in the Domain

The Domain, Mrs Macquarie's Road, Royal Botanic Gardens, CBD (www.carolsinthedomain.com). CityRail Circular Quay or Martin Place/ferry Circular Quay. **Map** p327 G/H5. **Date** wk before Christmas.
In case you thought Christmas wouldn't be Christmas in all the heat, you can join the 100,000 who fill the Domain for an evening of traditional carols by candlelight. The crowds are kept in tune by a 150-strong choir and a chorus of local and blow-in celebs, and the evening is sealed by the mandatory – for Sydney – firework display. Candles can be purchased (money goes to charity) and the event is televised live. Get there early to roll out your rug.

And they're off!

The biggest date on the Australian horse racing calendar is the Melbourne Cup, held at Melbourne's Flemington Racecourse on the first Tuesday in November at 3pm. The Aussie equivalent of the Grand National and Ascot rolled into one, the race is the peak of Victoria's Spring Racing Carnival and has been run every year since 1861, surviving even the world wars and the Depression. Even Mark Twain had something to say about it after he visited in 1895: 'Nowhere in the world have I encountered a festival of people that has such a magnificent appeal to the whole nation. The Cup astonishes me.'

Melbourneites may be able to see the event in the horseflesh, but, never keen on being upstaged by their southern rivals, Sydney has the afternoon off. Most businesses put on drinks or let their employees head down to central plazas or meeting places, where you will find TAB totalisator machines, beer on tap and champagne flowing. People get dressed up in fancy frocks or hats and suits as if they had tickets to the exclusive 'Birdcage' marquees at the actual event, and most everyone has a bet. Large screens are erected outdoors, at Martin Place, King Street Wharf and other locations, and crowds flock to Sydney's own Royal Randwick Racecourse for home-grown horsey action (*see p263*).

So if you're in town on the first Tuesday in November and wonder why everyone looks like they're going to a wedding, head to the nearest bookie's and place a bet. Australia is a gambling nation and with multi-million prize money at stake, it's a bonzer opportunity to have a punt at being a true-blue Aussie for the day.

Christmas Day on Bondi Beach

Bondi Beach. CityRail Bondi Junction then bus 381, 378, 380, L82/bus 378, 380, L82. **Map** p334. **Date** 25 Dec.

Thousands of travellers from around the world (especially Brits) gather on Bondi Beach each year for an impromptu party, some with their own sofa and Christmas tree. Since the council introduced an alcohol ban on the beach a few years ago, this traditional festivity has become more of a family affair and the backpacker crowd heads to the Bondi Pavilion for an all-day dance party. The sun will be just as fierce as usual, remember. **Photo** *p213*.

Sydney Hobart Yacht Race

Sydney Harbour (9363 9731/www.cyca.com.au). **Date** 26 Dec.

Hundreds of keen yachtsmen and supporters turn out on Boxing Day to watch the spectacular lunchtime start of this notoriously gruelling race to Hobart in Tasmania. It's sobering to remember that several sailors died in the 1998 race when wild seas tore yachts apart, but the sight of hundreds of sails filling the harbour as the racers make their way out to sea is stunning. The best viewing areas are coastal cliff spots around the harbour, such as Bradleys Head, Chowder Bay and Georges Heights on the west, Vaucluse Point, South Head and the Gap on the east, and North Head in the north. The yachts reach Hobart two days later.

New Year's Eve Fireworks

Sydney Harbour & Darling Harbour (9265 9757/www.sydneynewyearseve.com.au). **Date** 9pm & midnight 31 Dec.

When it comes to pyrotechnic experiences, New Year's Eve in Sydney takes the biscuit, in fact the whole damn cake. Each year the stakes to be the best in the world are raised, and Sydney usually wins. After a day of public spectacles, there are two fireworks displays, one at 9pm for families and then the midnight extravaganza. If you're lucky or cashed-up enough, you'll be on a boat in the harbour, and there are plenty of cruise companies offering New Year's Eve dos. But for landlubbers, some of the best views will simply cost you an all-day wait, as you'll have to get there very early to claim that front-row position – tens of thousands of others want it too.

Gates open at 8am for the popular Mrs Macquarie's Point, where alcohol is on sale but you won't be able to BYO. The area around the Opera House and Dawes Point in the Rocks gets very crowded and is popular with the younger crowd. On the North Shore crowds gather early at Milsons Point and McMahons Point, but Blues Point Reserve is probably the better option for a panoramic and less crushed view. For a 'village' feel, head over to Darling Street in Balmain and join the locals. For more information, visit the City of Sydney website (www.cityofsydney.nsw.gov.au), which lists details of all the major vantage points.

Sydney Festival

Various venues (8248 6500/www.sydneyfestival.org.au). **Date** Jan.

Launched in 1976 to celebrate the city and bring people into the CBD, the festival has branched out to include venues in Parramatta, showcasing the 'city of the west'. This is Sydney's major cultural event: held over the three-week period leading up to Australia Day (26 January), the festival brings dance, theatre, visual arts, opera and music, with acts from home and international arts superstars. Ticketed events are supplemented by an impressive free outdoor programme, including the popular Symphony & Jazz in the Domain evenings, and (appropriately avant-garde) firework displays.

Australia Day
Various venues (1 300 654 124/www.australia day.com.au). **Date** 26 Jan.
Festivities take place all over the city (and the rest of Australia) in the annual celebration of European settlement in Australia. Events focus around Hyde Park, the Rocks and Darling Harbour, with music, food, kids' entertainment and plenty of flag-waving. A morning 'Woggan-ma-gule' ceremony takes place in the Botanical Gardens to acknowledge the 'traditional owners', the local indigenous Gadigal people; weather permitting, the day culminates in a firework display over Darling Harbour.

Ferrython
Sydney Harbour (www.sydneyfestival.org.au). **Date** 26 Jan.
Thousands of spectators gather to watch four of Sydney's catamaran ferries race for the title of Ferry Champion, with the Harbour Bridge as the finishing line. The race, for which the First Fleet-class catamarans are elaborately decorated, is now a traditional part of the Sydney Festival's Australia Day celebrations, and is followed by a prize for best-dressed ferry. Good viewpoints are Milsons Point, McMahons Point, the Botanic Gardens and Mrs Macquarie's Chair. The race starts at 11am.

Chinese New Year
Chinatown, Haymarket (9265 9333/www.cityof sydney.nsw.gov.au). CityRail Central/LightRail or Monorail Paddy's Markets. **Map** p329 E7. **Date** varies, usually end Jan/early Feb.
Head to Chinatown for the traditional 15 days of Chinese New Year festivities, complete with firecrackers, markets, a colourful parade and dragon-boat racing on Darling Harbour.

Autumn

Gay & Lesbian Mardi Gras
Various venues (9568 8600/www.mardigras.org.au). **Date** Feb; ends 1st Sat in Mar.
The month of February sees Sydney celebrate all things queer. Sydney's gay, lesbian and transgender community swells with the arrival of thousands of international visitors to join in an extravaganza of shows, exhibitions, plays, art, film and sport. The finale to the festival is the parade, when marching boys and girls shimmy and strut their stuff down the 'Golden Mile' from Hyde Park down Oxford Street to the party venue at Fox Studios. For more details, *see p242* **New Mardi Gras**.

Royal Easter Show
Sydney Showground, Sydney Olympic Park, Homebush Bay (9704 1111/www.eastershow.com.au). CityRail Olympic Park. **Date** from Fri before Good Fri.
The Easter Show is a Sydney institution: for two weeks every year rural Australia is packaged up for the urbanites and attracts more than a million visitors. There are competitions galore, not just the livestock prizes and sheepdog trials you might expect,

but contests for bees (and beeswax candles), alpacas, rats, mice and Miss Showgirl (who must demonstrate her rural knowledge) – not to mention the popular women's wood-chopping contest.

Anzac Day March
Along George Street from Martin Place to Hyde Park. CityRail Circular Quay, Martin Place, Town Hall or Wynyard/ferry Circular Quay. **Map** (Martin Place) p327 F5–p329 F7. **Date** 25 Apr.
Sydneysiders pay their respects to the Australian and New Zealand troops killed at Gallipoli and in other wars by turning out in their thousands to watch the parade of veterans and Defence Force bands. A public holiday, the day starts with a dawn service at the Martin Place Cenotaph followed at 9am by a march along George Street and a 12.30pm service at the Anzac Memorial in Hyde Park. There are dawn services throughout Sydney and Australia. See the *Sydney Morning Herald* for full details of events for the day.

Sydney Writers' Festival
Various venues (9252 7729/www.swf.org.au). **Date** last wk in May.
From highbrow to pulp, fact to fiction, writers from around the world as well as home-grown talent come together for a week of debate and discussion. This is Sydney's biggest literary event, with readings, workshops and the chance to meet authors. Some events are free, some aren't, but all require booking.

Winter

Biennale of Sydney
Various venues (9368 1411/www.biennaleofsydney. com). **Date** June-Aug, even-numbered years only.
Each festival explores a specific subject or theme through the works of Australian and international artists – in 2006 the 'conceptual framework' was 'zones of contact'. Alongside what is claimed to be 'the southern hemisphere's largest collection of contemporary art' there are educational seminars, talks and screenings to complement the chosen theme.

Sydney Film Festival
Various venues (9280 0511/www.sydneyfilm festival.org). **Date** 3 wks in June.
Featuring the innovative and independent as well as mainstream movies, this fortnight of film aims to please all with cinema from Australia and around the world. For more details, *see p229*.

City to Surf Fun Run
From corner of Park & College Streets to Bondi Beach (1 800 555 514/http://city2surf.sunherald. com.au). **Date** mid Aug.
This 14km (8.75-mile) community fun run, first held in 1971, starts near Hyde Park in the city and finishes at Bondi Beach. Upwards of 50,000 runners participate, some world class, but most are amateur joggers and walkers, with a guaranteed chicken suit staggering up 'Heartbreak Hill'.

Arts & Entertainment

Children

Sea, sand, ferry rides and koalas to cuddle – what more could they want?

It's a breeze keeping children entertained in Sydney. Beaches, parks, entertainment venues and outdoor activities abound, and the climate makes it a pleasure to get the family out and about. Best tip: as soon as the kids start complaining, take them on a ferry trip across the harbour – it never fails!

Hats and sunblock are mandatory. The Australian sun is usually out and is extra-strong, particularly from November to February. Weather-wise, the best time to visit is in the spring (September to November), as the days are warm enough for swimming but you won't sizzle. When you hit the beach you'll notice that most local kids are wearing legionnaire-style hats that cover the head, neck and shoulders and 'rashies' – long-sleeved tops. You'll find sun-screening swimwear and hats at most department stores and pharmacies.

Pick up a copy of **Sydney's Child** (www.sydneyschild.com.au), a free monthly publication full of info on children's activities. You'll find it in libraries, museums, toy shops and health food shops, or call 8876 4880.

For shops that sell children's clothes, *see p199*; for toyshops, *see p209*.

Beaches

Beaches both with and without surf co-exist at **Manly** (*see p118* and *p138*), which also has pleasant walks and plenty of cheap places to eat. Head north for great playgrounds at **North Steyne** and **Queenscliff**. Head south along Fairy Bower, the waterfront pathway, and you'll find a paddling pool and safe swimming at **Shelly Beach** (*see p137*). The surf at **Bondi Beach** (*see p93* and *p135*) is usually too crowded and too strong for little ones, but there's a paddling pool and playgrounds at the north end, and lots of space for rollerblading. There's also a challenging skateboarders' ramp at the south end of the beach.

South of Bondi, sheltered **Bronte Beach** (*see p136*) has a large park with barbecue facilities, a fantastic playground and a mini steam train, plus great cafés and a wonderful fish and chip shop. **Balmoral Beach** (*see p135*) on the North Shore is good for picnics, and you can enjoy a cappuccino in the Balmoral Boatshed café while the kids play in the adjacent playground or swim in a netted area.

Of the northern beaches, the best options are **Dee Why Beach**, which has a good playground and a range of child-friendly eateries, and **Collaroy Beach** (*see p138*), which has a paddling pool, a large playground and barbecue facilities. Further north, **Clareville Beach** (*see p122*) is a secluded and safe swimming beach on the Pittwater (western) side of the peninsula; the water's too shallow for adults, but ideal for little kids.

Wherever you go, respect the surf and don't swim outside the marker flags. For other family-friendly beaches, *see pp133-139*.

Museums

As well as a fascinating assortment of animal skeletons, the **Australian Museum** (*see p71*) has lots of interactive exhibits, including Kids' Island, an indoor play and discovery area for under-sixes. There are also special activities in school holidays. The **Australian National Maritime Museum** has a playground as well as ships of all sorts to be explored, while the **Powerhouse Museum** (for both, *see p82*) fills a former power station with gadgets for curious visitors to try.

Sydney Children's Museum

Corner of Pitt & Walpole Streets, Merrylands (9897 1414/www.sydneykids.org). CityRail Merrylands. **Open** 10am-4pm daily. **Admission** $5.50 for all-day play; $4.40 concessions; $20 family; free under-2s. **No credit cards**.

This excellent museum of science and technology in the western suburbs will keep inquisitive kids aged five to ten absorbed for a day. The emphasis is on getting involved, with interactive displays including a space maze, TV studio, plasma ball, ultraviolet room and giant kaleidoscope.

Parks & playgrounds

For somewhere for the children to run around that's not a beach, head for **Centennial Park** (*see p92*) in Paddington. It's huge, beautiful and buzzing with activity: rollerblades, bikes and pedal cars can be hired from **Centennial Park Cycles** (*see p297*) at the Musgrave Avenue entrance. And, usefully, there's a café right next to a toddlers' playground.

Darling Harbour (*see p80*) is touristy, but has lots for kids of all ages, so it's ideal for whiling away a few hours. There's a giant playground at Tumbalong Park, conveniently surrounded by cafés, and also a fun water play area, paddle-boats and a merry-go-round – not to mention the Sydney Aquarium and an IMAX cinema. At weekends and during school holidays you'll see lots of street entertainers and may well chance upon an open-air concert.

The **Entertainment Quarter** (*see p92*), next to the Sydney Cricket Ground in Moore Park, has a great playground, an enormous open area where older kids can run wild, and lots of cinemas and child-friendly restaurants. Other attractions include an ice rink (winter only), the indoor play centre Lollipop's (9331 0811) and TV studio Channel [V] – a hot spot for teenagers. On Wednesday and Saturday there's an excellent farmers' market, and during school holidays a fairground with bouncy castles, a petting zoo and pony rides.

Services

Dial an Angel
9362 4225. **Phone enquiries** 8.30am-8.30pm daily. **Credit** MC, V.
Offers an excellent nanny or babysitting service, 24 hours a day. All carers are carefully screened.

Tresillian
9787 0855. **Phone enquiries** 24hrs daily.
A counselling service for help with unsettled babies, breastfeeding and any other parenting problems.

Theatre & film

The school holidays, especially Christmas, are the time for children's concerts and pantos, and there are more during the **Sydney Festival** (*see p214*) in January; check local newspapers and *Sydney's Child* for up-to-date details. At the **Sydney Opera House** (*see p68*), the Kids at the House programme offers a hands-on introduction to music, dance and theatre. The **IMAX cinema** (*see p227*) at Darling Harbour is great for rainy days, while the Palace and Hoyts cinema chains offer regular 'babes in arms' sessions for parents and infants.

Wildlife

Shark fans should head to **Sydney Aquarium** (*see p82*) and **Oceanworld Manly** (*see p120*). Both offer close encounters with sharks and stingrays, as well as hands-on experiences with starfish and sea urchins. Oceanworld Manly also has an interactive 'Dangerous Australian Animals' show and educational sleepover nights for kids (minimum 20). Sydney Aquarium offers an incredible range of marine life, including fairy penguins and seals.

Harbourside **Taronga Zoo** (*see p114*) has both native Australian and exotic animals on show. There are tours, presentations and a fantastic water play area that should keep kids happy all day (bring a change of clothes). The most scenic way to get there is by ferry – from the dock you can catch a cable car up the hill to the zoo's main entrance and work your way back down to the ferry. For more home-grown creatures, head west out of town to **Featherdale Wildlife Park** (*see p127*) near Blacktown, where kids can hand-feed a kangaroo, wallaby or emu and have their photo taken with a koala (for free). More koala cuddling is on offer at the **Koala Park Sanctuary** (*see below*).

A colony of flapping fruit bats inhabits the spacious **Royal Botanic Gardens** (*see p73*), on the harbour – it's also an ideal picnic spot and kids love the tour by 'trackless train'.

If you want to get out into the bush, there are several easy walks in and around Sydney, in particular at **Berry Island Reserve** (*see p115*), where you'll find a short track with informative plaques about the area's Aboriginal heritage. **Manly Dam Reserve**, off King Street, Manly Vale (catch a bus from Wynyard or Manly Wharf), has easy and very scenic walks, and you can swim safely. The **NSW National Parks & Wildlife Service** runs Discovery walks, talks and tours for children (1300 361 967, www.nationalparks.nsw.gov.au).

Australian Reptile Park
Gosford exit of Sydney-Newcastle Freeway, Somersby (4340 1022/www.reptilepark.com.au). CityRail Gosford then 10mins taxi ride. **Open** 9am-5pm daily. **Admission** $20; $10-$13 concessions; $52 family; free under-4s. **Credit** AmEx, MC, V.
An hour's drive north of Sydney lives this collection of cold-blooded critters, creepy-crawlies and native animals including koalas, echidnas, wombats and Tasmanian devils. There are lots of noisy, colourful birds too. Interactive exhibits include Spider World and the Lost World of Reptiles, and there are also shows and talks. On Sundays, stick around to see Eric the saltwater crocodile being fed at 1pm.

Koala Park Sanctuary
84 Castle Hill Road, West Pennant Hills (9484 3141/ www.koalaparksanctuary.com.au). CityRail Pennant Hills then bus 631, 632, 633. **Open** 9am-5pm daily. **Admission** $18; $8 concessions. **Credit** AmEx, DC, MC, V.
There's no denying that koalas are Australia's cutest native animal, and what kid wouldn't want to cuddle one? The main attractions are joined by their compatriots – emus, kangaroos, echidnas, dingoes and wombats – as well as some birds, including cockatoos and wedge-tailed eagles. Plus there are four hectares (ten acres) of lush rainforest, eucalyptus groves and native gardens to wander around.

Clubs

Prices down, indie in and watch out for those '80s flashbacks.

Toned down and sober have never been big words in Sydney clubland, but the ongoing credit crisis seems to be taking its toll on the way people party. While clubbing used to be an every-weekend affair for many, now people are saving their pennies for a once-a-month, let-the-dog-loose experience. In an attempt to lure punters back, door prices have been nipped, and small incentive schemes introduced, such as splashing complimentary champagne and two-for-one cocktails around. Organisers keep shifting their nights around to capture the newt-like attention spans of party-goers, while promoters continue a scatter-gun approach, inventing one-off events and outdoor festivals with big-name international DJs.

The current scene is a touch *Little Britain*, as London's retro electro/indie rock mood sweeps through the city, with the winds of cool blowing westwards. The inner-city mega-clubs, **Home** and **Tank**, still rule in terms of numbers, but two of the new favourites, **Purple Sneakers** and **Sly Fox**, take place in grungy inner-west pubs. **Mad Racket**, an irregular night-or-day event set up by four leading Sydney DJs, continues its roll as the DJs' in-club, where whoever gets on the turntables rules the way the session happens. It's held, improbably enough, out south-west at the Marrickville Bowling Club (corner of Sydenham Road and Fitzroy Street, Marrickville) – check www.madracket.com.au for the latest info.

With the new-style music comes a new-wear look. While partying in Sydney still means flesh and glitter, indie clubs are bringing op-shop retro onto the scene. For those old enough to remember 1980s fashion and music the first time around, it is at once vaguely disturbing yet strangely comforting to hear the pulse of the Human League while surrounded by a sea of slogan-bearing T-shirts and kinky boots. Glamour is definitely still in, but the notoriously exclusive and pricey clubs have had to thaw their ice-pick-cool policies.

As you would expect, most clubbers are in their teens and twenties, but there are still nights that those other side of 40 can happily slip into. As a general rule, think Sunday nights for slower grooves. For a more serious study of what's on, turn to the clubbing bible, magazine *3D World* (www.threedworld.com.au) – available for free in most record shops. Or visit www.inthemix.com.au to get a grip on what Sydney's spinning. For gay- and lesbian-oriented clubs, *see p240*.

Bars & clubs

Arq Sydney

16 Flinders Street, between Oxford & Taylor Streets, Darlinghurst (9380 8700/www.arqsydney.com.au). Bus 373, 377, 378, 380, 382, 391, 394, 396. **Open** 9pm-late Thur-Sun. **Admission** (after 10pm) $10 Fri; $20 Sat; $5 Sun. **No credit cards**. **Map** p329 H9.
The seven-tonne, million-dollar lighting rig is as much a part of the show as the people, who wear less here, perhaps, than anywhere else in Sydney. It's a multi-level flesh show, and the music gets more urgent the higher up the building you go. Friday is an anyone-goes affair; Saturday and Sunday remain true to the club's original gay theme (*see p240*). There's an ATM for when it's too late to care.

ArtHouse Hotel

275 Pitt Street, between Park & Market Streets, CBD (9284 1200/www.thearthousehotel.com.au). CityRail St James or Town Hall/Monorail Galeries Victoria. **Open** *Verge Bar, Gallery Bar & Dome Lounge* 11am-midnight Mon-Thur; 11am-3am Fri; 5pm-6am Sat. *Attic Bar* 5.30pm-late Tue-Sat. **Admission** *Kink* $20. **Credit** AmEx, DC, MC, V. **Map** p329 F7.
Saturday night's Kink transforms this former 19th-century school of art, which has also been a chapel and a theatre in its time, into a 21st-century nightclub. With an admission price about as lofty as the mile-high stilettoes that the wannabe models teeter in on, it makes for an expensive club night. Dress up, dress funky and praise be for dark corners to hide in, as this is a young, glamour-revved crowd. Great cocktails in the Attic Bar (*see p175*).

Beach Road Hotel

Corner of Beach Road & Glenayr Avenue, Bondi Beach (9130 7247). CityRail Bondi Junction then bus 380, 381, L82/bus 380, L82. **Open** *Club nights* 7pm-11pm Tue-Thur; 7pm-1am Fri-Sat; 4pm-10pm Sun. **Admission** free. **No credit cards**. **Map** p334.
While you will have to wear something more than your bikini top, this Bondi Beach pub is one of the few places where thongs (flip-flops) get through the door. School-night closing times keep extended frenzy under control, but it's still the perfect club option for those who want to hop from beach to disco in just a few bounds. Sort of like an ultra-glam RSL, it's easy to slip in and mix around the crowd – and best of all, it's free to get in. Live acts perform on Tuesday, Thursday and Sunday, but the hotel shifts

Spot-the-prince competition in the **Slip Inn**'s Garden Bar. *See p222.*

to dance mode on Friday and Saturday nights, with DJs playing anything from dub to house. Also a good spot for a game of pool (*see p182*).

Cargo Bar

52-60 The Promenade, King Street Wharf, Darling Harbour (9262 1777/www.cargobar.com.au). CityRail Wynyard/ferry Darling Harbour/Monorail Darling Park. **Open** *Bar* 11am-late daily. *DJs* 6pm-late Thur-Sun. **Credit** AmEx, DC, MC, V. **Map** p326 D6.

Cargo works hard to carry some music cred; it doesn't have the coolest crowd, but it does have one

of the best water views. It's a bar most of the time, with DJs shifting it into club mode at the end of the week. Arrive early on Thursday for the 6-8pm Chicago Gin Club, when complimentary G&Ts are slung from the bar – perfect for sunset sipping.

Club 77

77 William Street, between Crown & Yurong Streets, East Sydney (no phone/www.club77sydney.com). CityRail Kings Cross/bus 378, 380, 382. **Open** 8pm-3am Thur; 6pm-4am Fri; 7pm-4am Sat; 8pm-1am Sun. **Admission** $5-$10. **Credit** AmEx, DC, MC, V. **Map** p329 G7.

Naughty but nice

It's an interesting theory: the current outbreak of burlesque in Sydney could be down to international strife and the generally troubled state of the world. 'Look at Berlin just before Hitler took off – the arts were really amazing. That's when burlesque was big,' insists Glita Supernova, one of the creators of **Gurlesque** (www.gurlesque.com – *see p243*), a burlesque show for lesbians that has been running in the city for more than five years. 'It's so conservative at the moment, and burlesque is anti-establishment.'

There were tasters of things to come with the opening in 2003 of **Moulin Rouge** (*see p221*), a Kings Cross nightclub with fishnet-stockinged waitresses and cabaret-style furnishings. The club's patron saints are Aussie film director Baz Luhrmann and his production designer Catherine Martin, who channelled their own hyper-coloured, bent view of burlesque into their 2001 movie *Moulin Rouge!*; even Kylie has pushed the trappings of it with her recent 'Showgirl' tour.

Nevertheless, Sydney hadn't gone all the way until the arrival of **34b** (*photo*), a new burlesque club held on Fridays in Oxford Street's **Q Bar** (*see p221*). Acts range from the classic variety show Sugartime through to the all-guy troupe Man Jam. Christa Hughes,

original MC at 34b and long-time burlesque performer, remembers first 'getting her tits out' years ago at the Edinburgh Festival. 'I think it was just to get a response. I had moustaches painted across the nipples, but it wasn't meant to be, "Look at these amazing tits".' In the UK they understood it was about parody, but she was banned when she tried to do the same thing at Melbourne University. 'Australia just didn't get it.'

Sydney has strict laws when it comes to showing nipples and anything less than a G-string, so events remain on the safe side of full nudity. Still, audiences are often gobsmacked by Glita Supernova and her partner Sex Intents' take on the genre at Gurlesque. As well as lesbian-only nights, they have repackaged their troupe into an all-sexes act called Trip Tease that's leaving men's mouths wide open.

'It's like you took acid and went to a strip club,' says Glita. Performances to date have revolved around an overworked blue Smurfette stripper, the Three Little Pigs doing a chair routine and a half-human, half-chicken hybrid stripper called a 'Chickendale'. At last, it seems, Sydney is beginning to get the explosive mix of strip, humour and politics that burlesque has to offer.

Off the skids and so cool it doesn't bother to list itself in the phone book, Club 77 keeps it dark, underground and ultra-hip. Sydney's fashion trash turn up for the Bang Gang crew on Friday nights, while the long-running Club Kooky, on Sunday nights, shines its light on camp with art students a-go-go – it's also a big hit with the gay crowd (see p240). Live bands sometimes play too.

Home

Cockle Bay Wharf, Darling Harbour (9266 0600/infoline 9267 0674/www.homesydney.com). CityRail Town Hall/Monorail Darling Park/ferry Darling Harbour. **Open** *Bar* noon-late daily. *Club* 11pm-7am Fri; 11pm-6.30am Sat. **Admission** *Club* $25 Fri, Sat. **No credit cards**. Map p328 D7.
Rejuvenated by a recent face-lift, Home is still one of Sydney's best large-scale clubbing experiences. It sprawls over three levels and four bars, with chill-out areas, space-age lighting and a great view over Darling Harbour. Sublime on Friday spills over with everything from house to trance to drum 'n' bass and throws its finger at critics by remaining the longest-running club night in the city. Different events rock up on Saturday, and the club also hosts the occasional and self-explanatory Homesexual (see p244).

Lady Lux

2 Roslyn Street, between Darlinghurst Road & Ward Avenue, Kings Cross (9361 5361/www.ladylux. com.au) CityRail Kings Cross. **Open** 10pm-6am Wed-Sun. **Admission** $20. **No credit cards**. Map p330 J7.
One of the newer kids on the Kings Cross circuit, Lady Lux runs the gamut of what's currently happening in Sydney. Wednesday's Filth goes live with local and interstate bands, while Thursday's Grit brings hip hop. Friday's Lipstick channels cool and eclectic music to a media/fashion crowd, and Saturday aims for the masses with house plus remixed 1980s classics. Dark lighting and leather seating keep it warm and intimate, but beware Smut on Sundays, which pulls the toddler babes from Saturday night's Kink at ArtHouse (see p218).

Moulin Rouge

39 Darlinghurst Road, at Springfield Avenue, Kings Cross (8354 1711/www.moulinrougesydney.com.au). CityRail Kings Cross. **Open** 9pm-6am Fri, Sat; 10pm-6am Sun. **Admission** $10-$15. **Credit** AmEx, MC, V. Map p330 J7.
Think *Moulin Rouge!* the movie and you've got this club, part of the burgeoning burlesque scene in the city – see p220 **Naughty but nice**. The look is gaudy and red, while the waitresses in corsets and fishnets are matched only by the towering models this place attracts – pretty, pretty, in skyscraper shoes. Masks and feathers aren't unusual dress options, although the owner insists the dress code is reasonably relaxed. The dancefloor is almost a stage to the three split levels rising above. It's a bit like having a nightclub with a cabaret edge in your lounge, where you can drink absinthe while listening to laid-back funky breaks and disco.

Plan B

Bourbon, 24 Darlinghurst Road, at Macleay Street, Kings Cross (9358 1144/www.thebourbon.com.au). CityRail Kings Cross. **Open** 10pm-6am Fri-Sun. **Admission** $15 ($10 members) Fri, Sun; $20 ($15 members) Sat. **Credit** (bar only) AmEx, DC, MC, V. Map p330 J7.
There's something a little sad about the sleaze of Sydney giving way to the schmooze of style. The old Bourbon & Beefsteak, once the bastion of sailors on shore leave and all the Kings Cross skullduggery that accompanied them, is now simply the slick and shiny Bourbon (see p181), with its own club – Plan B. Leather ottomans seat a sleek clientele, there to groove to anything from R&B to relaxed, sexy house on Sundays. With the Bourbon restaurant serving medium-priced, bistro-style food, it makes for an easy night out with friends.

Purple Sneakers

Abercrombie Hotel, corner of Broadway & Abercrombie Street, Ultimo (9211 3486/ www.purplesneakers.com.au). CityRail Central. **Open** 8pm-late Fri. **Admission** $10. **No credit cards**. Map p328 D10.
Like the love child of the Killers and the Clash, Purple Sneakers is a strange little sideline on the club scene that's picking up on the London thing for indie/electro. Great fun, but vaguely disturbing if you experienced the 1980s the first time around. Dance in the basement of a grungy pub or hang out in the courtyard – this has all the hallmarks of having a party in someone's backyard. Lead singers of local rock bands often end up at the turntables. Dress down. See also p184.

Q Bar

Exchange Hotel, Level 3, 34-44 Oxford Street, between Riley & Liverpool Streets, Darlinghurst (9360 1375/www.qbar.com.au). Bus 352, 378, 380, L82. **Open** 9pm-late Wed-Sun. **Admission** $15 Fri; $20 Sat. **Credit** AmEx, MC, V. Map p329 G8.
It's hard to keep up with all the goings-on at busy, big Q Bar, which reinvents itself more often than Madonna. Currently, it has a dancefloor that swirls with funk and house, and becomes the burlesque club 34b on Friday nights (see p220 **Naughty but nice**). It's housed in the multi-level Exchange Hotel, a popular gay venue (see p240), which also offers the Phoenix club for more dancing, and Spectrum, which adds in live music. A mixed crowd keeps the mood party-friendly. **Photo** p222.

Sapphire Suite

2 Kellet Street, at Bayswater Road, Kings Cross (9331 0058/www.sapphiresuite.com.au). CityRail Kings Cross. **Open** 8pm-6am Thur-Sun. **Admission** after 9pm Fri-Sun $15. Map p330 J7.
In a vain attempt to bring a touch of Tank-style glamour to the Cross, Sapphire's interior designers have gone all out with a sapphire-inspired rock wall behind the long bar, with water trickling down its crevices. The effect is ice, ice baby – which is perhaps just as it should be for the sweaty dancers who

Q Bar's got a lot of balls and everyone is welcome. *See p221.*

come here for acid jazz on Thursday, live percussionists versus DJs on Friday, funky vocal house on Saturday and retro funk on Sunday. Arrive early on Thursday and Friday for complimentary champagne and cheap cocktails.

Slip Inn

111 Sussex Street, at King Street, CBD (8295 9999/www.merivale.com.au). CityRail Town Hall or Wynyard. **Open** *Slip Bar* noon-midnight Mon-Thur; noon-2am Fri; 5pm-2am Sat. *Sand Bar* 6pm-midnight Thur; 6pm-3am Fri; 9pm-3am Sat. *Garden Bar* noon-midnight Mon-Fri; 6pm-midnight Sat. *Chinese Laundry* 10pm-4am Fri; 10.30pm-4am Sat. *Cave* 11pm-4am Fri, Sat. **Admission** $15 Fri; $20 Sat. **Credit** AmEx, DC, MC, V. **Map** p327 E6.

The Slip Inn – famous locally as being the place where Aussie estate agent Mary Donaldson met her future husband, the Prince of Denmark – houses three bars (Slip, Sand and Garden) and two clubs (Chinese Laundry and the smaller Cave). Chinese Laundry splits itself into two nights: Break Inn on Fridays, and the pricier, pumped-up Laundry on Saturdays. Currently very popular is the Garden Bar – a huge, sun-filled courtyard at the rear that hosts a buzzing outdoor day club every Sunday. Its organisers also run other local and international events; details at www.sounds.net.au. **Photo** *p219.*

Sly Fox

199 Enmore Road, between Cambridge Street & Stanmore Road, Enmore (9557 1016). Bus 423, 426, 428. **Open** 10am-4am Mon-Thur; 10am-6am Fri; 10am-5am Sat; 10am-midnight Sun. **No credit cards.**

One of the strangest yet hottest little happenings in town, Sly Fox has fooled clubbers into believing it's something more than a local pub. Located at the grungier, western end of Enmore, it offers funk on

Thursday, drum 'n' bass on Friday and rotating DJs on Saturday. Wednesday brings lesbians and drag kings to the hugely popular girls' night (*see p239*). Once a month it gives itself up to goths or electronica. Cocktails cost $5 between 7pm and 9pm.

Tank

3 Bridge Lane, off Bridge Street, between George & Pitt Streets, CBD (9240 3094/www.tankclub.com.au). CityRail Circular Quay or Wynyard/ferry Circular Quay. **Open** 10pm-7am Fri, Sat. **Admission** $20 Fri; $25 Sat. **Credit** AmEx, DC, MC, V. **Map** p327 F4.

This high-columned über-club is the closest thing you'll get to a Studio 54 experience in Sydney. Big on style, Tank even credits the sound and lighting dudes on its website – it's nice to think the clubbers may care. The music itself has settled into comfortable funky/jazzy house on Friday and a chunkier sound on Saturdays, with loads of international DJs. And it's not as snooty as it once was: the fashion-heavy door policy has been relaxed and the VIP room has opened itself up for all to enter.

Yu at Soho Bar

Soho Bar, 171 Victoria Street, between Darlinghurst Road & Orwell Street, Potts Point (9358 4221/ www.yu.com.au). CityRail Kings Cross. **Open** *Bar* 10am-4am Mon-Thur, Sun; 10am-6am Fri, Sat. *Yu* 10pm-6am Fri-Sun. **Admission** $10 Sun; $15 Fri; $20 Sat. **Credit** (bar only) AmEx, DC, MC, V. **Map** p330 J7.

Friday nights attract the shiny young set at Art, while Saturday brings a 'who knows?' night, often with international DJs. Sunday's After Ours shifts to sophisticated grooves and a more mixed crowd. Yu's worth dressing up for, and its designers were thoughtful enough to install a sprung dancefloor. Prince Harry dropped in when he was in town.

Film

This city's as busy watching movies as it is making them.

Given their obsession with sport and the great outdoors, it's hard to fathom why Australians are such voracious movie-goers, but love film they do. In addition to their record take-up of DVD – the fastest per capita anywhere in the world – Aussies continue to flock to the cinema in ever-increasing numbers. Hollywood blockbusters typically dominate the box office (an Australian hit grosses in excess of $2 million, a big-budget American success ten times that), but home-grown films are thriving once more, both critically and commercially. Recent hits include *Wolf Creek*, *Look Both Ways* and the Nick Cave-scripted bushranger drama *The Proposition*.

The 'LA of the Antipodes' tag that Sydney enjoys, though, has as much to do with international hits being made at Rupert Murdoch's Fox Studios – the *Matrix* trilogy, *Moulin Rouge*, *Mission: Impossible II*, episodes II and III of *Star Wars*, *Superman Returns* – and the many stars who jet over for red-carpet premières. And lest we forget, Australian actors continue to shine in Hollywood and the rest of the world too – *see p226* **Lights, camera, Aussies!**

Reflecting this boom is the nature of cinema-going itself. Where once there was a series of independent cinemas dotted about town, now there are virtually none. Inevitably bowing to the teen-targeted multiplexes, the heritage-listed Randwick Ritz and Cremorne's Orpheum both screen mainstream fare. But despite the homogenisation, Sydney has a healthy appetite for art-house cinema, found at the Palace and Dendy theatres (though the Chauvel, the best art-house cinema in town, has closed). And the giant theatres – slick, comfortable affairs with stadium-sized sound systems – offer a luxurious touch, with Hoyt EQ's La Premiere and Bondi Junction's Gold Class options available at a price.

TICKETS AND INFORMATION

First-run movies open on Thursdays, with three to four premières a week. Unless it's a blockbuster, you can usually get a ticket without problem. Prices are around $15-$16 for adults, with concessions for children, senior citizens, students and the unemployed. Public holidays usually involve a $1 'surcharge', while Monday and Tuesday are traditionally bargain nights, when tickets are reduced to as little as $5. The major chains – Hoyts, Greater Union, Palace and Dendy – have websites with screening times, plus there are cinema ads in the entertainment sections of the *Sydney Morning Herald* and *Daily Telegraph*. Session times are also available through **Cinema Information Line** (1 902 263 456), albeit for a premium-rate call fee.

Cinemas

First-run

The multiplexes typically offer Hollywood blockbusters and kids' movies. Christmas, September school holidays and the Easter long weekend are key periods for distributors, who often hold back movies for that all-important opening weekend at these times.

Greater Union Bondi Junction

Westfield Bondi Junction, 500 Oxford Street, Bondi Junction (9300 1555/www.greaterunion. com.au). CityRail Bondi Junction/bus 352, 378, 380, L82. **Screens** 11. **Tickets** $15.50; $8.50-$12 concessions. **Credit** AmEx, DC, MC, V. **Map** p333 P11.

The newest addition in the ever-expanding multi-plex landscape (nearby Double Bay lost its art-house cinema because of it), this Bondi Junction cinema is located on the upper levels of Sydney's latest shopping mall. The cinema has digital surround sound, comfy seating, its own bar, a 'fine dining' food court right on its doorstep and harbour views to boot. Programmes feature a mix of blockbusters and the mainstream end of art-house. The complex stretches over six levels and takes up more than a block of land, so factor in navigation time. The Gold Class option, similar to Hoyt EQ's La Premiere, offers plush armchairs, a separate lounge and food and drink for twice the normal ticket price.

Greater Union George Street

505-525 George Street, between Bathurst & Liverpool Streets, CBD (9273 7431/www.greater union.com.au). CityRail Town Hall/Monorail World Square. **Screens** 17. **Tickets** $15.50; $8.50-$12 concessions. **Credit** AmEx, DC, MC, V. **Map** p329 F7.

The Greater Union chain's flagship cinema shows virtually every new commercial movie release as soon as it opens. Located in the heart of George Street's garish entertainment strip, it attracts throngs of noisy kids and can get a little edgy at night, so guard your valuables. The state-of-the-art auditoria with digital surround sound and comfy seats are especially popular with teens and out-of-towners, as you'll see from the queues.

Hoyts Broadway

Broadway Shopping Centre, Bay Street, at Greek Street, Glebe (9211 1911/www.hoyts.com.au). Bus 413, 431, 432, 433, 434, 436, 437, 438, 440. **Screens** 12. **Tickets** $15.50; $8.50-$12 concessions. **Credit** AmEx, DC, MC, V. **Map** p328 C9.

Situated on top of another shopping mecca, this huge complex (the largest auditorium has 379 seats) often wilts under the pressure of numbers, particularly on weekends with rowdy teens. Three of the theatres are 'cinemaxx' standard: high-backed seats, perfect sight lines, super-large screens and digital surround sound. As with the Palace chain's 'babes in arms' events, 'mums and bubs' sessions for movie-craving parents/grandparents/carers/nannies and their infants run every month.

Hoyts EQ

Bent Street, Entertainment Quarter, Driver Avenue, Moore Park (9332 1300/www.hoyts.com.au). Bus 339, 373, 374, 375, 376, 377, 393, 395, 396. **Screens** 12. **Tickets** $15.50; $8.50-$12 concessions. **Credit** AmEx, DC, MC, V. **Map** p332 K12.

Located in the Entertainment Quarter, part of the Fox Studios complex, this vast pseudo-retro complex boasts huge screens, stadium seating (total capacity 3,000) and clean facilities, and is a refreshing change

Art deco favourite **Ritz Cinema**.

from the pushing, shoving and traffic-choked thoroughfare of George Street. A classy extra package, popular with first-time daters, is La Premiere. For twice the cost of a usual ticket, you get a cosy, two-person sofa with unobstructed views, plus free soft drinks, tea, coffee and popcorn in the La Premiere lounge. There's also booze to buy, which you can take in with you, and a free cheese platter served with every bottle of vino.

Manly Twin Cinemas

43-45 East Esplanade, opposite Manly Wharf, Manly (9977 0644/www.manlycinema.com.au). Ferry Manly. **Screens** 2. **Tickets** $12.50; $8.50-$10.50 concessions. **No credit cards**. **Map** p334.

This modest two-screener features first-run mainstream movies and the odd art-house flick. Seats are adequate and the main screen has Dolby digital sound. It's located next to the ferry wharf and, not surprisingly, patronised by Manly locals.

Reading Cinemas

Market City, 9-13 Hay Street, entrance on Thomas Street, Haymarket (9280 1202/www.reading cinemas.com.au). CityRail Central/LightRail or Monorail Paddy's Markets. **Screens** 5. **Tickets** $15.50; $8.50-$10.50 concessions. **Credit** MC, V. **Map** p329 E8.

A youngish pup in the local market, the American-owned Reading chain has its Chinatown five-screener directly above Paddy's Market. Appropriately enough, it favours first-release mainstream and Asian movies (in Cantonese with English subtitles). Seats are comfortable and all screens have Dolby digital sound.

Ritz Cinema Randwick

39-47 St Paul's Street, at Avoca Street, Randwick (9399 5722/www.ritzcinema.com.au). Bus 314, 372, 373, 374. **Screens** 6. **Tickets** $8; $5-$7 concessions. **Credit** MC, V.

With its distinctive art deco design, recently restored to its former 1930s glory, and impressive sound system, the six-screen Ritz cinema is both a local landmark and an excellent venue for catching the latest mainstream releases. Signs explain the regulations – no alcohol/bare feet/smoking/laser lights/skateboards – which make sense if you hit the place in the afternoon after school's out. In the evening the place attracts a different crowd, including film geeks who seek out the Ritz for its great acoustics and old-fashioned flair. **Photo** *left*.

Art house

Both the Dendy and Palace cinema chains have great-value membership schemes, which are well worth the investment if you plan to go to the cinema regularly.

Cinema Paris

Bent Street, Entertainment Quarter, Driver Avenue, Moore Park (9332 1633/www.hoyts.com.au). Bus 339, 373, 374, 375, 376, 377, 393, 395, 396.

Outback horror movie **Wolf Creek**, an international hit for the Aussie film industry.

Screens 4. **Tickets** $15.50; $8.50-$12 concessions. **Credit** AmEx, DC, MC, V. **Map** p332 K12. Unassuming art-house cinema within Fox Studios' Entertainment Quarter, with a total seating capacity of 600. Also hosts several film festivals.

Dendy Newtown

261-263 King Street, between Mary & Church Streets, Newtown (9550 5699/www.dendy.com.au). CityRail Newtown. **Screens** 4. **Tickets** $14; $8-$10.50 concessions. **Credit** AmEx, DC, MC, V. **Map** p334.

Matching its Opera Quays sister (*see below*) for style if not setting, Dendy Newtown offers quality first releases, 562 super-comfortable seats, big screens, Dolby digital surround sound and a bar. There's free parking for film-goers in the Lennox Street car park behind the cinema – a definite plus in often jam-packed King Street.

Dendy Opera Quays

2 East Circular Quay, Circular Quay (9247 3800/ www.dendy.com.au). CityRail/ferry Circular Quay. **Screens** 3. **Tickets** $14; $8-$10.50 concessions. **Credit** AmEx, DC, MC, V. **Map** p327 G3.

A stone's throw from the Opera House, with great views across to the Harbour Bridge, this luxurious complex (total capacity: 579) usually offers a mix of middlebrow and art-house fare, and is fully licensed. Full disabled access to all screens.

Govinda's

112 Darlinghurst Road, between William & Hardie Streets, Darlinghurst (9380 5155/www.govindas. com.au). CityRail Kings Cross. **Screens** 1.

Tickets $10.90; $21.90 with meal; $15.90 concessions. **Credit** AmEx, MC, V. **Map** p330 J8.

Adored by its twenty- and thirtysomething regulars, this Krishna-operated restaurant-cum-quality art-house cinema is a must-visit film experience. After you've loaded up on the generous vegetarian buffet, sit (or lie) back on the cushions and bean bags and enjoy arty films, documentaries and classics in 35mm. You can watch and not eat, but diners are given preference and since there are only 65 seats in the cinema – roughly half the restaurant's capacity – it's best to buy your ticket early.

Hayden Orpheum Picture Palace

380 Military Road, between Winnie & Macpherson Streets, Cremorne (9908 4344/www.orpheum. com.au). Bus 143, 144, 151, 228, 229, 230, 243, 246, 247, 257. **Screens** 6. **Tickets** $15.50; $8.50-$12 concessions. **Credit** MC, V.

Without doubt the grandest cinema in Sydney, Cremorne's art deco picture palace is a stunning step back in time. Built in 1935 by George Kenworthy, the top theatrical architect of the period, today's version is even glitzier than the original, thanks to a $2.5-million restoration some years back by owner and local TV celeb Mike Walsh. Each of the six auditoria has its own colour scheme and decor, but the 744-seat Orpheum is the true star of the show. It even has a genuine Wurlitzer cinema organ, which rises out of a stage pit on weekend evenings, complete with flashing lights and grinning organist. Expect a mix of mainstream US, British and Australian fare, with some art house, special presentations and the occasional cabaret show.

Arts & Entertainment

Lights, camera, Aussies!

The Australian film industry may be small, but the talent is not. Here's a who's who of top Aussie actors.

MADE IT

Cate Blanchett

Willowy blonde NIDA (National Institute of Dramatic Art) graduate who trod a deliberately arty film path – *Elizabeth*, *Oscar and Lucinda*, *Charlotte Gray*, *Veronica Guerin* – before Oscar caught up with her for *The Aviator*. Helped revive Aussie industry with *Little Fish* before jumping back into the big-name pool.

Toni Collette

Burst on to the scene in spandex hot pants in Aussie hit *Muriel's Wedding*, but now works mainly overseas. Films include *The Sixth Sense*, *Velvet Goldmine*, *Emma*, *About a Boy*, *Shaft*, *Love Actually*, *In Her Shoes* and *The Night Listener*.

Russell Crowe

A Kiwi by birth, but grew up in Sydney. Notorious for his off-set antics, but his films – the epic *Gladiator*, brooding *A Beautiful Mind*, understated *Cinderella Man* and the recent *A Good Year* – speak for themselves.

Judy Davis

Lead and character actress who went to NIDA with Mel Gibson and was Oscar-nominated for David Lean's *A Passage to India* and Woody Allen's *Husbands and Wives*. Has also worked with David Cronenberg, Clint Eastwood, Sofia Coppola, and played Judy Garland to great acclaim.

Mel Gibson

Born in America but mostly considered an Aussie. Shot to fame with *Mad Max*, then *Gallipoli*, the *Lethal Weapon* films and Oscar-winning *Braveheart*, which he also directed. Received hate mail for directing the religious epic *The Passion of the Christ*. Downscaled somewhat with *Apocalypto*.

Rachel Griffiths

Tends to opt for sharp, thought-provoking, intelligent roles. Standouts include *Muriel's Wedding*, *Hilary and Jackie* (for which she was Oscar-nominated), *Me Myself I* and US TV hit *Six Feet Under*.

Arts & Entertainment

Palace Academy Twin Cinema

3A Oxford Street, between South Dowling & Verona Streets, Paddington (9361 4453/www.palacecinemas. com.au). Bus 352, 378, 380, L82. **Screens** 2. **Tickets** $15; $8.50-$12 concessions. **Credit** AmEx, DC, MC, V. **Map** p329 H9.

The Palace-owned Academy Twin has seen better days, with its facilities in dire need of refurbishment (don't go if you're tall – the seats have very little leg room). One of the city's longest-running art cinemas, it presents an eclectic mix of foreign, Australian and arty mainstream releases, plus a number of show-cases including the Mardi Gras Film Festival.

Palace Norton Street Cinema

99 Norton Street, between Marion Street & Parramatta Road, Leichhardt (9550 0122/ www.palacecinemas.com.au). Bus 436, 437, 438, 440, 445, 470, L38. **Screens** 4. **Tickets** $15; $8.50-$12 concessions. **Credit** AmEx, DC, MC, V.

Located in the heart of Little Italy, the sleek and styl-ish Norton Street Cinema is the cream of the Palace chain. Seats are plush, the air-con keeps you cool, and the sound and sight lines are excellent. You'll find an intelligent mix of offbeat Hollywood releases, foreign (including an Italian film festival) and Australian art-house fare. The 'babes in arms' sessions on Thursday mornings are popular: lights are turned up, sound down and breastfeeding is everywhere.

Palace Verona Cinema

17 Oxford Street, at Verona Street, Paddington (9360 6099/www.palacecinemas.com.au). Bus 352, 378, 380, L82. **Screens** 4. **Credit** AmEx, DC, MC, V. **Map** p329 H9.

Just a few doors down from the Palace Academy Twin (*see left*), the modern Verona is the eastern-suburbs equivalent to Norton Street. Paddington's intellectuals, gays and arty crowd attend with glee. The four screens are on the small side and the seats not quite as soft as you'd expect, but the movies are an enticing blend of quirky commercial, sexy foreign and the best of Australian.

Drive-ins

Given the state-of-the-art multiplex explosion of recent years, it's a wonder that old bastion of the date movie, the drive-in, survives at all in Sydney. The two remaining sites are a good hour's train ride or drive out of the city, deep in the western suburbs, and differ wildly: the one at Bass Hill is stunning and worth the trip, while the other, in a field at Blacktown, isn't. Both are run by Greater Union and usually screen double features, mainly new mainstream releases. At both, gates and snack bars open at 6.30pm, with screenings starting at 7.30pm.

Hugh Jackman
Displayed musical prowess with *Oklahoma!* in London's West End and *The Boy from Oz* on Broadway while pursuing leading-man status in Hollywood. His Wolverine persona in the *X-Men* franchise cemented his star power.

Nicole Kidman
'Our Nic' has proved herself in recent years with films like *The Others*, *The Hours* (an Oscar win) and *Moulin Rouge*. Remains a global star and gossip mags' dream.

Heath Ledger
Teen heart-throb in *10 Things I Hate About You*, then switched to hero roles in *The Patriot*, *A Knight's Tale* and *Four Feathers*, before channelling his inner Brando for *Brokeback Mountain*.

Guy Pearce
Four years in *Neighbours*, then a drag queen in *The Adventures of Priscilla, Queen of the Desert*, followed by a lucrative spell in Hollywood, first as a naive cop in *L.A. Confidential*, then a bloke with a terrifyingly short memory in *Memento* and, more recently,

as Andy Warhol in *Factory Girl* and an outlaw in the Nick Cave-scripted *The Proposition*.

Geoffrey Rush
Trod the national theatre boards for 23 years until he won an Oscar playing genius pianist David Helfgott in *Shine*. Now in his fifties, Rush's film career continues to soar, thanks to the *Pirates of the Caribbean* films and an uncanny portrayal of Peter Sellers for HBO. Among his many other films: *Shakespeare in Love*, *Quills*, *Lantana* and *Swimming Upstream*.

Naomi Watts
The Kent rose claimed by Aussies as their own – her family moved when she was 15 – is now, like pal Nicole Kidman, an undoubted star after a decade-long slog. David Lynch's *Mulholland Dr.* launched her, but it was *King Kong* that proved her worth to the world.

Hugo Weaving
Donned a frock for *Priscilla* and won AFI (Australian Film Institute) awards for further offbeat hits. Playing Agent Smith in the *Matrix* and Elrond in *The Lord of the Rings* trilogies increased his studied cool status. ▶

Greater Union Twin Drive-In Bass Hill
Johnston Road, between Arundle & Handle Streets, Bass Hill (9724 1289/www.greaterunion.com.au). **Screens** 2. **Tickets** $15.50; $9.50-$12 concessions. **Credit** AmEx, DC, MC, V.

Greater Union Twin Drive-In Blacktown
Cricketers Arms Road, between Reservoir Road & M4 motorway, Blacktown (9622 4170/www.greater union.com.au). **Screens** 2. **Tickets** $15.50; $9.50-$12 concessions. **Credit** AmEx, DC, MC, V.

IMAX

IMAX Sydney
31 Wheat Road, southern end of Darling Harbour, Pyrmont (9281 3300/www.imax.com.au). CityRail Town Hall/Ferry Darling Harbour/Monorail or LightRail Convention. **Tickets** $22.50-$18; $13-$19 concessions; $40-$55 family. **Credit** AmEx, MC, V. **Map** p328 D7.
The giant, eye-shaped IMAX theatre sticks out on the water in touristy Darling Harbour. The 540-seat theatre claims to have the world's largest screen, some eight storeys high, and screens around 12 films a day from 10am to 10pm. Expect a mixed bag of 2D and 3D affairs, with documentaries a common

feature. Hardly essential viewing, although the sheer impact of seeing a 3D film makes it a worthy stop for the uninitiated.

Open-air

Given the climate, it's hardly surprising that Sydneysiders flock outdoors whenever they can. Open-air screenings are a firm fixture on the summer social calendar, with three main inner-city offerings: a picnic-on-the grass affair in Centennial Park, a similar set-up in North Sydney Oval (with seats and cover if desired) and a sensational harbourside experience in the Domain. Weather permitting (screenings are cancelled only in gale-force conditions), all are great nights out. You may have to pay booking fees on top of the prices quoted below.

Moonlight Cinema
Belvedere Amphitheatre, Centennial Park, Woollahra (1300 511 908/www.moonlight.com.au). Bus 378, 380, L82. **Tickets** $14-$15; $10-$13 concessions. **Credit** AmEx, DC, MC, V. **Map** p333 N11. **Date** early Dec-mid Mar.
Now gone nationwide, the Moonlight's programme focuses heavily on current and recent mainstream releases, with customary classics *Grease* and *Breakfast at Tiffany's* (on Valentine's Day) popular

Lights, camera, Aussies! (continued)

ON THE RISE

Simon Baker

Former soap kid turned thirtysomething alternative hunk. After struggling in LA, became a TV star with *The Guardian*. Films include *The Affair of the Necklace*, *Book of Love* and *Land of the Dead*. Recently moved back home to Sydney.

Eric Bana

A Melbourne comic who was picked by toe-cutting gangster Mark 'Chopper' Read to play him in daring flick *Chopper*. Despite no acting training, Bana was explosive. Turned green for the lead role in Ang Lee's *The Hulk*, Greek for *Troy* and Israeli for Spielberg's *Munich*.

Joel Edgerton

The *Secret Life of Us* came first, but it was appearing in George Lucas's *Star Wars* episodes two and three that had the phones ringing. Went to LA for *Hellion*.

Melissa George

A high-school dropout at 16, the Perth pin-up found soapie fame in the early 1990s as Angel Brooks in *Home and Away*. Moving to LA and bit-parting led to starring roles in *Derailed*, *The Amityville Horror*, and *Turistas* before lead duties beckoned with *Three Days in Dublin*.

Anthony LaPaglia

The Adelaide-born actor ditched his Aussie accent for Hollywood but now owns a share of Sydney's new FC. Regular film work, including a brilliant turn in *Lantana*, complements US TV success with *Without a Trace*. Married to *My Big Fat Greek Wedding*'s Gia Carides.

Nathan Phillips

Despite starring in the worst-ever local release (*You and Your Stupid Mate*) and one of the best (*Wolf Creek*), the former *Neighbours* star (yes, another one) and all-round genial goof went stateside in 2005 for *Snakes on a Plane* with Samuel L Jackson.

Richard Roxburgh

Versatile theatre actor and great film baddie who co-starred as the sadistic villain in *Mission: Impossible II*, the rat-like Duke in *Moulin Rouge* and Dracula in *Van Helsing*.

---

fixtures. Films kick off at sunset and entry is via Woollahra Gate (Oxford Street) only. Bring a picnic, cushions and insect repellent, and arrive early. Limited Gold Grass tickets (at $30 a pop) guarantee a prime spot, 'bean bed' and a bottle of bubbly.

Open-Air Cinema

Mrs Macquarie's Chair, The Domain, CBD (1300 366 649/www.stgeorge.com.au/openair). CityRail Circular Quay or Martin Place/ferry Circular Quay. **Tickets** $20.50-$21.50; $18.50-$19.50 concessions. **Credit** AmEx, DC, MC, V. **Map** p330 J3. **Date** early Jan-mid Feb.

Part of the Sydney Festival, this is the ultimate outdoor movie-going experience, with the Harbour Bridge and Opera House in the background. You get several Sydney premières of mainstream movies, as well as a pick of current and classic fare. Films start at 8.30pm, but the gates open from 6.30pm – as do the stylish on-site bar and restaurant. Capacity is around 1,700.

Starlight Cinema

North Sydney Oval, Miller Street, North Sydney (9922 2755/www.starlightcinema.com.au). CityRail North Sydney. **Tickets** $15-$18; $7.50-$16 concessions. **Credit** AmEx, DC, MC, V. **Map** p311 C2. **Date** mid Jan-mid Mar.

The latest outdoor summer movie season (it started in 2003), the Starlight has a similar mix of movies to its Moonlight equivalent in Centennial Park, but with seating and covers if the weather turns nasty. There's an on-site bar and food, with waiter service and deckchairs for an additional fee.

Festivals

Festival of Jewish Cinema

Date Nov.

The annual screening of international Jewish films organised by the Melbourne-based Jewish Film Foundation, which often provides a useful sneak peek at future Oscar contenders. Check the local press for details of venues and timings.

Flickerfest

Information: PO Box 7416, Bondi Beach, NSW 2026 (9365 6888/www.flickerfest.com.au). **Date** early Jan.

Running for nine days after the New Year madness has subsided, Flickerfest is the only short-film festival in Australia to be recognised by the American Academy of Motion Picture Arts & Sciences as an Oscar-qualifying event. As a result, it's not only a serious event on the world film calendar, it's also one of the few forums in which local short-film-makers can directly compare their work with international fare. Bondi Pavilion on the edge Bondi Beach is the venue.

Arts & Entertainment

LOCAL STARS
Kerry Armstrong
Her tango-dancing, love-starved wife helped make *Lantana* into an international hit and won her Best Actress at the 2001 AFI awards, where she beat Nicole Kidman. Continues to work regularly in both TV and film.

Bryan Brown
The quintessential Aussie bloke had a taste of Hollywood back in the late 1980s opposite Tom Cruise in *Cocktail* and Sigourney Weaver in *Gorillas in the Mist*. Has since tended to stay closer to home with British actress wife Rachel Ward, most recently unearthing new talent for TV's *Twisted Tales*.

John Jarratt
Wolf Creek transformed the former character actor turned TV handyman into an international psychotic, with director Greg McLean gleefully nabbing him for 2007 follow-up *Rogue*.

Claudia Karvan
Starred opposite Judy Davis in *High Tide* at the age of 14. Didn't get on with Hollywood, but is considered one of Australia's leading actresses and a household name thanks to roles in TV series *The Secret Life of Us* and *Love My Way*.

Deborah Mailman
The stage star and former Australian *Play School* host became the first Aboriginal actor to win an AFI award, as the lead in *Radiance* in 1998. Since then, has starred in *Rabbit-Proof Fence*, TV's *The Secret Life of Us* and the erotic drama *The Book of Revelation*.

Miranda Otto
Daughter of an actor (Barry Otto), married to one (Peter O'Brien) and a true luvvie. Dipped her toe in the Hollywood pool in *The Thin Red Line*, *What Lies Beneath* and *Human Nature*. Also played Eowyn in *The Lord of the Rings* trilogy.

Sam Worthington
Yet to strike out beyond Oz, the quiet star of local hits *Somersault* and *M* carries a smouldering yet nonchalant screen presence. Was also shortlisted for Bond.

Mardi Gras Film Festival & queerDOC Festival
Information: Queer Screen, PO Box 1081, Darlinghurst, NSW 1300 (9332 4938/ www.queerscreen.com.au). **Date** *Mardi Gras* Feb; *queerDOC* Sept.
Part of Sydney's month-long gay and lesbian jamboree, the Mardi Gras Film Festival features mainly international gay movies, screened at the Palace Academy Twin Cinema (*see p226*) and other venues. In September, Queer Screen also puts on the queerDOC festival, the world's first dedicated entirely to queer documentaries.

Sydney Film Festival
Information: Level 5, Suite 501, 414-418 Elizabeth Street, Surry Hills, NSW 2010 (9280 0511/9660 3844/www.sydneyfilmfestival.org). **Date** early June.
A slick, high-profile, two-week orgy of international and Australian film, with up to 250 movies, opening on the Queen's Birthday weekend in early June. One of the oldest movie festivals in the world – it celebrated its half-century in 2003 – it seems to have addressed criticisms of elitism in recent years. Regular highlights include major retrospectives and meet-the-film-maker forums. The main venues are the grand State Theatre (*see p271*) and the Dendy Opera Quays (*see p225*).

Tropfest
Information: 62-64 Riley Street, East Sydney, NSW 2010 (9368 0434/www.tropfest.com.au). **Date** last Sun in Feb.
Instigated by actor-turned-director John Polson (*Swimfan*, *Hide and Seek*), this free outdoor festival of short films is held every February for just one day at Polson's old hangout, the Tropicana café (*see p171*) in Darlinghurst. The films are simulcast on giant screens in the Domain to an audience that runs into the tens of thousands, and to other cities around Australia. The festival is heavily frequented by actors, directors and writers, and its judging panel usually includes A-list celebs who are working in town: Samuel L Jackson, Russell Crowe and John Woo have all performed judging duties in the past. All films are under seven minutes, made specially for the festival and have to contain a reference to the year's Tropfest Signature Item (past items have included a bubble, an umbrella, a kiss, a coffee bean and chopsticks).

Women on Women
Information: PO Box 522, Paddington, NSW 2021 (9332 2408/www.wift.org). **Date** Oct, biennial.
Women in Film & Television (WIFT), a non-profit outfit committed to improving the lot of women in film, organises this festival of short and feature-length work by new and established female talents.

Galleries

Aboriginal, contemporary, modern classics – they're all here.

Sydney's visual arts scene continues to defy easy definition. Big-budget commercial galleries compete for attention with humbler (but sometimes more innovative) experimental spaces. Conventional media such as painting are the norm at several of the city's most esteemed art venues, such as **Eva Breuer Art Dealer**; others stake their industry-leading reputations on indigenous art or experimentation with new media. And though it remains the country's pre-eminent tourist draw, Sydney isn't necessarily considered the national arts leader – for many, that honour belongs to Melbourne. What is assured is Sydney's status as an always varied and interesting visual arts hub.

The city's gallery heartland is Paddington, where scores of spaces offer schmoozy opening nights and exhibitions that regularly feature the best in Australian contemporary art. This is the place to get a snapshot of what's driving the visual arts scene, even if time is limited. In one afternoon, you could see top-notch contemporary work by the likes of subversive photographer Tracey Moffatt at **Roslyn Oxley9**, cutting-edge new media at **Kaliman Gallery**, a diverse selection of Aboriginal art at **Hogarth Galleries** and an engaging local or international showing at the **Australian Centre for Photography**.

Not that the city's eclectic art scene is restricted to the eastern suburbs. Just south of the CBD, the increasingly gentrified suburb of Waterloo shines brightly on the art radar. That's thanks mainly to converted warehouse complex **2 Danks Street**, home to several important galleries.

The city centre also has its share of vibrant venues: you can see shows from likely future stars at **Mori Gallery** or sample established artists (and free drawing classes) at drinking spot-cum-exhibition space the **ArtHouse Hotel**.

Although it remains a fashionable pursuit among Sydney's most trend-conscious (and affluent) citizens, some of the scene's most vital components are refreshingly democratic – and free. High-profile public exhibitions that meld Sydney's fabled natural beauty with local artistic talent are the most reliable crowd-pullers. Perhaps most alluring is **Sculpture by the Sea** (*see p213*), a massively popular

event held each November in which artworks are displayed along the seductive stretch of coast between Bondi and Tamarama Beaches. **Art & About** (*see p212*), held in October, has several outdoor components, including a series of oversized photographs documenting local life set amid the fig trees in Hyde Park.

Look out too for the annual **Archibald Prize** at the **Art Gallery of New South Wales** (*see p70*), with the winner usually announced in late March. This portraiture competition is as entertaining for the fierce division of opinion it sparks as for the always varied works on show. A spoof portrait competition, the Bald Archies, is classic irreverence; announced soon after its more sober counterpart, it is shown in Sydney and other centres.

And don't miss the general collections at the Art Gallery of NSW and the other major public gallery, the **Museum of Contemporary Art** (*see p67*). The former offers a superb overview of Australian art, including a fine indigenous collection and works by luminaries such as John Olsen and the late **Brett Whiteley**, whose former studio is now a museum (*see p86*). The Art Gallery of NSW's regular international shows, which have recently featured the likes of Impressionist superstar Camille Pissarro, are just as noteworthy.

INFORMATION AND OPENING HOURS

For an excellent round-up of what's on, grab a copy of *Art Almanac* ($3, published 11 times a year) or *Art Gallery Guide Australia* ($3, published bi-monthly). The latter has a useful calendar of gallery openings and events. Both are available at bookshops, galleries and newsagents, as is the quarterly journal *Art & Australia* ($20), which takes a more in-depth look at visual arts news and exhibitions.

Many galleries are shut on Mondays, and many close for some period during Christmas and New Year, so call before you set out if you're in town at that time. Admission is free unless otherwise stated.

Central Sydney

ArtHouse Hotel
275 Pitt Street, between Park & Market Streets, CBD (9284 1200/www.thearthousehotel.com.au). CityRail St James or Town Hall/Monorail Galeries

See what lies behind the distinctive exterior of **Martin Browne Fine Art**.

Victoria. **Open** 11am-midnight Mon-Thur; 11am-3am Fri; 5pm-6am Sat. **Credit** AmEx, DC, MC, V. **Map** p329 F7.

This popular Sydney watering hole also doubles as an art gallery, holding about 30 shows – from photography to installation and sculpture – each year. Painters Mary Shackman and South-African born sculptor Marguerite Derricourt are among the established and up-and-coming artists to have exhibited here. If you fancy an art lesson with your aperitif, there are free life drawing classes each Monday: bring your own materials, model supplied.

Collins & Kent Fine Art

Shop 25, Opera Quays, 7 Macquarie Street, Circular Quay (9252 3993/www.collinskent.com.au). CityRail/ferry Circular Quay. **Open** 10am-8pm Mon-Sat; 10am-7pm Sun. **Credit** AmEx, DC, MC, V. **Map** p327 G4.

Part of Opera Quays, the smart shopping and dining strip between Circular Quay and the Sydney Opera House, this upmarket gallery shows works by European masters. Look out for originals by the likes of Chagall, Dali, Miró, Picasso and Matisse.

Legge Gallery

183 Regent Street, between Boundary Street & Henderson Road, Redfern (9319 3340/www.legge gallery.com). CityRail Redfern. **Open** 11am-6pm Tue-Sat. Closed mid Dec-early Feb. **Credit** MC, V.

Contemporary Australian painting, sculpture and some ceramics make up Legge Gallery's diverse collection. The mix of young and established artists includes Ingo Kleinert, known for his assemblage work, and abstract painter Derek O'Connor.

Liverpool Street Gallery

243A Liverpool Street, between Riley & Crown Streets, East Sydney (8353 7799/ www.liverpoolstreetgallery.com.au). CityRail Museum.

Open 10am-6pm Tue-Sat. **Credit** AmEx, DC, MC, V. **Map** p329 G8.

Behind its impressive glass façade, Liverpool Street Gallery showcases a diversity of Australian artists alongside modern international works. Painting – whether abstract, realist or figurative – predominates at this innovative space, but you might also find sculpture, works on paper and photography at the monthly shows.

Martin Browne Fine Art

57-59 Macleay Street, at Challis Avenue, Potts Point (9331 7997/www.martinbrownefineart.com). CityRail Kings Cross/bus 311, 312. **Open** 11am-6pm Tue-Sun. **Credit** MC, V. **Map** p330 J6.

The history of this gallery's setting – the distinctive Yellow House – is as compelling as the fine contemporary Australian and international art it now shows. The building is a former landmark of bohemian Kings Cross and one-time residence of iconic Australian artists including Brett Whiteley and Martin Sharp. Its eye-catching yellow paintwork is said to represent Van Gogh's unrealised ambition of having a home for artistic expression. Nowadays, it offers a reliably strong selection of works over two floors. **Photo** *above.*

Mori Gallery

168 Day Street, between Bathurst & Liverpool Streets, CBD (9283 2903/www.morigallery.com.au). CityRail Town Hall/Monorail World Square. **Open** 11am-6pm Wed-Sat. **No credit cards**. **Map** p329 E7.

Stephen Mori's gallery shows an eclectic mix of works from established young Australian names, including Susan Norrie, Raquel Ormella and Tim Johnson. He has also shown a talent for fostering new artists, exhibiting an interesting selection of art by impressive 'unknowns' over the years, including both new media and more traditional offerings.

Outback Centre

28 Darling Walk, 1-25 Harbour Street, Darling Harbour (9283 7477/www.outbackcentre.com.au). CityRail Town Hall/Monorail Darling Park. **Open** 10am-6pm daily. **Credit** AmEx, DC, MC, V. **Map** p329 E7.

Alongside its gift shop, the Outback Centre has a well-regarded Aboriginal art gallery, which includes works from the Central and Western Deserts, Arnhem Land and the Kimberleys.

Ray Hughes Gallery

270 Devonshire Street, between Bourke & Crown Streets, Surry Hills (9698 3200/www.rayhughes gallery.com). Bus 301, 302, 303, 305. **Open** 10am-6pm Tue-Sat. Closed 2wks from Christmas. **Credit** MC, V. **Map** p329 G11.

A colourful character on the Sydney art scene and former subject of the controversial Archibald portraiture competition held each year (entries always generate heated argument), Ray Hughes shows leading contemporary Australian and Chinese artists in his inner-city gallery. Names to look out for include landscape artist Joe Furlonger, Chinese painter Li Jin, Scottish ceramicist Stephen Bird and abstract artist Brett McMahon.

Robin Gibson Gallery

278 Liverpool Street, between Forbes & Darley Streets, Darlinghurst (9331 6692/www.robin gibson.net). CityRail Kings Cross. **Open** 11am-6pm Tue-Sat. **Credit** MC, V. **Map** p330 H8.

In an atmospheric three-storey Georgian sandstone house, Robin Gibson Gallery is known for varied, mainly Australian exhibitions that strike a balance between contemporary and traditional styles. The late sculptor Clement Meadmore and emerging Australian painters Gina Bruce and Catherine Fox feature on the long list of artists shown.

SH Ervin Gallery

National Trust Centre, Watson Road, next to the Observatory, The Rocks (9258 0173/www.nsw. nationaltrust.org.au/ervin.html). CityRail Circular Quay or Wynyard/ferry Circular Quay. **Open** 11am-5pm Tue-Sun. Closed mid Dec-mid Jan. **Admission** $6; $4 members/concessions. **Credit** AmEx, DC, MC, V. **Map** p327 E3.

A spectacular setting on Observatory Hill and an impressive line-up of annual exhibitions and themed shows are the drawcards at the National Trust gallery. It specialises in Australian art (painting, sculpture and works on paper), both contemporary pieces and historical surveys. Perhaps the gallery's strongest selling point is its popular annual shows. These include the 'Salon des Refusés', a selection of rejected works from the high-profile Archibald and Wynne art competitions. In November and December, 'The Year In Art' surveys works seen in Sydney galleries throughout the year.

Watters Gallery

109 Riley Street, at Stanley Lane, East Sydney (9331 2556/www.wattersgallery.com). CityRail
Museum. **Open** 10am-5pm Tue, Sat; 10am-7pm Wed-Fri. Closed mid Dec-early Jan. **Credit** AmEx, DC, MC, V. **Map** p329 G7.

Established in 1964, this Sydney institution maintains a loyal following among some of Australia's most significant artists. Established names are the focus, and most artists in the Watters stable have been showing at the gallery for more than two decades. Among the notables are leading sculptor Robert Klippel, figurative painter Vicki Varvaressos and renowned surrealist painter James Gleeson. Another Watters regular is Chris O'Doherty (aka Reg Mombassa) whose colourful, politicised images fuse fashion and art. O'Doherty also designs for popular sportswear label Mambo, where his iconic images showcase a strong larrikin streak.

Eastern Suburbs

Aboriginal Art Print Network

68 Oxford Street, between Crown & Riley Streets, Darlinghurst (9332 1722/www.aboriginalart prints.com.au). Bus 378, 380, 382. **Open** 9am-6pm Mon-Fri; 11am-6pm Sat. Closed Christmas-early Jan. **Credit** AmEx, MC, V. **Map** p329 G8.

Director Michael Kershaw says his collection of limited-edition Aboriginal prints is probably the largest in the world. A number of the country's best indigenous artists are represented here, among them Kimberley legend Rover Thomas and urban artist Sally Morgan. The signed and numbered prints are an excellent (and relatively affordable) way of making a first foray into quality Aboriginal art. The gallery's website has an extensive listing of works by title, artist and region.

Australian Centre for Photography

257 Oxford Street, between Ormond & William Streets, Paddington (9332 1455/www.acp.au.com). Bus 378, 380, 382. **Open** 11am-6pm Tue-Sun. Closed Christmas-early Jan. **Credit** AmEx, MC, V. **Map** p332 K10.

Impressive local and international photography and new media feature in the ACP gallery; innovative video works are an increasingly regular highlight. Aspiring photographers can enrol in the Centre's various courses and hone their skills in its digital suite or darkroom. ACP also publishes *Photofile* magazine, which includes a good round-up of photo-related events around town.

Blender Gallery

16 Elizabeth Street, between Oxford & Underwood Streets, Paddington (9380 7080/www.blender. com.au). Bus 378, 380, 382. **Open** 10am-6pm Mon-Sat. Closed Christmas-end Jan. **Credit** MC, V. **Map** p332 L10.

Expect mainly photography and, less regularly, sculpture, painting and mixed media over two floors in a converted Paddington terraced house. The annual exhibition of photography finalists in the national Walkley journalism awards is a highlight. A courtyard café adjoins the exhibition space.

Arts & Entertainment

How to buy Aboriginal art

Staggeringly diverse and almost always visually dazzling, Aboriginal art remains a favourite of committed collectors and casual purchasers alike. Leading works by big-name artists such as Emily Kame Kngwarreye and Rover Thomas reliably fetch top dollar, not to mention the $411,750 paid at a 2005 Sotheby's auction for a painting by Central Australian artist Clifford Possum. Many of Sydney's most reputable galleries stock, or even specialise in, indigenous paintings, prints, weavings and carved work.

But you don't have to be a big-league collector to acquire a piece of evocative, good-quality Aboriginal art. The best advice is to do some research and, crucially, exercise a degree of caution. Unscrupulous vendors keen to offload works of dubious provenance are, unfortunately, as much a feature of the Sydney art scene as outlets showcasing world-class works. Operators in tourist centres such as Darling Harbour and the Rocks hawking 'Aboriginal'-themed tea towels and drinks coasters are easy to avoid. Discerning reputable works from those with more questionable origins in a gallery setting can be a trickier proposition.

One way to guarantee authenticity is to consult a specialist. Members of the **Australian Indigenous Art Trade Association** (www.arttrade.com.au), including vendors in Sydney, must properly document any artwork's origins and ensure artists' rights are upheld. Find out if the trader belongs to that organisation or to the **Australian Commercial Galleries Association** (www.acga.com.au). It is also worth asking

for artist biographies. Be aware, also, that a dealer's explanation of an artwork's meaning or significance may only scratch the surface of a complex culture and value system.

Paintings on canvas, linen and board cost the most and are likely to increase in value the quickest. A more affordable, but equally authentic, alternative is a limited-edition print from a gallery like the **Aboriginal Art Print Network** (see p232). It represents several of Australia's leading Aboriginal artists, with limited-run works starting from around $350; original paintings by the same artists are likely to sell for at least ten times that. Fine craftwork or sculpture from emerging 'hotspots' such as the Tiwi Islands, found at vendors such as **Birrung Gallery** (see p235) and **Hogarth Galleries** (photo – see p234), are another more affordable entry point. The fact that weaving and carved works currently have less mainstream profiles than painting, for example, also makes them a more 'unique' acquisition.

The best way to get a taste for what's available – and what appeals to you – is to visit a handful of specialist spaces. If time is shorter, or for a broader overview, the **Museum of Contemporary Art** (see p67) and the **Art Gallery of New South Wales** (see p70) are major galleries with good exhibition track records. The latter's permanent collection includes first-class Aboriginal art.

Another highly recommended starting point is Susan McCulloch's excellent book *Contemporary Aboriginal Art*. It provides a detailed guide to Aboriginal art by region, and includes images and gallery listings.

Kimberley Under The Stars by Trevor Nickolls.

Coo-ee Aboriginal Art Gallery

31 Lamrock Avenue, at Chambers Avenue, Bondi Beach (9300 9233/www.cooeeart.com.au). CityRail Bondi Junction then bus 380, 381, 382, L82/ bus 380, L82. **Open** 11am-5pm Tue-Sat. **Credit** AmEx, MC, V. **Map** p334.

This highly regarded Aboriginal art gallery has been around for almost 30 years. It specialises in quality artworks from indigenous communities in the Northern Territory, Western Australia and the Torres Strait Islands.

Eva Breuer Art Dealer

83 Moncur Street, between Queen Street & Jersey Road, Woollahra (9362 0297/www.evabreuer artdealer.com.au). Bus 380, 382, 389. **Open** 9.30am-6pm Tue-Fri; 9.30am-5pm Sat; 1-5pm Sun. **Credit** AmEx, MC, V. **Map** p333 M10.

High-end 20th- and 21st-century Australian art is the focus here, with an emphasis on paintings by such home-grown greats as Arthur Boyd and Sidney Nolan. Its varied programme includes solo shows and arresting thematic exhibitions, and standards are always high.

Hogarth Galleries

7 Walker Lane, between Liverpool & Brown Streets, Paddington (9360 6839/www.aboriginalartcentres. com). Bus 378, 380, 382. **Open** 10am-5pm Tue-Sat. **Closed** 2wks from Christmas. **Credit** AmEx, DC, MC, V. **Map** p332 J9.

Tucked away down a Paddington side street, this highly regarded gallery features a diversity of Aboriginal art. Geographical variety is a particular strength: artists from the far north of Queensland, the Central and Western Deserts, Arnhem Land and Western Australia are all regularly represented. Expect bark paintings, prints, woven work and carvings. **Photo** *p233.*

Ivan Dougherty Gallery

Corner of Oxford Street & Greens Road, Paddington (9385 0726/www.cofa.unsw.edu.au/galleries/idg). Bus 378, 380, L82. **Open** 10am-5pm Mon-Sat. **No credit cards. Map** p332 J9.

Part of the University of NSW College of Fine Arts, the IDG is known for challenging and diverse shows and a focus on professional, not student, work. Themed exhibitions often include a range of media, from design to sketches on paper and video. Quirky installation works are another strong point: think sheds erected within the gallery or chocolate smeared on the walls. Those in search of student art will have to pick their moment: the only regular student (Master of Fine Arts) shows are in January and December.

Kaliman Gallery

56 Sutherland Street, at Cascade Street, Paddington (9357 2273/www.kalimangallery.com). Bus 378, 380, 382. **Open** 11am-5.30pm Tue-Sat. **Credit** AmEx, MC, V. **Map** p332 L9.

Expect a strongly experimental flavour and works from younger Australian artists at Kaliman.

Colourful painting, installation works and new media feature frequently.

Rex Irwin Art Dealer

1st Floor, 38 Queen Street, between Oxford Street & Halls Lane, Woollahra (9363 3212/ www.rexirwin.com). Bus 380, 382, 389. **Open** 11am-5.30pm Tue-Sat; and by appointment. Closed mid Dec-late Jan. **Credit** MC, V. **Map** p332 L11.

This compact gallery represents several of Australian art's leading names, including landscape artist Nicholas Harding, painter Peter Booth and renowned photographer Rex Dupain (son of iconic Australian photographer Max). The gallery also deals in works by emerging Australian artists such as ceramicist Prue Venables, as well as European works including British figurative painting and prints and drawings by Picasso.

Roslyn Oxley9 Gallery

8 Soudan Lane, off Hampden Street, Paddington (9331 1919/www.roslynoxley9.com.au). Bus 378, 380, 382. **Open** 10am-6pm Tue-Fri; 11am-6pm Sat. Closed Christmas-late Jan. **Credit** AmEx, MC, V. **Map** p332 L9.

Roslyn and Tony Oxley run one of Sydney's most visually striking galleries and arguably one of the country's finest. Top-flight Australian artists including renowned photographer Julie Rrap feature, as do sculptor James Angus, indigenous photographer Destiny Deacon and installation artist Lindy Lee. Big-name international artists of the likes of Tracey Emin have also shown here, and the gallery encourages up-and-coming offshore talent. The efficient and knowledgeable staff are a bonus.

Sherman Galleries

16-20 Goodhope Street, at Glenmore Road, Paddington (9331 1112/www.shermangalleries. com.au). Bus 380, 382, 389. **Open** 10am-6pm Tue-Fri; 11am-6pm Sat. Closed mid Dec-Jan. **Credit** AmEx, MC, V. **Map** p332 K9.

Sherman Galleries maintains a strong reputation on the Sydney art scene. You might find the work of established painters or emerging photographers and video artists, or Asian art – a particular interest, with regular shows by Chinese diaspora artists Guan Wei and Xu Bing. Acclaimed urban indigenous artist Clinton Nain is another regular exhibitor. Rotating sculpture and installation shows feature in the gallery's garden.

Stills Gallery

36 Gosbell Street, between Boundary Street & Neild Avenue, Paddington (9331 7775/www.stillsgallery. com.au). Bus 389. **Open** 11am-6pm Tue-Sat. Closed mid Dec-Jan. **Credit** AmEx, MC, V. **Map** p330 K8.

This large, bright exhibition space shows leading contemporary Australian photographers and some installation and video works. Represented artists include the highly regarded photojournalist Narelle Autio, Trent Parke and Petrina Hicks. Every five weeks there is a Saturday discussion by the artist whose work is on show at the time.

Get an eyeful at **Utopia Art Sydney**.

Inner West

Aboriginal & Pacific Art Gallery

2 Danks Street, at Young Street, Waterloo (9699 2211/www.2danksstreet.com.au). Bus 301, 302, 303, 305, 355. Closed mid Dec-mid Jan. **Credit** AmEx, MC, V.
Under the direction of long-time indigenous art specialist Gabriella Roy, this gallery shows traditional and contemporary Aboriginal works, specialising in Arnhem Land barks and carvings.

Annandale Galleries

110 Trafalgar Street, at Booth Street, Annandale (9552 1699/www.annandalegalleries.com.au). Bus 370, 470. **Open** 11am-5pm Tue-Sat. Closed mid Dec-mid Feb. **Credit** MC, V.
Disproving the theory that Sydney's best art spaces are confined to Paddington and the city, this inner-west stalwart represents leading contemporary Australian and international artists. Australian abstract painter Guy Warren and overseas artists such as Leon Kossoff and William Kentridge are some of the names to look out for. The gallery also has a strong selection of Aboriginal work, and some pieces by the likes of Chagall and Miró.

Birrung Gallery

70 Norton Street, between Parramatta Road & Marion Street, Leichhardt (9550 9964/www.world vision.com.au/birrung). Bus 435, 436, 437, 438, 440. **Open** 10am-5.30pm Tue-Fri; 11am-5pm Sat, Sun. **Credit** AmEx, MC, V.
Birrung Gallery's diverse Aboriginal art offerings include works in fibre from Arnhem Land, Western Deserts paintings and various works from the Tiwi Islands, off Australia's north coast near Darwin. The gallery is run by charity World Vision Australia, with profits directed into indigenous employment and leadership programmes.

Boomalli Aboriginal Artists' Co-op

55-59 Flood Street, between Marian & Myrtle Streets, Leichhardt (9560 2541/www.boomalli.org.au). Bus 435, 436, 437, 438. **Open** 10am-5pm Tue-Fri. **Credit** AmEx, DC, MC, V.
Boomalli's focus on contemporary urban Aboriginal art sets it apart from most indigenous galleries, which tend to prefer regional works. The gallery has associations, or past links, with many of Australia's foremost indigenous artists, including Jeffrey Samuels and Bronwyn Bancroft. Its focus is NSW artworks, which it exhibits in single shows, themed exhibitions and broad-ranging surveys.

Gallery Gondwana

7 Danks Street, at Bourke Street, Waterloo (8399 3492/www.gallerygondwana.com.au). Bus 301, 302, 303, 305, 355. **Open** by appointment Tue; 10am-5.30pm Wed-Sat. **Credit** AmEx, MC, V.
In conjunction with its sister gallery in Alice Springs, Gallery Gondwana sources works from leading Aboriginal artists including Dorothy Napangardi, Kudditji Kngwarreye and Betsy Lewis. Expect Central and Western Desert paintings as well as weaving and other craft. Two annual exhibitions, 'Big Country' and 'Divas of the Deserts', promote male and female indigenous artists respectively. The gallery also offers a consultancy service for collectors of Aboriginal art.

2 Danks Street

2 Danks Street, at Young Street, Waterloo (9698 2201/www.2danksstreet.com.au). Bus 301, 302, 303, 305, 355. **Open** 11am-6pm Tue-Sat. Closed mid Dec-mid Jan. **Credit** MC, V.
In a traditionally industrial but increasingly residential (and upwardly mobile) inner-city suburb, this former warehouse boasts seven permanent galleries and three spaces devoted to temporary shows. These include Aboriginal & Pacific Art (*see above*), Utopia Art Sydney (*see below*), the international Conny Dietzschold Gallery and the Brenda May Gallery, which shows modern, often experimental work in a variety of media. The popular Danks Street Depot café (*see p172*) is also here.

Utopia Art Sydney

2 Danks Street, at Young Street, Waterloo (9699 2900/www.2danksstreet.com.au). Bus 301, 302, 303, 305, 355. **Open** 10am-5pm Tue-Sat. Closed mid Dec-mid Jan. **Credit** AmEx, MC, V.
Utopia Art Sydney promotes Aboriginal artists from the Utopia and Papunya Tula regions of the Northern Territory alongside work by non-Aboriginal artists, including sculptor Marea Gazzard and the gallery's owner Christopher Hodges. Emily Kame Kngwarreye is among the leading indigenous artists regularly shown here. **Photo** *above*.

Gay & Lesbian

There's a big queer magnet buried under Sydney – how else do you explain it?

Sydney's reputation as one of the world's leading gay cities is well known, but it can give people exaggerated expectations. While you won't find a larger gay scene anywhere else in the southern hemisphere or this side of the Pacific, some tourists, used to the massive queer presence in some European and North American cities, express dismay when they first arrive. After checking out the rag-tag collection of bars, shops and dance clubs clustered around the city's gay strip, Oxford Street (also known as the 'Golden Mile'), visitors have been known to ask: 'Is that all there is?'

Fortunately, the answer is no. Gay Sydney is an amorphous kind of place, with few defined boundaries but several concentrated centres. That unmistakeable homosexual energy can be found at North Bondi beach, in the cafés of Potts Point and in the clubs and cafés of the inner western suburbs – especially Newtown and Erskineville – but you'll also find it popping up in places where you least expect it, such as the Blue Mountains.

Sydney acts as a magnet for gay men and lesbians from all around Australia, as well as New Zealand and Asia: they're drawn by the simple fact that gay life in the Emerald City is relatively hassle-free. Homosexuals in NSW are legally protected against discrimination, as are those living with HIV or AIDS and transgendered people. Same-sex sex is legal (the age of consent is 16 for everyone), and the state government recognises same-sex partnerships.

But part of gay Sydney's appeal. for locals and visitors alike, is the annual **Gay & Lesbian Mardi Gras**, held in late summer and culminating in a spectacular parade and even-more-spectacular party – for full details, *see p242* **New Mardi Gras**.

Back in 2002, the future of this much-loved event appeared uncertain when its organising body collapsed in a heap of bad debts. But a new group took over and staged a modestly successful event in 2003, and since then, Mardi Gras has been growing again.

It's the best time for the queer tourist to visit Sydney: the clubs pump, the beaches beckon, and excitement hangs in the air. Oxford Street and its surrounding areas come into their own.

Dyke visitors might find the venues around Darlinghurst, Surry Hills and East Sydney overwhelmingly patronised by gay men, but

fear not: the Newtown area has a strong concentration of lesbians and a plethora of flirty and cheap venues. Though Sydney's recent 'lesbian baby boom' means that you're just as likely to find dyke couples with toddlers in tow hanging out in cafés rather than clubs.

But gay Sydney's scene extends far beyond the pubs and clubs. There are lots of community groups covering every possible leisure activity, political bent, social cause or medical issue, so there's no need to be alone. For a full listing of the groups on offer, check out the website of the oldest-running gay community publication, the *Sydney Star Observer*, at www.ssonet.com.au.

WHERE TO STAY

It can safely be said that any 'international' hotel (glass front, big lobby, expensive cocktails) in Sydney will be gay-friendly. A large chunk of staff at any of these places will be 'family', so you should have no hassles. If you want the full ghetto-accommodation experience, check before arriving with the US-run **International Gay & Lesbian Travel Association** (www.iglta.com). Other good online sites for travel to and within Australia, including gay-friendly accommodation lists, are **Gay Australia Guide** (www.gayaustralia guide.com) or **Gay & Lesbian Tourism Australia** (www.galta.com.au).

PLAYING SAFE

While Sydney is one of the most tolerant places on earth for gays and lesbians, bashers and homophobes do exist. At night, be sensible. Stick to well-lit streets with your mates, walk quickly and with a sense of purpose and, if you're intoxicated or just nervous, play safe and catch a cab. Be aware that while the Mardi Gras season brings out huge numbers of homosexuals, it also flushes out the occasional homophobe, so don't let your guard down at this time of year. And if you are in trouble or feel threatened, just look out for the pink triangle. The Safe Place Program started in 1993 after concerns about violence directed against gays and lesbians. Gay-friendly businesses now place pink triangle stickers as conspicuously as possible outside, usually near the doorway. In addition, many police stations will have a Gay & Lesbian Liaison Officer, whom you can talk to if you get into trouble.

Arts & Entertainment

Safe sex is a way of life – 'if it's not on, then it's definitely not on', as the local slogan goes. Sydney is the epicentre of Australia's HIV pandemic and while a decade of safe sex campaigns has hugely reduced the incidence of new infection, the evil lurgy is still out there.

INFORMATION

For the latest on what's happening, ask the staff at the **Bookshop Darlinghurst** (*see p193*): they're approachable and their knowledge can't be bettered. Alternatively, check the queer press, available in gay outlets, bottle shops, newsagents, music venues and cinemas everywhere. The city's two free weekly gay newspapers, *Sydney Star Observer* and *SX*, have full, up-to-the-minute what's on and venue guides. Dykes will find the free monthly news magazine *Lesbians on the Loose* (www.lotl.com) required reading. For gay community groups, helplines and support networks, *see p300*.

Nightlife

Bars & pubs

Mars Lounge (*see p180*) in Surry Hills is popular with a gay, lesbian and straight crowd, particularly on Sunday nights when some of Sydney's top DJs, such as Alex Taylor, play.

Bank Hotel

324 King Street, between Newman & Wilson Streets, Newtown (9557 1692). CityRail Newtown. **Open** noon-late Mon-Sat; noon-midnight Sun. **No credit cards. Map** p334.

One of Newtown's most popular pubs, the Bank draws a smattering of gays and lesbians throughout the week, but traditionally gets overrun with lesbians on Wednesday nights. There's no dancefloor, but that doesn't deter the regulars from dancing about to the resident DJs, while others make use of Sleepers, the intimate cocktail bar out the back. Look out also for the pub's in-house (but outdoor) Thai restaurant – just go down the side stairs under the mounted elephant head. The place was undergoing renovation at time of writing, so things might have changed by the time you read this.

Colombian Hotel

Corner of Oxford & Crown Streets, Darlinghurst (9360 2151). Bus 352, 378, 380, L82. **Open** 10am-4am Mon-Thur; 9am-6am Fri, Sat; 9am-4am Sun. **Credit** AmEx, DC, MC, V. **Map** p329 G9.

The gay pub that more gay pubs should try to be like, the Colombian is a relative newcomer to the scene, having opened its doors for the 2002 Gay Games. Inside there are two levels of fun, all decorated in an 'art deco meets Aztec' design theme that succeeds against all the odds. The downstairs bar opens on to the street, and is great for people-watching, while the upstairs cocktail bar is more

Good clean fun at **Arq Sydney**. *See p240.*

sedate, with comfortable couches and lounges, although boogie fever breaks out later on Friday and Saturday nights. Both floors get crowded pec-to-pec on weekends, although it should be noted that the Colombian is also one of the Golden Mile's more lesbian-friendly establishments.

Imperial Hotel

35 Erskineville Road, at Union Street, Erskineville (9519 9899). CityRail Erskineville or Newtown. **Open** 3pm-midnight Mon-Wed; 3pm-late Thur; 3pm-6am Fri; 1pm-6am Sat; 1pm-midnight Sun. **Admission** $5 Fri, Sat. **No credit cards. Map** p334.

The Imperial is featured at the beginning of the movie *Priscilla, Queen of the Desert*, and the pub has honoured this by staging a succession of rude but hilarious Priscilla drag shows ever since (look out for flying ping-pong balls!). The front bar draws a crowd of locals during the day, but by night, the hotel swarms with gay men and lesbians. In addition to the front bar, there's a cocktail lounge, a back bar that intersperses dancing and drag shows, and a dark downstairs area that's perfect if you're up for a late-late-night boogie but don't want to go into town or Darlinghurst. It's the drag shows that really

Life's a drag

Sydney is arguably the drag queen capital of the world: there are almost as many drag shows per square mile as there are Thai restaurants. But Sydney queens do far more than put on some slap and tell old double-entendre jokes: the scene is rich and diverse, with something for everyone. Old-school drag hasn't gone away (think big wigs, Shirley Bassey numbers and a rich vein of double entendre), but there's also 'new school' drag (think boys who look like real girls, doing Britney Spears and Christina Aguilera numbers) and drag kings (girls who give the boys a taste of their own medicine).

The scene has its roots in the 1960s, when one of Sydney's most famous performers, Carlotta – now a full-blown TV personality, author and celebrity – headlined at drag supper club Les Girls in Kings Cross. But since the release of *The Adventures of Priscilla, Queen of the Desert* in 1994, drag has become positively mainstream: performers like Claire de Lune and Verushka Darling host their own shows on pay TV, drag queens took part in the closing ceremony of the 2000 Olympics and they are all the rage in TV commercials, advertising everything from coffee to mobile phones.

The hottest ticket on the drag scene is the one that gets you into the annual **Drag Industry Variety Awards**, or DIVAs for short (www.divaawards.com.au). The show is a veritable drag Oscars, with performers emerging from stretch limos on to a red carpet, dressed to the nines in big wigs, fur collars and vertiginous stilettos, with accompanying males to serve as handbags, naturally. In 2005 the 15th annual awards were held at Star City Casino, with an audience of 1,000, five hosts and six production numbers.

For the best drag shows in town, check out **Arq** (*see p240*), the **Imperial Hotel** (*see p237*), **Newtown Hotel** (*see p239*), **Sly Fox** (*see p239*) and the **Stonewall Hotel** (*see p241*). If you want a taste of dressing like a queen for the night, try **House of Priscilla** in Darlinghurst (1st floor, 47 Oxford Street, at Pelican Street, 9286 3023, www.houseof priscilla.com.au), where the friendly staff are well versed in decking out drag artists and party boys. Alternatively, you can always see Sydney through rose-tinted drag queen spectacles on a **Sydney by Diva** tour (9360 5557, www.sydneybydiva.com). This three-hour comedy bus tour of Sydney's tourist spots is hosted by one or two of the city's top divas and is an unforgettable ride. At most times of the year the tour operates on a Sunday afternoon, but additional services operate at peak periods such as Mardi Gras. There are economy and first-class fares, but be warned: if you choose economy, brace yourself for non-stop wisecracks.

pack them in, though, so get in early on Thursday, Friday or Saturday nights. The 'Bingay' event on Tuesdays (bingo hosted by a drag queen) is a fundraiser for the AIDS Council of New South Wales, and makes for a very fun, low-rent midweek mixer.

Manacle

Basement, rear of Taylor Square Hotel, 1 Patterson Lane, at Bourke Street, Surry Hills (9331 2950/ www.manacle.com.au). Bus 352, 378, 380, L82. **Open** 7am-2pm Mon; 7pm-3am Thur, Fri; 7am-4pm, 7pm-3am Sat; 7am-7pm, 8pm-late Sun. **Admission** $5 Mon; $7 Sat (day); $10 Sun (day). **No credit cards**. **Map** p329 H9.

Formerly known as the Barracks, Manacle is a down 'n' dirty bar for the fetish boys, located at the rear of the Taylor Square Hotel. Usually one or two separate bar areas are open (both with pool tables, and one with a small dancefloor), although on some special-event nights, other bars within the Taylor Square Hotel are opened up and 'absorbed' into Manacle. Don't go in wearing crop tops and sparkly hot pants: Manacle is a club for blokes who like other blokes. Think darkness, think leather, think a heavy cruising vibe; think of the Blue Oyster Bar from the *Police Academy* movies and you won't be far off the mark. Manacle bursts at the seams during its infamous big-party-weekend recovery events, and also provides a Sunday-daytime recovery during the warmer months of the year.

Middle Bar

Kinselas Hotel, 383-387 Bourke Street, at Taylor Square, Darlinghurst (9331 3100/www.middlebar. com.au). Bus 352, 378, 380, L82. **Open** 7pm-4am Thur-Sun. **Credit** AmEx, DC, MC, V. **Map** p329 H9. Looking for a more upmarket drinking experience? Middle Bar, located on the upper level of Kinselas Hotel, may be just the ticket. With an outdoor deck overlooking Taylor Square, it's the place to be on a hot summer night. It attracts a dressy crowd that encompasses straights, gay men and lesbians. The common denominator is a sense of style, and money: be prepared to shell out for fancy cocktails. There are plenty of plush sofas and funky DJs.

Newtown Hotel

Corner of King & Watkin Streets, Newtown (9517 1728). CityRail Newtown. **Open** 10am-midnight Mon-Sat; 10am-10pm Sun. **No credit cards**. **Map** p334.

A very friendly neighbourhood pub, patronised by a large crowd of locals. With its comfy assortment of leather chairs, and doors that open right on to King Street, the Newtown Hotel is a great spot to sit and watch the world go by. Downstairs is the kind of place where customers feel at ease sitting on their own, reading a paper, watching music videos or the large-screen TV or catching one of the many drag shows on throughout the week. The bar upstairs is a little more laid-back – perfect for a quiet drink or a secret tryst. Thankfully, the well-stocked gaming lounge is enclosed in its own room, allowing conversation in the main bar too.

Oxford Hotel

134 Oxford Street, at Taylor Square, Darlinghurst (9331 3467). Bus 352, 378, 380, L82. **Open** *Main bar* 24hrs daily. *Gilligans* 5pm-late Wed-Sun. *Gingers* 5pm-late Fri-Sun. **Credit** AmEx, MC, V. **Map** p329 H8.

A mainstay of the 'Golden Mile' for about as long as anyone can remember, the Oxford has undergone a few changes in recent years. The ground-floor pub used to be dark and cloistered, but renovations and additions have opened it up considerably. A wooden veranda now enables outdoor drinking over Taylor Square – extremely pleasant in the warmer months – while an additional space, O Lounge, has opened next door to provide more seating and somewhere to put those dreaded pokie machines.

But the best things about the place haven't changed: the main space is still a 24-hour bar, and still an almost universally gay male venue – it's the meeting spot for the Harbour City Bears (www.hcbears.com), who get together here on Friday nights. The vibe is quite sociable early on, but gets edgier as the evening wears on. Upstairs, past the beefy security, is Gilligans, also popular with Sydney's straight girls, who appreciate its comfortable banquettes, great views over Taylor Square and killer cocktail list. Upstairs again is a second cocktail bar, Gingers, which is open to the public only on Fridays and Saturdays.

Slide Lounge

41 Oxford Street, between Crown & Bourke Streets, Darlinghurst (9283 7884). Bus 352, 378, 380, L82. **Open** 6pm-3am Wed-Sun. **Credit** AmEx, DC, MC, V. **Map** p329 G8.

Slide opened its doors at the end of 2005. Like the Colombian (*see p237*) up the road, it occupies the site of a former bank – though it's hard to tell, given the slick fit-out and furnishings. In the early evening it functions as a restaurant, but the party mood becomes more pronounced as the night wears on. Expect a flashy, well-dressed crowd and impressive cocktails. The waiters all wear sexy skirts (including the boys). New gay bars in Sydney can be a risky venture, but Slide already seems to have found its niche as a more upmarket gay watering hole: in 2006 it was the official Mardi Gras Festival Bar, and Sophie B Hawkins graced it with a live show. **Photo** *p240*.

Sly Fox

199 Enmore Road, between Cambridge Street & Stanmore Road, Enmore (9557 1016). Bus 423, 426, 428. **Open** noon-4am Mon-Thur; noon-6am Fri; noon-5am Sat; noon-midnight Sun. **No credit cards**. From the outside, the Sly Fox looks like an average spit-and-sawdust Aussie pub, but get past security and you'll find one of Sydney's hottest lesbian bars. Wednesday night is the big night, with dancing, pool competitions and lots of shows. This is the home of Sydney's drag king scene, so expect to see some wild acts. Recently, the pub also ran its first-ever lesbian wet T-shirt competition. It's also got a fabulous cocktail menu, cheap shots and draws a very sexy crowd. *See also p222.* **Photo** *p241*.

Slide Lounge.
See p239.

Sol's Deckbar

191 Oxford Street, at Taylor Square, Darlinghurst (9360 8868). Bus 352, 378, 380, L82. **Open** 10am-5am Mon-Fri; 7am-6am Sat, Sun. **Credit** AmEx, DC, MC, V. **Map** p329 H9.

Deckbar's location – right on Taylor Square, on the site of the old Café 191 – makes it a prime spot for people-watching. A small, intimate kind of space, Deckbar draws a mixed crowd of an evening, and is a favoured spot for many people to meet for a drink before a night's clubbing.

Tilbury Hotel

12-18 Nicholson Street, at Forbes Street, Woolloomooloo (9368 1955). Bus 423, 426, 428. **Open** 8am-11.30pm Mon-Fri; 9am-11.30pm Sat; 10am-9.30pm Sun. **Credit** AmEx, MC, V. **Map** p330 H6.

Come Sunday afternoons and early evenings, the upstairs bar at the Tilbury swarms with a very spunky, very fashionable crowd of gay men. There's a pool table, which hardly gets touched, and a DJ, but not a lot of room for dancing. The place to be is on the veranda, which gets crowded with Sydney's most beautiful gay men. And don't they know it!

Clubs

Arq Sydney

16 Flinders Street, between Oxford & Taylor Streets, Darlinghurst (9380 8700/www.arqsydney.com.au). Bus 373, 377, 378, 380, 382, 391, 394, 396. **Open** 9pm-late Thur-Sun. **Admission** (after 10pm) $10 Fri; $20 Sat; $5 Sun. **No credit cards. Map** p329 H9.

Arq is the busiest club on the Sydney scene, and the first port of call for many a gay tourist. Its big nights are Saturday and Sunday, drawing a very Oxford Street crowd of bare-chested pretty boys. With two levels and a mezzanine walkway, it holds around 900 people when full – and it always is at weekends. Head for the upper floor for sensational lighting and uptempo house and trance music, delivered via an ultra-crisp sound system; the lower floor is more chilled, with lounges, pool tables and more funky music. Shows are a speciality, whether drag or song and dance numbers from pop stars (both aspiring and actual). The club goes into overdrive on long weekends, and its recovery parties are hugely popular. Look out also for Fomo, regular foam parties held every few months during the summer, when both dancefloors get awash with suds. *Photo p237.*

Club 77

77 William Street, between Crown & Yurong Streets, East Sydney (no phone/www.club77sydney.com). CityRail Kings Cross/bus 378, 380, 382. **Open** 8pm-3am Thur; 6pm-4am Fri; 7pm-4am Sat; 8pm-1am Sun. **Credit** AmEx, DC, MC, V. **Map** p329 G7.

Club Kooky is the Sunday night party at Club 77 and something of an underground institution. Conceived over ten years ago by queer and alternative Sydney DJs Seymour Butz and Gemma, it's a space for all those people who are left cold by the constant repetition of trance remixes and Kylie Minogue numbers in most gay venues in Sydney. The crowd is as alternative as the music, but you never know who you might spot on the dancefloor: Nick Cave, Rufus Wainwright and Jarvis Cocker all turned up when they were in town for the Sydney Festival.

Exchange Hotel

34-44 Oxford Street, between Riley & Liverpool Streets, Darlinghurst (9331 1936). Bus 352, 378, 380, L82. **Open** *Spectrum* 8pm-late Sat; 5pm-midnight Sun. *Phoenix* 11pm-late Thur-Sat. **Admission** *Spectrum* $15-$25. *Phoenix* $5 after 11pm; $5 Fri; $7 Sat. **Credit** AmEx, MC, V. **Map** p329 G8.

There are four floors of fun in this decade-old gay fave, but Spectrum and the subterranean Phoenix are of most interest to gay and lesbian visitors. Spectrum is a quiet cocktail bar that turns into a dance club later in the evening several nights a week. The Phoenix is a small, sweaty box of a club, renowned for a harder style of dirty house music and a crowd that skews a bit older and dirtier too. On Saturday nights the place is overrun with shirtless gay men, although the Phoenix also features lesbian DJs and the occasional dyke-dominated night.

Midnight Shift

85 Oxford Street, between Riley & Crown Streets, Darlinghurst (9360 4319). Bus 352, 378, 380, L82. **Open** noon-2am Mon-Wed; noon-4am Thur; noon-7am Sat, Sun. **Admission** $15 Fri; $20 Sat. **No credit cards. Map** p329 G8.

Another Sydney legend, but this one's really only for the boys: the 'no open-toed shoe' policy is a convenient if transparent way for women to be excluded. The Shift is really two clubs in one: at street level, it's a dark but friendly bar, with no cover charge, a wide range of punters and pool tables out the back. The large dancefloor is well utilised, particularly on Sunday evenings, when the resident DJs

Arts & Entertainment

play feel-good retro classics. Upstairs is the packed dance club, which has an entry fee and a crowd of wall-to-wall men, who bump and grind both on and off the dancefloor. If you can take your eyes off the washboard stomachs and bulging biceps, there are great lighting effects and frequent drag shows with the best production values in town. Pick up the local gay press to see details of the regular Indulgence parties, which feature leather and uniform-fetish dudes grooving away until dawn.

Palms on Oxford

124 Oxford Street, at Taylor Square, Darlinghurst (9357 4166). Bus 352, 378, 380, L82. **Open** 8pm-3am Wed-Sun. **No credit cards. Map** p329 H8.
We won't beat around the bush: Palms is probably gay Sydney's most tragically fun venue. Don't go expecting cutting-edge music and hipper-than-hip lighting effects, but do expect lots of Kylie/disco diva remixes and a friendly crowd out for a good time. Located a few doors down from the popular Oxford Hotel (*see p239*), Palms feels a bit like a 1980s gay bar – and that's just the way the punters like it.

Stonewall Hotel

175 Oxford Street, between Taylor Square & Palmer Street, Darlinghurst (9360 1963/www.stonewall hotel.com). Bus 352, 378, 380, L82. **Open** 11am-late daily. **No credit cards. Map** p329 G9.
A large, three-level pub and dance venue, much loved and always busy. The crowd tends towards younger gay men (wearing the latest-season fashions and spiky quiffs) and those that fancy them. The street-level bar has a chatty, pub-style atmosphere, with drag shows, karaoke contests, the occasional talent quest, a small dancefloor and sexy male dancers on the bar on weekends. Upstairs there are two lounge areas with more bars; it's a bit like partying in somebody's living room. The crowds pack in for the regular 'Malebox' nights, at which everyone is assigned a number, and messages can be left for punters you like the look of. The Stonewall also hosts various events, launches and parties during Gay Pride Week in June, which commemorates the Stonewall riots in New York in 1969.

Taxi Club

40-42 Flinders Street, between Taylor & Short Streets, Darlinghurst (9331 4256). Bus 373, 377, 378, 380, 382, 391, 394, 396. **Open** 9am-5am daily. **Credit** MC, V. **Map** p329 H9.
When everything else is closed, when desperation strikes, never fear – there's always the Taxi. This is the venue for night owls, serious drinkers or a combination of the two. It provides the cheapest drinks in queer Sydney and is open until 5am. Which is why it's a favourite with both drag queens – who stop here after a night's work – and some extremely intoxicated out-of-towners. There's also a restaurant and café on the ground floor, a gaming room, a TV area and lounge on the first floor, and a small dancefloor above that. It's a members' club, but you can get temporary membership on the door for free.

Dance parties

The highlight of the party calendar is the massive **Mardi Gras party**, a 12-hour affair that features top-name DJs, spectacular lighting, big shows and an extremely sexy crowd (*see p242* **New Mardi Gras**). But there are plenty of other parties throughout the year, including smaller, 'boutique' events such as **Toybox**, **Bad Dog** and **Fag Tag**, which cater for more specific musical and/or sexual tastes. Every public holiday long weekend is sure to feature at least one major event, and the bigger party weekends (New Year's Eve, Mardi Gras, the October long weekend) offer several, including pre-party parties, recovery parties and (yes) post-recovery parties.

Dance parties come and go as promoters emerge or fade from the scene, so the best way to keep in touch is to pick up the *Sydney Star Observer*, *SX* or *Lesbians on the Loose*, from venues and cafés around the city.

For many years, New Year's Eve was when gay and lesbian community group Pride staged its annual fund-raiser at Fox Studios, but

Sly Fox. *See p239.*

New Mardi Gras

Lots of big cities have gay pride parades, but few take them to heart like Sydney has Mardi Gras. It's gaudy, bawdy, irreverent and sexy – the perfect shorthand, then, for the city.

The Mardi Gras parade started as a series of demonstrations in the winter of 1978 commemorating New York's Stonewall Riots, and itself turned violent when police moved in. Several years later, the parade moved to the more comfortable season of early March, and then the Mardi Gras story was one of unparalleled growth: it became an empire, with a series of parties, a month-long arts festival and a reputation for sexual liberation that travelled around the world.

But in 2002, that empire crumbled. Falling attendances at fund-raising dance parties were blamed for the organising body's big financial losses, and it was forced into administration in August that year.

Sydney's gay and lesbian community was not going to lose its annual party so easily, though, and so arose New Mardi Gras to stage a parade, a party and a small festival in 2003. It was successful, and although finances remain tight, there are indications that the phoenix is still healthy. A three-year, $1.5 million sponsorship contract with the proprietors of dating website Gaydar, announced in late 2005, meant that, for the first time, New Mardi Gras could start to do some longer-term planning.

To the spectator, New Mardi Gras looks much the same as ever – especially the main public event, the parade, with its marching boys, drag queens in limos, disco lorries, dykes on bikes and masses of community groups including PFLAG (Parents & Friends of Lesbians & Gays) and even the NSW police.

Behind the scenes, though, New Mardi Gras has returned to the festival's roots, with a core aim of achieving equality for gay, lesbian, transgender and bisexual people. But don't worry it's gone po-faced – it's still very much a fun-filled, feathers-and-sequins affair.

WHAT AND WHEN

The Mardi Gras festival takes place over three or four weeks, ending on the last weekend in February or the first weekend in March. Although it's the parade and party on the final Saturday that get the publicity, it's worth joining the locals at as many of the pre-parade events as you can fit in.

Events kick off with the **Festival Launch** (usually on a Friday), which over the past few years has been held in Hyde Park. It's fun and a real gathering of the tribe: many bring a picnic and make a night of it. Entertainment comes in the form of speeches and a few snippets from Mardi Gras festival shows.

Other celebrations include the **Mardi Gras Film Festival**, art exhibitions, themed parties and nightly cabaret performances and stage shows in venues all over Sydney. **The Fair Day** in Victoria Park, Camperdown (held on the Sunday a fortnight before the final weekend), attracts more than 60,000 people and features an excellent high-camp pet show. Fair Day is the gay community's big day out, so expect to see everyone from lesbian mums to leather daddies. Another big event is **Shop Yourself Stupid**, organised by an HIV and AIDS charity, the Bobby Goldsmith Foundation. Oxford Street shops hand over a percentage of their takings to the BGF, and the pubs always get involved by putting on spectacular drag shows on the street.

declining popularity saw its cancellation in 2005. Instead, Fantasy, organised by New Mardi Gras, the Sydney Leather Pride Association and the Harbour City Bears, was given a run. Ticket sales were disappointing, so this concept is unlikely to be revisited – but gay Sydney will certainly celebrate New Year in some way: check the local gay press for more information nearer the time.

Azure

www.azureparty.com. **Date** end Feb/early Mar.
Azure is one of the hot party tickets of the year – and with good reason. Held beside Farm Cove against the stunning backdrop of Sydney Harbour,

this open-air event is held on the weekend before Mardi Gras (although it's not an official part of the Mardi Gras season). The cheaper tickets get snapped up months in advance; don't wait or you'll be spending over $150 to get in. Nominally a fund-raiser for the Gay & Lesbian Rights Lobby, the AIDS Trust of Australia and a number of other charities, Azure is primarily a way for the beautiful people to kick-start a week of Mardi Gras fun.

Bad Dog

Check local gay press for information.
Organised by a group of DJs and artists dismayed by the stodgy sameness of Sydney's gay clubs, the Bad Dog events, which happen every few months,

The **parade** itself begins at sunset. It starts at the corner of Hyde Park and Whitlam Square, heads up Oxford Street to Flinders Street and finishes at the party venue, the Entertainment Quarter in Moore Park. Crowds have been estimated at anything up to half a million. Many stake out their territory at least six hours before the parade starts, while hotels and restaurants along the route sell seats at ticket-only cocktail parties. Another comfortable option is the Bobby Goldsmith 'Glamstand' on Driver Avenue, which seats several thousand (for tickets and information, visit www.bgf.org.au or call 9283 8666). Many people head for Taylor Square – a really bad idea, since the crush can get ugly. Instead, a good viewing spot is right at the end of the parade, opposite the BGF seating – but get there early because the police cordon off the streets, making access difficult.

After the parade comes the **party**. Attracting some 17,000 revellers, it features top DJs and performers whose identities are usually kept secret until the night (don't expect Kylie, though: she hasn't come for years). As well as the crammed dance halls and outrageous drag shows, there are plenty of different areas in the Entertainment Quarter complex for drinking, eating and chilling out. There's also a hefty medical presence, just in case your night goes wrong.

INFORMATION AND TICKETS

To keep abreast of what's going on, contact **New Mardi Gras** (9568 8600, www.mardigras .org.au) or get the excellent, free programme, available from January from gay-friendly venues around Oxford Street and Newtown. You'll need to book accommodation and

tickets (at least for the major events) months ahead. Tickets for the main party are available from mid December and usually sell out at least a month in advance, so don't wait until you hit Sydney to buy them. Tickets are limited to four per person and can be purchased from Ticketek (9266 4800, www.ticketek.com.au) and also through accredited travel agents (booking fees apply).

are a refreshing alternative to the norm. The venues tend to be away from the Oxford Street Golden Mile (Waverley and Marrickville Bowling Clubs have been used in the past), while the parties are renowned for drawing a crowd that's high on friendliness and low on attitude.

Fag Tag

www.fagtag.com.au.

A much-needed innovation on the party scene, Fag Tag's premise is simple: each party sees a horde of lesbians and gay men descend on an otherwise straight venue and claim it for a night. But this is no guerrilla act: the venues are in on the joke, which means there's little risk of trouble from surprised

regulars. Venues that have been Fag Tagged in the past few years include the Bourbon & Beefsteak in Kings Cross and the Eastern Hotel in Bondi Junction, and there are plans for plenty more.

Gurlesque

www.gurlesque.com.

Five years old and showing no signs of maturity (thank goodness), the Gurlesque 'all-lezzo strip shows' continue to pack out venues and leave the dykes of Sydney gasping for more. Formed by dancers who were tired of stripping for men and wanted to 'give it to the girls', the Gurlesque events encourage all women to explore and interpret the art of striptease. The results, they say, have ranged

Arts & Entertainment

'from hilarious comedy and drag to seriously sexy, in-your-face pussy strutting'. With stunning costumes (just waiting to come off), raunchy routines and music from DJ Sveta, Gurlesque has truly brought something unique and unrivalled to the girls' scene. Catch them at the Marquee Club (128 Pyrmont Bridge Road, Camperdown, 9557 0221, www.themarqueerocks.com).

Homesexual

www.homesexual.com.au.
Homesexual is the regular gay and lesbian party at mega-club Home (*see p221*). Often held the night after another big party (such as New Year's Eve or Mardi Gras), it can be relied on for great drag shows and a dream team of Sydney DJs. With four floors and numerous dance spaces, it caters for a diverse range of musical tastes. Some complain that the place can get too packed when at its 2,200-person capacity, but organisers say they're working to improve the bottleneck areas. Don't forget to check out the beautiful balcony: sipping a cocktail while looking out over Darling Harbour and the city makes for a magical moment.

Inquisition

Entertainment Quarter, Driver Avenue, Moore Park (9319 2309/www.sydneyleatherpride.org). Bus 339, 373, 374, 376, 377, 393, 395, 396. **Date** May. **Map** p332 J/K12.
Inquisition brings the annual Leather Pride Week to its climax. Festivities usually include an art exhibition, workshops, the physique competition Love Muscle and the Forbes Street Fair (in Darlinghurst), but Inquisition is the party for punters of all kinds to fly their fetish flag for a night. Some die-hards have decried the influx of 'leather tourists' at the event, but it remains gay Sydney's premier fetish party, with a music policy that runs to the harder side of house, and some spectacular floor shows.

Queen's Birthday Ball

www.threesisterssocialgroup.org.
Date Queen's Birthday long weekend in June.
And now for something completely different. A fancy-dress ball on the long weekend of Queen Elizabeth II's birthday (a public holiday in Australia), organised by the Three Sisters Social Group. Held in various locations around the Blue Mountains, the ball is not a dance event in the conventional sense – more an old-style camp party with dressing-up, lots of tragic drag, dancing, silliness and merriment, attracting many locals as well as Sydney queens looking for something new.

Ruby

www.rubydance.com.au.
Sydney DJ Ruby (that's a bloke, by the way) decided to create his own dance parties back in the late 1990s, and they've grown in scope ever since. Each party is given a theme (*Alice Through the Looking Glass* and Enchanted Forest have been two of the more memorable), and no expense is spared in decorating

the various venues. But the parties are also renowned for their stunning light displays, ferocious uptempo music and the sexiness of the crowd.

Sleaze Ball

Entertainment Quarter, Driver Avenue, Moore Park (9568 8600/www.mardigras.org.au). Bus 339, 373, 374, 376, 377, 393, 395, 396. **Tickets** (plus booking fee) $120; $80 members, concessions. **Date** 1st Sat in Oct. **Map** p332 J12.
A Mardi Gras fund-raiser, Sleaze Ball is held on the Saturday night of the October long weekend. It features several halls, spectacular shows and a huge number of DJs. In the 1990s, attendance topped out at a staggering 17,000, but these days the party draws about half that number. Each year has a theme – some recent ones have been In Uniform, Beast and HomoSutra – and party-goers are urged to dress up accordingly.

Toybox

Check local gay press for information.
'Daytime is playtime!' That's the motto of the phenomenally successful Toybox parties, which have attracted many thousands of buff party boys and girls since 2003. Held every few months in various venues, the parties start in the early afternoon and continue until late. A number have been held at Luna Park as a recovery event after the Mardi Gras and Sleaze Ball parties, leading some of the faithful to abandon the main event and devote their energies to Toybox instead. Renowned for their awesome lighting, superior sound quality and high production values all round, these parties are a very hot ticket in gay Sydney right now.

Gyms

As in all large gay cities worthy of that mantle, there is a thriving culture of the body in Sydney. Below are just a few of the gyms popular with gay men and lesbians.

Bayswater Fitness

33 Bayswater Road, between Kellett Street & Ward Avenue, Kings Cross (9356 2555/www.bayswater fitness.com.au). CityRail Kings Cross. **Open** 6am-midnight Mon-Thur; 6am-11pm Fri; 7am-10pm Sat; 7am-9pm Sun. **Admission** $18. **Credit** AmEx, DC, MC, V. **Map** p330 J7.
Popular with locals from the Potts Point/Elizabeth Bay area, Bayswater Fitness offers aerobics classes and all the usual workout facilities.

City Gym Health & Fitness Centre

107-113 Crown Street, between William & Stanley Streets, East Sydney (9360 6247/www.citygym. com.au). CityRail Kings Cross/bus 323, 324, 325, 389. **Open** 24hrs 5am Mon-10pm Sat; 8am-10pm Sun. **Admission** $16. **Credit** MC, V. **Map** p329 G8.
A legendary venue, popular with gay men and the serious bodybuilding crowd. Full fitness facilities, extensive programme of classes and, for the men, a notoriously cruisy changing area (with steam room).

Gold's Gym

23 Pelican Street, between Oxford & Goulburn Streets, Darlinghurst (9264 4496/www.goldsgym .com/gymsites/au/sydney). CityRail Museum. **Open** 6am-midnight Mon-Fri; 5.30am-10pm Sat; 7am-9pm Sun. **Admission** $19.75. **Credit** AmEx, DC, MC, V. **Map** p329 G8.
A very busy franchise of the global gym brand, with a huge gay and lesbian clientele. Classes, solarium, massage and all the usual workout facilities.

Saunas & sex clubs

Sydney has plenty of men-only sex-on-premises venues, and most of them draw particular crowds. Take along a gym membership card if you have one: many establishments offer discounts for gym members. Most venues have signed up to a code of practice organised by the AIDS Council, meaning they distribute free condoms and lube to customers. Over-18s only.

Bodyline Spa & Sauna

10 Taylor Street, at Flinders Street, Darlinghurst (9360 1006/www.bodylinesydney.com.au). Bus 378, 380, L82. **Open** noon-7am Mon-Thur; 24hrs noon Fri-7am Mon. **Admission** $23; $12 concessions, noon-4pm Mon-Fri. *Gym members* $16 Mon-Thur. **Credit** AmEx, DC, MC, V. **Map** p329 H9.
Established in 1991, Bodyline was the first lawfully established sex-on-premises gay venue in NSW, and is still gay-owned and operated. It has a huge spa, steam room and sauna on the lower ground floor; a coffee lounge and cinema on the ground floor; private rooms and a video room on the first floor; and a great sun deck on the second floor. It's kept very clean and tends to attract the buff party crowd from many of the nearby nightclubs, including Arq.

HeadQuarters on Crown

273 Crown Street, at Campbell Street, Darlinghurst (9331 6217/www.headquarters.com.au). Bus 352, 378, 380, L82. **Open** 24hrs daily. **Admission** $10 before 7pm Mon-Fri; $15 after 7pm Mon-Fri; $17 Sat, Sun. **Credit** MC, V. **Map** p329 G9.
Sprawling over three large levels, HeadQuarters specialises in 'fantasy play areas' including a pig pen, a jail room and a wet area – you get the idea. It holds frequent fetish nights (including leather, Speedo and footy shorts parties) as well as the occasional all-nude evening – details in the local gay press. There's a coffee lounge and full air-con – thank goodness.

Ken's at Kensington

83 Anzac Parade, opposite Ascot Street, Kensington (9662 1359/www.kensatkensington.com.au). Bus 373, 377, 392, 394, 396. **Open** 11am-6am Mon-Thur; 24hrs 11am Fri-6am Mon. **Admission** $21; $16 5-11pm Sun; $11-$16 noon-5pm Mon-Fri, concessions. **No credit cards.**
Something of a legend in gay Sydney, Ken's at Kensington has been running for over 30 years, and just about everybody has trod its halls at some time or other. The upper level features a chill-out cinema,

a gym and a few private booths, while the lower includes a swimming pool, a steam room, a sauna, a spa and many private rooms. Look out for the glass ceiling over the pool. The regular 'Buck Naked' nude nights are extremely popular, while DJ Seymour Butz adds to the ambience on Sunday afternoon with an appropriately sexy soundtrack.

Sydney City Steam

357 Sussex Street, at Liverpool Street, CBD (9267 6766/www.sydneycitysteam.com.au). CityRail Town Hall. **Open** 10am-6pm Mon-Thur; 24hrs 10am Fri-6am Mon. **Admission** $17; $14 concessions; $12 10am-2pm Mon-Fri. **No credit cards.** **Map** p329 E8.
Gay-owned and operated, and located in the heart of Chinatown, Sydney City Steam features four floors of action and gets extremely busy. Facilities include a spa, steam room, sauna, two cinema spaces, a number of 'fantasy rooms', a coffee shop area and even the services of a non-sexual masseur.

Beach bums

Like most Sydneysiders, the gay and lesbian residents of the Emerald City take to the water like... well, like a duck takes to water. Outdated travel guides point the gay tourist in the direction of Tamarama, but today's savvy visitor knows that **North Bondi** (*see p135*) is the beach of choice for the gay boys. The area in front of the North Bondi Surf Life Saving Club is the most popular patch: this is where you'll find gay Sydney's most body-beautiful specimens, relaxing and chatting – all in the latest season's swimwear, of course. The main scene of action for the girls, meanwhile, centres around Coogee Women's Pool on **Coogee Beach** (*see p136*).

As for the harbour beaches, **Redleaf Pool**, just outside Double Bay on New South Head Road, is a popular spot; and some gay men let it all hang out at the nudist beaches of **Lady Jay Beach** (often called Lady Jane) and **Obelisk Beach**. For an indoor pool patronised by both gay men and lesbians, head to the aquatic centre at **Cook & Phillip Park** (*see p258*).

Music

Prick up your ears.

Rock, Roots & Jazz

Rock

Sydney has a long-standing tradition of live music, epitomised by the pubs and clubs that showcase up-and-coming talent and confirmed by the recent boom in concert revenues. Just a few years ago, for instance, only the mass international appeal of artists like Santana or Dylan could pack out an area as large as Centennial Park to its 20,000 capacity. Yet in 2005, introspective singer-songwriters Missy Higgins (from Melbourne) and Ben Lee (from Sydney) did just that. Aussie bands such as Wolfmother and the Morning After Girls also found an appreciative audience awaiting them in the US and the UK. Unlike the Vines, who conquered the UK before Australia, these bands were tried and tested on home ground before they'd barely recorded a note. Meanwhile, international acts continue to head Down Under in their droves, lured by the prospect of five-star beachside vacations, uninterrupted sunshine, appreciative crowds and the range of excellent venues at their disposal. Live music has, it seems, come of age.

Thirty years ago, the climate couldn't have been more different. Raised on a wholesome staple of TV shows *Six O'Clock Rock*, *Bandstand* and later *Countdown*, Aussies didn't know what to make of visiting bands they'd idolised on record but couldn't relate to in the flesh. Intimidated by the sheer bravado of overseas 'guests', audiences reacted in typical Aussie fashion: they fought back. Sinatra was famously blockaded in his hotel suite in 1974 by unions after he branded a journalist a 'whore', while an inebriated Eric Clapton slurred his way through a 1975 tour to jeers and condemnation. Pete Townshend vowed never to return after the 'humourless' reception the Who received from the media a few years earlier, and Joe Cocker was physically ejected from Australia for bad behaviour and told never to return.

Where people felt at ease – and where the heart of live music lay – was in the pubs. The Angels, Cold Chisel, Radio Birdman, Midnight Oil, and Hunters and Collectors all blossomed in beer barns that swelled with the music-hungry masses. Such behaviour dated back, interestingly enough, to the American GIs stationed in Sydney in the 1940s. They brought with them a rich tradition in song, and local dives began servicing them, creating a musical revolution of sorts in the process. By 1955, when the infamous 'six o'clock swill' (a 6pm close that ensured mass downings of beer) had been banished, Sydney was ready to embrace homespun rock 'n' roll and an ensuing teenage rebellion. When, in 1957, Johnny O'Keefe and Col Joye and the Joy Boys tore up the Town Hall for the inaugural Rock 'n' Roll Ball, popular music had arrived.

By the late 1970s and '80s, Sydney bands were flying high – literally – around the world, with AC/DC and INXS achieving the unthinkable: recognition on both sides of the Atlantic. But while MTV happily played Men at Work and the UK loved Kylie, the local scene suffered a recession as fire restrictions impinged and nightclubs took the place of pubs. The national passion for gambling (resulting in pubs being filled with poker machines) threatened to finish off the live scene altogether, but thanks to power acts such as You Am I, the mid/late 1990s saw a resurgence in band power that continues unabated.

The ever-resilient inner-city scene is buoyed by Sydney's dominance of the music industry. All the major record companies (domestic and international) have their headquarters in the city, and any band worth its salt must do the Sydney circuit to have any hope of getting signed. In addition, the ARIA (Australian Record Industry Association) awards are staged in Sydney every October as a typically glitzy televised affair. The huge success of reality

Ticket agencies

You can book tickets for all major venues through agencies **Ticketek** (9266 4800, www.ticketek.com.au) and **Ticketmaster** (136 100, www.ticketmaster.com.au), but both charge booking fees, even if you book online. For smaller shows, try **Moshtix** (9209 4614, www.moshtix.com.au).

Rock fave the **Metro**. *See p248.*

TV's *Australian Idol* (the finals of which were held at Sydney Opera House) also reawakened interest – in pop, at least – with winners and finalists scoring record deals. For the time being, reality and band power co-exist, although once the effect of iTunes kicks in properly (it only launched in Australia in mid 2005), a clearer picture may emerge in an ever-sophisticated market.

Annual festivals have blossomed too, with **Big Day Out** (www.bigdayout.com), held in Sydney and throughout Australia and New Zealand in January, continuing to be a major draw for overseas acts, despite draconian law enforcement. The all-Aussie **Homebake** (*see p213*), held in the Domain in December, pulls in huge crowds. There are also two new festivals: **The Great Escape** (www.thegreat escape.net.au), held near Olympic Park over Easter, and **Come Together** (www.come together.com.au) at Luna Park in June.

INFORMATION

ABC's national youth radio network **Triple J** (105.7 FM) still highlights new Aussie talent – past glories include Silverchair and Grinspoon, both still riding high in popularity – while **FBi Radio** (94.5 FM) has taken the mantle as the underground spot on the dial.

Free publications *Drum Media* and the *Brag* provide music news, reviews and listings, and are widely distributed in pubs and record shops. The *Sydney Morning Herald*'s Metro

The best Venues

For meeting the locals

Sweat- and star-soaked, the **Annandale Hotel** (*see p250*) is the place to see the latest hot young bands.

For real rock stars

The muso-savvy cool of the **Enmore Theatre** (*see right*) works a treat for rock's elite.

For a perfect setting

The indoor/outdoor **Opera Bar** (*see p253*), by the steps of the Opera House, screams style and class.

For jazz jivers

The long-running **Basement** (*see p253*) is always dependable.

For classical sounds

The **City Recital Hall** (*see p254*), the purpose-built pretender to the older Opera House.

section on Friday features news, reviews and listings, as does the pseudo-tabloid *Daily Telegraph* with its Sydney Live section every Thursday, with local versions of *Rolling Stone* and *Hot Press* targeting the monthly market.

Tickets often sell out far less quickly than you might expect, and you'll find many upcoming international bands in more intimate venues than you'd expect. Note that smoking isn't allowed in any indoor venue.

Major venues

Big Top

Luna Park, Milsons Point (9033 7600/www.bigtop sydney.com). CityRail/ferry Milsons Point. **Box office** 10am-6pm Mon-Thur, Sun; 10am-10pm Fri, Sat. **Tickets** $40-$120. **Credit** AmEx, MC, V.
Used as both a mid-sized band venue (capacity 2,950) and for glitzy awards nights, the indoor Big Top opened in 2004 as part of the much-delayed redevelopment of Luna Park (*see p111*). Since then the likes of Eels and Nick Cave have graced its stage to much acclaim. State-of-the-art sound and sight lines, great facilities and easy access make it popular with punters.

Enmore Theatre

130 Enmore Road, between Simmons & Reiby Streets, Newtown (9550 3666/www.enmoretheatre. com.au). CityRail Newtown. **Box office** 9am-6pm Mon-Fri; 10am-4pm Sat. **Tickets** $40-$110. **Credit** AmEx, DC, MC, V. **Map** p334.
The most atmospheric of the inner-city venues, this 1,600-seat theatre, dating from 1908, plays host to established local talent, overseas acts and big-name stand-up and theatre. Queens of the Stone Age, Kings of Leon and the Rolling Stones (doing a 'club night') have all strutted their stuff here. The acoustics and sight lines are excellent, the seats are often removed in the stalls for dancing, and the door and bar staff are ultra-friendly. Need we say more?

Hordern Pavilion

Driver Avenue, Moore Park (9921 5333/ www.playbillvenues.com.au). Bus 339, 373, 374, 376, 377, 393, 395, 396. **Box office** (in person) 2hrs before show. **Tickets** $70-$120. **Credit** AmEx, DC, MC, V. **Map** p332 J12.
A barn of a venue, yet with a typically relaxed Aussie vibe, the 5,500-capacity Hordern sits at the cool end of the Moore Park complex at Fox Studios. Built in 1924, it presents big-name local acts (Powderfinger, John Butler Trio) and overseas artists seeking financially viable intimacy (Oasis, Coldplay, the Strokes). The floor is usually standing only, there's tiered seating behind and on both sides, and it's air-conditioned.

Metro

624 George Street, at Central Street, CBD (9287 2000/www.metrotheatre.com.au). CityRail Town Hall/Monorail World Square. **Box office**

You'll find an array of sounds, and a restaurant, at the slick **Vanguard**. *See p252.*

10am-7pm Mon-Fri; noon-7pm Sat. **Tickets** $20-$75. **Credit** MC, V. **Map** p329 E7.
With its tiered, standing-only set-up – the stage is always in full view – the 1,200-capacity Metro is the archetypal muso hangout. Its central location, relatively intimate size and overwhelmingly vibey ambience keeps it constantly in demand. If a hot band's in town, chances are they'll sniff out the Metro first. **Photo** *p247.*

State Theatre
49 Market Street, between Pitt & George Streets, CBD (admin 9373 6852/www.statetheatre.com.au). CityRail St James or Town Hall/Monorail City Centre. **Box office** (in person) 9am-5pm Mon-Fri; and until 8pm on show days. **Tickets** $25-$120. **Credit** AmEx, DC, MC, V. **Map** p327 F6.
The first choice for older, 'serious' artists (think Elvis Costello, Lou Reed, Brian Wilson), this opulent palace, built in 1929, boasts massive chandeliers, abundant statuary, an imported marble staircase and enough gilt to challenge Versailles. It's a rococo-cum-deco delight, never short of atmosphere, and plays co-host to the Sydney Film Festival (*see p229*) in winter when gigs are scarce and occasional theatre pieces (*see p271*). It's got a capacity of 2,000, and seating is mandatory, with dancing restricted to the aisles – if security are friendly.

Sydney Entertainment Centre
35 Harbour Street, between Hay & Pier Streets, Darling Harbour (admin 9320 4200/ www.sydentcent.com.au). CityRail Central or Town Hall/Monorail/LightRail Paddy's Markets. **Box office** (in person) 9am-5pm Mon-Fri. **Tickets** $90-$180. **Credit** AmEx, DC, MC, V. **Map** p329 E8.
This 12,500-seater complex in Darling Harbour presents more A-list acts than any other. Built in 1983, it's a typical aircraft hangar that can accommodate crowds easily and safely and is convenient for transport and accommodation. Like most venues this size, though, it falls short on atmosphere, with heavy-handed security. Radiohead, REM, Kylie and the like play here to packed houses. Presents an array of other events when not in concert mode.

Sydney Opera House
For listings, see p254.
The Sydney icon's acoustics tend to work better for more 'refined' acts such as Norah Jones and Michael Buble than louder bands. That said, the powers that be have broadened the House's remit, so the main Concert Hall now houses anything from the final telecasts of *Australian Idol* to avant-garde artistes, while the smaller Studio opts for intimate, often acoustic-based shows. The steps are also used for music events, much to the dismay of local residents.

Sydney SuperDome
Edwin Flack Avenue, at Olympic Boulevard, Sydney Olympic Park, Homebush Bay (8765 4321/ www.superdome.com.au). CityRail Olympic Park/ RiverCat Homebush Bay then bus 401. **Box office** (in person) 1hr before show. **Tickets** varies. **Credit** AmEx, DC, MC, V.
Built for the 2000 Olympics, the SuperDome boasts a whopping 21,000-seat capacity and multiple configurations for anything from rock, pop and rap

The saviours of sound

The current vibrancy of Sydney's rock scene owes a lot to two brothers. Back in 2000, it was all very different. Australian music was at an all-time low, competing with an ever-stronger global market and changing tastes, and the **Annandale Hotel** (see below), the legendary champion of live bands, was closing its doors as a venue. The venue that had launched a thousand bands, from Midnight Oil to the Vines. The venue that was Sydney's musical heartbeat. Gone. In its place: poker machines. Lots of them.

'It was a total disaster,' recalls Matt Rule, who now co-owns the pub with his older brother, Dan. 'We were asked to step in as managers and resurrect it. So we put live music back on two or three nights a week – then we bought the place.'

The Rules patiently watched as the punters slowly came back and the talent returned, kickstarting the revival of the live rock scene across Sydney. Within a year, the Annandale was back on the map. These days, it's the bands who approach the Rules (the Strokes were a recent example). Matt recalls a particular jaw-dropping moment in 2004: 'The Big Day Out festival had wound up that night and we suddenly found ourselves with the Annandale as the unofficial official after-party. We had Metallica, the Strokes, Kings Of Leon, Basement Jaxx, the Mars Volta, Peaches, the Sleepy Jackson, Jet and all the Aussie bands in here. I had to stop and take it all in. It was unbelievable.'

The Rules' song, though, remains the same: to support established and new talent in the appropriate way. And it's not just bands either. 'We're now also running pub markets every Sunday,' says Matt, 'with a free gig afterwards, cult 16mm movies on Mondays, and a music trivia night every Tuesday with Rodney Todd – a little guy with a huge personality and a massive Afro. We're living in different times.' The pub's slogan – 'Fuck this, I'm going to the Annandale!' – which appears on its posters, website, T-shirts, stubby holders and DVDs, sums up the spirit of the place.

The Annandale still has an unfussy, home-grown feel to it – a dying trend in

(Mötley Crüe, Foo Fighters and 50 Cent have played here) to big-scale dance parties, monster truck shows, equestrian events and even psychics. It has enjoyed a surge in bookings of late, boosted by international recognition for its first-rate facilities.

Pubs & clubs

There are dozens – if not hundreds – of pubs (aka hotels) in Sydney where you can see bands perform. RSL (Returned Services League) clubs also offer regular gigs of all shapes and sizes. These have licensing laws that require all visitors, whatever their age, to show ID, so bring your passport and adhere to the dress code (no shorts, singlets or flip-flops, aka thongs) or you won't get in. Most serve good bar food too. The following are the bigger inner-city players.

@ Newtown RSL

52 Enmore Road, at Station Street, Newtown (9557 5044/www.atnewtown.com.au). CityRail Newtown. **Open** 11am-midnight Mon-Thur; 11am-3am Fri, Sat; 3-10pm Sun. **Admission** $10-$45. **Credit** AmEx, MC, V. **Map** p334.
The friendliest and most musically minded of the RSLs in Sydney, @ Newtown features everything from stand-up comedy to jazz to indie rock, with meal deals on Tuesday nights.

Annandale Hotel

Corner of Parramatta Road & Nelson Street, Annandale (9550 1078/www.annandalehotel. com.au). Bus 413, 435, 436, 437, 438, 440, 461. **Open** 11am-midnight Mon-Sat; 11am-10pm Sun. **Admission** $10-$30. **Credit** (phone & internet bookings only) AmEx, MC, V.
The legendary Annandale is the place to see hot up-and-coming bands, including visiting interstate acts, and to catch overseas talent performing 'secret' shows for fans. The sound is reasonable and the upper level at the rear is given over to tables and chairs for the terminally rocked out. A gallery of photos lines the walls in the second bar, with a large beer garden at the rear. The Annandale also hosts weekly cult movie nights, pub trivia and Sunday markets. *See also above* **The saviours of sound**.

Bar Broadway

Corner of Broadway & Regent Street, Haymarket (9211 2321/www.barbroadway.com.au). CityRail/ LightRail Central. **Open** 11.30am-4am Mon-Sat; noon-4am Sun. **Admission** $10-$20. **Credit** AmEx, MC, V. **Map** p329 E9/10.
This blond wood and stainless steel bar hosts everything from acoustic to ska and funk. The intimate upstairs space, with its low ceilings, cocktail bar and chat areas, doubles as a club. The downstairs bar has lighting dim enough to fake some prowess with a pool cue.

modern Sydney pubs and bars – and parades its glory years subtly, with photos scattered haphazardly about the place. The 'CBGB's of Sydney' as one industry type coined it, doesn't have to be on show: the bands are. It's all about the music, stupid.

Matt (left) and Dan Rule.

Bridge Hotel

119 Victoria Road, at Wellington Street, Rozelle (9810 1260/www.bridgehotel.com.au). Bus 500, 501. **Open** 24hrs Mon-Sat; until midnight Sun. **Admission** $5-$50. **No credit cards**.

Blues-oriented R&B acts and cover bands play the large room here (capacity 700), along with the odd thesp revue. Retro discos spin into action on many nights after 11pm. Popular with meat-marketeers, birthday bashers and suburban gals.

Cat & Fiddle Hotel

456 Darling Street, at Elliot Street, Balmain (9810 7931/www.thecatandfiddle.net). Bus 432, , 434, 442, 445, 446. **Open** 10am-midnight Mon-Sat; noon-10pm Sun. **Admission** $10. **No credit cards**.

Folk, bush, jazz and pop: all do the rounds at this seasoned, ever-reliable venue. Out-of-towners pick up work here, while old faves often play low-key shows for the faithful.

Gaelic Club

64 Devonshire Street, between Chalmers & Elizabeth Streets, Surry Hills (9211 1687/www.thegaelicclub. com). CityRail/LightRail Central. **Open** varies; call for details. **Admission** $20-$55. **No credit cards**. **Map** p329 F10.

Another barn of a room, with capacity not far off the four-figure mark, this place attracts local and international acts who can't – or don't want – to play the Metro (*see p248*). Located in the band-loving area of Surry Hills, it's booked solid through much of the year, with the Strokes, the Darkness and Shane McGowan all having appeared. The lack of any air-conditioning means it heats up fast, though.

Hopetoun Hotel

416 Bourke Street, at Fitzroy Street, Surry Hills (9361 5257/www.hopetounhotel.com.au). Bus 301, 302, 303. **Open** 2pm-midnight Mon-Sat; noon-10pm Sun. **Admission** $10-$20. **No credit cards**. **Map** p329 G10.

The other pub venue in Sydney that showcases live local talent on a weekly basis. More intimate than the Annandale (*see p250*), it also tends to book more left-field acts. A basement bar is open at weekends for musos taking an audio break, plus there's an upper level for lunchtime snacks.

Lansdowne Hotel

2-6 City Road, at Broadway, Chippendale (9211 2325/www.thelansdowne.com.au). Bus 426, 427, 428. **Open** 10am-3am Mon-Sat; noon-10pm Sun. **Admission** free. **Credit** AmEx, MC, V. **Map** p328 C10.

The Lansdowne has been refurbished as a band venue, but is still working on winning its punters back. A good spot for a laid-back Sunday afternoon, when you can see three bands on the same bill, it may yet prove to be a serious contender. Convenient after a Saturday stroll around nearby Glebe.

Arts & Entertainment

Rose of Australia

*1 Swanson Street, at Charles Street, Erskineville
(9565 1441). CityRail Erskineville.* **Open** 10am-
midnight Mon-Sat; 10am-10pm Sun. **Admission**
free. **Credit** AmEx, DC, MC, V. **Map** p334.

A stayer in the pub stakes, this low-key venue often
has something going on. It covers all angles, with
pop, rock and cover bands, as well as jazz.

Sandringham Hotel

*387 King Street, between Holt & Goddard Streets,
Newtown (9557 1254/www.sandringhamhotel.
net.au). CityRail Newtown.* **Open** 10am-midnight
Mon-Wed; 10am-2am Thur-Sat; 10am-10pm Sun.
Admission $5-$15. **No credit cards. Map** p334.

Rebooted a few years back as a band venue, the
Sandringham's upstairs space is small but cosy,
decked out in opulent red. Plenty of undiscovered
talent rocks up to a receptive brigade hungry for
fresh sounds. Local favourites Iotfi are often found
here on Thursday nights.

Spectrum

*Exchange Hotel, 34-44 Oxford Street, between
Riley & Liverpool Streets, Darlinghurst (9331
1936/www.pashpresents.com). Bus 352, 378, 380,
L82.* **Open** 8pm-late Sat; 5pm-midnight Sun.
Admission $15-$25. **Credit** AmEx, MC, V.
Map p329 G8.

Bringing music screaming into the 'pink strip' of
town, this intimate club has succeeded in showcasing hot new bands and attracting established talent
who want a central location that isn't a barn. Local
favourites Magic Dirt chose to launch their *Snow
White* album here over five nights in 2005. Also
hosts popular Bin Bang Bong club nights. Housed
in the four-level Exchange Hotel, a popular gay
venue (*see p240*).

Vanguard

*42 King Street, between Queen & Fitzroy Streets,
Newtown (9557 7992/www.thevanguard.com.au).
Bus 352, 422, 423, 426, 428.* **Open** 5pm-midnight
Tue-Sat; 4-10pm Sun. **Admission** $10-$30. **Credit**
AmEx, DC, MC, V. **Map** p334.

Opened in late 2003, the smart yet cosy Vanguard
adds to the inner west's push on the live music front.
Expect a range of rock, jazz and blues acts, in comfy
surroundings; there's a restaurant too. It's often
used for showcases of local and international touring acts. **Photo** *p249*.

Jazz

Although its appeal lies primarily with
the inner-city wine bar set, jazz enjoys an
undeniably solid presence in Sydney's live
music scene. Jazz audiences are fiercely loyal:
1980s hero Vince Jones – one of the few jazz
all-rounders to break out into the mainstream –
still sells out well in advance. Local legend
Jackie Orszaczky and his partner Tina Harrod
are among the most recognised faces of the

Sydney jazz scene, and are to be found at
various inner-city venues on a weekly basis.
Hard bop fans should catch Bernie McGann, a
craggy veteran who wrings emotion from his
alto sax and swings like a gorilla when hyped.
Trumpeter James Morrison is very much the
popular face of jazz in Australia. Technically
he's brilliant, although good taste can give way
to complex virtuosity.

Young experimentalists work independently
or in company with older but edgy players in
the vein of Mike Nock, John Pochee, Mark
Simmonds and Bob Bertles. These stalwarts
have helped bring an array of bands to the fore,
including Clarion Fracture Zone, Wanderlust,
the Catholics, the Necks, Ute, Australian Creole,
First Light, the Scott Tinkler Trio, Twentieth
Century Dog and Engine Room, some of whom
gained overseas exposure. 'Nu' jazz has also
proved a popular offshoot.

The avant-garde continues to influence
many bands, adding bite and a degree of
wildness to a prevailing world music influence.
Contemporary jazzers often earn their living
in rock, funk, Latin and blues bands and
have allowed these influences to colour their
playing. Champion of new talent **SIMA**
(Sydney Improvised Music Association,
www.sima.org.au) offers up an array of
innovative jazzers to watch. In addition, the
Jazzgroove Association (www.jazzgroove.
com) – a musicians' co-op dedicated to
promoting new jazz talent – helps organise
events and profile young players, including
the Gerard Masters Trio, Nicholas McBride
and the Nick Bowd Quartet.

More recent additions to the scene continue
to keep it fresh and eclectic. Singer-songwriter
Elana Stone from the Jazzgroove stable packs a
punch, as does Matt Baker's Transition Project,
Cin Cin, guitarist Ray Beadle and the Edwina
Blush Trio. Saxophonists Mark Taylor, Dale
Barlow and Tim Hopkins, vocalist Melanie
Oxley, keyboardist Chris Abrahams and
guitarist Ben Hughes show what can be done
with melodies and instrumentation, while fans
of hard-core free improvisers can get their
kicks from multi-instrumentalist Jim Denley
and turntable maniac Martin Ng.

Possibly the best place to see the bulk of
Sydney's jazz talent, and some top international
acts besides, is the ever-expanding **Manly
International Jazz Festival** (*see p212*). Held
over the long weekend in October, its musical
scope covers swing, blues, funk, Afro-Latin and
zydeco. To get the scoop on what's happening
jazz-time, tune into **Eastside Radio** (89.7 FM)
and Jazztrack (5-7pm Saturday and Sunday).
For a full guide to jazz on local and national
radio, visit www.jazzscene.com.au.

Jazz joint the **Wine Banq**. *See p253.*

Venues

Recent arrival the **Vanguard** (*see p252*) mirrors the modern-day vibe of the long-running Basement in style and content. Expect a mix of roots, blues, jazz and acoustic-based melodies. Other venues with occasional jazz nights include the **Bald Faced Stag** in Liechhardt (345 Parramatta Road, 9560 7188), with jam sessions and banks on Thursdays; and **Café Sydney** (9251 8683, www.cafesydney.com), an upmarket eaterie on the top floor of the Customs House at Circular Quay, which offers funk, jazz and world selections most Sunday lunchtimes – booking advised. Jazz acts also feature regularly at the popular weekend **Rocks Market** (*see p192*) to keep the tourist crowds jigging and grinning. R&B, guitar duos and the occasional classical string ensemble also mingle among the stalls.

Basement
29 Reiby Place, off Pitt Street, Circular Quay (9251 2797/www.thebasement.com.au). CityRail/ferry Circular Quay. **Open** noon-late Mon-Fri; 7.30pm-late Sat, Sun. **Admission** $25-$80. **Credit** AmEx, DC, MC, V. **Map** p327 F4.
One of the hippest clubs on the scene, this hugely popular jazz and blues venue near the Quay boasts a supper-club-style setting with tables, an adjacent

'blue room' and a bistro for cheap eats. Expect the likes of Tony Joe White or Roger McGuinn to turn up, along with world music maestros and established local jazz names.

Macquarie Hotel
42 Wentworth Avenue, at Goulburn Street, Surry Hills (8262 8888/www.macquariehotel.com). CityRail Central. **Open** 11am-2am Mon-Sat; noon-10pm Sun. **Admission** free. **Credit** AmEx, DC, MC, V. **Map** p329 F8.
An inner-city pub that does actually double as a hotel. It proudly touts itself as 'Sydney's new home of jazz & funk', with sessions from Wednesday through Sunday. Jackie Orszaczky has performed residencies in recent times.

Opera Bar
Lower Concourse Level, Sydney Opera House, Bennelong Point, Circular Quay (9247 1666/ www.operabar.com.au). CityRail/ferry Circular Quay. **Open** 11.30am-late daily. **Admission** free. **Credit** AmEx, DC, MC, V. **Map** p327 G3.
A mix of jazz and ambient DJs perform during the summer months in a setting that's hard to beat anywhere in Sydney. A mix of world, jazz and funk kicks off throughout the week from 8.30pm, and at weekends from 2.30pm. *See also p177.*

Sound Lounge
Seymour Centre, corner of City Road & Cleveland Street, Chippendale (box office 9351 7940/admin 9351 7944/www.seymour.usyd.edu.au). Bus 422, 423, 426, 428. **Open** from 8.30pm Fri, Sat. **Admission** $15; $12-$13 concessions. **Credit** MC, V. **Map** p328 C11.
With the Side On Café closing its doors in 2006, SIMA performances are now held here on Friday and Saturday nights, in what was the old restaurant area of this student-friendly arts centre. Capacity is kept low (never above 90), with pub grub and drinks served in a supper club environment.

Soup Plus
1 Margaret Street, at Clarence Street, CBD (9299 7728/www.soupplus.com.au). CityRail Wynyard. **Open** noon-midnight Mon-Sat. **Admission** $10-$15; $35 incl 2-course meal before 10pm Fri, Sat. **Credit** AmEx, MC, V. **Map** p327 E5.
Now re-established in its new, purpose-built home after 30 years on George Street, this long-standing trad jazz forum favours mainstream and bop stylists, as well as jam sessions that can vary wildly in quality, but are often entertaining. Worth a dinner date while you're in town. Music starts at 7.30pm.

Wine Banq
53 Martin Place, entrance on Elizabeth Street, CBD (9222 1919/www.winebanq.com.au). CityRail Martin Place. **Open** noon-late Mon-Fri; 6pm-late Sat. **Admission** free-$15. **Credit** AmEx, DC, MC, V. **Map** p327 E5.
This ultra-sophisticated wine and posing venue (*see p177*) is the new kid on the block of jazz. Trios and combos take the stage Fridays and Saturdays from

Arts & Entertainment

10pm and occasional weeknights from 9pm. During the annual Sydney Festival (*see p214*), the joint puts on nightly revels in the company of local big names and lesser-known imports from the US. **Photo** *p252*.

Woollahra Hotel

Corner of Moncur & Queen Streets, Woollahra (9363 2782/www.woollahrahotel.com.au). Bus 378, 380, 389. **Open** noon-midnight Mon-Sat; noon-10pm Sun. **Admission** free. **Credit** AmEx, DC, MC, V. **Map** p333 M10.

Not an ideal venue – it's on the snobbier side of the eastern suburbs and lacks the warmth of jazz's hallowed grounds – but its musical servings can still surprise. Jazz Juice sessions every Sunday (6-9.30pm) and Thursday (8-11pm). The French restaurant, Bistro Moncur (*see p158*), is a winner.

Classical & Opera

Sydneysiders are very enthusiastic when it comes to classical music. This is especially true when it's laid on in full-blown fashion in an outdoor, picnic-style setting. The orchestral and carol-singing sit-ins in the Domain pack in tens of thousands of families every year, although connoisseurs steer clear of such mainstream fare, which tends to favour well-worn classics.

The **Sydney Festival** (*see p214*) alleviates post-Christmas blues by running musical events throughout January – including the Sydney Symphony's free **Symphony & Jazz in the Domain**. The other main outdoor event, also free, is Opera Australia's **Opera in the Domain**, on the last Saturday in January or the first Saturday in February. ABC's TV and radio stations often broadcast live relays of opera performances, usually at weekends.

Venues

The **Eugene Goossens Hall** – named after the British composer and conductor who first suggested the idea of the Opera House back in 1954, and housed in the ABC headquarters in Ultimo – is often used by smaller ensembles playing contemporary music. **Sydney Town Hall** (*see p79*) also showcases contemporary music, plus free organ recitals, the SBS Youth Orchestra, the Sydney University Musical Society and Sydney Festival events. Churches are also popular if irregular venues for recitals, and a guide to church music can be found in the *SMH*'s Metro section. **St Andrew's Cathedral** (*see p79*) plays host to the Cathedral Singers & Orchestra, who perform choral classics, as well as jazz choirs and guest chamber music groups. The Historic Houses Trust of NSW offers classical (and jazz) concerts in the ballroom at **Government**

House (*see p71*). Drinks are served before the performances, giving you the chance to stroll through the grounds at sunset.

City Recital Hall

Angel Place, near Martin Place, CBD (admin 9231 9000/box office 8256 2222/www.cityrecitalhall.com). CityRail Martin Place. **Box office** 9am-5pm Mon-Fri; and 3hrs before show. **Tickets** free-$90. **Credit** AmEx, MC, V. **Map** p327 F5.

The 1,200-seat City Recital Hall in the centre of the CBD gives Sydney's orchestras room to roam, as well as hosting international names (including one David Helfgott). Created via a deal with the AMP Corporation, the two-tiered, horseshoe-shaped hall has a colour scheme borrowed from a Latvian baroque church (soft grey, soothing aubergine and twinkles of gold) and the architecture and acoustics have been designed for both chamber orchestras and solo performers. The acoustics are said to match Amsterdam's Concertgebouw.

Sydney Opera House

Bennelong Point, Circular Quay (box office 9250 7777/www.sydneyoperahouse.com). CityRail/ferry Circular Quay. **Box office** 9am-8.30pm Mon-Sat; and 2hrs before show Sun. **Tickets** *Opera Theatre* $50-$250; $52-$194 concessions. *Concert Hall* $40-$140; $33-$97 concessions. *Studio* $25-$35; $20-$25 concessions. **Credit** AmEx, DC, MC, V. **Map** p327 G3.

The largest shell of the Sydney icon houses the 2,700-seat Concert Hall (although it was originally intended for opera productions). Thanks to its purpose-built acoustics, symphonic music can be heard with a full, rich and mellow tone. Eighteen adjustable acrylic rings (aka the 'toilet seats') are suspended above the orchestra platform to reflect some of the sound back to the musicians. The hall also has the largest mechanical tracker-action organ in the world, with 10,154 pipes. The smaller, 1,500-seat Opera Theatre is used by Opera Australia, but has its problems (it can't do a real-time set change or a take a full-scale orchestra). The Studio (capacity 350) showcases anything from rap to percussion bands and spoken-word shows. The two other spaces are used for drama productions (*see p271*). **Photo** *p255*.

Orchestras & groups

Australian Brandenburg Orchestra

9328 7581/www.brandenburg.com.au.

Australia's first period-instrument group – baroque and classical periods, that is – has played to sell-out audiences from Tokyo to Germany. Formed by artistic director Paul Dyer in 1990, the orchestra now puts on regular seasons at the City Recital Hall. Its concerts are fashionable events – rich mixes of visual and musical experience.

Australian Chamber Orchestra

8274 3800/www.aco.com.au.

Under the flamboyant artistic directorship of high-profile young violinist Richard Tognetti, the ACO has injected some excitement into classical music. Formed in 1975, the Sydney-based orchestra is relatively youthful – most performers are under 40 – and Tognetti's programming is always provocative. He likes to mix periods, offer rarely heard works and blend period-instrument soloists with contemporary instruments. The results are invariably startling.

Musica Viva
8394 6666/www.musicaviva.com.au.
Musica Viva is the world's largest chamber music organisation, touring Australian and international groups around the country, as well as providing a schools programme in Australia and Singapore. The outfit, which turned 60 in 2005, tours famous choirs and caters to a wide range of musical sensibilities. A roll-call of the world's best ensembles, including the Emerson Quartet, the Beaux Arts Trio and Sydney stars the Tankstream Quartet, have all appeared on its impressive calendar.

Opera Australia
Opera Centre, 480 Elizabeth Street, between Devonshire & Belvoir Streets, Surry Hills (9699 1099/box office 9318 8200/www.opera-australia. org.au). CityRail/LightRail Central. **Open** *Box office* 9am-5pm Mon-Fri. *Tours* 10am, 11am, 2pm Mon-Fri. **Tickets** *Shows* $95-$230. *Tours* $18 incl tea; 11am tour $35 incl lunch. **Credit** AmEx, DC, MC, V. **Map** p329 F11.

Australia may be far from the great European opera houses, but the country's divas have been disproportionately represented in the ranks of global opera stars, among them Nellie Melba, Joan Hammond, Joan Sutherland, Elizabeth Whitehouse and Yvonne Kenny. And Opera Australia has the third-largest programme (after Covent Garden and the Vienna Staatsoper) of any opera company in the world. The company performs in the Opera Theatre of the Opera House for seven months of the year; from April to May and November to December it ups sticks to Melbourne.

As is usual in big arts organisations, the backstage manoeuvrings are often more interesting than what plays out front. OA's bare-bones production budgets, and the costs of storing and restaging productions from the past 30 years, have placed it under enormous financial stress. Conductor Simone Young presided over a music-led revival for three vibrant years until more infighting and cost-cutting saw her departure in late 2003; after a year's gap, Brit-born Richard Hickox stepped in as music director at the beginning of 2005. For the visiting punter, there are still 175 performances of more than a dozen operas in any given year, as well as 80 performances of four different ballets. The company's touring arm, OzOpera, performs year-round across Australia.

Visitors can also go behind the scenes at OA's headquarters in Surry Hills. The tour takes in the costume, millinery and wig-making departments, the props and storage departments, set design and building, and rehearsal spaces for singers and musicians. Tours are for groups (minimum 15 for

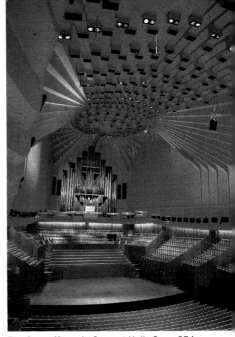

The **Opera House**'s Concert Hall. *See p254.*

the 11am tour, but only two for other tours), and must be booked about two weeks ahead.

Sydney Symphony
8215 4600/www.sydneysymphony.com.au.
Under the artistic directorship of conductor Gianluigi Gelmetti, the Sydney Symphony continues to be the flagship of a network of Australian state capital city orchestras. Established in 1932 as a radio broadcasting orchestra, it has grown into the biggest and best in the country, attracting the finest soloists from Australia and abroad. The orchestra presents more than 140 events a year.

Other ensembles

Look out for the **Sydney Philharmonia Choirs** (9251 2024, www.sydneyphilharmonia. com.au), which has been going strong for 80 years and continues to stun audiences with a lusty *Carmina Burana* or luscious *Missa Solemnis* several times a year. A capella outfit the **Song Company** (9251 1600, www.song company.com.au), Australia's premier vocal ensemble, perform early operas and oratorios. Other a cappella groups include Sydney's first world music choir, **Voices from the Vacant Lot** (www.voicesfromthevacantlot.net), while the **Sydney Gay & Lesbian Choir** (9360 7439) attracts an audience broader than its selection criteria might suggest. Local chamber group **Macquarie Trio** (www.macquarie trio.com.au) is also highly regarded.

Sport & Fitness

They love sport in Sydney. They love it! They love it all!

Sydney is a sporting mecca. The urban hub of a country blessed with weather that makes staying indoors virtually a criminal offence, its harbour, beaches and parks swarm with people taking an active approach to life. Even the more indolent folk holed up in the city's pubs are usually surrounded by walls of televised action and the throbbing murmur of passionate, sport-related conversation.

A few basics. Although football, in the Pommy version, is the fastest-growing sport in Australia – its popularity recently boosted by the new A-League and by the national side qualifying for the World Cup for the first time since 1974 – the term 'footy' here generally refers to the city's game of choice, rugby league. What the British call 'football' is generally known as 'soccer'. Passion for cricket, meanwhile, is undiminished by the country's historic Ashes defeat in 2005, while Aussie Rules – traditionally a Victorian sport – has soared in popularity since the Sydney Swans triumphed in the 2005 premiership.

For more active types, the city's outdoor pursuits range from walking and climbing to water sports and extreme thrills such as skydiving, all on offer in the most spectacular surroundings and with some of the most professional trainers on the planet.

Participation sports

Canoeing & kayaking

There's no fresher, or more original, way to take in the harbour than from water level, and for as little as $15 an hour you can hire a canoe from **Sydney Harbour Kayaks** (9960 4389, www.sydneyharbourkayaks.com) in Mosman. The company also runs guided tours. Further out of town, **Bundeena Kayaks** (9544 5294, www.bundeenakayaks.com.au) offers a wonderful kayaking experience on the waterways of southern Sydney's Royal National Park. If you feel up to braving the choppier waters (and sharks) of the Pacific, head north to **Blue Water Sea Kayaking** (0249 81 51 77, www.seakayaking.com.au) in Port Stephens.

For an overview of paddling opportunities in the state's lakes, rivers and ocean waters, contact **New South Wales Canoeing** (9660 4597, www.nswcanoe.org.au). The organisation also offers training for all ages and levels, from beginners' courses to white-water technique and navigation skills for sea kayakers.

Climbing

Sydney's surrounding areas, especially the Blue Mountains and Hunter Valley, offer plenty of natural resources for rock climbing and canyoning. **Outward Bound Australia** (1800 267 999, www.outwardbound.com.au) is a good first port of call for the novice, while the **Australian School of Mountaineering** (4782 2014, www.asmguides.com) caters for all levels. The latter is based in the Blue Mountains, a wilderness of canyons, plateaus and sandstone cliffs, and visits the Snowy Mountains in winter for ice-climbing trips.

Experts might want to go and talk the talk in **Paddy Pallin** (9264 2685, www.paddy pallin.com.au), a gear shop in the CBD. **The Edge Adventure Centre** (Hudson Avenue, Castle Hill, 9899 8228, www.edge-adventure.com.au) is a good indoor centre, with climb heights up to 18.5 metres (61 feet). You'll also find climbing walls at **Climb Fit** (12 Frederick Street, CBD, 9436 4600, www.climbfit.com.au) and **City Crag** at the back of Mountain Designs (499 Kent Street, CBD, 9267 3822).

If you want to combine climbing with a range of other adventurous sports, **Bush Sports** (9630 0587, www.bushsports.com.au) tackles the lot, including climbing, abseiling, canyoning, rafting and caving, as well as survival programmes, 'Amazing Races' – based on a reality TV format – and treasure hunts.

Cycling

First things first: cycle helmets are compulsory in Sydney, and bottled water a must. Also, local councils have been slow on the uptake with cycle paths, so it's well worth visiting recreational and commuter bike group **Bicycle NSW** (Level 5, 822 George Street, 9281 4099, www.bicyclensw.org.au) for a word of advice and a copy of *Cycling Around Sydney* ($30) before putting foot to pedal.

Competitive cyclists can speak to **Cycling NSW** (9738 5850, www.nsw.cycling.org.au) for the best info on local clubs, rides and racing, while off-roaders should approach **BMX NSW**

Mind those competitive urges if you go **kayaking** on the harbour. *See p256.*

(6367 5277, www.bmxnsw.com.au) for the latest on BMX facilities, tracks and events. For more advice on cycling and bike hire, *see p296.*

Fishing

If it involves water, Australians love it. To get involved with one of Sydney's biggest participation sports, you first need to buy a recreational licence ($6 for three days, $12 for one month, $30 for one year, $75 for three years). You can do this at various fishing shops and clubs, by phoning 1300 369 365 or online at www.dpi.nsw.gov.au/fisheries.

Next step is to find out the best spots: you'll find information on the state government website above, or call the government helpline on 1300 550 474. Alternatively, get nattering with the staff in tackle shops – the guys at **Compleat Angler** in the CBD (3rd Floor, Dymocks Building, 428 George Street, 9241 2080, www.compleatangler.com.au) are particularly happy to share their local expertise and offer demonstrations too.

For a dawn-to-midday session out in the harbour, try **Fishabout Tours** (9451 5420, www.fishnet.com.au/fishabout_tours): prices range from $430 for one person to $160 each for four. Boat, licence, equipment, hot and cold snacks, and drinks are all included.

At certain times in autumn and spring, big-game fishing is an option. A charter with Botany Bay-based sea dog Captain John Wright of **Game & Sport Fishing Charters** (0414 542 548, www.gamefisher.com) offers a thrilling day fishing marlin, tuna, shark and other big ocean fish. Prices for up to six people range from $1,450 for game fishing and $1,300 for sport fishing. No licence is required.

Golf

Many of Sydney's abundance of golf courses are private, but public courses near the CBD include **Moore Park Golf Course** (Cleveland Street, 9663 1064, www.mooreparkgolf.com.au). Club hire costs $40, lessons are around $50 per half-hour, and the course also has a three-level driving range. Also fairly central is the south-eastern suburbs' **Eastlake Golf Club** in Kingsford (Gardener Road, 9663 1374, www.eastlakegolfclub.com.au), where club hire is $28, and lessons $45 for half an hour. Contact the **NSW Golf Association** (9505 9105, www.nswga.com.au) for more locations.

Gyms & sports centres

Surprisingly, in a country so fixated on the outdoors, gyms are really popular in Australia – you're never too far from all the weights, circuit training and aerobics classes you could wish for. The ubiquitous **Fitness First** (9762 1600, www.fitnessfirst.com.au) is among the cheapest, and has branches all over the city. Membership, which can be used in any branch the world over, starts at $15 per week, while one-off visits cost $18. For gyms popular with gay men and lesbians, *see p244*.

Cook & Phillip Park

4 College Street, at William Street, CBD (9326 0444/ www.cookandphillip.com.au). CityRail Museum or St James. **Open** 6am-10pm Mon-Fri; 7am-8pm Sat, Sun. **Admission** *All facilities* $16; $8.50 concessions. *Pool only* $5.80; $4.20 concessions. **Credit** AmEx, MC, V. **Map** p329 G7.

This well-equipped aquatic and fitness centre has a 50m heated indoor swimming pool, a leisure pool with wave machine, hydrotherapy pools, basketball courts and a good gym, with physiotherapy also available. It hosts various classes and team sports; the aqua aerobics classes are especially popular.

Hang-gliding, skydiving & paragliding

For a bird's-eye view of the city and an adrenalin rush that'll last months, a tandem flight with **Sydney Hang Gliding Centre** (4294 4294, www.hanggliding.com.au) starts at $195, including in-flight photos.

Beginners can experience the thrill of skydiving in tandem with an instructor (along with a whole range of other hair-raising activities) through **Adrenalin Club** (80 McDougall Street, Kirribilli, 9959 3934, www.adrenalin.com.au). It costs $325. **Sydney Skydiving Centre** (1 800 805 997, 9791 9155, www.sydneyskydivers.com.au) also offers a pulse-racing accelerated free-fall (AFF) course: one day's training, followed by a jump that gives up to a minute of free fall before you pull the ripcord and enjoy a mellow five minutes floating on a cushion of air and taking in the Sydney coastline. Prices start at $427, including gear hire, training and membership.

If jumping off a cliff with only a parachute and an instructor to save your bones sounds like fun, **Sydney Paragliding Centre** (4294 9065, www.sydneyparagliding.com) offers tandem adventures from $175, about an hour out of the city. Contact the **Australian**

Lawn unto themselves

Ditch any preconceptions: in Australia, bowls is more a game for young hipsters than flannel-wearing septuagenarians. As a result, clubs in the trendier parts of town tend to offer 'barefoot' bowls, which means bowling with a less formal, more sociable slant. Some are so casual they even let you bring a music system and barbecue – though check with the club just how barefoot they're prepared to go. Good spots to try are **Balmain Bowling Club** (156 Darling Street, 9810 1071), the oldest club in NSW; **Camperdown Bowling & Recreation Club** (Mallett and Pidcock Streets, on the edge of Camperdown Park, 9519 7961); **Coogee Bowling Club** (Dolphin Street, 9665 5782, http://coogeebowlingclub.com); and **Paddington Bowling Club** (2 Quarry Street, next to Trumper Park, 9363 1150).

In early 2006, the **Royal NSW Bowling Association** (9283 4555, www.rnswba. org.au) climbed aboard when it launched a new initiative known as ModBowls to encourage younger generations to play on a social level, in casual clothes. The annual registration fee for a ModBowler is $25. Contact the association for more details.

If it's just a one-off quirky bowling experience you're after, **Rock 'n' Bowl** (9976 3109, www.rocknbowl.com.au) offers party-style classes in Manly and North Sydney.

Parachute Federation (6281 6830, www.apf. asn.au) for further information, safety advice or just a bit of reassurance.

Horse riding

The only horse-riding point in central Sydney is the old Sydney Showgrounds in Centennial Park. **The Centennial Parklands Equestrian Centre** (114-120 Lang Road, next to Fox Studios, 9332 2809, www.cp.nsw.gov.au) administers the site and offers lessons to novice or experienced riders of all ages. Prices start at $70, while simple rides in the park along the 3.6km (2.2 mile) bridleway cost $50 per person.

Rollerblading (in-line skating)

You won't walk far along the promenades at Manly and Bondi Beaches without encountering a group of rollerbladers. Centennial Park, with its flat roads and moderate traffic, also attracts more than its fair share of multi-wheeled pedestrians, and **Centennial Park Cycles** (9398 5027, www.cyclehire.com.au) hires out blades plus safety gear for $15 an hour or $30 for four hours. Skates can also be hired from some surf shops at the beaches.

Sailing

Sailing, fishing, houseboats, sea tours, function boat hire – you name it, if it's of a nautical nature, **Charter Boat Information Service** (9552 1827) will provide you info on it.

If you'd rather get your hands on the ropes than be a passenger, the **Pacific Sailing School** (9326 2399, www.pacificsailing school.com.au) in Rushcutters Bay is one of the many schools in the Sydney Harbour, Middle Harbour and Port Hacking areas. **Eastsail** (9327 1166, www.eastsail.com.au), also based in Rushcutters Bay, offers courses in crewing and sailing, with beginners' courses of four three-hour practical sessions, one three-hour theory session and one club race. Courses cost $475 each, with discounts for group bookings. The nationwide company **Ausail** (9960 5451, www.ausailsydney.com.au) also provides lessons, as well as luxury yacht charters.

For more companies and locations, try the **Yachting Association of NSW** (9660 1266, www.nsw.yachting.org.au).

Scuba diving

The Great Barrier Reef may be a few thousand kilometres north, but the diving opportunities around Sydney are magnificent. As well as its own reefs, the city's coast offers gobsmacking marine life – including non-threatening sharks and the freakishly unique weedy seadragon – sponge gardens and wrecks.

One of the most experienced diving companies in Australia, **Pro Dive** (1800 820 820, www.prodive.com.au), has scuba centres throughout Sydney. It organises day trips and entire scuba holidays, and its PADI Open Water Certification (which will allow you to dive pretty much anywhere in the world) includes classroom theory, pool skills training and ocean dives, and costs $395 per person. The linked outfits **Dive Centre Manly** (10 Belgrave Street, 9977 4355, www.divesydney.com) and **Dive Centre Bondi** (192 Bondi Road, 9369 3855, www.divebondi.com.au) also offer a variety of courses, for beginners to advanced.

If a training course isn't what you're after, you could just go snorkelling. Local dive shops will give you a rundown on their area as well as hiring you the right equipment. Rule number one? Making sure the gear fits snugly.

Surfing

Surfing is as integral a part of Sydney life as enjoying a drink in the sunshine. **Manly**, **Dee Why** and **Freshwater** have good waves for beginners, while **Bondi**, **Bronte**, **Cronulla** and any of the **northern beaches** tend to attract the more confident wave-rider. Most beaches have a surf lifesaving club to help you stay out of trouble and you can hire surfboards and body boards for around $15 an hour.

If you've never stood up on a board before, consider having some lessons first. Matt Grainger at **Manly Surf School** (9977 6977, www.manlysurfschool.com) has 20 years' experience of teaching novices. Beginner, intermediate and advanced courses cost $50 for a two-hour group session and $80 an hour for a one-to-one. **Let's Go Surfing** in Bondi (128 Ramsgate Avenue, 9365 1800, www.letsgo surfing.com.au), charges $69 per person for a group class, with three sessions for $165 or a one-to-one, 90-minute lesson for $130.

Long Reef Surf (www.longreefsailboards. com.au) – which has two locations, north (1012 Pittwater Road, Collaroy, 9971 1212) and south (116 Grand Parade, Brighton-le-Sands, 9599 2814) – offers lessons too, and **Surfing Australia** (6674 9888, www.surfing australia.com.au) also arranges courses in conjunction with local shops along the coast.

For the latest surf conditions, visit www.coastalwatch.com or www.realsurf.com. Also look for the excellent *Wave-Finder* (published by the Hedonist Surf Company), a mini guide to beaches around Australia, available from surf shops and bookshops.

Arts & Entertainment

Swimming

IN THE SEA

Different sections of beaches are marked for swimming each day. These are considered safe and are patrolled by professional surf lifesavers, so always swim between the red and yellow flags. For more advice on safety and details of Sydney's best beaches, *see pp133-39.*

IN OCEAN/HARBOUR POOLS

If you fancy sea water without the hostility of the waves, try one of Sydney's tidal swimming pools. **North Bondi** has two small paddling pools, while south Bondi has the lane-marked **Bondi Icebergs** pool, famous for the winter exploits of the Speedo-clad elderly men who have for years braved the freezing waters on Sunday mornings. **Wylie's Baths** in Coogee is the best-preserved of the seaside pools, and there are also women-only baths about 200 metres south of Wylie. You'll also find pools at Collaroy, Bronte, Cronulla, Palm Beach and Dee Why beaches, all of which get jammed in the summer. Some harbour beaches, including Clontarf, Balmoral, Nielsen Park and Double Bay, have enclosed swimming areas.

IN PUBLIC POOLS

One of the many grand sporting venues that graced Sydney for the 2000 Olympics is the **Sydney International Aquatic Centre** (*see p261*), a fantastic facility with wonderful play areas for kids, which is open to the public when there isn't a competition on.

If you'd rather stay in the city, there's a very swish 50 metre pool at **Cook & Phillip Park** (*see p258*) and similar-sized affairs in **Prince Alfred Park** (near Central Station, off Chalmers Street, 9319 7045) and at **Victoria Park** (near Sydney University, between City Road and Broadway, 9660 4181). Two beautiful, splendidly sited outdoor pools are the **North Sydney Olympic Pool** (*see p113*), beneath the northern end of the Harbour Bridge at Milsons Point, and the **Andrew (Boy) Charlton Pool** (*see p70*) at the edge of the Botanical Gardens.

The **NSW Swimming Association** (9552 2966, www.nswswimming.com.au) can tell you about the city's other pools.

Tennis

Public tennis courts are run by local councils and charge around $12-$20 an hour. Ever keen to promote the sport, **Tennis NSW** (9763 7644, www.tennisnsw.com.au) will happily advise you on courts in your area.

If you take your tennis seriously and/or would like it to be part of your social life, it may

be worth joining the **White City Tennis Club** (30 Alma Street, Paddington, 9360 4113, www.whitecitytennis.com), one of the best-known tennis clubs in central Sydney and the former host of the Sydney International. It costs $1,056 per year plus a $580 joining fee.

Waterskiing

Adding a shot of adrenalin to the visual thrill of exploring Sydney's waterways, this somewhat intimidating sport benefits from the Aussie 'too easy' attitude. The trainers at **Aquatic Leisure** (0407 200 562, www.aquaticleisure.com.au) are confident that they can get you on your feet, whatever your level.

Windsurfing

Opportunities for windsurfing – 'sailboarding' to water-sports purists – are abundant in the waters around Sydney. The **Balmoral Sailing School** (9960 5344, www.sailingschool.com.au) at Balmoral Beach is one of the best places to learn. Courses range from introductory to advanced; a basic four-hour course costs $175. The school also hires out fully rigged windsurfers (as well as dinghies, Hobie Cats and kayaks) for around $40 an hour.

Already know your stuff? In that case, for north-easterlies, the best spots are Pittwater at Palm Beach, Narrabeen Lake, Balmoral Beach, Rodd Point in the harbour and Botany Bay south of the airport. Silver Beach at Kurnell is good for westerlies, and southerlies favour the area around Captain Cook Bridge in Sutherland. Much of the enjoyment of windsurfing depends on weather and wind direction, so call the boating weather forecast (1 900 926 101 – beware the 77¢-a-minute call rate) before going.

The **NSW Boardsailing Association** (www.windsurfing.org) has more information.

Spectator sports

Venues

Since 2000, Homebush Bay has been Sydney's centre of gravity for top-level spectator sport. There, **Sydney Olympic Park** (*see p126*) comprises a cluster of venues for both national and local sporting events. **Telstra Stadium** (formerly Stadium Australia; *see p261*), the focal point of the park, is its pride and joy. The authorities are keen to use its massive capacity to recoup some of the money that went into building it, so a number of big events have been moved from Moore Park's **Sydney Cricket Ground** and **Aussie Stadium** (formerly Sydney Football Stadium; for both, *see p261*) to

this spot 20 kilometres (12.5 miles) west, in
Sydney's demographic centre, if not its heart.
   The **Sydney Olympic Park Visitor
Centre** (1 Showground Road, 9714 7888,
www.sydneyolympicpark.com.au) has info on
all the venues. Its website is a cyber-shrine to
sport in Sydney, well worth checking out.

TICKETS
Ticketek (9266 4800, www.ticketek.com) is the
main outlet for most sporting events in Sydney,
including those held at any of the Olympic
venues at Homebush Bay, but **Ticketmaster**
(13 6100, www.ticketmaster7.com) also sells
tickets for many fixtures. Both charge booking
fees. You can sometimes buy tickets at the
venue on the day, often for cash only.

Sydney Cricket Ground (SCG) & Aussie Stadium
*Driver Avenue, Moore Park (1 800 801 155/
9360 6601/tours 1300 724 737/www.sydneycricket
ground.com.au). Bus 372, 373, 374.* **Tours** 10am,
1pm Mon-Fri. **Tickets** $23.50; $15 concessions;
$62 family. **Map** p332 J/K11.
Book ahead for a two-hour tour.

Sydney International Aquatic Centre
*Olympic Boulevard, Sydney Olympic Park, Homebush
Bay (9752 3666/www.sydneyaquaticcentre.com.au).
CityRail Olympic Park/RiverCat Sydney Olympic
Park then bus 401.* **Open** 5am-8.45pm Mon-Fri;
6am-6.45pm/7.45pm Sat, Sun. **Tours** noon, 1pm,
2pm daily. **Admission** *Swim & spa* $6.20; $4.30-$5
concessions; $19.50 family. *Swim & gym* $18; $8.50
concessions. **Tours** $19; $9.50-11 concessions;
$52 family. **Credit** MC, V.
Having hosted the pool events during the Olympics,
this place is still home to high-quality international
meets and rather less illustrious inter-school competitions. Great venue for serious lane-pounders, and
impressive enough just to visit.

Sydney International Athletics Centre
*Edwin Flack Avenue, Sydney Olympic Park,
Homebush Bay (9752 3444/www.sydneyathletic
centre.com.au). CityRail Olympic Park/RiverCat
Sydney Olympic Park then bus 401.* **Open** *Visits*
3-8pm Mon-Fri; 8am-1pm Sat; 9am-1pm Sun.

Sydney International Tennis Centre
*Rod Laver Drive, Sydney Olympic Park, Homebush
Bay (8746 0777/www.sydneytennis.com.au).
CityRail Olympic Park/RiverCat Sydney Olympic
Park then bus 401.*

Sydney Olympic Park Sports Centre
*Olympic Boulevard, Sydney Olympic Park, Homebush
Bay (9763 0111/www.sports-centre.com.au). CityRail
Olympic Park/RiverCat Sydney Olympic Park then
bus 401.* **Open** *Visits* 7am-11pm daily.

It hosted tae kwon do and table tennis in the
Olympics and now is home to various indoor spectator sports including gymnastics, soccer, bad-
minton, volleyball, hockey and martial arts.

Sydney SuperDome
*Edwin Flack Avenue, at Olympic Boulevard,
Sydney Olympic Park, Homebush Bay (8765 4321/
www.superdome.com.au). CityRail Olympic Park/
RiverCat Sydney Olympic Park then bus 401.*

Telstra Stadium
*Olympic Boulevard, Sydney Olympic Park,
Homebush Bay (8765 2000/guided tours 8765 2300/
www.telstrastadium.com.au). CityRail Olympic Park/
RiverCat Sydney Olympic Park then bus 401.*
The stadium's stands were moved closer together
after the Olympics for visibility and atmosphere's
sake. Crowds fill almost half of its 83,500 capacity
at regular rugby league games, while it tends to be
nearly full for exhibition events, and you'll struggle
to get a ticket for rugby union tests or State of Origin
rugby league games. For information on tours, *see
p126* **Sydney Olympic Park**.

Athletics
Australians follow athletics with more of a
passionate roar than a thoughtful stroke of the
beard. The **Sydney International Athletics
Centre** (*see above*) is home to various major
events, including trials for Commonwealth and
Olympic Games. Contact **Athletics Australia**
(03 9820 3511, www.athletics.org.au) or, for
competition within the state, **Athletics NSW**
(9552 1244, www.nswathletics.org.au).

Aussie Rules
Forget its tooth-spitting image abroad – this
hybrid of soccer, rugby and Gaelic football is
a truly remarkable spectator sport, involving
great athleticism, strength and tactical prowess.
Sydneysiders used to have a lukewarm
relationship with the sport, as it was
traditionally played south of the state border:
it was invented in Melbourne around 1858, and
even the local team, the **Sydney Swans** (9339
9123, www.sydneyswans.com.au), were a South
Melbourne team until they relocated in 1982.
   For a long time, poor results meant that the
Swans didn't catch on in their new home.
However, slow but steady progress came to a
climax when they won a historic Australian
Football League premiership title in 2005.
Many of Sydney's unconverted turned fanatical,
and the team now regularly sells out the 42,000-
seat **Sydney Cricket Ground**; even for its
occasional matches at the city's huge **Telstra
Stadium** (for both, *see above*), Aussie Rules
fans make enough of a dent for there to be a
decent, family-based atmosphere.

The 83,500-capacity **Telstra Stadium** is Sydney's biggest Olympic relic. *See p261.*

The season is between March and September. If you're feeling perverse, go and support the Kangaroos of Melbourne – keen to make inroads into the Sydney market, they usually play about five 'home' games at the SCG.

Baseball

Baseball has a small but thriving scene in Sydney, with most areas having a team in the state's 'Major League'. The season runs from September to February, with games taking place on Wednesday and Thursday evenings and Sunday afternoons. Women's games are on Friday nights, and there is also a beginners' league and under-18s competition.

NSW Baseball League (9675 4522, www. nsw.baseball.com.au) has information, or for more general information about the sport in Australia, visit www.baseball.com.au.

Basketball

Sydney's two teams in the National Basketball League (www.nbl.com.au) are the **Sydney Kings** and relative newcomers the **West Sydney Razorbacks**. The Kings (9281 1777, www.sydneykings.com.au) play at the **Sydney Entertainment Centre** (*see p249*), and the Razorbacks, aka the Pigs (9740 6259, www.razorbacks.com.au), at Homebush's **Olympic Park Sports Centre** (*see p261*).

The **Sydney Flames** (9351 4960, www.sydney flames.com) are the city's women's NBL side. The season runs from September to February, and tickets start at $16.

For more information about the sport, contact the **NSW Basketball Association** (9746 2969, www.nswbasketball.net.au).

Cricket

Yes, they still love it. Australia may have been on the losing end of the most spectacular Ashes series in living memory in 2005, but, especially during the summer months, cricket – a national obsession for well over a century – enjoys a stranglehold on the sporting calendar, for both spectators and participants. If there's an international match on, a trip to the famous **Sydney Cricket Ground** (see *p261*) is a must for any visitor.

Matches involving Australia at the SCG are viewed – both live and on TV – with an almost religious obsession, and the highlight of the cricketing calender is the **Sydney Test**, played over five days against a touring side, usually in the first week of January. You can also expect a handful of one-dayers at the SCG in the afternoon and under lights in the evening: if you find drawn-out tests slow, the much faster one-day cricket, which always produces a winner, is the best option.

Getting tickets for the bigger matches can be difficult, but local games don't usually sell out. For information on matches, phone the SCG or visit www.baggygreen.com.au.

Hard-core fans craving the thwack of leather on willow when there are no internationals on can see the New South Wales cricket team, the **NSW Blues**, play around five matches at the SCG between October and March in the interstate Pura Cup competition. The early March final, should NSW reach it, always takes place in Sydney. The Blues also play other one-dayers at various locations around the city. Meanwhile, hundreds of fields around Sydney host cricket matches of all levels on summer Saturday afternoons. **Cricket NSW** (9339 0999, www.cricketnsw. com.au) has information on fixtures and venues.

Golf

Melbourne tends to get the bigger golf events, but Sydney's lusher, plusher courses usually get to host the odd match in the **PGA Tour of Australasia**, which pitches the best Australian players against a handful of overseas stars. Tickets can cost anything from $20 a day. You can see up-to-date match schedules at www.pgatour.com.au.

Greyhound racing

Wentworth Park Greyhound Track

Wentworth Park Road, Glebe (9552 1799/ www.wentworthparksport.com.au). LightRail Wentworth Park. **Open** 6-11pm Mon, Sat. **Admission** $5.50. **No credit cards.** **Map** p328 C8. Ten races each night.

Harness racing

Harold Park Paceway

Wigram Road, Glebe (9660 3688/www.harold park.com.au). LightRail Jubilee Park/bus 433. **Open** 1-5.30pm Tue; 7-11pm Fri. **Admission** $8. **No credit cards.** 'The trots' (think horse racing meets Ben Hur) are held most Friday nights and Tuesday afternoons.

Horse racing

There are race meetings in Sydney every Saturday as well as several midweek events. The **Australian Jockey Club** (9663 8400, www.ajc.org.au) runs meets at **Royal Randwick**, flanking Centennial Park at its southern edge, and in the southern suburbs at **Warwick Farm**. The **Sydney Turf Club** (9930 4000, www.theraces.com.au), meanwhile, organises programmes at **Rosehill Gardens** in Parramatta and in **Canterbury Park** to the south. Admission is $10-$11, $15-$30 for major races, with under-18s going free.

Evening racing is a regular weekday fixture at Canterbury from October to the end of February and makes a fantastic night out.

Major milestones on the Sydney racing calendar include the Australian Jockey Club's four-day carnival every Easter, which includes the down-under versions of **Doncaster Day** and **Derby Day**, and features $10 million in prize money. Other huge events are the **Golden Slipper** at Rosehill, usually held a week before Derby Day, and the **Spring Carnival** at Randwick. **Melbourne Cup Day**, the country's leading horse-racing event, held on the first Tuesday in November, is also the biggest day in Sydney in terms of crowds drawn to the day's meets at the Royal Randwick. Many people take the afternoon off work, and there's a party atmosphere all over town (*see p214* **And they're off!**).

Canterbury Park Racecourse *King Street, Canterbury (9930 4000). CityRail Canterbury then shuttle bus or bus 428.*
Rosehill Gardens Racecourse *Grand Avenue, Rosehill (9930 4000). CityRail Rosehill/RiverCat Parramatta then shuttle bus.*
Royal Randwick Racecourse *Alison Road, Randwick (9663 8400). Bus 372, 373, 374, 376, 377.*

Arts & Entertainment

The beaut game

Ten years ago, to associate the word 'football' with a round ball in Australia pretty much amounted to treason. But now the word officially – if not yet popularly – refers to the hands-off game so revered in Europe, South America and Asia. It's now the fastest-growing sport in the country, and with the Australian national team, the Socceroos, a genuine contender on the international footballing circuit since qualifying for the 2006 World Cup (for the first time in 32 years), the game's popularity can only soar higher.

Winter 2005 also saw the formation of the eight-team **A-League** (www.aleagueonline. com.au), the latest and greatest in a long line of attempts to get a popular national league under way. The signs are good: the football may not be of the highest standard – think second-tier level in the major European leagues – but it's improving steadily and can only get better. After all, the crowds are healthy, the sponsorship pretty meaty and the winner goes into the Asian version of the Champions League. No wonder several of the game's household names in Britain are considering a move down under.

The local side, **Sydney FC** (www.sydneyfc. com), have started with a bang, winning the A-League's inaugural season. The team's star – each team is allowed to pay one player English Premiership-level wages – is former Manchester United legend Dwight Yorke (*photo*). Sydney play most of their games at the **Aussie Stadium** (*see p261*) to a crowd of newly converted Aussies plus expats hitherto deprived of their footy fix and happy to support a different team away from home. The gently boisterous atmosphere is highly enjoyable, and tickets are good value at $15.

If you want to watch soccer on TV, opportunities are plentiful. As well as A-League matches, Foxtel (www.foxtel.com.au) shows four or five Premiership games – including a 3pm Saturday kick-off – most weekends, plus a highlights programme on Monday nights. SBS (www20.sbs.com.au) offers UEFA Champions League and English FA Cup games, as well as *The World Game*, a comprehensive magazine show, on Sunday afternoons. ESPN, shown at some pubs and available for an extra fee on a Foxtel subscription, offers Champions League and UEFA Cup games, plus domestic action from countries including Spain, Italy and Holland.

You'll struggle to find a pub in Sydney without a television screen, and there are some good options for football fans. In the CBD, you could try **Cheers Bar** (561 George Street, 9261 8313, www.cheersbar.com.au), **Jacksons on George** (176 George Street, 9247 2727, www.jacksonsongeorge.com.au) or long-standing fave **Scruffy Murphy's** (corner of Goulbourn & George Streets, 9211 2002, www.scruffymurphys.com.au). Darling Harbour has **One World Sport** (1-25 Harbour Street, 9264 5200), while bang on Bondi Beach is expats fave **Hotel Bondi** (178 Campbell Parade, 9310 3271, www.hotelbondi.com.au).

And for really homesick fans, there are a number of local supporters clubs for British teams, including Arsenal's **Ozarsenal** (www.ozarsenal.com), the **Manchester United Supporters Club of NSW** (www. manutdnsw.com), Tottenham Hotspur's **Ozspurs** (www.ozspurs.com) and Rangers' **Western Sydney Loyal Glasgow Rangers** (www.westernsydneyloyalgrsc.com).

Warwick Farm Racecourse *Hume Highway, Warwick Farm (9602 6199). CityRail Warwick Farm then shuttle bus.*

Rugby league

In Sydney, rugby league is the biggest of all the permutations of 'football'. Australia's domestic league, run by the **National Rugby League** (9232 7566, www.nrl.com.au), starts in March and culminates in a four-week finals series at the **Aussie Stadium** and **Telstra Stadium** (for both, *see p261*) in October. Adult tickets can cost well over $100 for a prime seat, but average at around $20.

The city's fixation with the sport won't waver any time soon, especially following the **Wests Tigers'** victory in the Grand Final of 2005. Russell Crowe's attempts to take over his favourite club, the fanatically supported and comically inept **South Sydney Rabbitohs**, also help keep the sport in the news.

Other big matches include the **State of Origin** series, when NSW takes on Queensland. To find out about the international doings of the **Kangaroos**, Australia's national team, contact the **Australian Rugby League** (9232 7566, www.australianrugbyleague.com.au).

Sydney teams

Canterbury-Bankstown Bulldogs *9789 2922/ www.bulldogs.com.au.*
Cronulla-Sutherland Sharks *9523 0222/ www.sharks.com.au.*
Manly Sea Eagles *9970 3000/ www.mightyeagles.com.*
Parramatta Eels *8843 0300/ www.parraeels.com.au.*
Penrith Panthers *4720 5555/ www.panthersworld.com.au.*
St George Illawarra Dragons *9587 1966/ www.dragons.com.au.*
South Sydney Rabbitohs *8306 9900/ www.souths.com.au.*
Sydney City Roosters *9386 3248/ www.sydneyroosters.com.au.*
Wests Tigers *8741 3300/www.weststigers.com.au.*

Rugby union

It may still be bridesmaid to rugby league, but union has enjoyed a steady rise in popularity in Australia thanks to World Cup victories in 1991 and 1999 and the country's successful hosting of the World Cup itself in 2003.

The **Tooheys New Super 14** competition pitches provincial teams from Australia, New Zealand and South Africa against each other. It runs from February to May, and involves a handful of home matches for the **NSW Waratahs** (www.waratahs.rugby.com.au) at the **Aussie Stadium** (*see p261*). The national

side, the **Wallabies**, play occasional test or tri-nation matches at the **Aussie Stadium** or **Telstra Stadium** (for both, *see p261*). More info is available from the **Australian Rugby Union** (9956 3444, www.rugby.com.au).

Surfing

Competitive surfing is a serious business in Sydney, and competitions take place at lots of the city's beaches every summer weekend, ranging from local inter-club meetings to junior tournaments to professional events involving the world's best surfers.

Contact the sport's governing body, **Surfing NSW** (9349 7055, www.surfingaustralia. com.au) for info on events and locations.

SURF LIFESAVING

A century after the country's first lifesaving club was founded at Bondi in 1906, there are now more than 115,000 registered surf lifesavers in Australia. According to a recent study, they would cost the authorities $1.5 billion a year in wages if they weren't volunteers. A series of competitions throughout the year helps develop and demonstrate the skills involved. For more information, contact **Surf Life Saving NSW** (9984 7188, www.surflifesaving.com.au). Its website has a comprehensive events calendar.

Swimming

Sydney is famously full of breathtaking places to have a dip, and swimming is also a massive spectator sport. Several World Cup swim meets take place in the city, and the **Sydney International Aquatic Centre** (*see p261*) in the Homebush Bay Olympic Park is the venue for most of the major local events.

A more alien spectacle to non-locals are the local beach swims, in which up to 500 local and international competitors embark on one- to three-kilometre swims in the ocean from different beaches around Sydney.

More details of all competitions are available from the **NSW Swimming Association** (9552 2966, www.nswswimming.com.au).

Tennis

The **Sydney International**, a warm-up event in January for the Australian Open in Melbourne, is held at the **Sydney International Tennis Centre** (*see p261*) in Homebush Bay. It's a prime opportunity to see world-class tennis in Sydney. For upcoming tournaments, contact **Tennis NSW** (9763 7644, www.tennisnsw.com.au).

Arts & Entertainment

Theatre & Dance

Opening nights and men in tights.

Every town with an arts scene has a perennial crisis about it. The razor of self-doubt slits into ideas of status, worth and value, with an infinite supply of nay-sayers touting self-serving fantasies of impossibly bright pasts. As such, it's pleasant to point out that Sydney's theatre scene has never been more thriving, more varied or more fun. It manages to sustain a thoroughly efficient and worthwhile high-end mainstream and, better still, the healthiest, biggest and most diverse fringe scene in the city's short, bloody and drunken history.

For mainstream theatre, the **Sydney Theatre Company** is usually reliable, **Ensemble Theatre Company** equally so, **Griffin Theatre Company** continues to showcase new Australian writing and, despite recent oddness, **Company B** is still usually where the action is. But if you want a cheaper and chancier artistic option, check out the big small four: the **Old Fitzroy Hotel**, the **Darlinghurst Theatre**, Griffin Theatre's **Stablemates** programme, and **B Sharp**, the fringe arm of Company B. It's rare to find performance and artistic standards so high in exchange for ticket prices so low. Like any good thing, it probably won't last, so catch them before they succumb to death by homogenisation.

Dance in Sydney is awaiting such cultural renovation. Old stayers like the **Australian Ballet** and the **Sydney Dance Company** continue with their reliable turns, while the irregularly performing **Bangarra** has some frisson. Often the best dance comes from touring interstate and overseas groups.

Sydney's current artistic strength may be the harbinger of some glorious future. Or it may be a last flicker of government-supported dissent before the encroaching darkness. Only time, and ticket stubs, will tell. But fun it remains – and is there a better place to debate the end of civilisation than a decent foyer with a reasonably priced bar?

INFORMATION AND TICKETS

For information on what's on where, when and how much it costs, check the 'Stage' pages of the Metro supplement in Friday's *Sydney Morning Herald*.

In general, tickets bought directly from theatre box offices offer the cheapest deal: you can view the seating plan and choose your price range. Alternatively, you can use a booking agency such as **Ticketek** (9266 4800, www.ticketek.com.au), **Ticketmaster** (13 6100, www.ticketmaster.com.au) or **MCA Ticketing** (1300 306776, www.mca-tix.com) though all charge booking fees.

Theatre

Companies

Australian Theatre for Young People
9251 3900/www.atyp.com.au.
Australia's premier theatre for the 'young' (generously defined) still manages to make often wonderful and essential work by and for the young and the young at heart. Under newish artistic director Timothy Jones, this long-established outfit has extended its reputation for worthwhile work, though there's still a whiff of star-factory fantasy about the company: Nicole Kidman is its patron, and its members (or their parents) pay stiff class fees.

Bell Shakespeare Company
9241 2722/www.bellshakespeare.com.au.
In 1970 actor-director John Bell founded the Nimrod company, widely regarded as spearheading the Australian theatre revival of that decade in Sydney. This all-Bard-all-the-time company (what, you got a better writer, punk?) is his current venture, featuring a regular ensemble of some of Australia's most talented young and less-young actors. It focuses on innovative, utterly comprehensible and intelligent remountings of the canon, with the unofficial motto 'Shakespeare with an Australian accent'. Based in Sydney, with regular seasons at the Opera House, Bell also tours all over Australia.

Company B
9698 3344/www.belvoir.com.au.
The most creative and iconic mainstream theatre group in Sydney, Company B specialises in bold readings of the classics and new Australian plays, with a strong history of exploring new indigenous voices and the Aboriginal experience in contemporary Australia. Many of the country's best actors and directors have created their strongest work in collaboration with the company. Its fringe arm, B Sharp, presents sometimes cutting- and bleeding-edge work. The company's usual home is the Belvoir Street Theatre (*see p268*), but until September 2006 it's operating out of the Seymour Centre (*see p270*) while Belvoir Street is being renovated.

Stranger in Between, at the **Stables Theatre**. *See p271.*

Ensemble Theatre Company

9929 8877/www.ensemble.com.au.
Founded in 1958 by American Hayes Gordon, the Ensemble is the oldest surviving professional theatre company in NSW, and Sandra Bates had her 20th anniversary as artistic director in 2006. It manages without government funding, though it always treads a fine line between cosseting and challenging the legion of loyal subscribers on whom it depends. Among its usual highlights are neglected classics from the American canon, with Arthur Miller almost the house speciality. It has its own theatre (*see p269*) in Kirribilli and also hires out the Opera House's Playhouse a couple of times a year.

Griffin Theatre Company

9332 1052/www.griffintheatre.com.au.
One of the essential engines of Sydney's theatre scene, Griffin is the city's only company solely dedicated to nurturing, developing and performing new Australian work. It produces four or five shows a year, and also manages the Stablemates programme, which gives over its desirable performance space to selected independent companies. Griffin also hosts writers' residencies and the annual Griffin Award for the best unproduced new Australian play.

New Theatre

9519 3403/www.newtheatre.org.au.
Established in 1932 as a workers' theatre, the New has (like Newtown, the once working-class inner-city suburb it resides in) changed substantially. Though still committed to political and socially enquiring work, the New has moved far from simplistic agit-prop and now ranges across classics, neglected Australian repertoire and contemporary European and American work. Technically amateur (the actors are unpaid), the New is at its best when mounting large-cast classics that are no longer considered economical anywhere else.

PACT Youth Theatre

9550 2744/www.pact.net.au.
Sydney's perennially edgy and way-cool youth theatre is where youngsters experiment with their own emerging identities, both theatrical and social. It specialises in contemporary performance technique and group-devised shows at its flexible Erskineville home (*see p270*).

Sidetrack Performance Group

9560 1255/www.sidetrack.com.au.
For several decades, Sidetrack has produced some of Sydney's most interesting contemporary plays and non-text work at its Marrickville base (*see p271*). The group is multilingual, multicultural and multi-skilled, with an increasing interest in the cracks, fissures and tensions beneath the surface success of Australian multiculturalism. Recently, they've also been exploring and reviving the forgotten genre of Australian Greek-language theatre from the 1950s and '60s.

Arts & Entertainment

House style

As Australia's best-known performing arts building, the **Sydney Opera House** (*see p271*) has always excelled at the top end of the arts scene. Typical high-art genre separation is even reflected in the names of the various spaces in 'the House': opera and ballet in the Opera Theatre; classical music in the Concert Hall; drama in the Drama Theatre; and plays in the Playhouse.

Lovers of such traditional forms certainly enjoy the House's standard fare – though as the years go by, this audience is developing a dreadful habit of dying off in numbers. So the hottest demographic is the elusive 'youth', often generously defined to mean anyone under 40.

The House's attempt to get a little bit funky and attract that audience is the **Studio**, an adaptable, two-level space that seats between 220 and 350. In the spirit of revolutionaries everywhere, amid the tepid white and beige of the rest of the Opera House, it's red. Very, very, red.

The Studio's executive producer, Virginia Hyam, reckons the key to success in attracting people who would usually never go near such a 'posh' venue is threefold – mixing genres, colliding the new and untried against old hands doing new work, and cheap tickets (most shows are $20-$30). 'It's targeted at people who are interested in more edgy, contemporary work, which they may not get to see in other places. It's really breaking down what is genre; it's about performance, it's about entertainment. A lot of stuff has a political slant as well.' Recent shows have included avant-garde dance from the Netherlands, New York 'cabaret terrorists', and an Indonesian-Australian mix of dance grooves and traditional percussion.

Mixing theatre, dance, comedy, music and all forms of cross-genre fertilisations in between, the Studio is certainly Sydney's most eclectic performance space. 'The idea is that if someone picks up the programme, out of 20 shows they might see five things that they really like, and the guy next to them will see five different things that he'll really like,' says Hyam. She's also proud of the renovations to the Studio's shared vestibule: 'You can even see the harbour now if you're in the foyer. That's pretty cool!'

Sydney Theatre Company (STC)

9250 1700/www.sydneytheatre.com.au.

Sydney's official state theatre company has been overseen by artistic director Robyn Nevin since 1999. Nevin made her name as one of Australia's finest actors before shifting into directing, and she's been extremely successful at luring some of the country's most famous actors back on to her boards – Judy Davis and Cate Blanchett, most notably. More than 80% of the company's income is derived from box office receipts and it has to stage sure-fire hits to balance the books, though the recent retirement of Australia's best-known (and tallest) social satirist, David 'Tribe' Williamson, will leave a hole in the repertoire: various attempts to find a new Williamson have failed spectacularly. The STC performs in several venues – its home at the Wharf Theatres (*see p272*), the Drama Theatre at the Opera House (*see p271*), and the new, snazzy Sydney Theatre (*see p272*).

Urban Theatre Projects

9707 2111/www.urbantheatre.com.au.

Urban Theatre Projects' mission is to work with Sydney's diverse cultures to make challenging and relevant contemporary theatre. Based in western Sydney, its work is produced through collaboration between artists and local residents, with a focus on storytelling, geographical identity and multimedia. UTP can be found performing in warehouses, railway stations, schools, shopping centres, town squares, private homes, buses and occasionally even in theatres.

Venues

The plush, 1,200-seat **Theatre Royal** in the CBD (MLC Centre, King Street, 9224 8444) once hosted major productions on a regular basis, but, thanks to having Sydney's least-capacious foyer and the perennial rumble from nearby undergound trains, is now rarely used. It does, however, see some brief action around Sydney Festival time. The **National Institute of Dramatic Art** (215 Anzac Parade, Kensington, 9697 7600, www.nida.edu.au), Australia's most self-eminent drama school – and the alma mater of the likes of Mel Gibson, Cate Blanchett and several thousand people you've never heard of – is also an occasional venue. Stand-up and some touring theatre shows put in an appearance at the **Enmore Theatre** in Newtown, though it's better known as a rock venue (*see p248*).

Belvoir Street Theatre

25 Belvoir Street, at Clisdell Street, Surry Hills (9699 3444/www.belvoir.com.au). CityRail/LightRail Central. **Box office** 9.30am-6pm Mon, Tue; 9.30am-7.30pm Wed-Fri; 12.30-7.30pm Sat; 4-7.30pm Sun. **Tickets** *Company B productions* $48; $30-$42 concessions. *Other productions* varies. **Credit** AmEx, MC, V. **Map** p329 F11.

Ensemble Theatre's production of *A View from the Bridge*.

This one-time tomato sauce factory, now owned by a non-profit consortium of performers, actors, writers and their supporters, is home to the innovative Company B (*see p266*), which has exclusive use of the brilliantly intimate 350-seat Upstairs Theatre. The even more intimate 80-seat Downstairs space hosts Belvoir's B Sharp fringe season. Belvoir Street attracts Sydney's most discerning and loyal theatre-goers, who can often be found maintaining their passion in the foyer bar (served by the city's best arts bar staff). At the time of writing, Belvoir Street was being renovated: the work should be finished by September 2006, and until then all performances and the box office are at the Seymour Centre (*see p270*).

Capitol Theatre

13 Campbell Street, between Pitt & George Streets, Haymarket (box office 1300 136166/admin 9320 5000/www.capitoltheatre.com.au). CityRail Central/LightRail Capitol Square. **Box office** 9am-5pm Mon-Fri. **Tickets** $47-$97; $37-$47 concessions. **Credit** AmEx, DC, MC, V. **Map** p329 E8.

Completed in 1893, the interior of the Capitol (originally known as the Hippodrome) was designed by an American theatre specialist to create the illusion of sitting outdoors under stars. Like most illusions, it generally fails. Once reduced to being a too-big porn cinema and then nearly derelict for years, the Capitol was expensively and extensively restored just as the fashion for gargantuan long-running musicals peaked. It's deeply kitsch, but if the occasional show's no good you can always marvel at the furnishings. Since the closure of *The Lion King* in 2005, it has remained pretty, but pretty dark.

Darlinghurst Theatre

19 Greenknowe Avenue, at Baroda Street, Elizabeth Bay (8356 9987/www.darlinghursttheatre.com). CityRail Kings Cross/bus 311, 312. **Box office** 6pm on performance days. *Phone bookings* 9.30am-6pm Mon-Sat. **Tickets** $28; $22 concessions. **Credit** (phone bookings only) AmEx, MC, V. **Map** p330 J6.

The Darlo is located on the edge of Kings Cross, and has comfortable, individually sponsored seats (with name-plates – which semi-famous actor will you sit on tonight?) and excellent sight lines. The theatre co-produces a variety of new work and updated classics in collaboration with a range of local and touring companies. One of Sydney's best-value theatres, with a happily eclectic programme.

Ensemble Theatre

78 McDougall Street, at Willoughby Street, Kirribilli (9929 0644/www.ensemble.com.au). CityRail Milsons Point/ferry Kirribilli. **Box office** 9.30am-8pm Mon-Sat; 10am-3pm Sun. **Tickets** $40-$59; $23-$39 concessions. **Credit** AmEx, DC, MC, V.

Hayes Gordon transformed an old boathouse into Sydney's first in-the-round space in the 1950s, but the theatre has since recovered from the fickle whims of offshore trendiness. The company (*see p267*) is now consistently commendable and has reclaimed its inner pros arch. Beautifully run since 1986 by Sandra Bates, it has one of Sydney's best foyers and a house style of honest, no-nonsense work. **Photo** *above*.

Lyric Theatre

Star City Casino, 80 Pyrmont Street, between Jones Bay Road & Union Street, Pyrmont (9777 9000/www.starcity.com.au). LightRail Star City/ferry

Founded in 1997 by a desperately hip yet talented collective of Sydney actors, and located under an old backpacker's pub (*see p183*), the Fitz programmes first-time playwrights, as well as contemporary takes on classics and whatever's currently hip, hot or happening. Quite probably the coolest theatre space in Sydney. The laksa is average, but the shows have the requisite level of spice. **Photo** *left*.

PACT Theatre
107 Railway Parade, at Sydney Street, Erskineville (9550 2744/www.pact.net.au). CityRail Erskineville. **Box office** 1hr before show. **Tickets** $15; $10 concessions. **No credit cards**. **Map** p334.
This old factory space (yeah, another one) is home to the oft-exciting PACT Youth Theatre (*see p267*) and occasionally hosts itinerant fringe companies of immensely varying quality.

Parramatta Riverside Theatres
Corner of Church & Market Streets, Parramatta (8839 3399/www.riversideparramatta.com.au). CityRail/RiverCat Parramatta. **Box office** 9am-5pm Mon-Fri; 9.30am-1pm Sat. **Tickets** $45-$55; $25-$35 concessions. **Credit** AmEx, MC, V.
This costly Bicentennial project is a council-mandated but difficult multi-theatre complex, perched beside the pleasant, if brownish, Parramatta River. It gets shows touring from more inner-Sydney venues and other states, and under recent management has somewhat recovered its reputation due to better programming and the annual and excellent Big Laugh Comedy Festival (late March/early April).

Performance Space
199 Cleveland Street, between George & Pitt Streets, Redfern (9698 7235/www.performancespace. com.au). CityRail Central or Redfern/LightRail Central/bus 352. **Box office** 10am-6pm Mon-Fri; and 1hr before show. **Tickets** $20-$25; $15 concessions. **Credit** MC, V. **Map** p329 E11.
A former Greek-language cinema and dance hall with a surviving sprung floor, the Performance Space is contemporary, funky and has the only foyer in Sydney where banging on about 'post-performative practice' won't earn you instant derision. Inconsistent for the best reasons, the P Space remains the best escape from the stultification of the post-post-another-signifier-for-'post' mainstream. Whatever, I'll have a Coopers.

Seymour Centre
Corner of City Road & Cleveland Street, Chippendale (box office 9351 7940/admin 9351 7944/ www.seymour.usyd.edu.au). Bus 422, 423, 426, 428. **Box office** 9am-5pm Mon-Fri; 11am-3pm Sat; 2hrs before performance. **Tickets** $15-$48; $10-$30 concessions. **Credit** AmEx, MC, V. **Map** p328 C11.
The Seymour Centre caters for a grab-bag of productions that have usually failed to find a better venue elsewhere. The main stage, designed with Tyrone Guthrie's open-stage model in mind, is a total flop. Apart from uni student work, it remains Sydney's premier space where good art goes to die.

Toby Schmitz's *Cunt Pi* at the **Old Fitzroy**.

Darling Harbour/bus 443. **Box office** 9am-5pm Mon-Sat; 11am-5pm Sun; later on show days. **Tickets** varies. **Credit** AmEx, DC, MC, V. **Map** p326 C6.
Designed for Lloyd-Webber musicals and similar fare, the Lyric is a state-of-the-art theatre that, like the Capitol, is suffering from the global decline in audiences for very expensive, beautifully marketed and generally content-free musicals. Of course, they occasionally lob into town, but the commercial failure of *The Producers* here in 2005 will reverberate for years to come.

New Theatre
542 King Street, between Angel & Knight Streets, Newtown (9519 3403/www.newtheatre.org.au). CityRail Newtown or St Peters/bus 422, 308, 370. **Box office** 9am-5pm Mon-Fri; and 1hr before show. **Tickets** $25; $20 concessions. **Credit** (phone bookings only) MC, V. **Map** p334.
An intimate 160-seater that's home to the New Theatre (*see p267*), Australia's most committed continuously producing company. Cheaper than chips and far more nourishing, the New is usually one of Sydney's best, and best-value, aesthetic options.

Old Fitzroy Hotel
129 Dowling Street, at Cathedral Street, Woolloomooloo (9294 4296/www.oldfitzroy.com.au). CityRail Kings Cross/bus 200. **Box office** from 6.30pm on show days. **Tickets** $27; $19 concessions; $33 beer/laksa/show. **Credit** MC, V. **Map** p330 H7.

Sidetrack Studio Theatre

142 Addison Road, at Illawarra Road, Marrickville (9560 1255/www.sidetrack.com.au). Bus 428. **Box office** 10am-5pm Mon-Fri; and 1hr before show. **Tickets** $22; $18 concessions. **Credit** MC, V.

Long-term home for multicultural ensemble Sidetrack Performance Group (*see p267*), this corrugated iron box is located right under the airport flight path. Not all resonant quaking is aesthetic, but this space often demonstrates how art can be improved via interrogation of regular stereotypes and regularly spaced, noisy jumbos.

Stables Theatre

10 Nimrod Street, at Craigend Street, Kings Cross (9361 3817/www.griffintheatre.com.au). CityRail Kings Cross. **Box office** (in person) 1hr before show. **Tickets** *Griffin productions* $39; $22-$29 concessions. *Other productions* varies. **Credit** AmEx, DC, MC, V. **Map** p330 J8.

Seating a closely packed and usually sweaty audience of 120 – after three decades of loved history, is functional air-con perhaps possible this millennium? – this actual ex-stables, complete with camp painted horses, is home to the Griffin company (*see p267*). New Oz is the house style, and fine productions and better acting make it a local treasure. **Photo** *p267*.

Star City Showroom

Star City Casino, 80 Pyrmont Street, between Jones Bay Road & Union Street, Pyrmont (9777 9000/www.starcity.com.au). LightRail Star City/ferry Darling Harbour/bus 443. **Box office** 9am-5pm Mon-Sat; 11am-5pm Sun; later on show days. **Tickets** varies. **Credit** AmEx, DC, MC, V. **Map** p326 C6.

It's big, it's brassy but at least you get bar service during the entertainment. Star City's 950-seat, cabaret-style room manages to recreate all the tackiness of Las Vegas. Often popular for jukebox musicals and stage versions of TV shows.

State Theatre

49 Market Street, between Pitt & George Streets, CBD (admin 9373 6852/www.statetheatre.com.au). CityRail St James or Town Hall/Monorail City Centre. **Box office** (in person) 9am-5pm Mon-Fri; and until 8pm on show days. **Tickets** $25-$120. **Credit** AmEx, DC, MC, V. **Map** p327 F6.

Designed at the dawn of talking pictures, the impossibly over-the-top State is Australia's only example of true rococo. All plaster and all fake, the State hosts the Sydney Film Festival (*see p229*) and rare theatre pieces too supersized to belong elsewhere. It's a good cinema and average sit-down music venue (*see p249*), but an awful live theatre, despite having more bad statuary per square inch than anywhere else on the planet.

Sydney Opera House

Bennelong Point, Circular Quay (box office 9250 7777/www.sydneyoperahouse.com). CityRail/ferry Circular Quay. **Box office** 9am-8.30pm Mon-Sat; and 2hrs before show Sun. **Tickets** *Opera Theatre* $50-$250; $52-$194 concessions. *Concert Hall* $40-$140; $33-$97 concessions. *Drama Theatre* $42-65; $43-$51 concessions. *Playhouse* $20-$50; $15-$35

Sydney Theatre, part of an expanding arts scene in Walsh Bay. *See p272.*

concessions. *Studio* $25-$35; $20-$25 concessions.
Credit AmEx, DC, MC, V. **Map** p327 G3.

Danish architect Jørn Utzon's difficult yet only famous child (we love it so much we let him go), the Opera House is a wonderful piece of sculpture masquerading as a functional arts venue. Despite the fact that it's best appreciated from the outside, experiencing the weirdness of Sydney's best-known built icon is probably essential. In addition to the Opera Theatre and the larger Concert Hall, it contains three theatre spaces: the Drama Theatre (oddly widescreen and distant), the smaller Playhouse (perhaps Sydney's worst mid-sized venue) and the Studio (a late attempt to reclaim the funk, a project that is still ongoing – *see p268* **House style**). Regardless of the building's drawbacks, the work can be good, with the STC (*see p268*), Ensemble (*see p267*) and Bell Shakespeare (*see p266*) all performing, plus touring shows. For music productions, *see p254*.

Sydney Theatre

22 Hickson Road, opposite Pier 6/7, Walsh Bay (9250 1999/www.sydneytheatre.org.au). CityRail/ferry Circular Quay then 15mins walk. **Box office** 9am-8.30pm Mon-Sat; 3-5.30pm Sun (show days only). **Tickets** $42-$80; concessions vary. **Credit** AmEx, MC, V. **Map** p327 E3.

New and nicely designed, the Sydney represents the acme of the city's lust for a well-done, stock-standard lyric theatre space. So after numerous tries, the town got one – with seating for nearly 900. Because it's programmed by the STC (*see p268*) the Sydney doesn't depend on the whims of commercial producers for its varying product. It often features good drama, and occasionally good dance, though its acoustic construction means you can't walk out before the interval without making a great deal of noticeable noise. Not that that stops anyone. It's almost opposite the Wharf Theatres. **Photo** *p271*.

Wharf Theatres

Pier 4/5, Hickson Road, Walsh Bay (9250 1777/ www.sydneytheatre.com.au). CityRail/ferry Circular Quay then 15mins walk. **Box office** 9am-7.30pm Mon; 9am-8.30pm Tue-Fri; 11am-8.30pm Sat; 2hrs before performance Sun. **Tickets** $42-$69; $51 concessions (not Fri, Sat). **Credit** AmEx, MC, V. **Map** p327 E2.

A converted wharf and warehouse on the western side of the Harbour Bridge, near the Sydney Theatre (*see above*). Surrounded by ever more swanky residential redevelopment, it houses the STC's (*see p268*) artistic, management and production staff, rehearsal space and a lovely restaurant, as well as two theatres, Wharf 1 and Wharf 2. The Sydney Dance Company (*see below*), Australian Theatre for Young People (*see p266*) and Bangarra (*see below*) also perform here. The complex also boasts Sydney's best foyer – on a summer's night, its G&T is well worth the view, if perhaps not the price. Get off at Circular Quay, walk through the Rocks and under the Bridge, and even before the show you'll experience aesthetic magic.

Dance

Keep an eye out for Gideon Obazarnek's once-groovy **Chunky Move** (www.chunky move.com). A Sydney-expat company based in Melbourne, the Chunksters usually visit Sydney once a year and are often worth catching.

Australian Ballet

1300 369 741/www.australianballet.com.au.

Australia's national classical ballet company is based in Melbourne and is a classic example of why static European art traditions don't always translate to new climes. The company usually performs two seasons of very stock-standard ballet a year at the Sydney Opera House (*see above*). People who care about ballet tend to become passionately attached to the company's offerings; for everyone else it's boiler-plate nostalgia with boiler-plate tutus. Attempts at modernising the repertoire are regularly howled down by the company's ageing fans, though they do try something vaguely modern most years. Along with Opera Australia (*see p255*), it's the only taxpayer-propped company that isn't required to programme new Australian work.

Bangarra Dance Theatre

9251 5333/www.bangarra.com.au.

Australia's leading contemporary indigenous dance company, Bangarra has been artistically directed by Stephen Page since 1991. Its value is in its mix of contemporary style with ancient Aboriginal traditions of physicality, movement and bodily storytelling. Consistently popular, Bangarra regularly tours the world and remains one of Australia's only distinctive arts exports. It is, like most things, cheaper at home.

National Aboriginal & Islander Skills Development Association

www.naisda.com.au.

NAISDA's work is based in traditional dance, but at its best becomes cross- (and often counter-) cultural. AIDT (Aboriginal & Islander Dance Theatre) and NAISDA's student ensemble regularly perform their fusion of traditional and contemporary dance around town – though this may change as they're planning to move out of Sydney, to Gosford on the Central Coast, in August 2006.

Sydney Dance Company

9221 4811/www.sydneydance.com.au.

In 2006 Graeme Murphy marked 30 years of running the Sydney Dance Company, which may show that you can have too much of a once-good thing. Wildly inconsistent, the SDC is always hoping that spotty international accolades will trump an increasingly obvious lack of ideas and failure of inspiration. The company finds its best successes these days with explorations of the vanilla edge of homo-erotica, but while it still has a loyal core of true believers and the occasional artistic success, the company is long overdue for a fresh blood transfusion.

Arts & Entertainment

Trips Out of Town

National Museum of Australia, Canberra. *See p288.*

Short Trips

Heavenly weekends away are essential to the Sydney life beautiful.

It's surprisingly easy to get away from bustling Sydney, and just a couple of hours' drive can reward you with spectacular new scenery. Head west for the **Blue Mountains**, historic towns and expanses of bushland; head north or south for pristine beaches, rainforest and national parks along the coasts. The wineries of the **Hunter Valley** are two hours' drive north of Sydney, while a trip south will take you to the gentle rolling hills and period villages of the **Southern Highlands**, and further on, **Canberra**, the federal capital.

The easiest way to travel about is by car – see p295 for car hire companies – but, where possible, we've also included details of local trains, buses and internal flights. Journey times are from central Sydney.

INFORMATION

CountryLink (central reservations 13 2232, www.countrylink.info) operates trains and coaches in NSW, around Canberra, and in Queensland and Victoria. Visit its website for details of its good-value multi-day train and tour packages to destinations in NSW.

For general information on areas around Sydney, visit the **Sydney Visitor Centre** (see p306). **Tourism New South Wales** (9931 1111, www.tourism.nsw.gov.au) will direct you to a regional tourist office.

Heading West

Blue Mountains

A mere two hours west of the CBD, the Blue Mountains are one of Australia's most popular natural playgrounds and a must-visit for any tourist. This spectacular wilderness covers over 10,000 square kilometres (almost 4,000 square miles) of breathtakingly beautiful and rugged country: in 2000 the **Blue Mountains National Park**, which covers nearly 2,500 square kilometres (965 square miles), was grouped together with six other nearby national parks to form the **Greater Blue Mountains World Heritage Area**. Most of it is so isolated from Sydney's urban sprawl to the east that it could hide a species of tree, the Wollemi pine, that was thought to have been extinct for 150 million years.

The Blue Mountains – in reality a maze of plateaus and dramatic gorges – are part of the Great Dividing Range, which separates the eastern seaboard and its cities from Australia's rural and desert heart. They only look blue from a distance, due to sunlight refracting through the eucalyptus oil that evaporates from the bush's legion of gum trees.

For decades after the first settlers arrived in Sydney, the Blue Mountains were thought to be impassable – but the very future of the colony depended on breaking through the dense bush and bridging its gaping canyons. With no sheep tracks to follow and river paths ending in crashing waterfalls, it took until 1813 before its secrets were finally unlocked and farmers had access to the sprawling fertile land beyond. Today the area is easily traversed by rail and car (thanks to the efforts of a group of prisoners who were offered pardons if they could complete the first road in a matter of months – they did).

The administrative region called the City of the Blue Mountains is a narrow strip of townships and villages snaking its way along a high plateau between vast tracts of virginal bush. The townships are usually deliberately picturesque, full of twee 'Olde Wares' shops and pricey 'Devonshire' teas. Lavishly restored cottages nestle amid English cold-climate gardens, though some residents are radically embracing native flora, often to the discomfort of older locals who like their traditional conifers, rose beds and topiary hedges.

With nature the area's star attraction, the best way to explore is by taking one or several of the numerous well-signposted and maintained bushwalks. These range from hour-long quickies to camping treks of several days' duration. Good advice on walks can be found at the **Blue Mountains Information Centre** (see p278). More adventurous types can enjoy rock climbing, abseiling and the thrill of riding mountain bikes in actual mountains.

Almost all Sydney-based tour companies offer a one-day bus trip for a quick look around, but the better (and cheaper) option is to catch a CityRail train from Sydney's Central Station. Trains depart hourly every day, and take around two hours to reach the upper mountains.

While most townships have their own bush trails, the centre of the action lies in the

It takes some imagination to see **Three Sisters**, but the mountains do look blue.

adjoining townships of **Katoomba** and **Leura**. One easy sightseeing option is the **Blue Mountains Explorer Bus** (4782 4807, www.explorerbus.com.au). It's a double-decker (for some reason painted in the livery of a red London bus) departing just across from Katoomba train station 11 times a day between 9.30am and 4.30pm ($29, $14.50-$25 concessions, $72.50 family). It stops at 30 resorts, galleries, tea rooms and general scenic attractions around Katoomba and Leura. You can get off and on as often as you like, and tickets are valid for up to seven days. CityRail also offers a combined train-plus-Explorer-bus ticket.

Katoomba is the most popular township for visitors thanks to its proximity to attractions such as the **Three Sisters** rock formation near Echo Point and **Scenic World** (see *p277*), where a range of gravity-defying vehicles grant spectacular views as you travel over and into the Jamison Valley. If you've got some time, descend the precipitous 841-step **Giant Staircase** next to the Sisters (only the genuinely athletic or masochistic should attempt to climb up it), and then do the two-and-a-half-hour easy walk through the Jamison Valley to the foot of the Scenic Railway for a sweat-free, mechanised ascent.

Katoomba is home to the Blue Mountains City Council, three pubs, a swathe of cafés and plenty of writers, artists and poets of steeply varying quality. Its chief built attractions are the 1880s **Carrington Hotel** (see *p277*) and the intimate and terribly 'heritage' **Paragon Café** (65 Katoomba Street, 4782 2928). There are also some excellent second-hand bookshops. The three best for dusty bibliophiles are **Brian's Books** (44 Katoomba Street, 4782 5115), **Mr Pickwicks** (86 Katoomba Street,

4782 7598) and **Blue Mountains Books** (92 Katoomba Street, 4782 6700).

Linked to Katoomba by bus, train, a panoramic cliff drive or a half-hour walk is Leura, with its more upmarket guesthouses, vastly smarter shops and manicured gardens: in local parlance, if Katoomba is Mount Penrith, Leura is Mount Paddington. One of the world's chintz capitals, Leura is a delight for all lovers of knick-knacks, baubles and ornamental flummery.

Further into the mountains beyond Katoomba, the **Hydro Majestic Hotel** (see *p277*) in Medlow Bath is popular for pricey coffee with an expansive view. More down to earth is the village of **Mount Victoria**, which is the starting point for many more fine mountain hikes.

On the northern side of the mountains, off the Bells Line of Road above the Grose Valley, is the quintessentially transplanted English hamlet of **Mount Wilson**. This charming village is best visited in spring or autumn, when some house-proud locals open their gardens for your viewing pleasure and herbaceous envy. It's also notable for **Withycombe** (corner of the Avenue and Church Avenue), the house where the parents of Australia's only Nobel literature laureate, Patrick White, lived for a time. For more natural splendour, try the hushed and majestic remnant rainforest grandiloquently named the **Cathedral of Ferns**.

Also in the area are the magnificent **Mount Tomah Botanic Gardens** (4567 2154, www.rbgsyd.nsw.gov.au).

You'll need to travel to the south-western edge of the Blue Mountains to reach the other main attraction in the area: the **Jenolan Caves** (6359 3311, www.jenolancaves.org.au).

Trips Out of Town

BLOODY RIPPER

That's Australian for **'frightfully good deal'**. It's why Red Spot is the local Australian car rental company that's taking the locals by storm. Red Spot offer ripper low prices and a non-rip-off policy of no hidden extras. The low rates are all-inclusive. Nothing more to pay. ● Free hotel delivery ● Airport collection and drop off ● Free touring guides ● Unlimited kilometers ● Latest model cars ● Book now on the web and your car will be waiting at the airport. When in Australia, do as the Aussies do. Rent your bloody car from Red Spot.

A tangled series of extraordinary underground limestone caverns, complete with stalagmites and stalactites, within a large and peaceful nature reserve, they're open 9am to 5pm daily ($17, $11.50 concessions, $44 family). The caverns come in two flavours – easy guided tours with walkways and steps, and various adventure caves requiring helmets, overalls and climbing (from $55). If you're less adventurous, a good two-cave tour is the Lucas Cave followed by the Orient Cave ($29.50, $20 concessions, $77 family).

Scenic World

Corner of Cliff & Violet Streets, Katoomba (4782 2699/www.scenicworld.com.au). **Open** 9am-5pm daily. **Tickets** *Skyway return trip* $16; $8 children; $40 family. *Cableway & Railway return trip* $16; $8 children; $40 family. **Credit** AmEx, DC, MC, V.

Views and vertigo are the main features of this collection of tourist transports. The Scenic Skyway – a cable-car system over the Jamison Valley – was renovated a few years ago. The new cars have glass floors, so now you can see it really is a long way down – 270m (890ft), in fact. The Scenic Railway features an old coal train reinvented as the world's steepest rail incline, which takes you down into the rainforested valley – as does the Scenic Cableway, another cable car ride. There's a 2km (1.25-mile) boardwalk between the lower Railway and Cableway stations, so you can go down on one and back on the other.

Where to stay & eat

Blue Mountains YHA

207 Katoomba Street, Katoomba (4782 1416/ fax 4782 6203/www.yha.com.au). **Rates** $24-$26 dorm; $72-$79 double; $116 family. **Credit** MC, V.

The Blue Mountains outpost of the YHA empire is an excellent modern hostel in a historic 1930s art deco building right in the centre of Katoomba. Won the gong for best backpacker accommodation in Oz at the 2005 Australian Tourism Awards.

Carrington Hotel

15-47 Katoomba Street, Katoomba (4782 1111/ fax 4782 7033/www.thecarrington.com.au). **Rates** from $190 B&B. **Credit** AmEx, DC, MC, V.

A gorgeous, rambling, old-style resort hotel with lots of antiques and oodles of 19th-century charm. Cocktails on the balcony are a must.

Hydro Majestic Hotel

Great Western Highway, Medlow Bath (4788 1002/ fax 4788 1063/www.hydromajestic.com.au). **Rates** from $195 midweek; $250 weekend. **Credit** AmEx, DC, MC, V.

An upmarket, beautifully restored historic hotel with astonishing views and a Victorian feel, once famous for its spa cures, hence the 'Hydro'. Worth a visit for tea and scones.

Take a tour

Plenty of tour operators run interesting and entertaining day trips in and around the Blue Mountains. Some tours start in Sydney, while others leave from Katoomba. The following outfits are recommended:

Australian School of Mountaineering

4782 2014/www.asmguides.com.

Based in Katoomba, ASM has provided outdoor training and guiding for more than two decades. It runs an impressive range of canyoning, rock climbing and abseiling trips: prices vary.

Fantastic Aussie Tours

4782 1866/1300 300 915/ www.fantastic-aussie-tours.com.au. **Prices** from $86.

A day tour to Jenolan Caves from Katoomba, with cave entrance. Cheaper tickets are offered for bushwalkers who just want a bus service to the caves.

High n Wild

4782 6224/www.high-n-wild.com.au. **Prices** from $95.

This Katoomba-based adventure outfit runs canyoning expeditions involving swimming, wading, and squeezing through tight spaces, and other outdoor fun options from bushwalking to ice climbing.

Oz Trek Adventure Tours

9360 3444/www.oztrek.com.au. **Prices** $55; $39 concessions.

A packed day trip from Sydney includes a visit to the Olympic site at Homebush, a tour of the major Blue Mountain sites and a one- to two-hour bushwalk.

Visitours

9499 5444/www.visitours.com.au. **Prices** from $84.

The Blue Mountains tour from Sydney also includes a stop at Featherdale Wildlife Park and the Olympic Park. Learn to throw a boomerang and play the didgeridoo.

Wonderbus

9555 9800/www.wonderbus.com.au. **Prices** from $65.

A range of tours to the Blue Mountains, including a day trip from Sydney that involves three hours of bushwalking and covers most of the area's main sites.

Trips Out of Town

Jenolan Caves House

Jenolan Caves (6359 3322/fax 6359 3227/www. jenolancavesresort.com.au). **Rates** (B&B plus dinner per person) from $75 midweek; $85 weekend. **Credit** AmEx, DC, MC, V.

Inside the caves complex, this dark, wood-panelled hotel with roaring fires has the feel of a grand English country house. Next door, the Gatehouse Jenolan offers four-bed dorms for $25 a head.

Lilianfels Blue Mountains

Lilianfels Avenue, Echo Point, Katoomba (4780 1200/fax 4780 1300/www.lilianfels.com.au). **Rates** from $330 midweek; $600 weekend. **Credit** AmEx, DC, MC, V.

This five-star pile perched just above Echo Point is the poshest accommodation in the mountains, with two famed restaurants and great views.

Getting there

By car

Springwood, Faulconbridge, Wentworth Falls, Leura, Katoomba & Mount Victoria Take Great Western Highway (Route 32) and/or Western Motorway (Route 4). It's 109km (68 miles) from Sydney to Katoomba – about 2hrs.
Kurrajong & Mount Tomah Take Great Western Highway (Route 32) or Western Motorway (Route 4); turn off to Richmond via Blacktown; then Bells Line of Road (Route 40). Mount Wilson is 6km (3.75 miles) off Bells Line of Road.
Jenolan Caves Take Great Western Highway (Route 32) via Katoomba and Mount Victoria; then turn south at Hartley; it's another 46km (29 miles) to the caves.

By train

Trains depart hourly from Central Station. It's about 2hrs to Katoomba.

Tourist information

Also check out the websites www.katoomba-nsw.com and www.bluemts.com.au.

Blue Mountains Information Centre

Echo Point Road, Katoomba (1300 653 408/ 4782 9865/www.australiabluemountains.com.au). **Open** 9am-5pm daily.

Heading North

Hawkesbury River

If you've ever wondered what the west coast of Scotland would look like without the rain, mist and midges, head to the stunning Hawkesbury River. It's like Argyll with sunshine. Skirting the outer edges of Australia's biggest city for much of its length, the great greenish-brown giant licks over 1,000 kilometres (620 miles) of

foreshore as it curls first north-east and then, from Wisemans Ferry, south-east towards the sea, emptying into an estuary at Broken Bay. The river's fjord-like saltwater creeks and inlets are ideal for exploring by boat, and houseboating holidays are popular.

The town of **Windsor** retains many of its original buildings, as well as its waterwheel and charm. Among the stalwarts is the oldest inn in Australia still being used for its original purpose (the Macquarie Arms, built in 1815), Australia's oldest courthouse (1822), St Matthew's Anglican Church, built by convict labour from a design by convict architect Francis Greenway (also in 1822), and the oldest Catholic primary school still in use (1836). Also of note is John Tebbutt's house and observatory, with its outsized telescope.

It's worth taking a cruise with **Hawkesbury Heritage Discovery Tours** (4577 6882, 0427 206 483), as you'll get the enthusiastic low-down on the area's history from a local guide.

Within easy reach of Windsor, there's more colonial architecture at **Richmond**, a tree-lined garden town whose railway station dates back to 1822, and **Ebenezer**, with Australia's oldest church (on Coromandel Road, built 1809).

The Hawkesbury's change of course is marked by an S-bend at **Wisemans Ferry**, another of the river's historic villages. It has Australia's oldest ferry service, which still runs 24 hours a day (and is one of the few remaining free rides in New South Wales). On the far side of the ferry is a section of the convict-built Great Northern Road, once 264 kilometres (164 miles) long, which shows just what sweat and toil really mean.

Up the road in the Macdonald River Valley, in the secluded hamlet of **St Albans**, is another colonial inn, the **Settlers Arms** (1 Wharf Street, 4568 2111). A couple of kilometres from here, in the Old Cemetery on Settlers Road, lies the grave of William Douglas, a First Fleeter who died in 1838. Rumours also suggest that St Albans was Windsor magistrates' preferred venue for illicit nooky over the years.

The lower reaches of the Hawkesbury are its most spectacular, with steep-sided forested banks and creeks branching off its wide sweep. Near the end of **Berowra Creek** (west of the Pacific Highway), at the foot of two deep, bush-covered hills, is beautiful **Berowra Waters**. There's not much here apart from a small car ferry, a cluster of bobbing boats and a few restaurants offering fine cuisine (including Hawkesbury oysters). Much of the remainder of the river, as it makes its way to the sea, is equally tranquil – notably the slender fingers of water that make up **Cowan Creek** (east of the Pacific Highway).

It's here, in the sweeping expanse of the **Ku-ring-gai Chase National Park**, that many people choose to cruise or moor for a spot of fishing.

If you haven't got time for houseboating, Australia's last **riverboat postman** may be the answer. The four-hour cruise from Brooklyn allows you to participate in the delivery of mail while taking in the scenery – an inside view that few see. The boat leaves Brooklyn Wharf at 9.30am weekdays, excluding public holidays: details on 9985 7566.

Otherwise, you could always hike from Berowra railway station down to Berowra Waters along a fascinating, well-marked bush track (part of the Great North Walk). A round trip takes about four hours.

Where to stay & eat

Able Hawkesbury Houseboats

3008 River Road, Wisemans Ferry (1800 024 979/ 4566 4308/www.hawkesburyhouseboats.com.au). **Rates** from $460 2 nights midweek. **Credit** MC, V.
Choose from seven different sizes of boat, ranging from 26ft to 48ft in length.

Berowra Waters Fish Café

199 Bay Road, Berowra (9456 4665). **Open** 9am-4pm Mon, Tue; 9am-9pm Wed-Sat; 8.30am-9pm Sun. **Main courses** $10-$15. **Credit** MC, V.
A great setting with views across the water. Serves fish and chips in various guises. BYO.

Court House Retreat

19 Upper Macdonald Road, St Albans (4568 2042/ fax 9871 0592/www.courthousestalbans.com.au). **Rates** from $160. **Credit** MC, V.

B&B accommodation (four double rooms) in a historic sandstone building that once housed a courtroom, police station and lock-up.

Retreat at Wisemans

Old Northern Road, Wisemans Ferry (4566 4422/ fax 4566 4613/www.wisemans.com.au). **Rates** from $95 midweek; $120 weekend. **Credit** AmEx, DC, MC, V.
Comfortable rooms with views of the golf course or river. The Riverbend Restaurant, serving Mod Oz food, is recommended (about $36 for two courses).

Ripples Houseboat Hire

87 Brooklyn Road, Brooklyn (9985 5534/www.ripples. com.au). **Rates** from $500 2 nights midweek. **Credit** MC, V.
Two kinds of boat, sleeping up to six or ten.

Getting there

By car

Richmond & Windsor It's 59km (37 miles) from Sydney to Windsor, and the journey takes 60-90mins. **Via Hornsby** Pacific Highway (Route 83) to Hornsby; Galston Road; then Pitt Town Road. **Via Pennant Hills** Epping Road (Route 2) to Pennant Hills; then Route 40. **Via Parramatta** Western Motorway (Route 4) to Parramatta; then Route 40.
Wisemans Ferry & St Albans Pacific Highway (Route 83) to Hornsby; Galston Road; then Old Northern Road.
Berowra Waters Pacific Highway (Route 83); 12km (7 miles) north of Hornsby, Berowra turn-off signed. The Brooklyn turn-off is 12km (7 miles) further north.

By train

Richmond & Windsor There's a regular train service to Windsor and the upper Hawkesbury River

The **Hawkesbury River** at Brooklyn.

area on the Richmond line (via Blacktown) from Central Station. Journey time is around 1hr.

Berowra Waters The main Sydney-Newcastle line from Central Station goes to Berowra Waters (via Berowra Station) and Brooklyn (via Hawkesbury River Station). The trip takes about 40mins (not all trains stop at both stations).

By bus

For details of coach services to the Hawkesbury region, contact the local tourist office (*see below*) or CountryLink NSW (13 2232, www.countrylink.info).

Tourist information

Hawkesbury River Information Centre

5 Bridge Street, Brooklyn (9985 7947). **Open** 9am-5pm Mon-Fri; 9am-4pm Sat; 10am-3pm Sun.

Tourism Hawkesbury

Ham Common, Windsor Road, Clarendon (4588 5895/www.hawkesburyweb.com.au). **Open** 9am-5pm Mon-Fri; 10am-3pm Sat; 10am-2pm Sun.

Hunter Valley

The second-most visited region in New South Wales after the Blue Mountains is the state's main wine-growing region – and that is the reason to visit. The area around the main town of **Pokolbin**, two hours north of Sydney, boasts more than 75 wineries (from the smallest boutiques to the big boys, such as Lindemans), which offer tastings and cellar-door sales of wine ranging from semillons and shirazes to buttery chardonnays. Mingled among the vineyards are award-winning restaurants and luxury hotels, but there are plenty of cheaper options too.

While such wine-based indulgence has put the Hunter firmly on the tourist map, the area's personality is, in contrast, also bound up with coal mining. The very waterway from which the region gets its name was originally known as the Coal River (it was renamed in 1797 after the then NSW governor, John Hunter), the founder of the Hunter's wine-making industry, Scottish civil engineer James Busby, arrived in Australia in 1824 partly to oversee coal-mining activities in nearby Newcastle. But while the Hunter Valley once boasted the largest shaft mine in the southern hemisphere, which held the world record for coal production in an eight-hour shift (Richmond Main Colliery, now a museum and open irregularly), all but two of its mines have now closed.

The wine industry sprouted from humble beginnings in the 1830s, but has fared rather better. The original vines were cuttings taken from France and pre-dated the phylloxera disease that tainted European wine. Thus

Australian grapes are now claimed to be more authentic than modern-day French wines, which use roots from American vines. Seeing out the tough 19th century, then the Depression of the 1930s and later fighting off competition from other antipodean wine regions, such as South Australia, the Hunter made it to the 1970s wine rush and ever since then it has done little but flourish.

Despite its small area – the main vineyard district north of the town of **Cessnock** is only a few kilometres square – the sheer number of wineries in the Lower Hunter Valley can present the wine tourist with a problem: where to start? Inevitably, familiarity leads many to the bigger, more established vineyards – which is a good way of gaining an insight into wine-growing traditions. Large family companies in Pokolbin, such as **Tyrrells** (Broke Road, 4993 7000), **Draytons** (Oakey Creek Road, 4998 7513) and **Tulloch** (Glen Elgin Estate, DeBeyers Road, 4998 7580) have been producing wine in the area for more than a century, while at **Lindemans** (McDonalds Road, 4998 7684) there's a museum exhibiting old wine-making equipment. Other big wineries, such as **Wyndham Estate** (Dalwood Road, Dalwood, 4938 3444), on the banks of the Hunter River itself and Australia's oldest continually operating winery, and **McGuigan Brothers** (McDonalds Road, 4998 7402), offer full on-site facilities, including galleries, museums, restaurants and cafés.

But it would be a shame to miss out on the smaller enterprises. Places such as **Oakvale** (set against the Brokenback Range, Broke Road, 4998 7520) offer the time and space for a more individual tasting experience. Many of these boutique wineries are set within picturesque surroundings. **Hungerford Hill** (Broke Road, 4998 7666) – formerly housed in a beautiful tiny converted church, and recently moved into a new landmark designer building – has some of the best 'stickies' (dessert wines and rich ports) in the area. The grounds of **Pepper Tree Wines** (Halls Road, 4998 7539) incorporate a former convent – the area's swishest guesthouse (*see p282*) – which was moved lock, stock and barrel to the Hunter for the purpose. Further afield, in Rothbury, the **Wandin Valley Estate** offers accommodation in villas, and has its own cricket ground. Talking of which, have a look at **Brokenwood** (McDonalds Road, 4998 7559) to enjoy its always cracking Cricket Pitch and Graveyard wines. And yes, they do both come from vines grown on cricket pitches and graveyards.

Look out for vintages produced in 1988, 2000 and 2003: these were the best years in the Hunter Valley for decades.

Since the Hunter is reasonably flat and compact, and the wineries are not far apart, it's a good place to ditch four-wheel transport. Bikes are available from some guesthouses for a small charge, while **Grapemobile** (0500 804038, 0418 404 039, 4991 2339, www.grapemobile.com.au) hires out bikes and also runs enjoyable day and overnight cycling and walking tours of the wineries from Cessnock. Finally, if you're not high enough already, see the regimented rows of vines from above with a sunrise balloon flight: try **Balloon Aloft** (1443 Wine Country Drive, North Rothbury, 1800 028 568, 4938 1955, www.balloonaloft.com) – prices vary based on the number of people and the season.

BARRINGTON TOPS

Although it's less than an hour's drive north of the Hunter Valley, the Barrington Tops is as different from the wine-growing district as it's possible to be. A national park with a world heritage listing, its upper slopes are thick with subtropical rainforest containing thousand-year-old trees, clean mountain streams and abundant wildlife. With its swimming holes, camping and bushwalking, the Barrington Tops is a domain for outdoor enthusiasts. The area can also be explored with mechanical help: try eco-specialist **Bush Track Tours** (0419 650 600, www.bushtracktours.com) – a full-day tour from Sydney costs from $172.50 per person for four people.

Further south are green hillocks and greener valleys, the sort of landscape that insists you jump out of bed straight on to the back of a horse or a mountain bike. If you have your own transport and three or four days to spare, you might consider visiting the triangle of attractions in this area – the Hunter Valley, Barrington Tops and Port Stephens. An excellent and unique place to base yourself is the award-winning **Eaglereach Wilderness Resort** (Summer Hill Road, Vacy, 4938 8233, www.eaglereach.com.au). Perched on a mountain top, you have vistas in all directions from your luxury log cabin (from $275 per person) set in 400 hectares (1,000 acres) of raw bushland. Despite the luxury, nature is on your doorstep – expect to see kangaroos at your window and giant lizards in the front yard.

Wine tours

While many vineyards offer tastings at the cellar door, the local cops rightly take exception to drink-driving, so the best idea may be to take an organised tour. You can travel in old-fashioned style in a horse-drawn carriage: **Pokolbin Horse Coaches** (4998 7305, 0408 161 133) offer regular tours and can custom-

design a tour (minimum four) to suit your needs. The **Hunter Valley Wine Country Visitor Centre** (see p282) has details of other outfits.

Activity Tours Australia

9904 5730/www.activitytours.com.au. **Rates** (with lunch) $95; $79 concessions.
Day trips from Sydney to the Hunter Valley, taking in five wineries, a tour to see how wine is made and a cheese factory. Maximum 19 people.

Hunter Vineyard Tours

4991 1659/www.huntervineyardtours.com.au. **Rates** $50; $75 with lunch.
Full-day tour in 12- or 22-seat buses, taking in five wineries (lunch optional) in the Cessnock area. Pick-up from local hotels.

Trekabout Tours

4990 8277/www.hunterweb.com.au/trekabout. **Rates** $35 half day (Mon-Fri only); $45 full day.
Half- or full-day winery tours for up to six people. The shorter tour visits four to five wineries; the full-day option gets to six or seven. You'll need to get yourself to the Hunter Valley – pick-up is from hotels in the Cessnock/Pokolbin area.

Where to stay & eat

Most Hunter Valley guesthouses will not take bookings for less than two nights, especially over weekends. Rates drop considerably midweek. There are more – and cheaper – hotels and motels in Cessnock.

Barrington Guest House

2940 Salisbury Road, 30mins drive from Dungog, Barrington Tops (4995 3212/fax 4995 3248/ www.barringtonguesthouse.com.au). **Rates** (full board, shared bathroom) from $95 per person. **Credit** MC, V.
Interesting guesthouse-style accommodation and luxury huts right on the edge of the rainforest. Semi-tame kangaroos stretch out on the lawns and the trees are thick with birds.

Barringtons Country Retreat

1941 Chichester Dam Road, 15mins drive from Dungog, Barrington Tops (4995 9269/fax 4995 9279/www.thebarringtons.com.au). **Rates** (minimum 2 nights) from $70 per person. **Credit** MC, V.
If you like to flirt with rural surroundings safe in the knowledge that modern comforts are close at hand, try this place. Log cabins overlooking the valley, spa baths and imaginative cooking at moderate rates.

Casuarina Restaurant & Country Inn

Hermitage Road, Pokolbin, Hunter Valley (4998 7888/fax 4998 7692/www.casuarinainn.com.au). **Rates** suite $285 Mon-Thur, Sun; $310 Fri, Sat. **Credit** AmEx, DC, MC, V.
Over-the-top themed suites are the thing here: pick from the Moulin Rouge, the Oriental, the Bordello,

Casanova's Loft, the Mariner's Suite, Out of Africa, Edwardian, Palais Royale and, finally, Romeo's Retreat. Plus a pool, tennis court and a pretty good Mediterranean-style restaurant.

Hunter Valley Gardens Lodge

Next to McGuigan Brothers Winery, corner of Broke Road & McDonalds Road, Pokolbin (4998 7600/fax 4998 7710/www.hvg.com.au). **Rates** B&B from $315 Mon-Thur, Sun; $710 Fri, Sat. **Credit** AmEx, DC, MC, V.

A pleasant place to lay your head, right in the heart of the wine area. The associated Harrigan's Irish Pub also has decent rooms from $235.

Peppers Convent Guest House

Grounds of Pepper Tree Wines, Halls Road, Pokolbin (4998 7764/fax 4998 7323/www.peppers.com.au). **Rates** (per person) from $186 Mon-Thur, Sun; from $189.50 Fri, Sat. **Credit** AmEx, DC, MC, V.

The ultimate indulgence, with lots of antiques and surrounding vineyards. One of the country's classiest restaurants, Robert's, is also here.

Wandin Valley Estate

Wilderness Road, Lovedale (4930 7317/fax 4930 7814/www.wandinvalley.com.au). **Rates** from $150. **Credit** AmEx, DC, MC, V.

Winery accommodation in four self-contained, well-appointed villas five minutes from Pokolbin.

Getting there

By car

Lower Hunter Valley Sydney-to-Newcastle Freeway (Route 1) to Freemans Interchange; then turn off to Cessnock (Route 82). Alternatively, leave Route 1 at Calga; head through Central Mangrove towards Wollombi; then turn off to Cessnock (Route 132). Journey time: 2hrs. The main wine-growing district around Pokolbin and Rothbury is about 12km (7 miles) north-west of Cessnock.
Barrington Tops The journey takes about 3hrs.
Direct route Sydney-to-Newcastle Freeway

(F3/Route 1) to Maitland turn-off on New England Highway (Route 15); Paterson Road; then turn right for Dungog approx 5km (3 miles) beyond Paterson.
Via Hunter Valley Follow signs from Cessnock to Maitland (via Kurri Kurri), then as above.

By train

Dungog, just south of Barrington Tops, is served by a few daily trains from Sydney (journey time just over 3hrs) via Newcastle (90mins). Some guesthouses will pick up from Dungog.

By bus

Rover Coaches (1800 801 012, 4990 1699, www.rover coaches.com.au) runs a daily service to the Hunter Valley from Sydney (departing at 7.30am, returning at 7.30pm), plus day and weekend tours of the region; call for departure points. Keans Travel (1800 043 339, 4990 5000) also operates a regular coach service (not Sat).

Tourist information

Gloucester Visitor Information Centre

27 Denison Street, Gloucester (6558 1408/www. gloucester.org.au). **Open** 8.30am-5pm Mon-Fri; 8.30am-3pm Sat, Sun.
For information on the Barrington Tops.

Hunter Valley Wine Country Visitor Centre

111 Main Road, Pokolbin (4990 4477/www.wine country.com.au). **Open** 9am-5pm Mon-Fri; 9.30am-5pm Sat; 9.30am-3.30pm Sun.
You can also book accommodation here.

Port Stephens

The third point in a triangle of northern attractions that includes the Hunter Valley and Barrington Tops, Port Stephens Bay is a beautiful stretch of water most famous for its whale and dolphin cruises. Two pods of

You can drink in more than the view in the **Hunter Valley**. *See p280.*

dolphins – around 70 individuals – inhabit the bay, and your chances of getting up close to them are very high. Whales come into the calmer waters of the bay on their migration route from Antarctica.

The main town in the area is **Nelson Bay**, on the northern bank of the harbour, where you'll find hotels, restaurants and takeaways.

Several operators run good dolphin- and whale-watching tours. Highly recommended is a cruise on **Imagine** (5104 Nelson Bay Road, Nelson, 4984 9000, www.imaginecruises.com.au), a luxury catamaran operated out of Nelson Bay Marina by Frank Future and Yves Papin. All year except June and July they offer a daily two-hour dolphin trip departing at 10.30am ($22, $14-$18 concessions), and a range of longer cruises departing from D'Albora Marina. There's a boom net on board, which is lowered over the edge for thrill-seekers to lie in and get really close to the dolphins. They also operate humpback whale cruises from June to mid November. You can also go looking for dolphins in a kayak with **Blue Water Sea Kayaking** (40 Victoria Parade, Nelson Bay, 4981 5177, www.seakayaking.com.au).

Another option for nature lovers is a visit to the **Tomaree National Park** (4984 8200, www.nationalparks.nsw.gov.au) on the southern shore of the inner harbour. Here, you can see low-flying pelicans skidding on to land on the water, and there's a large breeding colony of koalas at **Lemon Tree Passage**. And if you have access to a 4WD, you can't miss **Stockton Beach**, a 32-kilometre (19-mile) expanse of sand starting at Anna Bay, where you can drive through the waves or even take a shot at dune-bashing over the towering silica hills (providing you have someone to help tow you out when you get stuck – or overturn).

Fighter World (Medowie Road, Williamtown, 4965 1717, www.fighterworld. com.au, $7, $5 concessions, $20 family) is also worth a visit for those with kids or a military bent. An offshoot from the RAAF Williamtown airbase, it celebrates Australia's fighter-plane history with a wide variety of exhibits including Meteors, Mirages and Vampires.

Where to stay & eat

Peppers Anchorage Port Stephens
Corlette Point Road, Corlette (4984 2555/fax 4984 0300/www.peppers.com.au). **Rates** (per person) $142.50-$213.50 midweek; $184-$255 weekends (minimum 2 nights). **Credit** AmEx, DC, MC, V.
Part of the Peppers chain, this is a top-class resort right on the water. Private balconies offer sweeping views across the bay.

Port Stephens Motor Lodge
44 Mangus Street, Nelson Bay (4981 3366/fax 4984 1655). **Rates** $80-$155. **Credit** AmEx, DC, MC, V.
A motel-like place located a short stroll from the main township. There's also a swimming pool.

Salamander Shores
147 Soldiers Point Road, Soldiers Point (4982 7210/ fax 4982 7890/www.salamander-shores.com). **Rates** from $149 midweek. **Credit** AmEx, DC, MC, V.
A pleasant hotel with standard motel accommodation, lovely rooms with balconies and sea views, and a pretty garden. There's a good restaurant too.

Getting there

By car
Take Sydney-to-Newcastle Freeway (F3/Route 1); it's a 2.5hr drive.

By train
CityRail trains run almost hourly from Central Station to Newcastle. Buses connect with the trains for transfers to Port Stephens.

By bus
Port Stephens Coaches (1800 045 949, 4982 2940, www.pscoaches.com.au) runs a daily service to Nelson Bay, departing Eddy Avenue, Central Station, Sydney, at 2pm. It leaves Nelson Bay for the return trip daily at 9am. The journey takes 3.5hrs.

Tourist information

Port Stephens Visitor Information Centre
Victoria Parade, Nelson Bay (4980 6900/ www.portstephens.org.au). **Open** 9am-5pm daily.

Heading South

South Coast

According to most of the people who live there, particularly residents of the Shoalhaven region (which stretches 160 kilometres/100 miles south of the town of Berry), this is the area of New South Wales that has it all: wilderness galore, including large tracts of national park and state forest; beaches so long and white they make Bondi look like a house party at a sewage dump; some of the cleanest, clearest water in Australia; a bay 82 times the size of Sydney Harbour, with pods of crowd-pleasing dolphins; easy access to magnificent mountain vistas; heritage and antiques; 'surfing' kangaroos at Pebbly Beach, just south of Ulladulla; and the best fish and chips in the country at Bermagui (head for the marina and just follow the seagulls).

Trips Out of Town

Whale of a time

Each year, more than 3,000 humpback and southern right whales migrate north along the NSW coastline from their winter feeding grounds in the Antarctic to their summer breeding ground off the tropical Queensland coast. They are joined by a scattering of minke whales and pygmy killer whales. The migration starts in early June, and by the middle of the month has really hotted up. The peak month for the return trip is September, though you can see stragglers up to mid November. The best time of day for spotting whales is around midday, when glare off the water is at a minimum, though the sun at dawn can also help by backlighting the telltale spout.

The best place to see whales from land is where the coast juts out into deep water. Some great areas are **Byron Bay** (in the north of the state) and **Eden** (in the south), though there are also good spots nearer to Sydney: **North Head**, at the entrance to Sydney Harbour; the headlands either side of **Botany Bay**; and **Barrenjoey Head**, just past Palm Beach.

Whales love to pop into sheltered bays too, to feed and rest: **Jervis Bay** and off **Ulladulla** are exceptional whale-watching spots. **Dolphin Watch Cruises** (*see p285*) runs three-hour whale cruises to Jervis Bay in June, July and from mid September to mid November (departing at 9.30am, $43, $28-$37 concessions, $120 family).

Port Stephens is also on the migration route. **Imagine** (*see p283*) runs two daily cruises during June, July and the October school holidays (9.30am, 1.30pm, $55, $30-$50 concessions). From August to mid November, there's just one cruise, at 1.30pm. The trip lasts about four hours.

More and more whales are coming right into **Sydney Harbour** itself these days. A few years ago, a pair of them chose to mate right under the Harbour Bridge, upon which everyone left work and home to head for the harbour for a look. And an albino humpback dubbed Migaloo (Aboriginal for 'white fella') has been adopted by the city: reports on its movement when nearby are broadcast on TV and radio. Diving company **Pro Dive** (*see p259*) offers twice-daily, three-hour trips from Sydney in June and July ($95, $85 concessions; not recommended for children under ten).

If you're driving from Sydney along the Princes Highway (Route 1), take a quick detour towards Stanwell Park and drive along Hargrave Road between Coalcliff and Clifton to marvel at the spectacular new **Sea Cliff Bridge**, which twists and turns as it hugs the rocky coastline below and the ragged cliffs at your side. Back on the Princes Highway and beyond the Royal National Park, the first region you encounter is Illawarra, the administrative centre of which is the city of **Wollongong**. It's perhaps unfair to view Wollongong as one of the two ugly sisters on either side of Sydney (the other being Newcastle), but as you approach its smoking industrial surroundings it's hard not to.

The road then begins to slide prettily between the coast on one side and the beginnings of the Southern Highlands on the other (Illawarra comes from an Aboriginal word meaning 'between the high place and the sea'). The first seaside town worthy of a stop is **Kiama**. The town's main attraction is the **Blow Hole**, which spurts spray up to 60 metres (200 feet) into the air from a slatey, crenellated outcrop next to a comparatively tranquil harbour. Also by the harbour is a fresh fish market, while on the way into town there's a block of 1885 quarrymen's cottages that have been renovated and turned into restaurants and craft shops. On the way out, don't miss the wonderful sign 'Stan Crap – Funeral Director'.

Kiama is a good base for exploring the subtropical **Minammurra Rainforest**, the **Carrington Falls** and nearby **Seven Mile Beach**, an undeniably impressive caramel arc, backed by a hinterland of fir trees.

An alternative base is the tree-lined inland town of **Berry**, a little further south. It's an entertaining hybrid of hick town and quaint yuppie heaven, where earthy locals mix with weekending Sydneysiders in search of antiques and fine dining. The former are catered for by a couple of daggy pubs, while many of the latter bed down at the **Bunyip Inn Guest House** (*see p285*).

JERVIS BAY

Undoubtedly the Shoalhaven region's greatest attraction, and the one that drives normally restrained commentators to reach for their superlatives, is Jervis Bay. A huge place, it encompasses the wonderful **Booderee National Park** and 56 kilometres (34 miles) of shoreline. It also has a history of close shaves. First, in 1770, Captain Cook sailed straight past it on the way towards Botany Bay, recording it only as 'low-lying wetlands' and missing entirely its deep, wide natural harbour (which made it an ideal alternative to Sydney as fulcrum for the new colony). Later, this ecologically sensitive beauty spot was mooted as a possible port for Canberra and the ACT. And in 1975, Murrays Beach, at the tip of the national park, was chosen as a site for a nuclear reactor (a project thankfully defeated by public protest).

These narrow escapes and a fortuitous lack of population growth around Jervis Bay mean that this coastal area remains one of the most undisturbed and beautiful in Australia. Divers testify to the clarity of its waters; swimmers are sometimes literally dazzled by the whiteness of its sands (Hyams Beach is said to be the whitest in the world). It's not just popular with people: among its regularly visiting sea and bird life are fur seals, giant rays, whales (southern right, pilot and killer), sharks, sea eagles, penguins and many, many more.

A good way to get a feel for Jervis Bay and meet its resident bottlenose dolphins is to hook up with **Dolphin Watch Cruises** (50 Owen Street, Huskisson, 4441 6311, www.dolphin watch.com.au), which also runs whale cruises. **Huskisson**, the launching point for the cruises, is one of six villages on the shores of the bay. It's got a couple of accommodation options, two dive shops – **Deep6Diving** (64 Owen Street, 4441 5255, www.deep6divingjervisbay.com.au) and **Seasports** (47 Owen Street, 4441 5598, www.jbseasports.com.au) – wonderful fish and chips, and a pub with a bistro, the **Husky Pub** (4441 5001) on Owen Street. Just south of Jervis Bay there is excellent sailing, snorkelling and swimming at **St George's Basin**, and fishing at **Sussex Inlet**.

You could stay in Huskisson, but it's well worth bringing a tent to get a proper feel for the Booderee National Park (admission $10 per vehicle per day), which is jointly managed by the local Aboriginal community. The best place to camp is at **Caves Beach**, where you wake up to the calls of birds and eastern grey kangaroos. **Green Patch** has more dirt than grass, but better facilities and can accommodate camper vans as well. The Christmas/New Year period sees a ballot for places. Book through the park's visitor centre (*see p286*).

ULLADULLA

Despite all the stunning scenery around Jervis Bay, it can be worth venturing further south to the sleepy fishing town of Ulladulla for somewhere to stay. Ulladulla's protected harbour may not quite recall Sicily, but the town has a sizeable Italian fishing community (guaranteeing decent local pizzas and pasta), and the **Blessing of the Fleet** is an annual event on Easter Sunday. From here it's easy to access wilderness areas to the west and further

south – **Budawang** and **Murramarang National Parks** – plus yet more expansive beaches, such as **Pebbly Beach** (which is actually sandy) with its resident kangaroos.

Where to stay & eat

Bunyip Inn Guest House
122 Queen Street, Berry (4464 2064/fax 4464 2324). **Rates** from $50. **Credit** AmEx, DC, MC, V.
A National Trust-classified former bank with 13 individually styled rooms, one with a four-poster bed. There's also a swimming pool.

Huskisson Beach Tourist Resort
Beach Street, Huskisson (4441 5142/ www.huskissonbeachtouristresort.com.au). **Rates** from $30 camping; $85 cabin. **Credit** MC, V.
This resort offers various cabins (including self-catering ones) as well as plenty of camping spots right opposite the beach. There's a pool too.

Jervis Bay Guest House
1 Beach Street, Huskisson (4441 7658/fax 4441 7659/www.jervisbayguesthouse.com.au). **Rates** from $145. **Credit** AmEx, DC, MC, V.
This four-and-a-half-star guesthouse opposite a beach has just four rooms, with balconies overlooking the sea and the sunrise, and is a short walk to the shops and restaurants in Huskisson. All this makes it very popular, so book well ahead.

Ulladulla Guest House
39 Burrill Street, Ulladulla (1800 700 905/4455 1796/fax 4454 4660/www.guesthouse.com.au). **Rates** from $170. **Credit** AmEx, DC, MC, V.
A popular five-star option with great service and ten lovely rooms. It also has self-catering units, a pretty saltwater pool, sauna, spa, small gym, art gallery and an excellent French restaurant.

Getting there

By car
Take Princes Highway (Route 1). Allow at least 2hrs to Jervis Bay, 3hrs to Ulladulla and slightly longer to Pebbly Beach.

By train
There are regular trains from Central Station to Wollongong, Kiama, Gerringong, Berry and Bomaderry (for Nowra and Ulladulla), via the South Coast line, changing trains at Dapto. It's 3hrs to Bomaderry; from there a limited coach service operated by Premier Bus Services (13 3410, www.premierms.com.au) continues on through Nowra as far as Ulladulla.

By bus
Interstate coaches travelling the Princes Highway between Sydney and Melbourne stop at many of the towns mentioned above. There are also local bus and coach services along the coast. Contact the local tourist offices for more details.

Tourist information

Booderee National Park Visitors Centre
Jervis Bay Road, Jervis Bay (4443 0977/www. booderee.np.gov.au). **Open** 9am-4pm daily.

Shoalhaven Tourist Centres
www.shoalhaven.nsw.gov.au/region. Corner of Princes Highway & Pleasant Way, Nowra (1300 662 808/4421 0778). **Open** 9am-5pm daily. *Princes Highway, Civic Centre, Ulladulla (4455 1269).* **Open** 10am-5pm Mon-Fri; 9am-5pm Sat, Sun.

Tourism Kiama
Blowhole Point Road, Kiama (4232 3322/ www.kiama.com.au). **Open** 9am-5pm daily.

Southern Highlands

The Southern Highlands, known by wealthy 19th-century Sydneysiders as the 'sanatorium of the south' for its cool climes and fresh air, has recently experienced something of a renaissance as a tourist destination. It's easy to see why – just a two-and-a-half-hour train ride from Sydney, the area has well-preserved villages such as Berrima (founded 1831), fading stately homes such as Ranelagh House in Robertson and a range of cosy accommodation, all set in a gently undulating landscape so easy on the eye that it evokes a different country (even before the area was first settled, Governor Macquarie said it reminded him of England).

There's some truth to the local saying that the Southern Highlands are mostly for 'the newly-weds and the nearly-deads', but there is something here for most tastes: the highlands encompass tropical and subtropical rainforest, the second-largest falls in NSW and the edge of Morton National Park, where you can walk on the wild side.

Of the many pleasant approaches by car, two leading from the main coastal road (Princes Highway) stand out. The first is to take the Illawarra Highway (from Albion Park) through **Macquarie Pass National Park**; the second is to take the tourist drive from just beyond Berry. The route from Berry – rising, bending and finally dropping towards the **Kangaroo Valley** – is often romantically thick with mist, but on even a partly clear day it affords luscious views of the countryside.

Kangaroo Valley Village, despite its iron roofs and sandstone-pillared Hampden Bridge (built in 1897), is a little disappointing, but the walking and camping nearby are excellent, as are canoeing and kayaking on the **Kangaroo River** (contact Kangaroo Valley Tourist Park near the bridge, 4465 1310, www.holidayhaven.com.au/kangaroovalley).

Leaving Kangaroo Valley, the road rises and twists once more before leading you to the **Fitzroy Falls**. A short saunter from the impressive **Fitzroy Falls Visitor Centre** (4887 7270, open 9am-5.30pm daily) and you are amid scenery that's as Australian as Paul Hogan. There are five falls in the vicinity, but Fitzroy is the nearest and biggest, plummeting 81 metres (266 feet) into Yarunga Valley. Take any of the walks around the falls and you could encounter 48 species of gum tree, lyre birds and possibly a wombat.

Another way of exploring the top end of underrated **Morton National Park** is to use the town of **Bundanoon** as a base for bushwalking and cycling. Bundanoon, which means 'a place of deep gullies', is as Scottish in flavour as its name sounds. Every year in the week after Easter the town transforms itself into Brigadoon for a highland gathering, featuring traditional games, Scottish dancing and street parades. Bundanoon was also once known as the honeymoon centre of the Southern Highlands – in its heyday it had 51 guesthouses – but these days the bedsprings rarely squeak, as it has largely fallen out of fashion.

Slightly north of the forgettable town of Moss Vale is **Berrima**, considered Australia's finest example of an 1830s village. This is the town the railways forgot, so many of its early buildings remain in pristine condition. A highlight is the 1838 neo-classical **Court House** (corner of Wilshire and Argyle Street, 4877 1505, www.berrimacourthouse.org.au) with its sandstone portico and curved wooden doorways. Don't miss the reconstruction of the 1843 trial of the adulterous Lucretia Dunkley and her lover: particularly good is the judge's sentencing of the pair for the murder of her dull husband. Other historic buildings include **Harper's Mansion** and Australia's oldest continually licensed hotel, the **Surveyor General Inn** (*see p287*), both built in 1834.

An unexpected delight on the long road to Bowral is **Berkelouw's Book Barn** (Old Hume Highway, 4877 1370, open 9.30am-5pm daily), containing some 200,000 second-hand books. Bowral itself is attractive enough, especially during the spring Tulip Festival, but its biggest claim to fame is as the town that gave Australian cricket the late Donald Bradman. The great man is honoured in the **Bradman Museum** (St Jude Street, 4862 1247, www.bradman.org.au, open 10am-5pm daily, $8.50, $4-$7 concessions, $22 family) on the edge of the lush Bradman Oval, opposite the old Bradman home. If cricket doesn't captivate you, then take a trip up **Mount Gibraltar**, overlooking the surrounding countryside, and the view surely will.

About 60 kilometres (37 miles) west of the town of Mittagong (via part-dirt road), the mysterious and beautiful **Wombeyan Caves** feature a number of unique encrustations and deposits. You can take a guided tour, and there's on-site accommodation and camping: contact the **Wombeyan Caves Visitor Centre** (Wombeyan Caves Road, Taralga, 4843 5976, www.jenolancaves.org.au, open 8.30am-5pm daily) for details.

Destined to become the area's most famous village, and all because of a talking pig, is the sleepy hollow of **Robertson**, where the film *Babe* was shot. Almost the entire cast is on the breakfast menu at **Ranelagh House** (*see below*). On the way back to Sydney, be sure to take the road out of Robertson to the Princes Highway for some spectacular sea views as you twist and turn your way down the hillside.

Where to stay & eat

Briars Country Lodge & Inn

Moss Vale Road, Bowral (4868 3566/fax 4868 3223/www.briars.com.au). **Rates** from $150 midweek; $245 weekend. **Credit** AmEx, DC, MC, V.
A country retreat with 30 garden suites set in beautiful parkland. Adjacent to the lodge is the Georgian Briars Inn (c.1845), which has a true country atmosphere, with cosy bars and bistro food. You can even take in a bit of fly fishing in the hotel lake.

Bundanoon Country Hotel

Erith Street, Bundanoon (4883 6005/fax 4883 6745/www.countryinn.com.au). **Rates** (per person) $55-$73. **Credit** AmEx, DC, MC, V.
This creaky old hotel boasts a wonderful billiards table, Nea Hayes's famous pies and the occasional poetry reading.

Ranelagh House Guesthouse

Illawarra Highway, Robertson (4885 1111/fax 4885 1130/www.ranelagh-house.com.au). **Rates** (per person) from $55 midweek; $70 weekend. **Credit** AmEx, MC, V.
The best place in the area to take a leisurely cream tea. It also offers a 'country-style' lunch and has a good dinner menu.

Surveyor General Inn

Old Hume Highway, Berrima (4877 1226/fax 4877 1159/www.highlandsnsw.com.au/surveyorgeneral). **Rates** (per person) from $60 midweek; $80 weekend. **Credit** AmEx, MC, V.
The rooms are simple, with brass beds and a shared bathroom, but the inn oozes historical charm.

Getting there

By car

The inland route (120km/75 miles) via Hume Highway (Route 31) takes just under 2hrs. The coastal route is via Princes Highway (Route 60); then turn inland on Illawarra Highway (Route 48) by Albion Park. It's slightly longer (130km/80 miles) and slightly slower (just over 2hrs).

By train

Trains to the Southern Highlands depart from Sydney's Central Station every day. Most stop at Mittagong, Bowral, Moss Vale and Bundanoon. The journey takes about 2.5hrs.

By bus

Several bus companies serve the area, including Greyhound (13 2030, www.greyhound.com.au) and Priors Scenic Express (1800 816 234, 4472 4040).

Tourist information

Tourism Southern Highlands

62-70 Main Street, Mittagong (1300 657 559/ 4871 2888/www.southern-highlands.com.au). **Open** 9am-5pm Mon-Fri; 8.30am-4.30pm Sat, Sun.

Canberra

Canberra, sitting in its own Australian Capital Territory (ACT), was created in 1911 as the compromise choice of federal capital to end the squabbling between arch-rivals Sydney and Melbourne. It's always been dogged by bad press. It's the city that people from other Australian cities love to hate, the New Zealand of intra-Australian jokes ('a waste of a good sheep paddock'), regarded by detractors as a sterile, low-level metropolis full of also-(Canber)rans, a mundane mecca for politicians and bureaucrats. For those Australians who have visited the city, Canberra can also evoke some less than favourable memories of being escorted (by the ears if necessary) around endless exhibitions and galleries as a kid, or of getting lost in the car among the city's eccentric circles.

There's some truth to those clichés. Yet Canberra is also loved with a passion by many of its residents, who point to its space, clean air, tranquillity and proximity to unspoilt bushland. There were few trees on the plains around Canberra when white settlers came; hundreds of thousands have been planted since. New householders were given two trees to plant in front of their homes in exchange for not building walls or fences – perhaps a factor in the dreadful bushfires around Christmas 2002, when some 200 houses burned to the ground.

Whether you side with Canberra's detractors or defenders is partly a matter of taste and partly a matter of perception. On a clear day, viewed from **Mount Ainslie**, the **Telstra Tower** (Black Mountain Drive, Acton, 1800 806 718, 6219 6111) or the basket of a hot-air

Trips Out of Town

Canberra's **Parliament House** lets light into the business of government.

balloon (try **Balloon Aloft**, 7 Irving Street, Phillip, 6285 1540, www.balloon.canberra. net.au), Canberra can appear stately, elegant and positively Washingtonesque. Back on the ground, the city may seem less disorienting from the saddle of a bicycle. In fact, compared with the murderous streets of Sydney, Canberra is a cyclist's heaven, with relatively flat terrain, plenty of cycle paths, negligible traffic (riding is permitted on pavements, anyway) and most of the sights within easy pedalling distance.

Doing a circuit of the central artificial **Lake Burley Griffin** (a two-hour ride) might even win you over to the vision of 'the city beautiful' that Canberra's architect, Walter Burley Griffin, originally had in mind. The **National Capital Exhibition** (Regatta Point, Commonwealth Park, 6257 1068, www.national capital.gov.au, open 9am-5pm daily, free) is on a knoll overlooking the lake. The exhibition provides further insights into Griffin's competition-winning design for Canberra, eloquently drawn by his wife Marion Mahoney. There is also a model of the city, which makes it a good starting point for a tour.

Whatever Canberra's faults, as federal capital it can claim to have many of Australia's most important national monuments, buildings and galleries, the most significant (and visited) being Parliament House, the Australian War Memorial, the National Gallery of Australia and the **National Museum of Australia** (Lawson Crescent, Acton Peninsula, 6208 5000, www.nma.gov.au, 9am-5pm daily, free). The latter, which opened in 2001, is the first official museum dedicated to the nation of Australia. It utilises state-of-the-art technology and

hands-on exhibits to take visitors through Aboriginal and Torres Strait Islander cultures and histories, Australian society and its history since 1788, and the interaction of people with the Australian environment. It relies heavily on image and sound rather than actual objects, so might not be everyone's cup of tea.

Opened in 1988, **Parliament House** (6277 5399, www.aph.gov.au, 9am-5pm daily, free) might look like an oversized wigwam from afar – thanks to an 81-metre (265-foot) stainless-steel flagpole – but it's as imposing as it is humble, as human as it is functional. From its position on Capital Hill it dominates Canberra's landscape, yet its turfed roof allows people to stand above their elected representatives. The foyer, the Great Hall and both chambers (Senate and House of Representatives) are airy and refreshingly bathed in natural light, and there are displays of Australian art and photos. Interesting free guided tours take place every 30 minutes from 9am to 4pm – try to join one early, before the coaches arrive. You can also view the goings-on in both chambers from the public galleries when parliament is in session.

Beneath this comparative baby of a building, but far from eclipsed by it, stands the **Old Parliament House** (6270 8222, 9am-5pm daily, $2), Australia's seat of democracy from 1927 to 1988. Opposite the main entrance, somewhat incongruous among the manicured lawns and rose gardens, is the **Aboriginal Tent Embassy**, a haphazard collection of tents and wobbly-looking structures hung with flags and a campfire. It was established in 1972 in protest at the government's refusal to recognise Aboriginal land rights: the founders described the site as an embassy because of their sense of alienation from their own land. Since then, the Tent Embassy has been removed, rebuilt, demolished, threatened by fire and relocated – only to move back again. It was recognised by the Australian Heritage Commission in 1995, ensuring its future protection, though that has done nothing to reduce the controversy it provokes among both indigenous and non-indigenous people.

Old Parliament House is also home to the **National Portrait Gallery** (King George Terrace, Parkes, 1800 779 955, 6270 8236, www.portrait.gov.au, 9am-5pm daily) and the **National Archives** of **Australia** (Queen Victoria Terrace, Parkes, 6212 3600, www.naa.gov.au). With leather sofas and film noir-ish frosted windows embossed in gold lettering, the latter reeks of the machinations of Australia's political past. Just down the road, and reputedly once linked to Old Parliament House by a white line so that worse-for-wear politicians could find their way there at night, is the **Hotel Kurrajong** (6234 4444, www.hotelkurrajong.com.au). Once the Canberra home of prime ministers and other eminences, it's now a lovely boutique hotel and also home to the Australian International Hotel School.

Located nearby is Australia's foremost art institution, the **National Gallery of Australia** (Parkes Place, Parkes, 6240 6411, www.nga.gov.au, 10am-5pm daily, free), which houses good collections of international, Australian, Aboriginal and Torres Strait Islander art, as well as major exhibitions from overseas that often bypass Sydney. Next door is the innovative **Questacon National Science & Technology Centre** (King Edward Terrace, Parkes, 6270 2800, www.questacon.edu.au, 9am-5pm daily, $14, $8-$9.50 concessions), with hands-on exhibits and a fairly realistic earthquake simulation.

On the other side of the lake stands the **Australian War Memorial** (Treloar Crescent, top of Anzac Parade, Campbell, 6243 4211, 10am-5pm daily, free). Commemorating as it does the country's 102,000 war dead from 11 international military involvements since 1860, this is a poignant place – especially the Hall of Memory and the Tomb of the Unknown Soldier.

If you've ever wondered how Australia, with its relatively small population, is able to produce so many top-class athletes, a visit to the **Australian Institute of Sport** (Leverrier Crescent, Bruce, 6214 1111, www.ausport.gov.au) and its Sports Visitor Centre on the city's outskirts will shed some light. It's a university for the country's elite sportspeople, and a tour ($13, $10 concessions), led by one of the sleek and toned resident athletes, will probably leave you guiltily pondering your fat content.

The name Canberra is derived from an Aboriginal word for 'meeting place': local tribes used to gather to feast on bogong moths, which

The medium is the message at the spectacular **National Museum of Australia**. *See p288.*

can end up here in their millions after being blown off course (they migrate from the grassy plains further north to high spots along the Great Dividing Range where they hole up for the summer). While the range of Canberra's cuisine has obviously grown since then, it can still seem something of a gastronomic desert after Sydney. However, in the suburb of Manuka, near the Parliamentary Triangle, you'll find the city's café culture alongside a cluster of restaurants and clubs.

The capital rarely gets overcrowded, except during the annual **Celebrate Canberra Festival** (6207 5369, www.celebratecanberra. com), held over ten days in March. This colourful event marks the city's founding in 1913 and includes hot-air balloons, exhibitions, theatre, music and dance. There's also **Floriade** (6205 0044, 6205 0666), a big and cheery celebration of all things floral. It usually runs from mid September to mid October.

Where to stay & eat

Canberra has one of the highest room-occupancy rates in Australia, so book ahead.

Brassey Hotel
Belmore Gardens, Barton (6273 3766/fax 6273 2791/www.brassey.net.au). **Rates** from $132. **Credit** AmEx, DC, MC, V.
A historic boutique hotel within walking distance of most attractions.

Canberra City YHA
7 Akuna Street, Canberra City (6248 9155/ www.yha.com.au). **Rates** from $24 dorm; $70 double/twin. **Credit** MC, V.
Opened in 2006, Australia's newest YHA has its own pub, café, pool, spa and sauna.

The Chairman & Yip
108 Bunda Street, Civic (6248 7109). **Open** noon-2.30pm, 6-10.30pm Mon-Fri; 6-10.30pm Sat. **Main courses** $25-$29. **Credit** AmEx, DC, MC, V.
Popular with political bigwigs, the Chairman serves modern Asian food, with lots of fish.

food@therepublic
20 Allara Street, Civic (6247 1717). **Open** 7am-4.30pm Mon-Fri. **Main courses** $13-$22. **Credit** AmEx, DC, MC, V.
A top-class café offering great dining in cutting-edge surroundings.

Medina Classic Canberra
11 Giles Street, Kingston (6239 8100/fax 6239 7226/www.medinaapartments.com.au). **Rates** from $149. **Credit** AmEx, DC, MC, V.
Just minutes from Parliament House in fashionable Kingston, the Medina has comfortable and very good-value one-, two-, and three-bedroom suites. There's a heated pool, spa and gym too.

Mezzalira
Melbourne Building, 55 London Circuit, Canberra City (6230 0025). **Open** noon-2.30pm, 6-9pm Mon-Fri; 6-9pm Sat. **Main courses** $18-$26. **Credit** AmEx, MC, V.
Smart modern Italian food in a converted bank.

Olims Canberra Hotel
Corner of Ainslie & Limestone Avenues, Braddon (6243 0000/fax 6243 0001/www.olimshotel.com). **Rates** from $145. **Credit** AmEx, DC, MC, V.
Set in manicured lawns and just a short walk from the city, Olims has simple but comfortable enough rooms, with a couple of pleasant dining options.

Rydges Lakeside Canberra
London Circuit, at Edinburgh Street, Canberra City (1800 026 169/fax 6257 3071/www.rydges.com). **Rates** from $240. **Credit** AmEx, DC, MC, V.
This is the prime city address at which to stay, next to Lake Burley Griffin.

Tilley's Devine Café Gallery
Corner of Brigalow & Wattle Streets, Lyneham (6247 7753/www.tilleys.com.au). **Open** 9am-11pm Mon-Sat; 9am-6.30pm Sun. **Main courses** from $7.90. **Credit** AmEx, MC, V.
A huge bar and pavement café, and a major venue for touring music acts – it stays open later on Fridays and Saturdays if there's a band playing.

Getting there

By air
Canberra has a small domestic airport about 15mins drive from the city centre. Both Qantas (13 1313) and Virgin Blue (13 6789) fly there several times a day; the trip from Sydney takes 30-40mins.

By car
Canberra is 288km (179 miles) south of Sydney. Take M5 motorway connecting with the Hume Highway (Route 31); turn off to Canberra on Federal Highway beyond Goulburn. Journey time: 2.5hrs in a Ferrari, but allow up to 3.5hrs.

By train
CountryLink's very handy Xplorer train service (13 2232, www.countrylink.info) runs from Central Station to Canberra and back again three times a day. The trip takes just over 4hrs.

By bus
Most big firms run services to Canberra; try Firefly Express (1300 730 740, www.fireflyexpress.com.au) or Greyhound (13 2030, www.greyhound.com.au).

Tourist information

Canberra Visitor Centre
330 Northbourne Avenue, Dickson (1300 554 114/6205 0044/accommodation 1300 733 228/ www.canberratourism.com.au). **Open** 9am-5.30pm Mon-Fri; 9am-4pm Sat, Sun.

Directory

Features

Directory

Getting Around

Arriving & leaving

By air

Sydney Airport (9667 9111, www.sydneyairport.com.au) is on the northern shoreline of Botany Bay, nine kilometres (six miles) south-east of the city centre. Opened in 1920, it's one of the oldest continuously operating airports in the world. Since a swanky upgrade for the 2000 Olympics, it's now among the world's best – and quite proud of it.

There are three terminals: **T1** is for all international flights on all airlines and for QF (Qantas) flights 001-399; **T2** is a domestic terminal for Virgin Blue, Regional Express, Jetstar and QF flights 1600 and above; **T3** is the Qantas terminal for QF domestic flights 400-1599.

The international terminal is a great place to shop, with more than 100 outlets ranging from ordinary duty-free stores and international designer showcases to Aussie gear such as Mambo, Rip Curl and RM Williams, plus souvenir outlets selling Aboriginal artefacts and kitsch mementos.

GETTING TO AND FROM THE AIRPORT

Built for the Olympics, the **Airport Link rail service** (131 500, www.airportlink.com.au) between Sydney Airport and Central Station runs an efficient service every ten minutes from both international and domestic terminals. The line is a spur of the green CityRail line, so serves all the main inner-city interchanges. It takes ten minutes to reach Central Station from the domestic terminals and 13 minutes from the international one. Trains run from 5.19am to 12.30am Monday to Friday and from 5.09am to 12.46am Saturday and Sunday.

A single fare from the international terminal to Central Station costs $12.60 ($8.60 under-16s); it's $12 ($8.30 under-16s) from the domestic terminals. The rail link was put up for sale in 2006, so there may be changes afoot.

Bus-wise, the excellent **KST Sydney Airporter** (9666 9988, www.kst.com.au) shuttle runs a door-to-door service to all hotels, major apartment blocks and backpacker joints in the city, Darling Harbour and Kings Cross. A single costs $10 ($5 under-12s). Look for the white buses with a blue and red logo outside Bay 1 at T1 and directly outside both T2 and T3. Book three hours in advance for hotel pick-ups and give yourself plenty of time to get to the airport, as the shuttle will take twice as long as a taxi.

Each terminal has its own sheltered **taxi** rank, with supervisors in peak hours to ensure a smooth and hassle-free flow of taxis. You never have to wait for long, even in the vast sheep-pen-style queuing system of the international terminal, where 190 vehicles are on call. If you have any special needs – wheelchair access, child seats or an extra-large vehicle – go to the front of the queue and tell the supervisor, who will call you a specially fitted taxi. It takes about 25 minutes to get into the city, depending on the traffic and time of day, and costs around $25 plus $2 airport toll.

The main car rental companies all have desks at the airport; for more info on driving in Sydney, *see p295*.

AIRLINES: INTERNATIONAL

Around 40 airlines operate regular international flights into Sydney, including:

Air Canada 1300 655 767/ www.aircanada.com
Air New Zealand 13 2476/ www.airnewzealand.com.au
British Airways 1300 767 177/ www.britishairways.com
Cathay Pacific 13 1747/ www.cathaypacific.com
Emirates 1300 303 777/ www.emirates.com
Garuda Indonesia 1300 365 330/ www.garuda-indonesia.com
JAL (Japan Airlines) 9272 1111/ www.jal.co.jp

Malaysia Airlines 13 2627/ www.malaysiaairlines.com.my
Qantas 13 1313/ www.qantas.com.au
Singapore Airlines 13 1011/ www.singaporeair.com
Thai Airways 1300 651 960/ www.thaiair.com
United Airlines 13 1777/ www.ual.com
Virgin Atlantic 1300 727 340/ www.virgin-atlantic.com

AIRLINES: DOMESTIC
Jetstar 13 1538/www.jetstar.com.au
Qantas 13 1313/www.qantas.com.au
Regional Express (Rex) 13 1713/ www.regionalexpress.com.au
Virgin Blue 13 6789/ www.virginblue.com.au

By bus

Lots of bus companies operate throughout Australia. Handily, they all use the **Sydney Coach Terminal** located in Central Station as their main pick-up and drop-off point. National carrier **Greyhound** (13 2030, from abroad +61 7 4690 9950, www.greyhound.com.au), transports more than a million passengers a year.

By rail

The State Rail Authority's **CountryLink** (central reservations 13 2232, www.countrylink.info) operates out of Central Station with extensive user-friendly services to all main NSW and interstate destinations.

By sea

International cruise liners, including the *QE2*, dock at the **Overseas International Passenger Terminal** located on the west side of Circular Quay, or around the corner in **Darling Harbour**.

Public transport

To get around Sydney you'll probably use a combination of trains, ferries, buses and maybe the 'airborne' Monorail or the chic LightRail streetcars. As well as the Sydney Buses network (run by the State Transit Authority, STA), there are CityRail trains and Sydney Ferries. The other transport services are privately run and therefore generally more expensive. The centre of Sydney is so small that if you're in a large group, it's often cheaper to pool for a taxi.

Transport Infoline

13 1500/www.sta.nsw.gov.au.
Phone enquiries 6am-10pm daily. A great, consumer-friendly phone line and website offering timetable, ticket and fare information for STA buses, Sydney Ferries and CityRail, plus timetabling (only) for cross-city private bus services.

Fares & tickets

There are several combination travel passes covering the government-run transit system, and they're worth buying if you plan extensive use of public transport.

TravelPass

Unlimited seven-day, quarterly or yearly travel throughout the zones for which it has been issued, on buses, trains and ferries. These passes are aimed at commuters, but can be useful if you're in Sydney for any length of time. To find the right TravelPass for you, check the STA website or ask at any train station or bus information kiosk (where you can also buy them). Newsagents displaying a Sydney Buses Ticket Stop sign, and ticket offices or vending machines at Circular Quay and Manly also sell passes.

Passes are also available for a combination of buses and ferries, or for travel solely by bus, ferry or train. TravelPasses cannot be used on the STA premium Sydney Explorer and Bondi Explorer bus services, Sydney Ferry harbour cruises, JetCats or private buses.

SydneyPass

This one is specifically aimed at tourists. Unlimited travel on selected CityRail trains, buses (including premium services such as the Explorer buses) and ferries (including premium services such as JetCats and cruises). Valid for any three, five or seven days within an eight-day period. A three-day pass costs $100 ($50 concessions, $250 family); for a five-day pass it's $130 ($65 concessions, $325 family); and $150 ($75 concessions, $375 family) for a seven-day pass.

DayTripper

Unlimited one-day travel on buses, ferries and CityRail trains until 4am – but not on the Explorer buses or JetCats. It costs $15 ($7.50 under-16s) and is available on board buses, from STA offices and at Sydney Ferries ticket offices.

BusTripper

A pass offering unlimited all-day travel on buses only – except for the premium Explorer bus services. It costs $11.30 ($5.60 under-16s).

Buses

Buses are slow but fairly frequent, and offer a better way of seeing the city than the CityRail trains, which operate underground within the centre. Buses are the only option for transport to popular areas such as Bondi Beach, Coogee and the northern beaches (beyond Manly), which aren't served by either train or ferry. Sydney is divided into eight zones; the city centre is zone 1. The minimum adult fare is $1.70 (80c concessions), which covers two zones.

The bus driver will not stop unless you hold out your arm to request a ride. Pay the driver (avoid big notes) or validate your travel pass in the machine at the door.

The bus route numbers give you an idea of where they go. Buses **131-193** service Manly and the northern beaches; **200-296** the lower north shore (including Taronga Zoo) and the northern suburbs; **300-400** the eastern suburbs (including Bondi, Paddington, Darlinghurst and Sydney Airport); **401-500** the inner south and inner west suburbs, including Balmain, Leichhardt, Newtown and Homebush; and **501-629** the north-west including Parramatta and Chatswood. In general, the 100s and 200s start near Wynyard Station and the 300s-600s can be found around Circular Quay.

Bus numbers starting with an 'X' are express services, which travel between the suburbs and major centres on the way into the city. Stops are marked 'Express'. Limited-stop or 'L' services operate on some of the longer routes to provide faster trips to and from the city (mainly for commuters).

Buses in the central and inner suburbs run pretty much all night, but services from central Sydney to the northern beaches stop around midnight. **Nightrider** buses operate hourly services to outer suburban train stations after the trains have stopped running until 5am.

STA also runs the tourist-oriented **Sydney Explorer** and **Bondi Explorer** bus services. For full details of both these, and private bus tours, *see p56.*

CityRail

CityRail (www.cityrail.nsw. gov.au) is the passenger rail service covering the greater Sydney region (and the sister company to CountryLink, covering country and long-distance routes within NSW). The sleek, double-decker silver trains run underground on the central **City Circle** loop – Central, Town Hall, Wynyard, Circular Quay, St James and Museum stations – and overground to the suburbs (both Central and Town Hall stations provide connections to all the suburban lines). Although certainly quicker than the bus, trains are not as frequent as many would like and waits of 15 minutes, even in peak time, are not uncommon. For one of the best rides in Sydney, take the

Directory

train from the city to the north shore – it passes over the Harbour Bridge and the views are spectacular.

CityRail tickets can be bought at ticket offices or vending machines at rail stations. Expect huge queues in rush hour. A single ticket anywhere on the City Circle costs $2.20 ($1.10 under-16s); an off-peak return costs $2.60 ($2.20 under-16s).

For more details of CityRail services, call the **Transport Infoline** (*see p293*) or visit **www.cityrail.info**. For a map of the CityRail city network, *see p336*.

Ferries

No trip to Sydney would be complete without clambering aboard one of the picture-postcard green-and-yellow ferries that ply the harbour and are used daily by hundreds of commuters. All ferries depart from Circular Quay ferry terminal, where **Sydney Ferries** operates from wharves 2 to 5. These stately vessels are a great way to explore the harbour: there's plenty of room to take pictures from the outdoor decks or just to sit in the sun and enjoy the ride. JetCats – sleek, fast catamarans – operate a service to Manly, taking 15 minutes, as opposed to 30 minutes on an ordinary ferry.

Ticket prices vary, but a single from Circular Quay to destinations within the Inner Harbour costs $5 ($2.50 under-16s). A single JetCat fare is $7.50. If you plan to use the ferries a lot, the FerryTen pass covers ten rides within the Inner Harbour and costs $32.50 ($16.20 concessions); and $46.60 ($23.30 concessions) to Manly (by ferry only, not the JetCat). A JetCatTen costs $65.70.

Tickets are sold at ticket offices and vending machines at Circular Quay and Manly.

Tickets for Inner Harbour services can also be purchased from on-board cashiers. For a map of the ferry system, *see p335*. For details of Sydney Ferries' **sightseeing cruises**, *see p58*.

Sydney Ferries Information Centre

Opposite Wharf 4, Circular Quay (9207 3170/www.sydneyferries.info). CityRail/ferry Circular Quay. **Open** 6.45am-6.15pm Mon-Sat; 7.15am-6.15pm Sun. **Map** p327 F4.

Metro LightRail

In 1997 Sydney welcomed back its streetcars. Trams were abolished in the early '60s, but the privately run Metro LightRail, operated by Veolia Transport Sydney (which is also in charge of the Metro Monorail), now provides a slick 14-station service from Central Station via Darling Harbour, Pyrmont and Star City casino to the inner west. It's especially useful for visiting Darling Harbour, Paddy's Market, the excellent Sydney Fish Market, Glebe and the Powerhouse Museum.

Trams operate 24 hours a day, seven days a week, between Central and Star City stations, and from 6am to 11pm Monday to Thursday and Sunday, 6am to midnight Friday and Saturday, from Central all the way out to Lilyfield in the west. Trams run about every ten to 15 minutes from 6am to 11pm, and every 30 minutes outside these hours. The line is divided into two zones. Single tickets for zone 1 cost $3 ($1.80 concessions), and tickets for both zones cost $4 ($3 concessions). A Day Pass offers unlimited trips for $8.50 ($6.50 concessions). Tickets are available from Central Station or on board the train.

For more info, call 9285 5600 or visit **www.metro lightrail.com.au**.

Metro Monorail

Sydneysiders are not great fans of the noisy aerial monorail that runs anti-clockwise around the CBD at first-floor office level, but it's often the first thing tourists notice and does provide a fun, novelty ride between Darling Harbour, Chinatown and the city centre. It runs every three to five minutes, 7am to 10pm Monday to Thursday, 7am to midnight Friday and Saturday, 8am to 10pm Sunday.

The seven-station loop costs $4.50 (free under-5s) whether you go one stop or all the way. A Supervoucher Day Pass ($9) offers a full day of unlimited travel, plus some discounts on museum admissions. Tickets can be bought at station ticket offices or vending machines.

For more details, call 9285 5600 or visit **www.metro monorail.com.au**.

Taxis

It's quite easy to flag down a taxi in Sydney and there are many taxi ranks in the city centre, including ones at Central, Wynyard and Circular Quay. Staff in a restaurant or bar will also call a taxi for you. A yellow light indicates the cab is free, and it's common to travel in the front passenger seat alongside the driver. Drivers will often ask which of two routes you want to follow, or if you mind if they take a longer route to avoid traffic. But there are swags who don't know where they're going and will stop to check the map; if this happens, make sure they turn off the meter. Tipping is not expected, but passengers sometimes round up the bill.

The standard fare is $1.62 per kilometre from 6am to 10pm (add an extra 20 per cent from 10pm to 6am), plus a $2.80 hiring fee and, if relevant, a $1.40 telephone booking fee. If a cabby takes you across the Bridge, the $3 toll will be added to the fare, even if you travelled via the toll-free northbound route.

Taxi companies

Legion Cabs 13 1451/ www.legioncabs.com.au
Premier Cabs 13 1017/ www.premiercabs.com.au
RSL Cabs 9581 1111/ www.rslcabs.com.au
St George Cabs 13 2166/ www.stgeorgecabs.com.au
Silver Service Taxis 13 3100/ www.silverservice.com.au
Sydney's popular luxury taxi service; amazingly, the same price as a regular taxi, but often hard to book.
Taxis Combined Services 13 3300/www.taxiscombined.com.au
Wheelchair Accessible Taxis Service 1800 043 187

Water taxis

Great fun, but expensive. The cost usually depends on the time of day and the number of passengers, but the fare for two from Circular Quay to Doyles fish restaurant at Watsons Bay, which takes ten to 12 minutes, is around $60. The outfits below accept all major credit cards, and can be chartered for harbour cruises.

Beach Hopper Water Taxis

0412 400990/www.watertaxi.net.au.
If you want to be dropped off at a beach – literally on to the sand – call Sydney's only purpose-built beach-landing water taxi service. It also operates a summer 'Beach Safari' service: for $35 per person per day, you can hop on and off at any number of harbour beaches on its run.

Water Taxis Combined

9555 8888/www.watertaxis.com.au.
This company can pick you up from almost any wharf, jetty or pontoon provided there is enough water depth, and, in the case of private property, there is permission from the owner. The limousine taxis take up to 20 passengers.

Driving

Driving in Sydney can be hair-raising, not so much because of congestion (Sydneysiders may complain, but it's not at all bad for a major city), but primarily because of the fast and furious attitude of locals.

Under Australian law, most visitors can drive for as long as they like on their domestic driving licence without the need for any additional authorisation. A resident must apply for an Australian driving licence after three months, which involves a written test. You must always carry your driving licence and your passport when in charge of a vehicle; if the licence is not in English, you need to take an English translation as well as the original licence.

Driving is on the left. The general speed limit in cities and towns is 60kph (38mph), but many local and suburban roads have a 50kph (30mph) limit. The maximum speed on highways is 100kph (60mph), and 110kph (70mph) on motorways and freeways. Speed cameras are numerous and there are heavy penalties for speeding. The legal blood alcohol limit is 0.05 per cent for experienced drivers, zero for provisional or learner drivers. Seat belts are mandatory and baby capsules or child seats must be used for all children.

Fuel stations

Petrol stations are fairly plentiful, and easy to find on main roads, although you won't find so many in central Sydney. At the time of writing, the cost of petrol (regular unleaded) was 122c per litre.

Parking

In central Sydney parking is a pain and not recommended. In some suburbs, such as tree-lined Paddington, the quality of the road surface is poor, and narrow one-way streets with parking on both sides compound the problem. Note that you must park in the same direction as the traffic on your side of the road.

Rates at city-centre car parks range from $5 to $20 for one hour, with $30 to $65 the day rate. 'Early Bird' special rates often apply if you park before 9am and leave after 3.30pm. Look under 'Parking Stations' in the *Yellow Pages* for more car parks.

Secure Parking

155 George Street, at Alfred Street, CBD (9241 2973/www. secureparking.com.au). **Open** 7am-10.30pm Mon-Wed; 7am-11pm Thur; 7am-1am Fri; 8.30am-1am Sat; 9am-10pm Sun. **Credit** AmEx, DC, MC, V. **Map** p327 F4.
Other locations: Harris Street, Ultimo (9660 7068); 1 Martin Place, entrance on Pitt Street, CBD (9552 6318).

Wilson Parking – Cinema Centre

521 Kent Street, between Bathurst & Liverpool Streets, CBD (9264 5867/www.wilsonparking.com.au). **Open** 24hrs daily. **Credit** AmEx, DC, MC, V. **Map** p329 E7.
Other locations: City Group Centre, 2 Park Street, CBD (9261 4710); St Martin's Tower, Clarence Street, CBD (9261 5568).

Tolls

The toll for the Harbour Bridge and Tunnel is currently $3 for cars heading south (free for northbound cars). The toll for the 'eastern distributor' is $4.50 for northbound cars travelling into the city, free for those heading out or south. The Cross-City Tunnel (www. crosscity.com.au) running west to east opened in 2005 to ease congestion in the CBD, but at the time of writing has failed to attract drivers, so the toll has been slashed to $1.87 from its initial $3.56 – considered extortionate for a trip of just over two kilometres.

Vehicle hire

Most of the major car rental firms are situated near one another on William Street in Kings Cross, and also have outlets at Sydney Airport. Rates vary almost hourly and all offer discounted deals. What's given below is the rate for the cheapest hire car available for a one-day period quoted on a given day. Rates drop if the car is hired for a longer period. We list some of the major car hire companies below, but more outfits are listed in the *Yellow Pages* under 'Car &/or Minibus Rental'. Those offering ultra-cheap deals should be approached with caution, though: always read the small print before you sign.

You will need to show a current driver's licence and probably your passport. Credit cards are the preferred method of payment and are nearly always asked for to cover insurance costs, even if you do eventually pay by cash or travellers' cheque. A few firms will rent to 18-year-olds, but usually you have to be 21 and hold a full driving licence to rent a car in NSW. If you're under 25, you'll probably have to pay an extra daily surcharge, and insurance excesses will be higher.

Avis

200 William Street, at Dowling Street, Kings Cross (9357 2000/ www.avis.com.au). CityRail Kings Cross. **Open** 7.30am-6.30pm Mon-Thur, Sat, Sun; 7.30am-7pm Fri. **Rates** (unlimited km) from $58/day. **Credit** AmEx, DC, MC, V. **Map** p330 H7.
Other locations: Central Reservations (13 6333/9353 9000); Sydney Airport (8374 2847).

Budget

93 William Street, at Crown Street, Kings Cross (8255 9600/ www.budget.com.au). CityRail Kings Cross. **Open** 7.30am-6pm daily. **Rates** (unlimited km) from $64/day. **Credit** AmEx, DC, MC, V. **Map** p329 G7.
Other locations: Central Reservations (1300 362 848); Sydney Airport (9207 9160).

Hertz

Corner of William & Riley Streets, Kings Cross (9360 6621/www.hertz. com.au). CityRail Kings Cross. **Open** 7.30am-7pm daily. **Rates** (unlimited km) from $50/day. **Credit** AmEx, DC, MC, V. **Map** p329 G8.

Other locations: Central Reservations (13 3039); Sydney Airport (9669 2444).

Red Spot

202-210 Elizabeth Street, at Campbell Street, Surry Hills (1300 668 810/9211 1144/www.redspot rentals.com.au). CityRail/LightRail Central. **Open** 8am-6pm Mon-Fri; 8am-noon Sat, Sun. **Rates** (unlimited) $79/day. **Credit** AmEx, DC, MC, V. **Map** p329 F9.
Other locations: Sydney Airport (9352 7466/9317 2233).

Thrifty

75 William Street, at Riley Street, Kings Cross (8374 6177/www. thrifty.com.au). CityRail Kings Cross. **Open** 7.30am-6pm daily. **Rates** (unlimited km) from $52/day. **Credit** AmEx, DC, MC, V. **Map** p329 G8.
Other locations: Central Reservations (1300 367 227); Sydney Airport (1300 367 227).

Cycling

Sydney's steep hills, narrow streets and chaotic CBD make cycling a challenge, even for the most experienced of cycle couriers. However, Centennial Park and Manly both offer safe cycle tracks. Helmets are compulsory for all cyclists, including children carried as passengers. During the day a bicycle must have at least one working brake and a bell or horn. At night, you'll need a white light at the front and a red light at the rear, plus a red rear reflector. There are lots of other road rules, as cycles are considered to be vehicles: for full details, see **www.rta. nsw.gov.au**. You may get fined if you break the rules.

Cycle nuts are vocal in Sydney and are being heeded by the state-sponsored Bike Plan 2010, which promises the creation of a series of arterial cycle networks across NSW, resulting in 200 kilometres (125 miles) of bikeways being constructed across the state each year until 2010. The RTA provides 'Cycleways' maps for the Sydney metropolitan area. View them online at www.rta. nsw.gov.au or phone 1800 060 607 to get hard copies.

Centennial Park Cycles

50 Clovelly Road, between Avoca & Earls Streets, Randwick (9398 5027/www.cyclehire.com.au). Bus 339. **Open** 8.30am-5.30pm Mon-Fri; 8am-6pm Sat, Sun. **Rates** mountain bikes from $12/hr; children's bikes from $10/hr. **Credit** AmEx, MC, V. **Map** p333 N14.
Family-run, Sydney's largest cycle and rollerblade hire shop has been in operation for more than 30 years. They have everything here, from tandems to tricycles, pedal cars and scooters. They also provide a bicycle pick-up and delivery service. Credit card details and photo ID are required to hire equipment.

Manly Cycle Centre

36 Pittwater Road, at Denison Street, Manly (9977 1189/ www.manlycycles.com.au). Ferry Manly. **Open** 9am-6pm Mon-Wed, Sat; 9am-7pm Thur; 10am-5pm Sun. **Rates** $15/hr; $35/day. **Credit** AmEx, MC, V. **Map** p334.
Located a block from Manly Beach, this full-service bike shop hires out front-suspension mountain bikes, and even jogging pushchairs for ultra-fit mums and dads. Credit card details and photo ID are necessary.

Woolys Wheels

82 Oxford Street, at Greens Road, Paddington (9331 2671/www.woolys wheels.com). Bus 378, 380, L82. **Open** 9am-6pm Mon-Wed, Fri; 9am-8pm Thur; 10am-4pm Sat, Sun. **Rates** from $39/day. **Credit** AmEx, DC, MC, V. **Map** p332 J9.
A Paddo institution, hiring high-quality, 21-speed hybrid bikes, from one day up to a week. A $400 deposit is always required.

Walking

Walking is often the most practical – and enjoyable – way of getting around central areas, though there can be long waits for pedestrian lights. There are a number of marked scenic walks that you can do: ask at the **Sydney Visitor Centre** (*see p306*) for details. Some harbour and beachside walks are detailed in the Sightseeing chapters. For self-guided historical walks, *see p12* **Walk into history**.

For central Sydney street maps, *see pp326-334*. To buy street maps, travel guides and national park walking guides, visit **Map World** (*see p193*).

Resources A-Z

Addresses

Addresses begin with the apartment or unit number, if any, followed by the street number, followed by the street name. For example, Apartment 5, 50 Sun Street would be written as 5/50 Sun Street. This is followed by the locality and then by the state or territory and postcode – for instance, Paddington, NSW 2021. Postcodes cover a much larger area than their UK equivalents. Many residents and businesses have post office box numbers instead of personalised addresses.

Age restrictions

It is legal to buy and consume alcohol at 18. A learner's driving licence can be applied for at 16. A driving test can be taken at age 17, and if passed, drivers must then show a provisional 'P' plate (red P for one year, green P for two years), before being eligible for a full driving licence. Both gays and heterosexuals can have sex at 16 in NSW (though be warned, laws vary from state to state). It is illegal to sell cigarettes to anyone under 18, but there is no legal minimum age for smoking.

Business

Conventions & conferences

Sydney Convention & Exhibition Centre

Darling Harbour (9282 5000/ www.scec.com.au). Ferry Darling Harbour/Monorail/LightRail Convention. **Map** p328 D7.
This integrated centre has 30 meeting rooms and six exhibition halls, plus two business centres, in-house catering and audio-visual services, 24-hour security and parking for more than 900 cars.

Couriers & shippers

Australia Post (13 1318, www.auspost.com.au) has national and international courier services: **Messenger Post Courier** is the national service, while **Express Courier International (ECI)** dispatches to more than 180 countries. Other services you could try include **Allied Express** (13 1373, www.allied express.com.au) and **DHL Worldwide Express** (13 1406, www.dhl.com.au).

Office hire & business services

The multinational **FedEx Kinko's** chain (www.kinkos.net.au) has several branches around Sydney, some of which are open round the clock for internet access, self-service computers, photocopying and printing. The company also offers commercial shipping.

Servcorp

Level 17, BNP Centre, 60 Castlereagh Street, between King Street & Martin Place, CBD (9231 7500/www.servcorp.com.au). CityRail Martin Place. **Open** 8.30am-5.30pm Mon-Fri. **Credit** AmEx, DC, MC, V. **Map** p327 F6.
Servcorp offers prime office space in the CBD, North Sydney and North Ryde for one- to 15-person companies with full business services (minimum lease one month) – and it claims to be cheaper than a secretary. Especially geared to foreign clients, with a multilingual support team. It also provides 'virtual' receptionists and business addresses.

Secretarial services

AW Secretarial Services

Suite 3, Level 5, 32 York Street, between King & Market Streets, CBD (9262 6812). CityRail Town Hall. **Open** 8.30am-5pm Mon-Fri. **Credit** MC, V. **Map** p327 E6.
For word processing, CVs and spreadsheets.

Translators & interpreters

Commercial Translation Centre

Level 20, 99 Walker Street, North Sydney (1800 655 224/9954 4376/ www.ctc4.com). CityRail North Sydney. **Open** 9am-5pm Mon-Fri. **Credit** MC, V.
The worldwide CTC has 80 linguistic staff with languages that include Japanese, Mandarin, Korean, Thai, Malay, French, German, Spanish, Dutch and Swedish.

Useful organisations

Australian Stock Exchange

20 Bridge Street, CBD (13 1279/ 9227 0000/www.asx.com.au). CityRail Wynyard or Circular Quay. **Open** 10am-4.30pm Mon-Fri. **Map** p327 F4.

Australian Taxation Office

100 Market Street, CBD (13 2861/ www.ato.gov.au). CityRail St James. **Open** 8.30am-4.45pm Mon-Fri. **Map** p327 F6.

State Chamber of Commerce

Level 12, 83 Clarence Street, CBD (1300 137 153/www.thechamber.com.au). CityRail Wynyard. **Open** 9am-5pm Mon-Fri. **Map** p327 E6.

Consumer

The excellent and practical website of the **NSW Office of Fair Trading** (*see p298*) offers advice for consumers on how to avoid 'shady characters, scams and rip-offs' and for businesses on how to do the right thing. The **Traveller Consumer Helpline** (1300 552 001) provides a rapid response (including access to translators) for travellers who experience unfair employment schemes, problems with accommodation or car rental, faulty goods or overcharging.

NSW Office of Fair Trading

1 Fitzwilliam Street, Parramatta (13 3220/www.fairtrading.nsw. gov.au). Ferry/CityRail Parramatta. **Open** 8.30am-5pm Mon-Fri.

Customs

Before landing on Australian soil you will be given an immigration form to fill out, as well as customs and agriculture declaration forms. You will pass through either the Green (nothing to declare) channel or the Red (something to declare) channel. Your baggage may be examined by Customs, regardless of which channel you use.

Anyone aged 18 years or over can bring in $900 worth of duty-free goods ($450 for under-18s), 2.25 litres of alcohol and 250 cigarettes or 250 grams of other tobacco products. You must declare amounts of $10,000 or more. Visitors can bring items such as computers into Australia duty-free, provided Customs is satisfied that these items are intended to be taken away again on departure.

UK Customs & Excise (www.hmce.gov.uk) allows travellers aged 18 and over returning from outside the EU to bring home £145 worth of gifts and goods, 200 cigarettes or 250 grams of tobacco, one litre of spirits or two litres of fortified wine, 60ml perfume and 250ml toilet water. **US Customs** (www.customs. ustreas.gov) allows Americans to return from trips to Australia with goods valued up to US$800.

Quarantine

You must declare all food, plant cuttings, seeds, nuts or anything made from wood, plant or animal material that you bring into Australia. This includes many souvenirs and airline food. If you don't, you could face an on-the-spot fine of $220, or prosecution and fines of $60,000. Sniffer dogs will hunt out the tiniest morsel as they roam the airport with their handlers.

Quarantine officers use high-tech X-ray machines to check your luggage. Quarantine bins are provided at the airport for you to ditch any food and plants you may have about you before you reach immigration. Check the website of the **Australian Quarantine & Inspection Service** (www.aqis.gov.au) for details.

Australia also has quite strict laws prohibiting and restricting the export of native animals and plants, and items deemed 'moveable cultural heritage'. These include birds and their eggs, fish, reptiles, insects, plants, seeds, fossils and rock art. Products made from protected wildlife, such as hard corals and giant clam shells, are not allowed to be taken out of the country. If in doubt, check with the **Department of the Environment & Heritage** (6274 1900, www.deh.gov.au).

If you need to carry medicine for yourself in or out of the country, it is advisable to have a prescription or doctor's letter. Penalties for carrying illicit drugs in Australia are severe and could result in a jail term. Check the **Customs National Information Line** (1300 363 263, www.customs.gov.au).

Disabled

It was not until 1992 that building regulations required that provisions be made for the disabled, so some older venues do not have disabled access. Restaurants tend to fare better, as most have ramps.

New transport standards will require that people with disabilities have access to most public transport within 20 years. For the time being, many Sydney streets are far from wheelchair-friendly. Constant construction upheavals and the city's hills aside, the standard of pavement surfaces in the inner suburbs leaves a lot to be desired. Poor street lighting compounds the problem.

For more information, check out the excellent website of the **Disability Information Resource** (www.accessibility. com.au), which provides details on wheelchair access throughout the city, from music venues and restaurants to museums and public toilets. Or contact the following:

Travel advice

For up-to-date information on travel to a specific country – including the latest news on safety and security, health issues, local laws and customs – contact your home country government's department of foreign affairs. Most have websites packed with useful advice for would-be travellers.

Australia
www.smartraveller.gov.au

Canada
www.voyage.gc.ca

Republic of Ireland
http://foreignaffairs.gov.ie

New Zealand
www.mfat.govt.nz/travel

UK
www.fco.gov.uk/travel

USA
http://travel.state.gov

Directory

Disability Information & Referral Centre (DIRC)

Suite 208, 35 Buckingham Street, Surry Hills (9657 1796/www.dirc. asn.au). **Open** 8.30am-4.30pm Mon-Fri. **Map** p329 F10.
Provides information and referral on all disabilities for the whole of NSW and has a great, up-to-date database on eastern suburbs services.

Spinal Cord Injuries Australia

9661 8855/www.scia.org.au.
This organisation provides consumer-based support and rehabilitation services to help people with physical disabilities participate fully in society. Phone/internet enquiries only.

State Library of NSW Disability Information

State Library of NSW, corner of Macquarie Street & Cahill Expressway, CBD (9273 1583/ www.sl.nsw.gov.au/access). **Open** *Phone enquiries* 9am-5pm Mon-Fri. **Map** p327 G5.
Helpful info line that offers a great starting point for disabled visitors.

Drugs

Cannabis and harder drugs are illegal in Australia, but that hasn't prevented a huge drug culture – and problem – from developing. High-volume imports from Asia ensure cheap and dangerously pure strains of heroin on the streets, while cannabis, ecstasy, cocaine and ice (crystal meth) are the chosen poisons of the city's youth.

Kings Cross is the epicentre of drug dealing in Sydney and has been the target of a clean-up campaign by the local government. The future of the 'shooting gallery' safe injection room in the area hangs in the balance, as right-wing nay-sayers and enthusiastic project supporters argue over its success rates. Still, come nightfall it's not uncommon for addicts to shoot up on the streets, in the parks and even on beaches. Needle disposal bins are everywhere. *See also* p301 **Helplines**.

Electricity

The Australian domestic electricity supply is 230-240V, 50Hz AC. UK appliances work with just a basic plug adaptor, but US 110V appliances will need a more elaborate form of transformer as well.

Embassies & consulates

Canada

Level 5, Quay West Building, 111 Harrington Street, at Essex Street, CBD (9364 3000/visa information 9364 3050/www.canada.org.au). CityRail/ferry Circular Quay. **Open** 8.30am-4.30pm Mon-Fri. **Map** p327 E4.

Ireland

Level 30, 400 George Street, at King Street, CBD (9231 6999/www.dfa.ie). CityRail Wynyard. **Open** 10am-1pm, 2.30-4pm Mon-Fri. **Map** p327 F6.

New Zealand

Level 10, 55 Hunter Street, at Castlereagh Street, CBD (8256 2000/www.nzembassy.com). CityRail Martin Place or Wynyard. **Open** 9am-12.30pm, 1.30-5pm Mon-Fri. **Map** p327 F5.

South Africa

Rhodes Place, State Circle, Yarralumla, Canberra (6273 2424/ www.sahc.org.au). **Open** 8.30am-1pm, 2-5pm Mon-Fri.

United Kingdom

Level 16, The Gateway, 1 Macquarie Place, at Bridge Street, CBD (9247 7521/www.britaus.net). CityRail/ferry Circular Quay. **Open** *Phone* 9am-5pm Mon-Fri. *Counter* 10am-12.30pm, 1.30-4.30pm Mon-Fri. **Map** p327 F4.

USA

Level 59, MLC Centre 19-29 Martin Place, CBD (9373 9200/ http://sydney.usconsulate.gov/sydney). CityRail Martin Place. **Open** 8am-5pm Mon-Fri. **Map** p327 F5.

Emergencies

For the fire brigade, police or ambulance, dial **000**. It's a free call from any phone.

For hospitals, *see below* **Health**. For other emergency numbers, *see* p301 **Helplines**.

You can contact the **Poisons Information Centre** (open 24 hours daily) at 13 1126.

Gay & lesbian

The quickest way to find gay-related information is via weekly newspapers *Sydney Star Observer* (www.ssonet. com.au), the boysy *SX* (www. evolutionpublishing.com.au/ sxnews), or, for women, the excellent monthly mag *Lesbians on the Loose* (www.lotl.com). All are free from newsagents, clubs and bars all over town.

Help & information

For information on **STDs, HIV & AIDS**, *see* p300.

Gay & Lesbian Counselling Service of NSW

8594 9596. **Open** 5.30pm-10.30pm daily.
Information and phone counselling.

Gay & Lesbian Tourism Australia

08 8267 4634/0408 252 360/ www.galta.com.au.
A non-profit organisation dedicated to the welfare of gay and lesbian travellers in Australia.

Health

The universal government healthcare system, Medicare Australia, has a reciprocal agreement with Finland, Italy, Malta, the Netherlands, New Zealand, Norway, Republic of Ireland, Sweden and the UK, entitling residents of those countries to get necessary medical and hospital treatment for free. This agreement does not cover all eventualities (for example, ambulance fees or dental costs), and only applies to public hospitals and casualty departments.

If you have travel insurance, check the small print to see whether you need to register with Medicare before making a claim; if not, or if you don't

Directory

have insurance, you can claim a Medicare rebate by taking your passport and visa, together with the medical bill, to any Medicare centre.

For more information, phone or write to the information service below. *See also below* **Doctors** *and* **Prescriptions**.

Medicare Information Service
Postal address: PO Box 9822, Sydney, NSW 2001 (13 2011/ www.hic.gov.au). **Open** *Phone enquiries 9am-4.30pm Mon-Fri.*

Accident & emergency

In an emergency, call **000** for an ambulance.

Prince of Wales Hospital
Barker Street, Randwick (9382 2222). Bus 373, 374.

Royal North Shore Hospital
Pacific Highway, St Leonards (9926 7111). CityRail St Leonards.

Royal Prince Alfred Hospital
Missenden Road, Camperdown (9515 6111). Bus 412.

St Vincent's Public Hospital
Corner of Burton & Victoria Streets, Darlinghurst (8382 1111). CityRail Kings Cross/bus 378, 380, L82.

Complementary medicine

Australians are very open to complementary medicine and treatments; indeed, many conventional doctors take a holistic approach and combine mainstream treatments with complementary care. Look in the *Yellow Pages* under 'Alternative Health Services' for hundreds of practitioners. The following organisations may be of help.

Australian Natural Therapists Association
1800 817 577/www.anta.com.au.

Australian Traditional-Medicine Society
Postal address: PO Box 1027, Meadowbank, NSW 2114 (9809 6800/www.atms.com.au).

Contraception & abortion

FPA Health (Family Planning Association)
Clinics and advice: 1300 658 886/ www.fpahealth.org.au. **Open** 9am-5.30pm Mon-Fri.
Nurses provide free phone advice and practical help, including contraception and pregnancy testing.

Marie Stopes International
9764 4133/www.mariestopes.com.au. **Open** 8am-9pm Mon-Fri; 9am-2pm Sat.
Offers counselling, pregnancy termination, advice on contraception and other health issues.

Dentists

Dental treatment is not covered by Medicare, and therefore not by the reciprocal agreement (*see p299* **Health**). Be prepared for hefty fees. Check the *Yellow Pages* for listings, though it's a good idea to ask locals to recommend a dentist they know and trust.

Doctors

For listings of doctors, see the *Yellow Pages* under 'Medical Practitioners'. If your home country is covered under the reciprocal Medicare agreement, and your visit is for immediately necessary treatment, you can claim a refund from Medicare. Try to get to one of the increasingly rare 'bulk billing' medical practices, where your trip will be free. Otherwise you will only get back a proportion of the fee, which must be claimed in person.

Hospitals

Hospitals are listed in the *White Pages* at the front of the phone book in the 'Emergency,

Health & Help' section, with a location map. For hospitals with 24-hour A&E, *see above* **Accident & emergency**.

Opticians
See p209.

Pharmacies

Standard opening times for chemists are 9am to 5.30pm Monday to Friday, and usually 9am to 5.30pm Saturday, 10am to 5pm Sunday (though weekend opening times depend on the area). Many convenience stores and supermarkets stock over-the-counter drugs. *See also p209.*

Prescriptions

In Australia, prescription costs vary depending on the drugs being prescribed. On the Pharmaceutical Benefits Scheme (PBS) you shouldn't have to pay more than $28.60 – but to get this price you must have a Medicare card or temporary Medicare card, available to visitors from nations with a reciprocal health care agreement from any Medicare office, with your passport and visa.

STDs, HIV & AIDS

AIDS Council of NSW (ACON)
9 Commonwealth Street, Surry Hills (1800 063 060/9206 2000/ www.acon.org.au). CityRail Museum. **Open** 10am-6pm Mon-Fri.
Map p329 F9.
Information, advice and support.

HIV/AIDS Information
1800 451 600/9332 9700/www. sesahs.nsw.gov.au/albionstcentre. **Open** 8am-7pm Mon-Fri; 10am-6pm Sat.
Statewide information service.

Sydney Sexual Health Centre
Sydney Hospital, 8 Macquarie Street, opposite Martin Place, CBD (9382 7440). CityRail Martin Place.

Open *Phone enquiries* 9.30am-6pm Mon-Fri. *Open clinic* 10am-6pm Mon, Tue, Thur, Fri; 2-6pm Wed. **Map** p327 G5/6.
Government-funded clinic aimed at young people at risk, gay men and sex workers.

Helplines

Alcohol & Drug Information Service *1800 422 599/9361 8000.* **Open** 24hrs daily.
Crisis counselling, information, assessment and referrals.
Alcoholics Anonymous *9387 7788/www.alcoholicsanonymous. org.au.* **Open** 24hrs daily.
Manned by volunteers who are recovering alcoholics.
Child Abuse Line *13 2111/ www.community.nsw.gov.au.* **Open** 24hrs daily.
For immediate help, advice and action involving children at risk.
Domestic Violence Line *1800 656 463.* **Open** 24hrs daily.
Call 000 if in immediate danger, otherwise this service offers expert counselling and advice.
Gamblers Counselling Service *9951 5566/G-Line 1800 633 635/ www.wesleymission.org.au.* **Open** 9am-5pm Mon-Fri. *G-Line* 24hrs daily.
A face-to-face counselling service plus 24-hour telephone helpline.
Kids Helpline *1800 551 800/ www.kidshelp.com.au.* **Open** 24hrs daily.
Confidential, non-judgemental support for children and young people aged five to 18. Counsellors available by email or for real-time web counselling.
Law Access *1800 817 227/ www.lawaccess.nsw.gov.au.* **Open** 9am-5pm Mon-Fri.
Advice and information on all on legal issues.
Lifeline *13 1114.* **Open** 24hrs daily.
Help for people in crisis.
Rape Crisis Centre *1800 424 017/9819 6565.* **Open** 24hrs daily.
Rape counselling over the phone.
Salvation Army Salvo Care Line *9331 6000.* **Open** 24hrs daily.
Help for anyone in crisis or contemplating suicide.

Insurance

Getting some travel insurance is advisable, especially if you're aiming to stay in backpacker hostels, where thefts are common. Australia has reciprocal health care agreements with many countries; *see p299* **Health**.

Internet

Cybercafés are everywhere in Sydney. Look out for **Global Gossip**, which has locations all over town; try 790 George Street, CBD (9212 4444) or visit www.global gossip.com.au for others. Most backpacker hotels have internet links, and most libraries will provide access.

Language

Despite the country's history, contemporary vernacular Australian owes more to US English than the UK variety, so you may read about a 'color program', and 'pissed' means annoyed not drunk. Words that have a peculiarly Australian flavour include: *arvo* (afternoon); *bludger* (scrounger, as in 'dole bludger'); *daggy* (nerdy or goofy); *daks* (trousers); *doona* (duvet); *dunny* (lavatory/loo/toilet); *Manchester* (household linen); and *thongs* (flip-flops, not G-strings). Take special care when talking about your roots (*root* means shag/bonk/sexual encounter or just plain knacker – anything but your ancestry or blonde streaks in your hair).

You will probably hear 'G'day, mate' and 'Fair dinkum', but often said with a knowing wink.

Left luggage

There are left-luggage lockers for hire in the international terminal of **Sydney Airport** (call 9667 0926 for information). They cost $11 per bag for up to 24 hours.

Legal help

For embassies and consulates, *see p299*.

Law Access

1800 817 227/www.lawaccess. nsw.gov.au. **Open** 9am-5pm Mon-Fri. Advice and information on all on legal issues.

Lost property

For belongings lost on State Transit public transport, try phoning the main STA switchboard on 9245 5777, or 9379 341 for CityRail and CountryLink. For the Monorail and LightRail, phone 9285 5600. If you've left something behind in a cab, phone the relevant taxi company. For property lost on the street, contact the police on 9281 0000. For items lost at the airport, phone 9667 9583 or contact the airline.

Media

Newspapers

DAILIES
Sydney has two local papers, the broadsheet *Sydney Morning Herald* (www.smh. com.au, owned by Fairfax) and the tabloid *Daily Telegraph* (http://dailytelegraph.news. com.au, News International, owned by Rupert Murdoch). The *SMH* is an institution with an ego to match. Local stories prevail, with solid coverage of politics and events, but beware the comment columns. It is accompanied by *the (sydney) magazine*, a self-indulgent monthly freebie, filled with Versace and Porsche ads.

The *Daily Telegraph* puts out two editions, morning and afternoon, giving it the edge over the *SMH* for scoops. In true tabloid style, it also carries plenty of bitchy celebrity news in its 'Sydney Confidential' spread.

News International also produces a freebie newspaper, *MX* (www.mxnet.com.au), handed out at CityRail stations Monday to Friday.

The two national newspapers, the *Australian* (www.theaustralian.news. com.au, Murdoch) and the *Australian Financial Review* (http://afr.com, Fairfax), are both based in Sydney, and both have that bias in their coverage. The *Australian* has been trying to shake out its starchiness, but the result has been a rather bizarre mish-mash of armchair trendiness and what could be called a kind of 'gentle conservatism'. The *Review* offers excellent news coverage, plus business and politics.

WEEKEND
The weekend *Sydney Morning Herald* is vast, mainly due to a surfeit of classifieds. The *Saturday Telegraph* is not as thick, but still has supplements. The *Australian* aspires to stylish minimalism, with a slick, svelte weekend broadsheet on Saturday, accompanied by a print-heavy magazine. On Sundays there is Fairfax's tabloid *Sun-Herald*, designed to compete with the popular *Sunday Telegraph*.

Radio

AM stations
NewsRadio (ABC) 630 AM
Rolling news service with strong international content and daytime coverage of parliament.
Radio National (ABC) 576 AM
Intelligent, provocative talk shows, arts and current affairs.
Radio 2GB 873 AM
Veteran talk show radio station that feeds off local whingeing, humorous tirades and chatty hosts.
SBS Radio 1107 AM
Ethnic, multilingual programmes for Sydney's diverse communities.
2BL (ABC) 702 AM
The Australian Broadcasting Corp's popular talk station features non-commercial, non-ranting, reasonably intelligent banter.
2CH 1170 AM
Easy, yawn, listening.
2KY 1017 AM
Racing, racing and more racing.
2UE 954 AM
The home of Sydney's best-loved and hated talk show kings. These big mouths – including John Laws and Stan Zemanek – have egos as large as their bank balances.

FM stations
ABC Classic FM 92.9 FM
Classical music for non-purists, and some cool jazz.

MIX 106.5 FM
Celine Dion, Phil Collins, the Spice Girls – oh, and is that Lionel Ritchie?
Nova 96.9 FM
This relative newcomer is young, brash and cheeky.
SBS Radio 97.7 FM
Special-interest ethnic programming.
Triple J 105.7 FM
Well respected as the station most devoted to the discovery and spread of new music.
2DAY 104.1 FM
Made its name by taking women seriously. And the listeners flocked. Funny, that.
2000FM 98.5 FM
Ethnic specialist with community-driven shows.
2MMM (Triple M) 104.9 FM
Rock, ads and then more rock.
Vega 95.3 FM
Sydney's newest radio station, launched in 2005, targeting the baby-boomers with talk and music.
WSFM 101.7 FM
Classic hits from the 1960s to '80s, every one a singalong.

Television

The government-funded TV and radio networks are **ABC** (Australian Broadcasting Corporation) and **SBS** (Special Broadcasting Service). ABC has strong links with the BBC and tends to get first dibs on new BBC series. It also has a lot of homemade shows and is good for documentaries and current affairs. SBS has a remit to support multicultural programming and is woefully underfunded. It features foreign films (subtitled), has good world news at 6.30pm every night and is renowned for its documentaries, many commissioned from independent Australian producers. It's also where you'll find comprehensive European football coverage.

The other three networks – **Seven**, **Nine** and **Ten** – are commercial and, for the most part, populist, featuring a large dose of US TV, heaps of local lifestyle shows and ads seemingly every five minutes. Pay TV (satellite and digital) is growing, with (Murdoch-owned) **Foxtel** dominating the market so far.

Money

In 1966 Australia relinquished pounds, shillings and pence for the Australian dollar ($) and cent (c). Paper money comes in $100, $50, $20, $10 and $5 denominations. Coins come in bronze $2 and $1 pieces, and silver 50c, 20c, 10c and 5c pieces. At the time of writing, the tourist exchange rate was approximately $2.40 to £1, $1.40 to US$1 and $1.70 to €1.

ATMs

There are 24-hour ATMs all over town – outside banks, and increasingly in pubs, bottle shops and convenience stores.

Most banks will accept each other's cards, but will charge a fee. Some ATMs accept credit cards – check the card logos displayed. Be aware that withdrawing money on your credit card usually incurs interest straight away. Most ATMs also accept debit cards linked to international networks such as Cirrus, Connect and Barclays.

Banks

The banks below have branches throughout the city. All are open 9.30am to 4pm Monday to Thursday, and 9.30am to 5pm Friday.

ANZ
97 Castlereagh Street, CBD (13 1314/www.anz.com). CityRail St James. **Map** p327 F6.

Commonwealth Bank of Australia
48 Martin Place, CBD (9378 2000/ www.commbank.com.au). CityRail Martin Place. **Map** p327 F5.

National Australia Bank
75 Elizabeth Street, CBD (13 2265/ www.national.com.au). CityRail Martin Place. **Map** p327 F6.

Westpac
60 Martin Place, CBD (13 2032/ www.westpac.com.au). CityRail Martin Place. **Map** p327 F/G5.

Directory

Bureaux de change

American Express

105 Pitt Street, between Martin Place & Hunter Street, CBD (1300 139 060/www.americanexpress.com/ australia). CityRail Wynyard. **Open** 9-5pm Mon-Fri. **Map** p327 F5. **Other locations**: throughout the city.

Travelex

Queen Victoria Building, 455 George Street, between Market & Druitt Streets, CBD (9264 1267/ www.travelex.com). CityRail Town Hall. **Open** 9am-6pm Mon-Fri; 10am-3pm Sat. **Map** p327 E6. **Other locations**: throughout the city.

Credit cards

MasterCard (MC), Visa (V), Diners Club (DC) and American Express (AmEx) are widely accepted. You can also use credit cards to get cash from any bank (take your passport), and some ATMs. To report lost or stolen cards, call (free) these 24-hour numbers:

American Express 1300 132 639
Diners Club 1300 360 060
MasterCard 1800 120 113
Visa 1300 651 089

Tax & tax refunds

A ten per cent **GST** (Goods & Services Tax) is charged on some goods, food and services, including accommodation, and is included in the display price. Tourists can reclaim it on selected goods when they leave the country using the **Tourist Refund Scheme** (TRS). This scheme applies only to goods you carry as hand luggage or wear onto the aircraft or ship when you leave.

The refund can be claimed on goods costing a total of $300 or above (including GST) bought from one shop no more than 30 days before you leave. You can buy several lower-priced items from the same shop, either in one go or at different times, provided you've spent at least $300 total

within the 30-day period. And you can reclaim tax for items bought from any number of shops, as long you've spent at least $300 in each one.

To claim a refund, you must get a tax invoice from the shop or shops in question. You then claim your refund at a TRS booth, after passport control. Here you'll need to show the goods, the tax invoices, your passport and international boarding pass. Refunds are paid by cheque or credit to an Australian bank account, or to a credit card. Customs aims to post cheque refunds within 15 business days, while bank and credit card refunds are issued within five business days.

Full details are on the Australian Customs website, **www.customs.gov.au** – click on 'travellers'.

Natural hazards

With a dangerously thin ozone layer, the sun is Sydney's biggest natural hazard. The best way to avoid it is to 'slip, slap, slop' – slip on a T-shirt, slap on a hat, and slop on some sun-cream, preferably SPF 30.

For information about Sydney's wildlife hazards, *see p304* **Creature discomforts**.

Opening hours

Shops are usually open from 8.30am or 9am to 5pm or 6pm Monday to Saturday, and from 10am or 11am to 4pm or 5pm Sunday. Thursday is late-night opening (usually until 9pm). Some shops close at noon on Saturdays. Banks are usually open from 9.30am to 4pm Monday to Thursday, until 5pm on Friday, and closed at the weekend.

Police stations

To report an emergency, dial **000**. If it is not an emergency, call the police at **13 1444**. The **City Central Police**

Station is at 192 Day Street, CBD (9265 6499). More info at www.police.nsw.gov.au.

Postal services

Australia Post (13 1318, www.auspost.com.au) says about 90 per cent of letters within the metropolitan area arrive the next business day. Post is delivered once a day Monday to Friday, with no delivery on Saturdays or Sundays. Post to Europe takes four to ten days. Stamps for postcards to Europe and the USA cost $1.10; for letters it's $1.85 (up to 50 grams), and international aerogrammes cost 95c. Letters within Australia cost from 50c to $2.45.

Most post office branches open from 9am to 5pm Monday to Friday, but the GPO Martin Place branch is also open on Saturdays. Stamps can also be bought at some newsagents and general stores. Suburban post offices will receive post for you; otherwise have it sent Poste Restante (general delivery) to GPO Sydney, NSW 2000 – and collect it from the address below. Most post offices also rent out PO boxes, but only on an annual basis.

General Post Office

1 Martin Place, CBD (9244 3713). CityRail Martin Place or Wynyard. **Open** 8.15am-5.30pm Mon-Fri; 10am-2pm Sat. **Map** p327 F5/6.

Poste Restante

Level 2, Hunter Connection Building, 310 George Street, CBD (13 1318). CityRail Martin Place or Wynyard. **Open** 9am-5pm Mon-Fri. **Map** p327 F5.

Religion

Consult the *Yellow Pages* under 'Churches, Mosques and Temples' for places of worship.

Safety & security

Sydney is a fairly safe city, although car theft, vandalism

Creature discomforts

Australia's array of mini-creatures is legendary. And Sydney, being temperate and humid, is the perfect breeding ground for all things cold-blooded or with six or more legs. Most bugs, arachnids and reptiles are completely harmless, and most tend to bother residents rather than visitors in built-up areas, but there are a few nasties to look out for. The following are the critters you should be aware of.

SPIDERS

While many different types of spider tend to congregate in Sydney, there are two with a potentially fatal bite – the **funnel web** and the **redback**. The funnel web is a nasty, aggressive creature native to the Sydney bush. Reddish-brown and hairy, it lives in holes in the ground. If bitten, apply pressure and immobilise the wounded area, using a splint if possible, and get to a hospital (or dial 000) immediately. The redback, which is smaller and black with a red stripe on its body, lives mainly outside. Apply ice if bitten and seek immediate medical help.

SNAKES

Five of the ten most dangerous snakes in the world are said to live in Australia, with names like **king brown**, **taipan** and **tiger**. Most are more scared of you than you are of them, but a couple can be more aggressive – so it is sensible to play it safe: always wear boots when hiking through the bush, don't put your hands in any holes or crevices, and watch where you're walking. If someone with you is bitten, assume that the snake is venomous. Wrap the limb tightly, attach a splint and keep the victim still and calm, then seek immediate medical attention. Snake bites will not cause immediate death and antivenin is usually available from medical services.

COCKROACHES

They say the cockie would be the only thing to survive a nuclear holocaust – whether or not this is true, Sydneysiders will try anything short of napalm to wipe them out. Despite being nasty, the cockroaches (which seem to grow to the size of frogs during summer – perhaps a response to the chemical warfare being waged against them) are harmless.

FLIES AND MOSQUITOES

Flies and mozzies are a fact of Aussie life, but besides imparting an itchy bump (mozzies) and an irritable disposition (flies), they're not dangerous. There are also a couple of flies that bite, such as the **march fly** – but their bite is not poisonous, just a tad painful. Some people can experience nasty allergic reactions to bites – if this is you, try prescribed or over-the-counter antihistamines (ask the pharmacist for advice). Personal repellents, such as Rid, tend to be fairly effective, or you can buy coils to burn outdoors, or repelling candles. Mosquito nets and screens are a good idea in summer.

BUSHLAND BRUTES

If you plan to fit in a little bushwalking anywhere on Australia's east coast, there are a couple of creatures you need to watch out for besides snakes.

Ticks are very dangerous, if not removed immediately, as they excrete a toxin that can cause paralysis or, in extreme cases, even death. So each day after bushwalking check your body for lumps and bumps – they tend to like hairy areas, skin creases and ears – and slowly pull or lever any ticks out with sharp-pointed tweezers. **Leeches** are common bushland suckers – literally. However, they aren't dangerous and can easily be persuaded to let go by applying salt or heat.

---

and burglary are on the increase. That said, you will frequently read about drug-related shootings, and racial tension has heightened since the Bali bombings and the riots on Cronulla Beach in 2005. And while the stereotype of hot-blooded Aussie males ending an alcohol-fuelled evening with a pub brawl is not the norm, it does happen –

so steer clear of drunk rednecks at closing time.

In an emergency, dial **000**.

Smoking

Sydney is heavily anti-smoking, and you'll see crowds of smokers standing outside restaurants. Smoking is banned on public transport and in cafés, restaurants and a

wide range of enclosed spaces, such as theatres, shopping malls and community centres.

The NSW Workcover Occupational Health Act states that smoking should be eliminated from all indoor areas in the workplace, and you may not smoke on premises where facilities are being provided for children. Smoking in pubs and clubs is now restricted to one area only, usually around the pokies, and there are moves to ban it completely. There are fines for tossing cigarette butts out of car windows.

Study

Anyone can apply to study in Australia, but you must obtain a student visa before starting a course. For more details, visit the Department of Immigration's website at **www.immi.gov.au**. You'll be granted a student visa only for a full-time registered course.

Universities

University of NSW
Postal address: University of NSW, Sydney, NSW 2052 (9385 1000/ www.unsw.edu.au). Location: Anzac Parade, Kensington. Bus 302, 303, 391, 392, 393, 394, 395, 396, 397, 399, 400, 410.
The UNSW is one of the leading teaching and research universities in Australia. Almost 9,000 of its 40,000 students are foreign.

University of Sydney
Postal address: University of Sydney, NSW 2006 (9351 2222/www.usyd. edu.au). Location: City Road, Darlington, & Parramatta Road, Camperdown. City Road entrance: bus 422, 423, 426, 428/Parramatta Road entrance: bus 412, 413, 435, 436, 437, 438, 440, 461, 480.
Founded in 1850, this was Australia's first uni. It has around 46,000 students, of whom nearly 9,000 are international.

Macquarie University
Postal address: Macquarie University, NSW 2109 (9850 7111/ www.mq.edu.au). Location: Balaclava Road, North Ryde. Bus 288, 292.
Macquarie has more than 30,000 students, around 9,000 of them from overseas. The university is set in bushland north of Sydney, offering a rural alternative to city universities.

Telephones

Dialling & codes

The country code for Australia is **61**; the area code for NSW, including Sydney, is **02**. You never need to dial the 02 from within the state. Numbers

beginning 1800 are free when dialled within Australia; numbers beginning 13 or 1300 are charged at a 25c flat fee.

Making a call

To make an international call from Sydney, you dial an international access code – either **0011** or **0018** (*see below*) – followed by the country code, area code (omitting the initial 0 if there is one), and then the number.

The different international access codes give you different pricing systems. Telstra, the dominant Australian phone company, offers a choice of 0011 Minutes or 0018 Half Hours. The 0011 calls are for shorter chats, charged per second. The 0018 calls are for a long chat and you'll know exactly how much your call will cost up front. Warning beeps tell you when your half-hour is almost up.

The country code for the UK is **44**, for New Zealand **64**, for the United States **1**, for the Republic of Ireland **353** and for South Africa **27**.

Standard local calls are untimed flat-fee calls between standard fixed telephone services within a local service area. To check if local call charges apply, call 13 2200.

STD calls (national long-distance calls) are charged according to their distance, time and day, plus a fee. Each call starts with five pip tones.

Public phones

There are public phones dotted around the city, as well as in bars, cafés, railway stations and post offices. You can also make long-distance and international calls at many internet cafés. Most public phones accept coins ($1, 50c, 20c, 10c). Some also accept major credit cards. Cheap international phonecards are available from newsagents.

Directory enquiries

Dial **1223** to find a number within Australia, and **1225** for international directory enquiries.

Operator services

For operator-assisted national or international calls, phone **1234**.

Mobile phones

Australia's mobile phone network operates on dual-band 900/1800 MHz (megahertz). This means that if you're coming from the UK you should be able to use your own mobile phone – but that's not as simple as it sounds.

If you keep your UK SIM card in the phone, when you arrive your phone will register itself with a local network with which your UK service provider has an agreement. If you want to use this facility, check with your service provider before you go, as you may need to set your phone up to work abroad. This is the easiest method, but potentially very expensive: calling numbers in Australia will cost the same as calling back to the UK – ie a lot – and you'll have to pay to receive calls as well as to make them.

Another simple option is to to buy or rent a phone. Plenty of Sydney companies offer competitive mobile phone rentals with local networks, for a minimum of three days, billed to your credit card. Or you could just buy or rent a SIM card for an Australian network and put it in your UK phone (and top it up as required). However, your phone may have been 'locked' so that it works only with your UK service provider's SIM card. You're entitled to get the phone unlocked, and the service provider has to give you an unlocking code – for free – if you ask for it. Once you've unlocked your phone you can put any SIM card in it. In practice, service providers tend not to make this easy, and the process can be fraught with difficulties. Alternatively, any mobile phone repair shop will do it, for about $40.

If you're in Sydney for a year or more, you could get a phone or SIM card on a billed package. To get this kind of plan – usually 12 months minimum – you'll need an Australian credit rating, and it takes six months to get one.

To investigate further, look under 'Mobile Telephones & Accessories' in the *Yellow Pages* or try these places:

Paddington Phones

381 Riley Street, at Foveaux Street, Surry Hills (9281 8044/ www.paddington-phones.com.au). CityRail Central. **Open** 9am-5.30pm Mon-Fri. **Map** p329 G10.
Rentals, pre-paid and fixed-term deals are all available.

Vodafone Rentals

Arrivals Hall, T1 International Terminal, Sydney Airport (9700 8036/www.vodafone.com.au). **Open** 6.30am-9pm daily.
Rent or buy a phone or SIM card as soon as you arrive.
Other locations: Mid City Centre, Pitt Street (9231 2800); Westfield Bondi Junction (9389 9873).

Tickets

You can book tickets for all major venues (music, theatre, dance and so on) through agencies **Ticketek** (9266 4800, www.ticketek.com.au) and **Ticketmaster** (13 6100, www.ticketmaster.com.au). Also try **MCA Ticketing** (1300 306 776, www.mca-tix.com) or **Moshtix** (9209 4614, www.moshtix.com.au). All charge booking fees.

Time

New South Wales operates on **Eastern Standard Time** (GMT plus 10 hours). Between October and March, Daylight Saving Time comes into

operation, and the clocks go forward one hour. Australia has three time zones – the others are Western Standard Time (GMT plus 8 hours) and Central Standard Time (GMT plus 9.5 hours). Confusingly, Queensland doesn't recognise Daylight Saving Time.

Tipping

Tipping is appreciated but not expected in restaurants and cafés, where ten per cent is the norm. Locals never tip in taxis.

Toilets

There are plenty of free, well-maintained public lavatories in Sydney – in department stores, shopping centres, rail stations, beaches and parks. It is frowned upon to use the toilet in a bar if not buying a drink. And a note for women: Sydney's sewage pipes are a lot narrower and so more prone to blockage than elsewhere, tampons and sanitary towels being the main culprits. It's not something anyone tells you until you've got the plumber there and a hefty bill – use a bin instead!

Tourist information

As well as the visitor centres below, the City of Sydney's website – **www.cityof sydney.nsw.gov.au** – and Tourism NSW's site – **www. visitnsw.com.au** – have lots of useful information. If you're planning to travel elsewhere in the country, Australia's official website – **www.australia. com** – is packed with helpful ideas and information.

Sydney Visitor Centre

Level 2, corner of Argyle & Playfair Road, The Rocks (9240 8788/ www.sydneyvisitorcentre.com). CityRail/ferry Circular Quay. **Open** 9.30am-5.30pm daily. **Map** p327 F3.
Other locations: *33 Wheat Road, Darling Harbour (9240 8788). Ferry*

Darling Harbour/City Rail Town Hall/Monorail Darling Park. **Open** 9.30am-5.30pm daily. **Map** p328 D7. *Arrivals hall, T1 International Terminal, Sydney Airport (9667 6050).* **Open** 5.30am-11.30pm daily.
This is the main official information resource, with two city-centre locations – in the Rocks and in Darling Harbour – plus an office at the airport.

Cadman's Cottage/ Sydney Harbour National Park Information Centre

110 George Street, between Argyle Street & Mill Lane, The Rocks (9247 5033/www.nationalparks.nsw. gov.au). CityRail/ferry Circular Quay. **Open** 9am-4.30pm Mon-Fri; 10am-4.30pm Sat, Sun. **Map** p327 F3.

Manly Visitor & Information Centre

Manly Wharf, Manly (9976 1430/ www.manlytourism.com). Ferry Manly. **Open** 9am-5pm Mon-Fri; 10am-4pm Sat, Sun (5pm summer). **Map** p334.

Parramatta Heritage & Visitor Information Centre

346A Church Street, next to Lennox Bridge, Parramatta (8839 3311/ www.parracity.nsw.gov.au). CityRail/ ferry Parramatta then 10mins walk. **Open** 9am-5pm daily.

Visas & immigration

All travellers, including children – except for Australian and New Zealand citizens – must have a visa or an **ETA** (Electronic Travel Authority) to enter Australia. An ETA is sufficient for tourists from EC countries – including the UK and Ireland, except holders of GBN (British National Overseas) passports – the USA, Canada and Japan (but not South Africa), who are intending to stay for up to three months.

ETAs, available for straightforward tourist and business trips, are the simplest to arrange: your travel agent or airline or a commercial visa service can arrange one on the spot if you give them details or a copy/fax of your passport (no photo or ticket is required). You don't need a stamp in your passport: ETAs are confirmed electronically at your port of entry. Alternatively, you can apply for an ETA online via **www.eta.immi.gov.au**. The service costs $20, and you can be approved for entry in less than 30 seconds.

If your entry requirements are more complex or you want to stay longer than three months, you will probably need a non-ETA visa, which you apply for by post or in person to the relevant office in advance of your trip. For up-to-date information and details of the nearest overseas office where visa applications can be made, check **www.immi. gov.au**. For details on working visas, *see below* **Working in Sydney**.

Weights & measures

Australia uses the metric system.

When to go

Sydney has a moderate climate, with warm to hot summers, cool winters and rainfall all year round.

Spring brings blossoming flowers and clear blue days, with temperatures warm enough to shed the woollies, especially when the sun shines. In summer, Sydneysiders live in shorts. In January and February the sun bakes the city, and temperatures can top 30°C (90°F) – and even go over 40°C (104°F). In autumn, the city is swept by strong winds, while winter mornings and nights mean low temperatures that can – but rarely do – dip down to 6°C (43°F). Winter daily maximums tend to hover between 14°C (57°F) and 18°C (64°F), and on occasion snow falls in the Blue Mountains.

NSW public holidays

New Year's Day (1 January); Australia Day (26 January); Good Friday; Easter Monday; Anzac Day (25 April); the Queen's Birthday (2nd Monday in June); August Bank Holiday (1st Monday in August); Labour Day (1st Monday in October); Christmas Day (25 December); and Boxing Day (26 December).

Women

Chauvinism may still be alive even in Sydney, but Australian women more than hold their own. The nation was the second country to give women the vote (in 1894 in South Australia). In real terms

Australian women still do not earn the same as their male counterparts, and in many industries they're a long way off breaking the glass ceiling.

Sydney is pretty safe for women, but take care when leaving the hub of the city at night; you don't have to go far for it to feel remote.

Feminist Bookshop

Orange Grove Plaza, Balmain Road, Lilyfield (9810 2666/www.feminist bookshop.com). Bus 440, 445, 470. **Open** 10.30am-6pm Mon-Fri; 10.30am-4pm Sat. **Credit** AmEx, MC, V.
Open since 1974, the shop has a good stock of books, journals and mags by, for and about women.

Working in Sydney

If you want to work while in Sydney, you'll need to have a visa that allows this. The **Working Holiday Program** provides opportunities for people aged 18 to 30 from some countries (including Canada, Denmark, France, Germany, Ireland, Italy, Japan, the Netherlands, Norway, Sweden and the UK) to holiday in Australia and supplement their funds through incidental employment. The visa allows a stay of up to 12 months from the date of first entry to Australia, regardless of whether or not you spend the whole time in Australia. You are allowed to do any kind of work of a temporary or casual nature, but you cannot work for more than three months with any one employer.

Working holiday visas can be obtained by making an application on the internet at **www.immi.gov.au**, or by lodging a written application at an overseas visa office.

If you do not fit the working visa mould, you may still be able to work if you are sponsored by a company or if you apply for residency. Be warned though, the latter option is complex, expensive and takes a great deal of time.

Average climate

Month	Temperature (°C/°F)	Rainfall mm/in
January	19-26/66-79	89/3.5
February	19-26/66-79	102/4
March	17-24/63-76	127/5
April	14-22/58-72	135/5.3
May	11-19/52-67	127/5
June	9-16/49-61	117/4.6
July	9-16/49-61	117/4.6
August	9-17/49-63	76/3
September	11-19/52-66	74/2.9
October	13-22/56-72	71/2.8
November	16-24/61-75	74/2.9
December	17-25/63-77	74/2.9

Directory

Further Reference

Books

Non-fiction

Carlotta & McSween, Prue
I'm Not That Kind of Girl
Carlotta was part of of Les Girls,
a Kings Cross drag dance troupe,
and had Australia's first sex
change operation. Her fascinating
life story is told with warmth,
honesty and humour.

Clark, Manning *A History
of Australia*
Six-volume history of the white
settlement, with sympathy for the
underdog.

Dalton, Robin *Aunts Up the Cross*
Dalton's affectionate memoir of life in
Sydney's most raffish locale, Kings
Cross, from the 1920s to the '40s.

Drewe, Philip *Sydney Opera House*
An incisive and intellectual
examination of Utzon's building
as a piece of notable architecture.

Dupain, Max & Rex *Inside Sydney*
Max Dupain's 1920s and '30s
photographs reflected Sydney's
emergence as a modern city and its
body and beach culture; in the past
few decades his son Rex has picked
up where Max left off.

**Evans, Matthew & Thomson,
Simon** (eds) *The Sydney Morning
Herald Good Food Guide*
The *SMH*'s annual round-up of the
best restaurants, cafés and bars in
Sydney and beyond.

Facey, Albert *A Fortunate Life*
Enormously successful
autobiography tracing Facey's life
from Outback orphanage to Gallipoli,
the Depression and beyond.

Foster, David & others
Crossing the Blue Mountains
Accounts of journeys into the
interior from Sydney, including that
of Darwin in 1836.

Gill, Alan *Orphans of the Storm*
Shocking true story of the thousands
of people who came to Australia in
the 20th century as child migrants.

Graham, Lorrie *Sydneysiders*
A photojournalist's warm and gritty
album of Sydney characters.

Gregory's
Sydney Compact Street Directory
A bit of a brick, but the best guide
to Sydney's streets you'll find.
Covers central areas in great detail
and extends out to the suburbs.

Halliday, James *Australia
Wine Companion*
Good to take on a tour of vineyards.

**Hooke, Huon & Kyte-Powell,
Ralph** *The Penguin Good
Australian Wine Guide*
This long-running annual guide to
the Australian wine industry is

aimed mostly at enthusiasts, but
accessible to beginners as well.

Hughes, Robert *The Fatal Shore*
Epic tale of brutal early convict life,
by the Sydney-born New York art
critic; made into a TV series.

Hughes Turnbull, Lucy *Sydney,
Biography of a City*
Authoritative tome from way back
to now. Good reference material.

James, Clive *Unreliable Memoirs*
Ironic memoir of a Sydney childhood
by Britain's favourite Aussie.

Keneally, Thomas *The
Commonwealth of Thieves*
History of the colony in the time
of the first three fleets.

Ker Conway, Jill *The Road
from Coorain*
Moving account of growing up on
a remote NSW sheep farm, made
into a compelling TV series starring
Juliet Stevenson. Girlhood solitude,
despair during an eight-year drought
and dreams of a new destiny make
for gripping reading.

Moorhouse, Geoffrey *Sydney*
A new look at the city's history
by a distinguished travel writer.

Morgan, Sally *My Place*
Bestselling autobiography of an
Aboriginal woman from Western
Australia.

Pilger, John *A Secret Country*
Passionately critical account of
Australia by the expat journalist.

Walsh, Kate *The Changing
Face of Australia*
A pictorial chronology of a century
of immigration, underlining the shift
towards a multiculture.

Wheatley, Nadia *The Life and
Myth of Charmian Clift*
Well-crafted biography of one of
Australia's most undervalued
writers, who after a rich and
extraordinary life became a well-
loved newspaper columnist.

Fiction

Carey, Peter *Bliss, Illywhacker,
Oscar and Lucinda, The True
History of the Kelly Gang, Theft*
Booker Prize-winning novelist who
started life as an ad agent.

Courtenay, Bryce *Brother Fish,
Whitethorn*
Australia's bestselling writer,
though he doesn't always stick to
Oz-related subject matter.

Franklin, Miles *My Brilliant
Career*
Famous 1901 novel about a rural
woman who refuses to conform.

Gibbs, May *Snugglepot and
Cuddlepie*
Most famous of Gibbs's children's
books about the gumnut babies.

Grenville, Kate *The Secret River*
Convict settlers around the
Hawkesbury River and what they
do to Aboriginal locals.

Keneally, Thomas *Bring Larks
and Heroes*; *The Chant of Jimmy
Blacksmith*
Two novels about oppression – of
convicts in the former, Aboriginal
people in the latter.

Lawson, Henry *Joe Wilson and
His Mates*
Collection of short stories about
mateship and larrikinism by the
first Australian writer to be given
a state funeral (in 1922).

Lindsay, Norman *The Magic
Pudding*
Splendidly roguish children's tale –
as Australian as a book can get.
Made into a so-so movie.

Park, Ruth *The Harp in the South;
Poor Man's Orange*
Tales of inner-city struggle, written
in the 1940s. Park also wrote the
wonderful children's book *The
Muddle-Headed Wombat*.

Slessor, Kenneth *Selected Poems*
The quintessential Sydney poet. This
collection contains 'Five Bells' and
'Groaning to God in Darlinghurst'.

Spender, Dale (ed) *The Penguin
Anthology of Australian Women
Writers*
Female writers, past and present.

Stead, Christina *For Love Alone*
Evocative tale set in Sydney about
a creative young girl from an
unconventional family. Finally
she satisfies her wanderlust and
heads for London.

Winton, Tim *Cloudstreet;
That Eye, the Sky*
The best novels from a twice winner
of the Miles Franklin literary award.

Travel

Bryson, Bill *Down Under*
Amusing travel writer Bryson
dissects the Aussie character and
explores the brown land.

Dale, David *The 100 Things
Everyone Needs to Know About
Australia*
Essential background reading:
covers everything from Vegemite
to Malcolm Fraser's trousers.

Jacobson, Howard *In the
Land of Oz*
Parodic account of Jacobson's travels
down under. Sharp, insulting but
entertaining all the same.

Lambin, Ann & Davies, Djida
Sydney for Children
An excellent, comprehensive
practical guide for parents on how
to make the best of Sydney's child-
friendly resources.

Directory

Morris, Jan *Sydney*
Personal and highly readable account
of the city 'left on the shores of
history by Empire's receding tide'.
Park, Ruth & Champion, Rafe
Ruth Park's Sydney
Completely rewritten update of
Park's 1960s classic companion
Guide to Sydney. Covers the city
from La Perouse to Manly.
Smith, Seana *Sydney for
Under-Fives*
Solid reference book picking out the
best of Sydney for babies, toddlers
and pre-schoolers.
Sproule, Kristen *Sensual Sydney*
A little bit naughty, a little bit kitsch,
and a surprisingly useful guide to
Sydney's more pleasurable exploits.

Film

**The Adventures of Priscilla,
Queen of the Desert**
(Stephan Elliott, 1994)
Terence Stamp joins Guy Pearce and
Hugo Weaving in high heels for this
gritty high camp tale of Sydney drag
queens on tour in the bush.
Erskineville Kings
(Alan White, 1999)
Hugh Jackman in a gritty role in a
flawed but powerful tale of two
brothers and their abusive
upbringing in a Sydney suburb.
**He Died with a Felafel In His
Hand** (Richard Lowenstein, 2001)
Noah Taylor (*Shine*) is great as a
neurotic twentysomething who
ends up in Sydney.
Lantana (Ray Lawrence, 2001)
AFI award-winning thriller about
marriage and relationships, set
in Sydney. Stars Aussie actors
Geoffrey Rush, Kerry Armstrong
and Anthony LaPaglia.
Looking for Alibrandi
(Kate Woods, 2000)
An Italian-Australian battles with
her identity in Sydney's western
suburbs. Local star Pia Miranda
excels in the lead.
Mission: Impossible II
(John Woo, 2000)
Tom Cruise chose the home of his
then wife Nicole Kidman to film the
superspy sequel. The city features in
a big way in the opening sequences.
Moulin Rouge!
(Baz Luhrmann, 2001)
OTT love story for the MTV
generation from local boy Baz
Luhrmann, set in decadent,
turn-of-the-20th-century Paris and
filmed at Sydney's Fox Studios.
Newsfront (Phillip Noyce, 1978)
Rival news teams in 1950s Sydney
battle to shoot the best newsreel film.
The Proposition
(John Hillcoat, 2005)
Nick Cave-scripted drama of murder,
rape, rough justice and manhunt in
the 1880s Outback.

Rabbit-Proof Fence
(Phillip Noyce, 2002)
The 'stolen generations' seen
through the true 1930s story of three
Aboriginal children's awe-inspiring
struggle to get back to their mother.
The Sum of Us (Geoff Burton &
Kevin Dowling, 1994)
A youthful Russell Crowe plays a gay
plumber looking for love in Sydney.
Two Hands (Gregor Jordan, 1999)
Bryan Brown plays an underworld
Sydney crime boss, with Heath
Ledger as the hapless lad who's
entangled in his world. Watch out
for a sparky Bondi Beach scene.
Wolf Creek (Greg McLean, 2005)
Three backpackers get stuck in
the Outback, meet a helpful local,
unpleasantness follows. Influenced
not only by Bradley Murdoch's
murder of British traveller Peter
Falconio in 2001, but also by Ivan
Milat, a 1990s serial murderer of
backpackers in NSW.

Music

AC/DC Formed in Sydney in 1973.
Angus Young's schoolboy attire has
become one of rock's oddest brands.
Singer Bon Scott died in London in
1980 before the band completed its
milestone album *Back In Black*.
Most recent album was *Stiff Upper
Lip*, released in 2000.
INXS Sydney's ultimate rock star,
Michael Hutchence, headed this
international rock band of the 1980s
and '90s until his death in a Double
Bay hotel room in 1997.
Nick Cave Enigmatic, brooding
vocalist from the Bad Seeds. The
introspective, depressing *The
Boatman's Call* (1997) is considered
one of his finest works.
Delta Goodrem Latest popsicle to
make the break from *Neighbours*.
Writes her own stuff, plays the piano
and sang at the opening of the 2006
Commonwealth Games in Melbourne.
David Hirschfelder One of
Australia's most successful modern
composers: film scores for *Shine* and
Elizabeth were nominated for Oscars.
Natalie Imbruglia After leaving
soap *Neighbours*, Imbruglia moved to
London and launched a smash music
career helped by her winsome voice.
Her debut single 'Torn' (1997) was a
huge worldwide hit, and her 2005
album *Counting Down the Days* a UK
No.1, though only No.12 in Australia.
Ben Lee Released his solo debut
Grandpaw Would in 1995 aged just
16, for which he was dubbed 'the
greatest Australian songwriter of all
time'. Won four Australian Recording
Industry Association (ARIA) awards
in 2005 after releasing album *Awake
Is the New Sleep*.
Midnight Oil Began life as Farm
in Sydney in 1971 and became as

famous for its political activities
as its music. Reformed in 1976 as
Midnight Oil, and played gigs to
support Save the Whales and
Greenpeace. Album *Black Fella,
White Fella* (1986), about the plight
of indigenous Australians, produced
their most famous single, 'Beds Are
Burning'. The band effectively split
in 2002 when singer Peter Garrett
decided to concentrate on politics –
he's now a NSW Labor MP.
Rogue Traders Rock band that
incorporates bits of other people's
music into their own, rather than
sampling direct. Sort of another
Neighbours offshoot, as they're
fronted by Natalie Bassingthwaighte.
Album *Here Come the Drums* (2002)
hit No.2 in Oz.
Silverchair Fronted by Daniel
Johns (Mr Natalie Imbruglia), the
three-piece first performed in Europe
in 1995. Now back in Sydney, they
have a huge following. Worked with
classical pianist David Helfgott on
their 1999 hit album *Neon Ballroom*.
Diorama (2002) was another huge
hit and won them six ARIA awards,
but Daniel Johns's struggle with
arthritis that year stopped them
touring. Next studio album expected
late 2006 or early 2007.
The Whitlams After years of crap
venues and no money, frontman Tim
Freedman begged, borrowed and
finally scraped the funds for a last-
ditch CD. Its single 'No Aphrodisiac'
became the ARIA award-winning
monster hit of 1998. Double album
Little Cloud was released in 2006.

Websites

Backpackers Ultimate Guide
www.bugaustralia.com/sydney
Useful site for those travelling in
Sydney on a budget.
Bureau of Meteorology
www.bom.gov.au
Get the latest weather forecast.
City of Sydney
www.cityofsydney.nsw.gov.au
Weekly update of events happening
in the city, with full contact details.
City Search
http://sydney.citysearch.com.au
Guide to what's going on in Sydney
and elsewhere in Oz, with events,
restaurants and entertainment.
**De Groots Best Restaurants
of Australia**
www.bestrestaurants.com.au
Fulsome restaurant listings, with
photos and menus. The restaurant
reviews are uncritical, though, and
the layout confusing.
Eatability
www.eatability.com.au
More restaurant info, plus pubs,
cafés and bars. Includes user-
generated ratings and reviews – the
latter often wildly contradictory.

Index

Index

See the Sydney where Sydneysiders like to be seen

Once you've had your photograph taken in front of the Harbour Bridge and the Opera House, head to where Sydneysiders do their sightseeing. Westfield Bondi Junction is the ultimate shopping destination in town and so very Sydney. Get a taste of Australia's best designers like Leona Edmiston and enjoy international fashion icons like Hugo Boss and Polo Ralph Lauren at Aussie dollar prices. Visit the Concierge Desk on Level 3 when you arrive and we'll give you a free visitor's welcome pack. You'll find the locals are very friendly (and stylish) at Westfield Bondi Junction.

For more info, check out westfield.com/bondijunction

Westfield Bondi Junction

Street Index

Area name	PADDINGTON
Place of interest and/or entertainment	
Parks	
Hospital/university	
CityRail station	⇌
Monorail station	Ⓜ
LightRail station	LR
Steps	

Maps

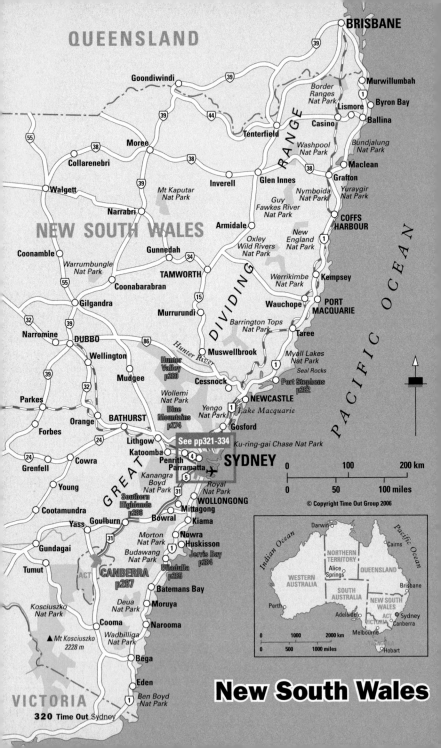

New South Wales

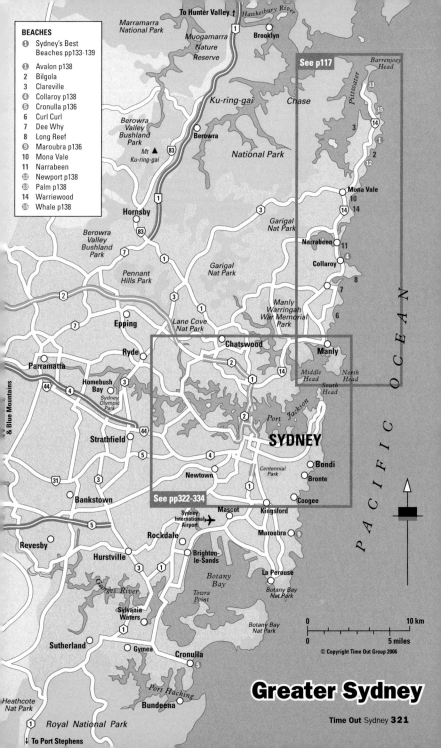

BEACHES

❶ Sydney's Best
   Beaches pp133-139

❶ Avalon p138
2 Bilgola
3 Clareville
④ Collaroy p138
⑤ Cronulla p136
6 Curl Curl
7 Dee Why
8 Long Reef
❾ Maroubra p136
10 Mona Vale
11 Narrabeen
⑫ Newport p138
⑬ Palm p138
14 Warriewood
⑮ Whale p138

See p117

See pp322-334

P A C I F I C   O C E A N

Greater Sydney

0 ____ 10 km

0 ____ 5 miles

© Copyright Time Out Group 2006

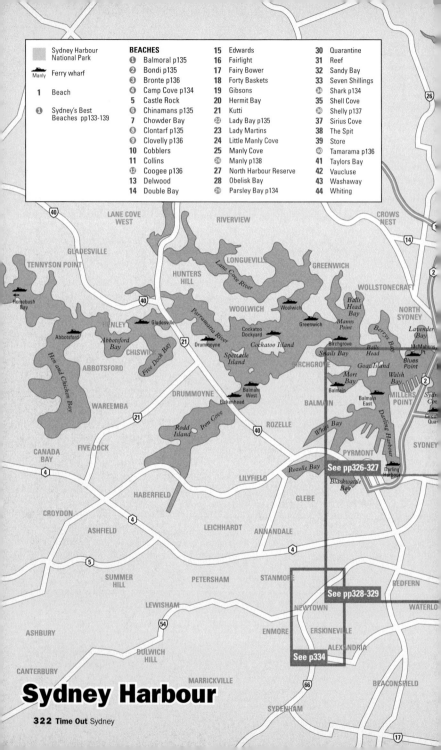

BEACHES

Legend		
■	Sydney Harbour National Park	
⛴ Manly	Ferry wharf	
1	Beach	
❶	Sydney's Best Beaches pp133-139	

BEACHES

❶	Balmoral p135	**15**	Edwards	**30**	Quarantine
❷	Bondi p135	**16**	Fairlight	**31**	Reef
❸	Bronte p136	**17**	Fairy Bower	**32**	Sandy Bay
❹	Camp Cove p134	**18**	Forty Baskets	**33**	Seven Shillings
5	Castle Rock	**19**	Gibsons	㉞	Shark p134
❻	Chinamans p135	**20**	Hermit Bay	**35**	Shell Cove
7	Chowder Bay	**21**	Kutti	㊱	Shelly p137
❽	Clontarf p135	㉒	Lady Bay p135	**37**	Sirius Cove
❾	Clovelly p136	**23**	Lady Martins	**38**	The Spit
10	Cobblers	**24**	Little Manly Cove	**39**	Store
11	Collins	**25**	Manly Cove	㊵	Tamarama p136
⑫	Coogee p136	㉖	Manly p138	**41**	Taylors Bay
13	Delwood	**27**	North Harbour Reserve	**42**	Vaucluse
14	Double Bay	**28**	Obelisk Bay	**43**	Washaway
		㉙	Parsley Bay p134	**44**	Whiting

See pp326-327

See pp328-329

See p334

Sydney Harbour

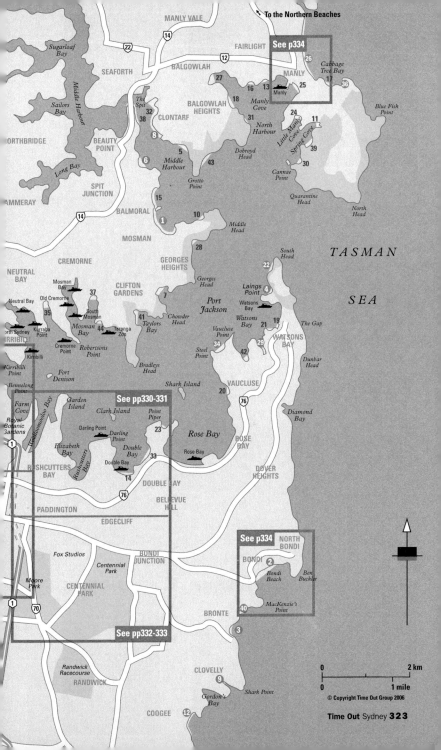

To the Northern Beaches

MANLY VALE

FAIRLIGHT

See p334

MANLY

Sugarloaf Bay

SEAFORTH

BALGOWLAH

Cabbage Tree Bay

Sailors Bay

Middle Harbour

BEAUTY POINT

BALGOWLAH HEIGHTS

Manly Cove

Little Manly Cove

Blue Fish Point

NORTHBRIDGE

CLONTARF

The Spit

North Harbour

Spring Cove

Long Bay

SPIT JUNCTION

Middle Harbour

Dobroyd Head

Cannae Point

Quarantine Head

North Head

CAMMERAY

BALMORAL

Grotto Point

MOSMAN

Middle Head

TASMAN

GEORGES HEIGHTS

South Head

SEA

NEUTRAL BAY

CREMORNE

CLIFTON GARDENS

Georges Head

Port Jackson

Laings Point

Watsons Bay

Neutral Bay

Mosman Bay

Old Cremorne

SOUTH MOSMAN

Chowder Head

Watsons Bay

The Gap

North Sydney

Kurraba Point

Mosman Bay

Taronga Zoo

Taylors Bay

Vaucluse Point

WATSONS BAY

KIRRIBILLI

Cremorne Point

Robertsons Point

Bradleys Head

Steel Point

Dunbar Head

Kirribilli Point

Fort Denison

Shark Island

VAUCLUSE

Bennelong Point

Woolloomooloo Bay

Garden Island

Clark Island

Point Piper

Rose Bay

Diamond Bay

Farm Cove

Royal Botanic Gardens

Darling Point

Double Bay

ROSE BAY

See pp330-331

Elizabeth Bay

Rushcutters Bay

Darling Point

Double Bay

Rose Bay

DOVER HEIGHTS

RUSHCUTTERS BAY

DOUBLE BAY

PADDINGTON

BELLEVUE HILL

EDGECLIFF

See p334

NORTH BONDI

Fox Studios

BONDI JUNCTION

BONDI

Centennial Park

Bondi Beach

Ben Buckler

Moore Park

CENTENNIAL PARK

Centennial Park

MacKenzie's Point

BRONTE

Randwick Racecourse

See pp332-333

RANDWICK

CLOVELLY

Shark Point

COOGEE

Gordon's Bay

2 km

1 mile

© Copyright Time Out Group 2006

Time Out Sydney **323**

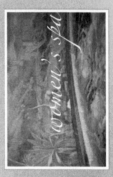

BABYLON
SAUNA AND SPA

巴比倫桑拿殿

BABYLON

Recover, relax and refresh at Babylon Sauna and Spa. Start with a sauna or steam, soak in a relaxing spa then revitalise and soothe the soul with anyone of Babylon's Massages.

Choose from a traditional Chinese Massage, Korean style, Aromatherapy, Body Scrub or a good old fashioned head and foot massage. With over 50 masseurs available every day, we will have a style to suit your needs.

They have separate area for men and women, with luxurious lound areas to relax. So when you're visiting Sydney, don't forget to take time out to recover, relax and refresh with a massage at Babylon Sauna and Spa.

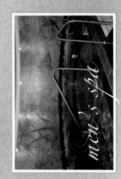

women's spa

men's spa

foot massage

massage

Level 2, Market City Shopping Centre, Haymarket, Chinatown, Sydney, 2000
Open 11am - 3am   7days   phone: 9281 8886

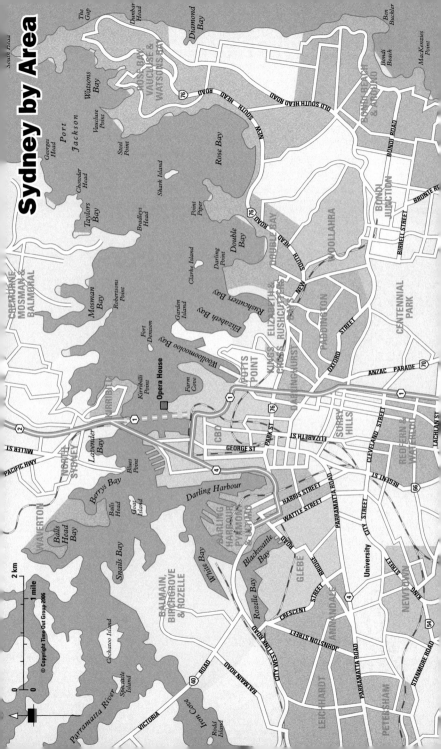

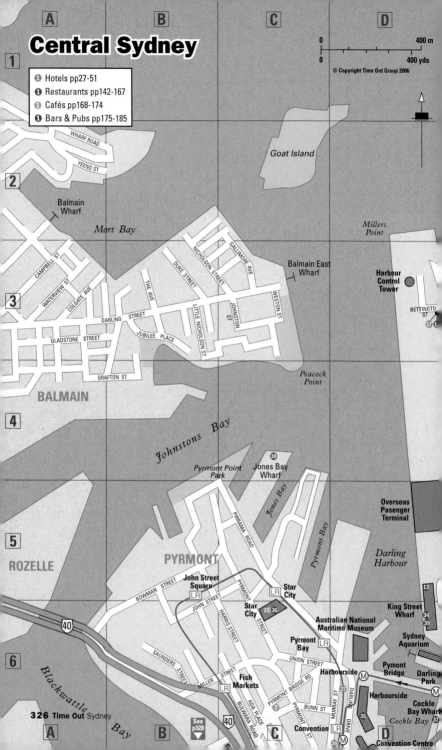

Central Sydney

❶ Hotels pp27-51
❶ Restaurants pp142-167
❶ Cafés pp168-174
❶ Bars & Pubs pp175-185

400 m
400 yds
© Copyright Time Out Group 2006

Goat Island

WHARF ROAD

YEEND ST

Balmain
Wharf

Mort Bay

*Millers
Point*

Balmain East
Wharf

**Harbour
Control
Tower**

BETTINGTO
ST

CAMPBELL ST

WATERVIEW ST

COLGATE AVE

THE AVE

DUKE STREET

NICHOLSON STREET

GALLIMORE AVE

JOHNSTON
ST

WESTON ST

LITTLE NICHOLSON ST

DARLING STREET

JUBILEE PLACE

GLADSTONE STREET

GRAFTON ST

BALMAIN

*Peacock
Point*

Johnstons Bay

Pyrmont Point
Park

Jones Bay
Wharf

Jones Bay

Pyrmont Bay

**Overseas
Pasenger
Terminal**

*Darling
Harbour*

ROZELLE

PYRMONT

John Street
Square

BOWMAN STREET

PIRRAMA ROAD

JOHN STREET

PYRMONT STREET

HARRIS STREET

**Star
City**

**Star
City**

25 36

**King Street
Wharf**

13

34
39

**Sydney
Aquarium**

**Australian National
Maritime Museum**

**Pyrmont
Bay**

**Pyrmont
Bridge**

**Darling
Park**

SAUNDERS STREET

MILLER STREET

Fish
Markets

ADA PLACE

BULWARRA ROAD

PYRMONT BRIDGE RD

UNION STREET

BUNN ST

PYRMONT ST

MURRAY ST

DARLING DRIVE

Harbourside

Harbourside

**Cockle
Bay Wharf**

Cockle Bay

*Blackwattle
Bay*

40

40

Convention

Convention Centre

See
p328

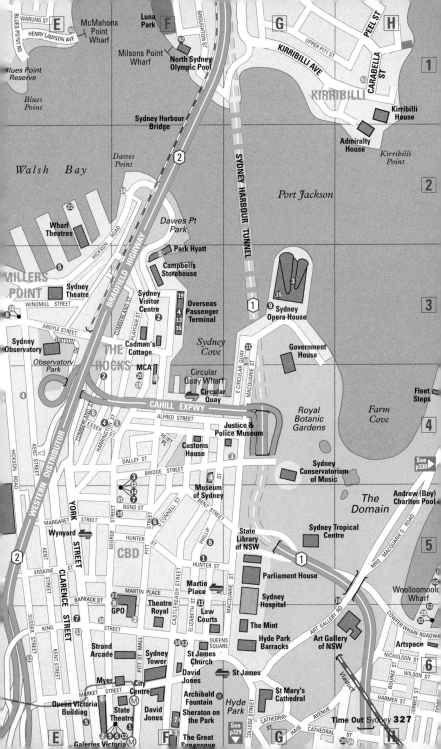

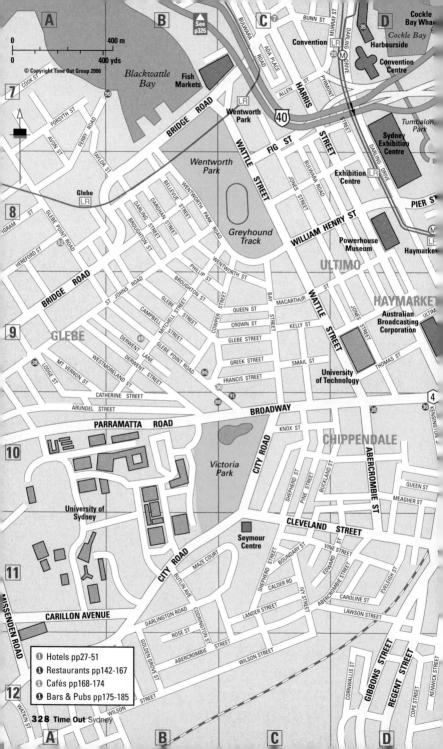

Maps

A | B | C | D

7

COOK ST
FORSYTH ST
AVON ST
FERRY ROAD
TAYLOR ST

0 | 400 m
0 | 400 yds

© Copyright Time Out Group 2006

Blackwattle Bay

BRIDGE ROAD

Fish Markets

90

See p326

BUXWARA ROAD

ADA PLACE

ALLEN ST

HARRIS STREET

BUNN ST
MURRAY ST
DARLING DRIVE

Convention

LR

Cockle Bay Wharf

Cockle Bay

Harbourside

Convention Centre

35

M

Wentworth Park

LR

PYRMONT ST

40

FIG ST

Sydney Exhibition Centre

Tumbalon Park

8

IGRAM ST
GLEBE POINT ROAD
HEREFORD ST

Glebe
LR

52

BRIDGE ROAD

DARLING STREET
DARGHAN STREET
BROUGHTON ST
BELLEVUE STREET
WENTWORTH PARK ROAD

Wentworth Park

Greyhound Track

WATTLE STREET

BUXWARA ROAD

JONES STREET

WILLIAM HENRY ST

Exhibition Centre

LR

PIER ST

M
LR

9

GLEBE

MT VERNON ST
LODGE ST
ST JOHNS ROAD
PHILLIP ST
BROUGHTON ST
CAMPBELL STREET
MITCHELL STREET
GLEBE STREET
DERWENT LANE
GLEBE POINT ROAD
DERWENT STREET
WESTMORELAND ST

WENTWORTH ST

COWPER STREET

QUEEN ST

CROWN ST

GLEBE STREET

GREEK STREET

FRANCIS STREET

49

38

86

30

91

88

BAY STREET

MACARTHUR ST

KELLY ST

SMAIL ST

WATTLE STREET

ST

JONES STREET

THOMAS ST

ULTIMO

Powerhouse Museum

Haymarket

HAYMARKET

Australian Broadcasting Corporation

ULTIM

University of Technology

10

PARRAMATTA ROAD

University of Sydney

BROADWAY

KNOX ST

Victoria Park

CITY ROAD

35

4

36

KENSINGTON ST

CHIPPENDALE

SHEPHERD ST
PINE STREET
BUCKLAND ST
ABERCROMBIE ST

QUEEN ST

MEAGHER ST

11

MISSENDEN ROAD

University of Sydney

CITY ROAD

MAZE COURT
BUTLIN AVE

Seymour Centre

CLEVELAND STREET

VINE STREET
EDWARD ST
ABERCROMBIE STREET
EVELEIGH ST

SHEPHERD STREET
BOUNDARY ST
CALDER RD
IVY STREET

CAROLINE ST

LAWSON STREET

12

WATKIN ST

CARILLON AVENUE

DARLINGTON ROAD
ROSE ST
ABERCROMBIE STREET
CODRINGTON ST
GOLDEN GROVE ST
WILSON STREET

LANDER STREET

CORNWALLIS STREET

COPE STREET

GIBBONS STREET

REGENT STREET

RENWICK STREET

❶ Hotels pp27-51
❶ Restaurants pp142-167
❶ Cafés pp168-174
❶ Bars & Pubs pp175-185

328 Time Out Sydney

A | B | C | D

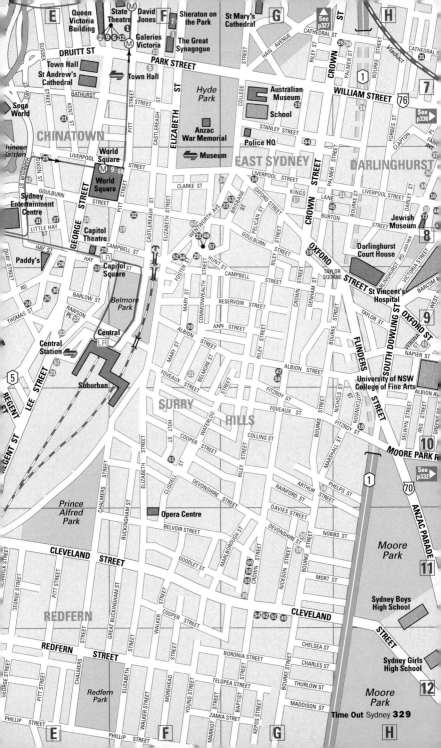

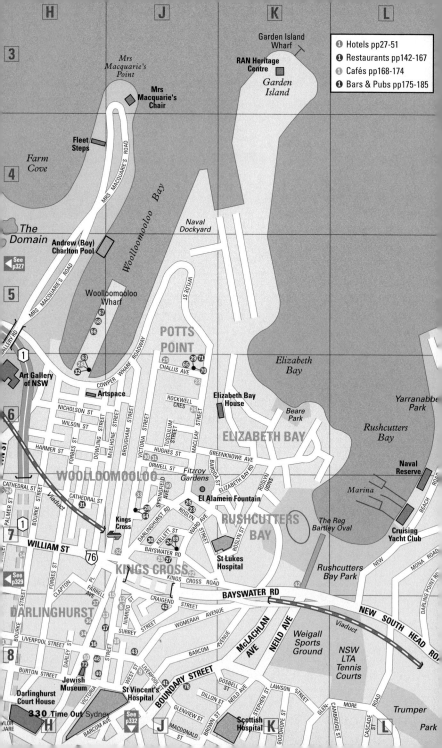

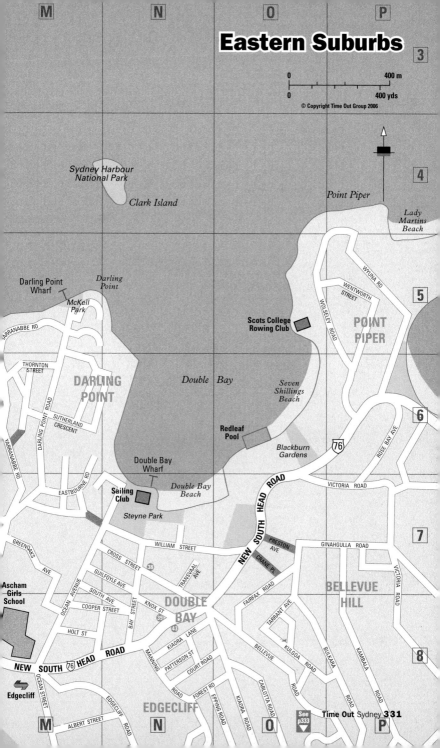

Eastern Suburbs

0   400 m
0   400 yds

© Copyright Time Out Group 2006

Sydney Harbour
National Park

Clark Island

Point Piper

Lady
Martins
Beach

Darling Point
Wharf

*Darling
Point*

McKell
Park

YARRANABBE RD

THORNTON
STREET

**DARLING
POINT**

DARLING POINT ROAD

SUTHERLAND
CRESCENT

YARRANABBE RD

EASTBOURNE RD

Scots College
Rowing Club

WOLSELEY ROAD

WYUNA RD

WENTWORTH
STREET

**POINT
PIPER**

Double   Bay

*Seven
Shillings
Beach*

ROSE BAY AVE

Redleaf
Pool

*Blackburn
Gardens*

76

Double Bay
Wharf

*Double Bay
Beach*

VICTORIA ROAD

Sailing
Club

Steyne Park

NEW SOUTH HEAD ROAD

76

WILLIAM   STREET

PRESTON
AVE

CRANE PL

GINAHGULLA   ROAD

VICTORIA ROAD

GREENOAKS
AVE

CROSS   STREET

38

TRANSVAAL
AVE

FAIRFAX   ROAD

**BELLEVUE
HILL**

**Ascham
Girls
School**

GUILFOYLE AVE

OCEAN AVENUE

SOUTH AVE

COOPER STREET

BAY   STREET

KNOX ST

**DOUBLE
BAY**

33

43

KIAORA LANE

TARRANT AVE

BELLEVUE

KULGOA   ROAD

BULKARA   ROAD

KAMBALA   ROAD

HOLT ST

MANNING   ROAD

KIAORA ROAD

PATTERSON ST

COURT ROAD

FOREST RD

EPPING ROAD

KIAORA   ROAD

CARLOTTA   ROAD

ROAD

NEW   SOUTH 76 **HEAD   ROAD**

OCEAN STREET

EDGECLIFF   ROAD

ALBERT STREET

EDGECLIFF

← Edgecliff

See
p333
▼

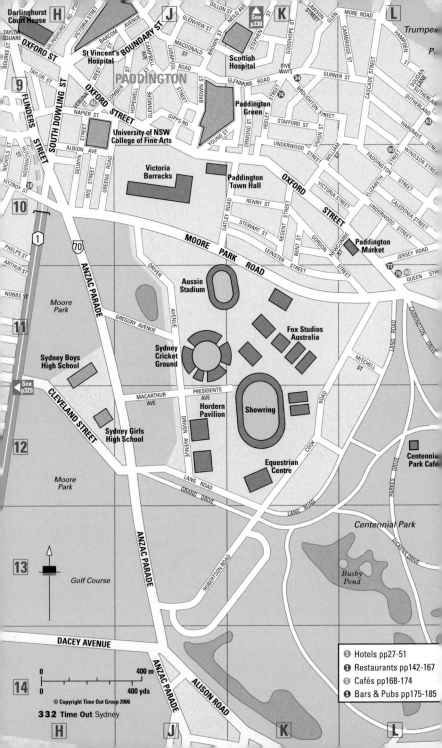

H   J   K   L

Darlinghurst
Court House

OXFORD ST

9
FLINDERS STREET

SOUTH DOWLING STREET

St Vincent's
Hospital

BOUNDARY ST

OXFORD STREET

PADDINGTON

Scottish Hospital

FIVE WAYS
34

Paddington
Green

GLENMORE ROAD

GURNER ST

University of NSW
College of Fine Arts

Paddington
Town Hall

OXFORD
STREET

Paddington
Market

10

Victoria
Barracks

MOORE   PARK   ROAD

11
Moore
Park

ANZAC PARADE

Aussie
Stadium

GREGORY AVENUE

Sydney Boys
High School

Sydney
Cricket
Ground

Fox Studios
Australia

MITCHELL ST

CLEVELAND STREET

MACARTHUR
AVE

PRESIDENTS
AVE

Hordern
Pavilion

Showring

12
Sydney Girls
High School

Moore
Park

LANG ROAD

GRAND DRIVE

Equestrian
Centre

Centennial
Park Café

Centennial Park

Busby
Pond

DICKENS DRIVE

13
Golf Course

ANZAC PARADE

14
DACEY AVENUE

0   400 m
0   400 yds

© Copyright Time Out Group 2006

ALISON ROAD

❶ Hotels pp27-51
❶ Restaurants pp142-167
❶ Cafés pp168-174
❶ Bars & Pubs pp175-185

H   J   K   L

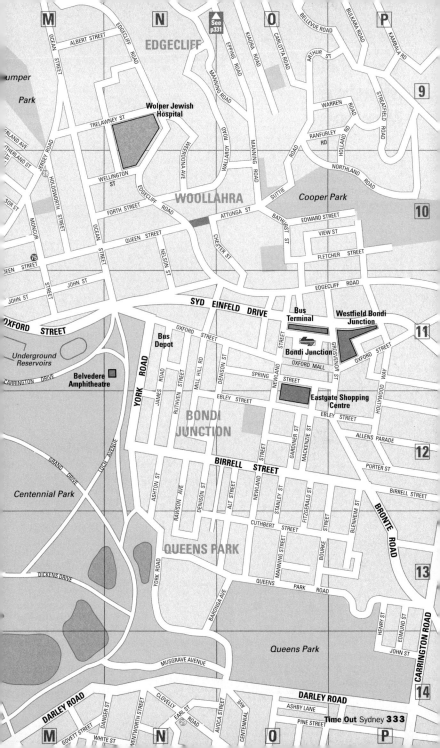

Bondi Beach
Manly &
Newtown

- ❶ Hotels pp27-51
- ❶ Restaurants pp142-167
- ❶ Cafés pp168-174
- ❶ Bars & Pubs pp175-185

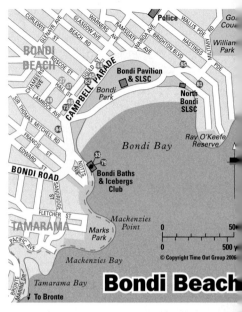

Bondi Beach

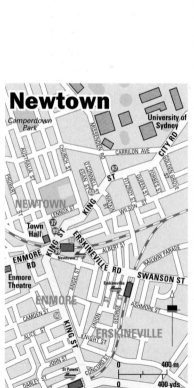

Newtown

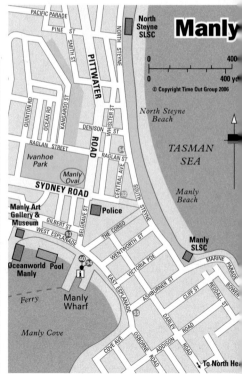

Manly

Sydney Ferries

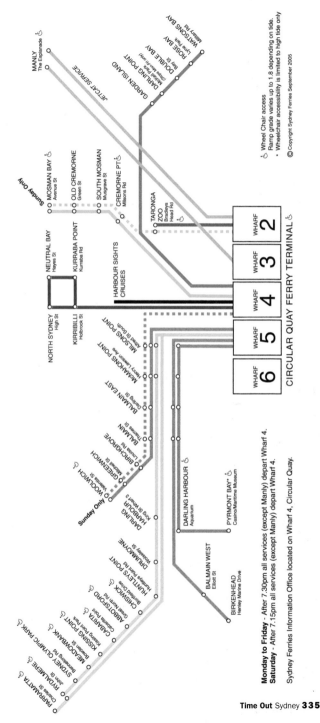

Monday to Friday - After 7.30pm all services (except Manly) depart Wharf 4.
Saturday - After 7.15pm all services (except Manly) depart Wharf 4.

Sydney Ferries Information Office located on Wharf 4, Circular Quay.

♿ Wheel Chair access
• Ramp grade varies up to 1.8 depending on tide.
• Wheelchair accessibility is limited to high tide only

© Copyright Sydney Ferries September 2005

CityRail's Sydney suburban network

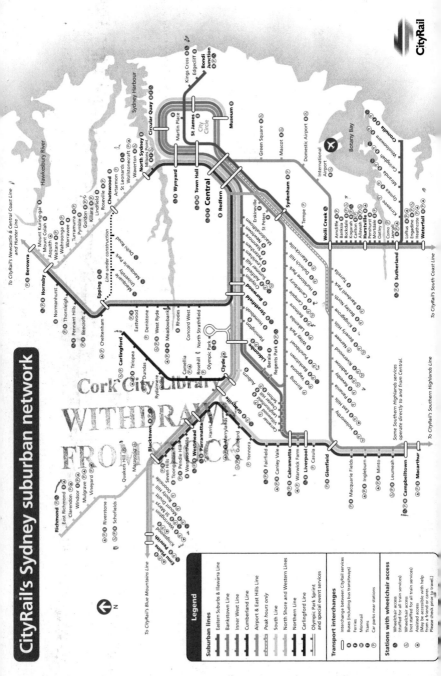

Legend

Suburban lines

- Eastern Suburbs & Illawarra Line
- Bankstown Line
- Inner West Line
- Cumberland Line
- Airport & East Hills Line
- Peak hours only
- South Line
- North Shore and Western Lines
- Northern Line
- Carlingford Line
- Olympic Park Sprint and special event services

Transport interchanges

- Interchange between CityRail services
- Buses (including bus transitways)
- Ferries
- Monorail
- Trams
- Car parks near stations

Stations with wheelchair access

- Wheelchair access (staffed for all train services)
- Wheelchair access (not staffed for all train services)
- Assisted access (May be accessible with help from a friend or carer. Please check prior to travel.)